ECONOI

REPORT

OF THE

PRESIDENT

TRANSMITTED TO THE CONGRESS

FEBRUARY 2011

TOGETHER WITH

THE ANNUAL REPORT

OF THE

COUNCIL OF ECONOMIC ADVISERS

UNITED STATES GOVERNMENT PRINTING OFFICE

WASHINGTON : 2011

For sale by the Superintendent of Documents, U.S. Government Printing Office
Internet: bookstore.gpo.gov Phone: toll free (866) 512-1800; DC area (202) 512-1800
Fax: (202) 512-2104 Mail: Stop IDCC, Washington, DC 20402-0001

ISBN 978-0-16-087664-6

C O N T E N T S

		Page
ECONOMIC REPORT OF THE PRESIDENT		1
ANNUAL REPORT OF THE COUNCIL OF ECONOMIC ADVISERS*		9
CHAPTER 1.	FROM CRISIS TO RECOVERY AND GROWTH	19
CHAPTER 2.	THE YEAR IN REVIEW AND THE YEARS AHEAD	29
CHAPTER 3	THE FOUNDATIONS OF GROWTH	53
CHAPTER 4.	THE WORLD ECONOMY	81
CHAPTER 5.	HEALTH CARE REFORM	111
CHAPTER 6.	TRANSITIONING TO A CLEAN ENERGY FUTURE	125
CHAPTER 7.	SUPPORTING AMERICA' S SMALL BUSINESSES	143
REFERENCES		157
APPENDIX A.	REPORT TO THE PRESIDENT ON THE ACTIVITIES OF THE COUNCIL OF ECONOMIC ADVISERS DURING 2010	165
APPENDIX B.	STATISTICAL TABLES RELATING TO INCOME, EMPLOYMENT, AND PRODUCTION	179

*For a detailed table of contents of the Council's Report, see page 13.

ECONOMIC REPORT
OF THE
PRESIDENT

ECONOMIC REPORT OF THE PRESIDENT

To the Congress of the United States:

As we begin a new year, the country is still emerging from the worst recession in generations. Across the nation, millions lost their jobs, their businesses, and their sense of security about the future. Many have had to put off their plans for a better life: going to college, buying a new home, or retiring after a long career.

At the same time, we've seen encouraging signs that the recovery is beginning to take hold. An economy that had been shrinking for a year is now growing again. After two years of job losses, our economy added more than one million private sector jobs in 2010. Yet, as we all are too well aware, the recovery is not happening fast enough. Millions of Americans—our neighbors, friends, family members—are still looking for jobs. This means that the most immediate task must be to get our fellow Americans back to work by accelerating economic growth and job creation by the private sector.

That's why, at the end of last year, I signed into law a measure to prevent taxes from rising on middle-class families and to create new incentives for businesses to create jobs. This bipartisan compromise cut payroll taxes for 155 million workers, prevented a $3,000 tax increase from going into effect on the typical working family, and extended important tax credits to help families make ends meet and send their kids to college. The law also extended unemployment insurance, preventing 7 million Americans from losing their benefits as they look for new work, and gave businesses two powerful incentives to invest and create jobs. These were 100 percent expensing of investment expenditures and an extension of the research and experimentation tax credit.

I proposed an up-front investment in building new roads, rails, and runways to upgrade our infrastructure and create new jobs. And last month, I laid out a commonsense approach to regulation that is pragmatic, based on evidence, and driven by data that will help lay the groundwork for economic growth and job creation while continuing to protect our health, safety, and environment. In addition, my Administration has moved aggressively to open markets abroad and boost exports of American goods and services.

These steps will help the economy this year. But it is also essential that we take stock and look to the future—to what kind of America we want to see emerge from this crisis and take shape for the generations of Americans to come.

We know what it takes to compete for the jobs and industries of our time. We know what we have to do to win the future. We need to out-innovate, out-educate, and out-build the rest of the world. We have to make America the best place on Earth to do business. We need to rein in deficits after a decade of rising debt, and reform our government. This is the way to robust and widely shared prosperity.

The first step in winning the future is encouraging American innovation. That is ultimately driven by free enterprise. But public support also plays an essential role in encouraging innovative research and development. It holds incredible promise for our future. That is why, throughout history our government has provided cutting-edge scientists and inventors with the support that they need. This is what planted the seeds for the Internet. This is what helped make possible breakthroughs like computer chips and GPS.

Two years ago, I set a goal for America: that we needed to reach a level of research and development we haven't seen since the height of the Space Race. And this year, my budget helps us meet that goal. We'll invest in biomedical research, information technology, and especially clean energy technology—an investment that will strengthen our security, protect our planet, and create countless new jobs for our people.

We've begun to reinvent our energy policy. We're telling America's scientists and engineers that if they assemble teams of the best minds in their fields, and focus on the hardest problems in clean energy, we'll fund the Apollo Projects of our time. We're doing this through investments in innovation hubs across America. These are teams of scientists focused on one difficult problem. We're also supporting the Advanced Research Projects Agency for Energy, modeled on a successful defense agency that has developed cutting-edge technologies for decades.

In addition, clean energy breakthroughs will only translate into clean energy jobs if businesses know there will be a market for what they're selling. So in my State of the Union, I called on Congress to join me in setting a new goal: by 2035, 80 percent of America's electricity will come from clean energy sources.

The second part of our strategy is education. Over the next ten years, nearly half of all new jobs will require education that goes beyond a high school degree. And yet, as many as a quarter of our students aren't even finishing high school. The quality of our math and science education lags behind many other nations. And so the question is whether all of us—as citizens, and as parents—are willing to do what's necessary to give every child a chance to succeed.

Of course, our schools share this responsibility. When a child walks into a classroom, it should be a place of high expectations and high performance. Yet too many schools in our country don't meet this threshold test. That's why we launched a competition called Race to the Top. Race to the Top is the most meaningful reform of our public schools in a generation. For less than one percent of what we spend on education each year, it has led over 40 states to raise their standards for teaching and learning.

Next, because an increasing number of jobs require more than a high school diploma, higher education must be within reach of every American. So we've ended the taxpayer subsidies that went to banks to act as a middleman in the student loan process, and used the savings to make college affordable for millions of students. And this year, we will work to make permanent our tuition tax credit—worth $10,000 for four years of college. We are also revitalizing America's community colleges, which will help us reach the goal I set two years ago: by the end of the decade, America will once again have the highest proportion of college graduates in the world.

The third step in winning the future is rebuilding America. To attract new businesses to our shores, we need the fastest, most reliable ways to move people, goods, and information—from high-speed rail to high-speed internet. That is why, over the last two years, we have begun rebuilding for the 21st century, a project that has meant thousands of good jobs for the hard-hit construction industry.

We will put more Americans to work repairing crumbling roads and bridges. We will make sure this is fully paid for, attract private investment, and pick projects based on what's best for the economy, not politicians. Within 25 years, our goal is to give 80 percent of Americans access to high-speed rail, which could allow you to go places in half the time it takes to travel by car. Routes in California and the Midwest are already underway.

And within the next five years, we will also make it possible for business to deploy the next generation of high-speed wireless coverage to 98 percent of all Americans.

All these investments—in innovation, education, and infrastructure—will make America a better place to do business and create jobs. But to help our companies compete, we also have to knock down barriers that stand in the way of their success.

To help businesses sell more products abroad, we set a goal of doubling our exports by 2014. My Administration has worked to knock down barriers our exporters face and advocated for U.S. exporters abroad—resulting in signing important deals to sell more American goods and services to China and India. And in December, we finalized a trade agreement with South Korea that will support at least 70,000 American jobs. This agreement has unprecedented support from business and labor, Democrats and Republicans, and I've asked Congress to pass it as soon as possible. Finally, we are also pursuing agreements with Panama and Colombia, and continuing our Asia Pacific and global trade talks.

To reduce barriers to growth and investment, I've ordered a review of government regulations. When we find rules that put an unnecessary burden on businesses, we will fix them. But I will not hesitate to create or enforce commonsense safeguards to protect the American people. That's what we've done in this country for more than a century, from child labor laws to protections for our air and water. It's why last year, we put in place consumer protections against hidden fees and penalties by credit card companies, and new rules to prevent another financial crisis. And it's why we passed reform that finally prevents the health insurance industry from exploiting patients.

The final step in winning the future is to make sure we aren't buried under a mountain of debt. We are living with a legacy of deficit-spending that began almost a decade ago. And in the wake of the financial crisis, some of that was necessary to keep credit flowing, save jobs, and put money in people's pockets.

That is why in my Budget, I've proposed that government live within its means while investing in the future. I have promised to veto any bill that contains earmarks. I've proposed freezing annual domestic spending for the next five years. This would reduce the deficit by more than $400 billion over the next decade, and will bring discretionary spending to the lowest share of our economy since Dwight Eisenhower was President.

Yet, at the same time, we cannot solve our fiscal problems on the backs of our most vulnerable citizens. And it would also be a mistake to cut the deficit by gutting our investments in innovation and education, which are so critical for our future prosperity. The fact is, priorities like education, innovation, and infrastructure have traditionally commanded bipartisan support. There are no inherent ideological differences that should prevent Democrats and Republicans from improving our economy. We are all Americans, and we are all in this race together—we can focus on what is necessary for America to win the future.

For as difficult as the times may be, the good news is that we know what the future could look like for the United States. We can see it in the classrooms that are experimenting with groundbreaking reforms, and giving children new math and science skills at an early age. We can see it in the wind farms, solar plants, and advanced battery plants that are opening across America. We can see it in the laboratories and research facilities all over this country that are churning out discoveries and turning them into new start-ups and new jobs.

Our job is simply to harness the potential that exists all across this country, and this economic report lays out the policies that will help our nation succeed by doing exactly that. In the subsequent chapters, we will look at the progress that has been made over the past year. In addition, this report will lay out many of the policies that will foster growth and make our economy more competitive. That is our great challenge today. And I am absolutely confident it is one we will meet.

THE WHITE HOUSE
FEBRUARY 2011

THE ANNUAL REPORT
OF THE
COUNCIL OF ECONOMIC ADVISERS

LETTER OF TRANSMITTAL

COUNCIL OF ECONOMIC ADVISERS
Washington, D.C., February 23, 2011

MR. PRESIDENT:

The Council of Economic Advisers herewith submits its 2011 Annual Report in accordance with the provisions of the Employment Act of 1946 as amended by the Full Employment and Balanced Growth Act of 1978.

Sincerely,

Austan Goolsbee
Chairman

Cecilia Elena Rouse
Member

CONTENTS

CHAPTER 1. FROM CRISIS TO RECOVERY AND GROWTH.... 19

The Year in Review and the Years Ahead.................................... 22
The Foundations of Growth.. 23
The World Economy 24
Health Reform 25
Energy Policy.. 25
Supporting America's Small Businesses................................. 26
CONCLUSION 27

**CHAPTER 2. THE YEAR IN REVIEW AND THE YEARS
AHEAD**... 29

DEVELOPMENTS IN 2010 AND THE NEAR-TERM OUTLOOK......... 30
Consumption and Saving... 30
Developments in Housing Markets....................................... 33
Business Fixed Investment.. 37
Business Inventories 38
Government Outlays, Consumption, and Investment.................. 40
State and Local Government... 43
Real Exports and Imports... 44
Labor Market Trends 45
Prices 49
Financial Markets 50
THE LONG-TERM OUTLOOK 51
CONCLUSION 52

CHAPTER 3. THE FOUNDATIONS OF GROWTH........................ 53

THE IMPORTANCE OF ECONOMIC GROWTH 53
SOURCES OF ECONOMIC GROWTH 55

INNOVATION AND ECONOMIC GROWTH 57
    Basic Research.. 58
    Intellectual Property Rights 60
    Antitrust and the Innovative Marketplace................................ 61
    The Research and Experimentation Tax Credit........................... 62
    Entrepreneurship 62
    National Priority Areas... 63
INFRASTRUCTURE AND ECONOMIC GROWTH............................ 64
    Roads, Railways, and Runways... 65
    Electricity Infrastructure.. 66
    Information Networks.. 67
SKILLS AND ECONOMIC GROWTH 69
    Early Childhood Education 72
    Elementary and Secondary Education..................................... 73
    Higher Education 76
    Job Training... 78
CONCLUSION 79

CHAPTER 4. THE WORLD ECONOMY 81

STATUS OF THE WORLD RECOVERY... 82
    Crisis Fading, But Challenges Remain.................................... 82
    The Rebound in World Trade.. 86
    Global Policy Coordination 87
THE EVOLUTION OF THE WORLD ECONOMY.............................. 89
    Global Imbalances... 89
    Determinants of Exports 94
    Evolving U.S. Trade Patterns 97
TRADE POLICY 103
    Negotiating to Open New Markets.. 103
    Encouraging Exports by Enforcing Existing Agreements............... 107
    Advocacy to Encourage Exporters, Credit, and Trade
    Facilitation... 109
CONCLUSION 110

CHAPTER 5. HEALTH CARE REFORM 111

ADDRESSING THE RISING COST OF MEDICAL CARE 114
    Trends in Aggregate Health Spending 114
    Technological Change and Increases in Health Spending............. 115

Market Imperfections and Increases in Health Care Spending.... 115
How the Affordable Care Act Promotes High-Value Medical Care.......... 116
IMPROVING THE HEALTH INSURANCE MARKET 118
Problems in the Market for Health Insurance.......... 119
How the Affordable Care Act Addresses the Insurance Market Failures 120
Employers and the Affordable Care Act 122
Expanding Medicaid 122
CONCLUSION 123

CHAPTER 6. TRANSITIONING TO A CLEAN ENERGY FUTURE 125

INITIAL STEPS TOWARD A CLEAN ENERGY ECONOMY.......... 128
Energy Investments in the Recovery Act 128
Further Steps Toward a Cleaner Economy 130
NEXT STEPS TOWARD A CLEAN ENERGY ECONOMY 134
A Federal Clean Energy Standard 134
Energy Efficiency 136
Transportation 138
Research and Development 139
CONCLUSION 140

CHAPTER 7. SUPPORTING AMERICA'S SMALL BUSINESSES... 143

IMPACT OF THE RECESSION ON SMALL BUSINESSES 144
Job Creation 144
Financing Small Business 145
Changes in Availability of Credit and Capital for Small Business 146
ADMINISTRATION POLICIES TO SUPPORT SMALL BUSINESS 150
Tax Cuts for Small Business 150
Initiatives to Increase Access to Credit 151
Policies to Encourage Greater Access to Capital 154
CONCLUSION 156

REFERENCES 157

APPENDIXES

A. Report to the President on the Activities of the Council of
    Economic Advisers During 2010 165
B. Statistical Tables Relating to Income, Employment, and
    Production 179

LIST OF FIGURES

1-1.   Unsustainable Expansion: Recent Boom vs. Past Booms.............. 20
1-2.   U.S. Export Growth Lagged Other Top Exporters, 2000–2005.... 21
1-3.   U.S. Investment Growth Lagged Other Major Economies,
       2000-2005... 22
2-1.   Real GDP Growth by Quarter... 29
2-2   Consumer Sentiment and the Stock Market................................. 30
2-3.   Consumption and Net Worth Relative to Disposable Personal
       Income (DPI) 31
2-4.   Banks' Willingness to Lend to Consumers................................... 32
2-5.   House Prices.. 34
2-6.   Share of Mortgages in Foreclosure 36
2-7.   Business Fixed Investment and Cash Flow 38
2-8.   Inventory Investment and its Contribution to Real GDP Growth   39
2-9.   Manufacturing and Trade Inventories... 40
2-10. Deficit as a Share of GDP... 42
2-11. U.S. Exports and World GDP.. 44
2-12. Path of Non-Census Employment in the Past Three Recessions.   45
2-13. Path of Non-Census Employment Since the End of the Recession 46
3-1.   Progress in U.S. Real Income Per Person Since 1820 54
3-2.   E-Commerce Share of Business-to-Business Manufacturing
       Shipments 67
3-3.   Broadband Adoption across OECD Countries.............................. 68
3-4.   Average Wage and Salary Income by Educational Group 71
4-1.   Real GDP Growth.. 83
4-2.   Unemployment Rate.. 85
4-3.   Import Volume Indexes 86
4-4.   Export Volume Indexes.. 87
4-5.   Current Account Deficits or Surpluses as a Share of World GDP   91
4-6.   U.S. Exports by Sector 95
4-7.   U.S. Trade in Services 96
4-8.   Share of U.S. Goods Exports to Mature Foreign Economies........ 98
4-9.   Share of U.S. Goods Exports to Major Emerging Economies...... 99

4-10.   Share of U.S. Goods Imports by Foreign Source 100
4-11.   U.S. Export Growth vs. Foreign GDP Growth,
          2009:Q2 – 2010:Q2 101
4-12.   Projected Share of U.S. Nominal Export Growth, 2009–14 102
4-13.   U.S. Trade Disputes at the WTO 108
5-1.   GDP and Health Spending 114
5-2.   Percent of Americans Uninsured 119
6-1.   U.S. Wind, Solar, and Geothermal Energy Generating Capacity   132
6-2.   State Renewable Energy Standards in 2025 136
7-1.   Births, Closures, and Bankruptcies of Firms 144
7-2.   Bank Lending to Small Business 146
7-3.   Most Important Problem Facing Small Businesses in 2009 147
7-4.   Venture Capital Investment 148
7-5.   U.S. Initial Public Offerings 149
7-6.   SBA-Backed Loan Approvals 152

LIST OF TABLES

2-1.   Administration Economic Forecast 51
2-2.   Components of Potential Real GDP Growth, 1953–2021 52
4-1.   Import Tariffs, Nontariff Measures, and Trade Restrictiveness,
          2008 104

LIST OF BOXES

3-1.   Technological Progress and the Advance of Health 56
3-2.   The Power of Market-Based Innovation 58
3-3.   The Social Gains from Innovation 59
3-4.   STEM Education and Educate to Innovate 75
3-5.   America's Universities: Leading the World 77
3-6.   Skills for America's Future 79
4-1.   What Do We Owe the Rest of the World? 92
4-2.   The Korea-United States Free Trade Agreement 105
5-1.   Early Provisions of the Affordable Care Act 113
6-1.   Energy Security Benefits of Reduced Oil Consumption 126
6-2.   Clean Energy Investments in the Recovery Act 129
6-3.   The Recovery Act and ARPA-E: Spurring Innovation to Transform
          the Energy Economy 131
6-4.   The Social Cost of Carbon: A Tool for Cost-Effective Policy 133

C H A P T E R   1

FROM CRISIS TO
RECOVERY AND GROWTH

The recession that began at the end of 2007 was both the longest and the worst since the Great Depression more than 75 years ago. By some measures, such as the total jobs lost, it was as deep as the past three recessions combined.

It was a breathtaking moment of free fall in the private sector. Capital markets collapsed. Credit to businesses froze. Banks failed. Foreclosures soared. National output fell at rates not seen in decades. And millions of people lost their jobs.

Policymakers in the Administration, Congress, and the Federal Reserve responded with aggressive, concerted actions to stop the crisis. Although there will likely be debates over the impact of each of those responses for decades to come, few can dispute that the economic climate has improved substantially from the darkest days at the end of 2008 and the beginning of 2009 in large part because of these actions. And the Nation's economy did not fall into depression.

As gross domestic product (GDP) has been recovering, and as the private sector has added more than 1.1 million jobs since the beginning of 2010, economic policy has shifted from crisis to recovery and fostering growth.

This year, the *Economic Report of the President* puts its primary focus on the particular moment in which the Nation now finds itself—a moment when the most important priority is reestablishing the primacy of broad-based growth to ensure the well-being of the American people and to keep America the premier economy on Earth.

Without question, growing our way out of the hole left by the crisis will take a determined effort across industries, states and localities, and the Federal Government. Data from many countries over many years document how painful the emergence from a deep financial crisis can be. The challenges today have been heightened by the need to confront multiple pressures, many of which are lingering effects of the crisis itself: financial woes in Europe, continued weakness in the U.S. housing market, depleted state and local government budgets, and the need to improve the Nation's long-term fiscal situation. And yet the American economy has now been growing for more than a year and a half. The private sector, as of this writing, has added jobs for 11 consecutive months. The economy must grow faster, but certainly this is movement in the right direction.

The challenge will be to shift the focus of the U.S. recovery away from the boom-and-bust cycles of the recent past toward more sustainable growth. In particular, from 2001 to 2005, the two overwhelming drivers of growth were increased consumer spending and investment in residential real estate. Each was unsustainable. Consumption spending grew faster than income, and the personal saving rate fell dangerously close to zero. The bursting of the housing bubble left millions of vacant homes and lowered home prices such that investment in the housing sector is still struggling to recover.

Figure 1-1
Unsustainable Expansion: Recent Boom vs. Past Booms

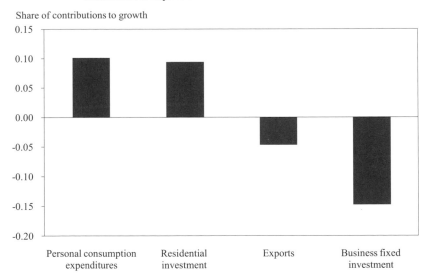

Note: The figure shows the share of contribution to GDP growth from 2001:Q1 to 2005:Q4 minus the share of contribution to growth from 1953:Q2 to 2001:Q1.
Source: Bureau of Economic Analysis, National Income and Product Accounts.

Figure 1-1 shows how imbalanced the early 2000s were relative to normal expansions in the second half of the 20th century. It illustrates the share that personal consumption, residential investment, exports, and nonresidential business fixed investment contributed to GDP growth during the five years following the business cycle peak in 2001:Q1, relative to the past averages. Consumption and residential investment were dramatically outsized contributors to GDP growth during the recent boom compared to the past. Business investment and exports were dramatically undersized.

U.S. nonresidential investment and exports during 2000–2005 were weak not only relative to our own history, but also relative to other major economies. Figure 1-2 shows that U.S. nonresidential investment barely grew at all over those years. Nonresidential investment grew faster in other G-7 countries than in the United States and grew even faster in a broader set of advanced economies.

Figure 1-2
U.S. Investment Growth Lagged Other Major Economies, 2000–2005

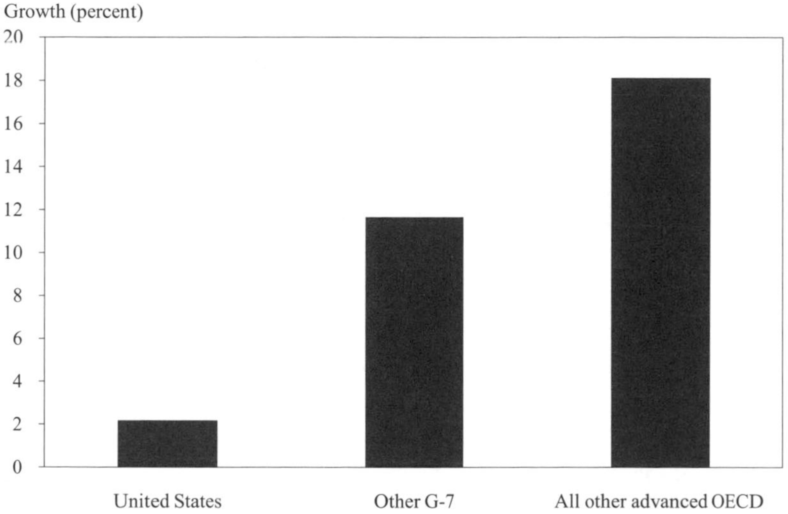

Growth (percent)

Note: Cumulative growth in real gross private nonresidential fixed capital formation, 2000–2005.
Sources: OECD Economic Outlook no. 88, Annex Table 6; CEA calculations.

Figure 1-3 shows the cumulative growth of exports from the United States during 2000–2005, compared with export growth in other high-income economies and other major exporters. Clearly, U.S. export growth in the early 2000s was weak relative to export growth in other major economies.

The Nation can do better, and the Administration has outlined a plan to enable it to do so. It is important to remember that the recent consumption and residential booms were aberrations. The goal now is to return to more sustainable sources of growth, where nonresidential business investment and exports take a more central role. To help business investment reclaim this role as a key driver of growth, the Administration has made extensive efforts to encourage businesses to invest at home—through tax policy, credit policy, and the public investments that make the United States an attractive place to do business. With the momentum of the recovery building among our trading partners, the Administration also believes that we should turn to greater exports as an important source of growth going forward.

Figure 1-3
U.S. Export Growth Lagged Other Top Exporters, 2000–2005

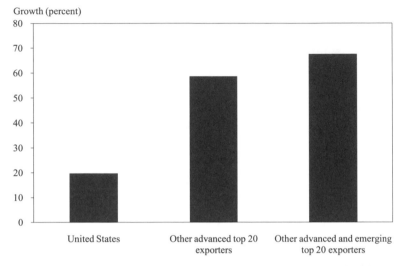

Notes: Cumulative growth in exports of goods and services, 2000–2005. This analysis of the top 20 exporters excludes Belgium due to lack of data prior to 2002.
Sources: World Bank, World Development Indicators; CEA calculations.

The United States established itself as the premier economic power in the world based on the energy and ingenuity of its people, and the Administration will continue to reinforce this foundation of our growth—educating workers, investing in science, and building the infrastructure that American companies need to succeed. As the President says, with the policies in place to support innovation and sustained economic growth, the United States will "win the future."

This *Economic Report* follows these themes in greater detail and also examines other key aspects of the economy, as described below.

The Year in Review and the Years Ahead

Coming out of the deepest recession since the 1930s, the economy completed its sixth consecutive quarter of recovery by the end of 2010, as described in Chapter 2. Real GDP grew 2.8 percent during the four quarters of 2010, up from 0.2 percent a year earlier. During 2010, stress in financial markets eased, the stock market gained 13 percent, and the economy added 1.1 million private sector jobs.

Recent growth in consumer spending reflects improvements in sentiment, in the stock market, and in banks' willingness to lend to consumers, thus easing many of the adverse shocks received during the recession. The increase in consumer spending has been achieved without a significant decline in the personal saving rate.

Housing prices have stabilized, but construction activity and most aspects of the housing market remain weak, about one-quarter of mortgages are under water, and the foreclosure rate remains high.

Equipment and software investment grew rapidly during 2010, but investment in business structures did not. Cash flow is strong. The inventory investment contribution to real GDP growth has moderated. Export growth has been strong.

Government policy has supported the recovery during 2009 and 2010, and the Tax Relief, Unemployment Insurance Reauthorization, and Job Creation Act, the compromise tax framework signed into law by the President on December 17, 2010, will help the economy in 2011. The position of state and local governments, however, remains difficult. At the same time, long-run fiscal responsibility is crucial, and the Administration has taken a number of steps to reduce deficits in coming years.

Private sector employment grew in each of the final 10 months of 2010, and the unemployment rate fell during 2010. The Recovery Act, the Hiring Incentives to Restore Employment Act, and the Education Jobs and Medicaid Assistance Act all helped to increase employment.

The Administration's economic forecast reflects the view that the U.S. economy is operating substantially below its potential level, as indicated by the elevated unemployment rate. Although the Administration estimates that the potential growth rate of real GDP is 2.5 percent, it believes that real GDP can grow faster over the next six years as the gap between actual and potential GDP declines. Reflecting this above-trend growth, the Administration projects that the unemployment rate will continue to fall over time.

The Foundations of Growth

As the United States begins to shift from crisis to recovery and growth, the Nation needs to make critical investments in innovation, infrastructure, and skills. Chapter 3 details Administration policies in these areas that are designed to deliver rapid, sustained, and broad-based economic growth and quality jobs in the years ahead.

The historical rise in American standards of living, in broad measures of income per person, in health and longevity, and in the variety of goods and services that Americans consume, demonstrates the power of long-run trends over short-run economic cycles in determining Americans' economic prosperity. Physical capital (investment), human capital (skills), and innovation are the primary sources of economic growth but have been neglected for years. To foster innovation, the Administration is proposing critical investments in basic research, intellectual property rights, antitrust enforcement, research tax credits, entrepreneurship, and national priority areas, such as biotechnology and nanotechnology, health information technology, and clean energy. These investments work to ensure that the private sector, the Nation's engine of innovation, is not saddled by market failures but can forcefully and efficiently drive America's economic growth. Chapter 3 also discusses the role of infrastructure—including 21st-century transportation, electricity, and information networks—as a critical platform for growth.

Emphasizing the core importance of skills to U.S. economic growth and to the quality jobs of today and tomorrow, Administration policy focuses on enhancing early childhood education, elementary and secondary schooling, higher education, and job training. These efforts not only help U.S. citizens live up to their potential and compete in a global economy, but also work to reverse the Nation's rising wage inequality and declining rates of educational attainment relative to other countries.

The World Economy

The world economy saw sustained progress toward economic recovery in 2010, but growth during the recovery has been unevenly distributed between advanced and emerging economies.

As part of a broader shift toward growth in the United States that relies more on exports and investment, the President has set a goal of doubling nominal U.S. goods and services exports in five years: from $1.57 trillion in 2009 to $3.14 trillion a year by the end of 2014. Through the first three quarters of 2010, exports increased by 17 percent relative to the same period in 2009, representing a significant step toward that goal. A sizable portion of that growth came from increasing exports to emerging markets. Chapter 4 details the ways in which a changing world economy will affect this goal, as well as the U.S. role in the world economy.

The President's National Export Initiative has identified several areas in which U.S. trade policy can complement the forces already at work in the evolving global economy to help achieve this export goal. The Administration is committed to a trade policy that opens new markets for U.S. exporters by reducing foreign government–imposed tariffs and nontariff barriers. The

Administration is also actively enforcing commitments taken on by its trading partners and assisting U.S. exporters with gaining access to trade credit and streamlining the exporting process.

Health Reform

A signature effort of the Administration has been to ensure the security and affordability of health insurance coverage while extending coverage to millions of uninsured Americans. The Affordable Care Act, which President Obama signed into law in March 2010, is the latest chapter in nearly a century-long history of efforts to ensure comprehensive health insurance coverage for more Americans, coupled with major steps in the quest for high value in health spending. For decades, the policy problem posed by tens of millions of uninsured Americans has overshadowed the underlying economic challenge of how to control costs while preserving the high quality of the American medical care system. In addition to implementing policies to cover the uninsured, the Affordable Care Act introduces a framework for moving the medical care system toward high-value care.

Chapter 5 describes how the Affordable Care Act controls costs and improves quality by strengthening physician and hospital incentives to improve the quality of care and provide care more efficiently. These delivery system reforms are paired with reforms that create new coverage options through competitive state marketplaces for insurance, ensure access to affordable coverage through the provision of tax credits for small businesses and individuals, and put in place individual and employer responsibility requirements. Over the next decade, these reforms are expected to expand coverage to 32 million Americans, make health care more affordable, and improve the quality of care. The Affordable Care Act is also fiscally responsible. The Congressional Budget Office has estimated that the law will reduce projected deficits by $230 billion during 2012–21 and by more than $1 trillion in the subsequent decade.

Energy Policy

Energy plays a critical role in the economy, and Chapter 6 outlines key steps the Administration is taking to transition the Nation toward cleaner sources of energy that have the potential to support new industries, exports, and high-quality jobs; to improve air quality and reduce the dangers of climate change; and to enhance America's energy security and international competitiveness.

As an initial step, the Recovery Act directed over $90 billion in public investment and tax incentives to increasing renewable energy sources such as wind and solar power, weatherizing homes, and boosting R&D for new technologies. Looking forward, the President has proposed a Federal Clean Energy Standard to double the share of electricity produced by clean sources to 80 percent by 2035, a substantial commitment to cleaner transportation infrastructure, and has increased investments in energy efficiency and clean energy R&D.

These programs are interconnected in important ways. They are all motivated by the fact that the national benefits from clean energy go beyond its immediate producers or consumers. The programs focus on different parts of the clean energy supply chain—innovation, manufacturing, generation, and use—and thus complement one another. And in the end, the Administration's clean energy programs are linked by the goal that in coming years Americans will breathe cleaner air, enjoy better health, face reduced risks from climate change, and work and do business in an economy based on a safer and more secure energy supply.

Supporting America's Small Businesses

America's small businesses are an essential building block to economic growth and prosperity, in part because entrepreneurs create a disproportionate share of net new jobs in the U.S. economy. Chapter 7 examines the heavy toll the recession took on small businesses, dramatically reducing the availability of credit and capital needed to add capacity, hire more workers, and develop new products. In response to these challenges, the Administration has taken several important steps, most notably through the Recovery Act, the Small Business Jobs Act, and the Startup America initiative, to increase the flow of credit and capital to small business.

The Administration has enacted 17 tax cuts for small businesses to support America's entrepreneurs. It has also enacted policies to make health insurance more affordable for small businesses and entrepreneurs and to facilitate small business exports to new markets overseas. Taken together, these efforts have improved the outlook for American small business and created a stronger environment for entrepreneurship.

Conclusion

The past year has seen crucial improvement in the American economy. Although the recession generated devastating job losses and an output decline of historic proportions, the economy is no longer on the brink of a depression. Growth has resumed, jobs are returning, and unemployment is falling. Now is the time to chart the course for an economy that will provide jobs, new and revitalized industries, and rising living standards for Americans. This *Report* lays out the central elements of the path forward.

C H A P T E R   2

THE YEAR IN REVIEW AND THE YEARS AHEAD

Following the deepest recession since the Great Depression, the U.S. economy completed its sixth consecutive quarter of recovery at the end of 2010. The recovery began in the second half of 2009 and the first half of 2010, but real gross domestic product (GDP) then decelerated around midyear before growth quickened again to 3.2 percent at an annual rate in the fourth quarter of 2010 (Figure 2-1). Private sector employment also decelerated during the summer, before picking up in the fourth quarter. With the financial crisis now well behind us, and considerable slack remaining in employment and resources, the U.S. economy has tremendous potential to grow without reigniting inflation.

Figure 2-1
Real GDP Growth by Quarter

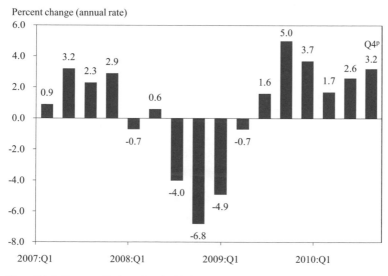

Note: Q4ᴾ indicates preliminary data for 2010:Q4.
Sources: Bureau of Economic Analysis, National Income and Product Accounts.

Consumption and Saving

Consumer spending composes about 70 percent of GDP and, as is typical, has been less volatile than the overall economy during this recession and recovery. Consumption made up about 40 percent of the decline in GDP during the recession and about 54 percent of the recent rebound. Movements in this important component of spending reflect changes in consumer sentiment, household wealth and income, credit availability, government income support programs, and taxes.

Measures of consumer sentiment fell to their lowest levels of the recession from November 2008 through February 2009 and rebounded sharply through May 2010. Confidence slipped a few points around midyear 2010 and then was roughly stable through October before picking up toward the end of the year. Nevertheless, sentiment remains well below pre-recession levels.

Figure 2-2
Consumer Sentiment and the Stock Market

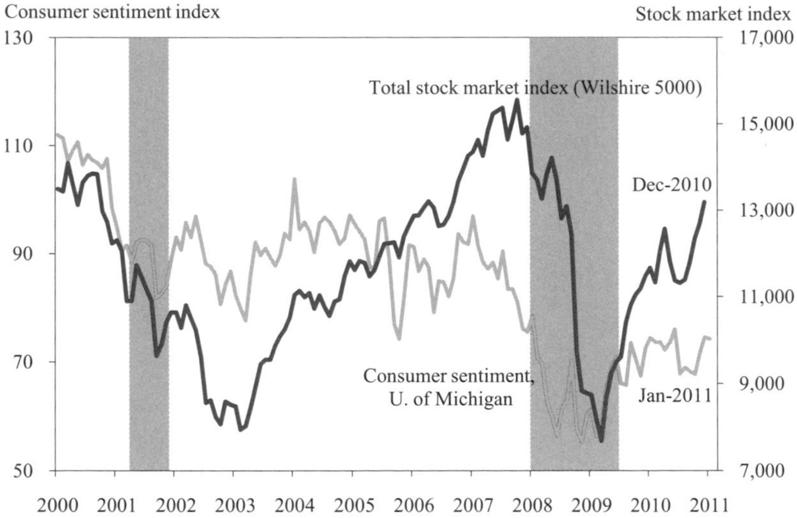

Note: Grey areas represent recessions.
Sources: Wilshire Associates Incorporated; Thompson Reuters (University of Michigan Surveys of Consumers).

Stock market fluctuations closely parallel those of consumer sentiment (Figure 2-2), with a few notable exceptions, such as during 2007, when sentiment started falling a year earlier than the stock market did. Nevertheless, sentiment and the stock market have shown similar rebounds during the recovery, recapturing by December 2010, 95 percent and 76 percent (respectively) of their recessionary decline since the December 2007 business-cycle peak. Thus, although sentiment and the stock market sometimes move independently, both have supported the 2010 growth in consumer spending.

Figure 2-3
Consumption and Net Worth Relative to Disposable Personal Income (DPI)

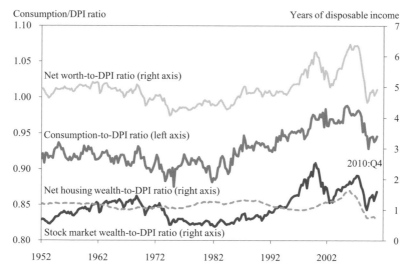

Note: Wealth components for 2010:Q4 were estimated by the CEA.
Sources: Bureau of Economic Analysis, National Income and Product Accounts; Federal Reserve Board; CEA calculations.

After consumer sentiment, a second prime determinant of consumer spending is household wealth (also called net worth). As can be seen in Figure 2-3, the consumption rate (the share of disposable income consumed) tends to fluctuate with the wealth-to-income ratio. A one dollar drop in wealth appears to reduce annual consumer spending by two to four cents. The decline in the wealth-to-income ratio from its 2007 average to its low point in the first quarter of 2009 amounted to 1.8 years of income. (In other words, household wealth declined by the amount of income earned in 1.8 years.) This was the deepest decline since compilation of these data began in 1952. Of this 1.8 year-of-income decline, 1.1 years of income was lost from stock market wealth, and about 0.6 year from housing wealth (net of mortgage debt owed). (Components of wealth aside from stock market wealth and housing wealth edged down slightly relative to income.) Since 2009:Q1, the wealth-to-income ratio has recovered about 0.4 year of income, with the rebound entirely due to stock market gains as housing and the other forms of wealth have edged a bit lower relative to disposable income. After netting out this rebound, the drop in wealth from 2007 through end-of-year 2010 has been about 1.3 years of income. A decline in wealth of this magnitude can be expected to set off an adjustment process that raises the saving rate by about 4.3 percentage points. With the saving rate having risen from an average of 1.9 percent during 2005–07 to 5.8 percent in 2010, the adjustment of personal saving to the lower level of household net worth is now in line with the fundamentals, taking the historical relationships as a guide.[1]

Another influence on consumer spending is the willingness of financial institutions to lend to households. Households prepare for lean times by saving out of regular income or by planning to draw on bank credit such as credit cards. When bank credit becomes less readily available, some households react by saving more so that they can build up their buffer stocks, and other households, who had been planning to draw on their credit lines, become unable to do so because credit is not available. The sharp decline in banks' willingness to lend during the recession (Figure 2-4) is among the reasons why the saving rate increased. During 2010, however, the Federal Reserve's Senior Loan Officers Survey shows that banks became somewhat more willing to lend to consumers.

Figure 2-4
Banks' Willingness to Lend to Consumers

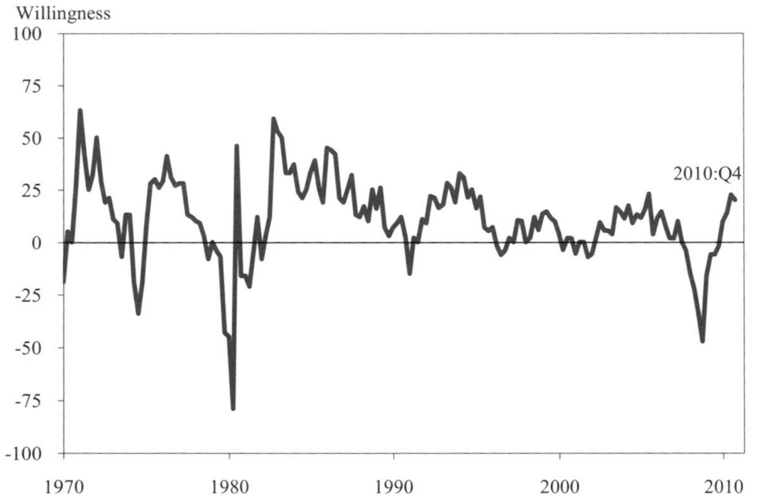

Note: Willingness = the net percentage of domestic respondents reporting increased willingness to make consumer installment loans.
Source: Federal Reserve Board, Senior Loan Officer Opinion Survey on Bank Lending Practices.

---

[1] The model was described in the 2010 *Economic Report*, pp. 117–20.

Various income support programs have also likely influenced consumer spending during the past year. Extended unemployment benefits and emergency unemployment benefits totaled $43 billion in 2009 and $65 billion in 2010, up from $8 billion in 2008. These benefits stabilized consumer spending relative to the path that it would have taken otherwise.

Consumer spending has also been sustained by other policies such as the Making Work Pay (MWP) tax credit, which provides up to $400 ($800 for working married couples) for those with earned income up to $75,000 ($150,000 for couples), and progressively less for those with income above these limits. For the economy as a whole, MWP lowered tax liabilities (and boosted disposable income) by roughly $50 billion and $57 billion in calendar years 2009 and 2010, respectively. For 2011, MWP is being replaced—by provisions of the Tax Relief, Unemployment Insurance Reauthorization, and Job Creation Act enacted by Congress at the end of 2010 (discussed more fully later in this Chapter). Provisions included a 2 percentage point, one-year reduction in the payroll tax that funds Social Security, reducing tax liabilities by about $112 billion. In addition, the new law supports consumer spending by continuing the extension of unemployment insurance through 2011. This new law was proposed, legislated, and signed after the Administration economic forecast was finalized, and so its effects are not included in that forecast.

Although purchases of durable goods, such as motor vehicles and household appliances, are regarded as consumption in the national income and product accounts, they can also be considered a form of investment because they are long-lasting and provide services for the duration of ownership. Consumer durable purchases are typically more volatile than other purchases, declining faster than overall consumption during a cyclical downturn and growing faster than overall consumption during cyclical recovery periods (for example, durable goods purchases grew at an 11.1 percent annual rate during the four quarters of 2010). Rapid growth of durables purchases may pull down the saving rate temporarily at some point during the early part of the recovery.

Developments in Housing Markets

As shown in Figure 2-5, the CoreLogic home price index, a comprehensive and closely watched measure of existing home prices, dropped 32 percent from the peak of the housing market in April 2006 to the trough in March 2009, following the bursting of the housing bubble that built up between 2002 and 2005. The United States had never before suffered such a sharp drop in national house prices. Although house prices fell about 30 percent in nominal terms during the Great Depression, general price levels at that time fell 25 percent. As a result, the real house price decline during the Great Depression was only about 7 percent. During the current episode, the overall inflation rate has slowed but not turned negative, making the recent decline in house prices far larger in real terms than that during the Depression.

Figure 2-5
House Prices

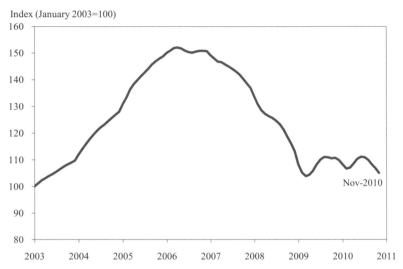

Index (January 2003=100)

Sources: First American CoreLogic National House Price Index including distressed sales; CEA calculations.

House prices have generally stabilized since March 2009, fluctuating around a roughly flat trend line. Nonetheless, house prices have been volatile over the past year, because of unusual market conditions such as the large supply of distressed homes on the market and the short-term impetus to demand from temporary tax credits for homebuyers. Among the factors that continue to keep sales and starts below their long-run trend levels are modest income growth, slower household formation, and tighter mortgage underwriting standards, as well as heightened uncertainty among potential homebuyers and the large "shadow inventory" of foreclosed and other distressed properties on (or soon to be on) the market.

The bursting of the housing bubble has posed serious challenges to homeowners. Houses are typically leveraged assets (that is, financed with debt); according to the Census Bureau's American Housing Survey, about 68 percent of owner-occupied houses carry a mortgage. Leverage amplifies the effects of price changes on household net worth because price changes affect asset values while leaving outstanding debt unchanged. Because mortgage debt does not change when house prices fall, declines in prices cause even larger declines in home equity (that is, the house value less total mortgage debt). For example, the owner of a $100,000 house with an $80,000 mortgage would have $20,000 in home equity. If prices fell 10 percent, the house would be worth $90,000 and home equity would fall to $10,000—a 50 percent decline in equity from a 10 percent decline in prices. The higher the leverage, the larger will be the decline in home equity for a given decline in the value of the house. For that reason, the 32 percent decline in house prices led to a 56 percent decline in home equity, resulting in a loss of about $7.5 trillion in net housing wealth over three years.

For many of the most highly leveraged households—in particular those who bought their homes near the peak of the market with no or low down payments—the decline in the value of their home was larger than their equity, meaning that their houses were worth less than their mortgages. Many of these underwater borrowers subsequently defaulted on their mortgage payments, often because they could not keep up with payments after losing income during the recession and could not sell their homes for enough to cover the mortgage debt. Although home prices in many parts of the country have stabilized, about a quarter of homeowners with mortgages remain underwater. Total negative equity is estimated to be roughly $750 billion. In the states with the highest shares of households underwater—Nevada, Arizona, Florida, Michigan, and California—a third or more of homeowners with mortgages have negative equity (in Nevada, the share is about two-thirds). These homeowners are the most likely to default on their loans: according to CoreLogic, the rate of foreclosure initiation rises steadily as negative equity increases, reaching about 14 percent for homeowners whose homes are worth less than half their mortgage balance.

As Figure 2-6 shows, although the foreclosure rate fell in 2010, it remains extraordinarily high by historical standards. The rate has stayed high partly because of long lags in the foreclosure timeline (a bank may take months or even years to resell a house after its original owner defaults on the mortgage) and partly because falling house prices exacerbated the recession, leading to job losses that fed back into more foreclosures. Problems with foreclosure paperwork that came to light last fall have contributed to the slower rate of new foreclosures as lenders take extra time to verify that foreclosures are properly documented.

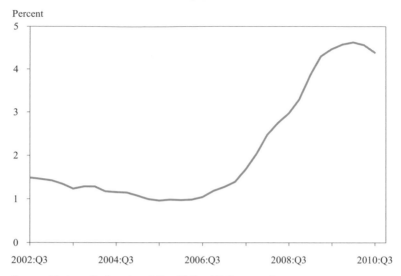

Figure 2-6
Share of Mortgages in Foreclosure

Percent

Source: Mortgage Bankers Association, National Delinquency Survey.

The Obama Administration, as well as the previous Administration and the Federal Reserve, took extraordinary policy actions in response to the enormous damage done by the collapse of housing markets. In September 2008, to keep the flow of new mortgage credit open, the Treasury placed the government-sponsored enterprises (GSEs), Fannie Mae and Freddie Mac, into conservatorship and committed sufficient capital to allow them to keep funding new mortgages. The Federal Housing Administration (FHA) also ramped up its lending substantially, offering new mortgages to many house-holds who could otherwise not obtain them. At the height of the boom, the combined market share of the GSE, FHA, and Veterans Administration loans was about 36 percent of new originations; today the share is about 90 percent. Meanwhile, from early 2009 through the first quarter of 2010, the Federal Reserve purchased $1.25 trillion—and the Treasury, more than $200 billion—of mortgage-backed securities guaranteed by Fannie Mae, Freddie Mac, and the Government National Mortgage Association (Ginnie Mae) on the open market, helping to push mortgage rates to record low levels. Many households were thus able to refinance their mortgages and reduce their monthly payments.

Nonetheless, weakness in the housing market has remained, resulting in continued foreclosures. The Administration's housing programs, including the Home Affordable Refinance Program (HARP), the Housing Affordable Modification Program (HAMP), and funds allocated to state and local housing finance agencies in the hardest-hit areas, have helped many borrowers achieve more affordable mortgages, but the housing market remains under stress in many areas, hampering the economic recovery.

Business Fixed Investment

Overall nonresidential investment grew at a rapid 10 percent annual rate during the four quarters of 2010, but its two main components diverged sharply. Equipment and software investment grew 16 percent, while investment in nonresidential structures fell 6 percent.

More than a third of the growth in equipment and software investment during 2010 was in information-processing equipment and software, which grew 11 percent. A bit less than a third was in transportation equipment, which grew 55 percent (with most of the strength in motor vehicles). Investment in industrial equipment also grew notably, 15 percent (accounting for more than an eighth of equipment and software investment growth).

Within the nonresidential structures category, investment in buildings fell in 2010, but that decline was partially offset by rapid growth of investment in structures for petroleum and natural gas drilling (51 percent at an annual rate). Declines in the buildings component were widespread, from health care facilities, to office buildings, shopping centers, factories, and power generation plants. Because of the long lead time required, investment in structures tends to lag cyclical turning points.

Overall business investment may be poised to grow rapidly because firms now appear to have plenty of internal funds. Corporate profits have rebounded almost to their pre-recession level. As a result, corporate cash flow, a measure of internal funds available for investment that includes undistributed profits and depreciation, has also risen substantially during the recovery. Ordinarily, nonresidential investment exceeds corporate cash flow (Figure 2-7), and the corporate sector as a whole must borrow to finance its investments. (Noncorporate entities are also responsible for some investment.) But because of the corporate sector's recent strong growth, net corporate cash flow today is in the unusual position of exceeding investment. A large share of these investable funds has been channeled to financial investments rather than to new physical capital, as can be seen by the rising level of liquid assets held by nonfinancial corporations.

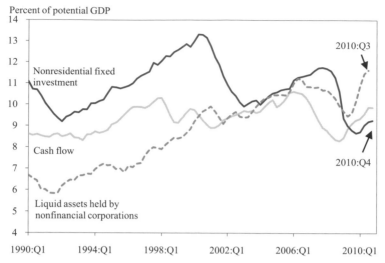

Figure 2-7
Business Fixed Investment and Cash Flow

Percent of potential GDP

Notes: Potential GDP is a CBO estimate. Cash flow is from the National Income and Product
Accounts, and nonfinancial liquid assets are plotted using their three-quarter moving averages.
Sources: Bureau of Economic Analysis, National Income and Product Accounts; Federal
Reserve Board (Flow of Funds L.102); Congressional Budget Office.

Another contribution to investment growth is the forecast increase in real GDP growth in 2011 because the level of investment is often related to the growth rate of GDP. Also spurring investment during 2011 will be the provision of the Tax Relief, Unemployment Insurance Reauthorization, and Job Creation Act allowing full expensing for tax purposes of equipment investment put in place during the year.

Business Inventories

Inventory investment played a large role in the initial stages of recovery. Inventory investment—that is, the change in inventories—is one of the components of GDP, so the change in inventory investment (the change in the change in inventories) affects the growth of GDP. Inventory investment was increasingly negative in the first and second quarters of 2009 (the light blue bars in Figure 2-8), and the inventory contribution to GDP growth was negative (the blue bars). Inventory investment started to rise in the third quarter of 2009, from a negative value to a less-negative one, and that rise contributed positively to GDP growth through the third quarter of 2010. During the first three quarters of 2010, inventory investment

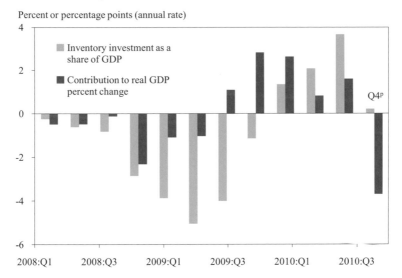

Figure 2-8
Inventory Investment and its Contribution to Real GDP Growth

Percent or percentage points (annual rate)

Notes: Inventory investment as a share of GDP is computed as 4 x [real inventory investment / real GDP(-1)]. Q4ᴾ indicates preliminary data for 2010:Q4.
Source: Bureau of Economic Analysis, National Income and Product Accounts; CEA calculations.

contributed an average of 1.7 percentage points at an annual rate to real GDP and accounted for more than half of the period's real GDP growth. Inventory investment commonly accounts for a high share of growth during the early stages of recovery.

By the third quarter, this recent increase in inventory investment had raised the stock of inventories, returning it to a more normal level relative to sales. The sharp fourth-quarter rise in final sales (7.1 percent at an annual rate according to preliminary data) exceeded the rise in production, and inventory investment dropped off sharply, subtracting more than 3 percentage points from GDP. Although inventories remain lean with respect to sales, they are less so than they were earlier in the recovery (Figure 2-9) so that inventory investment may play a smaller part in GDP growth over the next year than it did during the past two years.

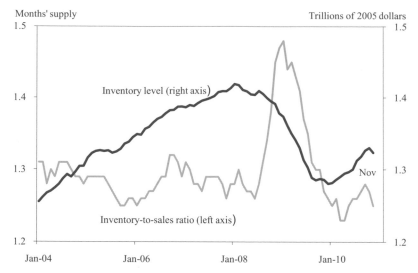

Figure 2-9
Manufacturing and Trade Inventories

Months' supply   Trillions of 2005 dollars

Inventory level (right axis)

Inventory-to-sales ratio (left axis)

Nov

Jan-04   Jan-06   Jan-08   Jan-10

Note: The real inventory level is from the National Income and Product Accounts, and the
inventory-to-sales ratio is from the Census Bureau.
Sources: Bureau of Economic Analysis, National Income and Product Accounts; Census Bureau.

Government Outlays, Consumption, and Investment

The Federal budget deficit on September 30, the end of fiscal year
2010, was $1.29 trillion, down about 8.5 percent from $1.41 trillion the
year before. As a share of GDP, the deficit fell from about 10 percent in FY
2009 to 8.9 percent in FY 2010. With the recovery beginning to take hold,
Federal receipts rose about 3 percent during 2010, while spending fell about
2 percent. Corporate tax receipts, in particular, increased nearly 39 percent
as taxable profits rose. Despite their pickup in 2010, corporate tax receipts
are still about half what they were in FY 2007—a measure of the depth of the
budget hole created by the recession. Receipts from individual income taxes
and payroll taxes continued to fall in FY 2010, in part because of lower labor
market activity linked to the recession and in part because of tax cuts for
households implemented as part of the Recovery Act of 2009.

The Recovery Act was enacted when U.S. real GDP was contracting
at an annual rate of more than 6 percent and employment was falling by
more than 700,000 jobs a month. The Recovery Act's spending provisions,
tax cuts, and aid to states and individuals were designed to cushion the
fall in demand caused by the financial crisis and the subsequent decline in
consumer and business confidence, household wealth, and access to credit.
As of the third quarter of 2010, the Council of Economic Advisers (CEA)
estimates that the Recovery Act has raised the level of GDP, relative to what

it otherwise would have been, by 2.7 percent and raised employment, relative to what it otherwise would have been, by between 2.7 million and 3.7 million jobs.[2]

According to the Congressional Budget Office (CBO 2010), net Federal outlays arising from the financial crisis—including the Troubled Assets Relief Program (TARP), Federal deposit insurance payouts, and Treasury payments to the government-sponsored enterprises Fannie Mae and Freddie Mac—were $367 billion lower in 2010 than in 2009, because of lower spending and additional repayments of TARP loans. Repayments by banks under TARP accounted for a large share of the additional receipts. In 2009, the Administration estimated that TARP would cost $341 billion. These estimates have steadily decreased, and following recent developments such as repayments from the insurance company AIG and sales of government-owned shares of stock in General Motors and Citigroup, the President's 2012 Budget estimates TARP's deficit cost will be $48 billion. Recent estimates from the CBO are even lower. By contrast, short-term recession-related spending increased during 2010; spending on defense and entitlement programs such as Social Security and Medicare also rose, though at a slower pace than its average over the past five years. Overall, spending fell from about 25 percent of GDP in 2009 to 23.8 percent in 2010. Excluding short-term expenditures, spending relative to GDP was about 21 percent in 2010, roughly the same as its average over the past 30 years.

Deficits are expected to decline quickly over the coming years as the recovery picks up, short-term countercyclical measures wind down, and the Administration's proposed budget cuts occur. As shown in Figure 2-10, the Administration projects that the deficit as a share of GDP will fall from 10.9 percent in FY 2011 to 4.6 percent in FY 2013, and to 3.2 percent in FY 2015.

Nonetheless, major long-term fiscal challenges remain. Even before the financial crisis and ensuing recession, the long-run budget outlook was problematic, in part because a series of policy choices over the past decade had reduced projected revenue while increasing projected spending. At the same time, trying to balance the budget all at once would be counterproductive because the recovery of the private sector is still fragile and would likely be imperiled by a sharp and immediate fiscal contraction.

The 2010 Tax Relief, Unemployment Insurance Reauthorization, and Job Creation Act, passed in December 2010, extended tax cuts for all Americans for two years. As a result of the new law, families will not see their taxes increase in 2011 and 2012, as had been scheduled. It also introduces a 2 percentage point payroll tax cut that will provide about $112 billion of

---

[2] See CEA (2010b). The CEA uses two methods of estimating the impact of the Recovery Act on employment. The multiplier approach yields 2.7 million jobs, while the statistical projection approach yields 3.7 million.

tax relief to working Americans in 2011. In addition, the new law continues the extension of unemployment insurance so that workers who lost their job through no fault of their own will continue to receive support through 2011. Together, the tax cuts and additional unemployment insurance payments will boost consumption. The new law also introduces strong incentives to firms to invest in 2011 by allowing them to expense the full cost of their equipment investment.

Figure 2-10
Deficit as a Share of GDP

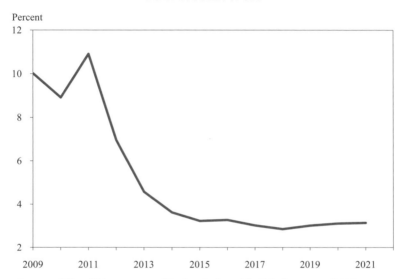

Sources: Office of Management and Budget, *Budget of the U.S. Government* (2011);
Bureau of Economic Analysis, National Income and Product Accounts.

In the absence of new tax legislation, the simultaneous expiration of the Making Work Pay tax cuts and of the tax cuts enacted between 2001 and 2003 would have reduced real GDP growth over the four quarters of 2011 by 0.9–2.8 percentage points, according to the Congressional Budget Office (CBO 2011). The positive impact of the new law exceeded what most private forecasters had been expecting for fiscal policy, leading them to increase their estimates of 2011 growth. At the same time, the package is constructed to be temporary (including one- and two-year provisions) so that its effect on the long-term deficit is minimal.

Still, the need for medium- and long-term fiscal consolidation is clear. For the medium term, President Obama has announced an ambitious goal of cutting the deficit in half by 2013. To help meet that target, the Administration has proposed a number of new initiatives to help restore fiscal discipline, including a five-year freeze on nonsecurity discretionary spending, a two-year freeze on Federal wages, a slowdown in the growth of defense spending, and eliminating earmarks from the appropriations process. These proposals build on a number of steps that the Administration has already taken to reduce deficits in coming years, the most important of which is enactment of the Patient Protection and Affordable Care Act of 2009. If the cost-control provisions of the law are followed over the next several decades, they will have a profound effect on the budget. A second critical step was the enactment of the Statutory Pay-As-You-Go Act, which requires Congress to offset most spending increases with tax increases or reduced spending elsewhere, an important move toward fiscal responsibility. In addition, economic growth will affect the long-run ratio of debt to GDP. Steps to spur that growth are discussed in depth in Chapter 3.

State and Local Government

The operating deficit of state and local government has improved during the recovery but remains precarious because of the severity of the downturn. In addition, while funds from the Recovery Act helped to support state and local revenues during 2009 and 2010, that support is scheduled to diminish. The continuing distress is evident from the 414,000 jobs that the sector lost between August 2008, the peak of state and local employment, and December 2010. The state and local sector's direct contribution to real GDP growth was negative during the four quarters of 2009 and remained so through the first quarter of 2010. Its GDP contribution was close to zero during the final three quarters of 2010.

State and local tax revenues reached a low point in the second quarter of 2009 but then grew 8 percent for the five quarters through the third quarter of 2010, recovering $103 billion, or most of their nominal decline during the preceding four quarters. Almost half of the recovery in tax receipts ($47 billion) came from corporate taxes, a source that usually provides only about 4 percent of state and local tax revenues. Sales and property taxes, by contrast, grew more slowly than the overall economy. Federal grants-in-aid (mostly for Medicaid and education) generally increased during 2009 and 2010 because of the Recovery Act, which provided a cumulative $147.1 billion in such grants through 2010:Q3.

Current state and local government expenditures—which include transfers to individuals as well as government consumption—have grown slowly since the business-cycle trough in the second quarter of 2009, at a 3.0 percent annual rate through the third quarter of 2010, compared with a 4.0 percent growth rate of nominal GDP. The combination of restrained spending growth, a recovery in tax revenues, and increased Federal transfers moved the current operating position of state and local governments from a maximum deficit of $67 billion at an annual rate in the third quarter of 2008 to a surplus of $45 billion in the third quarter of 2010.

Real investment by state and local governments (which is not part of current expenditures) fell over the four quarters of 2009 and the first quarter of 2010 but edged up in the second and third quarters of 2010. The gain in investment spending likely reflects the recent increase in capital transfers for transportation under the Recovery Act.

During 2011 and 2012, state and local governments will have to make tough budget decisions. The sector is likely to show little spending growth as Federal transfers diminish and past declines in house prices restrain growth in the property tax base, which accounts for about a third of tax collections. One point of relative strength in the near term, however, is state and local construction spending (for example, on roads and bridges), as the longer-lived portions of the Recovery Act investments are translated into public infrastructure capital.

Real Exports and Imports

Real exports grew 9 percent during the four quarters of 2010, a rebound following a 3 percent contraction in 2008 and no change in 2009. The rebound coincides with a general recovery of non-U.S. GDP beginning in mid-2009 (Figure 2-11). In addition to its sensitivity to the economic strength of our trading partners, U.S. export performance also reflects movements in relative prices across countries. The broad index of the real value of the dollar rose during the recession—compounding the effect of falling world demand—but has generally fallen since March 2009, depreciating a total of 3 percent during the 12 months of 2010.

Figure 2-11
U.S. Exports and World GDP

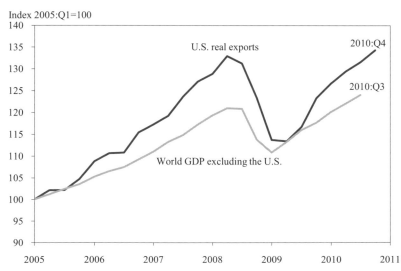

Sources: Bureau of Economic Analysis, National Income and Product Accounts; country sources; CEA calculations.

Shrinking exports subtracted from GDP growth in each quarter between 2008:Q3 and 2009:Q2, but real exports have added to GDP in every quarter since, including adding 1.1 percent to real GDP growth over the four quarters of 2010. In the coming years, a combination of strong growth in many key export markets should allow for continued growth in real exports (see Chapter 4 for a detailed discussion of the recovery of U.S. exports).

Real imports grew 11 percent during the four quarters of 2010. Although they grew faster than real exports, they had also fallen more steeply than real exports during 2008 (6 percent) and 2009 (7 percent). The pattern in real imports parallels, but is sharper than, the general shape of the contraction and rebound in overall U.S. personal consumption spending. Because imports tend to be concentrated more in goods than is overall consumer spending, real imports move more closely with goods consumption—which is cyclically sensitive—than with consumption overall. And because business equipment investment includes imported capital goods, real imports track this cyclically sensitive series as well.

Labor Market Trends

The recession's impact on the labor market was severe, and it will take time before the labor market regains full strength. Figure 2-12 illustrates the pattern of employment (excluding jobs associated with the decennial Census) from its peak for each of the previous three recessions. The figure

Figure 2-12
Path of Non-Census Employment in the Past Three Recessions

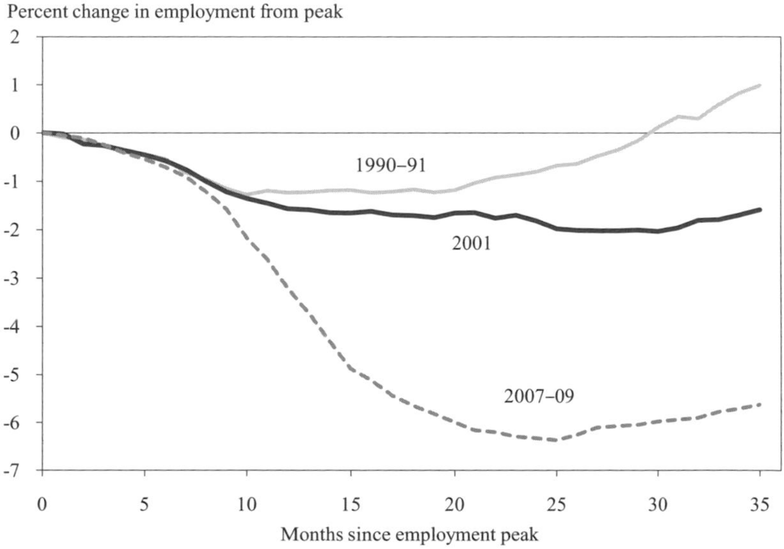

Sources: Bureau of Labor Statistics, Current Employment Statistics; CEA calculations.

shows that the first several months of job losses associated with the 2007–09 recession (the dashed line) followed a pattern almost identical to those of the two previous recessions, those of 1990–91 and 2001.[3] Beginning in summer 2008, however, job losses became more severe, resulting in a much longer and deeper recession.[4] By the time President Obama took office in January 2009, the economy was shedding more than 700,000 jobs a month, and employment reached its trough in February 2010. Between the peak of employment in January 2008 and the trough, the economy lost 8.75 million nonfarm jobs—almost as many as were lost in the past three recessions (1981–82, 1990–91, and 2001) combined, adjusting for growth in the size of the economy. Job losses as a share of the economy were the largest the United States has experienced in 65 years.

Despite these historic employment losses, sustained albeit modest job growth began relatively quickly after the recession officially ended. Figure 2-13 compares the path of non-Census employment following this recession with those of the previous two recoveries, normalized to the level of employment at the official end date of each recession. As can be seen, job losses

Figure 2-13
Path of Non-Census Employment Since the End of the Recession

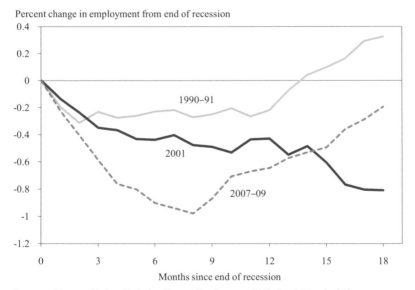

Sources: Bureau of Labor Statistics, Current Employment Statistics; CEA calculations.

[3] Figures 2-12 and 2-13 show non-Census jobs. The Census hired and subsequently laid off more than half a million temporary workers in 2010. These month-to-month changes affect headline numbers but are less reflective of labor market fundamentals. Thus, we exclude Census jobs from this employment series.

[4] The official end date of the 2007–09 recession was June 2009, a full 18 months after the recession officially began. In contrast, both the 2001 and 1990–91 recessions officially lasted 8 months.

continued after the end of each recession, with the most recent recovery continuing to experience the deepest losses. However, in the recovery from the 2007–09 recession (dashed line), non-Census job growth began 9 months into the recovery and continued in each month through December 2010 (the 18th month after the end of the recession). By comparison, the 1990–91 recovery (light blue line) was somewhat delayed, experiencing no net job creation until 12 months into the recovery. In sharp contrast, the 2001 recovery (dark blue line) continued to lose jobs throughout the comparable time period, and sustained job growth did not begin until 22 months after the official end date of the recession. Thus, while the 2007–09 recession lasted longer and job losses were much deeper than in either the recession of 1990–91 or 2001, recovery in the labor market began sooner.

Beyond these trends, 2010 also saw improvements along other margins of labor adjustment. Generally speaking, one would expect the workweek and the use of temporary help to grow before total employment begins to grow, because firms can lengthen the workweek and use temporary help to increase labor input without having to bear the fixed costs, such as benefits, associated with hiring a permanent worker. During the recession, the workweek for production and nonsupervisory employees lost 0.8 hour. However, it gained back nearly two-thirds of that loss in the next 13 months, reaching 33.5 hours in July 2010, and maintained that level throughout the second half of the year. This gain is important, because a 0.1 hour gain for employed workers is roughly equivalent in terms of labor input to an increase in employment of more than 300,000 jobs. Likewise, temporary help services, which lost about 800,000 jobs during the recession, began to grow toward the end of 2009 and saw strong gains in 2010. The industry has now gained back more than half its losses.

Most important, private sector employment has grown in every month since March of 2010, adding a total of 1.1 million jobs during 2010 and recording the strongest private sector job growth since 2006. Total nonfarm employment fared nearly as well, adding more than 900,000 jobs during 2010, though this job growth was tempered by a loss of 243,000 jobs in local government.

However, it is clear that the economy still has a long way to go before it fully recovers. Recessions resulting from a financial crisis tend to be deeper than other types of recessions, and recovery from them is more difficult (Reinhart and Reinhart 2010; Reinhart and Rogoff 2009). State and local governments continue to face substantial budget shortfalls that have led to cuts in public sector employment. The national unemployment rate, which fell 0.7 percentage point from its peak to December, remains elevated, with more than 6 million people in long-term unemployment (defined as having been jobless and searching for work for 27 weeks or more) as of December 2010.[5] Further, although the number of job seekers per job opening had fallen to 4.7 in December (from a high of more than 6), it remains unacceptably high.

Policy Responses to Support the Labor Market. The Administration's first major step in addressing the severe contraction of the labor market was the Recovery Act, which kept the employment situation from getting substantially worse. In fact, the CEA has previously estimated that in the absence of the Recovery Act, non-Census employment growth would not have begun until the third quarter of 2010 (or roughly 14 months from the official end date of the recession; see Figure 2-13), which would have placed the current recovery more in line with the slower employment responses of the previous two recessions.

In addition, in March of 2010, President Obama signed the Hiring Incentives to Restore Employment (HIRE) Act, which cuts payroll taxes for employers hiring workers who have been unemployed for at least 60 days. The law contains two key provisions. First, it exempted employers from paying their share of Social Security taxes (6.2 percent of wages) on qualified workers hired from February 4, 2010 to December 31, 2010, and offset these losses to the Social Security Trust Fund with general fund revenues; this provision of the law ended in 2010. Second, for each hire that is retained for at least one year, the law gives the employer a general business tax credit equal to 6.2 percent of that employee's yearly wages, up to a maximum of $1,000. According to the Department of the Treasury, from February to November of 2010, an estimated 11.8 million workers who had been unemployed for eight weeks or longer were hired, qualifying their employers for the HIRE Act payroll tax exemption.

In August 2010, in response to the continuing job losses in state and local government, the President signed the Education Jobs and Medicaid Assistance Act, which provided $10 billion to states to prevent layoffs of teachers. According to CEA estimates, this critical assistance supported 160,000 teacher jobs during the 2010–11 academic year.

---

[5] The unemployment rate is a prominent, but incomplete, measure of labor market well-being. If workers are encouraged or discouraged by labor market conditions, they may enter or exit the labor force, moving the unemployment rate in the opposite direction of the economy's momentum. However, thus far in the recession and recovery, other measures of labor underutilization (for example, the employment-to-population ratio or measures including those working part-time for economic reasons) have shown patterns similar to the unemployment rate.

In addition, the Administration made several efforts over the past year to help small businesses and promote entrepreneurship. The measures included passing numerous tax cuts for small business, signing the Small Business Jobs Act, and launching Startup America in early 2011. These policies are discussed in detail in Chapter 7.

All of these policy responses were designed to put jobless Americans back in the workplace as quickly as possible, both for their own well-being and also for that of the nation as a whole. The labor market growth seen thus far is encouraging, especially compared with the recoveries following the 1990–91 and 2001 recessions, but obviously is only a start. More robust job creation is needed.

Prices

Price inflation as measured by the consumer price index excluding food and energy (known as the core CPI) moved lower in 2010, dropping to 0.8 percent from 1.8 percent during the two preceding years. The GDP price index excluding food and energy edged up slightly to a still-low 1.1 percent. (The GDP price index is the broadest index of what is produced in the United States including investment, exports, and government services in addition to consumer goods and services.)

There have been higher rates of inflation at some early stages of goods processing, but restrained growth of unit labor costs arising from a combination of low capacity utilization, elevated unemployment, and strong productivity growth have overwhelmed other influences as commodities are processed and moved down the supply chain toward the final consumer. Further, these commodity and materials prices make up only a small share of overall goods prices. Labor costs now make up about 58 percent of costs in the nonfarm business sector, and labor costs per unit of real output fell in 2009 and 2010.

The Administration's inflation forecast reflects three balancing forces: persistent downward pressure on inflation from the high levels of economic slack, a further expected pickup in economic growth, and fairly stable inflation expectations. The Administration's projected rise in CPI inflation to 1.4 percent in 2011 moves in the direction expected by the consensus of professional forecasters.

Financial Markets

From December 2009 through December 2010, stock market values rose, and yields on Treasury notes fell, but the movements were volatile in both cases. Long-term interest rates fell during these 12 months, also with some notable fluctuations.

Stock market values—as measured by the Standard and Poor's 500 Composite Index—rose 13 percent in 2010, following a 23 percent gain in 2009. Despite the back-to-back gains, the index at year's end was still 20 percent below its October 9, 2007, peak. Corporate profits rose rapidly in 2009 and 2010, and the gains in the stock market have not kept up with the gains in earnings. As a consequence, the price-to-earnings ratio for the S&P 500 had fallen by year's end to about 17, slightly below the average of the 50 years through 2007.

Indicators of financial stress improved dramatically during 2009 and changed little during the 12 months of 2010. The spread between the 3-month interbank lending rates and 3-month Treasury bill rates was only 16 basis points (or 0.16 percentage point) by December, considerably below its 2000–07 average of 45 basis points. Similarly the spread between AA- and B-rated corporate bonds had fallen to only 3.6 percentage points, somewhat below its 2000–2007 average of 4.1 percentage points. Also during 2010, banks eased standards on commercial and industrial loans.

Yields on 10-year Treasury notes in December 2010 were 3.29 percent, down from 3.59 percent in December 2009. Ten-year yields rose early in the year but fell more than a full percentage point from April to October, likely reflecting slow economic growth and a flight to quality triggered by concerns abroad. Falling inflation expectations may also have been a factor in the mid-year decline, as suggested by the premium paid for Treasury Inflation-Protected Securities (TIPS). During the last two months of 2010, long-term rates reversed part of their earlier decline. Despite the uptick at year's end, yields on 10-year Treasury notes were still at the low end of their historical range. Real rates (that is, after subtracting inflation expectations) were also low, as indicated by the TIPS market where rates around the 10-year horizon were about 1 percent.

When the Administration's economic forecast was finalized in mid-November 2010, the projected path for 91-day Treasury bills over the next two years was calibrated from rates in the market for federal funds futures, which suggested that rates would remain extremely low in 2011 and then edge up slightly in 2012.

Table 2-1
Administration Economic Forecast

	Nominal GDP	Real GDP (chain-type)	GDP price index (chain-type)	Con-sumer price index (CPI-U)	Un-employ-ment rate (percent)	Interest rate, 91-day Treasury bills (percent)	Interest rate, 10-year Treasury notes (percent)	Nonfarm payroll employ-ment (average monthly change, Q4-to-Q4, thou-sands)
	Percent change, Q4-to-Q4				Level, calendar year			
2009 (actual)	0.6	0.2	0.5	1.5	9.3	0.2	3.3	-44
2010	4.0	2.5	1.5	1.0	9.6	0.1	3.2	76
2011	4.3	3.1	1.2	1.4	9.3	0.2	3.0	146
2012	5.7	4.0	1.6	1.9	8.6	0.9	3.6	194
2013	6.2	4.5	1.6	1.9	7.5	2.6	4.2	275
2014	6.0	4.2	1.7	2.0	6.6	3.7	4.6	277
2015	5.4	3.6	1.7	2.0	5.9	4.0	4.9	224
2016	5.1	3.2	1.8	2.1	5.5	4.1	5.2	182
2017	4.5	2.7	1.8	2.1	5.3	4.1	5.3	138
2018	4.3	2.5	1.8	2.1	5.3	4.1	5.3	113
2019	4.4	2.5	1.8	2.1	5.3	4.1	5.3	99
2020	4.3	2.5	1.8	2.1	5.3	4.1	5.3	97
2021	4.3	2.5	1.8	2.1	5.3	4.1	5.3	93

Notes: Based on data available as of November 17, 2010. Interest rate on 91-day T-bills includes secondary market discount basis. The figures do not reflect the upcoming BLS benchmark revision, which is expected to reduce 2009 and 2010 job growth by a cumulative 366,000 jobs.
Sources: Department of Commerce (Bureau of Economic Analysis and Economics and Statistics Administration); Department of Labor (Bureau of Labor Statistics); Department of the Treasury; Office of Management and Budget; CEA calculations.

THE LONG-TERM OUTLOOK

Looking ahead, the Administration projects moderate GDP growth of 3.1 percent in 2011, with growth then rising to an average rate of 4.1 percent during the next four years. Table 2-1 reports the Administration's forecast used in preparing the President's fiscal year 2012 Budget. (The long lead time for the budget process necessitates completing the forecast by mid-November, which was before the year-end agreement on the Tax Relief, Unemployment Insurance Reauthorization, and Job Creation Act of 2010.) The Administration estimates that potential GDP growth—the rate of growth of real GDP that could be sustained with the economy at full employment and steady inflation—will be roughly 2.5 percent a year (Table 2-2, line 8). During 2011, projected GDP growth is slightly stronger than potential growth, and the unemployment rate is projected to tick down. Monthly payroll employment is expected to increase each year in 2011,

2012, and 2013. In the Administration forecast, real GDP grows faster than its potential rate through 2017, gradually closing the gap between the actual and the potential level of GDP.

The growth rate of the economy over the long run is determined by the growth rate of its supply-side components, which include population, labor force participation, the ratio of nonfarm business employment to household employment, the workweek, labor productivity, and the ratio of real GDP to nonfarm business output. The Administration's forecast for the contribution of the growth rates of these supply-side factors to potential real GDP growth is shown in Table 2-2. Together, the sum of all of these components equals the growth rate of potential real GDP, which is projected at 2.5 percent a year.

Table 2-2
Components of Potential Real GDP Growth, 1953–2021

	Growth rate	
Component	1953:Q2 to 2007:Q4	2010 to 2021
1 Civilian noninstitutional population aged 16+	1.4	1.0
2 Labor force participation rate	0.2	-0.3
3 Employment rate	0.0	0.0
4 Ratio of nonfarm business employment to household employment	0.0	0.0
5 Average weekly hours (nonfarm business)	-0.3	-0.1
6 Output per hour (productivity, nonfarm business)	2.1	2.3
7 Ratio of real GDP to nonfarm business output	-0.2	-0.4
8 SUM: potential real GDP	3.2	2.5
9 Memo: actual real GDP	3.2	3.2

Note: All contributions are in percentage points at an annual rate. 1953:Q2 and 2007:Q4 are business-cycle peaks. Nonfarm business employment, workweek, and productivity come from the productivity and cost database maintained by the Bureau of Labor Statistics.
Sources: Department of the Treasury; Office of Management and Budget; CEA calculations.

CONCLUSION

The U.S. economy today has substantial excess capacity and therefore vast potential to grow without igniting an increase in inflation. The overall trend of economic data toward the end of 2010 has been encouraging. The Administration's efforts to continue tax cuts for the middle class, extend unemployment insurance, and provide incentives for business investment strengthen prospects for continued recovery in 2011.

CHAPTER 3

THE FOUNDATIONS OF GROWTH

As the United States economy shifts from crisis to recovery and growth, policy must also be rebalanced to emphasize the foundations of growth that promise Americans a stronger and more prosperous future. Policy must move beyond the short-run demands of the business cycle to support the broader economic environment that ensures rapid, broad-based, and sustained economic growth, bringing Americans greater income, higher-quality jobs, and longer and healthier lives.

At the core of the Nation's economic growth is our capacity to innovate, educate, and build. Innovation, drawing on a long tradition of American ingenuity, has made American workers and businesses world leaders in productivity. With private sector investments in the lead, U.S. marketplaces provide the test beds in which new ideas are proven and the means by which successful ideas spread. At the same time, the creation and diffusion of new ideas require essential public inputs in education, infrastructure, and the national innovation system, which all work together to sustain and accelerate U.S. economic growth. This chapter considers the foundations of that economic growth and the public policies that will ensure America's continuing economic success.

THE IMPORTANCE OF ECONOMIC GROWTH

Rapid and sustained economic growth is a defining feature of U.S. history. Figure 3-1 shows the rise of real U.S. income per person from the Industrial Revolution in the early 19th century to the present. Adjusted for inflation, income per person in 2007 was double its level in 1971. Income per person in 1971 was double its level in 1940, and income per person in 1940—even after a decade of the Great Depression—was double its level in 1896. All told, average income per person in the United States today is 25 times what it was in 1820 (Maddison 2008). Income does not rise in every year, and it can fall sharply, but over the longer run the upward trend clearly dominates short-run cycles. The experience of the American economy in the past two years has been especially difficult, but Figure 3-1 also makes clear that, if America can capitalize on its long-run legacy of growth, then the Nation can expect to grow beyond its current challenges and reach new economic heights.

Figure 3-1
Progress in U.S. Real Income Per Person Since 1820

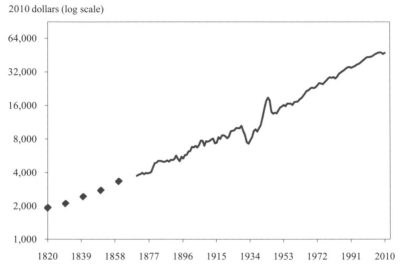

Sources: Maddison (2008); Bureau of Economic Analysis, National Income and Product Accounts.

Beyond the summary measure of income per person, the progress in American standards of living can be seen in how we live our lives—and how long those lives are. Life expectancy in the United States in the early to mid-1800s was approximately 40 years. Fifteen percent of children did not survive their first year of life, and over 30 percent did not reach their fifth birthday in many American cities (Haines 2001). Today, life expectancy is 78, and infant mortality has fallen by a factor of 20. In the early 1800s, primary school was the height of most Americans' educational attainment. Telegraphs and telephones had not been invented, let alone e-mail and wireless communications. There were no automobiles, no airplanes. There were no washing machines, dishwashers, air conditioners, or electric refrigerators. Indeed, there was no electrification—no light bulbs, radios, televisions, computers, or Internet—and none of the associated services that Americans now enjoy.

Overall, the economic growth imperative is clear. The improvements in income, health, and the variety and quality of products Americans consume all demonstrate the remarkable increase in prosperity the United States has enjoyed throughout its history. If the United States continues the same, sustained growth rate it has averaged since 1870, Americans can look forward to real incomes that are twice as high per person by 2046 and five and a half times higher in 2100, with new opportunities, higher-paying jobs, better educations, and healthier, longer lives.

Sources of Economic Growth

Any assessment of the appropriate role of growth policy starts with an analysis of how economic growth works, that is, how economies increase their output per person. Most directly, economists analyze the sources of growth by asking how the "inputs" workers use increase their output per unit of time. Economics offers three key ingredients for growth.

First, physical capital inputs, such as machines, tools, and infrastructure, make workers more productive. For example, investments in telecommunications equipment allow information to be exchanged rapidly, making wide arrays of workers, from emergency personnel to business managers, more productive. One source of growth, then, is this "physical capital deepening," investments that increase the amount of physical capital per worker.

Second, skill formation makes workers more productive. Investments in skill formation, or "human capital," include general education but also education specific to certain occupations, such as engineering, medicine, and law, as well as training to use certain types of machines and tools. For example, investment in training telecommunications engineers pays off in improved communication services. Thus, another source of growth is this deepening of human capital investments that raise the skills of workers.

Third, growth in advanced economies like the United States ultimately depends on technological progress, interpreted broadly to mean the creation and diffusion of new ideas. To continue the communications example, the advent of the telephone transformed people's ability to communicate, but once fixed-line telephones had spread across America, increasing the number of telephones per person had no such transformational power. Further progress awaited the invention of better communications technologies—the fax machine, the mobile telephone, the Internet—which have spurred additional investment in capital and further increased worker productivity. Technological progress drives capital deepening and creates new avenues to increased prosperity.

The foundational role of underlying technological progress can be inferred by considering the advance of major sectors of the U.S. economy. For example, advances in transportation were made possible by the invention and diffusion of numerous technologies, including engines, trains, automobiles, and airplanes. People and goods can now cross the country in six hours instead of months. This improvement was achieved through the invention of ever more advanced technologies. Box 3-1 considers an additional example—the advance of human health—at greater length.

Unfortunately, there are cracks in the foundations of America's growth that need to be addressed. The Nation's innovation system relies largely on the private sector but also depends on critical public inputs. For example, basic scientific breakthroughs in engineering, genetics, chemistry, and many other fields underpin commercial innovation but provide little or no direct profit themselves, so basic scientific research relies heavily on public support. Yet publicly funded research and development fell steadily from the early 1960s until recently.

Box 3-1: Technological Progress and the Advance of Health

Improvements in health have been possible through numerous medical advances. Polio, smallpox, diphtheria, and other debilitating or deadly viruses have been checked by vaccines. Bacterial infections, following the discovery of penicillin in 1928, are now treated by a wide range of antibiotics. Advances in controlling infection, bleeding, and pain made modern surgery possible, allowing surgeons to save and improve lives. Meanwhile, advances in the understanding of anatomy, molecular and cell biology, genetics, chemical synthesis, nuclear physics, and other areas have produced cascades of innovations for the diagnosis and treatment of disease. From laser eye surgery to X-ray, MRI, and ultrasound imaging technologies, to effective chemotherapies for particular cancers and pharmaceuticals that manage blood pressure, insulin levels, asthma, and many other chronic conditions, human health technologies have taken enormous leaps.

Health improvements raise workers' productivity, and increasing longevity can both extend working lives and encourage higher education. These mechanisms work to enhance economic growth. But much of the benefit of improved health—whether the decline in infant mortality or the direct enjoyment of longer lives—cannot be measured simply by tracking income per person. Thus, the benefits brought by these technological advances stand largely in addition to the 25-fold increase in U.S. per capita income since 1820.

Meanwhile, U.S. investments in infrastructure no longer lead the world, either in traditional physical infrastructure or in new information networks. American households rank only 14th among advanced countries in the adoption of high-speed Internet, for example, and average advertised download speeds in the United States rank 24th. Failure to provide American workers and businesses with efficient, modern infrastructure raises costs and disrupts the marketplace, making it increasingly difficult for the American economy to provide world-leading productivity and innovation.

In skill formation, the United States once led the world in the proportion of college graduates. It now ranks ninth in this measure among adults aged 25 to 34. Meanwhile, the quality of the Nation's primary and secondary education substantially lags other countries, especially in science and mathematics. These educational challenges are among the factors associated with stagnating wages among less-educated workers and with widening wage inequality, and they are further associated with unequal access to important goods and services, including health care. Furthermore, these challenges present obstacles to American workers and businesses seeking the high-productivity, high-wage jobs in the 21st-century global economy.

Making America more competitive and growing the economy is a preeminent goal of the Obama Administration. The rest of this chapter identifies the path forward, focusing on critical public policies and investments—in the Nation's innovation system and infrastructure and in the skills of individual Americans—that support rapid, broad-based, and sustained increases in America's prosperity.

Innovation and Economic Growth

Innovation, the introduction of new or improved goods, services, or practices into the economy, depends critically on private sector interest. Businesses, operating in a competitive market system, have numerous advantages in the creation and implementation of useful new ideas (Box 3-2). At the same time, the social rewards to innovation often exceed the private rewards to the original innovator, so the private sector may fall short in providing innovations and economic growth (Box 3-3). The Obama Administration is working to shore up the foundations of our national innovation system through critical public investments that will accelerate our future prosperity.

Box 3-2: The Power of Market-Based Innovation

Good ideas come from many quarters and from surprising directions, so their nature and source are fundamentally hard to foresee. The market system draws on American ingenuity from the ground up, relying on those individuals with close proximity to particular goods, services, or practices to develop the next-generation idea. Innovation can come from established firms, which developed the transistor, laser, and smartphone, for example, and from entrepreneurs, who led the creation of airplanes, personal computers, and Internet search engines.

Markets provide the crucible in which innovations are tested, then improved or discarded. Ultimately, it is buyers—consumers and other firms—who decide whether a new or improved good or service is worth paying for. The market system, with its price signals about costs and consumer demand, helps businesses direct their innovative efforts to high-value areas.

Once an idea is successfully demonstrated in the market, the market system invites other innovators to build on these ideas. For example, the laser turned out to have applications—in surgical devices and manufacturing tools, in computer printers, barcode scanners, and DVD players—far beyond those its early creators imagined. Early and uncertain visions of a large market for personal computers were realized only through a torrent of marketplace innovations across a vast array of established and entrepreneurial firms.

The market system also works to spread the best ideas, because competitive pressures favor the expansion of those firms with the most efficient methods and most desirable products. Flexible capital and labor markets pivot scarce resources toward the best ideas, constantly reinventing the American economy.

Basic Research

Basic scientific research typically has little direct commercial return, so its costs are not easily borne by firms. Yet downstream, commercial innovation is dependent on achievements in basic science. The biotechnology industry builds on Watson and Crick's discovery of the structure of DNA. The Web-based innovations and storefronts of the new economy build on government and university development of the Internet. Americans draw on achievements in basic science throughout their daily lives—in driving a car, using an electronic device, taking modern medications, talking on a telephone, or finding information online.

Box 3-3: The Social Gains from Innovation

The social gains from innovation typically extend well beyond the profits earned by the innovative enterprise. Telephones, light bulbs, subway trains, dishwashers, antibiotics, lasers, computers, Web browsers, and smartphones, for example, all offer large and ongoing social gains for Americans that far outstrip any commercial return to the original innovators. There are several reasons for this tendency. First, users will pay for an innovation only if its benefits exceed its price. These benefits in excess of the price—the "consumer surplus"—mean that much of the innovation's immediate value will accrue to the users rather than to the innovator. Second, the innovating business will face pressures to lower prices as other businesses imitate the successful innovation, especially once any intellectual property rights expire, transferring the innovation's value more fully to the user. Finally, a successful innovation often launches additional innovations, the benefits of which are not captured by the original innovator and additionally spill over to users.

Given that these users are workers or consumers, the social gains from innovation largely accrue through rising labor compensation, new workforce opportunities, and the higher quality and increasing variety of Americans' consumption. On average, the private firm may capture only a small percentage of the social gain from innovation. Thus, all Americans have an important stake in the innovation system. At the same time, because technological advances can be biased toward educated workers, investments in human capital become critical to ensure that the gains from workplace innovations remain widely shared, as discussed at the end of this chapter.

Given the importance of basic research, coupled with its low private return, the American innovation system relies on public support of university and government researchers who work to develop scientific breakthroughs and make these breakthroughs publicly available. This open science model for basic research expands collective knowledge and allows anyone with a good idea to tap these advances. Whether discovering fundamental properties of nature, developing understandings of disease that open new pathways for treatment, or creating the breakthroughs in nanotechnology that may revolutionize modern manufacturing, basic science will continue to create new foundations for future progress.

In 2009, the Obama Administration put in place the largest funding increase in basic science in U.S. history with an $18.3 billion contribution from the American Recovery and Reinvestment Act. More broadly, the Administration is committed to doubling the long-term funding for three key basic science agencies, the National Science Foundation, the Department of Energy's Office of Science, and the National Institute of Standards and Technology laboratories. With these commitments and others, the Administration is working towards those frontiers that promise new industries and new growth. In clean energy and electric vehicles, nanotechnology, advanced manufacturing, biotechnology, wireless communications, and other promising fields, the Administration is deploying resources to create fundamental breakthroughs at the beginning of the innovation pipeline. These priority areas are discussed further below.

Intellectual Property Rights

Effective protection of intellectual property rights, including patents and copyrights, is an essential role of government in encouraging innovation. Innovation typically requires substantial investments in the labor and materials necessary to create, develop, and test a new idea and then see it through to the marketplace. If others can steal the idea once it is proven, undermining the ability of the creator to recoup the costs of the innovative investment, then the incentive to innovate is reduced. Intellectual property rights address this problem by giving the innovator a limited-duration right to exclude others' use, thus helping to ensure that the private sector has the incentives to make innovative investments. In President Lincoln's words, the patent system adds "the fuel of interest to the fire of genius."

Intellectual property rights are particularly important to industries that make substantial investments in research and development (R&D), and R&D-intensive industries are leaders in driving U.S. growth and competitiveness. For example, among U.S. industries that produce internationally tradable goods and services, industries with above-average R&D levels generated more than twice the output and sales per employee, accounted for about 60 percent of exports, and accounted for five of the six U.S. industries that generated a trade surplus during the 2000–2007 period (Pham 2010).

Recognizing the importance of intellectual property, the Obama Administration is determined to improve the function of the patent system. The United States Patent and Trademark Office (USPTO) currently faces a backlog of 719,000 patent applications, and the average delay between patent application and patent grant has risen to 35 months. These delays are untenable for businesses, especially entrepreneurial businesses, which often rely on licensing their patents to generate revenue. The Obama Administration has begun to implement a five-year plan to improve the quality and timeliness of patent issuance. This strategic plan includes steps to redesign the agency's information technology infrastructure, reform the reward system for patent examiners, and hire 1,000 additional examiners, while a new pilot program is also opening the USPTO's first branch office. The Administration is also seeking legislative authority to give the USPTO greater capacity to meet its ever-increasing workload and improve patent quality. Legislative priorities include letting the USPTO set and keep its patent fees, so that it can expand its operations to meet its workload, and allowing "post-grant review," which can help limit errors in patent issuance and thus reduce costly litigation and market uncertainty.

The Administration is also working aggressively to protect against copyright and patent infringement. The Nation's first Intellectual Property Enforcement Coordinator, working within the Executive Office of the President, has released a Joint Strategic Plan to coordinate U.S. government actions to combat unauthorized use of intellectual property, both domestically and internationally, and is facilitating voluntary cooperative efforts by the private sector to reduce infringement. The Department of Justice and the Department of Homeland Security have increased law enforcement activity, including shutting down Web sites trafficking in infringing content, prosecuting theft of innovative trade secrets, and coordinating global law enforcement sweeps against counterfeit drugs. In addition, the United States Trade Representative has negotiated the first international enforcement agreement, the Anti-Counterfeiting Trade Agreement, to limit global trade in counterfeited goods and pirated copyrighted works.

Antitrust and the Innovative Marketplace

The U.S. antitrust agencies evaluate the extent to which a merger between existing competitors can reduce the degree of competition in a market. In situations where firms actively innovate to improve their position vis-à-vis their competitors, the agencies must consider whether those innovations would still be pursued should the merger go forward. Given the importance of innovation to economic growth, sound merger enforcement policy aims to promote innovation by approving mergers that are likely to create efficiencies and potentially spur innovation, while preventing mergers that may inhibit innovation through a reduction in competition.

In August 2010, the Antitrust Division of the Department of Justice and the Federal Trade Commission issued new Horizontal Merger Guidelines, which describe the merger enforcement policies of the two agencies. The new guidelines include, for the first time, a section explaining how the agencies assess whether a merger is likely to inhibit innovation by, for example, reducing a firm's incentive to continue a product development effort or initiate new product development.

The Research and Experimentation Tax Credit

Even with well-functioning intellectual property rights and markets, and with public support for basic scientific research, commercial innovation incentives still tend to fall short of the social benefits. The Research and Experimentation (R&E) tax credit is therefore an important tool to enhance private sector innovation incentives and accelerate economic growth. In 2007, the R&E tax credit supported 12,548 corporations and 56,000 individual taxpayers with $8.8 billion in credits. Recent studies find that research tax credits translate dollar-for-dollar into increases in current research spending, especially over the longer run as businesses develop their research enterprises (Hall and Van Reenen 2000; Bloom, Griffith, and Van Reenen 2002). Unfortunately, because the R&E credit is temporary and must be renewed periodically, uncertainty about the credit's availability reduces its incentive effect, especially in planning projects that will not be initiated and completed before the credit's expiration.

The Obama Administration has proposed to expand, simplify, and permanently extend the R&E tax credit. The proposal will expand the credit by approximately 20 percent, making a commitment of $100 billion over the next 10 years, which represents the largest commitment in the tax credit's history. The Administration also proposes to make the credit easier to use, providing a simple 17 percent credit rate to businesses, and to make the credit permanent, ensuring that businesses can count on the credit as they plan research investments that span multiple years.

Entrepreneurship

The United States has long recognized the role of entrepreneurship in tapping American ingenuity to develop new products and solve problems. Small firms typically produce more patents per dollar of R&D than do large firms. New businesses are also engines of job growth, with small firm births creating 40 million U.S. jobs between 1992 and 2005. Yet entrepreneurs face special challenges. Raising funds is difficult for firms that are new and have little collateral or no established reputation, even if they have a great idea. Moreover, disclosing ideas in pursuit of funding can risk losing the idea to established firms. Should a startup be capable of financing the initial innovative investment, long administrative delays in patent issuance typically delay licensing opportunities and may cause the startup to fail.

Government support for entrepreneurship can help ensure that good ideas from all sources enter markets, thereby boosting economic growth. For example, the Small Business Innovation Research (SBIR) program, which is managed by the Small Business Administration and supported by 11 federal agencies, assists small entrepreneurial businesses to compete for federal research and development awards. A recent report shows that during the 10-year period ending in 2006, businesses participating in the SBIR program frequently accounted for more than 20 of R&D Magazine's top 100 high-technology products of the year. The Administration's new Startup America initiative will facilitate entrepreneurship across the country, investing $2 billion in capital for entrepreneurs, improving the regulatory environment for young businesses, and increasing connections between entrepreneurs and high-quality business mentors. Meanwhile, on a different dimension, the Affordable Care Act will remove obstacles to entrepreneurship by enabling Americans to start and join new businesses without giving up access to health coverage, both by allowing workers with preexisting conditions to maintain their health insurance and by allowing Americans under age 26 to remain on their parents' insurance. Chapter 7 considers small business challenges and Administration policies in greater detail.

National Priority Areas

For national priorities where innovation is critical but market failures impede progress, government can help spur technological advances. Priority areas include developing clean energy sources, using information technology to improve health care and reduce costs, and nurturing the bio- and nanotechnology revolutions. The Administration is harnessing mechanisms, from basic research to government procurement, to help spark American ingenuity in these areas, driving economic growth and building the future industries that can provide American workers with quality jobs in the future global economy.

In clean energy, the Department of Energy's Advanced Research Projects Agency-Energy (ARPA-E) has awarded nearly $400 million to more than 120 research projects that seek fundamental breakthroughs in energy technologies. The Administration's fiscal year 2012 Budget will more than double total funding to date for ARPA-E. It will also double, from three to six, the number of Energy Innovation Hubs, bringing innovative thinkers from different disciplines together to create research breakthroughs on tough problems. One new Energy Innovation Hub will focus on improving batteries and energy storage, with applications to advanced vehicles. Overall, the FY 2012 Budget will significantly expand R&D investments in critical electric vehicle components while transforming the existing $7,500 tax credit for electric vehicles into a rebate available to all consumers at the point of sale. Building on existing initiatives like the Advanced Technology Vehicles Manufacturing loan program, which has invested over $2.4 billion to support three electric car factories in California, Delaware, and Tennessee, these initiatives are working to meet the President's goal of putting 1 million advanced vehicles on the road by 2015. Meanwhile, Department of Energy tax credits have leveraged gigawatts of private sector investments in wind, solar, and geothermal technologies, and the U.S. Navy is driving demand for new fuels by committing to convert half of the fuel used for powering its planes, ships, and vehicles to alternative fuels by 2020.

In health care, advances in information technology can help prevent medical errors; improve delivery of care for patients, doctors, and nurses; lower costs; and create data platforms to encourage further innovation. The Administration is making investments to accelerate the adoption of electronic health records, develop standards for secure exchange of health information over the Internet, and promote mobile and Web-based health technologies. The Strategic Health IT Advance Research Projects (SHARP) program is funding potentially game-changing advances to overcome obstacles to the adoption of health information technology.

The Administration has been making critical investments in biotechnology, nanotechnology, and advanced manufacturing. Through the Recovery Act, the Administration has invested in sequencing 1,800 complete human genomes, more than a 50-fold increase over the 34 genomes sequenced before Recovery Act funding, creating new capacity for understanding many diseases while also driving down DNA sequencing costs. The National Nanotechnology Initiative is developing a strategic plan to coordinate federal investments in nanotechnology fields, including investments to promote health, energy, materials, electronics and other applications. The FY 2012 Budget also increases investments at key science agencies to catalyze breakthroughs for advanced manufacturing applications and provides funding to initiate the Advanced Manufacturing Technology Consortia Program, a public-private partnership that will help spur innovation in manufacturing systems and shorten the time needed for innovations to reach the market.

INFRASTRUCTURE AND ECONOMIC GROWTH

Public investments in infrastructure reduce production and trade costs, enhance capital and labor mobility, and provide platforms to stimulate innovation. During the 1900s, America's infrastructure investments focused on the Nation's transportation systems and public utilities, including electrification, which provided a platform for the birth of major new industries and better opportunities for the American workforce. Today, as demand continues to grow and existing infrastructure decays, significant and renewed investment in our transportation and electricity systems is required.

The 21st century also calls for critical investments in the information and communication technology (ICT) infrastructure, including broadband Internet and wireless spectrum investments, that increasingly underpins the economy and provides abundant opportunities for further innovation and growth. Telecommunications investments have historically predicted substantial growth among advanced countries, and rapid adoption of ICT was associated with faster U.S. growth during the early Internet years. Of the world's 250 largest ICT companies today, 75 have their home in the United States; these 75 companies generated total revenues of more than $1 trillion in 2009. Additionally, ICT accounts for about 50 percent of U.S. venture capital spending, a key element in transforming innovative ideas into commercial applications (OECD 2010). Annual private investment in information processing equipment and software in the United States doubled between 1995 and 2009, growing 2.5 times faster than other U.S. private fixed investment.

Roads, Railways, and Runways

The United States has a rich history of government investment in transportation infrastructure leading to long-term economic benefits. The interstate highway system represents one example. Research has shown that well-designed infrastructure investments can raise economic growth, productivity, and land values, while also providing significant positive spillovers to economic development, energy efficiency, public health, and manufacturing.

In September 2010, President Obama announced a plan to renew and expand America's transportation infrastructure and increase government efficiency in making infrastructure investments. The plan includes a $50 billion investment to renew 150,000 miles of depreciating roads, construct and maintain 4,000 miles of passenger rail, and rehabilitate 150 miles of runways. Overall, the FY 2012 Budget seeks a six-year surface transportation reauthorization package totaling $556 billion, more than a 60 percent increase above the previous six-year package. The Administration is also seeking to modernize the transportation infrastructure to help people and goods move efficiently and keep American markets competitive. For example, the FY 2012 Budget provides $53 billion over the next six years for passenger rail, including the development of a high-speed rail system that will be accessible by 80 percent of Americans within 25 years, and $1.24 billion for the Next Generation Air Transportation System, a multiyear effort to improve efficiency, safety, and capacity of the Nation's aviation infrastructure.

The President's infrastructure plan also calls for the creation of a National Infrastructure Bank to leverage private capital and select projects of greatest national significance. The infrastructure bank, to be funded at $30 billion over six years, would depart from the Nation's traditional infrastructure decisionmaking process and instead weigh projects of national and regional significance against each other and fund those judged to have the greatest return to American taxpayers.

Electricity Infrastructure

Successful electrification across the United States in the early 1900s provided a general purpose technology upon which many further innovations would build, from lighting and household appliances to radio and television to computers and information technology. With rising carbon pollution and growing worldwide demand for scarce energy resources, the U.S. electricity infrastructure now faces new challenges. The Administration is currently taking numerous steps to modernize the Nation's electric grid and provide cleaner, more efficient, and more secure energy sources, largely through Smart Grid projects and transmission infrastructure financing.

The National Institute of Standards and Technology is coordinating Smart Grid standards, and the Recovery Act provided $4.1 billion for related Smart Grid investments. By providing a two-way flow of information, a Smart Grid promises to enable homes and businesses to manage electricity consumption based on need and price, thus reducing their utility bills. For example, energy usage and billing data can be provided nearly in real time to the consumer through smart meters or other technologies. Such data services can enable smart thermostats and smart home appliances to adjust their energy cycles based on price signals. Smart Grid technologies also include those that enable the broader electricity transmission infrastructure to operate more reliably and effectively, preventing brown-outs and other disruptions that can undermine the efficiency of the electric grid. Overall, Smart Grid technologies promise to lower consumer costs, increase the reliability of the electric grid, and facilitate the adoption of other innovative technologies, such as renewable energy resources and electric vehicles.

Smart Grid investments alone are not expected to alleviate fully the need for increased high-voltage transmission capacity. The Recovery Act also increased the borrowing authority of the power marketing agencies within the Department of Energy by $6.5 billion to finance new transmission investments that can accommodate increased generation to meet future energy demand, enhance grid reliability, and integrate location-constrained renewable energy resources. Taken together, investments in Smart Grid and electricity distribution and transmission will help modernize the Nation's electric grid, making electricity delivery to U.S. citizens more efficient, secure, and reliable.

Information Networks

In less than a decade, broadband (or high-speed) Internet access has transformed the American economy. The explosion in business-to-business (Figure 3-2), business-to-consumer, and government-to-consumer "e-commerce" has dramatically reduced transactions costs by reducing geographic and time constraints. Households can comparison shop, register their cars, and pay their bills online, saving time and money. Many workers can save hours of commuting time through telecommuting. More generally, broadband has expanded the ability to communicate ideas and information, a key to faster problem solving and innovation. The great potential for high-speed, low-cost information networks to trigger continued economic growth lies in their role as a general purpose technology that businesses and households can use in creative ways—some not yet imagined—to further transform their productive capacities.

Figure 3-2
E-Commerce Share of Business-to-Business Manufacturing Shipments

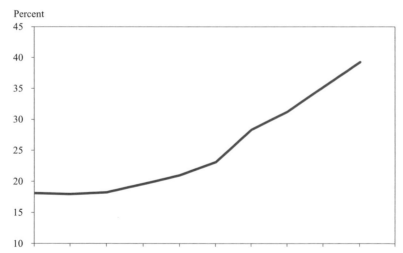

Sources: Census Bureau, Annual Survey of Manufacturers and the Economic Census.

In 2000, about 3 percent of Americans aged 18 and older had broadband at home. By 2010, the share had grown to about 66 percent.[1] Despite this tremendous progress, evidence suggests that the United States trails behind a substantial number of other advanced countries in broadband

---

[1] Smith 2010. Similar adoption rates are found in other studies; see Department of Commerce 2010.

adoption. One international comparison of broadband subscriptions per 100 inhabitants shows the United States ranking 14th (Figure 3-3) (OECD 2010).

Figure 3-3
Broadband Adoption across OECD Countries

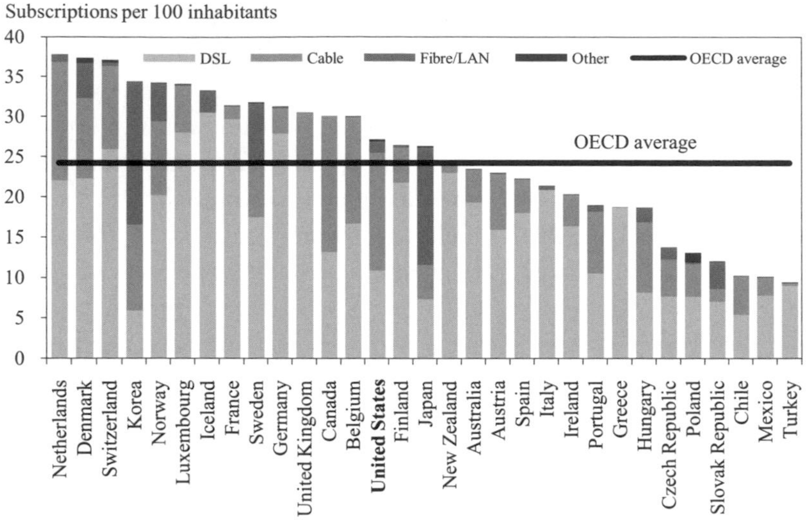

Subscriptions per 100 inhabitants

Source: OECD Information Technology Outlook (2010).

Jobs increasingly require Internet skills, but while 97 percent of schools are connected to the Internet, more than 50 percent of teachers say slow or unreliable Internet access presents obstacles to their use of technology in the classroom (FCC 2010). Additionally, broadband adoption is relatively low among certain groups of Americans, including poor households, African American and Hispanic households, and rural households (Department of Commerce 2010). As broadband becomes essential to learning, working, and improving productivity, these gaps in broadband adoption create a "digital divide" in the opportunities available to different groups of Americans.

To expand broadband Internet availability and strengthen this critical platform for the Nation's economic growth, the Administration has awarded $6.9 billion through the Recovery Act. These funds in part support the National Telecommunications and Information Administration's Broadband Technology Opportunities Program, which is deploying "middle-mile" infrastructure in areas with nearly 40 million households and 4 million businesses, bringing broadband to approximately 24,000 institutions, including schools, libraries, health care facilities, and public safety entities. These funds also support the Rural Utilities Service's Broadband Initiatives Program, which is bringing broadband access to approximately 2.8 million households, 364,000 businesses, and 32,000 community anchor institutions like hospitals and schools in rural America.

Spectrum policy is another critical component in managing the Nation's information infrastructure. More and more Americans are connecting wirelessly to broadband Internet services using computers, smartphones, and e-book readers, and increasing numbers of smart machines, such as smart parking meters and remote patient health monitoring systems, rely on wireless infrastructure. Smartphone penetration among Americans increased almost threefold between 2006 and 2009 by one measure, a trend that has multiplied wireless data traffic. The rapid expansion of wireless technologies may contribute substantially to future American productivity and economic growth, but additional gains will require allocating more electromagnetic spectrum for commercial and government use.

On behalf of the American people, the Federal Government manages the rights to electromagnetic spectrum, a scarce national resource. Today, the United States has provided just over 500 megahertz of spectrum for mobile communication. Experts believe that the United States will require hundreds of megahertz more of spectrum in coming years, yet only 50 megahertz are in the pipeline for commercial use. The Administration has committed to developing 500 megahertz of additional wireless spectrum and ensuring that spectrum is allocated to its highest-value uses.

Freeing additional spectrum to avoid "spectrum crunch" is essential to nurturing the next generation of high-speed wireless services and further innovations that businesses and entrepreneurs are beginning to deploy. However, more spectrum alone will not guarantee secure and interoperable systems that can support critical applications, such as public safety, or the extension of these essential wireless platforms to Americans living in remote rural areas. The Administration has budgeted over $18 billion to catalyze deployment of a nationwide, interoperable public safety wireless network, to invest in research solutions to overcome wireless technology obstacles, and to help businesses extend the next generation of wireless services to 98 percent of all Americans, including those in remote rural areas.

SKILLS AND ECONOMIC GROWTH

Ensuring that future economic growth is rapid, sustained, and broadly based requires investments in Americans' skills. Education is the pathway to higher-income jobs and the growing industries of the 21st century. Education is also needed to train the next generation of researchers and innovators, who will drive future technological progress. For both reasons,

Americans' skills are critical to future economic prosperity. The Obama Administration is working to ensure that our educational system is internationally competitive, comprehensive, and innovative in preparing our workforce for an increasingly knowledge-intensive economy.

The rapid technological changes of the 20th century not only enhanced productivity and created new industries but also increased demand for skilled labor (Goldin and Katz 2007). Higher education is the key to many modern occupations, and over the years Americans have correspondingly raised their educational attainment, with average years of schooling at age 30 rising 6.2 years between 1900 and 2000. But American gains in educational attainment are slowing. Average schooling duration in the final quarter of the 20th century increased at only about one-third of its previous pace. Compared with other countries, American educational attainment also appears to be falling behind.

While growth in educational attainment has slowed, the demand for skilled workers continues to increase. According to the Bureau of Labor Statistics, 14 of the 30 fastest-growing occupations in the United States require at least a bachelor's degree, with 7 others requiring either an associate's degree or a postsecondary vocational certificate or award. Moreover, over the past 30 years, the return to a college education has also risen, further suggesting that increasing demand for high-skilled workers is outstripping their supply. Figure 3-4 shows wage and salary income by degree attainment from 1963 to 2009. In 2009, workers with a bachelor's degree or more earned more than twice as much as those with only a high school diploma, while those with some college or an associate's degree earned 25 percent more. These wage premiums have risen 72 percentage points and 10 percentage points, respectively, since 1963. Although not shown in the figure, the returns to postgraduate education have risen even more steeply. In the mid-1960s, those with postgraduate degrees earned about 50 percent more than high school graduates; by 2009, this wage premium had more than tripled to 159 percent.

While earnings of workers who have attended college have risen, the annual income of those with only a high school degree or less has fallen since the 1970s, even before the declines during the recent recession. High school dropouts have fared the worst among all workers, with earnings falling 12 percent, in real terms, since 1963. These workers currently earn 30 percent less than high school graduates. This trend mirrors a broader pattern of rising wage and income inequality in the United States, with gains from economic growth concentrated in some segments of the population. In the past 20 years, real income for the top 20 percent of all households has grown by 20 percent, while incomes for households in the bottom half of the distribution have been essentially flat. By contrast, in other periods of economic growth, such as that from World War II to the mid-1970s, advances in labor income were spread roughly evenly throughout the wage distribution (Goldin and Katz 2007). A leading hypothesis about the causes of rising income inequality over the past 30 years points to technological advances that have increased the demand for high-skilled workers, while the supply of these workers has not accelerated to meet the demand (Katz and Murphy 1992). Institutional factors, such as declines in unionization and the real minimum wage, may also have played a role in increased wage inequality (DiNardo, Fortin, and Lemieux 1996).

Figure 3-4
Average Wage and Salary Income by Educational Group

Total wage and salary income (2009 dollars)

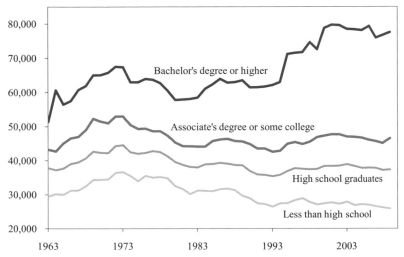

Notes: Calculations are for full-time workers aged 25–65 who worked 50–52 weeks in the calendar year. Before 1991, education groups are defined based on the highest grade of school or year of college completed. Beginning in 1991, groups are defined based on the highest degree or diploma earned. Incomes are deflated using the CPI-U.
Source: Bureau of Labor Statistics, March Current Population Survey, 1964–2010.

Further, the overall data on educational attainment mask large disparities by race and socioeconomic status. Whereas 49 percent of non-Hispanic whites aged 25 to 34 hold a postsecondary degree, only 29 percent of African Americans and 19 percent of Hispanics do. In addition, children from high-income households are almost four times as likely to obtain a postsecondary degree by age 24 as those from low-income families.

Finally, achievement lags in science, technology, engineering, and mathematics (STEM) fields, all areas that show high wage returns to training and underpin future innovation. Recent test results in primary and secondary education suggest that American schoolchildren are lagging behind in math and science. The 2009 Programme for International Student Assessment survey, for example, showed that American students placed 17th of 34 developed countries in science and 25th in math.[2]

President Obama recognizes that education is not only a driver of growth but also the surest way for individuals to share in the gains from growth. The challenge in developing a world-leading workforce involves both increasing educational attainment and enhancing the quality of education in this country. That is why the President has established a goal for the United States to resume world leadership in college degree attainment by 2020. To reach this goal, the Nation must raise its college completion rate from 40 percent to 60 percent. That requires 8 million additional young people to graduate from America's colleges and universities over the next 10 years.

The Administration has put forward a two-pronged strategy that, first, seeks to ensure that higher education is accessible and affordable to all individuals and, second, promotes innovative reform to ensure educational quality. The Administration's strategy gives states incentives to innovate toward comprehensive education reform as well as to adopt college- and career-ready standards of achievement. Effective education requires support from cradle to career. Reforms are needed at every level to produce a strong and competitive workforce.

Early Childhood Education

The years before kindergarten are among the most significant in shaping a child's foundation for learning and school success. Research shows that high-quality early learning programs help children arrive at kindergarten ready to succeed in school and in life, reducing achievement gaps that first appear at early ages. Disadvantaged students who have access to such programs realize positive gains in their cognitive, social, emotional, and language skills (Cunha et al. 2006). Investments in early childhood education can improve academic attainment, reduce the need for special education, and increase future graduation rates. Early childhood education also has been shown to reduce future crime and teenage pregnancy for disadvantaged children. Furthermore, investments in high-quality early childhood learning programs have been shown to be extremely cost-effective, with lasting returns to society as high as 17 percent per year (Belfield et al. 2006).

Recognizing the benefits of early childhood learning, the Administration's FY 2012 Budget proposes to establish a new, competitive Early Learning Challenge Fund (ELCF). States would compete for grant

---

[2] Results of the most recent National Assessment for Educational Progress show that, although American students have improved in math over the past 30 years, only 26 percent of 12th graders are "proficient" or better in math.

aid from this fund by establishing systems of early learning that set high standards and ensure that more children enter kindergarten with the skills necessary for success. The fund would promote evidence-based evaluation of programs, strategies for families and parents to assess the quality of early learning programs, and the creation of age-appropriate curricula and assessment systems.

Elementary and Secondary Education

Just as early childhood education is important to prepare children for primary education, the K–12 system is crucial to prepare students for college and the workplace. Too many students leave high school with inadequate academic preparation. In the 2007–08 school year, one in five first-year college students took remedial courses, a costly situation for both the student and society. The need for remedial work is also a warning sign that the student is more likely to drop out without completing his or her degree (Adelman 1998). The task of improving college and labor market preparedness thus begins well before a student reaches college or the labor market.

The Administration is committed to fostering innovation that will improve educational outcomes. The Recovery Act created Race to the Top, the largest-ever federal competitive investment in school reform. Race to the Top is designed to spur state and local reforms in K–12 education by allowing states to innovate and formulate their own solutions. The program provides competitive grants to encourage and reward states that have taken action to improve teacher quality, adopt college- and career-ready standards, incorporate better data into decisionmaking, and improve student achievement in low-performing schools.

Encouraged by the Race to the Top initiative, 48 states worked together to create a voluntary set of college- and career-ready standards, which establish a shared set of clear educational guidelines for language arts and mathematics education. As of December 2010, 40 states and the District of Columbia had adopted these standards. Many states also pledged to undertake a variety of innovative measures, including allowing more charter schools and promoting the use of better student achievement data to inform teacher evaluations. In August 2010, nine states and the District of Columbia were named Phase 2 winners of Race to the Top, joining Phase 1 winners Delaware and Tennessee. The program will benefit all of America's students, whether or not they live in a state that was awarded a grant. By providing incentives for all states to institute reforms, the program has spurred reform across the country. Thirty-four states have changed state education laws or policies to make them more conducive to reform that will provide higher-quality instruction and give students in low-performing schools access to the education that they deserve.

Another focus of the Administration's reform efforts is improving low-performing schools. As established in the Recovery Act, School Improvement Grants provide a total of $3.5 billion to transform the lowest-performing schools so that disadvantaged students receive the instruction and resources they need to succeed in the college or career of their choice. Already more than 700 schools are participating in this program.

The theme of giving states incentives to undertake reforms, adopt national standards of achievement, and improve the lowest-performing schools is embodied in the Administration's Blueprint for Reform in K–12, released in March 2010. Building on the success of Race to the Top, the Blueprint seeks to bring innovative strategies and meaningful standards to all 50 states. This plan will fix No Child Left Behind's accountability system with a new federal framework built around five key priorities: implementing college- and career-ready standards, placing effective teachers and leaders in every school, providing equity and opportunity for all students, rewarding states and school districts that excel, and promoting innovation and continuous improvement. Recognizing the importance of finding and supporting local solutions, the Blueprint proposes federal funding to support state and local school district efforts in tackling these goals. The FY 2012 Budget proposes consolidating dozens of redundant programs from No Child Left Behind, providing resources to help schools focus on results. The Blueprint's framework is centered on rewarding success and providing greater flexibility to local actors in developing school improvement plans.

In today's global economy, it is essential that all students be prepared academically for whatever career path they choose. The Administration has specifically targeted improving education in STEM subjects to maintain a skilled, innovative workforce in these growing fields (Box 3-4). In addition, the Obama Administration dramatically increased funding for the Teacher Incentive Fund, which supports efforts to develop and implement performance-based teacher and principal compensation systems in high-need schools. In September 2010, grants were awarded to school districts and state education departments that had developed "rigorous, transparent, and fair" teacher and principal evaluation systems, as measured by both higher achievement for students and classroom observations.

Box 3-4: STEM Education and Educate to Innovate

Training in science, technology, engineering, and mathematics (STEM) fields is an important pathway to high-quality jobs, and STEM education is also critical to producing future innovators who will develop new products and ideas. Recognizing the importance of teachers in K–12 education and especially in STEM fields, the President has set a goal of training an additional 100,000 effective STEM teachers over the next 10 years. The Administration's proposed FY 2012 Budget includes $100 million devoted to this task.

The Administration's Educate to Innovate campaign focuses specifically on improving children's education in STEM fundamentals in the classroom and beyond. Key elements of the campaign are harnessing public-private partnerships that build support around science and math teachers, connecting kids to the wonder of invention and discovery, and raising the profile of science through initiatives like the White House Science Fair. The Educate to Innovate campaign hopes to increase STEM literacy; move American students to the top of the international pack in STEM performance; and expand awareness, especially among under-represented groups, of STEM career opportunities.

As part of this campaign, the President announced the launch of Change the Equation in September 2010. This nonprofit organization was formed by the business community in response to the President's spring 2009 "call to action" at the National Academy of Sciences for all Americans to join in elevating STEM education as a national priority. In its first year of operation, Change the Equation will work with member companies to spread effective STEM education programs to sites across the country. It will also create a scorecard to assess the condition of STEM education in all 50 states, building a baseline from which to measure progress in coming years. Furthermore, Change the Equation will identify and share principles for effective business involvement in STEM education, helping its member companies judge and improve the effectiveness of their own programs through robust self-evaluation tools.

The immediate goal of Change the Equation is to replicate, within one year, successful privately funded programs in 100 high-need schools and communities. These programs include robotics competitions and improved professional development for math and science teachers. With leadership from the President and the private sector, a membership of more than 100 CEOs, and funding of $5 million for its first year of operations, Change the Equation is well positioned to promote its three key goals: great teaching, inspired learners, and a committed Nation.

Advancements in education technology have the potential to improve K–12 education by personalizing the learning experience and reducing the time needed for students to gain new knowledge. The Administration supports several programs, as well as the launch of an Advanced Research Projects Agency for Education, which will promote education technology innovations. With broadband, cloud computing, digital devices, and software, these technologies can spread widely and allow both the identification and adoption of best practices.

Higher Education

American universities remain a renowned strength of the Nation's educational system (Box 3-5). To reach the President's goal of leading the world in college completion by 2020 and to provide the skilled workforce needed for the economy to thrive, the Administration has prioritized making the college and university system accessible and affordable to all.

The Health Care and Education Reconciliation Act (HCERA), signed in March 2010, helps build a more reliable and effective financial aid system by making all federal loans—Stafford loans, PLUS loans, and consolidation loans—available directly to students, ending subsidies once paid to third-party administrators. By saving $68 billion in subsidies over the next 11 years, the direct loan program allows for deficit reduction and for greater investments in college affordability.

To make college more affordable to low-income students, the Administration also has greatly expanded the Pell Grant program. In addition to Recovery Act support for the Pell Grant program, HCERA invests more than $40 billion in Pell Grants, raising the maximum Pell award from $4,730 in 2008 to $5,550 in 2010 and to an estimated $5,975 in 2017. Pell Grants can be applied toward traditional college expenses as well as to vocational and adult education programs.

The impact of these efforts is already evident, with nearly 8 million Pell Grant recipients in the 2009–10 academic year. That is more than double the figure from 10 years earlier and is 26 percent above the 2008–09 level. Furthermore, the average award of $3,646 is 25 percent larger than the average award in 2008–09.

In addition, the American Opportunity Tax Credit (AOTC), established in the Recovery Act, provides up to $2,500 a year for college tuition and related expenses for American families. The AOTC is refundable, thereby also reaching lower-income families. The tax credit increased tax incentives for higher education by more than 90 percent and benefited 8.3 million students and their families in 2009. In December 2010, the President signed an extension of the AOTC through the end of 2012, and he has proposed making it permanent.

Box 3-5: America's Universities: Leading the World

Despite the relative decline in educational attainment in the United States, America's universities remain the strongest in the world. According to the *Times Higher Education* rankings for 2010–11, the United States boasts 15 of the top 20 universities in the world. In addition, American institutions remain the most popular destination for foreign graduate and undergraduate students. Of students traveling out of their country of residence for tertiary education, 19 percent go to the United States, more than the combined share of those who go to the next two most popular countries, the United Kingdom and Germany. The remarkable diversity of America's graduate programs has been shown to increase innovation and research productivity (Stuen, Maskus, and Mobarak 2010), making these programs even more attractive to both domestic and international students.

Universities play the dual role of creating new ideas and training high-skill workers, and American universities lead the world on this front. Since 1960, 63 percent of Nobel Prize winning research has been performed in the United States, mostly at universities. The diversity of the Nation's colleges and universities is a great strength: 31 percent of the U.S. Nobel Prize winners since 1960 were foreign born, and 44 percent of these immigrants received their graduate degrees in the United States.

Furthermore, American universities give students world-class training for the high-skill jobs of the future. University students in the United States have the opportunity to learn from the world's leading scientists and scholars, ensuring that the best new ideas enter the American workforce. Preparing the American workforce for the 21st century depends on taking innovative ideas from the laboratory to the workforce, and universities provide that bridge.

Federal efforts to increase financial aid, particularly the Pell Grant program, are the primary reason that net tuition (tuition minus grant aid) has fallen at all types of colleges and universities over the past five years, even as published tuition has risen substantially. To make higher education more accessible to all students, the HCERA provides $2.6 billion over the next decade to strengthen Minority-Serving Institutions (including Historically Black Colleges and Universities) nationwide. These schools play a key role in educating low- and middle-income students, enrolling nearly 60 percent of the Nation's 4.7 million minority undergraduate students and accounting for nearly one-third of all degree-granting institutions in higher education. These steps will ensure that minority students are given every chance to earn degrees and to enter (or return to) the workforce with the skills they need to succeed.

Job Training

In addition to traditional education pathways, job training programs provide vital opportunities for workers to gain new skills well suited to today's economy. Skill upgrading can be especially important for displaced workers whose skills might otherwise erode while they search for new job opportunities. Training is provided by a diverse set of institutions, including proprietary (for-profit) schools, four-year colleges, community-based organizations, labor unions, and public vocational and technical schools. Studies have documented that well-designed training and adult education programs can improve participants' labor market outcomes, increasing earnings and the probability of employment (CEA 2009). These improvements appear to be especially strong in training programs with a targeted focus on specific sectors, such as technical or high-growth sectors, and in programs that operate with a high level of employer involvement (Maguire et al. 2010). The Skills for America's Future initiative encourages and promotes these types of partnerships (Box 3-6).

The Administration has acted to promote career training for displaced workers, giving them the new skills they need to meet the demands of a competitive economy. HCERA provides $2 billion to fund the Trade Adjustment Assistance Community College and Career Training Grant Program, which provides grants to institutions of higher education to improve and expand programs suited to help workers affected by trade. Under the program, competitive funds will be made available to community colleges over the next four years to help increase completion of degrees, certificates, and other industry-recognized credentials. In addition, the Affordable Care Act, passed in March 2010, makes investments in workforce training in the high-growth field of health care, providing funding to train additional doctors, dentists, physicians' assistants, and much-needed nurses.

Finally, the Administration has called on Congress to reauthorize and modernize the Workforce Investment Act (WIA). The aim is to fuel the development and replication of effective practices in job training, adult education, and vocational rehabilitation. The Recovery Act provided nearly $4 billion for WIA programs, including $500 million for adult employment and training activities, nearly $1.5 billion to train displaced workers, and $750 million for a program of competitive grants for worker training and placement in the high-growth sectors of health care and clean energy. About 35 percent of workers receiving job training through WIA programs attend community colleges, putting those institutions on the front lines of training America's workforce for the jobs of tomorrow.

Box 3-6: Skills for America's Future

In October 2010, President Obama announced the creation of the Skills for America's Future (SAF) initiative to foster collaborative efforts between the private sector, community colleges, labor unions, and other institutions, with a commitment to scaling up meaningful and measurable solutions. The goal is to build a nationwide network of stakeholders who will work to maximize workforce development strategies, job training programs, and job placement.

SAF will identify and highlight characteristics of successful training programs that can be replicated and scaled up to reach more workers and institutions. The initiative already has the commitment of private sector leaders, along with innovative institutions, to advance these efforts. Actively engaging private employers, with expertise and knowledge of required credentials as well as local labor market conditions, is critical to the success of training programs. Building and encouraging collaborative efforts between private employers and public community colleges and other institutions is one of the cornerstones of the Skills for America's Future initiative.

In conjunction with SAF, the President also established the Skills for America's Future Task Force, cochaired by top-level Administration policymakers, to coordinate federal efforts to ensure that the private sector is well poised to work with and leverage federal training and education efforts.

CONCLUSION

Throughout its history, the United States has demonstrated a remarkable capacity to innovate and generate substantial increases in American standards of living. With the private sector in the lead and appropriate public investments where markets fall short, Americans will continue to see rapid, broad-based, and sustained economic growth. The Obama Administration is making investments in our national innovation system, infrastructure, and skills to provide the right foundations for prosperity. These foundations will ensure that, year after year, America's greatest resource—its people—can build a brighter future.

CHAPTER 4

THE WORLD ECONOMY

Like the U.S. economy, the world economy moved toward recovery in 2010 with positive economic growth reestablished in most regions and rebounding world trade. Emerging-market economies made substantial contributions to world growth, demonstrating their increasing importance to the world and U.S. economies. International policy coordination continued to play an important role: two leaders' summits of the Group of Twenty (G-20) were held in 2010, and significant agreements were reached on important global challenges such as ensuring a strong, sustainable, and balanced global recovery and setting core elements of a new financial regulatory framework, including bank capital and liquidity standards.

The world economy, however, must not only recover but also shift away from its pre-crisis pattern of growth that was too dependent on U.S. consumption. Global imbalances narrowed significantly during the crisis. Now, a fundamental challenge is to restore growth without restoring the old growth model and patterns of demand that led to those imbalances. Even without the economic crisis, however, the world economy would be undergoing substantial change. China has grown from the sixth- to the second-largest economy in just a decade, and the Group of Seven (G-7) advanced countries' share of the world economy continues to shrink as numerous emerging markets grow onto the world stage. These changes are generating shifts in world production and trade, but the growth of emerging markets need not portend a de-industrialization of advanced economies or a fall in the standard of living of Americans. The United States is home to many of the most innovative firms in the world, universities that attract more students than any other country, and the most productive workers of any major economy. In addition, output per capita is higher in the United States than in any of the other G-7 nations and much higher than in any emerging economy. These shifts do require, however, that the United States evolve to meet both new opportunities and new challenges. The same forces described in Chapter 3 on long-run growth—innovation, education, and infrastructure investment—coupled with a smart trade policy are crucial to the evolving role of the U.S. economy in the world.

The United States, both **as part** of the economic recovery and as part of its engagement with the global economy, must increase its exports over time. Substantial import growth in rapidly growing regions around the world helped drive U.S. exports at a fast pace in 2010, moving the United States closer to the Administration's goal of doubling exports by the end of 2014. Emerging-market economies are playing a growing part in U.S. trade relationships, and that role will only strengthen in the coming years. Robust enforcement of market access agreed to in previous trade accords, new trade agreements to guarantee access to these important emerging markets, and encouragement of balanced growth around the world will all help spur faster export growth. A range of additional policy initiatives—advocacy, export credit, and improvements in the U.S. transportation and supply chain infrastructure—can also contribute to export growth.

STATUS OF THE WORLD RECOVERY

The world economy in 2008–09 faced its most wrenching economic crisis in a generation. The recovery from that crisis has been quite rapid in many regions, leading to a rebound in world economic growth and trade. Many challenges remain, however. Regions are growing at different paces, and many countries are facing some combination of slow growth, a need for fiscal consolidation, or complications from rising prices or increased capital inflows. Fortunately, institutions like the G-20, which were platforms for increased economic cooperation during the crisis, have been able to continue to play a positive role in the world economy.

Crisis Fading, But Challenges Remain

The world economy has experienced both a remarkable setback and rebound in the past three years. The global contraction in the second half of 2008 and first quarter of 2009 was sharp but relatively short-lived. By the second quarter of 2009, the world's growth rate (the weighted average of the growth rate of countries' real gross domestic product or GDP) was positive, and by the third quarter, the average growth rate had returned to its 2007 levels. The International Monetary Fund (IMF) projects that, for the four quarters of 2010, the world economy grew more than 4 percent and will continue at that pace in 2011 (IMF 2010).

Although average growth coming out of the crisis has been rapid, it has not been evenly distributed, as Figure 4-1 demonstrates. The financial market shocks of the recession were concentrated in the advanced economies, and those economies have rebounded more slowly. Most emerging-market economies rebounded quickly; some, in fact, never saw a contraction, just a slowdown in their rapid growth. In the first half of 2010, real GDP in the emerging-market countries of the G-20 grew 7.9 percent on average (at an annual rate), compared with 3.3 percent for the G-7 countries (growth slowed slightly in both groups in the third quarter).[1] The IMF projects that substantially faster emerging-market growth will persist, predicting growth of 7 percent in emerging and developing economies in 2010 and 2011, compared with roughly 2.5 percent in advanced economies.

Figure 4-1
Real GDP Growth

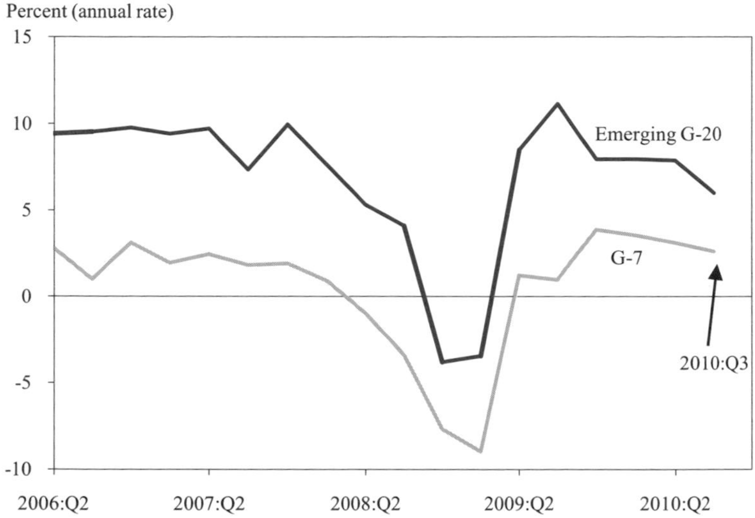

Percent (annual rate)

Sources: Country sources; CEA calculations.

It is not surprising to see advanced economies grow more slowly than emerging ones. Emerging markets tend to have faster population growth—and hence a growing labor supply—and can converge toward advanced economies through rapid productivity growth as they upgrade the education of their workforce and the technology they use. Still, a gap of roughly 4.5

[1] The G-20 is made up of 19 major economies plus the European Union. The G-7 includes the largest 7 advanced economies of that group (by size of economy, the United States, Japan, Germany, the United Kingdom, France, Italy, and Canada). The remaining members of the G-20 are Australia and South Korea along with major emerging-market nations: Argentina, Brazil, China, India, Indonesia, Mexico, Russia, Saudi Arabia, South Africa, and Turkey. Throughout this chapter, division of countries into emerging and advanced is based on IMF definitions.

percentage points in the growth rates of emerging and advanced economies is unusually large. Such a gap existed in the years immediately preceding the crisis, but between 1980 and 2007, the gap was much narrower: emerging and developing economies grew at an average of 4.4 percent, whereas the average for advanced economies was 2.8 percent.

Several serious challenges to sustained global growth remain. The unemployment rate in many advanced nations is still unacceptably high. As Figure 4-2 shows, the unemployment rate in the euro area is still at its peak, and the U.S. rate is trending down only very slowly. At the same time, many advanced economies face substantial fiscal deficits. The U.S. Federal fiscal deficit in 2010 was 8.9 percent of GDP, the euro-area deficit was 6.3 percent, and Japan's was 7.7 percent. Over the next few years, those deficits will have to come down. They will likely fall significantly because of the business cycle (deficits tend to shrink as economies recover), but further fiscal consolidation will be needed over time. Maintaining sufficient growth to lower the unemployment rate while simultaneously implementing credible medium-term fiscal consolidation will be a challenge in many countries. Further, some euro-area countries have faced pressure from financial markets in the form of rising yields on their debt, forcing them to lean toward faster consolidation. Because the advanced economies are operating below capacity, their inflation rates have been low. Core rates were close to 1 percent in the United States and the euro area, and deflation continued in Japan. Thus far, central banks have maintained an accommodative monetary policy stance, with the Federal Reserve and Bank of Japan adding new quantitative easing measures in 2010, and the Bank of England and the European Central Bank keeping policy rates low.

In contrast, rising inflation is a concern in emerging-market countries where growth has been faster. The 12-month change in consumer prices in China breached 5 percent (above the 3 percent target for 2010, and China is now reported to have raised its target to 4 percent for 2011); wholesale price inflation in India rose above 10 percent during the spring and summer of 2010; and inflation rates began to creep up in 2010 in many other emerging-market countries. Many central banks have raised policy rates or taken other action to calm inflation. The contrast between fast growth with rising interest rates in the emerging world and slower growth with lower interest rates in advanced economies has put pressure on capital flows and exchange rates. After depreciating during the crisis, the currencies of emerging-market nations of the G-20 appreciated 5 percent on average over the first 10 months of 2010 on a real trade-weighted basis, and capital flows into these countries increased as well.[2] Thus far, emerging nations have responded

---

[2] Net portfolio investment flows into emerging-market G-20 countries turned negative at the peak of the crisis but rebounded in 2009 and 2010.

with a varying mix of currency appreciation, currency intervention, and capital controls. Total foreign exchange holdings by emerging and developing countries rose by roughly $500 billion in the first three quarters of 2010 (more than double the amount in the first three quarters of 2009 after adjusting for valuation changes), reflecting increased currency intervention aimed at slowing or preventing appreciation.

Figure 4-2
Unemployment Rate

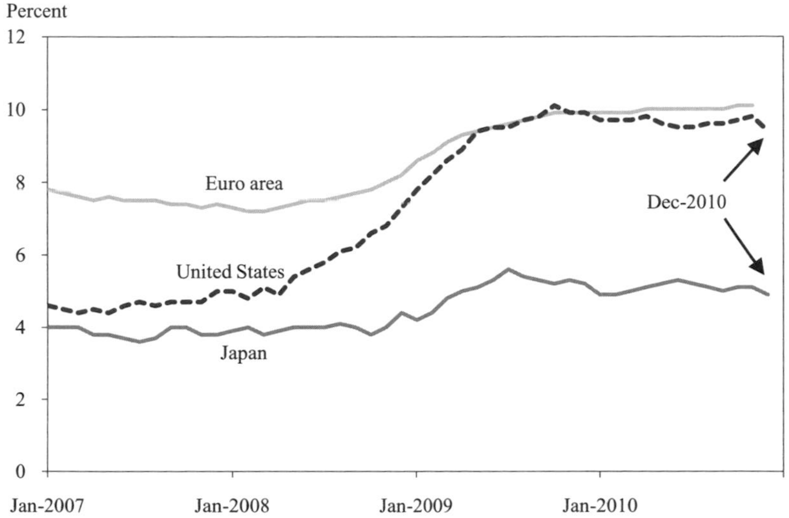

Sources: Country sources; CEA calculations.

While overall world growth has rebounded, another crucial challenge to the world economy is to make up for the output lost during the recession. By the end of June 2010, the world economy had recovered to the level of output before the recession, but world GDP remains considerably below the output trend it was on before the crisis struck. Research suggests that financial recessions are long and deep, and whether the output lost is completely recovered is an important issue.[3] For the world economy to return to its previous output trend, several years of above-average growth will be necessary.

---

[3] Reinhart and Rogoff (2009) demonstrate that financial recessions are longer and deeper than other kinds of recessions, but the authors do not comment on whether the output loss is permanent. IMF (2009) argues that, on average, countries do face a medium-term output loss and thus never recover to the pre-crisis trend level, but that study (which looked at earlier recessions) found wide variation in outcomes, with the top quarter of countries more than 5 percent above their pre-crisis output trend seven years after a banking crisis. In addition, a variety of methodological choices may bias the IMF results toward finding a permanent loss. Other work finds that most countries recover all output lost in a financial recession over the medium term (see, for example, Cecchetti, Kohler, and Upper 2009).

The Rebound in World Trade

A particular difficulty during the recession was the collapse in world trade. Even countries with little connection to the financial aspects of the recession were nonetheless affected as demand for imports plummeted and financing conditions for export credit tightened (Baldwin 2009). Trade fell even faster than GDP: the unprecedented collapse of world trade during the last quarter of 2008 and the first quarter of 2009 saw an almost simultaneous, precipitous decline of exports and imports across all major regions of the world.

Trade has recovered more quickly than GDP has: exports and imports picked up during the second and third quarters of 2009 and continued the V-shaped recovery in 2010, advancing significantly ahead of expectations. In October 2009, the IMF expected real world trade (adjusted for prices) to grow just 2.5 percent in 2010. Only months later, the Organisation for Economic Co-operation and Development projected a 6 percent increase. In April 2010, the IMF forecast a 7 percent increase, and in the fall of 2010, both institutions expected over 11 percent growth for the year.

Figure 4-3
Import Volume Indexes

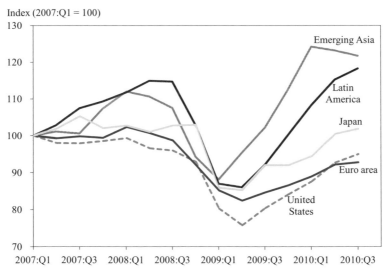

Sources: CPB World Trade Monitor; CEA calculations.

Important regional differences mark both the contraction in trade during the recession and the expansion of imports and exports during the recovery. Figure 4-3 shows the import volume (adjusted for prices) and Figure 4-4 the export volume of various regions relative to their levels in the first quarter of 2007. Asia's emerging economies experienced a sharp decline of imports and exports, but they were among the quickest to recover and were the first in 2010 to reach their pre-crisis levels. Japan, whose exports plunged nearly 40 percent from peak to trough in the crisis, also rebounded in 2010, closing the year with exports less than 10 percent below the pre-crisis peak. Japan's imports fell by only half as much as its exports, and they too were recovering but had not attained their pre-crisis levels by the end of 2010.

Figure 4-4
Export Volume Indexes

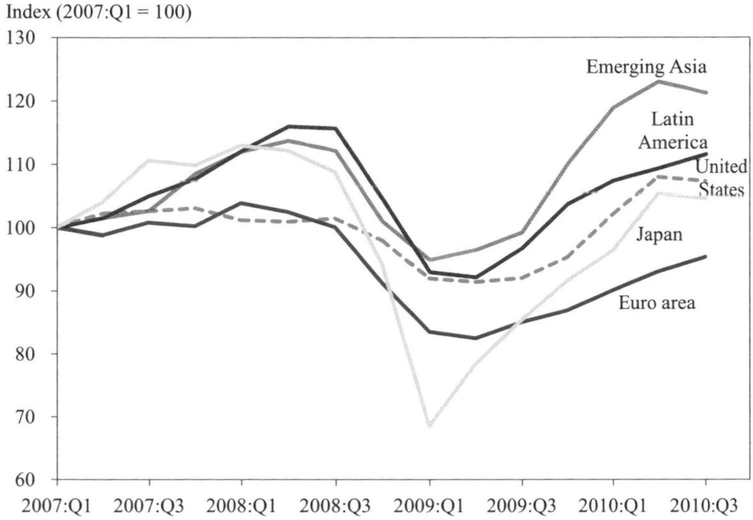

Index (2007:Q1 = 100)

Emerging Asia

Latin America

United States

Japan

Euro area

2007:Q1   2007:Q3   2008:Q1   2008:Q3   2009:Q1   2009:Q3   2010:Q1   2010:Q3

Sources: CPB World Trade Monitor; CEA calculations.

The export decline in the United States was similar to that in the euro-area countries, but U.S. exports have recovered more quickly. U.S. imports initially declined more sharply than those in the euro area, but they also have rebounded substantially. Among all of the major regions of the world, the euro area has had the slowest resumption in import growth.

Finally, despite the substantial progress in the V-shaped trade recovery, as of the third quarter of 2010, none of these economies had yet achieved the level of trade that had been projected to take place had pre-crisis trends continued in the absence of the 2008–09 trade collapse.

Global Policy Coordination

During the crisis, world leaders established the G-20 as the premier international body for international economic coordination. The G-20, whose members account for nearly 90 percent of world GDP, continued to play a pivotal role in 2010, holding two leaders' summits as well as finance ministers' and deputies' meetings, along with continual staff work.

At the leaders' summit in Pittsburgh in 2009, under U.S. leadership, the G-20 committed to work toward strong, balanced, sustainable global growth. In Toronto in June 2010, leaders made commitments to boost demand where needed and to strengthen public finances and financial systems. In Seoul in November 2010, they agreed to undertake macro-economic policies to ensure ongoing recovery and sustainable growth, including making exchange rates more market-determined and adopting other policies to temper global imbalances.

The G-20 also followed up on significant commitments to reform the international financial system and its institutions. Through the Basel Committee on Banking Supervision, nations around the globe negotiated a new framework for banking supervision that is intended to improve the ability of the global financial system to absorb shocks and reduce the risk of spillover from the financial sector to the real economy. The framework involves raising capital standards, broadening the coverage of supervision, introducing global liquidity standards, and promoting the buildup of capital buffers in good times.

G-20 nations also followed through on their commitment to change the governance structure of the two major international financial institu-tions: the IMF and the World Bank. The governance structure of these two organizations was heavily weighted toward advanced countries, and each is now being changed to incorporate more leadership from major emerging-market countries, including changes to quota shares and board seats.

Finally, policy coordination has continued as various financial diffi-culties have appeared throughout the year. The focus of much of the concern during 2010 has been on sovereign debt in Europe. First, central banks, including the Federal Reserve, coordinated to ensure sufficient liquidity across markets. More importantly, in May, European leaders worked with the IMF to create a European Financial Stabilization mechanism with up to $1 trillion committed to stabilizing the debt markets for various euro-area nations. The funds were first used in Greece to provide a necessary backstop as that country tried to rebalance a precarious fiscal situation. Toward the end of the year, the mechanism was used to backstop Ireland as it struggled with the costs of its banking system.

THE EVOLUTION OF THE WORLD ECONOMY

The world economy has begun a transformation. Rapidly growing emerging-market countries and some advanced countries with high savings will need to provide more demand to the world economy, and countries that are borrowing too much will need to save more. Changes are already taking place in the composition of U.S. exports as services play a larger role, but there will likely be continuity as well, as the United States maintains its exports of products that rely on sound legal institutions, an innovative economy, and the high skills and productivity of U.S. workers. More of those products, though, are likely to be headed toward rapidly growing emerging markets, a change that will be essential if the U.S. economy is to meet the Administration's goal of doubling exports in five years.

Global Imbalances

As the G-20 actions show, world leaders have recognized that more balanced growth is essential to the world economy. The United States had a large current account deficit before the crisis, and the Administration has been clear that the United States must find a more balanced growth model, one that involves more exports and investment. The trade balance, or net exports, represents the bulk of the current account (net income on overseas assets and unilateral transfers such as foreign aid and remittances make up the rest). At the same time, the current account represents the net lending of a country to the rest of the world because if a country exports less than it imports, it must either borrow or sell foreign assets to pay for that consumption from abroad.

The issue of global imbalances is a problem not just for the United States but for all nations. A single country's saving behavior can affect saving and investment around the globe. A large deficit, for example, can take up too much world savings and crowd out borrowing in other countries. Conversely, a current account surplus means a country is not contributing as much to world demand as it is to world supply and may be lowering world interest rates and encouraging deficits in other countries. Surpluses become particularly contentious when global output is below potential output. Thus, the macroeconomic behavior and outcomes of different countries are linked.[4] Before the crisis, when the United States was too reliant on consumption, other countries around the world were also too reliant on U.S. consumption and exports to the United States.

---

[4] Current account deficits or surpluses are not always a bad thing. Where many productive opportunities exist, a country may borrow to invest more than its savings allow and may therefore want a deficit; alternatively, a country may temporarily have an excess of savings. However, large persistent surpluses or deficits can be a sign of more structural imbalances in an economy.

The United States accounts for roughly one-quarter of the world economy, and consumption has historically accounted for roughly two-thirds of the U.S. economy. Thus, one might normally expect 16–17 percent of world aggregate demand growth to come from U.S. consumers. But emerging and developing economies often grow faster than more mature economies. Thus, a larger portion of world growth would be expected to come from emerging economies than their share of the world economy would warrant.

From 1996 to 2006, though, U.S. consumption played an outsized role in the world economy, with roughly 22–23 percent of the growth in the world economy coming from growth in U.S. consumption. This level was simply not sustainable. During this period, U.S. consumption rose to 70 percent of the U.S. economy, personal saving fell to very low levels, and U.S. business equipment and software investment growth lagged behind GDP growth. At the same time, the fiscal position of the U.S. Federal Government moved from substantial surpluses at the end of the 1990s to substantial deficits in the mid-2000s. These deficits also contributed to lower national saving. Such macroeconomic behavior had important implications for the world economy. The rapid growth in consumption and decline in saving (both personal and government) meant that the United States increasingly borrowed from the world and had a growing current account deficit.

At the same time that consumption was outpacing income in the United States, many other countries had export growth well in excess of GDP growth. Falling transport prices and the rise of globally integrated production supply chains mean that the production of a single good may generate far more recorded exports and imports than the value of the final good itself. To illustrate, consider a smartphone whose various parts may be traded across many borders at different stages of production before final assembly and sale of the phone. Each time a component crosses a border to move to the next stage of processing, it counts as an import for one country and an export for another. As a result, the total value of exports and imports for various countries from that one phone will likely exceed the total final value of the phone, leading to faster export growth than GDP growth when one more phone is made. From 1998 to 2008, exports grew faster than GDP in nearly every major economy. Of the largest 20 exporters, though, the United States had the lowest rate of export growth—96 percent, compared with an average of 243 percent among the other top 20 exporters. Even among other advanced countries, the average was 143 percent. The United States still exports more goods and services than any other country in the world, but over the past decade, it relied too much on domestic consumption to drive growth and not enough on the rest of the world. As a result its export growth lagged and its lead shrunk significantly.

Some countries, such as India and Brazil, opened up to the world economy and saw both their exports and imports rise substantially over the decade before the crisis. Their exports as a share of GDP increased, but they were not dependent on external demand for growth because they were both selling to and buying from the world. Yet other countries experienced the mirror image of the U.S. model of the 2000s. Rather than imports and consumption rising faster than incomes, exports and savings increased so that both exports and the trade surplus continued to grow as a share of their economies. These surplus countries thus effectively funded the borrowing of deficit countries and provided less demand support to the world economy. From 2000 to 2008, China's current account rose from a surplus of 2 percent of GDP to 10 percent, while Germany's moved from a deficit to a 7 percent surplus. While Germany's surplus rose, other countries in the euro area (France, Greece, Italy, Portugal, and Spain) experienced rising deficits.

Figure 4-5 shows that as the decade of the 2000s wore on, the global imbalances worsened. The U.S. deficit and the Chinese and German surpluses grew not just as a share of their own GDP but as a share of world GDP as well. By 2007, the U.S. deficit was shrinking as a share of both U.S. and world GDP, but China's surplus continued to rise as a share of world GDP, and the euro-area deficit countries' combined current account deficit was expanding as well.

Figure 4-5
Current Account Deficits or Surpluses as a Share of World GDP

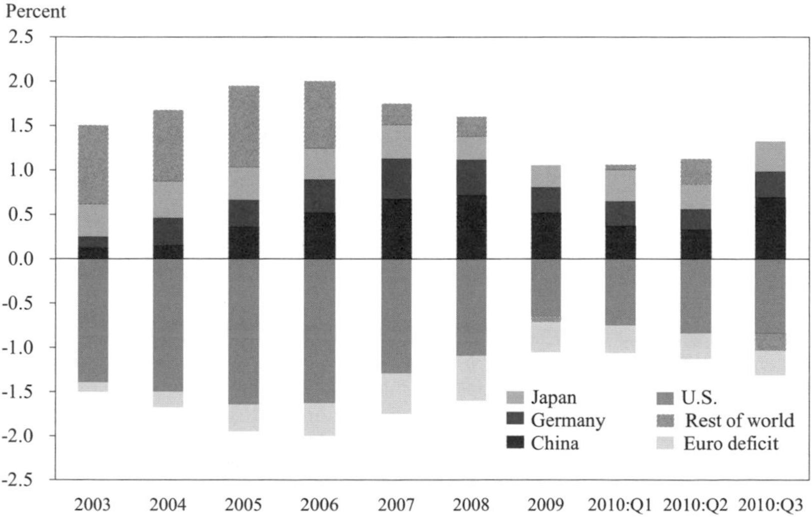

Notes: "Euro deficit" represents France, Greece, Ireland, Portugal and Spain. "Rest of world" represents all other countries not shown here plus the statistical discrepancy.
Sources: Country sources; CEA calculations.

The crisis brought about a sharp change in these imbalances.[5] The U.S. current account deficit shrank from 5 percent of its GDP to less than 3 percent in 2009. At the same time, China's surplus fell from 9.6 percent of its GDP in 2008 to 5.9 percent in 2009. Still, as is clear from the figure, imbalances remain and have begun once again to widen, albeit slowly. The U.S. current account deficit is still less than 4 percent of U.S. GDP and, given that the United States is growing somewhat slower than the world as a whole, this deficit is shrinking further as a share of world GDP. The surpluses in both Germany and China remain above 5 percent, however. Furthermore, when a fast-growing country such as China has a constant surplus as a share of its GDP, that implies the surplus is growing as a share of the world's GDP. Also, while U.S. borrowing in the early 2000s was larger than the surpluses in Germany, Japan, and China combined, over time the current account surpluses in these countries grew, and by the third quarter of 2010, their combined total was considerably larger than the U.S. current account deficit. As noted, the G-20 continues to work on how to reorient countries' policies so they are more mutually consistent and growth is more balanced and sustainable.

Box 4-1: What Do We Owe the Rest of the World?

Because the current account represents net borrowing in a year, it indicates the net capital flows (such as securities purchases, bank deposits, and direct investment) into a country. Along with adjustments for changes in exchange rates and asset prices, the current account measures the change in a country's net foreign wealth (all of the assets its investors own abroad minus all the claims on its economy by foreign investors). Net borrowing by U.S. residents over the past decade has left a negative net international investment position of roughly 20 percent of U.S. GDP. Relative to other countries, this negative position is still fairly small as a share of GDP.[a]

Box 4-1, continued on next page

---

[5] U.S. personal consumption increased to more than 23 percent of the world economy in 2001 and 2002, measured in current dollars, but over time, that share began to shrink. A depreciating real exchange rate and rapid growth in emerging markets meant that by 2007, U.S. consumption as a share of the world economy had declined to 18 percent. Despite growing by 6 percent in 2007, U.S. imports as a share of the world economy fell that year. The simple fact that emerging markets often grow faster suggested that U.S. consumers and U.S. imports could not continue to absorb such a large share of the world economy. The crisis abruptly and sharply changed the relationships, but they were already shifting well before the crisis erupted.

Box 4-1, continued

In addition, foreign investors own only about 11 percent of the overall financial assets in the U.S. economy. This fact is sometimes obscured by foreign investors' preference for U.S. Treasury bills. Because so much of U.S. net foreign debt is concentrated in one asset class, the United States is often viewed as a massive debtor to the world. Foreign investors own roughly one-third of U.S. Treasury securities (roughly one-half if Treasury securities held by government trust funds—such as the Social Security Trust Fund—are excluded) (see box figure). China is the largest foreign holder of U.S Treasuries, but China's investors own just 7 percent of the total—one-fifth as much as U.S. bondholders (some foreign holdings may be misclassified if, for example, China buys Treasuries through a London investment bank that buys them from the United States).

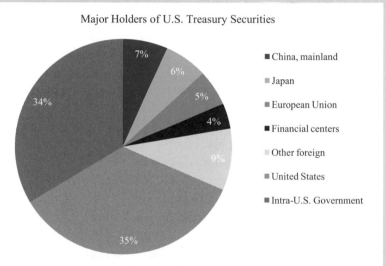

Major Holders of U.S. Treasury Securities

- China, mainland
- Japan
- European Union
- Financial centers
- Other foreign
- United States
- Intra-U.S. Government

Notes: Financial centers include Caribbean banking centers, Hong Kong, Luxembourg, Singapore, and Switzerland.
Sources: Treasury International Capital data, October 2010; Department of the Treasury, Monthly Statement of the Public Debt of the United States.

ᵃ The U.S. net international investment position has not become as negative as one might have expected based on the amount of borrowing over the 2000s. In addition to borrowing in any given year, the values of U.S. foreign assets and liabilities change in response to changes in market conditions. Over the past decade, the United States has had, on net, positive "valuation effects" (Lane and Milesi-Ferretti 2009). Strong asset performance in the United States and changes in currency may have led to a decline in the net international investment position in 2010.

Determinants of Exports

The United States is well positioned to spur growth through exports, even if the precise composition of the goods and services America will sell to the world in the future is not known today. The pattern of trade between one economy and another, quite different, economy is determined in part by the forces of comparative advantage, that is, what it is that differentiates the two economies. Comparative advantage can lie in differences in labor productivity, the relative availability of a country's natural and physical resources, the educational priorities that help to determine the skill sets of its people, and even the institutions that can create different conditions across national markets. For example, the United States exports high-tech machinery to other countries that may not have the high-skill labor or advanced technology required to make those goods. Also, high judicial quality and good contract enforcement give the United States an advantage in the production of goods and services that require businesses to invest to tailor products to particular consumer needs. Thus, the United States has a comparative advantage in highly complex products that are difficult to commoditize. Such products may require teamwork in the design and production process and substantial financial investment in research and development (R&D) and hence commitment to the protection of intellectual property.

But comparative advantage does not explain the determinants of and benefits to the back-and-forth trade of similar products (intraindustry trade), especially that taking place between similar economies. A modern-day example is trade in smartphones. Beginning in the late 1990s, a Canadian firm was a first entrant to the wireless communications market, and U.S. business consumers flocked to import a mobile device that could send and receive e-mail messages. Soon thereafter, U.S. firms innovated and engineered different varieties of these mobile products with additional features that increasingly appealed to individual consumers as well. Consumers in other countries (including Canada) imported substantial quantities of these U.S.-designed smartphones. The ability to trade internationally let these firms produce for multiple markets and take advantage of scale economies, and it encouraged their entrepreneurship and innovation by providing a larger potential market. But manufacturers are not the only ones that gain; consumers in the United States and Canada also benefit through access to foreign-designed varieties of the product in addition to those that are conceived and produced domestically.

Product quality is also important to understanding the determinants of intraindustry exports. Generally speaking, richer countries tend to specialize in higher-quality goods within the same product type, while developing and emerging economies tend to focus on goods further down the quality ladder. For example, Italy may import low-cost T-shirts from China, but it is a leader in exporting high-quality, high-fashion shirts to the world. Those products that have wide variation in quality allow advanced-country firms to differentiate their goods and services away from imported varieties from low-wage countries.

Manufacturing Exports. While the United States is still the largest combined exporter of goods and services, America has slid from being the world's leading exporter of goods at the beginning of the century to the third position, behind China and Germany. Nevertheless, the United States continues to export over $1 trillion of goods annually, more than three-quarters of which are manufactured, and these exports support more than one-fourth of the manufacturing jobs in the United States. As Figure 4-6 indicates, manufacturing and agriculture goods combine to make up more than two-thirds of total U.S. exports.

Figure 4-6
U.S. Exports by Sector

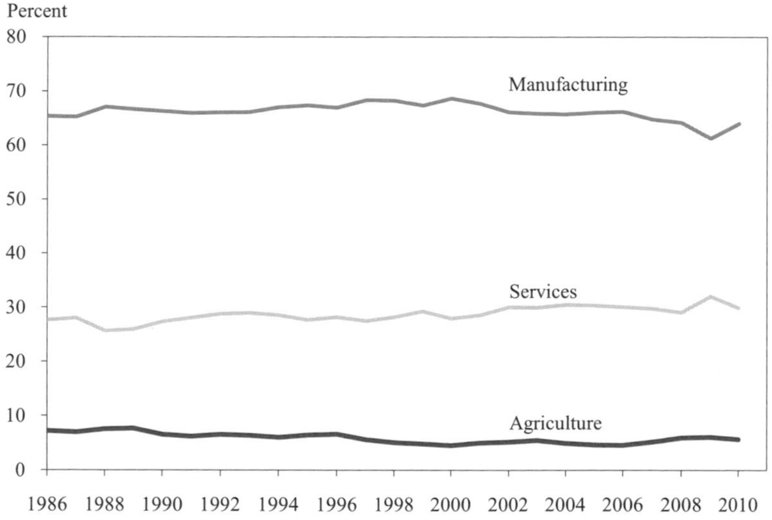

Note: 2010 data are through October.
Sources: Bureau of Economic Analysis / Census Bureau, U.S. International Trade in Goods and Services.

Experience from other high-income countries shows that a shift in the world share of exported goods does not mean a shift entirely out of manufacturing and into a service-only economy. Germany, the second-place goods exporter, maintains a substantial share of manufacturing in its economy and exports many of these products (including to emerging markets). Manufacturing is also a larger share of the economy in Japan than it is in the United States. Like the United States, these countries have a floating currency and highly paid, high-skilled workers. The rise of emerging markets—with lower wages but also lower productivity—has not forced these high-income countries out of manufacturing. Richer countries do tend to produce and consume more services than do emerging-market countries. Nevertheless, manufacturing, especially of complex products, continues to play a substantial role in advanced economies, including the U.S. economy.

Services Exports. Services are of increasing importance to high-income economies. Some services are nontraded, such as restaurant meals, live entertainment, and cleaning services. But services such as consulting, finance, architecture, accounting, law, and tourism are traded. With improvements in communications technology as well as infrastructure, many services are becoming increasingly tradable. As noted, nearly one-third of total U.S. exports annually are in services. Figure 4-7 shows the rapid growth of U.S. services exports as well as the growing surplus in U.S. services trade.

Figure 4-7
U.S. Trade in Services

Source: Census Bureau, U.S. International Trade in Goods and Services.

Some of the largest and fastest-growing U.S. services exports are in business, professional, and technical services. Other important categories are insurance, finance, and education services. Analogous to the case of goods exports, U.S. service exports are in sectors where U.S. firms and employees offer world-class, high-quality performance and thus give the United States a strong comparative advantage.

Changing Composition of Goods and Services Exports. Economic forces have traditionally allowed the United States to produce and export many of the goods and services in which it had a comparative advantage at that point in time. There is no reason to think that those forces will cease to operate going forward.

As the next section documents in more detail, the growth in U.S. exports is coming from new demand, much of it from emerging economies. Some emerging markets are quickly urbanizing and shifting away from subsistence agriculture, thus increasing foreign demand for U.S.-grown farm exports such as soybeans, corn, and wheat. These emerging economies are developing a sizable middle class, newly able to afford the higher-quality goods and services that they may not have been able to buy in the past. And the expansion of home-grown businesses in emerging economies creates new demand for R&D-intensive, highly complex products, such as aircraft, turbojets, oil and gas field machinery, electronic integrated circuits, and medical instruments. These products frequently sit at the top of the U.S. export list, and U.S. exports of these products will likely sit at the top of the quality ladder.

The details may be impossible to forecast accurately, but past experience suggests that the U.S. export industry is likely to be built on high-quality goods and services that tap into entrepreneurial talents and that reflect the United States' commitment to reward an innovative workforce. Many of the policies and programs described in Chapter 3 as essential to long-run innovation and growth are also critical to the successful evolution of the United States as it adjusts to changes in the world economy.

Evolving U.S. Trade Patterns

Even before the global economic crisis and recession of 2007–09, the United States had been in the midst of a longer-term reorientation of its international trade patterns. Understanding the relative shift in these trade patterns is as important as coming to terms with the shifting trends in the underlying goods and services that the United States produces and exports. While historical trading partners such as Canada, Japan, and the European Union continue to be a strong component of overall U.S. trade, the new and most dynamic sources of U.S. trading relationships are coming from other places in the world.

Increasing Trade with Emerging Economies. The share of total U.S. exports sent to mature trading partners has been declining for decades. The share of total U.S. goods exports consumed by the 27 countries of the European Union (EU) dropped from nearly one-third (31 percent) in 1948 to one-fifth (21 percent) in 2009, even though these economies have

grown increasingly wealthy. The share of total U.S. goods exports to historically important high-income economies like Japan and Canada has also
shown signs of decline (Figure 4-8). But the European Union, Canada, and
Japan are not buying less from the United States than they did in the past.
Rather, U.S. exporters are now shipping an increasing amount of goods to
other, faster-growing economies, in addition to maintaining their historical
trading relations (Figure 4-9).

Figure 4-8
Share of U.S. Goods Exports to Mature Foreign Economies

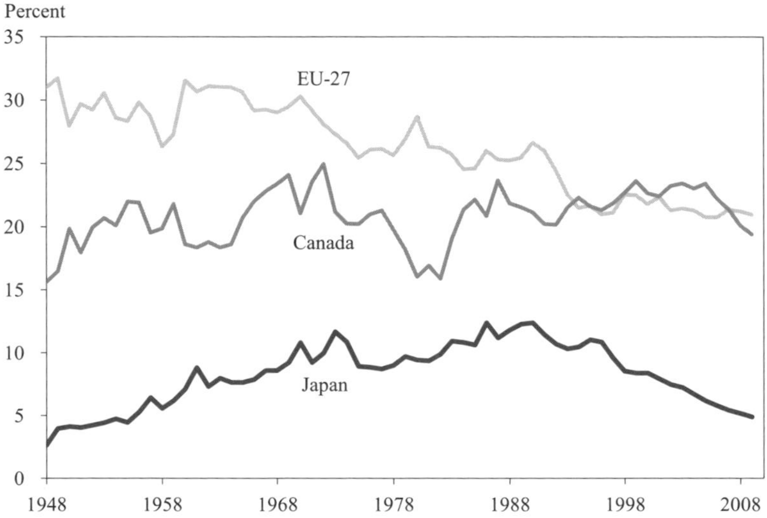

Sources: IMF Direction of Trade Statistics; CEA calculations.

U.S. trade with China exemplifies this story. As late as 2000, the year
before China joined the World Trade Organization (WTO) and substantially
opened its market to imports, only 2 percent of all U.S. goods exports went
to China. By 2009, after a decade of rapid growth, China had become the
fourth-largest destination market for U.S. goods exports after the European
Union, Canada, and Mexico. Mexico is another prime example. Mexico's
import tariffs in 1982 averaged 16 percent with a maximum rate of 100
percent (de la Torre and González 2005). Mexico signed onto the General
Agreement on Tariffs and Trade (GATT) in 1986, and by 1992 it had cut
those tariffs under the GATT to an average of 11 percent with a maximum
rate of only 20 percent. In recent years, the share of total U.S. goods exports
to Mexico has remained steady at 12 percent, nearly double its level in the
early 1980s before Mexico liberalized its economy, signed onto the GATT,
and negotiated the North American Free Trade Agreement (NAFTA).

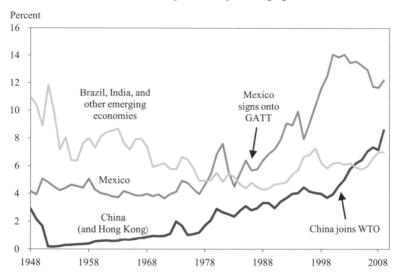

Figure 4-9
Share of U.S. Goods Exports to Major Emerging Economies

Percent

Brazil, India, and other emerging economies

Mexico signs onto GATT

Mexico

China (and Hong Kong)

China joins WTO

Sources: IMF Direction of Trade Statistics; CEA calculations.

U.S. exports to several other emerging economies still have room to grow. The share of total U.S. goods exports going to Brazil, India, and a number of other emerging economies (see Figure 4-9) has increased slightly from its mid-1980s low point, hitting a recent peak in the mid-1990s when some of these economies went through an initial phase of trade liberalization. U.S. export growth to these economies has since leveled off. Whether future U.S. export growth to these other emerging economies replicates the experience of earlier U.S. export expansions into China and Mexico—and even to Japan through the 1980s (see Figure 4-8)—depends partly on the extent to which these other emerging economies commit to liberalizing their import markets. A key item on the Administration's trade agenda is therefore continued work to open these markets through the Doha Round of WTO negotiations.

U.S. import patterns are also experiencing a reorientation. At the end of the 1940s, Japan and the European Union countries were still devastated by World War II and far from being the mature economies they are now. After these economies rebuilt, however, they quickly became large sources for U.S. imports. The European economies peaked at supplying nearly 30 percent of U.S. goods imports in the late 1960s; Japan peaked at roughly 20 percent of U.S. imports in the mid-1980s. Imports from Canada peaked at nearly 30 percent around 1970. U.S. imports from Canada, the European Union, and Japan continue to grow, but the share of U.S. imports from these countries has declined as imports from fast-growing export markets, including China and Mexico, have increased (Figure 4-10).

Figure 4-10
Share of U.S. Goods Imports by Foreign Source

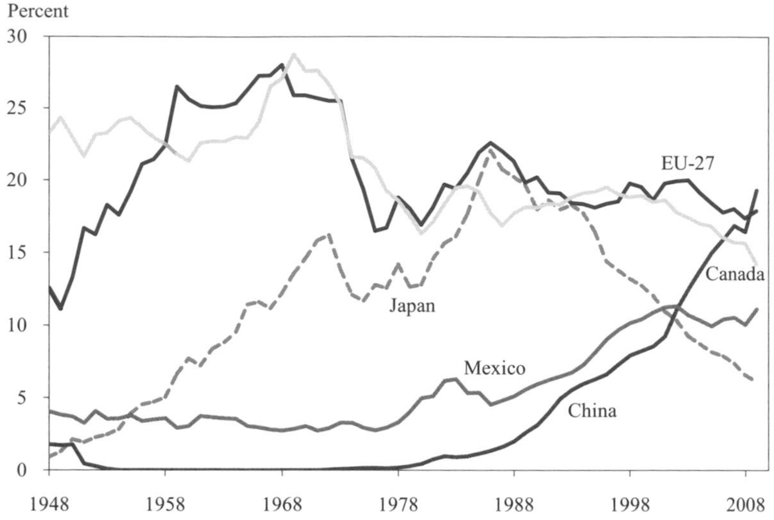

Percent

Sources: IMF Direction of Trade Statistics; CEA calculations.

Doubling U.S. Exports. In his January 2010 State of the Union address, the President established a goal of doubling U.S. exports of goods and services in five years, meaning that nominal exports would double from their 2009 level of $1.57 trillion to an annual level of $3.14 trillion by the end of 2014. To meet that goal, U.S. exports need to grow an average of 15 percent a year. So far, exports are on track to meet or exceed that pace. Through the first three quarters of 2010, U.S. exports of goods and services increased by 17 percent relative to the same period in 2009. Doubling exports over five years will increase the number of jobs supported by exports, and importantly, these are, on average, higher-paying jobs.

Goods exports have been rising faster than total exports, increasing 22 percent through the first three quarters of 2010. But that total masks significant variation in exports to different regions. U.S. goods exports to the Pacific Rim (East Asia and Oceania) increased by 32 percent, to Latin America by 29 percent, to Canada and Mexico by 26 percent, but to Europe by only 9 percent. This slow export growth to Europe means that even though it is a key export partner, the European market contributed very little to export growth in 2010. Some of this variation is attributable to the longer term, pre-crisis trends in which U.S. exports to many emerging economies were already increasing.

The extent to which a region drives U.S. export growth is not simply a function of the growth rate of U.S. exports to the region. The size of the trading relationship matters. Even though exports to our NAFTA partners grew more slowly than those to the Pacific Rim, exports to Canada and Mexico contributed more to total export growth because they represented roughly a third of all U.S. exports. Still, increasing demand from emerging markets is essential to the growth of U.S. exports. Emerging markets accounted for 43 percent of U.S. goods exports during the first nine months of 2010, but they generated half of the export growth during that period and might have generated even more than half had not excellent U.S. export performance to Canada and Korea helped keep up export growth to advanced regions. Faster growth of exports to emerging economies means their share of U.S. exports will rise over time.

Figure 4-11
U.S. Export Growth vs. Foreign GDP Growth, 2009:Q2 – 2010:Q2

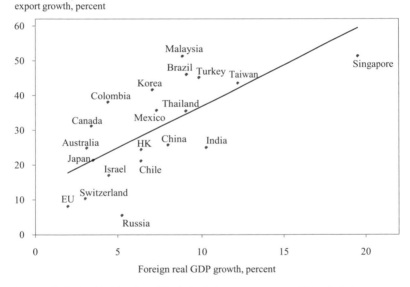

Sources: IMF Monthly Direction of Trade Statistics; country sources; CEA calculations.

A crucial determinant of U.S. export growth to a region is the pace at which that market is growing, that is, the speed and depth of trading partners' domestic economic recoveries. Figure 4-11 illustrates this fact by showing the strong positive relationship between growth in foreign real GDP and nominal growth in U.S. goods exports between the second quarter of 2009 and the second quarter of 2010. The relationship suggests that each percentage point of economic growth in a country is correlated with more than 2 percentage points of additional U.S. bilateral export growth. Eliminating Singapore, the sole outlier, leads to a relationship of roughly three to one.[6] Thus, growth abroad is good for the United States—the global economy is not a zero-sum game.

Figure 4-12
Projected Share of U.S. Nominal Export Growth, 2009–14

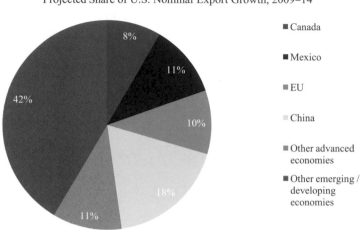

- Canada
- Mexico
- EU
- China
- Other advanced economies
- Other emerging / developing economies

Sources: IMF, World Economic Outlook, October 2010; Bureau of Economic Analysis / Census Bureau, U.S. International Trade in Goods and Services; CEA calculations.

U.S. export growth also benefits from changes in relative prices caused by faster inflation in growing emerging markets because faster inflation abroad means U.S. goods are cheaper on world markets relative to goods from these countries. These price and growth relationships suggest that if the United States is to double exports, an overwhelming portion of that new export growth will come from faster-growing emerging and developing economies. Figure 4-12 shows the share of projected growth of U.S. nominal exports by region using IMF forecasts for GDP and price growth in different regions. Trade with America's traditional partners will remain important. For example, trade with the European Union is likely still to be roughly 20 percent of U.S. exports by 2014, and growth in exports to EU countries will be roughly 10 percent of U.S. export growth over the five-year period. But more than 70 percent of U.S. export growth is projected to come from Mexico, China, and other emerging and developing countries. Growth in

[6] These findings are consistent with standard results on aggregate relationships across countries, which suggest that growth of real exports increases roughly 2 percent for every 1 percent of world real GDP growth; see Chinn (2005) and IMF (2007). In addition, one would expect U.S. export prices to rise in fast-growing markets, so the result that nominal growth of U.S. goods exports rose at a faster pace than the anticipated real growth is also to be expected.

these countries and active engagement in trade with them will be essential to meeting the Administration's goal of doubling U.S. exports in five years.

TRADE POLICY

Recent economic research has focused on U.S. firm productivity and the fixed cost of exporting as fundamental determinants of which U.S. businesses are able to enter new markets and export successfully (Bernard et al. 2007). Some costs to firms of market entry are well known—for example, learning about customer-specific attributes and tailoring products accordingly, establishing new distribution networks to reach a market, and targeting advertising to attract those new customers. Nevertheless, U.S. businesses that seek to enter a new foreign market sometimes have to overcome additional costs, such as foreign import tariffs. Another such cost is nontariff barriers, including foreign requirements that the exporting firm undertake a costly modification of its export product to fit local standards, even in the absence of any recognized technical, safety, or customer benefit for doing so.

Appropriately tailored government policy can reduce some of the costs that firms must incur to export to new foreign markets. In particular, the President's National Export Initiative includes several policy instruments aimed at reducing these costs. These instruments include negotiating the reduction of foreign tariffs and removal of nontariff barriers to trade, enforcing existing market access agreements, and increasing advocacy and access to credit for U.S. exporters.

Negotiating to Open New Markets

Any import tariff in a foreign market is an additional cost to market entry that U.S. firms must factor into their export decisions. Despite the trade liberalization of the past few decades, U.S. exporters still encounter substantial unevenness in the tariff treatment they receive.

For example, U.S. exporters enjoy low tariffs and open markets in U.S. NAFTA partners Mexico and Canada. Equally important are the relatively open markets of several high-income economies with which the United States has partnered for more than 60 years under the WTO and the GATT before it. As Table 4-1 shows, the European Union and Japan offer U.S. exporters most-favored-nation (MFN) tariff rates that are on average only moderately higher than the average rate the United States applies toward their exports. The applied import tariffs of these high-income economies are also quite close to their "bound" rates—that is, the upward limits that their applied tariffs cannot legally exceed without compensation to their trading partners. The third column of the table provides an alternative and more sophisticated measure of import "restrictiveness," the overall trade restrictiveness index (OTRI), that takes into account not only import tariffs but also some nontariff measures and the potential responsiveness of imports and exports (elasticities) to changes in trade barriers (Kee, Nicita, and Olarreaga 2009); it does not take into account trade distortions caused by undervalued exchange rates. The United States is also quite open based on this index, but Japan's OTRI is nearly twice as large, indicating that its nontariff measures are an important constraint to the ability of trading partners to export to its market.

Table 4-1
Import Tariffs, Nontariff Measures, and Trade Restrictiveness, 2008

Economy	Import regime			Conditions facing exporters
	Applied MFN Tariff (simple average, %)	Bound MFN Tariff (simple average, %)	Overall Trade Restrictiveness Index (OTRI)	Foreign Trade Restrictiveness Index (MA-OTRI)
United States	3.5	3.5	6.3	10.3
European Union	5.6	5.5	6.4	9.1
Japan	5.4	5.4	11.3	7.9
Korea	12.2	17.0	--	9.8
Colombia	12.5	42.9	19.9	8.1
Panama	7.2	23.5	--	12.6
China	9.6	10.0	9.8	9.2
Brazil	13.6	31.4	20.3	12.3
India	13.0	49.0	18.0	8.5
Russia	10.8	--	19.0	4.0

Notes: Russia's tariffs are not bound because it is not a WTO member. Dashes indicate data are not available. The most recently available year's data are reported where OTRI and MA-OTRI for 2008 are not available.
Sources: Tariff data from WTO (2009); OTRI and MA-OTRI from World Bank, World Trade Indicators.

There are substantial differences between the openness of these particular high-income economies and other important U.S. trading partners, however. First, consider Korea, a country with which the United States recently concluded negotiations on a trade agreement, as well as Colombia and Panama, countries with which the United States is seeking free trade agreements. Relatively high tariffs in these countries (see Table 4-1) are likely to remain in place until trade agreements negotiated with them are ratified and implemented. Completion of these agreements has the potential to lower and secure these import tariffs for U.S. exporters at rates much closer to zero and also to remove many other burdensome nontariff measures (Box 4-2). However, these gains will be realized only if the agreements address these burdensome measures in a sustainable way, which is why the Administration is committed to supporting only agreements that secure serious concessions and that overall are in the interest of U.S. workers and the U.S. economy.

Box 4-2: The Korea-United States Free Trade Agreement

In December 2010, the Administration announced the successful resolution of the outstanding issues with the Korea-United States free trade agreement (KORUS). The agreement is the most economically significant free trade pact that the United States has negotiated and signed in nearly 20 years. A study by the U.S. International Trade Commission estimated that the agreement could boost U.S. annual goods exports to Korea, including agriculture products and autos, by as much as $11 billion. The agreement also includes Korean commitments expected to result in considerable expansion of U.S. services exports.

Table 4-1 highlights why agreements like KORUS are especially critical for the competitiveness of U.S. exporters. In its absence, U.S. exporting firms face an average Korean import tariff of 12.2 percent; under the agreement, this rate will eventually reach zero and will help U.S. exports compete in Korea against Korean firms. Without KORUS, U.S. exporters would also be at a competitive disadvantage with other foreign competitors that also export to Korea. The European Union has signed a similar trade agreement with Korea, scheduled to be implemented in July 2011, that would give its exports a leg up. Indeed, in little more than 10 years, the United States has already fallen from being the number one exporter to Korea to being the fourth-largest supplier, trailing China, Japan, and the European Union. Implementation of KORUS and the lowering of Korea's tariffs toward U.S. exporters are expected to help stem further erosion.

The KORUS may also result in changes to the composition and source of U.S. imports. Korea's exporters already face a relatively low average U.S. tariff of 3.5 percent even without the agreement. KORUS would eventually lower that rate to the level enjoyed by the United States' other free trade partners, including Canada and Mexico.

Second, the major emerging economies also tend to have more restrictive import regimes than the high-income economies. Economic growth in China, India, and Brazil has surged in part because these nations lowered their import tariffs significantly from their levels of 20 years ago. U.S. firms have responded to those reductions by increasing exports to these new markets over the past 15 years, providing these economies with key goods and services that contribute to their growth. Nevertheless, Table 4-1 indicates that the import tariffs that remain in these economies are still relatively high.

Just as U.S. trade shows a reorientation toward emerging economies, U.S. trade liberalization negotiations have turned toward these same emerging economies, especially through forums such as the WTO's Doha Round of multilateral negotiations. Dubbed the Doha Development Agenda, the negotiations are focused in part on the power of trade liberalization to enhance the development prospects of low-income countries. The Administration is pushing for an ambitious set of trade liberalization commitments under the Doha Round not only to enhance opportunities for U.S. exporters of manufactured goods, services, and agricultural products, but also to increase opportunities for development-enhancing trade among developing countries. Emerging economies such as China, India, and Brazil will have a particular responsibility to further reduce and bind their import tariffs to produce such an outcome.

The need for partners to commit to additional trade liberalization is confirmed by evidence from the last column of Table 4-1, which reports a separate World Bank index (the market access-overall trade restrictiveness index, or MA-OTRI) of the average trade restrictiveness facing a country's exporters from all of its foreign markets combined. The index is based on tariff levels and some nontariff measures that trading partners impose (again, not including an undervalued exchange rate), and the importance of those measures is weighted by the composition of the exporting country's exports in addition to the exporter's and its trading partners' responsiveness (elasticities) to trade. Lower numbers reflect fewer trade barriers confronting the country's exporters. By this measure, the average U.S. exporter faces trade restrictions surpassed only by those facing exporters from Panama and Brazil. One reason for this high index number for the United States (and a main driver of it for Brazil and Panama) is that it is a major agricultural exporter and agricultural trade barriers around the world remain high: they need to be negotiated and reduced. Nevertheless, U.S. exporters face trade barriers that are higher than they are for Japan, the European Union, and other important competitors in global export markets. The Administration is therefore committed to negotiating better terms for U.S. exporters to help level the playing field. In addition to completion of free trade agreements with Korea, as well as Colombia and Panama, and a successful conclusion of the Doha Round, the Administration is placing increased emphasis on persuading Asian economies to reduce trade barriers and open themselves to U.S. exporters through the Trans-Pacific Partnership.

Encouraging Exports by Enforcing Existing Agreements

The Administration works to increase U.S. exports through regular engagement in bilateral and regional trade policy forums in a way that encourages trading partners to live up to their international commitments and obligations. These trade dialogues facilitate policy reforms, yield additional foreign market access, and level the playing field for American workers and companies. For example, in December 2010, the Administration worked with China through the Joint Commission on Commerce and Trade to improve China's intellectual property rights protection, better ensure non-discriminatory treatment of foreign suppliers and products, and provide fair treatment for new technologies. Similar successes are occurring through other dialogues, notably in other emerging economies throughout Asia, Africa, and Latin America.

Nevertheless, enforcement of existing trade agreements sometimes means that the U.S. Government resorts to dispute settlement provisions to resolve trade frictions, whether under a free trade agreement or more commonly under the WTO's multilateral auspices. The total number of disputes the United States has filed at the WTO has declined over time, dropping from 68 initiated between 1995 and 2000 to only 29 initiated between 2001 and 2010. As trading partners increasingly commit to open their markets to U.S. exporters, enforcement becomes increasingly important to ensure that trading partners live up to their agreements. Enforcement is a fundamental role for the Federal Government; under WTO rules, exporting firms themselves cannot challenge another country's trade actions. As such, U.S. Trade Representative Ronald Kirk has frequently stated the Administration's commitment to step up enforcement on behalf of U.S. exporting interests.[7]

A growing share of the complaints the United States has filed with the WTO is now being filed against emerging economies. As Figure 4-13 shows, nearly two-thirds of all disputes the United States brought between 2001 and 2010 were against emerging economies, up from roughly one-third between 1995 and 2000. This increase is not surprising given the importance the United States places on maintaining current and future trade with these emerging economies. During the 2008–09 crisis, for example, the number of import restrictions imposed on U.S. exporters by emerging markets increased substantially relative to those imposed by high-income trading partners (Bown 2010). Historically, many U.S. disputes allege that some element of a newly imposed import restriction that is obstructing U.S. exports is inconsistent with WTO rules.

---

[7] See, for example, his speech at Georgetown University on April 23, 2009.

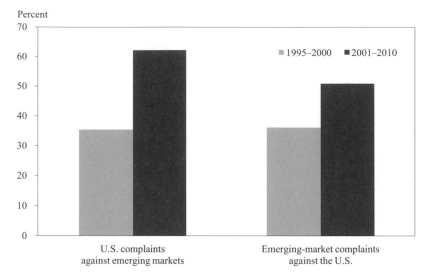

Figure 4-13
U.S. Trade Disputes at the WTO

Notes: Percentages are for the number of disputes initiated during the period. Disputes are broken down into bilateral (respondent/complainant) pairs.
Sources: WTO (2010); CEA calculations.

At the same time, as Figure 4-13 indicates, the share of disputes filed against the United States by foreign exporters in emerging economies attempting to protect their access to the U.S. import market has also grown. Because an increasing share of U.S. imports derives from emerging markets, these economies are now the most frequent challengers to U.S. trade policy.

Two additional points regarding the U.S. Government role in WTO disputes are worth highlighting. First, use of the WTO dispute resolution mechanism represents attempts to resolve differences between trading partners through rulings based on the application of agreed international trade rules. During 1995–2000, when more U.S. exports were destined for high-income economies, most U.S. disputes filed at the WTO were lodged against these economies, even though they were and continue to be strategic allies. The process was designed to prevent trade issues from escalating in a manner that would increase barriers to international trade.

Second, despite the growing importance of enforcement to keep foreign markets open to U.S. export interests, the U.S. Government's enforcement role has become ever more complex. The production process of many goods is increasingly fragmented into supply chains that cross international borders. As a result, domestic stakeholders often have varied interests with respect to the issues that may arise in a particular dispute.

When the U.S. exporter facing a new foreign trade barrier is also a multi-national firm with significant affiliate activity in that foreign market, that firm may be hesitant to publicly support U.S. Government actions to have the trade impediment removed. The company could face many forms of reprisal from the foreign government in ways that the U.S. Government is legally unable to help fight and that may cost the company more than it loses under the trade restriction. The complexities facing U.S. enforcement of the rights of U.S. exporters and the interests of the U.S. workforce are likely to continue to escalate as technology improves, transport costs continue to fall, and production processes continue to be integrated among operations in various nations.

Advocacy to Encourage Exporters, Credit, and Trade Facilitation

Part of the fixed cost of exporting can be learning about a market or making the necessary investments in building relationships. In many cases, the Federal Government may already have that information and can thus lower the cost of exporting by sharing it. As such, several WTO-consistent policies may help boost the visibility of U.S. exports, especially those produced by small- and medium-size firms, and lower the hurdle that each firm faces in entering new markets.

One approach, contained in the President's National Export Initiative, is for the U.S. Government to improve advocacy abroad. For example, trade fairs can showcase export-ready enterprises that may be too small or too young to be a part of the larger industry associations that often organize promotions. Advocacy could also involve better support from consular offices abroad, such as providing exporters with contacts and buyer-seller information.

The government can facilitate trade by offering trade credit to match the terms available to firms in other countries. Investments in the U.S. transportation and supply chain infrastructure are critical to enabling U.S. exporters to move their goods to ports quickly and inexpensively. The Administration is also committed to negotiating agreements on trade facilitation abroad so that U.S. exports can be shipped to foreign customers more efficiently. At an even more basic level, the Government, through the Small Business Administration, the Export-Import Bank, or the International Trade Administration, can work with U.S. firms (especially small businesses) to help them navigate the process of exporting.

In the end, the decision whether to export to a given country is a private market decision made every day by thousands of U.S. firms. Nevertheless, the National Export Initiative sets out an ambitious agenda by which the Federal Government can play a more constructive role for U.S. businesses and their workforce.

CONCLUSION

As the United States orients its economy toward more exports and more investment, growth in exports will be determined by U.S. interactions with a complex and changing world economy. Trade relationships of today look little like those of 50 years ago, when different countries led the world economy and played leading roles in U.S. trade. Recognizing those changes and engaging constructively with the world as it is today can be a significant source of growth for the U.S. economy for decades to come.

C H A P T E R   5

HEALTH CARE REFORM

On March 23, 2010, President Obama signed into law landmark legislation that extends health insurance coverage to millions of uninsured Americans, ensures the security and affordability of coverage for many more, and reduces the Nation's budget deficit. The Affordable Care Act is the latest chapter in nearly a century-long history of efforts to ensure comprehensive health insurance coverage for more Americans.[1] At the same time, the new law marks an important new chapter in the quest for high value in health spending. For decades, the policy problem posed by millions of uninsured Americans has overshadowed the underlying economic challenge of how to control health care costs while preserving the high quality of the American medical care system. In addition to extending coverage to the uninsured and reforming insurance markets to ensure that Americans with pre-existing conditions have access to affordable coverage, the Affordable Care Act introduces a framework for moving the medical care system toward higher-value care.

Broadly, the Affordable Care Act controls costs and improves quality by strengthening physician and hospital incentives to improve the quality of care and provide care more efficiently. These delivery system reforms are paired with coverage reforms that create new coverage options through competitive state marketplaces for insurance, ensure access to affordable coverage through the provision of tax credits for small businesses and individuals, and put in place individual and employer responsibility requirements. Over the next decade, these reforms are expected to expand coverage to 32 million Americans, make health care more affordable, and improve the quality of care.

---

[1] We use the term "Affordable Care Act" to mean the Patient Protection and Affordable Care Act (P.L. 111-148, enacted March 23, 2010) and the provisions of the Health Care and Education Reconciliation Act of 2010 (P.L. 111-152, enacted March 30, 2010) that are related to health care.

Many reforms that afford significant protection to consumers have already taken effect (Box 5-1). These reforms, in conjunction with those that will go into effect in a few years' time, provide Americans with unprecedented security, giving individuals and families freedom from worry about losing their insurance or having their coverage capped unexpectedly when they are sick. The Affordable Care Act also represents a significant tax cut for individuals and businesses purchasing health insurance; already, many small business owners who provided insurance to employees in 2010 are eligible for tax credits to offset the cost of this coverage, helping them make new hires and strengthening our economy. Beginning in 2014, additional tax credits for individuals and households will help millions of middle-class Americans afford health insurance. As a result of the Affordable Care Act, 1.2 million young adults up to age 26 now qualify for insurance under their parents' health plans. The Affordable Care Act also provides new benefits to America's seniors, improving the coverage of preventive care in Medicare and lowering the cost of prescription drugs under Medicare Part D by closing the "donut hole."

The Affordable Care Act is also fiscally responsible. The Congressional Budget Office has estimated that the law will reduce projected deficits by $230 billion during 2012–21 and by more than $1 trillion in the subsequent decade. The Affordable Care Act improves the financial status of the Medicare program by extending the solvency of the Hospital Insurance Trust Fund by 12 years. It provides unprecedented new authorities for fighting fraud, thus potentially returning hundreds of millions of dollars to the Medicare trust funds.

This chapter offers an economic analysis of how the Affordable Care Act will achieve the long-run goals of expanding coverage and making health care affordable once its major provisions take effect in 2014. The discussion is not meant to be exhaustive, and it necessarily excludes many parts of the law.[2] The focus is on the major provisions to promote value in the delivery of medical care and to expand insurance coverage. The measures aimed at controlling costs focus on promoting the provision of high-value medical care and improving the quality of care provided. Measures that expand coverage rely primarily on private markets. In both areas—controlling costs and expanding coverage—the discussion highlights the imperfections in markets for medical care and health insurance that are addressed by the Affordable Care Act. The aim is to explain how these policies work with, rather than against, the underlying economic forces that drive consumers and firms.

---

[2] Significant investments in health care workforce development and in community health centers are just a few important elements of the reform bill that this chapter does not discuss.

Box 5-1: Early Provisions of the Affordable Care Act

Although some of the Affordable Care Act's major provisions—such as the Health Insurance Exchanges and health insurance premium tax credits for individuals and families—do not go into effect until 2014, many provisions take effect much sooner, expanding coverage and making care more affordable.

Effective within 100 days of enactment

- The **Pre-Existing Condition Insurance Plan** provides coverage to individuals with pre-existing conditions who would otherwise be unable to obtain coverage.
- The **Early Retiree Reinsurance Program** helps employers with the cost of providing health insurance coverage for early retirees with unusually high medical spending.
- Rebate checks for $250 go to eligible beneficiaries to help **close the Medicare Part D coverage gap (the "donut hole").** The donut hole will be eliminated entirely by 2020.
- A Web portal—**www.HealthCare.gov**—enables consumers to search for the best plan for their needs at the lowest cost.
- A **Small Business Health Care Tax Credit** offsets the costs of offering health insurance for small firms with low-wage workers (applies to tax years beginning on or after January 1, 2010).

Effective for insurance plan years beginning six months after enactment

- **Consumer protections** prohibit insurance industry practices such as rescinding coverage, imposing lifetime caps on benefits, imposing unreasonable annual dollar limits on essential health benefits, and denying coverage for children based on pre-existing conditions.
- Private insurance plans covering dependent children must provide **coverage for adult children up to age 26 on a parent's plan.**
- New private insurance plans must provide **100 percent coverage with no additional out-of-pocket costs for preventive care and medical screening,** such as smoking cessation programs and blood pressure screening in adults, given an A or B rating by the U.S. Preventive Services Task Force.

Addressing the Rising Cost of Medical Care

Trends in Aggregate Health Spending

Health care spending has increased dramatically over the past half-century, both in absolute terms and as a share of gross domestic product (GDP) (Figure 5-1), placing increasing pressure on household finances, government budgets, and businesses' bottom line. Total spending in the U.S. health care sector was $2.5 trillion in 2009, representing 17.6 percent of GDP—almost twice its share in 1980.

Figure 5-1
GDP and Health Spending

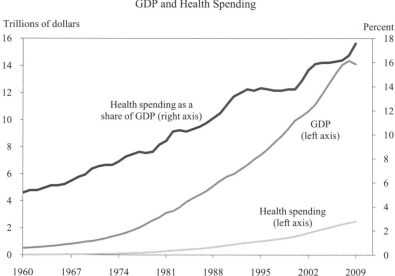

Sources: Centers for Medicare and Medicaid Services, National Health Expenditure Accounts; Bureau of Economic Analysis, National Income and Product Accounts.

These trends have given rise to concern that the Nation cannot sustain such high spending growth and must "bend the curve" of health spending. The challenge is to do so by transforming the Nation's health care system so that it rewards providers for delivering high-quality, high-value care and discourages the provision of low-quality, low-value care. Meeting that challenge is a much more complex task than simply slowing the growth of spending, but the benefits of a system that delivers high-value care are much greater than the benefits of one that simply delivers low-cost care.

Technological Change and Increases in Health Spending

Most health economists agree that increases in health spending are driven largely by the breathtaking pace of technological innovation in health care. The question is whether the benefits of these new technologies are worth their high cost. Economists have thought about that question in two different ways and have generally concluded that these technological breakthroughs are absolutely worth the cost.

The first approach is to estimate directly the costs and benefits associated with increases in health spending. Recent economic analyses of this kind confirm that the advance of technology in medicine is indeed "worth it" in terms of health benefits provided (Cutler and McClellan 2001; Cutler, Rosen, and Vijan 2006). Murphy and Topel (2006) estimate that discovering a cure for cancer, for example, would be worth about $50 trillion; a breakthrough that lowers cancer mortality permanently by even 1 percent would be worth almost $500 billion.

A second approach involves opportunity costs: what are we giving up to be able to spend so much on medical care? In this context, it is important to keep in mind that spending on health has risen during a period of overall economic growth. Health may be a "superior good" in the economic sense that as GDP rises, more and more resources go to health because other material needs are largely satisfied. Hall and Jones (2007) use a personal analogy: "[A]s we get older and richer, which is more valuable: a third car, yet another television, more clothing—or an extra year of life?" In fact GDP has grown so much over the past 50 years that increases in health spending, as large as they have been, have generally not reduced spending on nonhealth items. Rather than falling, real per capita spending on all nonhealth items more than doubled between 1960 and 1999 (Chernew, Hirth, and Cutler 2003).

Market Imperfections and Increases in Health Care Spending

Although increased spending on health delivers tremendous benefits on average, some medical spending is almost certainly of low value. Economists often attribute some of this low-value spending to a phenomenon known as moral hazard: at the point of service, most insured consumers pay only a fraction of the cost of their care, which gives them reason to opt for more, and sometimes less effective, care than they would choose if they were paying the full cost themselves. Unavoidably, the protection that insurance affords households against the risk of catastrophically high medical spending carries with it the "side effect" of some unnecessary spending (Pauly 1968).

The market for medical care also suffers from multiple information problems that contribute to rising costs. The first is incomplete information: simply put, there is considerable uncertainty for all—patients and providers alike—about the effectiveness of different medical treatments. And information in the medical care market is not only incomplete but also asymmetric. Patients know much less than providers (doctors and hospitals) do about what treatment is appropriate for a particular condition. Third-party payers such as insurance companies and state or Federal Government programs are also at an informational disadvantage relative to providers. These information asymmetries give rise to a principal-agent problem in which the less-informed party or "principal"—in this case, either the patient or the third-party payer—would like to hire the better-informed party or "agent"—in this case, the provider—to provide treatment but cannot be sure what to ask the provider to do or how much the provider should be paid. The result is that some health spending yields low value.

According to economic theory, one way to mitigate the principal-agent problem is to structure incentives so that it is in the interest of the agent to do what is best for the principal. Commissions, for example, give sales associates an incentive to work hard in situations where a supervisor might not be able to monitor their effort directly. In medical care, the challenge is to design payment mechanisms that reward providers for delivering high-quality, high-value care and discourage them from providing low-quality, low-value care while continuing to ensure that patients have control over their care and are never denied the care they need, expect, and deserve. As noted, the task is much more complex than simply reducing spending, but the potential benefits of having a system that delivers high-value care are tremendous.

How the Affordable Care Act Promotes High-Value Medical Care

Designing reimbursement systems that reward high-value care, discourage low-value care, and put patients in control represents a key challenge for reform. In addition, what may be high-value care for one individual may not be for another, because the efficacy of treatments may vary with an individual's characteristics. Rather than imposing a single solution to promoting high-value care—one that might get it wrong—the Affordable Care Act approaches the task from three different directions to create the conditions under which the right answers will emerge. It invests in better information about what treatments work best, while ensuring that all treatment options remain available to patients. It experiments with new approaches to delivering and paying for care. And it empowers patients to make informed decisions about their providers and their care.

Better Information about What Works: The Patient-Centered Outcomes Research Institute. The Affordable Care Act supports research through a private, not-for-profit Patient-Centered Outcomes Research Institute, governed by a multistakeholder group and expert advisory panels, whose task is to identify priorities for research. The Institute will continue the work of the Federal Coordinating Council for Comparative Effectiveness Research created by the American Recovery and Reinvestment Act in February of 2009. The Institute's research findings cannot be used to mandate coverage or reimbursement policy. The information the findings provide will enable patients, providers, employers, and insurers to choose high-value care.

New Approaches to Delivering and Paying for Care. The Affordable Care Act includes a host of new programs and demonstration projects designed to identify effective ways to encourage the provision of high-value care. Two illustrative examples are "bundled payments" and a delivery system reform that reduces hospital-acquired conditions.

Bundled payments are one-time reimbursements to providers for the costs of treating a patient's condition across multiple settings. For example, the hospital, the cardiologist, the primary care physician, and any other care-giver for a patient undergoing coronary artery bypass graft surgery would receive one payment. Bundled payments create incentives for providers to coordinate care and keep to a minimum any treatments that are of little or no value. Providers who keep patients healthy, and thus spend less, make a profit, and those who spend more lose money. The approach builds on the success of Medicare's inpatient prospective payment system, introduced during the 1980s, which has been adopted by many private insurance companies.

Hospital-acquired conditions (HACs) are generally avoidable health problems caused by medical treatment; they are considered indicators of poor-quality care. Examples include surgical site infections and urinary tract infections associated with catheters. Since 2008, Medicare has not reimbursed most hospitals for costs associated with treating these conditions in hospitalized patients. The Affordable Care Act increases the incentive to prevent these conditions by reducing Medicare reimbursement for *all* conditions in hospitals that have high rates of HACs and by extending the nonpayment policy to the Federal share of the Medicaid program. These changes will reduce Federal health spending through Medicare and Medicaid and will provide a roadmap to reduced spending for private insurers and employers. They also create a high-powered incentive for hospitals to prevent these conditions in the first place. The result—lowering spending *and* improving patient outcomes—is a classic win-win solution.

Bundled payments and nonpayment for HACs are just two examples of Affordable Care Act delivery system reforms that will result in higher value for patients; other promising reforms include Accountable Care Organizations and a program that reduces Medicare payments to hospitals with relatively high rates of preventable readmissions. In this same area, the Affordable Care Act also establishes the Center for Medicare and Medicaid Innovation (also known as the Innovation Center), which will identify, test, disseminate, and evaluate new models of delivering and paying for care. The Innovation Center will ensure that Medicare and Medicaid have the flexibility to test new incentive and delivery systems to keep pace with technological innovation in medical care. It will also seek to enlist the participation of private third-party payers to align provider incentives and accelerate the adoption of successful delivery system models.

Better Information on Provider Quality. One more way to drive the system to high-value care is to empower patients with better information on provider quality. The Affordable Care Act creates a quality-reporting program for physicians that will collect performance data on physicians who participate in Medicare and publish it on a Web site similar to the existing Hospital Compare and Nursing Home Compare Web sites. Research has shown that quality report cards influence consumer choice in health care and lead to higher-quality care (Bundorf et al. 2009; Mukamel et al. 2008; Werner, Stuart, and Polsky 2010). Reimbursement mechanisms that explicitly reward quality will be reinforced by patients "voting with their feet" in response to information on the quality of their providers.

Improving the Health Insurance Market

The ranks of the uninsured have grown steadily in the United States over the past decade, as shown in Figure 5-2. Almost 51 million Americans—16.7 percent of the population—lacked health insurance coverage in 2009 (DeNavas-Walt, Proctor, and Smith 2010). An increasing body of credible evidence has documented that being uninsured has negative consequences for health, access to medical care, and financial security (Asplin et al. 2005; Card, Dobkin, and Maestas 2009; Cooke, Dranove, and Sfekas 2010; McWilliams et al. 2004). The failure of the United States—unlike other industrialized nations—to ensure access to basic care for all its citizens, together with our Nation's continuing mediocre record on measures such as life expectancy and infant mortality, compared with other industrialized nations, has made the need for reform increasingly urgent.

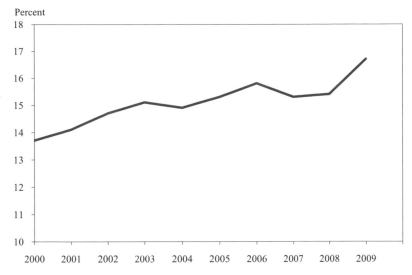

Figure 5-2
Percent of Americans Uninsured

Source: DeNavas-Walt, Proctor, and Smith (2010).

Problems in the Market for Health Insurance

Complicating the policy problem posed by the many uninsured Americans are long-standing market failures in the individual and small group health insurance markets. The most important such market failure is adverse selection. In the context of health insurance, adverse selection means that individuals or families with poorer health and thus high expected medical spending are more likely than their healthier counterparts to buy coverage at a given price. The selection of more high-cost people into coverage triggers a vicious cycle. To cover the health needs of this costly group, the insurer raises the premium, generating still more adverse selection into coverage. In the extreme case, the market simply does not function. In practical terms, some people are uninsured because the only policies available to them do not seem to be a good deal (although they might be a good deal for someone in worse health). Many more people pay higher prices than they should in order to get coverage at all.

A second failure contributing to dysfunction in health insurance markets is the problem of missing markets; in particular, there is no market for multiyear health insurance contracts that would protect individuals throughout their lives from the risk of becoming sick and having to pay much higher insurance premiums or lose their coverage altogether. The missing market problem contributes to multiple inefficiencies. Individuals with high medical spending may be "locked in" to a policy for fear that their premiums will increase if they change their coverage, particularly in the individual market. The decision not to seek new coverage may reduce competition in health insurance markets. Labor markets too suffer negative consequences when workers who want to change jobs—especially entrepreneurs who want to start new businesses—stay in their old jobs for fear of losing insurance.

Health insurance markets are also characterized by the high search costs they impose on consumers. Largely unaided, consumers must gather and evaluate comparative information about the prices and quality of an array of complex health insurance plans. The high cost of conducting that search reduces competition and may result in prices that are higher than the competitive level. One effective way to reduce search costs is through information systems that assist consumers in comparison shopping. In the market for life insurance, for example, greater use of price comparison Web sites has led to substantial reductions in premiums and gains in consumer surplus (Brown and Goolsbee 2002). For reasons that are not entirely clear—but may be related to the multiple other market failures—health insurance markets have been slow to adopt these innovations.

Health insurance markets are also highly concentrated; in all but four states, the three largest insurers control half of the market or more (Robinson 2004). Such concentration raises the possibility that insurers may have market power to set prices above the competitive level, and recent evidence suggests that increased concentration leads to higher premiums, consistent with that possibility (Dafny, Duggan, and Ramanarayanan 2010).

A final market failure is the "Samaritan's dilemma"; because hospitals and other health care providers offer charity care, some people do not purchase insurance (Coate 1995). Indeed, multiple studies document that the availability of charity care reduces the rate of private insurance coverage, suggesting that there is some "free riding" on the system (Herring 2005; Rask and Rask 2000).

How the Affordable Care Act Addresses the Insurance Market Failures

Exchanges. The Affordable Care Act extends insurance coverage to the uninsured and makes insurance markets work more effectively for those who already have coverage. To achieve these goals, it establishes Health Insurance Exchanges, organized marketplaces in every state that enable individual consumers without access to affordable employer-sponsored coverage to shop easily for coverage and receive any tax credits or reduced cost-sharing for which they are eligible. The Affordable Care Act also establishes Small Business Health Options Program (SHOP) Exchanges, similar marketplaces in each state for small group coverage. Private insurance companies will offer plans for sale through the Exchanges beginning in 2014. Beginning in 2017, states can choose to expand their Exchanges to larger employers as well.

Minimum Benefits and Coverage Tiers. Every plan available in these marketplaces must include a specified set of minimum essential benefits and will be categorized as platinum, gold, silver, or bronze depending on the extent of consumer cost-sharing. For platinum coverage—the most comprehensive—on average, consumers will pay only 10 percent of the cost of covered services as cost-sharing at the point of service. Consumers who choose this option can expect to pay a higher premium up front for the increased cost-sharing protections. The next three types of coverage— gold, silver, and bronze—feature progressively higher point-of-service cost-sharing corresponding to 20 percent, 30 percent, and 40 percent of the total cost of covered services. Consumers can expect to pay lower premiums up front for these categories of coverage, with bronze plans being the least expensive.

Online Choice Tools. Online tools will enable consumers to choose coverage based on the characteristics that are most important to them: premium costs, cost-sharing, or plan quality ratings, for example. The HealthCare.gov Web portal, which launched on July 1, 2010, is one such tool. Beginning in 2014, Exchanges will leverage these technologies to allow consumers to make informed choices among multiple plans. The Affordable Care Act has already provided states $49 million in funding to plan and develop their Health Insurance Exchanges, including information technology systems that will enable consumers to search for plans that best suit their needs and preferences.

Tax Credits for Premiums. Beginning in 2014, individuals and families without access to adequate, affordable coverage will receive tax credits for premiums purchased in the Exchange. These tax credits, which are available to households with incomes between 100 and 400 percent of the federal poverty level, limit the amount that an individual or family must pay for health insurance coverage as a share of household income.[3] The income share ranges from 2 percent for families at the low end of the eligibility threshold to 9.5 percent for those at the upper end. Some families eligible for a premium tax credit also receive cost-sharing assistance that limits their out-of-pocket spending at the point of service.

---

[3] The Federal poverty level in 2011 is $22,350 for a family of four living in the contiguous 48 states or the District of Columbia; 400 percent of the poverty level for such a family would be $89,400.

Coverage Responsibility. Creating Health Insurance Exchanges and developing online choice tools are significant steps toward making individual and small group health insurance markets more competitive, transparent, sensible, and affordable. By themselves, however, these steps do not address the critical problem of adverse selection. Correcting that market failure requires changing the current practices of both insurers and consumers. To that end, the Affordable Care Act provides a new protection for consumers called "guaranteed issue," which prohibits insurers from denying coverage to anyone who wants to buy it. The law also prohibits insurers from charging higher premiums for individuals in poor health. For their part, consumers who can afford coverage are required to have coverage or pay a penalty, except for specified exemptions such as individuals with religious objections. Any remaining incentives that insurers may have to try to attract healthier consumers will be offset through risk adjustment that transfers payments from insurers with relatively healthy enrollees to those with sicker enrollees. This framework largely solves the adverse selection problem.

Employers and the Affordable Care Act

Most employers already offer health insurance; 95 percent of employers with 50 to 199 employees and 99 percent of employers with 200 or more employees do so (Kaiser Family Foundation and Health Research and Educational Trust 2010). The Affordable Care Act imposes financial penalties of approximately $2,000 per full-time worker on the very few employers with 50 or more workers who do not offer coverage if their workers obtain premium tax credits for the purchase of coverage in an Exchange. The first 30 full-time employees are exempt for purposes of this calculation. Fewer than 10,000 firms, or 0.2 percent of American businesses, are likely to be affected by the penalty. Small employers (those with fewer than 50 workers) face no such penalties. On the contrary, the Affordable Care Act includes a tax credit to help businesses with fewer than 25 full-time workers and average annual wages below $50,000 afford health insurance for their workers, as described in Chapter 7. Together with the SHOP Exchanges described above, which allow small employers to join a larger pool of buyers and purchase coverage that has the same fair prices and low administrative cost that large employers have historically enjoyed, this tax credit will level the playing field for small and large employers in the area of health benefits.

Expanding Medicaid

In addition to expanding private coverage through the Exchanges, the Affordable Care Act expands public coverage. Specifically, it extends Medicaid eligibility to all individuals in families with incomes at or below

133 percent of the Federal poverty level. Expanding Medicaid eligibility provides a critical coverage option for the most economically vulnerable citizens. The Affordable Care Act also allocates resources to states to offset their added costs for newly eligible individuals (100 percent of the costs for the first three years, phasing to 90 percent permanently). The Administration has also proposed additional resources that will help states design and implement streamlined enrollment systems to make obtaining health insurance a seamless process.

CONCLUSION

In the end, the Affordable Care Act will benefit both those who now have health coverage and those who are uninsured. The more than 30 million uninsured Americans who will gain insurance coverage will reap the benefits of longer life and better health conferred by innovations in medical technology. The newly insured will also enjoy relief from the economic insecurity of lacking coverage; no longer will American families have to worry about being one illness away from bankruptcy. Americans who are now insured will benefit from lower premiums because they will no longer pay a "hidden tax" associated with the costs of providing uncompensated care to the uninsured. They will enjoy greater security of coverage because the law prevents insurance companies from canceling their coverage unexpectedly if they are in an accident or become sick. The insured will also be free from the worry that they will exhaust the limits of their coverage, because the new law prohibits annual and lifetime coverage limits. And the law ensures that they will have 100 percent coverage for important preventive care services with no additional out-of-pocket costs.

Insurance market reforms and the new Exchanges will make it possible for all Americans who lack access to employer-based insurance to obtain coverage, and thus feel greater economic security, during periods of labor market transition or instability. The Affordable Care Act will smooth the transition from school to work for young adults, who have historically been uninsured at very high rates. The law will also mitigate the consequences of job loss because losing a job will no longer entail losing all access to affordable insurance.

Moreover, the Affordable Care Act levels the playing field for small employers, who will be able to compete for workers by offering benefits that are comparable in price and generosity to those offered by large employers. Potential entrepreneurs will be able to pursue their dreams without having to worry about where they will get health insurance at a fair price, thus tapping new reserves of creativity for the American economy. And all employers—large, small, and in-between—will benefit from reduced uncertainty about health spending as a result of the larger and more stable private insurance pool that the Affordable Care Act will create. Reforming insurance markets will transform American business in subtle but far-reaching ways, improving the bottom line for both workers and employers.

The benefits of delivery system reform will be even more widely shared. Improvements in health care quality, such as reductions in hospital-acquired conditions, should, within just a few years, yield measurable benefits that will touch the lives of most, if not all, Americans. The transition to a uniformly high-quality, high-value system of medical care will take longer, but by improving the quality and value of health care while freeing up resources that can be used for other productive purposes, will lay the foundation for future economic growth.

CHAPTER 6

TRANSITIONING TO A CLEAN ENERGY FUTURE

American prosperity depends on a continuous supply of safe and reliable energy. Energy heats, cools, and lights homes and businesses; transports workers to jobs, customers to stores, and families to relatives; and runs the factories that manufacture the goods Americans consume and export. It is increasingly clear, however, that existing energy supplies pose risks to national security, the environment, the climate, and the economy. To counter those risks, while recognizing the continued importance of safe, responsible oil and gas production to the economy, the Administration is committed to moving the Nation toward use of cleaner sources of energy with the potential to support new industries, exports, and high-quality jobs; to improve air quality and protect the climate; and to enhance America's energy security and international competitiveness.

A future with cleaner energy sources promises numerous benefits. Innovation in cleaner energy will reduce U.S. dependence on oil—over half of which is imported—decreasing the vulnerability of the U.S. economy to supply disruptions and price spikes (Box 6-1). Cleaner energy will improve the quality of the air American families breathe, because energy use accounts for the vast majority of air pollution such as nitrogen oxides, sulfur dioxide, and carbon monoxide. Cleaner energy is essential for the United States to make progress toward its pledge, as part of the United Nations Climate Change Conferences in Copenhagen and Cancun, to cut carbon dioxide (CO_2) and other human-induced greenhouse gases by roughly 17 percent below 2005 levels by 2020, and to meet its long-term goal of reducing emissions by more than 83 percent by 2050. Finally, supported by well-designed policies, clean energy can make an important contribution to America's ability to compete internationally using innovative new technologies, while also having ancillary economic benefits like lower risks from accidents at coal mines and oil wells.

Box 6-1: Energy Security Benefits of Reduced Oil Consumption

Combustion of all fossil fuels generates pollution to varying degrees. But because more than half of the petroleum consumed in the United States is imported, it creates an additional set of costs for the American economy.

First, although 20 percent of U.S. imports come from Canada, America's biggest supplier, many of the most accessible reserves are concentrated in unstable regions, leading to fears of supply-related world price fluctuations. The risk may have declined over time, because the U.S. economy has become less energy intensive and the Strategic Petroleum Reserve is now filled to capacity with 727 million barrels of crude oil—more than two months of net imports. Nevertheless, petroleum still plays a key role in the United States, accounting for 37 percent of energy use and over 7 percent of personal consumption expenditures.

The second cost relates to the missed opportunity for the United States to lower world oil prices by decreasing its own demand for oil. Because the United States is the world's largest consumer of crude oil, decreased U.S. demand results in lower world prices. Lower prices benefit petroleum purchasers and harm petroleum producers, with no overall global benefit. Because the United States is a net importer, the offsetting effects would on balance favor U.S. interests.

The third component of the energy security cost of oil involves policy expenses borne by U.S. taxpayers. Among such expenses are military costs associated with protecting oil supply routes and maintenance costs of the Strategic Petroleum Reserve.

The Environmental Protection Agency and the National Highway Traffic Safety Administration estimated that the fuel economy and greenhouse gas emissions standards for cars and light trucks, issued in May 2010, have energy security benefits of $7 a barrel of oil in saved macroeconomic disruption costs in 2015 (in 2009 dollars), or about $0.16 a gallon of gasoline. This estimate depends on predictions about future oil prices, supply disruptions, OPEC behavior, and the elasticities of global oil supply and demand. The estimate does not include the demand-side market power benefit, which represents a transfer from exporters to importers. Nor does it include the U.S. policy expenses, because it is difficult to know how much of them to allocate to an incremental change in oil consumption. By comparison, one U.S. government estimate of the global social cost of the CO_2 emissions associated with one barrel of oil is $9.52 in 2010, going up to $20 in 2050 (Box 6-4).

These same security, environmental, and economic risks confront all the countries of the world to varying degrees. And many, like the United States, have embarked on efforts to transition to cleaner sources of energy. As a consequence, the clean energy sector is likely to be a vibrant source of innovation, growth, and international trade worldwide. Innovation is an engine of the American economy and a key to long-term job creation and economic growth. Those nations that invest first, and whose transition efforts are most successful, are likely to lead the world in exporting equipment and expertise as the rest of the world's countries seek the same secure, clean, affordable energy. The number of clean energy patents worldwide grew about 20 percent per year from 1997 through 2007, and the United States was home to 18 percent of the clean energy patents issued between 1988 and 2007, behind Japan with 30 percent (UNEP, EPO, and ICTSD 2010). The Obama Administration's commitment to clean energy represents an effort to ensure that the United States does not slip behind but instead leads the world in this critical sector.

The benefits of transitioning to clean energy—energy security, cleaner air, fewer risks from climate change, and enhanced economic competitiveness—are enjoyed by everybody, not just the producers or consumers of the clean energy. As a consequence, the benefits are not fully represented in market prices. Examples of these benefit spillovers abound. Clean energy innovators reap only part of the overall rewards for their efforts—the rest spill over to others who build on their work. The payments that solar and wind power generators receive for the electricity they supply do not reflect the benefits that spill over to the rest of the economy. Energy users reap only part of the benefits from weatherizing their homes and driving electric vehicles. These spillover benefits are substantial. A peer-reviewed report prepared by the EPA estimates that for the year 2010 alone, the Clean Air Act Amendments of 1990 yielded net benefits of $1.2 trillion—everything from lives saved to healthier kids to a more productive workforce (EPA 2010). These spillovers mean that market rewards for switching to clean energy production are lower than the societywide benefits, market costs of switching to clean energy consumption are higher than the societywide costs, and markets alone provide less clean energy than is optimal.

Because there are many types of clean energy benefit spillovers, the path to a clean energy future includes many possible policies. Existing fossil fuel consumption can be made cleaner by increasing the efficiency of combustion, by capturing and sequestering CO_2 emissions, or by switching within the fossil fuel sector to lower-emitting natural gas. Cleaner fossil fuel technologies and nonfossil sources of energy, such as wind, solar, geothermal, natural gas, and nuclear power, can supply a larger share of the Nation's energy consumption with the help of a Federal Clean Energy Standard. Energy use by homes and vehicles can become more efficient. And more energy-efficient technologies, some of which may have yet to be discovered, can be supported as they are developed and brought to market. Transitioning to a clean energy future and progressing toward America's carbon pollution reduction goals will be best accomplished by pursuing cost-effective, well-coordinated public policies.

This chapter highlights some of the important steps the Administration has already taken or is proposing to take to ensure that the economy makes the important transition to clean energy. The list of policies discussed here is not exhaustive but rather serves to demonstrate the economic rationale that motivates ongoing work on these programs. The policies include assisting with residential and commercial energy efficiency; increasing vehicle efficiency; increasing the share of electricity generated by clean sources; recording, reporting, and accounting for the cost of greenhouse gas emissions; funding transportation infrastructure including expanded transit and high-speed rail; assisting with manufacturing and adoption of electric vehicles; and providing incentives for clean energy research and development (R&D).

INITIAL STEPS TOWARD A CLEAN ENERGY ECONOMY

The Administration's first task in January 2009 was to end the deepest recession since the 1930s, and while doing so, it made major initial investments to help turn the economy in a new, cleaner direction. Many of those initiatives were integral to the recovery effort; others were distinct but concurrent.

Energy Investments in the Recovery Act

The American Recovery and Reinvestment Act (Recovery Act) directed about $800 billion in Federal expenditures and tax relief to investments and job creation, with a primary objective of reversing the collapsing economic conditions of early 2009. As part of that effort, the law contained over $90 billion in public investment and tax incentives targeted at increasing sources of clean energy and reducing America's dependence on fossil fuels (Box 6-2).

These clean energy investments directly targeted the beneficial spillovers that provide an economic rationale for promoting clean energy. One example is the Recovery Act funds directed to the Weatherization Assistance Program. The funds helped retrofit more than 300,000 low-income homes by the end of November. A recent study by the Oak Ridge National

Laboratory estimated that the annual average savings for homes weatherized by the program include $437 in heating and cooling costs and 2.65 tons of reduced CO_2 emissions (Eisenberg 2010). Another example of Recovery Act spending targeted at home energy efficiency is the Smart Grid funds that electric companies are using to test various types of electricity metering, enabling customers to monitor and adjust their electricity use to save power and money. Still other Recovery Act investments in transit, electric vehicles, and high-speed rail create construction jobs and will provide energy savings and other benefits to Americans for generations.

Box 6-2: Clean Energy Investments in the Recovery Act

The more than $90 billion in Recovery Act expenditures aimed at reducing American fossil fuel use fell into eight categories:

- $30 billion for energy efficiency, including retrofits for low-income homes
- $23 billion for renewable generation, such as wind turbines and solar panels
- $18 billion for transportation and high-speed rail
- $10 billion for Smart Grid technologies to improve the efficiency of electricity use and distribution
- $6 billion for domestic production of advanced batteries, vehicles, and fuels
- $4 billion for green innovation and job training
- $3 billion for carbon capture and sequestration
- $2 billion in clean energy equipment manufacturing tax credits

As an example of the programs that make up these categories, the top category, energy efficiency, includes the following:

- $5 billion for the Weatherization Assistance Program
- $3.1 billion for the State Energy Program
- $2.7 billion for Energy Efficiency and Conservation Block Grants
- $454 million for retrofit ramp-ups in energy efficiency
- $346 million for energy-efficient building technologies
- $300 million for energy-efficient appliance rebates / Energy Star®
- $256 million for the Industrial Technologies Program
- $104 million for national laboratory facilities
- $18 million for small business clean energy innovation projects

---

Another part of the Recovery Act addressed the positive spillovers that R&D generates for others by subsidizing a wide variety of investments in clean energy R&D. These investments included several billion dollars for

R&D directly related to clean energy. Roughly $3.4 billion has been awarded for research, development, and deployment of carbon capture and storage technologies. Another portion has funded R&D on potentially transformative, next-generation clean energy and efficiency-enhancing technologies, including advanced materials and building systems, vehicle efficiency, solar power, biofuels, and wind turbines. Recovery Act funds have also been awarded to finance clean energy research at universities as part of a larger $2 billion effort, managed by the Department of Energy, to support basic scientific research.

Funding for the Advanced Research Projects Agency-Energy (ARPA-E) within the Department of Energy represents an especially innovative R&D component of the Recovery Act. ARPA-E is modeled after the 50-year-old Defense Advanced Research Projects Agency (DARPA), which is credited with the initial innovations underlying the Internet, navigation satellites, and stealth technology for aircraft. ARPA-E aims to attract America's best scientists to focus on creative, transformational energy research that the private sector by itself cannot support but that could provide dramatic benefits for the nation (Box 6-3).

Full details of the Recovery Act and its economic effects, including the law's clean energy components, can be found in the CEA's quarterly reports to Congress.

Further Steps Toward a Cleaner Economy

In addition to the clean energy investments in the Recovery Act, the Administration has taken several other steps to lay the groundwork for cleaner energy. Among the most significant of these are new vehicle standards; increased electricity generation from renewable sources; and programs to record, report, and account for the cost of greenhouse gas emissions.

Vehicle Standards. In May 2010, the Environmental Protection Agency and the National Highway Traffic Safety Administration issued standards that will raise the combined car and light truck fuel economy from 30.1 miles per gallon in 2012 to 35.5 miles per gallon in 2016 and that are projected to reduce combined car and light truck tailpipe CO_2 emissions from 295 grams a mile in 2012 to 250 grams a mile in 2016. As a result of these rules, vehicles to be sold during model years 2012 to 2016 are projected to use 1.8 billion fewer barrels of oil over their lifetimes, and by 2030 the entire light-duty vehicle fleet will emit 21 percent less carbon pollution. The reduced fuel costs will save consumers $66 billion per year by 2030, in 2009 dollars, after taking into account the increase in the purchase price of vehicles.

Box 6-3: The Recovery Act and ARPA-E: Spurring Innovation to Transform the Energy Economy

The Advanced Research Projects Agency-Energy (ARPA-E) was developed to support innovations with the potential to create new clean energy jobs, businesses, and industries. It attracted thousands of proposals and has funded over 100 projects that have the potential to radically transform the energy sector.

One small startup company is developing a new way to manufacture the key part in solar panels—silicon wafers—for less than 20 percent of current costs. If successful, the technology could be used to increase domestic clean energy production and add many new jobs in the solar photovoltaic industry. A second startup is developing an inexpensive and versatile means of storing energy, using a new type of catalyst to separate pure hydrogen and oxygen from ordinary water. That technology could allow renewable energy to be used even at times or places where wind or sun is not available. Another company has partnered with Argonne National Laboratory to create lithium-ion batteries with the highest energy density in the world. The technology has the prospect of increasing U.S. leadership in advanced batteries and boosting the performance of hybrid/electric vehicles. Yet another small company is developing a new type of wind turbine that generates more energy than existing models and is cheaper to produce and operate. The turbine is compact enough to use in urban locations and could hasten the growth of wind power in the United States.

ARPA-E funds have enabled companies to pursue their innovative research, to attract additional financing from private investors, and to increase the odds of a dramatic breakthrough that would accelerate the development of American clean energy.

Doubling Renewable Electricity Generation. Early in his Administration, the President announced a goal of doubling the amount of electricity generated in the United States by wind, solar, and geothermal energy. Toward this goal, tax credits have assisted both the production of electricity from renewable sources and the manufacture of equipment (such as solar panels and wind turbines) used in that generation. As Figure 6-1 shows, the United States is on track to achieve that goal, adding more wind, solar, and geothermal capacity in 4 years than in the previous 30. Yet as the figure also shows, those particular sources of energy still account for only a small fraction of the Nation's overall electricity generating capacity. To build on the progress made to date, the President has proposed a Federal Clean Energy Standard to obtain 80 percent of electricity from these and other clean sources of electricity by 2035, expanding the range of sources from which clean energy is generated. The standard will double the share of electricity generated by this broader group of clean sources in 25 years, and will provide utilities with incentives to generate clean energy, along with the associated spillover benefits, at the lowest possible cost (see "Next Steps," below).

Figure 6-1
U.S. Wind, Solar, and Geothermal Energy Generating Capacity

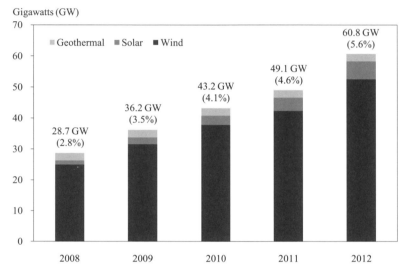

Notes: Net summer generating capacity of wind, solar, and geothermal energy. Percentages are shares of total net summer electricity generating capacity.
Sources: Energy Information Administration, Annual Energy Outlook 2011; CEA calculations.

Information Provision and Disclosure. In addition to these concrete, tangible steps that increase the efficiency of vehicles and the share of renewable sources used for electricity generation, the Administration has taken two significant steps that involve collecting and analyzing information. These two disclosure and information-gathering endeavors will inform and guide future Federal climate and energy policy.

The first of these was an interagency study to estimate the "social cost of carbon" (SCC), a set of values for the climate-related damages from incremental changes in carbon pollution. These estimates enable Federal agencies to consistently quantify the benefits of reduced CO_2 emissions when analyzing the costs and benefits of their regulatory actions, similar to the way all Federal agencies use consistent discount rates for trading off current and future costs and benefits. Based on the SCC described in Box

6-4, the CO_2 reductions in 2030 resulting from the new car and light truck standards described above are expected to save an estimated \$3.1 billion to \$31.8 billion, in 2009 dollars, in the form of reduced damages from climate change. The ability to quantify benefits consistently across agencies in this manner is critical for assessing the cost-effectiveness of rules and regulations.

Box 6-4: The Social Cost of Carbon: A Tool for Cost-Effective Policy

In 2010, an interagency task force that included the Council of Economic Advisers produced an important white paper called "Social Cost of Carbon for Regulatory Impact Analysis" (Interagency Working Group 2010). The goal was to measure the present value of benefits from reducing CO_2 emissions by an extra ton. The report suggests four values for this social cost of carbon (SCC): \$5, \$22, \$36, and \$67 a ton, in 2009 dollars. The first three average SCC estimates across various models and scenarios and differ based on the rate at which future costs and benefits are discounted (5, 3, and 2.5 percent, respectively). The fourth value, \$67, comes from evaluating the worst 5 percent of modeled outcomes, discounted at 3 percent. All four values rise over time as more carbon in the atmosphere exacerbates the damages from each additional ton. For example, the central value of \$22 rises to \$46 in 2050. These estimates provide guidance for assessing the costs and benefits of agencies' rule-makings that reduce incremental carbon pollution.

Why is it important for agencies to agree on a common range for the SCC? A key advantage of market-based regulations such as pollution fees or tradable permit schemes is that they are cost-effective. By putting a common price on emissions, these types of polices give each source of pollution equal private incentives to avoid paying that price by abating. The incremental cost of abating pollution will thus be equal across sources, meaning that it will not be possible to reduce collective compliance costs by abating less from some sources and more from others.

While most regulations do not involve a price on carbon, and the SCC is not itself a price, setting a common SCC range allows policymakers to explicitly compare the benefits and costs of emissions reductions across a wide range of regulations, and to mimic the cost-effectiveness of a true market-based policy. The Administration will periodically reassess whether the four SCC values are appropriate for evaluating U.S. policies; meanwhile, the SCC helps guide Federal agencies in the direction of consistent and cost-effective policymaking.

The second information-gathering step the Administration has taken has been to require major sources of carbon pollution to publicly report their annual emissions. The Mandatory Reporting of Greenhouse Gases Rule, published in October 2009, covers 85–90 percent of U.S. emissions from roughly 10,000 facilities. Data collection began in January 2010 for stationary sources, including electricity generators, large industrial facilities, and suppliers of fossil fuels. For cars and light trucks, engine manufacturers are required to report emissions beginning with model year 2011. This important step will be instrumental in helping identify cost-effective opportunities to reduce carbon pollution as well as ways to target regulations efficiently.

NEXT STEPS TOWARD A CLEAN ENERGY ECONOMY

In his 2011 State of the Union address and in his 2012 Budget, the President outlined a series of proposals that build on current efforts to transition to an economy based on cleaner sources of energy. Among these are a Federal Clean Energy Standard for electricity; further investments in energy efficiency; a substantial commitment to transportation infrastructure, including a major investment in high-speed rail and steps to achieve the Administration's goal of 1 million electric and hybrid vehicles on the streets by 2015; and increased investments in clean energy R&D.

A Federal Clean Energy Standard

The President has proposed a goal of generating 80 percent of the Nation's electricity from clean energy sources, defined broadly to include renewables and nuclear power as well as partial credit for fossil fuels with carbon capture and sequestration and efficient natural gas. To meet this goal, the Administration is proposing a Clean Energy Standard (CES) that would require electric utilities to obtain an increasing share of delivered electricity from clean sources—starting at the current level of 40 percent and doubling over the next 25 years. Electricity generators would receive credits for each megawatt-hour of clean energy generated; utilities with more credits than needed to meet the standard could sell the credits to other utilities or bank them for future use. By ensuring flexibility through a broad definition of clean energy and by allowing trading among utilities, the program is designed to meet the overall target cost-effectively. The Administration's proposal emphasizes the importance of protecting consumers and accounting for regional differences.

The proposed Federal CES will provide a critical complement to the Administration's investment in clean energy R&D, by creating a stable market for new technologies. Funding for R&D provides a "push" to technological innovation by helping to promote basic and applied research and addressing the market spillovers associated with private research efforts. A CES would create economic incentives for deployment of clean energy that can help "pull" new technologies coming out of R&D into the market. Importantly, a CES would not pick particular clean technologies, but instead let markets and businesses determine the most cost-effective technologies to achieve the target share of clean energy.

The Administration's proposed CES will build on the national progress depicted in Figure 6-1, as well as on a range of existing efforts at the state level. By the end of 2010, 31 states plus the District of Columbia had enacted renewable energy standards (RES), which specify the minimum amount of electricity that utilities are required to generate or purchase from renewable sources—typically solar, wind, geothermal, and biomass (Figure 6-2). Five additional states have also recognized specific renewable energy goals. The laws range from modest departures from the overall business-as-usual forecast to requirements that 33 percent of power come from renewable sources in California by 2020 and 40 percent in Hawaii by 2030. Together, the states that have binding RES policies currently account for nearly two-thirds of all national retail electricity sales.

Most RES laws incorporate market-based regulatory flexibility by allowing some utilities to meet the minimum renewable shares by purchasing renewable energy credits (RECs) from other utilities that exceed the standard. Because utilities can sometimes purchase energy and RECs across state borders, the patchwork of state standards depicted in Figure 6-2 can achieve some, but not all, of the cost-effectiveness benefits of a national standard. Although states have led the way, making significant advances in the use of renewable energy sources, a coordinated Federal action could achieve even greater benefits with lower costs. A Federal standard with nationally tradable credits would ensure that renewable power and other clean energy sources are deployed in those locations where they can be most cost-effective. By covering the whole country and including a wider array of sources, a Federal CES has the potential to accelerate the transition to clean energy at significantly lower cost.

Figure 6-2
State Renewable Energy Standards in 2025

Figure 6-2
State Renewable Energy Standards in 2025

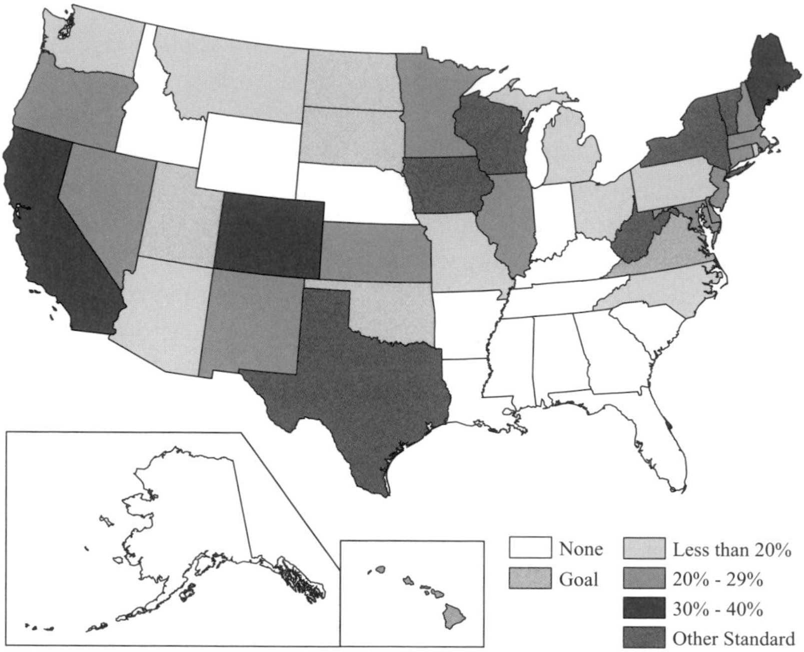

Notes: Percentages are renewable energy standards that are binding on utilities. In some states, the standards are binding only on investor-owned and/or large utilities.
Sources: North Carolina Solar Center, Database of State Incentives for Renewable Energy; various state sources.

Energy Efficiency

One certain approach to reducing energy-related pollution and America's reliance on fossil fuels would be to consume less energy. Americans have many opportunities to make energy efficiency-enhancing investments—in their homes, their vehicles, and their businesses. Examples include weatherizing buildings, replacing old appliances with new energy-efficient models, and switching to compact fluorescent light bulbs. For a variety of reasons, however, people tend to under-invest in these types of simple energy-saving measures where up-front costs would be paid back in the form of reduced energy bills.

There are numerous explanations for this energy paradox. People may simply not have the information necessary to evaluate the tradeoffs between current costs and future savings. Some energy efficiency decisions are made by landlords who have diminished incentives to invest in energy efficiency because their tenants pay the electricity bills. In other cases, people may plan to sell their homes before they would have enough time to reap the energy savings and might not expect those energy-saving investments to be reflected in resale prices. And some individuals simply do not have access to the funds to invest in energy efficiency, even if they know they would earn that investment back many times over. Existing Federal programs designed to address this energy paradox include the Energy Star program, which labels appliances, consumer electronics, and building products, providing the information consumers need to make cost-effective choices, and the Weatherization Assistance Program, which helps cash-strapped low-income families conserve energy and reduce their energy bills.

To build on existing efforts to address the energy paradox and the beneficial spillovers from energy efficiency, and to help boost job creation in the construction and manufacturing industries, the Obama Administration has proposed two new programs to help retrofit buildings: Homestar for residences, and the Better Buildings Initiative for commercial properties.

Homestar. The Homestar Energy Efficiency Retrofit Program would provide point-of-sale rebates to homeowners who make efficiency-enhancing improvements to their homes. Rebates of $1,000 to $1,500 would be paid for 50 percent of the costs of straightforward retrofits, including insulation, water heaters, windows and doors, and air conditioners. Other rebates of $3,000 would help pay for home energy audits and follow-up retrofits that reduce energy costs by 20 percent. Included in the proposal is an oversight program to ensure that contractors are qualified and that efficiency-improving work is done properly. The program aims to create tens of thousands of jobs and save homeowners hundreds of dollars a year in energy costs.

Better Buildings. For the commercial real estate that is currently responsible for roughly 20 percent of U.S. energy consumption, the President has proposed a Better Buildings Initiative. The initiative encourages retrofits of commercial buildings so that they become 20 percent more energy efficient over the next 10 years and save an estimated $40 billion a year in energy costs. The program calls for replacing the current tax deduction for commercial building upgrades with a more generous tax credit; promotes energy efficiency loans to small business, hospitals, and schools; and provides competitive "Race to Green" grants to state and local governments for programs that encourage energy-efficient commercial upgrades.

Together, Homestar and Better Buildings would complement the energy efficiency progress already made under the Recovery Act, help homeowners and businesses save energy costs, and help the Nation capitalize on the beneficial spillovers from energy efficiency investments.

Transportation

Transportation accounts for more than one-fourth of energy consumption in the United States, so the transition to a clean energy future must enable Americans to choose more energy-efficient vehicles, such as electric and hybrid cars, and to use less energy-intensive modes of transportation, including public transit and high-speed trains.

Vehicles. The President has challenged the Nation to become the first country in the world to have 1 million electric vehicles on its roads, and to do so by 2015. To achieve that goal, several obstacles must be overcome. One obstacle is what the industry calls its "chicken and egg" problem: many drivers will not purchase fully electric vehicles unless an infrastructure of charging stations is ready to support them, and businesses will not invest in charging stations without a sufficiently large base of electric vehicle owners as customers. A second obstacle involves the standard R&D innovation spillover—some of the gains from efforts to develop the first generation of electric vehicles will be earned by producers of subsequent generations of cars.

To help achieve the million-car goal, over $2.4 billion in Advanced Technology Vehicle Manufacturing loans are already supporting three of the world's first electric car factories, located in Delaware, Tennessee, and California. To make further progress, the 2012 Budget proposes to provide a $7,500 point-of-sale rebate to customers who buy electric vehicles; to invest $580 million toward research, development, and deployment of electric vehicles; and to fund a new $200 million competitive grant program to reward communities that invest in infrastructure to support electric vehicles.

Americans who continue to choose gasoline-powered vehicles can still make progress toward a clean energy future when those vehicles become more fuel-efficient. The new fuel economy and greenhouse gas emissions standards for cars and light trucks for model years 2012 to 2016 is a step in that direction. To make further progress, the National Highway Traffic Safety Administration and the Environmental Protection Agency have announced plans to develop standards for new cars and light trucks for model years 2017 and beyond, along with the first proposed requirements to increase fuel economy and reduce greenhouse gas emissions from medium- and heavy-duty trucks and buses.

Alternatives to Automobiles. Another way to reduce transportation-related energy use is to provide more Americans with the opportunity to choose alternative, cleaner forms of mobility such as railways for inter-city travel and commuting, and bicycles and walking for short local trips. However, all transportation systems require infrastructure investment: automobiles require roads, trains need tracks, and airplanes need airports and air traffic control systems. Throughout U.S. history, public investment in transportation infrastructure has led to long-term benefits, from the Erie Canal to the transcontinental railroad to the interstate highway system. As Chapter 3 notes, these types of infrastructure investments have been shown to have broad economic spillovers, including increased economic growth, productivity, and land values. Some transportation infrastructure investments, such as public transit, high-speed rail, and improved air traffic control, can also have significant energy efficiency benefits.

For intercity travel, the 2012 Budget proposes enhancements to train and air travel that will reduce energy demands. The United States already has the world's most extensive freight rail network. To extend that expertise to passenger trains, the Administration is proposing to invest $53 billion over six years to fund the development of a national passenger rail network, including high-speed trains, accessible to 80 percent of Americans by 2035. And for air travel, the budget includes continued investment in the NextGen satellite-based air traffic control system that will reduce delays, improve air safety, and yield significant energy savings.

For short local trips, the Administration is undertaking a number of measures to promote alternative modes of mobility, such as public transit, bicycles, and walking. The 2012 Budget allocates $119 billion for transit programs over six years, more than doubling the commitment to transit in previous budgets. As part of that, the Administration is proposing $28 billion in new grants over six years for projects supporting interconnections between various transportation modes and improving streets to make room for pedestrians, bicycles, and mass-transit alternatives.

Research and Development

Finally, a crucial, forward-looking part of clean energy policy involves R&D. As already described, market incentives produce less R&D than would be optimal because innovators create social benefits in excess of their private market returns. These positive spillovers affect every level of R&D, from basic science all the way through demonstration and deployment of existing technologies.

In the past, industries that have invested heavily in R&D have led the United States in creating high-quality jobs and exports. As Chapter 3 notes, R&D-intensive industries are characterized by higher sales per employee and more exports than comparable industries selling internationally trad-able goods and services. For the future, the energy sector is a large potential source of R&D-intensive industries—along with the associated high-quality jobs and exports they produce. Other countries around the world face the same energy-related threats to their prosperity as those confronting the United States, and global demand for new clean energy technologies is increasing. But given the spillovers associated with all R&D, those countries that make public investments in clean energy R&D are likely be the first to develop those new industries. To address those spillovers, and help ensure that the United States leads the world in this important growth industry, the President has called for more than $8 billion for clean energy research, development, and deployment incentives.

Research and development funding is often most productive when scientists collaborate across disciplines and institutions. To facilitate that cooperative work, the Department of Energy has launched three Energy Innovation Hubs. Each brings together top researchers from academia, industry, and government to work on a particular energy-related technology. The first three hubs focus on deriving fuel from sunlight, increasing energy efficiency in buildings, and improving nuclear reactors. The 2012 Budget proposes three additional hubs targeted at rare earths and other critical materials, vehicle batteries, and Smart Grid technology for energy transmission. Such funding for research and development will help make future innovations possible, yielding novel ways to produce clean energy and to store and use energy more efficiently.

Conclusion

To guide the United States toward a clean energy future, the Administration has enacted and proposed a wide variety of programs, including manufacturing loan guarantees, tax credits and rebates, R&D subsidies, weatherization assistance, new vehicle standards, information reporting requirements, significant investment in transit infrastructure, and a new Clean Energy Standard for electric utilities. The programs are connected in important ways. They are all motivated by the same fundamental economic rationale: the problem that the full social benefits of clean energy R&D, production, and consumption—including energy security, cleaner air and reduced carbon pollution, and enhanced international competitiveness and economic growth—are not reflected in private markets.

Moreover, the programs focusing on different parts of the clean energy supply chain—innovation, manufacturing, generation, and use—are complementary. The benefits from putting 1 million electric vehicles on the road will be fully realized only if the electricity used to charge those vehicles can be generated by clean sources. R&D creates technologies that will be valuable only if they are manufactured and deployed, which is why the Administration has proposed a Clean Energy Standard to create incentives for utilities to use new clean sources of energy. The Clean Energy Standard in turn is complemented by the Administration's programs to enhance energy efficiency.

In the end, all of the Administration's clean energy programs are united by the overriding goal that in the decades to come American families will prosper in a cleaner, safer world. Today's investments in clean energy R&D will lead to innovations and new industries with high-quality jobs. Clean sources of energy will mean that Americans breathe cleaner air, enjoy better health, face reduced risks from climate change, and work and do business in an economy facing lower risks from energy-related disruptions—a clean energy future.

CHAPTER 7

SUPPORTING AMERICA'S SMALL BUSINESSES

Ensuring the prosperity and growth of our Nation's small businesses and creating a climate conducive to entrepreneurship are critical to strengthening the American economy. The spirit of entrepreneurship has been intertwined with the Nation's history from the early entrepreneurs who laid the foundation for modern American commerce. Entrepreneurs built the industrial companies that helped to transform our Nation into an economic power, and today innovative startup companies proliferate across the country in a wide range of industries. Not only do small businesses now employ approximately half of the private sector workforce, nearly every American business starts small, implying that entrepreneurs play a critical role in economic growth and job creation.

Small businesses, defined by the Small Business Administration (SBA) Office of Advocacy as independent businesses having 500 or fewer employees, account for more than half of nonfarm private gross domestic product (GDP). These 27.5 million businesses, many of them family-owned companies, are a key part of the U.S. economy. The economic challenges of the past few years, however, have proved difficult for owners of small businesses. Between 2008 and 2009, the number of new businesses founded is estimated to have dropped 11.8 percent, from 626,400 to 552,600, and the number of bankruptcies rose 40 percent, from 43,546 to 60,837 (Figure 7-1).

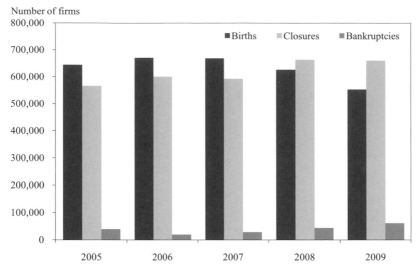

Figure 7-1
Births, Closures, and Bankruptcies of Firms

Notes: Births and closures in 2008 and 2009 are SBA estimates.
Births and closures include only employer firms. Bankruptcies include both employer and
nonemployer firms. Employer firms have paid employees while nonemployer firms do not.
Sources: SBA, Office of Advocacy.

In response, the Administration has taken several actions to support small business, such as reducing taxes and improving access to capital and credit. Through the American Recovery and Reinvestment Act (Recovery Act), the Hiring Incentives to Restore Employment (HIRE) Act, the Small Business Jobs Act (SBJA), and the Tax Relief, Unemployment Insurance Reauthorization, and Job Creation Act, the Administration cut taxes for small businesses 17 times and improved their access to credit and capital. This chapter briefly reviews the impact of the recession on small firms and details how Administration policies have built a solid foundation for the future growth and prosperity of American small business.

IMPACT OF THE RECESSION ON SMALL BUSINESSES

Job Creation

One particularly important contribution of small firms to the Nation's well-being is the jobs they create. According to the SBA's Office of Advocacy, small firms accounted for 9.8 million of the 15 million net new private sector jobs created between 1993 and 2009—nearly two out of every three of the period's net new jobs. In normal times, new small businesses account disproportionately for employment growth. Although many new firms fail, surviving firms create enough jobs to offset those lost to firm exits, so that most jobs created by firm births persist. A recent Kauffman Foundation study, for example, shows that startup firms created 3.1 million gross jobs in the United States in 2000. By 2005, about half of the initial firms had failed, but the survivors still employed 2.4 million people (Kane 2010).

During the recession, small businesses hired fewer workers than usual. According to Business Employment Dynamics statistics, between 2001 and 2007, businesses with fewer than 250 employees hired an average of 18.2 million workers a year, but those numbers fell to 16.5 million and 15.1 million in 2008 and 2009. Furthermore, some evidence suggests that small businesses have found it harder to recover from this recession than from past downturns. According to a Bureau of Labor Statistics report released in November 2010, new firms created a seasonally adjusted 1.1 million jobs during the three quarters before March 2010, or 31 percent fewer than during the comparable period after the 2001 recession.

Financing Small Business

Access to credit and capital enables owners of small businesses to start, support, and expand their companies. During the recession, both credit and capital availability for small businesses declined sharply, hampering entrepreneurs' efforts to finance operations and start new businesses. Although larger businesses typically rely on banks for only 30 percent of their financing, small firms receive 90 percent of their financing from banks (SBA 2009). Importantly, community banks—those with less than $1 billion in risk-weighted assets—provide 38 percent of small business and farm loans (COP 2010).

The capital structure of small business is typically roughly half equity and half debt, and the equity comes mainly from friends, family, or the founder themself. Unlike larger public companies, which routinely submit extensive financial documentation to the Securities and Exchange Commission, small firms cannot easily provide verified data to potential investors. These information asymmetries and other market frictions tend to slow the flow of credit and capital to promising small businesses. Many researchers have found evidence of these "liquidity constraints," which limit the funding that small business owners can raise from the market.[1]

Over the years, various institutions have arisen to help surmount this challenge in small business finance. One key to overcoming information issues is long-term relationships between small firms and commercial banks, whose officers not only can observe whether each small business is servicing

---

[1] This discussion draws from Berger and Udell, 2002; Peterson and Rajan, 1994; Evans and Jovanovic, 1989; and Holtz-Eakin, Joulfaian, and Rosen, 1994.

its loans, but also can collect additional information about its creditworthiness. To that end, one major aim of the SBA credit and capital programs is to overcome the market failures involved in financing small firms. The purpose of SBA loan programs, for example, is to support commercial loans to firms that would be considered good credit risks were it not for these information asymmetries. And the goal of SBA investment programs, such as the Small Business Investment Company program, is to overcome frictions in capital markets by encouraging the flow of venture and growth capital to small businesses.

Changes in Availability of Credit and Capital for Small Business

The recession complicated the already challenging financing landscape for small business in credit and capital markets. Commercial banks reduced their outstanding small loans (which are generally assumed to go disproportionately to small businesses) by more than $14 billion, or almost 2 percent, between June 30, 2008, and June 30, 2009, and the number of new loans to small business declined sharply (Duke 2010) (Figure 7-2).

Figure 7-2
Bank Lending to Small Business

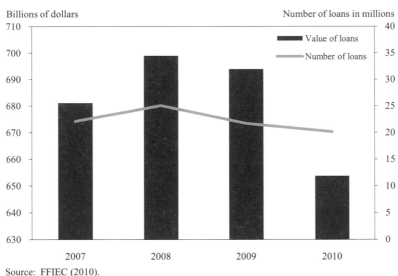

Source: FFIEC (2010).

Commercial and industrial loans, including loans to small businesses, fell an estimated 24 percent during the same period. This precipitous decline can be explained by changes in both demand and supply. First, the recession caused a drop in aggregate demand, reducing the ability of and incentives for small businesses to invest in new capital equipment or hire new employees.

As a result, the drop in demand for new loans contributed in part to the decline in lending to small business. Indeed, an additional 63.5 percent of bank senior loan officers reported lower demand in the second quarter of 2009 than reported higher or no change in demand, with smaller net differences throughout the rest of 2009 and early 2010. Furthermore, surveys from the National Federation of Independent Business indicated that in 2009 small business owners were far more concerned about poor sales than about tight credit (Figure 7-3).

Figure 7-3
Most Important Problem Facing Small Businesses in 2009

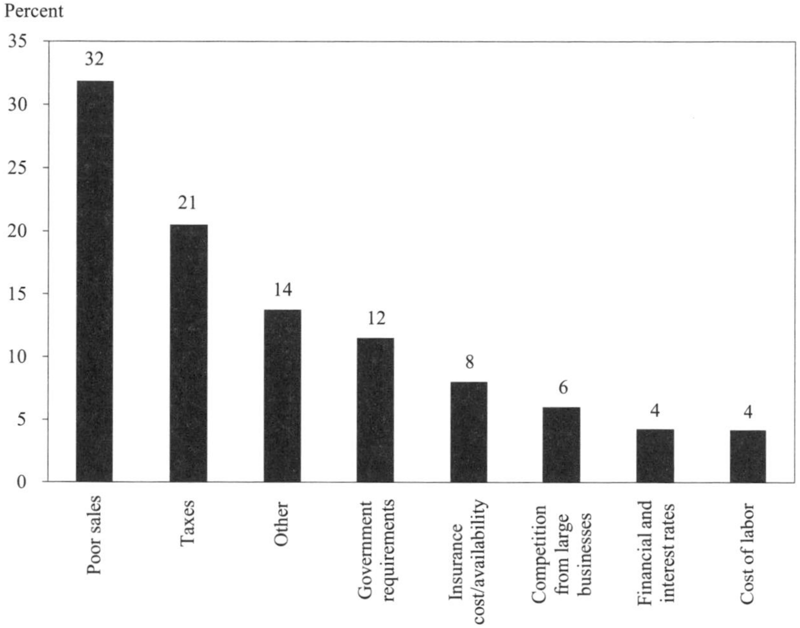

Notes: "Other" includes issues such as inflation and quality of labor. Data are an average of monthly National Federation of Independent Business surveys from 2009.
Sources: Dunkelberg and Wade (2010); CEA calculations.

But, falling demand was not the only problem. Firms that wanted to borrow and invest faced an especially grave situation during the recession. Specifically, the declining quality of existing loan portfolios for commercial banks led them to reduce or eliminate lines of credit and curtail new loans to small businesses. According to the Federal Reserve's Senior Loan Officer Opinion Survey on Bank Lending Practices, standards for lending to small businesses tightened, and interest rate spreads—the difference between rates charged to small businesses and a bank's prime customers—on loans between $100,000 and $1 million increased by 1 percentage point to its highest level in more than 10 years.

The sharp drop in both residential and commercial real estate prices also likely contributed to the deteriorating lending environment for many small businesses. The value of real estate assets is important to small businesses. According to the Federal Reserve's 2007 Survey of Consumer Finances, nearly 11 percent of all households owned and managed a small business, and 18 percent of these households used personal assets, such as their home, as collateral for loans.

Despite signs of overall economic recovery, the lending environment for small business may take some time to recover completely. Following the 1990 and 2001 recessions, for example, commercial lending continued to decline—falling 13.3 percent between 1990 and 1994, and 20.4 percent between 2001 and 2004 (COP 2010). Support for the small business lending market may thus continue to be necessary even as economic growth resumes.

The recession generated problems not only in the small business credit market but also in the angel and venture capital markets that allocate funds to promising new small businesses with high growth potential. Angel investors are wealthy individuals or small groups who invest in entrepreneurial ventures, often in the early stages of development. In 2009, these angel investors provided $17.6 billion (down 8.3 percent from 2008) in funding to 57,225 entrepreneurial ventures (Sohl 2010).

Figure 7-4
Venture Capital Investment

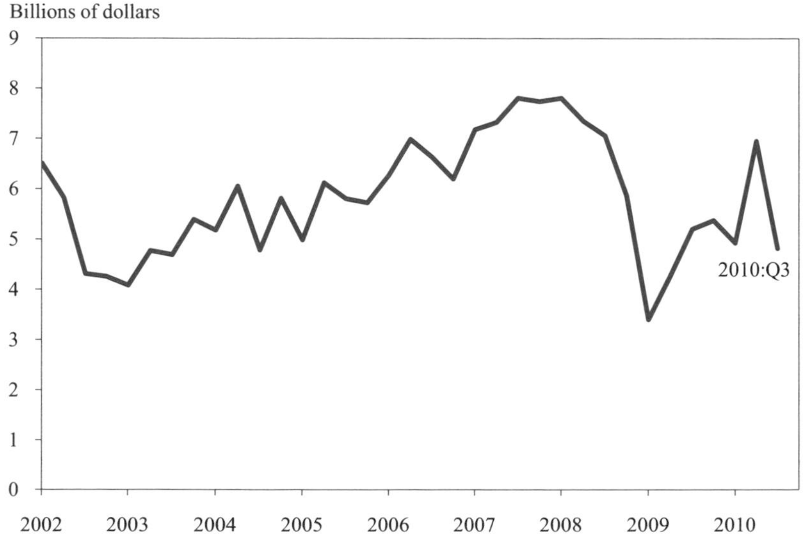

Source: PricewaterhouseCoopers and National Venture Capital Association (2010).

Venture capital firms raise funds from institutional investors and other limited partners to invest in privately held companies. Although venture capital firms fund less than 1 percent of new startups, firms that have received venture capital investments provide disproportionate growth, accounting for more than 12 million jobs and approximately $3 trillion in revenue in 2008. Venture capital has been especially important in spawning industries such as biotechnology, which has produced life-saving medicines and tens of thousands of American jobs (BIO 2008).

The venture capital market grew tremendously during the late 1990s, but fundraising has declined in recent years, and fewer venture capital firms are focusing on early-stage firms (Figure 7-4). Venture capital investment has never completely regained its strength since the end of the dot-com boom in the early 2000s, for at least three interrelated reasons: a decrease in such capital invested in early-stage startups; difficult economic conditions, including a weak initial public offering market (Figure 7-5); and asset reallocation away from venture capital funds by institutional investors. On average, $6.2 billion of venture capital was invested per quarter between 2001 and 2009. In the third quarter of 2010, however, venture capital investments fell 31 percent to $4.8 billion, according to a recent report from the National Venture Capital Association. The decline in access to capital for new firms exacerbated the more general financing challenges facing small firms.

Figure 7-5
U.S. Initial Public Offerings

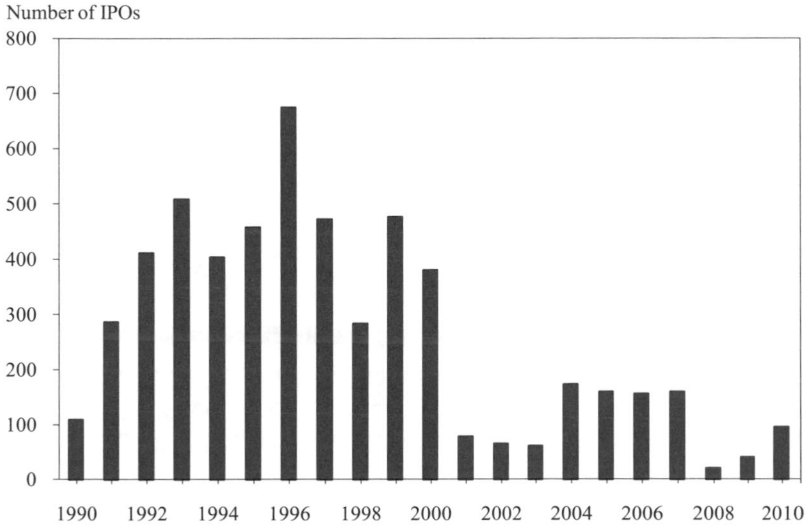

Number of IPOs

Source: Ritter (2010).

Administration Policies to Support Small Business

To address the challenges for small businesses and entrepreneurs arising from the recession, the Administration has taken measures that can be grouped under two broad headings: reducing the tax burden for small business and improving access to credit and capital. Both sets of policies are designed to increase the funds available to small business owners to hire workers, invest in new equipment, expand operations, or attract new customers. It should also be noted that the stimulus provided by the Recovery Act increased aggregate demand, a key concern mentioned in surveys of small business owners. The Financial Stability Plan, administered by the Department of Treasury, was designed to restore stability and confidence in the financial market. Both of these policies addressed the macroeconomic conditions affecting small businesses.

In addition, to further spur demand for the products and services provided by small business, the President issued a memorandum on April 26, 2010, calling for an Interagency Task Force on Federal Contracting Opportunities for Small Business. The task force released 13 specific recommendations in September 2010 aimed at increasing contracting opportunities for small business. Those recommendations are now being implemented by the Office of Management and Budget, the SBA, and other Federal agencies.

Tax Cuts for Small Business

Since taking office in January 2009, President Obama has signed into law 17 tax cuts targeted to small business. Each has given relief to business owners who struggled to stay afloat during the financial crisis and subsequent recession.

As noted, hiring by small businesses slowed during 2008 and 2009. In response, the HIRE Act was enacted in the spring of 2010, to spur job creation across the economy, including in small businesses. The law provided a two tiered tax incentive to employers who hire and retain jobless workers. The first part of the incentive exempted employers from paying their share of Social Security taxes (6.2 percent of the first $106,800 of wages) on qualified employees. The second part was a general business tax credit of up to $1,000 for each new employee retained for more than one year. Both of these targeted tax cuts provided an incentive for small businesses to hire new workers and retain them, helping to revive an important engine of job growth in the American economy.

In addition, the Affordable Care Act responded to small business owners' concerns about high health care costs by giving eligible employers a tax credit of up to 35 percent of health insurance premium costs, increasing to 50 percent for any two years starting in 2014. Moreover, would-be entrepreneurs are sometimes discouraged from starting new firms for fear of losing health insurance coverage provided by their employer. In response, the SBJA allows 2 million self-employed individuals to deduct the cost of health insurance in 2010 for themselves and their family from their self-employment taxes, saving these workers an estimated $1.9 billion.

Administration policy also aimed to increase incentives for small business investment. These incentives included a Recovery Act provision, which was extended in the later SBJA, that allowed 50 percent bonus depreciation for new investments. The Tax Relief, Unemployment Insurance Reauthorization and Job Creation Act expanded this same incentive through a provision allowing businesses to expense 100 percent of their investments from September 2010 through the end of 2011. It is estimated that this provision will benefit up to 2 million businesses. The Administration also doubled, from $125,000 to $250,000, the capital investment and new equipment purchases that small businesses could write off in 2009 and increased that limit to $500,000 in 2010 and 2011. It is estimated that 4.5 million small businesses qualify for this provision. Taken together, these measures reduce the cost of capital for small business, providing significant incentives to invest in new machinery and equipment.

Finally, the Administration has taken key steps to facilitate the startup of new businesses and encourage equity investments in existing small businesses. The Recovery Act permitted 75 percent of capital gains on qualified small business investments to be excluded from taxation. The SBJA temporarily raised that exclusion to 100 percent for key small business investments held for at least five years, a benefit that is estimated to go to 1 million firms—and which the Administration has proposed to make permanent.

Initiatives to Increase Access to Credit

Aside from these important tax cuts for small business, the President also signed legislation that has helped small businesses access credit to hire employees and expand. The Recovery Act provided $730 million to the SBA to eliminate fees on SBA-backed loans and raise the guarantee to 90 percent on certain loans. Furthermore, the Administration expanded the Microloan program and the Surety Bond Guarantee program and provided funds to improve the efficiency of the SBA's lending and oversight processes. Combined with measures taken under the Financial Stability Plan to unfreeze the secondary markets on which SBA loans are bought and sold, the Recovery Act SBA loan provisions have supported $30 billion in lending to more than 70,000 small businesses through October 2010. These measures were critical to the rebound of SBA-backed loans through 2009 and early 2010 (Figure 7-6).

Figure 7-6
SBA-Backed Loan Approvals

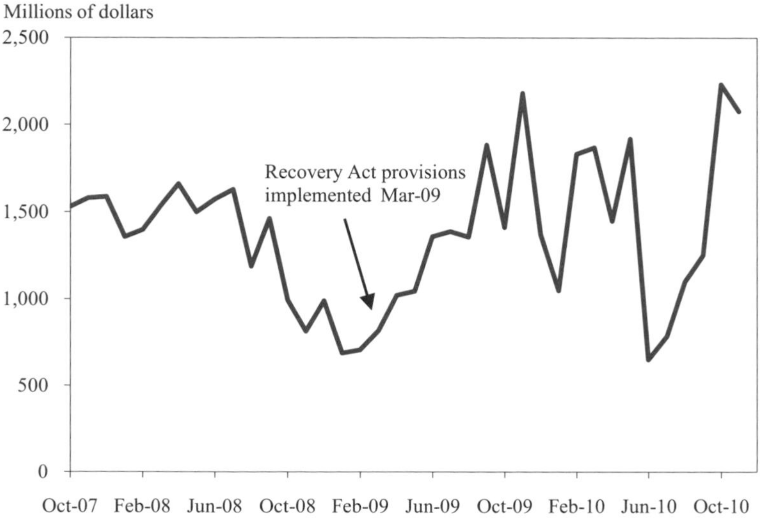

Millions of dollars

Recovery Act provisions
implemented Mar-09

Source: SBA.

The SBJA went even further to increase the amount of loans to small businesses. It provided $505 million to the SBA to support up to $14 billion in new lending for small business while extending Recovery Act provisions to increase loan guarantees and reduce fees, thus ensuring continued access to more affordable credit for small business owners. From February 2009 through December 2010, the SBA has supported more than $42 billion of loans to nearly 82,000 small businesses.

The Administration also took several new steps to increase access to credit. For example, as small businesses grow, they typically need to borrow more to finance more expensive equipment, to increase their real estate holdings, and to hire more skilled workers. In addition to extending Recovery Act SBA lending initiatives, the SBJA also permanently increased the maximum size of SBA 7(a) program loans from $2 million to $5 million, raised the lending limit in the SBA 504 manufacturing-related loan program from $4 million to $5.5 million, and temporarily increased the SBA Express program limit from $350,000 to $1 million.

Small Business Lending Fund. The Administration's efforts also focused on increasing small business lending more broadly. As noted, community banks are a critical source of credit for small businesses. These banks struggled during the financial crisis and sharply cut back their small business lending, though less dramatically than did larger institutions. To support these community banks and encourage more lending, the Administration created a Small Business Lending Fund to be administered by the Treasury Department and tailored to the specific needs of each state. Under this plan, the Federal Government is authorized to lend up to $30 billion in capital to community banks in return for preferred stock. The dividend rate that banks are required to pay back to the Treasury depends on how much they increase their loans to small business, with a dividend rate as low as 1 percent for lenders that increase loans by 10 percent or more.

State Small Business Credit Initiative. As part of the SBJA, the Administration also took action to boost small business lending by establishing a State Small Business Credit Initiative. Several states have already implemented loan programs to support small businesses, and the Administration is working with other states to create similar programs. Capital Access Programs, for example, create loan-loss reserves to which lenders and state governments contribute funds. Across a range of states, these funds have historically leveraged $10 to $30 from every $1 of public funds. The credit initiative will provide $1.5 billion to shore up state programs that faced difficulties during the economic downturn and to spur private sector lending to small businesses. This initiative will require a minimum leverage of 10 to 1—$10 for every $1 received from the Treasury Department, thus designed to support a total of $15 billion in lending across the nation.

National Export Initiative. Another important program to benefit small business is the National Export Initiative (NEI), launched through an executive order issued by the President on March 11, 2010. The NEI calls for a national outreach campaign both to identify small businesses that may be able to increase their exports and to raise awareness generally among the nation's small businesses about export opportunities. The NEI, working through a number of agencies, including the Commerce Department's International Trade Administration, will also provide training and other kinds of technical assistance to help small businesses prepare to become exporters. In addition, the NEI proposes to set up a pilot program to match small businesses with export intermediaries and outlines several measures to support small businesses with trade assistance programs once they begin to export to new markets. In the 11 months before August 2010, the Export-Import bank increased its approvals for small business loans nearly 14 percent, from $3.6 billion to $4.1 billion.

Policies to Encourage Greater Access to Capital

In addition to providing tax cuts and increasing credit for existing small firms, the Administration also has introduced important policies to provide access to capital and to encourage the formation of new businesses. In particular, the Administration has launched several important initiatives to facilitate the flow of venture and growth capital to small businesses and create more supportive conditions for the launch of new ventures.

Small Business Investment Company (SBIC) Program. SBICs are private venture and later-stage capital firms that register with the SBA and make equity investments in small companies. They raise equity capital from private sources, raise debt backed by SBA guarantees, and deploy this capital in private companies. Since 1958, SBICs have invested more than $56 billion in more than 100,000 small businesses. Today, approximately 338 SBICs manage more than $17 billion.

Just as the Administration took action to counteract the decline in small business credit availability, it worked to counter the decline in the funding of new small businesses. To reverse the precipitous fall in venture capital fundraising during 2008 and early 2009, provisions in the Recovery Act permanently increased the effectiveness of SBICs in providing capital to high-growth firms. The Recovery Act first made SBICs eligible for increased SBA guaranteed funding. It then required them to increase their investments in smaller companies.

In 2010, SBIC financing to small firms totaled $1.6 billion, an increase of 23 percent over its average for the previous four years. In addition, processing time fell from more than a year to less than six months, allowing the SBA to increase markedly the number of new SBICs that it licensed.

Promoting Entrepreneurship in Regional Clusters. The SBA also launched its Innovative Economies Initiative to spur the development of entrepreneurship in regional clusters. The SBA provided $6 million to 10 regional economies across the nation to nurture and grow small businesses in critical industry supply chains. In one instance, the SBA provided funds to its Small Business Development Centers in the Philadelphia region to link local small businesses to the Energy Regional Innovation Cluster initiative on green buildings.

Startup America. The Administration has also promoted the success of new small businesses with high growth potential. On January 31, 2011, it launched Startup America to encourage high-growth entrepreneurial ventures such as those that have revolutionized the nation's software, semi-conductor, life science, and energy sectors, among others. Startup America includes both specific federal policies and a public-private partnership to promote entrepreneurship. The primary goal is to increase the number of high-growth startups that create broad-based economic growth and jobs. A second goal is to celebrate and honor entrepreneurship as a core American value and give more Americans the opportunity to start their own business.

Startup America features policy initiatives in four areas: access to capital, entrepreneurship education and mentoring, commercialization of university and federal laboratory research, and reductions of barriers to growth for new ventures. To improve access to capital, the SBA will work with the private sector, through its SBIC Impact Fund program, to guarantee investments totaling $1 billion over the next five years in high-growth small businesses in underserved regions. The SBIC Innovation Fund program will guarantee an additional $1 billion of investment over several years in early-stage innovative companies. This initiative also calls for an extension of the 100 percent exemption of capital gains from qualified investments in small businesses and expands the New Markets tax credit program from $3.5 billion to $5 billion a year.

In the area of education and mentoring, the Department of Energy, the SBA, and the Department of Veterans Affairs will provide support to expand successful business mentorship programs for veterans of the wars in Iraq and Afghanistan and for clean energy entrepreneurs around the nation. In addition, private sector partners have committed to more than $350 million in investments for entrepreneurial education and mentoring. The third set of initiatives in Startup America will invest in strategies to bring innovative ideas from federal labs and universities into the commercial marketplace, both by establishing and disseminating best practices for commercializa-tion and by funding regional "proof of concept" centers. In the fourth set of initiatives on reducing barriers to growth, the U.S. Patent and Trademark Office has announced that it will pursue a more efficient "Three Track" patent examination process, creating benefits for entrepreneurs seeking more certainty over the timing of important intellectual property protection. Startup America will also ask Federal agencies to identify barriers to high-growth entrepreneurship and launch a listening tour for Administration officials to travel the nation and meet with entrepreneurs to solicit their recommendations for improving the environment for entrepreneurship.

CONCLUSION

Small businesses, the foundation of the American economy, are critical to economic growth and job creation. Entrepreneurs, in part because of their reliance on commercial banks, were especially hard hit during the financial crisis and subsequent recession. A swift and comprehensive policy response was thus essential. The Administration has advanced important initiatives to lower taxes and make health insurance more affordable for small businesses, to increase their access to credit and capital, and to provide stronger incentives for job creation and investment. Taken together, these steps have stabilized the small business economy and placed it on a stronger footing for future growth.

REFERENCES

Chapter 2
The Year In Review And The Years Ahead

CBO (Congressional Budget Office). 2010. "Monthly Budget Review: A Congressional Budget Office Analysis." November.

———. 2011. "The Budget and Economic Outlook: Fiscal Years 2011 to 2021." January.

CEA (Council of Economic Advisers). 2010a. *Economic Report of the President*. February.

———. 2010b. "The Economic Impact of the American Recovery and Reinvestment Act of 2009." Fifth Quarterly Report to Congress. November.

Reinhart, Carmen M., and Vincent R. Reinhart. 2010. "After the Fall." NBER Working Paper 16334. Cambridge, MA: National Bureau of Economic Research. September.

Reinhart, Carmen M., and Kenneth S. Rogoff. 2009. "The Aftermath of Financial Crises." *American Economic Review* 99, no. 2: 466–72.

Chapter 3
The Foundations of Growth

Adelman, Clifford. 1998. "The Kiss of Death? An Alternative View of College Remediation." *National Crosstalk* 6, no. 3: 11.

Belfield, Clive R., et al. 2006. "The High/Scope Perry Pre-School Program: Cost-Benefit Analysis Using Data from the Age-40 Follow-Up." *Journal of Human Resources* 41, no. 1: 162–90.

Bloom, Nick, Rachel Griffith, and John Van Reenen. 2002. "Do R&D Tax Credits Work? Evidence from a Panel of Countries 1979–1997." *Journal of Public Economics* 85, no. 1: 1–31.

CEA (Council of Economic Advisers). 2009. "Preparing the Workers of Today for the Jobs of Tomorrow." July.

Cunha, Flavio, et al. 2006. "Interpreting the Evidence on Life Cycle Skill Formation." In *Handbook of the Economics of Education*, edited by E. A. Hanushek and F. Welch. Amsterdam: North-Holland.

Department of Commerce. 2010. "Exploring the Digital Nation: Home Broadband Internet Adoption in the United States." November.

DiNardo, John, Nicole M. Fortin, and Thomas Lemieux. 1996. "Labor Market Institutions and the Distribution of Wages, 1973–92: A Semiparametric Approach." *Econometrica* 64, no. 5: 1001–44.

FCC (Federal Communications Commission). 2010. "Connecting America: The National Broadband Plan."

Goldin, Claudia, and Lawrence F. Katz. 2007. "Long-Run Changes in the Wage Structure: Narrowing, Widening, Polarizing." *Brookings Papers on Economic Activity* 2:135–65. Washington, DC: Brookings Institution.

Haines, Michael. 2001. "The Urban Mortality Transition in the United States, 1800–1940." Historical Working Paper 134. Cambridge, MA: National Bureau of Economic Research. July.

Hall, Bronwyn, and John Van Reenen. 2000. "How Effective Are Fiscal Incentives for R&D? A Review of the Evidence." *Research Policy* 29, no. 4-5: 449–69.

Katz, Lawrence, and Kevin Murphy. 1992. "Changes in Relative Wages, 1963–1987: Supply and Demand Factors." *Quarterly Journal of Economics* 57: 35–78.

Maddison, Angus. 2008. *Historical Statistics of the World Economy: 1–2008 AD*. Gronigen: Gronigen Growth and Development Centre.

Maguire, Sheila, et al. 2010. "Tuning in to Local Labor Markets: Findings from the Sectoral Employment Impact Study." Philadelphia, PA: Public/Private Ventures.

OECD (Organisation for Economic Co-operation and Development). 2010. "OECD Information Technology Outlook 2010." Paris.

Pham, Nam D. 2010. "The Impact of Innovation and the Role of Intellectual Property Rights on U.S. Productivity, Competitiveness, Jobs, Wages, and Exports." Washington, DC: NDP Consulting. April.

Smith, Aaron. 2010. "Home Broadband 2010." Internet and American Life Project. Washington, DC: Pew Research Center.

Stuen, Eric T., Keith E. Maskus, and Ahmed Mushfiq Mobarak. 2010. "Skilled Immigration and Innovation: Evidence from Enrollment Fluctuations in U.S. Doctoral Programs." Discussion Paper 7709. London: Centre for Economic Policy Research. February.

CHAPTER 4
THE WORLD ECONOMY

Baldwin, Richard E., ed. 2009. *The Great Trade Collapse: Causes, Consequences and Prospects.* VoxEU.org E-book.

Bernard, Andrew B., et al. 2007. "Firms in International Trade." *Journal of Economic Perspectives* 21, no. 3: 105–30.

Bown, Chad P. 2010. "Taking Stock of Antidumping, Safeguards, and Countervailing Duties, 1990–2009." Working Paper 5436. Washington, DC: World Bank. September.

Cecchetti, Stephen, Marion Kohler, and Christian Upper. 2009. "Financial Crises and Economic Activity." Working Paper 15379. Cambridge, MA: National Bureau of Economic Research. September.

Chinn, Menzie. 2005. "Doomed to Deficits? Aggregate U.S. Trade Flows Re-Examined." *Review of World Economics* 141, no. 3: 460–85.

de la Torre, Luz Elena Reyes, and Jorge G. González. 2005. "Antidumping and Safeguard Measures in the Political Economy of Liberalization: The Mexican Case." In *Safeguards and Antidumping in Latin American Trade Liberalization: Fighting Fire with Fire*, edited by J. Michael Finger and Julio J. Nogués. New York, NY: World Bank and Palgrave MacMillan.

IMF (International Monetary Fund). 2007. "Exchange Rates and the Adjustment of External Imbalances." In *World Economic Outlook: April 2007.* Washington, DC.

————. 2009. "What's the Damage? Medium-Term Output Dynamics after Financial Crises." In *World Economic Outlook: October 2009.* Washington, DC.

————. 2010. "Global Prospects and Policies." In *World Economic Outlook: October 2010.* Washington, DC.

Kee, Hiau Looi, Alessandro Nicita, and Marcelo Olarreaga. 2009. "Estimating Trade Restrictiveness Indices." *Economic Journal* 119, no. 534: 172–99.

Lane, Philip R., and Gian Maria Milesi-Ferretti. 2009. "Where Did All the Borrowing Go? A Forensic Analysis of the U.S. External Position." *Journal of the Japanese and International Economies* 23, no. 2: 177–99.

Reinhart, Carmen M., and Kenneth S. Rogoff. 2009. *This Time Is Different: Eight Centuries of Financial Folly.* Princeton University Press. Princeton.

WTO (World Trade Organization). 2009. World Tariff Profiles 2009. Geneva.

————. 2010. *WTO Disputes by Country/Territory* (www.wto.org/english/tratop_e/dispu_e/dispu_by_country_e.htm).

CHAPTER 5
HEALTH CARE REFORM

Asplin, Brent R., et al. 2005. "Insurance Status and Access to Urgent Ambulatory Care Follow-up Appointments." *Journal of the American Medical Association* 294, no. 10: 1248–54.

Brown, Jeffrey R., and Austan Goolsbee. 2002. "Does the Internet Make Markets More Competitive? Evidence from the Life Insurance Industry." *Journal of Political Economy* 110, no. 3: 481–507.

Bundorf, Kate M., et al. 2009. "Do Markets Respond to Quality Information? The Case of Fertility Clinics." *Journal of Health Economics* 28, no. 3: 718–27.

Card, David, Carlos Dobkin, and Nicole Maestas. 2009. "Does Medicare Save Lives?" *Quarterly Journal of Economics* 124, no. 2: 597–636.

Chernew, Michael E., Richard A. Hirth, and David M. Cutler. 2003. "Increased Spending on Health Care: How Much Can the United States Afford?" *Health Affairs* 22, no. 4: 15–25.

Coate, Stephen. 1995. "Altruism, the Samaritan's Dilemma, and Government Transfer Policy." *American Economic Review* 85, no.1: 46–57.

Cook, Keziah, David Dranove, and Andrew Sfekas. 2010. "Does Major Illness Cause Financial Catastrophe?" *Health Services Research* 45, no. 2: 418–36.

Cutler, David M., and Mark McClellan. 2001. "Is Technological Change in Medicine Worth It?" *Health Affairs* 20, no. 5: 11–29.

Cutler, David M., Allison B. Rosen, and Sandeep Vijan. 2006. "The Value of Medical Spending in the United States, 1960–2000." *New England Journal of Medicine* 355, no. 23: 920–27.

Dafny, Leemore, Mark Duggan, and Subramaniam Ramanarayanan. 2010. "Paying a Premium on Your Premium? Consolidation in the U.S. Health Insurance Industry." Working Paper 15434. Cambridge, MA: National Bureau of Economic Research. August.

DeNavas-Walt, Carmen, Bernadette D. Proctor, and Jessica C. Smith. 2010. *Income, Poverty, and Health Insurance Coverage in the United States: 2009.* Department of Commerce, Census Bureau.

Hall, Robert E., and Charles I. Jones. 2007. "The Value of Life and the Rise in Health Spending." *Quarterly Journal of Economics* 122, no. 1: 39–72.

Herring, Bradley. 2005. "The Effect of the Availability of Charity Care to the Uninsured on the Demand for Private Health Insurance." *Journal of Health Economics* 24, no. 2: 225–52.

Kaiser Family Foundation and Health Research and Educational Trust. 2010. *Employer Health Benefits: 2010 Annual Survey.* Menlo Park, CA, and Chicago, IL: Henry J. Kaiser Family Foundation and Health Research and Educational Trust.

McWilliams, J. Michael, et al. 2004. "Health Insurance Coverage and Mortality among the Near-Elderly." *Health Affairs* 23, no. 4: 223–33.

Mukamel, Dana B., et al. 2008. "Publication of Quality Report Cards and Trends in Reported Quality Measures in Nursing Homes." *Health Services Research* 43, no. 4: 1244–62.

Murphy, Kevin M., and Robert H. Topel. 2006. "The Value of Health and Longevity." *Journal of Political Economy* 114, no. 5: 871–904.

Pauly, Mark V. 1968. "The Economics of Moral Hazard: Comment." *American Economic Review* 58, no. 3: 531–37.

Rask, Kevin N., and Kimberly J. Rask. 2000. "Public Insurance Substituting for Private Insurance: New Evidence Regarding Public Hospitals, Uncompensated Care Funds, and Medicaid." *Journal of Health Economics* 19, no. 1: 1–31.

Robinson, James C. 2004. "Consolidation and the Transformation of Competition in Health Insurance." *Health Affairs* 23, no. 6: 11–24.

Werner, Rachel, Elizabeth Stuart, and Daniel Polsky. 2010. "Public Reporting Drove Quality Gains at Nursing Homes." *Health Affairs* 29, no. 9: 1706–13.

CHAPTER 6
TRANSITIONING TO A CLEAN ENERGY FUTURE

Eisenberg, Joel F. 2010. "Weatherization Assistance Program Technical Memorandum Background Data and Statistics." ORNL/ TM-2010/66. Oak Ridge National Laboratory.

EPA (Environmental Protection Agency). 2010. "The Benefits and Costs of the Clean Air Act: 1990 to 2020." Washington, DC.

Interagency Working Group on Social Cost of Carbon. 2010. "Technical Support Document: Social Cost of Carbon for Regulatory Impact Analysis under Executive Order 12866." February. (www.epa.gov/oms/climate/regulations/scc-tsd.pdf).

UNEP (United Nations Environment Program), EPO (European Patent Office), and ICTSD (International Center for Trade and Sustainable Development). 2010. "Patents and Clean Energy: Bridging the Gap Between Evidence and Policy." (www.epo.org/topics/issues/clean-energy/study.html).

CHAPTER 7
SUPPORTING AMERICA'S SMALL BUSINESSES

Berger, Allen N., and Gregory F. Udell. 2002. "Small Business Credit Availability and Relationship Lending: The Importance of Bank Organizational Structure." *Economic Journal* 112, no. 477, Features, F32–F53.

BIO (Biotechnology Industry Organization). 2008. *Guide to Biotechnology* (www.bio.org/speeches/pubs/er/).

COP (Congressional Oversight Panel). 2010. "May Oversight Report: The Small Business Credit Crunch and the Impact of the TARP" (http://cop.senate.gov/reports/library/report-051310-cop.cfm).

Duke, Elizabeth A. 2010. "Small Business Lending." Testimony before the Committee on Financial Services and Committee on Small Business, House of Representatives, February 26 (www.federalreserve.gov/newsevents/testimony/duke20100226a.htm).

Dunkelberg, William C., and Holly Wade. 2010. "NFIB Small Business Economic Trends." National Federation of Independent Business. (http://nfib.com/Portals/0/PDF/sbet/sbet201001.pdf)

Evans, David, and Boyan Jovanovic. 1989. "An Estimated Model of Entrepreneurial Choice under Liquidity Constraints." *Journal of Political Economy* 102, no. 4: 808–27.

FFIEC (Federal Financial Institutions Examination Council). 2010. Consolidated Reports of Condition and Income. Federal Deposit Insurance Corporation (www.ffiec.gov/reports.htm).

Holtz-Eakin, Douglas, David Joulfaian, and Harvey S. Rosen. 1994. "Sticking It Out: Entrepreneurial Survival and Liquidity Constraints." *Journal of Political Economy* 102, no. 1: 53–75.

Kane, Tim. 2010. "The Importance of Startups in Job Creation and Job Destruction." Kauffman Foundation Research Series: Firm Formation and Economic Growth. Kansas City, Mo. July. (www.kauffman.org/.../firm_formation_importance_of_startups.pdf).

Petersen, Mitchell A., and Raghuram G. Rajan. 1994. "The Benefits of Lending Relationships: Evidence from Small Business Data." *Journal of Finance* 49, no. 1: 3–37.

PricewaterhouseCoopers and National Venture Capital Association. 2010. "Money Tree Report" (www.pwcmoneytree.com/MTPublic/ns/index/jsp).

Ritter, Jay R. 2010. "Initial Public Offerings: Tables Updated through 2010." Table 1: Mean First-Day Returns and Money Left on the Table, 1990–2010 (http://bear.warrington.ufl.edu/ritter/IPOs2010Statistics.pdf).

SBA (Small Business Administration) and Treasury Department. 2009. "Report to the President: Small Business Financing Forum." (www.wipp.org/resource/resmgr/...to.../Small_Business_Financing_For.pdf) or (http://archive.sba.gov/smallbusinessforum/index.html).

Sohl, Jeffrey. 2010. "The Angel Investor Market in 2009: Holding Steady but Changes in Seed and Startup Investments." Center for Venture Research, University of New Hampshire. March 31. (www.unh.edu/news/docs/2009angelanalysis.pdf).

A P P E N D I X   A

REPORT TO THE PRESIDENT ON THE ACTIVITIES OF THE COUNCIL OF ECONOMIC ADVISERS DURING 2010

LETTER OF TRANSMITTAL

COUNCIL OF ECONOMIC ADVISERS
Washington, D.C., December 31, 2010

MR. PRESIDENT:

The Council of Economic Advisers submits this report on its activities during calendar year 2010 in accordance with the requirements of the Congress, as set forth in section 10(d) of the Employment Act of 1946 as amended by the Full Employment and Balanced Growth Act of 1978.

Sincerely,

Austan Goolsbee, *Chairman*
Cecilia Elena Rouse, *Member*

Council Members and Their Dates of Service

Name	Position	Oath of office date	Separation date
Edwin G. Nourse	Chairman	August 9, 1946	November 1, 1949
Leon H. Keyserling	Vice Chairman	August 9, 1946	
	Acting Chairman	November 2, 1949	
	Chairman	May 10, 1950	January 20, 1953
John D. Clark	Member	August 9, 1946	
	Vice Chairman	May 10, 1950	February 11, 1953
Roy Blough	Member	June 29, 1950	August 20, 1952
Robert C. Turner	Member	September 8, 1952	January 20, 1953
Arthur F. Burns	Chairman	March 19, 1953	December 1, 1956
Neil H. Jacoby	Member	September 15, 1953	February 9, 1955
Walter W. Stewart	Member	December 2, 1953	April 29, 1955
Raymond J. Saulnier	Member	April 4, 1955	
	Chairman	December 3, 1956	January 20, 1961
Joseph S. Davis	Member	May 2, 1955	October 31, 1958
Paul W. McCracken	Member	December 3, 1956	January 31, 1959
Karl Brandt	Member	November 1, 1958	January 20, 1961
Henry C. Wallich	Member	May 7, 1959	January 20, 1961
Walter W. Heller	Chairman	January 29, 1961	November 15, 1964
James Tobin	Member	January 29, 1961	July 31, 1962
Kermit Gordon	Member	January 29, 1961	December 27, 1962
Gardner Ackley	Member	August 3, 1962	
	Chairman	November 16, 1964	February 15, 1968
John P. Lewis	Member	May 17, 1963	August 31, 1964
Otto Eckstein	Member	September 2, 1964	February 1, 1966
Arthur M. Okun	Member	November 16, 1964	
	Chairman	February 15, 1968	January 20, 1969
James S. Duesenberry	Member	February 2, 1966	June 30, 1968
Merton J. Peck	Member	February 15, 1968	January 20, 1969
Warren L. Smith	Member	July 1, 1968	January 20, 1969
Paul W. McCracken	Chairman	February 4, 1969	December 31, 1971
Hendrik S. Houthakker	Member	February 4, 1969	July 15, 1971
Herbert Stein	Member	February 4, 1969	
	Chairman	January 1, 1972	August 31, 1974
Ezra Solomon	Member	September 9, 1971	March 26, 1973
Marina v.N. Whitman	Member	March 13, 1972	August 15, 1973
Gary L. Seevers	Member	July 23, 1973	April 15, 1975
William J. Fellner	Member	October 31, 1973	February 25, 1975
Alan Greenspan	Chairman	September 4, 1974	January 20, 1977
Paul W. MacAvoy	Member	June 13, 1975	November 15, 1976
Burton G. Malkiel	Member	July 22, 1975	January 20, 1977
Charles L. Schultze	Chairman	January 22, 1977	January 20, 1981
William D. Nordhaus	Member	March 18, 1977	February 4, 1979
Lyle E. Gramley	Member	March 18, 1977	May 27, 1980

Council Members and Their Dates of Service

Name	Position	Oath of office date	Separation date
George C. Eads	Member	June 6, 1979	January 20, 1981
Stephen M. Goldfeld	Member	August 20, 1980	January 20, 1981
Murray L. Weidenbaum	Chairman	February 27, 1981	August 25, 1982
William A. Niskanen	Member	June 12, 1981	March 30, 1985
Jerry L. Jordan	Member	July 14, 1981	July 31, 1982
Martin Feldstein	Chairman	October 14, 1982	July 10, 1984
William Poole	Member	December 10, 1982	January 20, 1985
Beryl W. Sprinkel	Chairman	April 18, 1985	January 20, 1989
Thomas Gale Moore	Member	July 1, 1985	May 1, 1989
Michael L. Mussa	Member	August 18, 1986	September 19, 1988
Michael J. Boskin	Chairman	February 2, 1989	January 12, 1993
John B. Taylor	Member	June 9, 1989	August 2, 1991
Richard L. Schmalensee	Member	October 3, 1989	June 21, 1991
David F. Bradford	Member	November 13, 1991	January 20, 1993
Paul Wonnacott	Member	November 13, 1991	January 20, 1993
Laura D'Andrea Tyson	Chair	February 5, 1993	April 22, 1995
Alan S. Blinder	Member	July 27, 1993	June 26, 1994
Joseph E. Stiglitz	Member	July 27, 1993	
	Chairman	June 28, 1995	February 10, 1997
Martin N. Baily	Member	June 30, 1995	August 30, 1996
Alicia H. Munnell	Member	January 29, 1996	August 1, 1997
Janet L. Yellen	Chair	February 18, 1997	August 3, 1999
Jeffrey A. Frankel	Member	April 23, 1997	March 2, 1999
Rebecca M. Blank	Member	October 22, 1998	July 9, 1999
Martin N. Baily	Chairman	August 12, 1999	January 19, 2001
Robert Z. Lawrence	Member	August 12, 1999	January 12, 2001
Kathryn L. Shaw	Member	May 31, 2000	January 19, 2001
R. Glenn Hubbard	Chairman	May 11, 2001	February 28, 2003
Mark B. McClellan	Member	July 25, 2001	November 13, 2002
Randall S. Kroszner	Member	November 30, 2001	July 1, 2003
N. Gregory Mankiw	Chairman	May 29, 2003	February 18, 2005
Kristin J. Forbes	Member	November 21, 2003	June 3, 2005
Harvey S. Rosen	Member	November 21, 2003	
	Chairman	February 23, 2005	June 10, 2005
Ben S. Bernanke	Chairman	June 21, 2005	January 31, 2006
Katherine Baicker	Member	November 18, 2005	July 11, 2007
Matthew J. Slaughter	Member	November 18, 2005	March 1, 2007
Edward P. Lazear	Chairman	February 27, 2006	January 20, 2009
Donald B. Marron	Member	July 17, 2008	January 20, 2009
Christina D. Romer	Chair	January 29, 2009	September 3, 2010
Austan D. Goolsbee	Member	March 11, 2009	
	Chairman	September 10, 2010	
Cecilia Elena Rouse	Member	March 11, 2009	

REPORT TO THE PRESIDENT ON THE ACTIVITIES OF THE COUNCIL OF ECONOMIC ADVISERS DURING 2010

The Council of Economic Advisers was established by the Employment Act of 1946 to provide the President with objective economic analysis and advice on the development and implementation of a wide range of domestic and international economic policy issues. The Council consists of a Chairman and two members appointed by the President and confirmed by the United States Senate.

THE CHAIR OF THE COUNCIL

Austan D. Goolsbee, who had been a Member of the Council since 2009, was appointed Chairman of the Council on September 10, 2010. Chairman Goolsbee is on a leave of absence from the University of Chicago, where he is the Robert P. Gwinn Professor of Economics at the Booth School of Business. He also served as the Chief Economist and Staff Director of the President's Economic Recovery Advisory Board for the duration of its existence from 2009 to 2011.

The Chairman is a member of the President's Cabinet and is responsible for communicating the Council's views on economic matters directly to the President through personal discussions and written reports. Chairman Goolsbee represents the Council at the Presidential economic briefings, daily White House senior staff meetings, budget meetings, Cabinet meetings, a variety of inter-agency meetings, and meetings with the President, the Vice President, and other senior government officials. He also meets frequently with members of Congress as well as with business, academic and labor leaders to discuss ideas about the economy.

Christina D. Romer resigned as Chair in September 2010 to return to the University of California, Berkeley, where she is the Class of 1957 -Garff B. Wilson Professor of Economics.

The Members of the Council

Cecilia Elena Rouse was nominated by the President on January 20, 2009, confirmed by the Senate on March 10, and took her oath of office on March 11. Dr. Rouse is on a leave of absence from Princeton University, where she is the Theodore A. Wells '29 Professor of Economics and Public Affairs. Dr. Rouse represents the Council at a wide variety of meetings and frequently attends meetings with the President and the Vice President. Dr. Rouse works closely with the Chairman on all issues before the Council, and especially on those related to labor, education, housing, and international trade.

Areas of Activity

Macroeconomic Policies

A central function of the Council is to advise the President on all major macroeconomic issues and developments. The Council is actively involved in all aspects of macroeconomic policy. In 2010, the central macroeconomic issues included formulating targeted measures to spur job creation; evaluating the effects of the policies and the economy's response; reforming financial regulation; monitoring the financial and economic recovery; providing analysis on the economic effects of the American Recovery and Reinvestment Act of 2009; innovation and infrastructure; and setting priorities for the budget. The Council works closely with various government agencies, the Office of Management and Budget, the National Economic Council, White House senior staff, and other officials.

The Council prepares for the President, the Vice President, and the White House senior staff a daily economic briefing memo analyzing current economic developments, and almost-daily memos on key economic data releases. It also issues reports periodically on economic issues.

The Council, the Department of Treasury, and the Office of Management and Budget—the Administration's economic "troika"— are responsible for producing the economic forecasts that underlie the Administration's budget proposals. The Council initiates the forecasting process twice each year, consulting with a wide variety of outside sources, including leading private sector forecasters and other government agencies.

The Council continued its efforts to improve the public's understanding of economic developments and of the Administration's economic policies through briefings with the economic and financial press, discussions with outside economists, presentations to outside organizations, and regular updates on major data releases on the CEA blog. The Chairman and Members also regularly met to exchange views on the macroeconomy with the Chairman and Members of the Board of Governors of the Federal Reserve System.

Microeconomic Policies

Throughout the year, the Council was an active participant in the analysis and consideration of a broad range of microeconomic policy issues. As with macroeconomic policy, the Council works closely with other agencies and White House senior staff on these issues. Among the specific microeconomic issues that received particular attention in 2010 were unemployment insurance, health insurance reform, financial regulatory reform, housing finance, education, access to post-secondary education, small business lending, foreclosure mitigation and prevention, the role of cost-benefit analysis in regulatory policy, and the economic effects of the Gulf Coast oil spill.

International Economic Policies

The Council was involved in a range of international trade and finance issues, with a particular emphasis on the consequences of the international financial crisis and the related global economic slowdown. The Council was an active participant in discussions at global and bilateral levels. Council Members and staff regularly met with economists, policy officials, and government officials of other countries to discuss issues relating to the global economy and participated in the Strategic and Economic Dialogue with China in May 2010.

The Council was particularly active in examining policies that could help the global economy recover from the crisis. It carefully tracked world economic developments and considered the potential medium-run impacts of the current crisis. The Council's role also included policy development and planning for the G-20 Summits in Toronto and Seoul.

The Council is a leading participant in the Organisation for Economic Co-operation and Development (OECD), an important forum for economic cooperation among high-income industrial economies. The Council coordinated and oversaw the OECD's review of the U.S. economy. Dr. Goolsbee is chairman of the OECD's Economic Policy Committee, and Council staff participates actively in working-party meetings on macroeconomic policy and coordination.

On the international trade front, the Council was an active participant in the trade policy process, occupying a seat on the Trade Policy Staff Committee and the Trade Policy Review Group. The Council provided analysis and opinions on a range of trade-related issues involving the enforcement of existing trade agreements, reviews of current U.S. trade policies, and consideration of future policies. The Council was also an active participant on the Trade Promotion Coordinating Committee, helping to examine the ways in which exports may support economic growth in the years to come. In the area of investment and security, the Council participated on the Committee on Foreign Investment in the United States (CFIUS), examining individual cases before the committee. The Council also provided empirical analysis of the pending free trade agreement with Korea.

THE STAFF OF THE COUNCIL OF ECONOMIC ADVISERS

The staff of the Council consists of the senior staff, senior economists, staff economists, research assistants, analysts, and the administrative and support staff. The staff at the end of 2010 were:

Senior Staff

Senior staff play key managerial and analytical roles at the Council. They direct operations, perform central Council functions, and represent the Council in meetings with other agencies and White House offices. The Executive Director oversees the research staff, as well as the development, drafting, and production of the *Economic Report of the President*.

Executive Director
Nan M. Gibson

Chief of Staff
Adam Hitchcock

Chief Economist
Jay C. Shambaugh

Director of Macroeconomic Forecasting   *Director of Statistical Office*
Steven N. Braun   Adrienne Pilot

Senior Economists

Senior economists are Ph.D. economists on leave from academic institutions, government agencies, or private research institutions. They participate actively in the policy process, represent the Council in inter-agency meetings, and have primary responsibility for the economic analysis and reports prepared by the Council, including this *Report*.

Chad P. Bown .... International Trade and Investment
Aaron Chatterji .... Entrepreneurship, Innovation
Benjamin Jones .... Macroeconomics, Innovation
Lisa B. Kahn .... Labor, Education
Arik Levinson .... Environment, Regulation
Helen G. Levy .... Health
Matthew Magura .... Industrial Organization, Regulation
Paul A. Smith .... Housing, Tax, Budget, Retirement

Staff Economists

Staff economists are typically graduate students on leave from their Ph.D. training in economics. They conduct advanced statistical analysis, contribute to reports, and generally support the research and analysis mission of the Council.

Sayeh S. Nikpay .... Health
James O'Brien .... Energy, Environment
Jamin D. Speer .... Labor, Education
Reid B. Stevens .... Macroeconomics
Owen Zidar .... Housing, Finance, Public Finance

Research Assistants

Research assistants are typically college graduates with significant coursework in economics. They conduct statistical analysis and data collection, and generally support the research and analysis mission of the Council. Both staff economists and research assistants contribute to this *Report* and play a crucial role in ensuring the accuracy of all Council documents.

Ravi P. Deedwania .... Health, Labor
Nicholas W. Hagerty .... Environment, Education, Infrastructure
Kia J. McLeod .... Macroeconomics, Housing, Innovation
Pedro Spivakovsky-Gonzalez ... International Economics
Julia Hanna Yoo .... Macroeconomics

Statistical Office

The Statistical Office gathers, administers, and produces statistical information for the Council. Duties include preparing the statistical appendix to the *Economic Report of the President* and the monthly publication *Economic Indicators*. The staff also creates background materials for economic analysis and verifies statistical content in Presidential memoranda. The Office serves as the Council's liaison to the statistical community.

Brian A. Amorosi .... Program Analyst
Dagmara A. Mocala .... Program Analyst

Administrative Office

The Administrative Office provides general support for the Council's activities. This includes financial management, ethics compliance, human resource management, travel, operations of facilities, security, information technology, and telecommunications management support.

Rosemary M. Rogers .... Administrative Officer
Doris T. Searles .... Information Management Specialist

Office of the Chairman

Meryl Holt .... Special Assistant to the Chairman and Director of Strategic Initiatives
Andres Bustamante .... Special Assistant to the Member and Research Economist
Eric Lesser .... Director of Strategic Planning

Staff Support

Lisa D. Branch .... Executive Assistant
Sharon K. Thomas .... Administrative Support Assistant

Editorial Staff

Brenda Szittya and Martha Gottron were the editors, and Andres Bustamante provided research and editorial assistance in the preparation, of the 2011 *Economic Report of the President*.

Interns

Student interns provide invaluable help with research projects, day-to-day operations, and fact-checking. Interns during the year were: Matthew L. Aks; Ian R. Appel; Michael D. Arena; Laura I. Blum; Kathleen A. Choi; Greg D. Dyer; Kenneth Friede; Benjamin J. Gettinger; David S. Gobaud; Max R. Harris; Michael P. Hupp; Peter L. Kerkhof; Michael C.

Levinson; Devin K. Mattson; Joshua Porter; Ceron J. Rhee; NaYoung Rim; and Cole L. Scandaglia.

DEPARTURES IN 2010

Andrew Metrick left his position as Chief Economist of the Council in July to return to Yale University, where he is the Deputy Dean for Faculty Development and Theodore Nierenberg Professor of Corporate Finance in the Yale School of Management. Michael B. Greenstone, Chief Economist of the Council until January, returned to the Massachusetts Institute of Technology, where he is the 3M Professor of Environmental Economics.

The senior economists who resigned (with the institutions to which they returned after leaving the Council in parentheses) were: Elizabeth O. Ananat (Duke University); Christopher D. Carroll (Johns Hopkins University); Mark G. Duggan (University of Maryland, College Park); W. Adam Looney (Brookings Institution); Jesse M. Rothstein (Department of Labor; University of California, Berkeley); and Ann Wolverton (Environmental Protection Agency).

The staff economists who departed were Sharon E. Boyd; Gabriel Chodorow-Reich; Laura J. Feiveson; Joshua K. Goldman; Sarena F. Goodman; Joshua K. Hausman; Zachary D. Liscow; William G. Woolston; and Jacqueline T. Yen. Those who served as research assistants at the Council and departed were Peter N. Ganong, Clare M. Hove, and Michael P. Shapiro. C. Bennett Blau and Gabrielle A. Elul served as staff assistants.

Archana A. Snyder left her position as Financial Officer to join the Federal Deposit Insurance Corporation as Financial Management Analyst. Julia B. Siegel was Special Assistant to the Chair and resigned to join the Office of Management and Budget as Confidential Assistant.

PUBLICATIONS OF THE COUNCIL

The Council's annual *Economic Report of the President* is an important vehicle for presenting the Administration's domestic and international economic policies. It is available for purchase through the Government Printing Office and is viewable on the Internet at www.gpo.gov/erp.

The Council prepared numerous reports in 2010, and the Chairman and Members gave numerous public speeches and testified to Congress. The reports, texts of speeches, and written statements accompanying testimony are available at the Council's website, www.whitehouse.gov/cea.

Finally, the Council publishes the monthly *Economic Indicators*, which is available on-line at www.gpo.gov/economicindicators.

STATISTICAL TABLES RELATING TO INCOME, EMPLOYMENT, AND PRODUCTION

C O N T E N T S

NATIONAL INCOME OR EXPENDITURE

Page

B–1. Gross domestic product, 1962–2010 188

B–2. Real gross domestic product, 1962–2010 190

B–3. Quantity and price indexes for gross domestic product, and percent changes, 1962–2010 192

B–4. Percent changes in real gross domestic product, 1962–2010 193

B–5. Contributions to percent change in real gross domestic product, 1962–2010 ... 194

B–6. Chain-type quantity indexes for gross domestic product, 1962–2010 196

B–7. Chain-type price indexes for gross domestic product, 1962–2010 198

B–8. Gross domestic product by major type of product, 1962–2010 200

B–9. Real gross domestic product by major type of product, 1962–2010 201

B–10. Gross value added by sector, 1962–2010 202

B–11. Real gross value added by sector, 1962–2010 203

B–12. Gross domestic product (GDP) by industry, value added, in current dollars and as a percentage of GDP, 1979–2009 204

B–13. Real gross domestic product by industry, value added, and percent changes, 1979–2009 206

B–14. Gross value added of nonfinancial corporate business, 1962–2010 208

B–15. Gross value added and price, costs, and profits of nonfinancial corporate business, 1962–2010 209

B–16. Personal consumption expenditures, 1962–2010 210

B–17. Real personal consumption expenditures, 1995–2010 211

B–18. Private fixed investment by type, 1962–2010 212

B–19. Real private fixed investment by type, 1995–2010 213

B–20. Government consumption expenditures and gross investment by type, 1962–2010 214

B–21. Real government consumption expenditures and gross investment by type, 1995–2010 215

B–22. Private inventories and domestic final sales by industry, 1962–2010 216

B–23. Real private inventories and domestic final sales by industry, 1962–2010 217

B–24. Foreign transactions in the national income and product accounts, 1962–2010 218

NATIONAL INCOME OR EXPENDITURE—*Continued*

B–25. Real exports and imports of goods and services, 1995–2010 219

B–26. Relation of gross domestic product, gross national product, net national product, and national income, 1962–2010 220

B–27. Relation of national income and personal income, 1962–2010 221

B–28. National income by type of income, 1962–2010 222

B–29. Sources of personal income, 1962–2010 224

B–30. Disposition of personal income, 1962–2010 226

B–31. Total and per capita disposable personal income and personal consumption expenditures, and per capita gross domestic product, in current and real dollars, 1962–2010 227

B–32. Gross saving and investment, 1962–2010 228

B–33. Median money income (in 2009 dollars) and poverty status of families and people, by race, selected years, 1998–2009 230

POPULATION, EMPLOYMENT, WAGES, AND PRODUCTIVITY

B–34. Population by age group, 1933–2010 231

B–35. Civilian population and labor force, 1929–2010 232

B–36. Civilian employment and unemployment by sex and age, 1964–2010 234

B–37. Civilian employment by demographic characteristic, 1964–2010 235

B–38. Unemployment by demographic characteristic, 1964–2010 236

B–39. Civilian labor force participation rate and employment/population ratio, 1964–2010 237

B–40. Civilian labor force participation rate by demographic characteristic, 1970–2010 238

B–41. Civilian employment/population ratio by demographic characteristic, 1970–2010 239

B–42. Civilian unemployment rate, 1964–2010 240

B–43. Civilian unemployment rate by demographic characteristic, 1970–2010 241

B–44. Unemployment by duration and reason, 1964–2010 242

B–45. Unemployment insurance programs, selected data, 1980–2010 243

B–46. Employees on nonagricultural payrolls, by major industry, 1965–2010 244

B–47. Hours and earnings in private nonagricultural industries, 1964–2010 246

B–48. Employment cost index, private industry, 1997–2010 247

B–49. Productivity and related data, business and nonfarm business sectors, 1960–2010 248

B–50. Changes in productivity and related data, business and nonfarm business sectors, 1960–2010 249

PRODUCTION AND BUSINESS ACTIVITY

B–51. Industrial production indexes, major industry divisions, 1962–2010 250

B–52. Industrial production indexes, market groupings, 1962–2010 251

B–53. Industrial production indexes, selected manufacturing industries, 1967–2010 252

B–54. Capacity utilization rates, 1962–2010 253

B–55. New construction activity, 1965–2010 254

B–56. New private housing units started, authorized, and completed and houses sold, 1964–2010 255

B–57. Manufacturing and trade sales and inventories, 1969–2010 256

B–58. Manufacturers' shipments and inventories, 1969–2010 257

B–59. Manufacturers' new and unfilled orders, 1969–2010 258

PRICES

B–60. Consumer price indexes for major expenditure classes, 1967–2010 259

B–61. Consumer price indexes for selected expenditure classes, 1967–2010 260

B–62. Consumer price indexes for commodities, services, and special groups, 1967–2010 262

B–63. Changes in special consumer price indexes, 1967–2010 263

B–64. Changes in consumer price indexes for commodities and services, 1939–2010 264

B–65. Producer price indexes by stage of processing, 1965–2010 265

B–66. Producer price indexes by stage of processing, special groups, 1974–2010 267

B–67. Producer price indexes for major commodity groups, 1965–2010 268

B–68. Changes in producer price indexes for finished goods, 1970–2010 270

MONEY STOCK, CREDIT, AND FINANCE

B–69. Money stock and debt measures, 1970–2010 271

B–70. Components of money stock measures, 1970–2010 272

B–71. Aggregate reserves of depository institutions and the monetary base, 1980–2010 274

B–72. Bank credit at all commercial banks, 1972–2010 275

B–73. Bond yields and interest rates, 1933–2010 276

B–74. Credit market borrowing, 2002–2010 278

B–75. Mortgage debt outstanding by type of property and of financing, 1952–2010 280

B–76. Mortgage debt outstanding by holder, 1952–2010 281

B–77. Consumer credit outstanding, 1959–2010 282

GOVERNMENT FINANCE

B–78. Federal receipts, outlays, surplus or deficit, and debt, fiscal years, 1944–2012 .. 283

B–79. Federal receipts, outlays, surplus or deficit, and debt, as percent of gross domestic product, fiscal years 1938–2012 284

B–80. Federal receipts and outlays, by major category, and surplus or deficit, fiscal years 1944–2012 285

B–81. Federal receipts, outlays, surplus or deficit, and debt, fiscal years 2007–2012 ... 286

B–82. Federal and State and local government current receipts and expenditures, national income and product accounts (NIPA), 1962–2010 287

B–83. Federal and State and local government current receipts and expenditures, national income and product accounts (NIPA), by major type, 1962–2010 288

B–84. Federal Government current receipts and expenditures, national income and product accounts (NIPA), 1962–2010 289

B–85. State and local government current receipts and expenditures, national income and product accounts (NIPA), 1962–2010 290

B–86. State and local government revenues and expenditures, selected fiscal years, 1944–2008 291

B–87. U.S. Treasury securities outstanding by kind of obligation, 1972–2010 292

B–88. Maturity distribution and average length of marketable interest-bearing public debt securities held by private investors, 1972–2010 293

B–89. Estimated ownership of U.S. Treasury securities, 1997–2010 294

CORPORATE PROFITS AND FINANCE

B–90. Corporate profits with inventory valuation and capital consumption adjustments, 1962–2010 295

B–91. Corporate profits by industry, 1962–2010 296

B–92. Corporate profits of manufacturing industries, 1962–2010 297

B–93. Sales, profits, and stockholders' equity, all manufacturing corporations, 1968–2010 298

B–94. Relation of profits after taxes to stockholders' equity and to sales, all manufacturing corporations, 1960–2010 299

B–95. Historical stock prices and yields, 1949–2003 300

B–96. Common stock prices and yields, 2000–2010 301

AGRICULTURE

B–97. Farm income, 1950–2010 302

B–98. Farm business balance sheet, 1952–2010 303

B–99. Farm output and productivity indexes, 1950–2008 304

B–100. Farm input use, selected inputs, 1950–2010 305

AGRICULTURE—*Continued*

B–101. Agricultural price indexes and farm real estate value, 1975–2010 306

B–102. U.S. exports and imports of agricultural commodities, 1950–2010 307

INTERNATIONAL STATISTICS

B–103. U.S. international transactions, 1952–2010 308

B–104. U.S. international trade in goods by principal end-use category, 1965–2010 310

B–105. U.S. international trade in goods by area, 2002–2010 311

B–106. U.S. international trade in goods on balance of payments (BOP) and Census basis, and trade in services on BOP basis, 1981–2010 312

B–107. International investment position of the United States at year-end, 2003–2009 313

B–108. Industrial production and consumer prices, major industrial countries, 1984–2010 314

B–109. Civilian unemployment rate, and hourly compensation, major industrial countries, 1984–2010 315

B–110. Foreign exchange rates, 1990–2010 316

B–111. International reserves, selected years, 1982–2010 317

B–112. Growth rates in real gross domestic product, 1992–2011 318

General Notes

Detail in these tables may not add to totals because of rounding.

Because of the formula used for calculating real gross domestic product (GDP), the chained (2005) dollar estimates for the detailed components do not add to the chained-dollar value of GDP or to any intermediate aggregate. The Department of Commerce (Bureau of Economic Analysis) no longer publishes chained-dollar estimates prior to 1995, except for selected series.

Unless otherwise noted, all dollar figures are in current dollars.

Symbols used:
^{p} Preliminary.
... Not available (also, not applicable).

Data in these tables reflect revisions made by the source agencies through January 28, 2011. In particular, tables containing national income and product accounts (NIPA) estimates reflect revisions released by the Department of Commerce in July 2010.

Table B–1. Gross domestic product, 1962–2010

[Billions of dollars, except as noted; quarterly data at seasonally adjusted annual rates]

Year or quarter	Gross domestic product	Personal consumption expenditures			Gross private domestic investment						
		Total	Goods	Services	Total	Fixed investment					Change in private inventories
						Total	Nonresidential			Residential	
							Total	Structures	Equipment and software		
1962	585.7	363.3	189.0	174.4	88.1	82.0	53.1	20.8	32.3	29.0	6.1
1963	617.8	382.7	198.2	184.6	93.8	88.1	56.0	21.2	34.8	32.1	5.6
1964	663.6	411.5	212.3	199.2	102.1	97.2	63.0	23.7	39.2	34.3	4.8
1965	719.1	443.8	229.7	214.1	118.2	109.0	74.8	28.3	46.5	34.2	9.2
1966	787.7	480.9	249.6	231.3	131.3	117.7	85.4	31.3	54.0	32.3	13.6
1967	832.4	507.8	259.0	248.8	128.6	118.7	86.4	31.5	54.9	32.4	9.9
1968	909.8	558.0	284.6	273.4	141.2	132.1	93.4	33.6	59.9	38.7	9.1
1969	984.4	605.1	304.7	300.4	156.4	147.3	104.7	37.7	67.0	42.6	9.2
1970	1,038.3	648.3	318.8	329.5	152.4	150.4	109.0	40.3	68.7	41.4	2.0
1971	1,126.8	701.6	342.1	359.5	178.2	169.9	114.1	42.7	71.5	55.8	8.3
1972	1,237.9	770.2	373.8	396.4	207.6	198.5	128.8	47.2	81.7	69.7	9.1
1973	1,382.3	852.0	416.6	435.4	244.5	228.6	153.3	55.0	98.3	75.3	15.9
1974	1,499.5	932.9	451.5	481.4	249.4	235.4	169.5	61.2	108.2	66.0	14.0
1975	1,637.7	1,033.8	491.3	542.5	230.2	236.5	173.7	61.4	112.4	62.7	–6.3
1976	1,824.6	1,151.3	546.3	604.9	292.0	274.8	192.4	65.9	126.4	82.5	17.1
1977	2,030.1	1,277.8	600.4	677.4	361.3	339.0	228.7	74.6	154.1	110.3	22.3
1978	2,293.8	1,427.6	663.6	764.1	438.0	412.2	280.6	93.6	187.0	131.6	25.8
1979	2,562.2	1,591.2	737.9	853.2	492.9	474.9	333.9	117.7	216.2	141.0	18.0
1980	2,788.1	1,755.8	799.8	956.0	479.3	485.6	362.4	136.2	226.2	123.2	–6.3
1981	3,126.8	1,939.5	869.4	1,070.1	572.4	542.6	420.0	167.3	252.7	122.6	29.8
1982	3,253.2	2,075.5	899.3	1,176.2	517.2	532.1	426.5	177.6	248.9	105.7	–14.9
1983	3,534.6	2,288.6	973.8	1,314.8	564.3	570.1	417.2	154.3	262.9	152.9	–5.8
1984	3,930.9	2,501.1	1,063.7	1,437.4	735.6	670.2	489.6	177.4	312.2	180.6	65.4
1985	4,217.5	2,717.6	1,137.6	1,580.0	736.2	714.4	526.2	194.5	331.7	188.2	21.8
1986	4,460.1	2,896.7	1,195.6	1,701.1	746.5	739.9	519.8	176.5	343.3	220.1	6.6
1987	4,736.4	3,097.0	1,256.3	1,840.7	785.0	757.8	524.1	174.2	349.9	233.7	27.1
1988	5,100.4	3,350.1	1,337.3	2,012.7	821.6	803.1	563.8	182.8	381.0	239.3	18.5
1989	5,482.1	3,594.5	1,423.8	2,170.7	874.9	847.3	607.7	193.7	414.0	239.5	27.7
1990	5,800.5	3,835.5	1,491.3	2,344.2	861.0	846.4	622.4	202.9	419.5	224.0	14.5
1991	5,992.1	3,980.1	1,497.4	2,482.6	802.9	803.3	598.2	183.6	414.6	205.1	–.4
1992	6,342.3	4,236.9	1,563.5	2,673.6	864.8	848.5	612.1	172.6	439.6	236.3	16.3
1993	6,667.4	4,483.6	1,642.3	2,841.2	953.3	932.5	666.6	177.2	489.4	266.0	20.8
1994	7,085.2	4,750.8	1,746.6	3,004.3	1,097.3	1,033.5	731.4	186.8	544.6	302.1	63.8
1995	7,414.7	4,987.3	1,815.5	3,171.7	1,144.0	1,112.9	810.0	207.3	602.8	302.9	31.2
1996	7,838.5	5,273.6	1,917.7	3,355.9	1,240.2	1,209.4	875.4	224.6	650.8	334.1	30.8
1997	8,332.4	5,570.6	2,006.8	3,563.9	1,388.7	1,317.7	968.6	250.3	718.3	349.1	71.0
1998	8,793.5	5,918.5	2,110.0	3,808.5	1,510.8	1,447.1	1,061.1	275.1	786.0	385.9	63.7
1999	9,353.5	6,342.8	2,290.0	4,052.8	1,641.5	1,580.7	1,154.9	283.9	871.0	425.8	60.8
2000	9,951.5	6,830.4	2,459.1	4,371.2	1,772.2	1,717.7	1,268.7	318.1	950.5	449.0	54.5
2001	10,286.2	7,148.8	2,534.0	4,614.8	1,661.9	1,700.2	1,227.8	329.7	898.1	472.4	–38.3
2002	10,642.3	7,439.2	2,610.0	4,829.2	1,647.0	1,634.9	1,125.4	282.8	842.7	509.5	12.0
2003	11,142.1	7,804.0	2,727.4	5,076.6	1,729.7	1,713.3	1,135.7	281.9	853.8	577.6	16.4
2004	11,867.8	8,285.1	2,892.3	5,392.8	1,968.6	1,903.6	1,223.0	306.7	916.4	680.6	64.9
2005	12,638.4	8,819.0	3,073.9	5,745.1	2,172.2	2,122.3	1,347.3	351.8	995.6	775.0	50.0
2006	13,398.9	9,322.7	3,221.7	6,100.9	2,327.2	2,267.2	1,505.3	433.7	1,071.7	761.9	60.0
2007	14,061.8	9,806.3	3,357.7	6,448.6	2,295.2	2,266.1	1,637.5	524.9	1,112.6	628.6	29.1
2008	14,369.1	10,104.5	3,379.5	6,725.0	2,096.7	2,137.8	1,665.3	582.4	1,082.9	472.5	–41.1
2009	14,119.0	10,001.3	3,230.7	6,770.6	1,589.2	1,716.4	1,364.4	451.6	912.8	352.1	–127.2
2010 p	14,660.2	10,351.9	3,427.6	6,924.3	1,821.4	1,752.8	1,412.5	381.8	1,030.7	340.4	68.5
2007: I	13,789.5	9,632.8	3,293.8	6,339.0	2,277.4	2,260.4	1,579.6	479.5	1,100.1	680.7	17.0
II	14,008.2	9,753.2	3,343.4	6,409.8	2,329.6	2,282.1	1,624.9	512.3	1,112.6	657.2	47.5
III	14,158.2	9,850.8	3,369.8	6,481.1	2,313.4	2,274.0	1,660.7	545.5	1,115.1	613.3	39.4
IV	14,291.3	9,988.4	3,423.8	6,564.6	2,260.4	2,247.9	1,684.6	562.2	1,122.4	563.3	12.6
2008: I	14,328.4	10,065.7	3,415.4	6,650.3	2,198.8	2,212.5	1,695.4	567.1	1,128.3	517.1	–13.7
II	14,471.8	10,183.0	3,458.7	6,724.3	2,170.9	2,194.1	1,697.5	584.4	1,113.2	496.6	–23.3
III	14,484.9	10,202.0	3,450.0	6,751.9	2,111.3	2,140.8	1,678.2	590.4	1,087.9	462.5	–29.4
IV	14,191.2	9,967.2	3,194.0	6,773.3	1,905.8	2,003.8	1,590.1	587.9	1,002.2	413.7	–98.0
2009: I	14,049.7	9,913.0	3,158.4	6,754.6	1,640.4	1,782.3	1,415.2	507.5	907.8	367.0	–141.9
II	14,034.5	9,920.1	3,175.4	6,744.7	1,530.2	1,709.8	1,367.5	464.0	903.5	342.2	–179.5
III	14,114.7	10,040.7	3,276.1	6,764.6	1,548.5	1,691.8	1,343.8	436.6	907.2	348.0	–143.3
IV	14,277.3	10,131.5	3,312.9	6,818.6	1,637.7	1,681.9	1,330.9	398.2	932.7	351.0	–44.2
2010: I	14,446.4	10,230.8	3,380.0	6,850.9	1,739.7	1,689.8	1,349.6	380.1	969.5	340.2	50.0
II	14,578.7	10,285.4	3,377.5	6,907.9	1,841.8	1,761.4	1,404.2	381.5	1,022.7	357.2	80.4
III	14,745.1	10,366.3	3,419.6	6,946.7	1,907.2	1,768.6	1,438.8	380.9	1,057.9	329.8	138.6
IV p	14,870.4	10,525.2	3,533.3	6,991.8	1,796.7	1,791.5	1,457.2	384.7	1,072.5	334.3	5.2

See next page for continuation of table.

TABLE B–1. Gross domestic product, 1962–2010—*Continued*

[Billions of dollars, except as noted; quarterly data at seasonally adjusted annual rates]

Year or quarter	Net exports of goods and services			Government consumption expenditures and gross investment					Final sales of domestic product	Gross domestic purchases[1]	Addendum: Gross national product[2]	Percent change from preceding period	
	Net exports	Exports	Imports	Total	Federal			State and local				Gross domestic product	Gross domestic purchases[1]
					Total	National defense	Non-defense						
1962	4.1	29.1	25.0	130.1	75.2	61.1	14.1	54.9	579.6	581.6	589.7	7.5	7.7
1963	4.9	31.1	26.1	136.4	76.9	61.0	15.9	59.5	612.1	612.8	622.2	5.5	5.4
1964	6.9	35.0	28.1	143.2	78.4	60.2	18.2	64.8	658.8	656.7	668.6	7.4	7.2
1965	5.6	37.1	31.5	151.4	80.4	60.6	19.8	71.0	709.9	713.5	724.4	8.4	8.6
1966	3.9	40.9	37.1	171.6	92.4	71.7	20.8	79.2	774.1	783.8	792.8	9.5	9.9
1967	3.6	43.5	39.9	192.5	104.6	83.4	21.2	87.9	822.6	828.9	837.8	5.7	5.7
1968	1.4	47.9	46.6	209.3	111.3	89.2	22.0	98.0	900.8	908.5	915.9	9.3	9.6
1969	1.4	51.9	50.5	221.4	113.3	89.5	23.8	108.2	975.3	983.0	990.5	8.2	8.2
1970	4.0	59.7	55.8	233.7	113.4	87.6	25.8	120.3	1,036.3	1,034.4	1,044.7	5.5	5.2
1971	.6	63.0	62.3	246.4	113.6	84.6	29.1	132.8	1,118.6	1,126.2	1,134.4	8.5	8.9
1972	−3.4	70.8	74.2	263.4	119.6	86.9	32.7	143.8	1,228.8	1,241.3	1,246.4	9.9	10.2
1973	4.1	95.3	91.2	281.7	122.5	88.1	34.3	159.2	1,366.4	1,378.2	1,394.9	11.7	11.0
1974	−.8	126.7	127.5	317.9	134.5	95.6	39.0	183.4	1,485.5	1,500.3	1,515.0	8.5	8.9
1975	16.0	138.7	122.7	357.7	149.0	103.9	45.1	208.7	1,644.0	1,621.7	1,650.7	9.2	8.1
1976	−1.6	149.5	151.1	383.0	159.7	111.1	48.6	223.3	1,807.5	1,826.2	1,841.4	11.4	12.6
1977	−23.1	159.4	182.4	414.1	175.4	120.9	54.5	238.7	2,007.8	2,053.2	2,050.4	11.3	12.4
1978	−25.4	186.9	212.3	453.6	190.9	130.5	60.4	262.7	2,268.0	2,319.1	2,315.3	13.0	13.0
1979	−27.5	230.1	252.7	500.7	210.6	145.2	65.4	290.2	2,544.2	2,584.8	2,594.2	11.7	11.5
1980	−13.1	280.8	293.8	566.1	243.7	168.0	75.8	322.4	2,794.5	2,801.2	2,822.3	8.8	8.4
1981	−12.5	305.2	317.8	627.5	280.2	196.2	83.9	347.3	3,097.0	3,139.4	3,159.8	12.1	12.1
1982	−20.0	283.2	303.2	680.4	310.8	225.9	84.9	369.7	3,268.1	3,273.2	3,289.7	4.0	4.3
1983	−51.7	277.0	328.6	733.4	342.9	250.6	92.3	390.5	3,540.4	3,586.3	3,571.7	8.7	9.6
1984	−102.7	302.4	405.1	796.9	374.3	281.5	92.7	422.6	3,865.5	4,033.6	3,967.2	11.2	12.5
1985	−115.2	302.0	417.2	878.9	412.8	311.2	101.6	466.1	4,195.6	4,332.7	4,244.0	7.3	7.4
1986	−132.5	320.3	452.9	949.3	438.4	330.8	107.6	510.9	4,453.5	4,592.6	4,477.7	5.8	6.0
1987	−145.0	363.8	508.7	999.4	459.5	350.0	109.6	539.9	4,709.2	4,881.3	4,754.0	6.2	6.3
1988	−110.1	443.9	554.0	1,038.9	461.6	354.7	106.8	577.3	5,081.9	5,210.5	5,123.8	7.7	6.7
1989	−87.9	503.1	591.0	1,100.6	481.4	362.1	119.3	619.2	5,454.5	5,570.0	5,508.1	7.5	6.9
1990	−77.6	552.1	629.7	1,181.7	507.5	373.9	133.6	674.2	5,786.0	5,878.1	5,835.0	5.8	5.5
1991	−27.0	596.6	623.5	1,236.1	526.6	383.1	143.4	709.5	5,992.5	6,019.1	6,022.0	3.3	2.4
1992	−32.8	635.0	667.8	1,273.5	532.9	376.8	156.1	740.6	6,326.0	6,375.1	6,371.4	5.8	5.9
1993	−64.4	655.6	720.0	1,294.8	525.0	363.0	162.0	769.8	6,646.5	6,731.7	6,698.5	5.1	5.6
1994	−92.7	720.7	813.4	1,329.8	518.6	353.8	164.8	811.2	7,021.4	7,177.9	7,109.2	6.3	6.6
1995	−90.7	811.9	902.6	1,374.0	518.8	348.8	170.0	855.3	7,383.5	7,505.3	7,444.3	4.7	4.6
1996	−96.3	867.7	964.0	1,421.0	527.0	354.8	172.2	894.0	7,807.7	7,934.8	7,870.1	5.7	5.7
1997	−101.4	954.4	1,055.8	1,474.4	531.0	349.8	181.1	943.5	8,261.4	8,433.7	8,355.8	6.3	6.3
1998	−161.8	953.9	1,115.7	1,526.1	531.0	346.1	184.9	995.0	8,729.8	8,955.3	8,810.8	5.5	6.2
1999	−262.1	989.3	1,251.4	1,631.3	554.9	361.1	193.8	1,076.3	9,292.7	9,615.6	9,381.3	6.4	7.4
2000	−382.1	1,093.2	1,475.3	1,731.0	576.1	371.0	205.0	1,154.9	9,896.9	10,333.5	9,989.2	6.4	7.5
2001	−371.0	1,027.7	1,398.7	1,846.4	611.7	393.0	218.7	1,234.7	10,324.5	10,657.2	10,338.1	3.4	3.1
2002	−427.2	1,003.0	1,430.2	1,983.5	680.6	437.7	242.9	1,302.7	10,630.3	11,069.5	10,691.4	3.5	3.9
2003	−504.1	1,041.0	1,545.1	2,112.6	756.5	497.9	258.5	1,356.1	11,125.8	11,646.3	11,210.8	4.7	5.2
2004	−618.7	1,180.2	1,798.9	2,232.8	824.6	550.8	273.9	1,408.2	11,802.8	12,486.4	11,959.0	6.5	7.2
2005	−722.7	1,305.1	2,027.8	2,369.9	876.3	589.0	287.3	1,493.6	12,588.4	13,361.1	12,735.5	6.5	7.0
2006	−769.3	1,471.0	2,240.3	2,518.4	931.7	624.9	306.8	1,586.7	13,339.0	14,168.2	13,471.3	6.0	6.0
2007	−714.0	1,661.7	2,375.7	2,674.2	976.3	662.3	314.0	1,697.9	14,032.7	14,775.8	14,185.1	4.9	4.3
2008	−710.4	1,843.4	2,553.8	2,878.3	1,079.9	737.3	342.5	1,798.5	14,410.2	15,079.5	14,543.6	2.2	2.1
2009	−386.4	1,578.4	1,964.7	2,914.9	1,139.6	771.6	368.0	1,775.3	14,246.3	14,505.4	14,265.3	−1.7	−3.8
2010 *p*	−515.5	1,837.1	2,352.6	3,002.3	1,214.4	817.8	396.6	1,788.0	14,591.6	15,175.6	....	3.8	4.6
2007: I	−725.1	1,575.5	2,300.6	2,604.4	944.0	637.6	306.4	1,660.3	13,772.5	14,514.6	13,859.8	5.3	5.4
II	−730.7	1,619.1	2,349.8	2,656.0	968.7	657.0	311.7	1,687.3	13,960.6	14,738.8	14,087.6	6.5	6.3
III	−704.4	1,690.3	2,394.7	2,698.4	992.1	674.7	317.4	1,706.4	14,118.8	14,862.6	14,302.9	4.4	3.4
IV	−695.7	1,761.8	2,457.5	2,738.2	1,000.6	679.9	320.7	1,737.6	14,278.8	14,987.0	14,489.9	3.8	3.4
2008: I	−738.5	1,819.9	2,558.4	2,802.3	1,033.4	702.1	331.3	1,768.9	14,342.1	15,066.8	14,520.7	1.0	2.1
II	−751.9	1,925.3	2,677.2	2,869.8	1,065.2	724.9	340.3	1,804.6	14,495.1	15,223.7	14,647.3	4.1	4.2
III	−763.1	1,927.3	2,690.4	2,934.7	1,105.5	762.1	343.4	1,829.2	14,514.3	15,248.0	14,689.2	.4	.6
IV	−588.4	1,700.9	2,289.3	2,906.5	1,115.4	760.2	355.1	1,791.2	14,289.2	14,779.5	14,317.2	−7.9	−11.7
2009: I	−375.7	1,521.2	1,896.9	2,872.0	1,103.2	743.9	359.4	1,768.8	14,191.6	14,425.4	14,172.2	−3.9	−9.2
II	−335.2	1,520.2	1,855.3	2,919.3	1,139.8	769.9	369.8	1,779.5	14,214.0	14,369.6	14,164.2	−.4	−1.5
III	−408.3	1,582.1	1,990.5	2,933.8	1,155.4	787.3	368.1	1,778.4	14,258.0	14,523.0	14,281.9	2.3	4.3
IV	−426.4	1,689.9	2,116.3	2,934.5	1,159.9	785.4	374.5	1,774.7	14,321.5	14,703.7	14,442.8	4.7	5.1
2010: I	−479.9	1,757.8	2,237.6	2,955.7	1,178.1	796.3	381.8	1,777.6	14,396.4	14,926.3	14,637.6	4.8	6.2
II	−539.3	1,817.9	2,357.1	2,990.8	1,206.7	813.0	393.7	1,784.1	14,498.3	15,118.0	14,774.0	3.7	5.2
III	−550.5	1,848.9	2,399.4	3,022.2	1,233.9	830.8	403.1	1,788.2	14,606.5	15,295.6	14,933.6	4.6	4.8
IV *p*	−492.2	1,923.9	2,416.0	3,040.7	1,238.7	831.0	407.7	1,802.0	14,865.2	15,362.6	....	3.4	1.8

[1] Gross domestic product (GDP) less exports of goods and services plus imports of goods and services.
[2] GDP plus net income receipts from rest of the world.

Source: Department of Commerce (Bureau of Economic Analysis).

TABLE B–2. Real gross domestic product, 1962–2010

[Billions of chained (2005) dollars, except as noted; quarterly data at seasonally adjusted annual rates]

Year or quarter	Gross domestic product	Personal consumption expenditures			Gross private domestic investment							
		Total	Goods	Services	Total	Fixed investment						Change in private inventories
						Total	Nonresidential				Residential	
							Total	Structures	Equipment and software			
1962	3,072.4	1,911.2			332.0							
1963	3,206.7	1,989.9			354.3							
1964	3,392.3	2,108.4			383.5							
1965	3,610.1	2,241.8			437.3							
1966	3,845.3	2,369.0			475.8							
1967	3,942.5	2,440.0			454.1							
1968	4,133.4	2,580.7			480.5							
1969	4,261.8	2,677.4			508.5							
1970	4,269.9	2,740.2			475.1							
1971	4,413.3	2,844.6			529.3							
1972	4,647.7	3,019.5			591.9							
1973	4,917.0	3,169.1			661.3							
1974	4,889.9	3,142.8			612.6							
1975	4,879.5	3,214.1			504.1							
1976	5,141.3	3,393.1			605.9							
1977	5,377.7	3,535.9			697.4							
1978	5,677.6	3,691.8			781.5							
1979	5,855.0	3,779.5			806.4							
1980	5,839.0	3,766.2			717.9							
1981	5,987.2	3,823.3			782.4							
1982	5,870.9	3,876.7			672.8							
1983	6,136.2	4,098.3			735.5							
1984	6,577.1	4,315.6			952.1							
1985	6,849.3	4,540.4			943.3							
1986	7,086.5	4,724.5			936.9							
1987	7,313.3	4,870.3			965.7							
1988	7,613.9	5,066.6			988.5							
1989	7,885.9	5,209.9			1,028.1							
1990	8,033.9	5,316.2			993.5							
1991	8,015.1	5,324.2			912.7							
1992	8,287.1	5,505.7			986.7							
1993	8,523.4	5,701.2			1,074.8							
1994	8,870.7	5,918.9			1,220.9							
1995	9,093.7	6,079.0	1,898.6	4,208.2	1,258.9	1,235.7	792.2	342.0	493.0	456.1		32.1
1996	9,433.9	6,291.2	1,983.6	4,331.4	1,370.3	1,346.5	866.2	361.4	545.4	492.5		31.2
1997	9,854.3	6,523.4	2,078.2	4,465.0	1,540.8	1,470.8	970.8	387.9	620.4	501.8		77.4
1998	10,283.5	6,865.5	2,218.6	4,661.8	1,695.1	1,630.4	1,087.4	407.7	710.4	540.4		71.6
1999	10,779.8	7,240.9	2,395.3	4,852.8	1,844.3	1,782.1	1,200.9	408.2	810.9	574.2		68.5
2000	11,226.0	7,608.1	2,521.7	5,093.3	1,970.3	1,913.8	1,318.5	440.0	895.8	580.0		60.2
2001	11,347.2	7,813.9	2,600.9	5,218.7	1,831.9	1,877.6	1,281.8	433.3	866.9	583.3		–41.8
2002	11,553.0	8,021.9	2,706.6	5,318.1	1,807.0	1,798.1	1,180.2	356.6	830.3	613.8		12.8
2003	11,840.7	8,247.6	2,829.9	5,418.4	1,871.6	1,856.2	1,191.0	343.0	851.4	664.3		17.3
2004	12,263.8	8,532.7	2,955.3	5,577.6	2,058.2	1,992.5	1,263.0	346.7	917.3	729.5		66.3
2005	12,638.4	8,819.0	3,073.9	5,745.1	2,172.2	2,122.3	1,347.3	351.8	995.6	775.0		50.0
2006	12,976.2	9,073.5	3,173.9	5,899.7	2,230.4	2,171.3	1,453.9	384.0	1,069.6	718.2		59.4
2007	13,228.9	9,289.5	3,261.6	6,028.3	2,161.6	2,132.7	1,552.0	438.2	1,109.0	584.2		27.7
2008	13,228.8	9,265.0	3,180.3	6,082.3	1,957.3	1,997.0	1,556.6	464.2	1,082.0	444.2		–37.6
2009	12,880.6	9,153.9	3,117.4	6,032.7	1,515.7	1,630.7	1,290.8	369.6	916.3	342.7		–113.1
2010 P	13,248.7	9,315.7	3,251.8	6,065.4	1,769.3	1,692.1	1,362.2	317.7	1,054.8	332.5		60.4
2007: I	13,089.3	9,235.2	3,241.1	5,994.4	2,146.1	2,127.7	1,499.0	404.8	1,093.0	631.3		17.3
II	13,194.1	9,270.5	3,252.4	6,018.3	2,195.1	2,147.2	1,539.1	430.6	1,104.6	611.4		44.9
III	13,268.5	9,310.0	3,271.9	6,038.7	2,178.9	2,140.8	1,574.1	454.6	1,112.6	570.6		36.1
IV	13,363.5	9,342.3	3,281.0	6,061.7	2,126.1	2,114.9	1,595.9	462.9	1,125.7	523.3		12.6
2008: I	13,339.2	9,324.1	3,232.6	6,090.6	2,074.3	2,081.6	1,603.7	462.7	1,134.0	482.2		–8.2
II	13,359.0	9,326.2	3,235.2	6,090.2	2,033.8	2,057.3	1,597.0	471.2	1,116.5	464.4		–20.6
III	13,223.5	9,243.5	3,171.4	6,070.0	1,967.2	1,993.3	1,561.5	466.9	1,084.1	435.6		–27.4
IV	12,993.7	9,166.3	3,082.3	6,078.5	1,753.8	1,855.6	1,464.2	456.1	993.3	394.7		–94.3
2009: I	12,832.6	9,154.1	3,095.7	6,053.6	1,529.5	1,663.4	1,313.7	399.7	903.4	352.7		–125.8
II	12,810.0	9,117.0	3,084.0	6,027.7	1,453.2	1,619.6	1,288.3	377.8	903.8	333.9		–161.8
III	12,860.8	9,161.6	3,138.2	6,020.7	1,494.5	1,622.4	1,282.9	365.5	913.1	342.4		–128.2
IV	13,019.0	9,182.9	3,151.8	6,028.7	1,585.7	1,617.1	1,278.3	335.3	944.7	341.7		–36.7
2010: I	13,138.8	9,225.4	3,195.4	6,029.6	1,690.2	1,630.5	1,302.6	319.3	989.7	330.7		44.1
II	13,194.9	9,275.7	3,222.6	6,053.4	1,791.5	1,702.5	1,355.3	318.9	1,046.0	350.1		68.8
III	13,278.5	9,330.6	3,255.2	6,076.9	1,855.1	1,708.8	1,388.0	316.0	1,084.2	323.3		121.4
IV P	13,382.6	9,431.2	3,334.1	6,101.9	1,740.3	1,726.6	1,403.1	316.7	1,099.5	326.0		7.2

See next page for continuation of table.

[Billions of chained (2005) dollars, except as noted; quarterly data at seasonally adjusted annual rates]

Year or quarter	Net exports of goods and services			Government consumption expenditures and gross investment					Final sales of domestic product	Gross domestic purchases [1]	Addendum: Gross national product [2]	Percent change from preceding period	
	Net exports	Exports	Imports	Total	Federal			State and local				Gross domestic product	Gross domestic purchases [1]
					Total	National defense	Non-defense						
1962	....	104.0	126.7	971.1	....	....	....	....	3,064.9	3,119.0	3,096.8	6.1	6.3
1963	....	111.5	130.1	996.1	....	....	....	....	3,202.6	3,248.8	3,232.8	4.4	4.2
1964	....	124.6	137.0	1,018.0	....	....	....	....	3,393.7	3,426.3	3,420.4	5.8	5.5
1965	....	128.1	151.6	1,048.7	....	....	....	....	3,590.7	3,659.2	3,639.5	6.4	6.8
1966	....	137.0	174.1	1,141.1	....	....	....	....	3,806.6	3,910.2	3,873.1	6.5	6.9
1967	....	140.1	186.8	1,228.7	....	....	....	....	3,923.3	4,018.2	3,971.1	2.5	2.8
1968	....	151.1	214.7	1,267.2	....	....	....	....	4,119.4	4,225.6	4,164.1	4.8	5.2
1969	....	158.4	226.9	1,264.3	....	....	....	....	4,248.6	4,358.6	4,291.6	3.1	3.1
1970	....	175.5	236.6	1,233.7	....	....	....	....	4,287.9	4,352.0	4,299.4	.2	-.2
1971	....	178.4	249.2	1,206.9	....	....	....	....	4,407.4	4,506.9	4,446.0	3.4	3.6
1972	....	191.8	277.2	1,198.1	....	....	....	....	4,640.6	4,755.8	4,682.9	5.3	5.5
1973	....	228.0	290.1	1,193.9	....	....	....	....	4,888.2	4,991.2	4,964.5	5.8	5.0
1974	....	246.0	283.5	1,224.0	....	....	....	....	4,874.1	4,926.2	4,944.0	-.6	-1.3
1975	....	244.5	252.0	1,251.6	....	....	....	....	4,926.3	4,872.0	4,921.4	-.2	-1.1
1976	....	255.1	301.3	1,257.2	....	....	....	....	5,120.2	5,189.2	5,191.2	5.4	6.5
1977	....	261.3	334.2	1,271.0	....	....	....	....	5,344.9	5,464.4	5,433.7	4.6	5.3
1978	....	288.8	363.2	1,308.4	....	....	....	....	5,639.7	5,763.2	5,733.2	5.6	5.5
1979	....	317.5	369.2	1,332.8	....	....	....	....	5,841.2	5,903.3	5,930.2	3.1	2.4
1980	....	351.7	344.7	1,358.8	....	....	....	....	5,870.7	5,780.6	5,913.4	-.3	-1.9
1981	....	356.0	353.8	1,371.2	....	....	....	....	5,959.5	5,944.7	6,052.5	2.5	2.7
1982	....	328.8	349.3	1,395.3	....	....	....	....	5,923.3	5,865.4	5,939.1	-1.9	-1.3
1983	....	320.3	393.4	1,446.3	....	....	....	....	6,172.9	6,208.3	6,202.3	4.5	5.8
1984	....	346.4	489.1	1,494.9	....	....	....	....	6,495.6	6,745.4	6,639.8	7.2	8.7
1985	....	357.0	520.9	1,599.0	....	....	....	....	6,838.9	7,045.3	6,893.9	4.1	4.4
1986	....	384.4	565.4	1,696.2	....	....	....	....	7,098.7	7,303.3	7,116.5	3.5	3.7
1987	....	425.7	598.9	1,737.1	....	....	....	....	7,296.2	7,518.4	7,342.2	3.2	2.9
1988	....	493.9	622.4	1,758.9	....	....	....	....	7,607.8	7,758.8	7,650.4	4.1	3.2
1989	....	550.6	648.8	1,806.8	....	....	....	....	7,867.5	7,990.9	7,924.0	3.6	3.0
1990	....	600.2	673.0	1,864.0	....	....	....	....	8,032.7	8,104.6	8,081.8	1.9	1.4
1991	....	640.0	672.0	1,884.4	....	....	....	....	8,034.8	8,034.6	8,055.6	-.2	-.9
1992	....	684.0	719.2	1,893.2	....	....	....	....	8,284.3	8,309.6	8,326.4	3.4	3.4
1993	....	706.4	781.4	1,878.2	....	....	....	....	8,515.3	8,592.9	8,563.2	2.9	3.4
1994	....	768.0	874.6	1,878.0	....	....	....	....	8,809.2	8,976.0	8,900.5	4.1	4.5
1995	-98.8	845.7	944.5	1,888.9	704.1	476.8	227.5	1,183.6	9,073.2	9,189.0	9,129.4	2.5	2.4
1996	-110.7	916.0	1,026.7	1,907.9	696.0	470.4	225.7	1,211.1	9,412.5	9,542.0	9,471.1	3.7	3.8
1997	-139.8	1,025.1	1,165.0	1,943.8	689.1	457.2	231.9	1,254.3	9,782.6	9,992.8	9,881.8	4.5	4.7
1998	-252.6	1,048.5	1,301.1	1,985.0	681.4	447.5	233.7	1,303.8	10,217.1	10,539.9	10,304.0	4.4	5.5
1999	-356.6	1,094.3	1,450.9	2,056.1	694.6	455.8	238.7	1,361.8	10,715.7	11,141.1	10,812.1	4.8	5.7
2000	-451.6	1,188.3	1,639.9	2,097.8	698.1	453.5	244.4	1,400.1	11,167.5	11,681.4	11,268.8	4.1	4.8
2001	-472.1	1,121.6	1,593.8	2,178.3	726.5	470.7	255.5	1,452.3	11,391.7	11,825.7	11,404.6	1.1	1.2
2002	-548.8	1,099.2	1,648.0	2,279.6	779.5	505.3	273.9	1,500.6	11,543.5	12,107.7	11,606.9	1.8	2.4
2003	-603.9	1,116.8	1,720.7	2,330.5	831.1	549.2	281.7	1,499.7	11,824.8	12,449.2	11,914.2	2.5	2.8
2004	-688.0	1,222.8	1,910.8	2,362.0	865.0	580.4	284.6	1,497.1	12,198.2	12,952.5	12,358.5	3.6	4.0
2005	-722.7	1,305.1	2,027.8	2,369.9	876.3	589.0	287.3	1,493.6	12,588.4	13,361.1	12,735.5	3.1	3.2
2006	-729.2	1,422.0	2,151.2	2,402.1	894.9	598.4	296.6	1,507.2	12,917.1	13,705.7	13,046.1	2.7	2.6
2007	-654.9	1,554.4	2,209.3	2,434.2	906.1	611.8	294.2	1,528.1	13,200.0	13,883.9	13,344.4	1.9	1.3
2008	-504.1	1,647.7	2,151.7	2,602.7	971.8	657.7	314.0	1,532.6	13,268.1	13,729.4	13,388.7	.0	-1.1
2009	-363.0	1,490.7	1,853.8	2,542.6	1,027.6	693.0	334.6	1,518.8	12,992.8	13,233.6	13,014.7	-2.6	-3.6
2010 P	-421.1	1,665.4	2,086.6	2,570.1	1,077.0	720.3	356.8	1,499.0	13,179.5	13,662.7	....	2.9	3.2
2007: I	-696.4	1,496.4	2,192.7	2,406.7	883.6	595.3	288.2	1,522.9	13,071.1	13,786.2	13,155.8	.9	.9
II	-696.2	1,521.3	2,217.5	2,426.8	898.9	607.3	291.5	1,527.8	13,146.4	13,891.2	13,269.0	3.2	3.1
III	-666.6	1,578.0	2,244.6	2,447.9	919.7	622.3	297.3	1,528.4	13,230.4	13,935.8	13,404.4	2.3	1.3
IV	-560.4	1,622.0	2,182.4	2,455.3	922.2	622.4	299.8	1,533.3	13,352.2	13,922.4	13,548.5	2.9	-.4
2008: I	-529.9	1,644.7	2,174.6	2,469.2	937.6	632.7	304.8	1,532.2	13,346.2	13,866.9	13,516.8	-.7	-1.6
II	-493.8	1,696.6	2,190.4	2,489.4	955.3	643.4	311.9	1,535.1	13,382.4	13,850.1	13,519.7	.6	-.5
III	-514.8	1,675.0	2,189.8	2,521.5	987.5	673.0	314.2	1,536.2	13,249.6	13,737.2	13,408.7	-4.0	-3.2
IV	-477.7	1,574.5	2,052.2	2,530.7	1,006.9	681.6	325.2	1,526.8	13,094.1	13,463.3	13,109.5	-6.8	-7.7
2009: I	-389.2	1,451.6	1,840.8	2,511.5	994.1	666.8	327.3	1,520.1	12,964.2	13,212.6	12,945.5	-4.9	-7.2
II	-342.0	1,447.8	1,789.9	2,549.3	1,029.2	693.2	335.9	1,523.8	12,971.4	13,143.7	12,929.4	-.7	-2.1
III	-390.8	1,490.0	1,880.8	2,559.3	1,043.5	708.3	335.2	1,520.0	12,984.5	13,239.8	13,013.8	1.6	3.0
IV	-330.1	1,573.5	1,903.6	2,550.3	1,043.6	703.8	339.8	1,511.2	13,051.1	13,338.2	13,170.1	5.0	3.0
2010: I	-338.4	1,616.4	1,954.8	2,540.2	1,048.4	704.4	344.0	1,496.8	13,085.5	13,467.6	13,313.0	3.7	3.9
II	-449.0	1,652.1	2,101.1	2,564.9	1,071.5	717.1	354.5	1,499.1	13,114.7	13,637.7	13,372.7	1.7	5.1
III	-505.0	1,679.3	2,184.3	2,589.6	1,094.3	731.8	362.6	1,501.7	13,145.3	13,777.6	13,449.3	2.6	4.2
IV P	-392.2	1,713.9	2,106.1	2,585.8	1,093.9	728.1	365.9	1,498.4	13,372.6	13,767.8	....	3.2	-.3

[1] Gross domestic product (GDP) less exports of goods and services plus imports of goods and services.
[2] GDP plus net income receipts from rest of the world.

Source: Department of Commerce (Bureau of Economic Analysis).

TABLE B–3. Quantity and price indexes for gross domestic product, and percent changes, 1962–2010

[Quarterly data are seasonally adjusted]

Year or quarter	Index numbers, 2005=100					Percent change from preceding period [1]				
	Gross domestic product (GDP)			Personal consumption expenditures (PCE)		Gross domestic product (GDP)			Personal consumption expenditures (PCE)	
	Real GDP (chain-type quantity index)	GDP chain-type price index	GDP implicit price deflator	PCE chain-type price index	PCE less food and energy price index	Real GDP (chain-type quantity index)	GDP chain-type price index	GDP implicit price deflator	PCE chain-type price index	PCE less food and energy price index
1962	24.310	19.071	19.062	19.023	19.525	6.1	1.4	1.4	1.2	1.4
1963	25.373	19.273	19.265	19.245	19.778	4.4	1.1	1.1	1.2	1.3
1964	26.841	19.572	19.563	19.527	20.081	5.8	1.6	1.5	1.5	1.5
1965	28.565	19.928	19.919	19.810	20.335	6.4	1.8	1.8	1.4	1.3
1966	30.426	20.493	20.484	20.313	20.795	6.5	2.8	2.8	2.5	2.3
1967	31.195	21.124	21.115	20.824	21.432	2.5	3.1	3.1	2.5	3.1
1968	32.705	22.022	22.012	21.636	22.351	4.8	4.3	4.2	3.9	4.3
1969	33.721	23.110	23.099	22.616	23.400	3.1	4.9	4.9	4.5	4.7
1970	33.786	24.328	24.317	23.674	24.498	.2	5.3	5.3	4.7	4.7
1971	34.920	25.545	25.533	24.680	25.651	3.4	5.0	5.0	4.2	4.7
1972	36.775	26.647	26.634	25.525	26.480	5.3	4.3	4.3	3.4	3.2
1973	38.905	28.124	28.112	26.901	27.492	5.8	5.5	5.5	5.4	3.8
1974	38.691	30.669	30.664	29.703	29.673	-.6	9.0	9.1	10.4	7.9
1975	38.609	33.577	33.563	32.184	32.159	-.2	9.5	9.5	8.4	8.4
1976	40.680	35.505	35.489	33.950	34.114	5.4	5.7	5.7	5.5	6.1
1977	42.550	37.764	37.751	36.155	36.303	4.6	6.4	6.4	6.5	6.4
1978	44.924	40.413	40.400	38.687	38.731	5.6	7.0	7.0	7.0	6.7
1979	46.328	43.773	43.761	42.118	41.550	3.1	8.3	8.3	8.9	7.3
1980	46.200	47.776	47.751	46.641	45.356	-.3	9.1	9.1	10.7	9.2
1981	47.373	52.281	52.225	50.810	49.318	2.5	9.4	9.4	8.9	8.7
1982	46.453	55.467	55.412	53.615	52.501	-1.9	6.1	6.1	5.5	6.5
1983	48.552	57.655	57.603	55.923	55.220	4.5	3.9	4.0	4.3	5.2
1984	52.041	59.823	59.766	58.038	57.513	7.2	3.8	3.8	3.8	4.2
1985	54.194	61.633	61.576	59.938	59.695	4.1	3.0	3.0	3.3	3.8
1986	56.071	63.003	62.937	61.399	61.945	3.5	2.2	2.2	2.4	3.8
1987	57.866	64.763	64.764	63.589	64.300	3.2	2.8	2.9	3.6	3.8
1988	60.244	66.990	66.988	66.121	67.088	4.1	3.4	3.4	4.0	4.3
1989	62.397	69.520	69.518	68.994	69.856	3.6	3.8	3.8	4.3	4.1
1990	63.568	72.213	72.201	72.147	72.838	1.9	3.9	3.9	4.6	4.3
1991	63.419	74.762	74.760	74.755	75.673	-.2	3.5	3.5	3.6	3.9
1992	65.571	76.537	76.533	76.954	78.218	3.4	2.4	2.4	2.9	3.4
1993	67.441	78.222	78.224	78.643	80.068	2.9	2.2	2.2	2.2	2.4
1994	70.188	79.867	79.872	80.265	81.836	4.1	2.1	2.1	2.1	2.2
1995	71.953	81.533	81.536	82.041	83.721	2.5	2.1	2.1	2.2	2.3
1996	74.645	83.083	83.088	83.826	85.346	3.7	1.9	1.9	2.2	1.9
1997	77.972	84.554	84.555	85.395	86.981	4.5	1.8	1.8	1.9	1.9
1998	81.367	85.507	85.511	86.207	88.242	4.4	1.1	1.1	1.0	1.4
1999	85.295	86.766	86.768	87.596	89.555	4.8	1.5	1.5	1.6	1.5
2000	88.825	88.648	88.647	89.777	91.111	4.1	2.2	2.2	2.5	1.7
2001	89.783	90.654	90.650	91.488	92.739	1.1	2.3	2.3	1.9	1.8
2002	91.412	92.113	92.118	92.736	94.345	1.8	1.6	1.6	1.4	1.7
2003	93.688	94.099	94.100	94.622	95.784	2.5	2.2	2.2	2.0	1.5
2004	97.036	96.769	96.770	97.098	97.788	3.6	2.8	2.8	2.6	2.1
2005	100.000	100.000	100.000	100.000	100.000	3.1	3.3	3.3	3.0	2.3
2006	102.673	103.263	103.257	102.746	102.292	2.7	3.3	3.3	2.7	2.3
2007	104.672	106.301	106.296	105.564	104.696	1.9	2.9	2.9	2.7	2.4
2008	104.672	108.598	108.619	109.061	107.151	.0	2.2	2.2	3.3	2.3
2009	101.917	109.618	109.615	109.258	108.774	-2.6	.9	.9	.2	1.5
2010 ᵖ	104.829	110.664	110.654	111.123	110.203	2.9	1.0	.9	1.7	1.3
2007: I	103.568	105.366	105.349	104.311	103.905	.9	4.4	4.4	4.0	2.9
II	104.398	106.188	106.169	105.212	104.344	3.2	3.2	3.2	3.5	1.7
III	104.985	106.709	106.706	105.813	104.901	2.3	2.0	2.0	2.3	2.2
IV	105.737	106.940	106.943	106.919	105.633	2.9	.9	.9	4.2	2.8
2008: I	105.545	107.454	107.416	107.954	106.301	-.7	1.9	1.8	3.9	2.6
II	105.702	108.295	108.330	109.185	106.998	.6	3.2	3.4	4.6	2.6
III	104.630	109.488	109.539	110.367	107.569	-4.0	4.5	4.5	4.4	2.2
IV	102.811	109.154	109.216	108.736	107.735	-6.8	-1.2	-1.2	-5.8	.6
2009: I	101.537	109.465	109.484	108.290	107.973	-4.9	1.1	1.0	-1.6	.9
II	101.358	109.555	109.558	108.810	108.583	-.7	.3	.3	1.9	2.3
III	101.760	109.759	109.750	109.598	108.990	1.6	.7	.7	2.9	1.5
IV	103.012	109.693	109.665	110.333	109.551	5.0	-.2	-.3	2.7	2.1
2010: I	103.960	109.959	109.952	110.901	109.887	3.7	1.0	1.1	2.1	1.2
II	104.403	110.485	110.488	110.888	110.171	1.7	1.9	2.0	.0	1.0
III	105.065	111.060	111.045	111.102	110.318	2.6	2.1	2.0	.8	.5
IV ᵖ	105.888	111.153	111.118	111.602	110.436	3.2	.3	.3	1.8	.4

[1] Quarterly percent changes are at annual rates.

Source: Department of Commerce (Bureau of Economic Analysis).

TABLE B–4. Percent changes in real gross domestic product, 1962–2010

[Percent change from preceding period; quarterly data at seasonally adjusted annual rates]

Year or quarter	Gross domestic product	Personal consumption expenditures			Gross private domestic investment				Exports and imports of goods and services		Government consumption expenditures and gross investment		
					Nonresidential fixed								
		Total	Goods	Services	Total	Structures	Equipment and software	Residential fixed	Exports	Imports	Total	Federal	State and local
1962	6.1	4.9	5.1	4.7	8.7	4.6	11.6	9.6	5.0	11.4	6.2	8.5	3.1
1963	4.4	4.1	4.0	4.2	5.6	1.2	8.4	11.8	7.2	2.7	2.6	.1	6.0
1964	5.8	6.0	6.0	6.0	11.9	10.4	12.8	5.8	11.8	5.3	2.2	−1.3	6.8
1965	6.4	6.3	7.1	5.5	17.4	15.9	18.3	−2.9	2.8	10.6	3.0	.0	6.7
1966	6.5	5.7	6.3	5.0	12.5	6.8	16.0	−8.9	6.9	14.9	8.8	11.1	6.3
1967	2.5	3.0	2.0	4.1	−1.3	−2.5	−.7	−3.1	2.3	7.3	7.7	10.0	5.1
1968	4.8	5.8	6.2	5.3	4.5	1.4	6.2	13.6	7.9	14.9	3.1	.8	5.9
1969	3.1	3.7	3.1	4.5	7.6	5.4	8.8	3.0	4.8	5.7	−.2	−3.4	3.4
1970	.2	2.3	.8	3.9	−.5	.3	−1.0	−6.0	10.7	4.3	−2.4	−7.4	2.8
1971	3.4	3.8	4.2	3.5	.0	−1.6	1.0	27.4	1.7	5.3	−2.2	−7.7	3.1
1972	5.3	6.2	6.5	5.8	9.2	3.1	12.9	17.8	7.5	11.3	−.7	−4.1	2.2
1973	5.8	5.0	5.2	4.7	14.6	8.2	18.3	−.6	18.9	4.6	−.4	−4.2	2.9
1974	−.6	−.8	−3.6	1.9	.8	−2.2	2.6	−20.6	7.9	−2.3	2.5	.9	3.8
1975	−.2	2.3	.7	3.8	−9.9	−10.5	−9.5	−13.0	−.6	−11.1	2.3	.3	3.7
1976	5.4	5.6	7.0	4.3	4.9	2.4	6.3	23.5	4.4	19.6	.4	.0	.7
1977	4.6	4.2	4.3	4.1	11.3	4.1	15.1	21.5	2.4	10.9	1.1	2.1	.4
1978	5.6	4.4	4.1	4.7	15.0	14.4	15.2	6.3	10.5	8.7	2.9	2.5	3.3
1979	3.1	2.4	1.6	3.1	10.1	12.7	8.7	−3.7	9.9	1.7	1.9	2.4	1.5
1980	−.3	−.4	−2.5	1.5	−.3	5.9	−3.6	−21.2	10.8	−6.6	1.9	4.7	−.1
1981	2.5	1.5	1.2	1.8	5.7	8.0	4.3	−8.0	1.2	2.6	.9	4.8	−2.0
1982	−1.9	1.4	.7	1.9	−3.8	−1.6	−5.2	−18.2	−7.6	−1.3	1.8	3.9	.0
1983	4.5	5.7	6.4	5.2	−1.3	−10.8	5.4	41.4	−2.6	12.6	3.7	6.6	1.2
1984	7.2	5.3	7.2	3.9	17.6	13.9	19.8	14.8	8.2	24.3	3.4	3.1	3.6
1985	4.1	5.2	5.3	5.2	6.6	7.1	6.4	1.6	3.0	6.5	7.0	7.8	6.2
1986	3.5	4.1	5.6	3.0	−2.9	−11.0	1.9	12.3	7.7	8.5	6.1	5.7	6.4
1987	3.2	3.1	1.8	4.0	−.1	−2.9	1.4	2.0	10.8	5.9	2.4	3.6	1.4
1988	4.1	4.0	3.7	4.2	5.2	.7	7.5	−1.0	16.0	3.9	1.3	−1.6	3.7
1989	3.6	2.8	2.5	3.0	5.6	2.0	7.3	−3.0	11.5	4.4	2.7	1.6	3.7
1990	1.9	2.0	.6	3.0	.5	1.5	.0	−8.6	9.0	3.6	3.2	2.0	4.1
1991	−.2	.1	−2.0	1.5	−5.4	−11.1	−2.6	−9.6	6.6	−.1	1.1	−.2	2.1
1992	3.4	3.4	3.2	3.6	3.2	−6.0	7.3	13.8	6.9	7.0	.5	−1.8	2.2
1993	2.9	3.6	4.2	3.2	8.7	−.6	12.5	8.2	3.3	8.6	−.8	−3.9	1.5
1994	4.1	3.8	5.3	3.0	9.2	1.8	11.9	9.7	8.7	11.9	.0	−3.8	2.6
1995	2.5	2.7	3.0	2.5	10.5	6.4	12.0	−3.3	10.1	8.0	.6	−2.7	2.7
1996	3.7	3.5	4.5	2.9	9.3	5.7	10.6	8.0	8.3	8.7	1.0	−1.2	2.3
1997	4.5	3.7	4.8	3.1	12.1	7.3	13.8	1.9	11.9	13.5	1.9	−1.0	3.6
1998	4.4	5.2	6.8	4.4	12.0	5.1	14.5	7.7	2.3	11.7	2.1	−1.1	3.9
1999	4.8	5.5	8.0	4.1	10.4	.1	14.1	6.3	4.4	11.5	3.6	1.9	4.5
2000	4.1	5.1	5.3	5.0	9.8	7.8	10.5	1.0	8.6	13.0	2.0	.5	2.8
2001	1.1	2.7	3.1	2.5	−2.8	−1.5	−3.2	.6	−5.6	−2.8	3.8	4.1	3.7
2002	1.8	2.7	4.1	1.9	−7.9	−17.7	−4.2	5.2	−2.0	3.4	4.7	7.3	3.3
2003	2.5	2.8	4.6	1.9	.9	−3.8	2.5	8.2	1.6	4.4	2.2	6.6	−.1
2004	3.6	3.5	4.4	2.9	6.0	1.1	7.7	9.8	9.5	11.0	1.4	4.1	−.2
2005	3.1	3.4	4.0	3.0	6.7	1.4	8.5	6.2	6.7	6.1	.3	1.3	−.2
2006	2.7	2.9	3.3	2.7	7.9	9.2	7.4	−7.3	9.0	6.1	1.4	2.1	.9
2007	1.9	2.4	2.8	2.2	6.7	14.1	3.7	−18.7	9.3	2.7	1.3	1.2	1.4
2008	.0	−.3	−2.5	.9	.3	5.9	−2.4	−24.0	6.0	−2.6	2.8	7.3	.3
2009	−2.6	−1.2	−2.0	−.8	−17.1	−20.4	−15.3	−22.9	−9.5	−13.8	1.6	5.7	−.9
2010 ᵖ	2.9	1.8	4.3	.5	5.5	−14.0	15.1	−3.0	11.7	12.6	1.1	4.8	−1.3
2007: I	.9	2.4	2.3	2.4	6.8	10.7	5.1	−16.4	6.4	4.6	−.5	−4.8	2.1
II	3.2	1.5	1.4	1.6	11.1	28.0	4.3	−12.0	6.8	4.6	3.4	7.1	1.3
III	2.3	1.7	2.4	1.4	9.4	24.3	2.9	−24.1	15.8	5.0	3.5	9.6	.2
IV	2.9	1.4	1.1	1.5	5.7	7.4	4.8	−29.3	11.6	−10.6	1.2	1.1	1.3
2008: I	−.7	−.8	−5.8	1.9	2.0	−.1	3.0	−27.9	5.7	−1.4	2.3	6.9	−.3
II	.6	.1	.3	.0	−1.6	7.5	−6.0	−14.0	13.2	2.9	3.3	7.8	.8
III	−4.0	−3.5	−7.7	−1.3	−8.6	−3.6	−11.1	−22.6	−5.0	−.1	5.3	14.2	.3
IV	−6.8	−3.3	−10.8	.6	−22.7	−8.9	−29.5	−32.6	−21.9	−22.9	1.5	8.1	−2.4
2009: I	−4.9	−.5	1.8	−1.6	−35.2	−41.0	−31.6	−36.2	−27.8	−35.3	−3.0	−5.0	−1.7
II	−.7	−1.6	−1.5	−1.7	−7.5	−20.2	.2	−19.7	−1.0	−10.6	6.1	14.9	1.0
III	1.6	2.0	7.2	−.5	−1.7	−12.4	4.2	10.6	12.2	21.9	1.6	5.7	−1.0
IV	5.0	.9	1.7	.5	−1.4	−29.2	14.6	−.8	24.4	4.9	−1.4	.0	−2.3
2010: I	3.7	1.9	5.7	.1	7.8	−17.8	20.4	−12.3	11.4	11.2	−1.6	1.8	−3.8
II	1.7	2.2	3.4	1.6	17.2	−.5	24.8	25.7	9.1	33.5	3.9	9.1	.6
III	2.6	2.4	4.1	1.6	10.0	−3.5	15.4	−27.3	6.8	16.8	3.9	8.8	.7
IV ᵖ	3.2	4.4	10.1	1.7	4.4	.8	5.8	3.4	8.5	−13.6	−.6	−.2	−.9

Note: Percent changes based on unrounded data.

Source: Department of Commerce (Bureau of Economic Analysis).

TABLE B–5. Contributions to percent change in real gross domestic product, 1962–2010

[Percentage points, except as noted; quarterly data at seasonally adjusted annual rates]

Year or quarter	Gross domestic product (percent change)	Personal consumption expenditures			Gross private domestic investment						
						Fixed investment					Change in private inventories
							Nonresidential				
		Total	Goods	Services	Total	Total	Total	Structures	Equipment and software	Residential	
1962	6.1	3.10	1.68	1.42	1.81	1.24	0.78	0.16	0.61	0.46	0.57
1963	4.4	2.56	1.29	1.27	1.00	1.08	.50	.04	.46	.58	−.08
1964	5.8	3.69	1.91	1.78	1.25	1.37	1.07	.36	.71	.30	−.13
1965	6.4	3.91	2.26	1.66	2.16	1.50	1.65	.57	1.07	−.15	.66
1966	6.5	3.50	2.02	1.48	1.44	.87	1.29	.27	1.02	−.43	.58
1967	2.5	1.82	.62	1.21	−.76	−.28	−.15	−.10	−.05	−.13	−.49
1968	4.8	3.51	1.92	1.59	.90	.99	.46	.05	.41	.53	−.10
1969	3.1	2.29	.95	1.34	.90	.90	.78	.20	.58	.13	.00
1970	.2	1.44	.24	1.19	−1.04	−.31	−.06	.01	−.07	−.26	−.73
1971	3.4	2.37	1.27	1.10	1.67	1.10	.00	−.06	.07	1.10	.58
1972	5.3	3.81	1.97	1.84	1.87	1.81	.93	.12	.81	.89	.06
1973	5.8	3.08	1.57	1.51	1.96	1.47	1.50	.31	1.19	−.04	.50
1974	−.6	−.52	−1.12	.60	−1.31	−1.04	.09	−.09	.18	−1.13	−.27
1975	−.2	1.40	.20	1.20	−2.98	−1.71	−1.14	−.43	−.70	−.57	−1.27
1976	5.4	3.51	2.08	1.43	2.84	1.42	.52	.09	.43	.90	1.41
1977	4.6	2.66	1.28	1.38	2.43	2.18	1.19	.15	1.04	.99	.25
1978	5.6	2.77	1.22	1.56	2.16	2.04	1.69	.54	1.15	.35	.12
1979	3.1	1.48	.47	1.02	.61	1.02	1.23	.53	.71	−.21	−.41
1980	−.3	−.22	−.74	.52	−2.12	−1.21	−.03	.27	−.30	−1.17	−.91
1981	2.5	.95	.34	.62	1.55	.39	.74	.40	.34	−.35	1.16
1982	−1.9	.86	.19	.67	−2.55	−1.21	−.50	−.09	−.42	−.71	−1.34
1983	4.5	3.65	1.74	1.91	1.45	1.17	−.17	−.57	.41	1.33	.29
1984	7.2	3.43	1.97	1.47	4.63	2.68	2.05	.60	1.45	.64	1.95
1985	4.1	3.32	1.41	1.90	−.17	.89	.82	.32	.50	.07	−1.06
1986	3.5	2.62	1.49	1.13	−.12	.20	−.36	−.50	.15	.55	−.32
1987	3.2	2.01	.48	1.53	.51	.09	−.01	−.11	.10	.10	.42
1988	4.1	2.64	.98	1.66	.39	.53	.58	.02	.55	−.05	−.14
1989	3.6	1.86	.66	1.20	.64	.47	.61	.07	.54	−.14	.17
1990	1.9	1.34	.16	1.18	−.53	−.32	.05	.05	.00	−.37	−.21
1991	−.2	.10	−.51	.61	−1.20	−.94	−.57	−.39	−.18	−.37	−.26
1992	3.4	2.27	.78	1.49	1.07	.79	.31	−.18	.50	.47	.29
1993	2.9	2.37	1.02	1.35	1.21	1.14	.83	−.02	.85	.31	.07
1994	4.1	2.57	1.29	1.27	1.94	1.30	.91	.05	.86	.39	.63
1995	2.5	1.81	.73	1.08	.48	.94	1.08	.17	.91	−.14	−.46
1996	3.7	2.35	1.09	1.26	1.35	1.33	1.01	.16	.85	.33	.02
1997	4.5	2.48	1.16	1.33	1.95	1.41	1.33	.21	1.12	.08	.54
1998	4.4	3.50	1.61	1.90	1.65	1.70	1.38	.16	1.22	.32	−.05
1999	4.8	3.68	1.90	1.78	1.50	1.52	1.24	.00	1.24	.28	−.02
2000	4.1	3.44	1.29	2.15	1.19	1.24	1.20	.24	.96	.05	−.05
2001	1.1	1.85	.77	1.09	−1.24	−.32	−.35	−.05	−.30	.03	−.92
2002	1.8	1.85	.99	.86	−.22	−.70	−.94	−.58	−.36	.24	.48
2003	2.5	1.97	1.11	.86	.55	.49	.10	−.10	.20	.40	.06
2004	3.6	2.42	1.08	1.34	1.55	1.13	.61	.03	.58	.52	.42
2005	3.1	2.34	.97	1.37	.92	1.05	.69	.04	.65	.36	−.13
2006	2.7	2.01	.78	1.22	.46	.39	.84	.27	.58	−.45	.07
2007	1.9	1.65	.66	.99	−.53	−.30	.75	.46	.29	−1.05	−.23
2008	.0	−.18	−.60	.41	−1.53	−1.02	.03	.22	−.19	−1.05	−.51
2009	−2.6	−.84	−.46	−.38	−3.24	−2.69	−1.96	−.81	−1.15	−.74	−.55
2010 ᵖ	2.9	1.27	1.00	.27	1.84	.46	.53	−.43	.97	−.07	1.38
2007: I	.9	1.64	.56	1.08	−.65	−.15	.75	.35	.40	−.91	−.49
II	3.2	1.08	.34	.74	1.51	.62	1.23	.88	.35	−.62	.90
III	2.3	1.20	.57	.62	−.46	−.18	1.06	.82	.24	−1.24	−.28
IV	2.9	.98	.27	.71	−1.53	−.76	.67	.28	.39	−1.43	−.77
2008: I	−.7	−.54	−1.42	.88	−1.47	−.98	.25	.00	.25	−1.23	−.49
II	.6	.08	.08	.00	−1.17	−.69	−.16	.30	−.46	−.53	−.48
III	−4.0	−2.46	−1.86	−.59	−1.95	−1.83	−1.00	−.14	−.86	−.84	−.12
IV	−6.8	−2.26	−2.57	.30	−6.32	−4.01	−2.84	−.36	−2.47	−1.18	−2.31
2009: I	−4.9	−.34	.41	−.75	−6.80	−5.71	−4.49	−1.99	−2.50	−1.22	−1.09
II	−.7	−1.12	−.32	−.79	−2.30	−1.26	−.72	−.76	.04	−.54	−1.03
III	1.6	1.41	1.62	−.21	1.22	.12	−.13	−.41	.28	.25	1.10
IV	5.0	.69	.42	.27	2.70	−.12	−.10	−1.01	.91	−.02	2.83
2010: I	3.7	1.33	1.29	.03	3.04	.39	.71	−.53	1.24	−.32	2.64
II	1.7	1.54	.79	.75	2.88	2.06	1.51	−.01	1.52	.55	.82
III	2.6	1.67	.94	.74	1.80	.18	.93	−.09	1.02	−.75	1.61
IV ᵖ	3.2	3.04	2.26	.78	−3.20	.50	.43	.02	.41	.08	−3.70

See next page for continuation of table.

[Percentage points, except as noted; quarterly data at seasonally adjusted annual rates]

| Year or quarter | Net exports of goods and services | | | | | | | Government consumption expenditures and gross investment | | | | |
| | Net exports | Exports | | | Imports | | | Total | Federal | | | State and local |
		Total	Goods	Services	Total	Goods	Services		Total	National defense	Non-defense	
1962	−0.21	0.25	0.17	0.08	−0.47	−0.40	−0.07	1.36	1.07	0.63	0.44	0.29
1963	.24	.35	.29	.06	−.12	−.12	.00	.58	.01	−.25	.26	.57
1964	.36	.59	.52	.07	−.23	−.19	−.04	.49	−.17	−.39	.23	.65
1965	−.30	.15	.02	.13	−.45	−.41	−.04	.65	−.01	−.19	.19	.66
1966	−.29	.36	.27	.09	−.65	−.49	−.16	1.87	1.24	1.21	.03	.63
1967	−.22	.12	.02	.10	−.34	−.17	−.16	1.68	1.17	1.19	−.02	.51
1968	−.30	.41	.30	.10	−.71	−.68	−.03	.73	.10	.16	−.06	.63
1969	−.04	.25	.20	.05	−.29	−.20	−.09	−.05	−.42	−.49	.06	.37
1970	.34	.56	.44	.12	−.22	−.15	−.07	−.55	−.86	−.83	−.03	.31
1971	−.19	.10	−.02	.11	−.29	−.33	.04	−.50	−.85	−.97	.12	.36
1972	−.21	.42	.43	−.01	−.63	−.57	−.06	−.16	−.42	−.60	.18	.26
1973	.82	1.12	1.01	.11	−.29	−.34	.05	−.08	−.41	−.39	−.02	.33
1974	.75	.58	.46	.12	.18	.17	.00	.52	.08	−.05	.13	.44
1975	.89	−.05	−.16	.10	.94	.87	.07	.48	.03	−.06	.09	.45
1976	−1.08	.37	.31	.05	−1.45	−1.35	−.10	.10	.00	−.02	.03	.09
1977	−.72	.20	.08	.11	−.92	−.84	−.07	.23	.19	.07	.12	.04
1978	.05	.82	.68	.15	−.78	−.67	−.11	.60	.22	.05	.16	.38
1979	.66	.82	.77	.06	−.16	−.14	−.02	.37	.20	.17	.03	.17
1980	1.68	.97	.86	.11	.71	.67	.04	.38	.39	.25	.14	−.01
1981	−.15	.12	−.09	.21	−.27	−.18	−.09	.19	.42	.38	.04	−.23
1982	−.60	−.73	−.67	−.06	.12	.20	−.08	.35	.35	.48	−.13	.01
1983	−1.35	−.22	−.19	−.03	−1.13	−1.01	−.13	.76	.63	.50	.13	.13
1984	−1.58	.63	.46	.17	−2.21	−1.83	−.39	.70	.30	.35	−.05	.40
1985	−.42	.23	.20	.02	−.65	−.52	−.13	1.41	.74	.60	.14	.67
1986	−.30	.54	.26	.28	−.84	−.82	−.02	1.27	.55	.47	.08	.71
1987	.16	.77	.56	.21	−.61	−.39	−.22	.51	.35	.35	.00	.17
1988	.82	1.24	1.04	.20	−.43	−.36	−.07	.26	−.16	−.03	−.12	.42
1989	.52	.99	.75	.24	−.48	−.38	−.09	.55	.14	−.03	.17	.41
1990	.43	.81	.56	.26	−.38	−.26	−.13	.64	.18	.00	.18	.46
1991	.64	.63	.46	.16	.02	−.04	.05	.22	−.02	−.07	.05	.24
1992	−.05	.68	.52	.16	−.72	−.78	.06	.10	−.16	−.32	.16	.26
1993	−.57	.32	.23	.10	−.90	−.85	−.05	−.16	−.33	−.31	−.02	.17
1994	−.43	.85	.67	.19	−1.28	−1.18	−.10	.00	−.30	−.27	−.04	.30
1995	.11	1.03	.85	.19	−.92	−.86	−.06	.11	−.20	−.19	−.01	.30
1996	−.15	.90	.68	.22	−1.04	−.94	−.10	.19	−.08	−.06	−.02	.27
1997	−.32	1.30	1.11	.19	−1.62	−1.44	−.17	.34	−.07	−.13	.06	.41
1998	−1.18	.26	.18	.08	−1.43	−1.21	−.22	.38	−.07	−.09	.02	.45
1999	−.99	.47	.29	.18	−1.45	−1.31	−.14	.63	.12	.07	.04	.51
2000	−.85	.91	.82	.08	−1.76	−1.52	−.24	.36	.03	−.02	.05	.33
2001	−.20	−.61	−.48	−.13	.41	.39	.02	.67	.24	.14	.09	.43
2002	−.65	−.20	−.25	.05	−.46	−.42	−.04	.84	.44	.28	.15	.40
2003	−.45	.15	.12	.03	−.60	−.55	−.04	.42	.43	.36	.07	−.01
2004	−.66	.89	.55	.34	−1.55	−1.29	−.26	.26	.28	.26	.02	−.02
2005	−.27	.67	.52	.15	−.94	−.87	−.07	.06	.09	.07	.02	−.03
2006	−.05	.93	.68	.25	−.98	−.80	−.18	.26	.15	.07	.07	.11
2007	.57	1.02	.75	.28	−.45	−.42	−.04	.25	.09	.10	−.02	.17
2008	1.18	.72	.53	.19	.46	.52	−.07	.54	.51	.36	.15	.04
2009	1.13	−1.18	−1.04	−.15	2.32	2.20	.12	.32	.43	.27	.16	−.11
2010 ᵖ	−.48	1.34	1.12	.22	−1.82	−1.72	−.09	.23	.39	.22	.17	−.16
2007: I	−.02	.71	.95	−.24	−.73	−.89	.16	−.09	−.33	−.34	.01	.25
II	.01	.76	.58	.17	−.75	−.65	−.10	.64	.48	.38	.10	.16
III	.87	1.71	.98	.74	−.84	−.72	−.12	.66	.64	.47	.18	.02
IV	3.21	1.32	.78	.54	1.89	1.78	.11	.24	.08	.01	.07	.16
2008: I	.84	.67	.78	−.11	.18	.42	−.24	.44	.47	.32	.15	−.04
II	1.04	1.61	1.24	.37	−.57	−.75	.18	.65	.55	.34	.21	.10
III	−.63	−.66	−.41	−.25	.03	.15	−.12	1.04	1.00	.93	.07	.04
IV	1.50	−3.03	−2.65	−.38	4.53	4.82	−.29	.31	.61	.28	.33	−.30
2009: I	2.88	−3.61	−3.14	−.47	6.48	5.95	.53	−.61	−.40	−.45	.06	−.21
II	1.47	−.08	−.26	.18	1.55	1.23	.33	1.24	1.11	.85	.26	.13
III	−1.37	1.30	1.29	.01	−2.67	−2.64	−.03	.33	.45	.48	−.03	−.12
IV	1.90	2.56	2.19	.37	−.66	−.68	.02	−.28	.01	−.13	.14	−.29
2010: I	−.31	1.30	1.09	.21	−1.61	−1.41	−.20	−.32	.15	.02	.13	−.48
II	−3.50	1.08	.93	.15	−4.58	−4.46	−.12	.80	.72	.40	.32	.08
III	−1.70	.82	.49	.33	−2.53	−2.16	−.37	.79	.71	.46	.25	.09
IV ᵖ	3.44	1.04	.85	.19	2.40	2.29	.11	−.11	−.01	−.11	.10	−.10

Source: Department of Commerce (Bureau of Economic Analysis).

TABLE B–6. Chain-type quantity indexes for gross domestic product, 1962–2010

[Index numbers, 2005=100; quarterly data seasonally adjusted]

Year or quarter	Gross domestic product	Personal consumption expenditures			Gross private domestic investment					
					Total	Fixed investment				
							Nonresidential			
		Total	Goods	Services		Total	Total	Structures	Equipment and software	Residential
1962	24.310	21.671	20.915	21.554	15.283	15.190	11.666	51.393	6.017	28.756
1963	25.373	22.564	21.750	22.470	16.309	16.367	12.315	51.986	6.524	32.145
1964	26.841	23.908	23.047	23.807	17.654	17.948	13.777	57.399	7.356	34.013
1965	28.565	25.420	24.679	25.122	20.131	19.781	16.177	66.553	8.705	33.020
1966	30.426	26.862	26.245	26.367	21.905	20.915	18.200	71.109	10.098	30.065
1967	31.195	27.667	26.758	27.451	20.903	20.530	17.955	69.313	10.031	29.119
1968	32.705	29.263	28.415	28.915	22.120	21.962	18.756	70.299	10.656	33.089
1969	33.721	30.359	29.283	30.204	23.409	23.329	20.181	74.096	11.598	34.066
1970	33.786	31.071	29.514	31.385	21.871	22.838	20.073	74.300	11.482	32.028
1971	34.920	32.255	30.749	32.469	24.365	24.568	20.074	73.082	11.596	40.811
1972	36.775	34.239	32.760	34.346	27.250	27.522	21.917	75.359	13.092	48.064
1973	38.905	35.935	34.457	35.974	30.443	30.037	25.106	81.520	15.494	47.756
1974	38.691	35.637	33.200	36.664	28.200	28.159	25.316	79.755	15.890	37.897
1975	38.609	36.445	33.425	38.040	23.205	25.135	22.814	71.355	14.377	32.977
1976	40.680	38.475	35.766	39.672	27.893	27.613	23.931	73.073	15.276	40.743
1977	42.550	40.094	37.301	41.312	32.107	31.582	26.632	76.079	17.577	49.490
1978	44.924	41.862	38.842	43.234	35.978	35.406	30.618	87.058	20.253	52.606
1979	46.328	42.857	39.464	44.555	37.125	37.404	33.702	98.098	22.022	50.676
1980	46.200	42.705	38.464	45.241	33.047	34.974	33.613	103.837	21.230	39.952
1981	47.373	43.353	38.919	46.053	36.019	35.756	35.528	112.161	22.133	36.749
1982	46.453	43.958	39.190	46.950	30.972	33.249	34.190	110.325	20.982	30.077
1983	48.552	46.471	41.684	49.407	33.857	35.673	33.748	98.404	22.111	42.527
1984	52.041	48.935	44.688	51.341	43.833	41.698	39.704	112.125	26.497	48.839
1985	54.194	51.484	47.039	53.996	43.425	43.891	42.336	120.095	28.180	49.612
1986	56.071	53.572	49.670	55.602	43.129	44.402	41.126	106.935	28.714	55.699
1987	57.866	55.225	50.564	57.818	44.458	44.646	41.096	103.859	29.107	56.811
1988	60.244	57.451	52.442	60.272	45.504	46.118	43.245	104.539	31.302	56.235
1989	62.397	59.075	53.766	62.098	47.330	47.504	45.660	106.616	33.596	54.528
1990	63.568	60.281	54.099	63.942	45.736	46.512	45.885	108.187	33.607	49.823
1991	63.419	60.371	53.025	64.899	42.016	43.496	43.425	96.150	32.743	45.035
1992	65.571	62.430	54.696	67.212	45.421	46.075	44.811	90.354	35.129	51.267
1993	67.441	64.647	56.969	69.363	49.481	50.024	48.723	89.768	39.515	55.454
1994	70.188	67.115	59.973	71.433	56.204	54.703	53.207	91.405	44.227	60.845
1995	71.953	68.931	61.765	73.249	57.955	58.226	58.801	97.235	49.519	58.854
1996	74.645	71.336	64.530	75.394	63.082	63.448	64.293	102.744	54.782	63.554
1997	77.972	73.970	67.607	77.719	70.932	69.302	72.053	110.280	62.315	64.756
1998	81.367	77.849	72.175	81.145	78.034	76.822	80.707	115.911	71.358	69.737
1999	85.295	82.106	77.924	84.469	84.903	83.969	89.129	116.049	81.451	74.098
2000	88.825	86.270	82.034	88.654	90.704	90.178	97.864	125.101	89.976	74.839
2001	89.783	88.603	84.611	90.837	84.333	88.470	95.137	123.191	87.073	75.263
2002	91.412	90.962	88.050	92.568	83.185	84.726	87.593	101.377	83.397	79.210
2003	93.688	93.520	92.060	94.314	86.162	87.464	88.398	97.514	85.516	85.724
2004	97.036	96.754	96.141	97.084	94.753	93.884	93.743	98.571	92.141	94.136
2005	100.000	100.000	100.000	100.000	100.000	100.000	100.000	100.000	100.000	100.000
2006	102.673	102.886	103.251	102.692	102.678	102.309	107.913	109.180	107.434	92.679
2007	104.672	105.335	106.105	104.929	99.509	100.490	115.193	124.578	111.389	75.380
2008	104.672	105.057	103.462	105.870	90.105	94.096	115.532	131.976	108.681	57.324
2009	101.917	103.797	101.416	105.006	69.778	76.835	95.804	105.064	92.035	44.220
2010 ᴾ	104.829	105.632	105.788	105.576	81.450	79.729	101.107	90.322	105.952	42.908
2007: I	103.568	104.719	105.437	104.340	98.798	100.254	111.257	115.080	109.783	81.468
II	104.398	105.119	105.808	104.756	101.054	101.176	114.234	122.401	110.948	78.895
III	104.985	105.568	106.440	105.110	100.309	100.875	116.829	129.246	111.756	73.633
IV	105.737	105.933	106.737	105.512	97.874	99.653	118.450	131.584	113.069	67.526
2008: I	105.545	105.727	105.163	106.014	95.494	98.082	119.026	131.551	113.906	62.228
II	105.702	105.752	105.245	106.007	93.629	96.940	118.533	133.949	112.151	59.929
III	104.630	104.813	103.171	105.655	90.563	93.924	115.899	132.731	108.890	56.206
IV	102.811	103.938	100.271	105.803	80.735	87.437	108.673	129.672	99.775	50.934
2009: I	101.537	103.800	100.709	105.370	70.410	78.380	97.501	113.638	90.745	45.515
II	101.358	103.379	100.328	104.919	66.901	76.316	95.618	107.399	90.786	43.089
III	101.760	103.885	102.092	104.797	68.800	76.447	95.216	103.911	91.716	44.185
IV	103.012	104.126	102.533	104.936	73.000	76.198	94.879	95.310	94.895	44.092
2010: I	103.960	104.608	103.952	104.952	77.811	76.826	96.677	90.761	99.408	42.670
II	104.403	105.178	104.837	105.366	82.474	80.219	100.592	90.649	105.067	45.177
III	105.065	105.801	105.898	105.775	85.400	80.517	103.019	89.848	108.898	41.719
IV ᴾ	105.888	106.942	108.465	106.211	80.118	81.356	104.142	90.031	110.434	42.068

See next page for continuation of table.

[Index numbers, 2005=100; quarterly data seasonally adjusted]

Year or quarter	Exports of goods and services			Imports of goods and services			Government consumption expenditures and gross investment				
								Federal			State and local
	Total	Goods	Services	Total	Goods	Services	Total	Total	National defense	Non-defense	
1962	7.971	7.494	9.141	6.248	4.843	14.954	40.977	60.488	74.623	33.377	28.818
1963	8.541	8.083	9.605	6.416	5.039	14.943	42.032	60.526	72.838	36.946	30.552
1964	9.547	9.190	10.180	6.757	5.372	15.328	42.958	59.725	69.951	40.157	32.626
1965	9.815	9.239	11.215	7.476	6.132	15.779	44.250	59.697	68.481	42.878	34.813
1966	10.495	9.880	11.986	8.587	7.099	17.783	48.149	66.303	78.306	43.320	36.998
1967	10.737	9.927	12.932	9.213	7.473	19.957	51.844	72.903	88.567	42.913	38.868
1968	11.580	10.713	13.925	10.586	9.016	20.315	53.472	73.491	90.001	41.897	41.168
1969	12.140	11.274	14.442	11.189	9.510	21.596	53.347	70.969	85.556	43.019	42.557
1970	13.445	12.560	15.729	11.666	9.882	22.722	52.059	65.738	77.800	42.567	43.738
1971	13.674	12.511	16.942	12.289	10.711	22.075	50.926	60.677	68.981	44.575	45.077
1972	14.700	13.856	16.835	13.672	12.168	23.011	50.556	58.197	63.588	47.722	46.068
1973	17.471	17.038	18.025	14.306	13.027	22.235	50.379	55.748	60.061	47.429	47.381
1974	18.852	18.391	19.432	13.982	12.665	22.210	51.648	56.243	59.595	49.891	49.164
1975	18.732	17.964	20.626	12.428	11.069	21.247	52.812	56.426	59.030	51.594	50.970
1976	19.550	18.817	21.236	14.858	13.572	22.714	53.049	56.453	58.828	52.085	51.346
1977	20.021	19.063	22.606	16.483	15.226	23.846	53.630	57.647	59.511	54.324	51.532
1978	22.132	21.193	24.496	17.911	16.591	25.546	55.210	59.092	60.019	57.700	53.216
1979	24.326	23.697	25.250	18.208	16.876	25.897	56.241	60.519	61.845	58.309	53.998
1980	26.946	26.521	26.826	16.999	15.623	25.319	57.337	63.390	64.541	61.573	53.958
1981	27.277	26.234	29.683	17.446	15.945	26.778	57.860	66.420	68.628	62.396	52.873
1982	25.193	23.863	28.860	17.220	15.544	28.205	58.876	68.989	73.814	59.402	52.898
1983	24.543	23.177	28.380	19.400	17.656	30.483	61.027	73.561	79.110	62.471	53.514
1984	26.546	25.009	30.911	24.122	21.927	38.126	63.078	75.829	82.971	61.279	55.444
1985	27.352	25.931	31.279	25.687	23.299	41.026	67.471	81.771	90.002	64.900	58.879
1986	29.451	27.263	35.820	27.883	25.687	41.488	71.573	86.407	95.766	67.130	62.669
1987	32.619	30.286	39.390	29.532	26.878	46.378	73.300	89.477	100.301	67.081	63.575
1988	37.844	35.992	42.939	30.693	27.966	47.954	74.220	88.010	99.826	63.499	65.933
1989	42.193	40.281	47.375	32.045	29.171	50.278	76.240	89.379	99.335	68.795	68.340
1990	45.989	43.671	52.372	33.191	30.020	53.564	78.655	91.185	99.305	74.465	71.112
1991	49.042	46.685	55.505	33.142	30.156	52.173	79.514	91.000	98.214	76.170	72.585
1992	52.410	50.177	58.496	35.466	32.999	50.768	79.885	89.351	93.351	81.218	74.156
1993	54.127	51.812	60.437	38.532	36.301	52.124	79.253	85.842	88.401	80.687	75.244
1994	58.847	56.853	64.275	43.129	41.149	54.901	79.245	82.555	84.072	79.525	77.197
1995	64.805	63.505	68.316	46.580	44.855	56.556	79.705	80.353	80.936	79.207	79.247
1996	70.186	69.106	73.101	50.631	49.060	59.514	80.507	79.423	79.856	78.577	81.090
1997	78.550	79.042	77.436	57.450	56.130	64.687	82.020	78.641	77.618	80.737	83.980
1998	80.343	80.805	79.303	64.165	62.780	71.721	83.759	77.758	75.978	81.374	87.291
1999	83.849	83.880	83.857	71.550	70.609	76.569	86.761	79.270	77.386	83.095	91.179
2000	91.054	93.182	86.102	80.871	80.086	84.955	88.519	79.661	76.986	85.066	93.744
2001	85.946	87.414	82.534	78.596	77.530	84.292	91.917	82.901	79.908	88.945	97.236
2002	84.224	84.268	84.115	81.270	80.409	85.837	96.192	88.953	85.782	95.357	100.473
2003	85.574	85.773	85.107	84.857	84.363	87.474	98.336	94.839	93.243	98.071	100.408
2004	93.698	93.025	95.237	94.231	93.660	97.252	99.668	98.710	98.535	99.067	100.234
2005	100.000	100.000	100.000	100.000	100.000	100.000	100.000	100.000	100.000	100.000	100.000
2006	108.962	109.416	107.935	106.086	105.904	107.059	101.359	102.127	101.588	103.237	100.910
2007	119.106	120.087	116.885	108.951	109.028	108.539	102.713	103.399	103.867	102.420	102.311
2008	126.255	127.649	123.095	106.113	105.189	111.167	105.605	110.900	111.653	109.326	102.611
2009	114.228	112.377	118.303	91.418	88.615	106.461	107.287	117.266	117.648	116.467	101.688
2010 <i>p</i>	127.613	128.772	125.143	102.898	101.594	110.203	108.449	122.906	122.289	124.194	100.361
2007: I	114.659	115.940	111.753	108.133	108.250	107.509	101.552	100.828	101.066	100.325	101.960
II	116.567	118.095	113.108	109.354	109.518	108.471	102.401	102.582	103.103	101.492	102.288
III	120.914	121.704	119.127	110.690	110.886	109.642	103.292	104.950	105.645	103.500	102.334
IV	124.286	124.609	123.554	107.624	107.458	108.535	103.606	105.236	105.655	104.363	102.661
2008: I	126.025	127.500	122.674	107.240	106.567	111.006	104.191	106.995	107.419	106.119	102.585
II	130.003	131.899	125.697	108.019	107.780	109.302	105.042	109.014	109.230	108.578	102.781
III	128.343	130.445	123.586	107.988	107.501	110.634	106.400	112.686	114.255	109.383	102.852
IV	120.649	120.753	120.424	101.204	98.908	113.727	106.787	114.906	115.707	113.223	102.225
2009: I	111.229	108.793	116.551	90.780	87.429	108.622	105.977	113.444	113.195	113.952	101.777
II	110.941	107.760	117.905	88.266	85.015	105.533	107.569	117.447	117.684	116.946	102.024
III	114.174	112.474	117.933	92.752	90.324	105.915	107.991	119.085	120.237	116.687	101.770
IV	120.569	120.484	120.822	93.874	91.691	105.772	107.613	119.091	119.477	118.283	101.179
2010: I	123.858	124.495	122.533	96.401	94.321	107.766	107.185	119.634	119.582	119.738	100.213
II	126.592	127.939	123.708	103.613	102.690	108.916	108.228	122.276	121.732	123.410	100.367
III	128.679	129.762	126.380	107.718	106.881	112.601	109.270	124.882	124.233	126.236	100.541
IV <i>p</i>	131.324	132.890	127.951	103.861	102.485	111.529	109.113	124.833	123.610	127.393	100.323

Source: Department of Commerce (Bureau of Economic Analysis).

TABLE B–7. Chain-type price indexes for gross domestic product, 1962–2010

[Index numbers, 2005=100, except as noted; quarterly data seasonally adjusted]

Year or quarter	Gross domestic product	Personal consumption expenditures			Gross private domestic investment					
		Total	Goods	Services	Total	Fixed investment				
						Total	Nonresidential			Residential
							Total	Structures	Equipment and software	
1962	19.071	19.023	29.404	14.090	26.548	25.465	33.788	11.537	53.878	13.003
1963	19.273	19.245	29.648	14.306	26.463	25.391	33.784	11.636	53.581	12.901
1964	19.572	19.527	29.971	14.573	26.613	25.545	33.955	11.801	53.558	13.003
1965	19.928	19.810	30.286	14.846	27.037	25.981	34.342	12.143	53.607	13.372
1966	20.493	20.313	30.953	15.277	27.592	26.528	34.854	12.580	53.749	13.857
1967	21.124	20.824	31.499	15.786	28.320	27.271	35.741	12.973	54.940	14.339
1968	22.022	21.636	32.597	16.468	29.378	28.367	36.999	13.621	56.416	15.100
1969	23.110	22.616	33.860	17.326	30.770	29.767	38.527	14.518	57.985	16.144
1970	24.328	23.674	35.152	18.287	32.072	31.047	40.348	15.473	60.119	16.666
1971	25.545	24.680	36.208	19.285	33.671	32.611	42.246	16.664	61.905	17.632
1972	26.647	25.525	37.135	20.103	35.077	34.009	43.673	17.863	62.651	18.703
1973	28.124	26.901	39.350	21.078	36.972	35.888	45.355	19.247	63.716	20.359
1974	30.669	29.703	44.261	22.868	40.648	39.422	49.733	21.910	68.414	22.460
1975	33.577	32.184	47.837	24.836	45.666	44.361	56.581	24.534	78.523	24.547
1976	35.505	33.950	49.709	26.558	48.190	46.932	59.718	25.741	83.143	26.124
1977	37.764	36.155	52.363	28.560	51.805	50.616	63.805	27.973	88.083	28.759
1978	40.413	38.687	55.576	30.779	56.030	54.891	68.078	30.675	92.731	32.281
1979	43.773	42.118	60.832	33.353	61.099	59.866	73.606	34.238	98.610	35.902
1980	47.776	46.641	67.644	36.805	66.836	65.468	80.098	37.421	107.032	39.789
1981	52.281	50.810	72.669	40.558	73.154	71.551	87.832	42.567	114.681	43.036
1982	55.467	53.615	74.650	43.712	76.899	75.468	92.670	45.927	119.155	45.340
1983	57.655	55.923	75.997	46.433	77.706	75.349	91.843	44.757	119.406	46.380
1984	59.823	58.038	77.435	48.850	77.256	75.790	91.621	45.147	118.364	47.714
1985	61.633	59.938	78.677	51.053	78.047	76.744	92.340	46.219	118.221	48.944
1986	63.003	61.399	78.309	53.378	79.737	78.579	93.908	47.106	120.094	50.994
1987	64.763	63.589	80.827	55.413	81.263	80.036	94.753	47.863	120.750	53.079
1988	66.990	66.121	82.958	58.127	83.120	82.111	96.857	49.895	122.256	54.913
1989	69.520	68.994	86.150	60.844	85.107	84.099	98.890	51.848	123.786	56.680
1990	72.213	72.147	89.678	63.812	86.747	85.808	100.783	53.522	125.389	58.011
1991	74.762	74.755	91.870	66.586	87.981	87.082	102.341	54.491	127.178	58.771
1992	76.537	76.954	92.978	69.240	87.672	86.831	101.488	54.502	125.681	59.486
1993	78.222	78.643	93.786	71.299	88.673	87.838	101.540	56.103	124.408	61.890
1994	79.867	80.265	94.740	73.205	89.828	89.023	102.029	58.089	123.695	64.069
1995	81.533	82.041	95.625	75.370	90.840	90.060	102.247	60.601	122.265	66.403
1996	83.083	83.826	96.676	77.479	90.455	89.817	101.054	62.141	119.323	67.828
1997	84.554	85.395	96.563	79.817	90.120	89.589	99.775	64.516	115.788	69.557
1998	85.507	86.207	95.106	81.695	89.109	88.756	97.587	67.480	110.641	71.412
1999	86.766	87.596	95.603	83.515	88.989	88.700	96.173	69.559	107.406	74.151
2000	88.648	89.777	97.520	85.824	89.954	89.751	96.219	72.298	106.114	77.415
2001	90.654	91.488	97.429	88.428	90.748	90.553	95.788	76.087	103.603	80.994
2002	92.113	92.736	96.430	90.807	91.118	90.924	95.363	79.292	101.494	83.002
2003	94.099	94.622	96.380	93.692	92.411	92.301	95.355	82.174	100.287	86.953
2004	96.769	97.098	97.867	96.687	95.632	95.541	96.834	88.441	99.897	93.296
2005	100.000	100.000	100.000	100.000	100.000	100.000	100.000	100.000	100.000	100.000
2006	103.263	102.746	101.508	103.411	104.371	104.419	103.534	112.922	100.194	106.081
2007	106.301	105.564	102.946	106.973	106.211	106.256	105.505	119.780	100.326	107.613
2008	108.598	109.061	106.262	110.566	106.977	107.053	106.984	125.460	100.083	106.361
2009	109.618	109.258	103.634	112.233	104.873	105.260	105.700	122.187	99.620	102.736
2010 ᵖ	110.664	111.123	105.409	114.159	103.023	103.613	103.711	120.409	97.710	102.356
2007: I	105.366	104.311	101.626	105.754	106.195	106.237	105.393	118.548	100.659	107.793
II	106.188	105.212	102.798	106.510	106.220	106.287	105.586	119.067	100.728	107.480
III	106.709	105.813	102.997	107.330	106.164	106.221	105.499	120.038	100.220	107.500
IV	106.940	106.919	104.362	108.298	106.264	106.279	105.541	121.466	99.696	107.681
2008: I	107.454	107.954	105.670	109.191	106.211	106.267	105.686	122.516	99.476	107.296
II	108.295	109.185	106.929	110.412	106.482	106.617	106.248	123.978	99.668	107.012
III	109.488	110.367	108.807	111.234	106.981	107.365	107.431	126.424	100.320	106.268
IV	109.154	108.736	103.643	111.428	108.235	107.961	108.571	128.922	100.868	104.867
2009: I	109.465	108.290	102.039	111.579	107.111	107.140	107.726	127.071	100.461	104.094
II	109.555	108.810	102.974	111.894	105.259	105.575	106.162	123.006	99.953	102.503
III	109.759	109.598	104.403	112.355	103.656	104.294	104.768	119.654	99.344	101.637
IV	109.693	110.333	105.120	113.102	103.466	104.030	104.144	119.017	98.721	102.712
2010: I	109.959	110.901	105.784	113.620	102.952	103.661	103.639	119.291	97.954	102.869
II	110.485	110.888	104.812	114.116	102.765	103.487	103.636	119.887	97.764	102.030
III	111.060	111.102	105.058	114.314	102.895	103.523	103.689	120.755	97.574	101.994
IV ᵖ	111.153	111.602	105.982	114.584	103.480	103.782	103.883	121.705	97.547	102.531

See next page for continuation of table.

[Index numbers, 2005=100, except as noted; quarterly data seasonally adjusted]

Year or quarter	Exports and imports of goods and services		Government consumption expenditures and gross investment					Final sales of domestic product	Gross domestic purchases [1]		Percent change [2]		
	Exports	Imports	Total	Federal			State and local		Total	Less food and energy	Gross domestic product	Gross domestic purchases [1]	
				Total	National defense	Non-defense						Total	Less food and energy
1962	27.940	19.706	13.398	14.202	13.897	14.783	12.743	18.920	18.654		1.4	1.3	
1963	27.877	20.088	13.690	14.506	14.209	15.037	13.028	19.125	18.871		1.1	1.2	
1964	28.107	20.512	14.070	14.995	14.620	15.798	13.293	19.424	19.175		1.6	1.6	
1965	29.001	20.797	14.444	15.379	15.024	16.104	13.662	19.781	19.507		1.8	1.7	
1966	29.877	21.281	15.044	15.914	15.535	16.708	14.334	20.346	20.054		2.8	2.8	
1967	31.022	21.364	15.671	16.386	15.994	17.215	15.137	20.978	20.637		3.1	2.9	
1968	31.698	21.689	16.520	17.287	16.834	18.327	15.945	21.880	21.508		4.3	4.2	
1969	32.771	22.254	17.517	18.226	17.757	19.284	17.013	22.968	22.563		4.9	4.9	
1970	34.027	23.570	18.945	19.699	19.116	21.143	18.411	24.182	23.778		5.3	5.4	
1971	35.283	25.017	20.421	21.383	20.810	22.746	19.720	25.394	25.000		5.0	5.1	
1972	36.928	26.770	21.989	23.471	23.209	23.892	20.896	26.494	26.112		4.3	4.4	
1973	41.784	31.423	23.594	25.080	24.911	25.231	22.495	27.968	27.623		5.5	5.8	
1974	51.478	44.957	25.977	27.315	27.223	27.245	24.970	30.493	30.459		9.0	10.3	
1975	56.738	48.699	28.586	30.158	29.880	30.505	27.410	33.389	33.300		9.5	9.3	
1976	58.600	50.165	30.469	32.302	32.057	32.549	29.114	35.320	35.208		5.7	5.7	
1977	60.987	54.586	32.583	34.742	34.486	34.993	31.005	37.582	37.586		6.4	6.8	
1978	64.703	58.440	34.670	36.888	36.908	36.514	33.042	40.232	40.252		7.0	7.1	
1979	72.490	68.434	37.575	39.727	39.853	39.100	35.976	43.576	43.797		8.3	8.0	
1980	79.843	85.240	41.669	43.900	44.179	42.906	40.002	47.557	48.408		9.1	10.5	
1981	85.744	89.822	45.768	48.165	48.542	46.917	43.975	52.029	52.864		9.4	9.2	
1982	86.138	86.794	48.775	51.434	51.953	49.825	46.786	55.233	55.859	55.358	6.1	5.7	
1983	86.478	83.541	50.717	53.218	53.775	51.501	48.857	57.414	57.817	57.517	3.9	3.5	3.9
1984	87.280	82.820	53.319	56.358	57.603	52.779	51.034	59.573	59.854	59.650	3.8	3.5	3.7
1985	84.609	80.100	54.974	57.635	58.696	54.574	53.002	61.414	61.553	61.521	3.0	2.8	3.1
1986	83.342	80.097	55.977	57.938	58.642	55.915	54.577	62.802	62.948	63.407	2.2	2.3	3.1
1987	85.451	84.948	57.541	58.642	59.236	56.953	56.849	64.552	64.923	65.447	2.8	3.1	3.2
1988	89.876	89.011	59.074	59.884	60.326	58.679	58.621	66.807	67.159	67.839	3.4	3.4	3.7
1989	91.373	90.956	60.924	61.504	61.882	60.497	60.654	69.338	69.706	70.282	3.8	3.8	3.6
1990	91.993	93.563	63.405	63.548	63.917	62.568	63.474	72.040	72.540	72.977	3.9	4.1	3.8
1991	93.212	92.783	65.606	66.070	66.222	65.672	65.443	74.592	74.917	75.470	3.5	3.3	3.4
1992	92.833	92.856	67.276	68.101	68.522	67.034	66.856	76.371	76.724	77.450	2.4	2.4	2.6
1993	92.808	92.144	68.949	69.830	69.712	70.002	68.494	78.057	78.339	79.156	2.2	2.1	2.2
1994	93.842	93.009	70.819	71.725	71.438	72.267	70.351	79.707	79.962	80.873	2.1	2.1	2.2
1995	95.997	95.557	72.753	73.717	73.161	74.830	72.252	81.379	81.674	82.647	2.1	2.1	2.2
1996	94.727	93.891	74.488	75.763	75.431	76.406	73.806	82.953	83.150	84.001	1.9	1.8	1.6
1997	93.103	90.627	75.854	77.047	76.517	78.095	75.219	84.449	84.397	85.266	1.8	1.5	1.5
1998	90.972	85.748	76.879	77.931	77.328	79.120	76.320	85.443	84.962	86.093	1.1	.7	1.0
1999	90.408	86.250	79.337	79.886	79.225	81.188	79.036	86.720	86.304	87.384	1.5	1.6	1.5
2000	91.999	89.963	82.513	82.524	81.821	83.907	82.482	88.623	88.463	89.163	2.2	2.5	2.0
2001	91.627	87.762	84.764	84.201	83.484	85.612	85.019	90.631	90.123	90.769	2.3	1.9	1.8
2002	91.253	86.784	87.003	87.318	86.624	88.689	86.810	92.089	91.422	92.300	1.6	1.4	1.7
2003	93.216	89.796	90.650	91.024	90.659	91.774	90.425	94.089	93.550	94.177	2.2	2.3	2.0
2004	96.517	94.144	94.531	95.335	94.895	96.234	94.062	96.759	96.400	96.762	2.8	3.0	2.7
2005	100.000	100.000	100.000	100.000	100.000	100.000	100.000	100.000	100.000	100.000	3.3	3.7	3.3
2006	103.447	104.144	104.842	104.107	104.421	103.468	105.276	103.266	103.380	103.157	3.3	3.4	3.2
2007	106.902	107.531	109.863	107.753	108.249	106.743	111.112	106.308	106.428	105.963	2.9	2.9	2.7
2008	111.874	118.685	115.009	111.119	112.109	109.077	117.349	108.608	109.813	108.668	2.2	3.2	2.6
2009	105.877	105.987	114.644	110.895	111.342	109.984	116.892	109.647	109.614	109.422	.9	–.2	.7
2010 *p*	110.309	112.851	116.815	112.745	113.519	111.159	119.279	110.713	111.086	110.572	1.0	1.3	1.1
2007: I	105.319	104.892	108.223	106.849	107.113	106.321	109.033	105.371	105.297	105.138	4.4	4.4	3.8
II	106.465	105.936	109.453	107.773	108.191	106.926	110.445	106.200	106.118	105.662	3.2	3.2	2.0
III	107.154	106.671	110.245	107.882	108.434	106.755	111.644	106.720	106.653	106.161	2.0	2.0	1.9
IV	108.672	112.623	111.529	108.509	109.259	106.969	113.326	106.941	107.644	106.890	.9	3.8	2.8
2008: I	110.719	117.728	113.500	110.230	110.975	108.695	115.451	107.460	108.693	107.706	1.9	4.0	3.1
II	113.553	122.345	115.290	111.515	112.673	109.122	117.555	108.310	109.887	108.561	3.2	4.5	3.2
III	115.137	122.999	116.391	111.958	113.245	109.294	119.075	109.539	110.953	109.261	4.5	3.9	2.6
IV	108.089	111.669	114.853	110.772	111.544	109.198	117.313	109.123	109.720	109.146	–1.2	–4.4	–.4
2009: I	104.841	103.127	114.356	110.979	111.562	109.794	116.356	109.466	109.163	109.096	1.1	–2.0	–.2
II	105.031	103.719	114.516	110.743	111.063	110.096	116.779	109.579	109.326	109.324	.3	.6	.8
III	106.212	105.879	114.635	110.716	111.153	109.822	116.998	109.809	109.702	109.429	.7	1.4	.4
IV	107.424	111.222	115.067	111.141	111.590	110.222	117.434	109.736	110.265	109.839	–.2	2.1	1.5
2010: I	108.771	114.514	116.358	112.375	113.046	110.997	118.760	110.020	110.838	110.274	1.0	2.1	1.6
II	110.060	112.234	116.606	112.615	113.377	111.053	119.014	110.552	110.852	110.491	1.9	.1	.8
III *p*	110.122	109.892	116.706	112.756	113.529	111.170	119.083	111.117	111.034	110.613	2.1	.7	.4
IV *p*	112.282	114.764	117.589	113.234	114.124	111.415	120.258	111.163	111.618	110.910	.3	2.1	1.1

[1] Gross domestic product (GDP) less exports of goods and services plus imports of goods and services.
[2] Quarterly percent changes are at annual rates.

Source: Department of Commerce (Bureau of Economic Analysis).

TABLE B–8. Gross domestic product by major type of product, 1962–2010

[Billions of dollars; quarterly data at seasonally adjusted annual rates]

Year or quarter	Gross domestic product	Final sales of domestic product	Change in private inventories	Goods							Services[2]	Structures
				Total			Durable goods		Nondurable goods			
				Total	Final sales	Change in private inventories	Final sales	Change in private inventories[1]	Final sales	Change in private inventories[1]		
1962	585.7	579.6	6.1	247.4	241.3	6.1	102.0	3.4	139.3	2.7	270.4	67.8
1963	617.8	612.1	5.6	258.5	252.9	5.6	108.6	2.6	144.3	3.0	286.6	72.7
1964	663.6	658.8	4.8	277.8	273.0	4.8	119.3	3.8	153.7	1.0	307.4	78.4
1965	719.1	709.9	9.2	304.3	295.1	9.2	131.6	6.2	163.5	3.0	330.1	84.7
1966	787.7	774.1	13.6	337.1	323.5	13.6	145.4	10.0	178.0	3.6	362.6	88.0
1967	832.4	822.6	9.9	345.4	335.5	9.9	150.0	4.8	185.5	5.0	397.5	89.6
1968	909.8	900.8	9.1	370.8	361.7	9.1	162.8	4.5	198.9	4.5	439.1	100.0
1969	984.4	975.3	9.2	397.6	388.4	9.2	175.7	6.0	212.7	3.2	478.6	108.3
1970	1,038.3	1,036.3	2.0	408.7	406.7	2.0	178.6	−.2	228.2	2.2	519.9	109.7
1971	1,126.8	1,118.6	8.3	432.6	424.4	8.3	186.7	2.9	237.7	5.3	565.8	128.4
1972	1,237.9	1,228.8	9.1	472.0	462.9	9.1	208.4	6.4	254.5	2.7	619.0	146.9
1973	1,382.3	1,366.4	15.9	547.1	531.2	15.9	243.6	13.0	287.6	2.9	672.2	162.9
1974	1,499.5	1,485.5	14.0	588.0	574.0	14.0	262.4	10.9	311.7	3.1	745.8	165.6
1975	1,637.7	1,644.0	−6.3	628.6	634.8	−6.3	293.2	−7.5	341.6	1.2	842.4	166.7
1976	1,824.6	1,807.5	17.1	706.6	689.5	17.1	330.9	10.8	358.6	6.3	926.8	191.2
1977	2,030.1	2,007.8	22.3	773.5	751.2	22.3	374.6	9.5	376.6	12.8	1,029.9	226.8
1978	2,293.8	2,268.0	25.8	872.6	846.8	25.8	424.9	18.2	422.0	7.6	1,147.2	273.9
1979	2,562.2	2,544.2	18.0	977.2	959.2	18.0	483.9	12.8	475.3	5.2	1,271.7	313.3
1980	2,788.1	2,794.5	−6.3	1,035.2	1,041.5	−6.3	512.3	−2.3	529.2	−4.0	1,431.6	321.3
1981	3,126.8	3,097.0	29.8	1,167.3	1,137.5	29.8	554.8	7.3	582.6	22.5	1,606.9	352.6
1982	3,253.2	3,268.1	−14.9	1,148.8	1,163.7	−14.9	552.5	−16.0	611.2	1.1	1,759.9	344.5
1983	3,534.6	3,540.4	−5.8	1,226.9	1,232.6	−5.8	592.3	2.5	640.3	−8.2	1,939.1	368.7
1984	3,930.9	3,865.5	65.4	1,402.2	1,336.8	65.4	665.9	41.4	670.9	24.0	2,102.9	425.8
1985	4,217.5	4,195.6	21.8	1,452.8	1,431.0	21.8	727.9	4.4	703.1	17.4	2,305.9	458.7
1986	4,460.1	4,453.5	6.6	1,491.2	1,484.7	6.6	758.3	−1.9	726.4	8.4	2,488.7	480.1
1987	4,736.4	4,709.2	27.1	1,570.7	1,543.6	27.1	785.3	22.9	758.3	4.2	2,668.0	497.6
1988	5,100.4	5,081.9	18.5	1,703.7	1,685.2	18.5	863.3	22.7	821.9	−4.3	2,881.7	515.0
1989	5,482.1	5,454.5	27.7	1,851.9	1,824.2	27.7	939.7	20.0	884.5	7.7	3,101.2	529.0
1990	5,800.5	5,786.0	14.5	1,923.1	1,908.5	14.5	973.2	7.7	935.3	6.8	3,343.9	533.5
1991	5,992.1	5,992.5	−.4	1,943.5	1,943.9	−.4	967.6	−13.6	976.3	13.2	3,548.6	499.9
1992	6,342.3	6,326.0	16.3	2,031.5	2,015.1	16.3	1,010.7	−3.0	1,004.4	19.3	3,788.1	522.7
1993	6,667.4	6,646.5	20.8	2,124.2	2,103.4	20.8	1,072.9	17.1	1,030.4	3.7	3,985.1	558.1
1994	7,085.2	7,021.4	63.8	2,290.7	2,226.9	63.8	1,149.8	35.7	1,077.1	28.1	4,187.2	607.3
1995	7,414.7	7,383.5	31.2	2,379.5	2,348.3	31.2	1,225.9	33.6	1,122.4	−2.4	4,396.7	638.5
1996	7,838.5	7,807.7	30.8	2,516.3	2,485.5	30.8	1,321.0	19.1	1,164.5	11.7	4,625.5	696.7
1997	8,332.4	8,261.4	71.0	2,701.2	2,630.2	71.0	1,430.7	40.0	1,199.5	31.0	4,882.5	748.6
1998	8,793.5	8,729.8	63.7	2,819.2	2,755.5	63.7	1,524.2	39.3	1,231.3	24.4	5,159.7	814.5
1999	9,353.5	9,292.7	60.8	2,990.1	2,929.3	60.8	1,633.8	37.4	1,295.5	23.4	5,485.1	878.2
2000	9,951.5	9,896.9	54.5	3,124.5	3,070.0	54.5	1,734.4	35.6	1,335.6	19.0	5,878.0	949.0
2001	10,286.2	10,324.5	−38.3	3,077.6	3,115.9	−38.3	1,731.5	−44.4	1,384.4	6.2	6,208.7	999.9
2002	10,642.3	10,630.3	12.0	3,101.2	3,089.1	12.0	1,678.9	17.7	1,410.3	−5.6	6,535.5	1,005.7
2003	11,142.1	11,125.8	16.4	3,170.1	3,153.7	16.4	1,694.2	13.0	1,459.5	3.3	6,891.7	1,080.4
2004	11,867.8	11,802.8	64.9	3,333.9	3,269.0	64.9	1,748.0	37.3	1,521.1	27.6	7,319.3	1,214.5
2005	12,638.4	12,588.4	50.0	3,472.9	3,422.9	50.0	1,855.9	35.2	1,567.0	14.7	7,802.1	1,363.4
2006	13,398.9	13,339.0	60.0	3,660.7	3,600.7	60.0	1,951.5	25.9	1,649.3	34.0	8,285.5	1,452.7
2007	14,061.8	14,032.7	29.1	3,836.9	3,807.8	29.1	2,058.2	11.2	1,749.6	17.9	8,792.1	1,432.8
2008	14,369.1	14,410.2	−41.1	3,763.5	3,804.6	−41.1	2,031.8	−25.7	1,772.9	−15.4	9,251.0	1,354.5
2009	14,119.0	14,246.3	−127.2	3,687.3	3,814.5	−127.2	1,915.9	−114.4	1,898.6	−12.8	9,320.5	1,111.3
2010 ᵖ	14,660.2	14,591.6	68.5	4,064.7	3,996.1	68.5	2,025.9	41.8	1,970.3	26.7	9,571.3	1,024.2
2007: I	13,789.5	13,772.5	17.0	3,748.0	3,731.0	17.0	2,010.4	11.4	1,720.6	5.6	8,608.1	1,433.4
II	14,008.2	13,960.6	47.5	3,839.2	3,791.7	47.5	2,051.3	5.8	1,740.3	41.7	8,720.7	1,448.3
III	14,158.2	14,118.8	39.4	3,869.5	3,830.1	39.4	2,063.1	7.5	1,767.0	31.9	8,849.3	1,439.4
IV	14,291.3	14,278.8	12.6	3,891.1	3,878.5	12.6	2,108.1	19.9	1,770.4	−7.4	8,990.1	1,410.1
2008: I	14,328.4	14,342.1	−13.7	3,834.1	3,847.8	−13.7	2,088.0	−19.4	1,759.9	5.7	9,123.2	1,371.0
II	14,471.8	14,495.1	−23.3	3,836.8	3,860.1	−23.3	2,072.4	−33.1	1,787.6	9.8	9,256.0	1,379.0
III	14,484.9	14,514.3	−29.4	3,799.9	3,829.4	−29.4	2,041.1	−2.4	1,788.2	−27.0	9,326.5	1,358.4
IV	14,191.2	14,289.2	−98.0	3,583.2	3,681.3	−98.0	1,925.5	−48.0	1,755.8	−50.0	9,298.4	1,309.6
2009: I	14,049.7	14,191.6	−141.9	3,609.3	3,751.2	−141.9	1,901.1	−143.3	1,850.1	1.4	9,258.2	1,182.2
II	14,034.5	14,214.0	−179.5	3,621.9	3,801.4	−179.5	1,906.4	−144.5	1,895.0	−35.0	9,296.5	1,116.1
III	14,114.7	14,258.0	−143.3	3,691.6	3,834.8	−143.3	1,920.7	−109.6	1,914.1	−33.7	9,326.8	1,096.3
IV	14,277.3	14,321.5	−44.2	3,826.5	3,870.7	−44.2	1,935.5	−60.2	1,935.2	16.0	9,400.4	1,050.4
2010: I	14,446.4	14,396.4	50.0	3,970.1	3,920.1	50.0	1,974.2	26.7	1,945.9	23.2	9,466.2	1,010.1
II	14,578.7	14,498.3	80.4	3,994.2	3,913.8	80.4	1,993.2	55.3	1,920.6	25.1	9,548.2	1,036.3
III	14,745.1	14,606.5	138.6	4,120.6	3,982.0	138.6	2,026.3	77.4	1,955.7	61.2	9,605.3	1,019.2
IV ᵖ	14,870.4	14,865.2	5.2	4,173.9	4,168.7	5.2	2,109.8	7.8	2,058.9	−2.6	9,665.3	1,031.2

[1] Estimates for durable and nondurable goods for 1996 and earlier periods are based on the Standard Industrial Classification (SIC); later estimates are based on the North American Industry Classification System (NAICS).

[2] Includes government consumption expenditures, which are for services (such as education and national defense) produced by government. In current dollars, these services are valued at their cost of production.

Source: Department of Commerce (Bureau of Economic Analysis).

[Billions of chained (2005) dollars; quarterly data at seasonally adjusted annual rates]

Year or quarter	Gross domestic product	Final sales of domestic product	Change in private inventories	Goods Total — Total	Goods Total — Final sales	Goods Total — Change in private inventories	Durable goods — Final sales	Durable goods — Change in private inventories[1]	Nondurable goods — Final sales	Nondurable goods — Change in private inventories[1]	Services[2]	Structures
1962	3,072.4	3,064.9	21.9	649.3							2,007.2	554.2
1963	3,206.7	3,202.6	20.3	675.1							2,090.3	591.7
1964	3,392.3	3,393.7	17.3	720.3							2,189.4	631.5
1965	3,610.1	3,590.7	32.9	780.7							2,299.1	663.1
1966	3,845.3	3,806.6	47.1	848.6							2,441.0	663.9
1967	3,942.5	3,923.3	33.9	850.9							2,576.9	654.2
1968	4,133.4	4,119.4	30.8	884.9							2,712.7	694.5
1969	4,261.8	4,248.6	30.3	915.4							2,800.8	703.3
1970	4,269.9	4,287.9	5.6	907.7							2,858.2	673.0
1971	4,413.3	4,407.4	25.0	934.7							2,926.8	735.5
1972	4,647.7	4,640.6	25.7	998.5							3,034.7	790.2
1973	4,917.0	4,888.2	39.0	1,104.7							3,125.5	807.1
1974	4,889.9	4,874.1	29.1	1,094.1							3,194.6	723.4
1975	4,879.5	4,926.3	–12.8	1,066.8							3,309.1	657.6
1976	5,141.3	5,120.2	34.3	1,150.5							3,400.2	719.2
1977	5,377.7	5,344.9	43.1	1,205.8							3,517.0	787.2
1978	5,677.6	5,639.7	45.6	1,286.8							3,651.5	862.8
1979	5,855.0	5,841.2	28.0	1,340.0							3,740.1	887.4
1980	5,839.0	5,878.7	–9.3	1,328.3							3,811.2	823.0
1981	5,987.2	5,959.5	39.0	1,388.2							3,887.4	811.9
1982	5,870.9	5,923.3	–19.7	1,316.8							3,956.9	742.6
1983	6,136.2	6,172.9	–7.7	1,373.7							4,120.1	796.3
1984	6,577.1	6,495.6	78.3	1,544.0							4,234.1	903.9
1985	6,849.3	6,838.9	25.4	1,581.0							4,448.8	951.0
1986	7,086.5	7,098.7	8.5	1,627.1							4,635.2	965.1
1987	7,313.3	7,296.2	33.2	1,692.7							4,785.3	969.3
1988	7,613.9	7,607.8	21.9	1,798.0							4,961.3	967.6
1989	7,885.9	7,867.5	30.6	1,900.2							5,114.8	961.0
1990	8,033.9	8,032.7	16.6	1,920.1							5,269.3	941.9
1991	8,015.1	8,034.8	–1.4	1,887.6							5,363.0	869.1
1992	8,287.1	8,284.3	17.9	1,964.7							5,521.7	902.4
1993	8,523.4	8,515.3	22.3	2,040.3							5,647.9	930.5
1994	8,870.7	8,809.2	69.3	2,183.8							5,781.2	978.4
1995	9,093.7	9,073.2	32.1	2,264.0	2,241.1	32.1	1,023.0	31.4	1,260.0	–3.3	5,902.5	988.9
1996	9,433.9	9,412.5	31.2	2,387.7	2,363.9	31.2	1,110.9	17.9	1,286.7	12.5	6,045.3	1,053.1
1997	9,854.3	9,782.6	77.4	2,573.9	2,509.8	77.4	1,222.7	40.2	1,309.9	36.1	6,208.3	1,097.8
1998	10,283.5	10,217.1	71.6	2,723.0	2,663.0	71.6	1,341.5	40.6	1,334.3	29.5	6,421.7	1,155.1
1999	10,779.8	10,715.7	68.5	2,914.0	2,855.8	68.5	1,476.4	39.5	1,385.0	27.7	6,663.6	1,202.2
2000	11,226.0	11,167.5	60.2	3,056.3	3,002.8	60.2	1,590.5	37.7	1,411.8	21.4	6,918.7	1,245.3
2001	11,347.2	11,391.7	–41.8	3,006.9	3,043.6	–41.8	1,614.7	–46.4	1,428.2	7.3	7,095.4	1,254.1
2002	11,553.0	11,543.5	12.8	3,059.2	3,047.4	12.8	1,596.7	18.1	1,451.9	–6.4	7,275.6	1,223.2
2003	11,840.7	11,824.8	17.3	3,164.0	3,146.1	17.3	1,656.3	13.5	1,490.5	3.6	7,416.0	1,263.6
2004	12,263.8	12,198.2	66.3	3,326.2	3,260.9	66.3	1,740.4	38.1	1,520.6	28.1	7,613.1	1,325.6
2005	12,638.4	12,588.4	50.0	3,472.9	3,422.9	50.0	1,855.9	35.2	1,567.0	14.7	7,802.1	1,363.4
2006	12,976.2	12,917.1	59.4	3,652.7	3,593.5	59.4	1,964.4	25.2	1,629.2	34.1	7,985.0	1,341.1
2007	13,228.9	13,200.0	27.7	3,803.3	3,775.7	27.7	2,101.6	10.8	1,675.8	16.9	8,169.6	1,267.0
2008	13,228.8	13,268.1	–37.6	3,784.4	3,829.9	–37.6	2,119.8	–23.4	1,710.9	–14.7	8,291.4	1,166.9
2009	12,880.6	12,992.8	–113.1	3,642.4	3,766.9	–113.1	2,005.3	–106.7	1,754.8	–9.6	8,278.2	973.6
2010 ᴾ	13,248.7	13,179.5	60.4	4,045.4	3,971.2	60.4	2,155.7	37.9	1,813.3	23.1	8,345.9	904.7
2007: I	13,089.3	13,071.1	17.3	3,723.0	3,706.4	17.3	2,033.8	11.1	1,672.8	6.1	8,097.1	1,276.3
II	13,194.1	13,146.4	44.9	3,779.9	3,732.4	44.9	2,082.4	5.7	1,651.8	38.6	8,136.7	1,286.1
III	13,268.5	13,230.4	36.1	3,810.8	3,773.4	36.1	2,115.3	7.1	1,660.6	28.5	8,197.4	1,270.9
IV	13,363.5	13,352.2	12.6	3,899.6	3,890.7	12.6	2,174.8	19.2	1,718.1	–5.8	8,247.1	1,234.9
2008: I	13,339.2	13,346.2	–8.2	3,887.6	3,898.4	–8.2	2,162.2	–17.8	1,737.6	8.4	8,276.9	1,195.0
II	13,359.0	13,382.4	–20.6	3,886.2	3,914.6	–20.6	2,170.8	–29.3	1,745.2	6.6	8,298.8	1,194.4
III	13,223.5	13,249.6	–27.4	3,776.9	3,807.9	–27.4	2,134.2	–1.6	1,677.0	–24.4	8,294.7	1,165.3
IV	12,993.7	13,094.1	–94.3	3,587.0	3,698.8	–94.3	2,012.2	–44.9	1,684.0	–49.2	8,294.9	1,112.8
2009: I	12,832.6	12,964.2	–125.8	3,565.5	3,711.3	–125.8	1,980.7	–133.7	1,724.2	3.5	8,262.9	1,010.8
II	12,810.0	12,971.4	–161.8	3,562.3	3,740.2	–161.8	1,987.6	–135.3	1,745.4	–29.8	8,280.2	975.0
III	12,860.8	12,984.5	–128.2	3,621.2	3,758.4	–128.2	2,016.4	–102.1	1,737.1	–28.5	8,276.3	974.9
IV	13,019.0	13,051.1	–36.7	3,820.4	3,857.8	–36.7	2,036.4	–55.6	1,812.4	16.3	8,293.2	933.5
2010: I	13,138.8	13,085.5	44.1	3,994.7	3,937.8	44.1	2,091.0	24.4	1,839.0	20.0	8,293.4	895.8
II	13,194.9	13,114.7	68.8	3,987.0	3,900.7	68.8	2,118.0	50.0	1,780.3	19.8	8,331.5	918.7
III	13,278.5	13,145.3	121.4	4,058.5	3,913.9	121.4	2,157.7	69.9	1,758.6	52.3	8,367.9	900.0
IV ᴾ	13,382.6	13,372.6	7.2	4,141.7	4,132.4	7.2	2,256.1	7.0	1,875.4	.5	8,390.8	904.4

[1] Estimates for durable and nondurable goods for 1996 and earlier periods are based on the Standard Industrial Classification (SIC); later estimates are based on the North American Industry Classification System (NAICS).

[2] Includes government consumption expenditures, which are for services (such as education and national defense) produced by government. In current dollars, these services are valued at their cost of production.

Source: Department of Commerce (Bureau of Economic Analysis).

Table B–10. Gross value added by sector, 1962–2010

[Billions of dollars; quarterly data at seasonally adjusted annual rates]

Year or quarter	Gross domestic product	Business [1]			Households and institutions			General government [3]			Adden-dum: Gross housing value added
		Total	Nonfarm [1]	Farm	Total	House-holds	Nonprofit institu-tions serving house-holds [2]	Total	Federal	State and local	
1962	585.7	463.9	445.5	18.4	51.0	37.0	14.0	70.7	36.5	34.2	46.0
1963	617.8	488.0	469.5	18.5	54.3	39.1	15.2	75.5	38.4	37.1	48.9
1964	663.6	524.9	507.5	17.3	57.7	41.2	16.5	81.1	40.7	40.4	51.6
1965	719.1	570.7	550.7	19.9	61.8	43.6	18.2	86.6	42.4	44.2	54.9
1966	787.7	624.3	603.5	20.8	66.6	46.2	20.4	96.8	47.2	49.6	58.2
1967	832.4	653.6	633.5	20.1	71.8	49.1	22.7	107.0	51.5	55.5	62.1
1968	909.8	713.5	693.0	20.5	77.5	51.9	25.6	118.8	56.3	62.5	65.9
1969	984.4	769.1	746.3	22.8	85.4	56.0	29.4	130.0	59.9	70.0	71.3
1970	1,038.3	802.2	778.5	23.7	92.6	59.8	32.8	143.5	64.0	79.5	76.7
1971	1,126.8	868.3	842.9	25.4	102.2	65.5	36.7	156.4	67.7	88.6	83.9
1972	1,237.9	957.1	927.5	29.7	111.4	70.8	40.5	169.4	71.5	97.9	91.1
1973	1,382.3	1,077.4	1,030.6	46.8	121.7	76.5	45.2	183.2	73.9	109.3	98.3
1974	1,499.5	1,164.5	1,120.3	44.2	133.6	83.0	50.6	201.3	79.6	121.8	106.8
1975	1,637.7	1,265.8	1,220.1	45.6	147.5	90.8	56.7	224.5	87.3	137.2	117.2
1976	1,824.6	1,420.7	1,377.7	43.0	160.5	98.7	61.8	243.5	93.8	149.7	126.6
1977	2,030.1	1,590.0	1,546.5	43.5	175.5	107.9	67.6	264.6	102.0	162.6	140.5
1978	2,293.8	1,809.4	1,758.7	50.7	196.9	121.3	75.6	287.5	109.7	177.8	155.5
1979	2,562.2	2,028.5	1,968.4	60.1	220.8	136.0	84.8	313.0	117.6	195.4	172.9
1980	2,788.1	2,186.1	2,134.7	51.4	253.5	156.5	97.0	348.5	131.2	217.3	199.8
1981	3,126.8	2,454.0	2,389.0	65.0	287.5	177.8	109.7	385.3	147.4	237.9	228.8
1982	3,253.2	2,514.9	2,454.5	60.4	319.3	196.7	122.7	419.0	161.2	257.7	255.7
1983	3,534.6	2,741.1	2,696.2	44.9	348.2	212.5	135.6	445.4	171.2	274.1	277.7
1984	3,930.9	3,065.5	3,001.3	64.2	380.3	231.0	149.3	485.1	192.1	293.1	301.3
1985	4,217.5	3,283.9	3,220.5	63.4	410.1	250.3	159.8	523.4	205.0	318.4	333.1
1986	4,460.1	3,461.5	3,402.1	59.5	442.3	268.0	174.3	556.3	212.6	343.7	359.7
1987	4,736.4	3,662.0	3,600.5	61.5	482.8	288.0	194.8	591.5	223.3	368.2	385.5
1988	5,100.4	3,940.2	3,879.4	60.7	529.7	313.1	216.6	630.6	234.8	395.8	415.3
1989	5,482.1	4,235.7	4,162.0	73.8	574.2	337.2	237.0	672.2	246.4	425.8	443.4
1990	5,800.5	4,453.9	4,376.6	77.3	624.0	363.3	260.6	722.7	258.8	463.9	477.8
1991	5,992.1	4,558.6	4,488.0	70.6	665.9	383.7	282.2	767.6	274.8	492.8	508.1
1992	6,342.3	4,829.2	4,748.9	80.4	711.1	405.3	305.9	801.9	282.0	519.9	538.6
1993	6,667.4	5,084.1	5,012.7	71.4	752.1	428.3	323.8	831.2	285.2	546.0	562.9
1994	7,085.2	5,425.2	5,341.3	83.9	800.0	461.3	338.7	859.9	285.2	574.7	602.6
1995	7,414.7	5,677.8	5,608.7	69.1	852.1	492.2	359.9	884.8	283.6	601.2	640.7
1996	7,838.5	6,030.2	5,936.9	93.3	897.0	519.8	377.2	911.3	287.6	623.7	671.3
1997	8,332.4	6,442.8	6,354.9	87.9	949.2	550.9	398.3	940.3	290.0	650.3	708.6
1998	8,793.5	6,810.8	6,731.6	79.2	1,010.1	583.9	426.3	972.5	292.2	680.3	745.3
1999	9,353.5	7,249.0	7,177.8	71.2	1,082.9	628.4	454.5	1,021.6	300.4	721.2	798.3
2000	9,951.5	7,715.5	7,641.9	73.6	1,157.2	673.5	483.7	1,078.8	315.1	763.7	849.9
2001	10,286.2	7,913.6	7,837.4	76.2	1,232.9	719.5	513.4	1,139.6	324.9	814.7	904.4
2002	10,642.3	8,132.8	8,060.5	72.3	1,298.0	746.0	552.1	1,211.4	351.8	859.6	932.5
2003	11,142.1	8,502.8	8,410.3	92.4	1,347.2	762.7	584.5	1,292.2	382.9	909.3	938.2
2004	11,867.8	9,084.6	8,966.4	118.3	1,423.8	806.0	617.7	1,359.3	412.0	947.3	988.7
2005	12,638.4	9,695.5	9,593.5	102.0	1,506.4	864.4	642.0	1,436.5	438.7	997.7	1,054.0
2006	13,398.9	10,284.1	10,191.1	93.1	1,602.9	924.8	678.1	1,512.0	460.6	1,051.3	1,130.8
2007	14,061.8	10,771.4	10,656.5	114.9	1,685.8	968.1	717.8	1,604.6	486.0	1,118.6	1,200.6
2008	14,369.1	10,863.5	10,732.3	131.1	1,808.0	1,048.8	759.2	1,697.6	517.1	1,180.5	1,302.6
2009	14,119.0	10,520.8	10,416.8	104.0	1,838.1	1,059.0	779.1	1,760.2	551.7	1,208.5	1,331.7
2010 ᵖ	14,660.2	11,018.7	10,893.5	125.2	1,840.4	1,043.0	797.4	1,801.0	579.2	1,221.8	1,323.4
2007: I	13,789.5	10,559.6	10,449.9	109.7	1,650.8	946.9	703.8	1,579.2	481.2	1,097.9	1,168.6
II	14,008.2	10,748.6	10,639.1	109.5	1,665.0	953.0	712.0	1,594.5	484.8	1,109.8	1,182.4
III	14,158.2	10,851.5	10,739.1	112.4	1,694.5	973.0	721.5	1,612.3	487.6	1,124.6	1,209.5
IV	14,291.3	10,925.9	10,797.9	128.0	1,733.1	999.4	733.7	1,632.4	490.5	1,141.9	1,242.0
2008: I	14,328.4	10,895.2	10,750.3	144.9	1,768.0	1,020.6	747.4	1,665.2	505.9	1,159.3	1,265.9
II	14,471.8	10,986.5	10,852.8	133.7	1,799.0	1,045.7	753.3	1,686.3	513.6	1,172.7	1,294.8
III	14,484.9	10,952.9	10,822.4	130.5	1,823.0	1,060.1	762.8	1,709.0	520.7	1,188.3	1,317.0
IV	14,191.2	10,619.1	10,503.7	115.5	1,842.1	1,068.8	773.4	1,729.9	528.2	1,201.7	1,332.9
2009: I	14,049.7	10,471.6	10,368.2	103.4	1,833.3	1,066.4	766.9	1,744.8	543.0	1,201.7	1,335.1
II	14,034.5	10,442.6	10,342.0	100.6	1,829.9	1,052.2	777.6	1,762.0	551.9	1,210.1	1,324.4
III	14,114.7	10,508.0	10,407.8	100.3	1,843.0	1,060.5	782.5	1,763.6	553.1	1,210.5	1,335.1
IV	14,277.3	10,660.9	10,549.3	111.6	1,846.1	1,056.8	789.3	1,770.3	558.6	1,211.7	1,332.2
2010: I	14,446.4	10,823.2	10,710.6	112.6	1,833.8	1,046.4	787.4	1,789.4	572.7	1,216.7	1,324.2
II	14,578.7	10,938.2	10,822.2	116.0	1,836.8	1,044.7	792.1	1,803.7	580.6	1,223.1	1,323.8
III	14,745.1	11,102.7	10,973.2	129.5	1,840.4	1,041.0	799.4	1,802.0	579.9	1,222.1	1,322.4
IV ᵖ	14,870.4	11,210.8	11,067.8	142.9	1,850.7	1,039.9	810.7	1,808.9	583.5	1,225.4	1,323.4

[1] Gross domestic business value added equals gross domestic product excluding gross value added of households and institutions and of general government. Nonfarm value added equals gross domestic business value added excluding gross farm value added.
[2] Equals compensation of employees of nonprofit institutions, the rental value of nonresidential fixed assets owned and used by nonprofit institutions serving households, and rental income of persons for tenant-occupied housing owned by nonprofit institutions.
[3] Equals compensation of general government employees plus general government consumption of fixed capital.

Source: Department of Commerce (Bureau of Economic Analysis).

TABLE B–11. Real gross value added by sector, 1962–2010

[Billions of chained (2005) dollars; quarterly data at seasonally adjusted annual rates]

| Year or quarter | Gross domestic product | Business [1] | | | Households and institutions | | | General government [3] | | | Adden-dum: Gross housing value added |
		Total	Nonfarm [1]	Farm	Total	House-holds	Nonprofit institu-tions serving house-holds [2]	Total	Federal	State and local	
1962	3,072.4	2,092.6	2,058.9	24.9	368.9	217.9	146.6	721.3	393.2	338.5	265.9
1963	3,206.7	2,189.2	2,155.2	25.7	384.0	226.9	152.6	742.8	396.7	356.1	278.9
1964	3,392.3	2,328.0	2,299.7	24.9	399.9	236.0	159.4	768.4	400.7	377.5	291.6
1965	3,610.1	2,492.3	2,462.6	26.5	419.7	246.9	168.6	794.2	403.4	400.5	307.1
1966	3,845.3	2,661.0	2,638.6	25.5	438.9	256.8	178.5	843.9	429.9	424.2	320.9
1967	3,942.5	2,712.0	2,684.1	27.6	457.1	267.1	186.6	888.7	457.9	442.1	335.6
1968	4,133.4	2,846.8	2,824.8	26.6	480.1	274.6	204.9	923.6	465.7	468.6	348.3
1969	4,261.8	2,934.0	2,910.9	27.5	501.2	285.9	214.9	947.2	467.1	490.0	364.6
1970	4,269.9	2,933.3	2,907.7	28.3	510.2	292.6	216.7	950.8	447.1	511.7	376.6
1971	4,413.3	3,046.0	3,018.2	29.8	531.7	305.9	224.5	952.4	426.5	532.5	393.6
1972	4,647.7	3,242.1	3,218.8	29.8	554.8	319.1	234.4	950.6	405.8	550.9	412.5
1973	4,917.0	3,469.4	3,454.8	29.5	574.6	330.6	242.7	954.9	390.7	570.2	427.8
1974	4,889.9	3,417.5	3,404.1	28.8	597.7	345.0	251.0	974.4	389.4	590.9	448.5
1975	4,879.5	3,385.6	3,348.6	34.3	617.9	354.2	262.5	990.1	387.3	608.9	462.2
1976	5,141.3	3,609.2	3,583.4	32.7	628.2	360.9	265.8	998.7	387.9	616.9	469.3
1977	5,377.7	3,810.1	3,783.0	34.5	637.5	365.0	271.3	1,009.2	389.0	626.4	481.2
1978	5,677.6	4,050.1	4,032.5	33.3	666.4	387.4	276.7	1,028.5	393.9	641.0	503.2
1979	5,855.0	4,184.6	4,159.7	36.3	695.3	405.0	287.8	1,039.5	393.5	652.4	523.0
1980	5,839.0	4,137.4	4,114.9	35.2	730.9	430.6	297.1	1,054.4	399.7	661.2	555.0
1981	5,987.2	4,252.5	4,202.5	46.5	754.1	444.1	306.8	1,060.2	405.9	660.9	576.7
1982	5,870.9	4,123.7	4,066.9	48.8	778.9	452.1	324.3	1,071.0	412.5	665.2	592.3
1983	6,136.2	4,345.8	4,328.5	31.9	801.0	460.5	338.5	1,077.9	422.0	662.5	605.4
1984	6,577.1	4,723.2	4,684.5	43.3	826.8	476.4	348.3	1,091.3	431.6	666.4	624.6
1985	6,849.3	4,942.5	4,886.4	52.9	841.2	487.4	351.2	1,122.5	443.9	685.6	649.1
1986	7,086.5	5,126.9	5,076.1	50.8	863.4	493.7	368.0	1,150.1	451.8	705.4	661.1
1987	7,313.3	5,295.7	5,245.2	51.3	895.8	506.8	388.0	1,175.3	463.6	719.0	676.8
1988	7,613.9	5,522.7	5,484.5	45.6	937.2	525.7	411.1	1,205.8	469.3	743.6	696.4
1989	7,885.9	5,727.3	5,678.1	52.3	974.8	542.0	432.9	1,234.6	475.1	766.4	712.2
1990	8,033.9	5,815.3	5,759.9	56.0	1,009.6	555.7	454.9	1,266.2	483.8	789.2	730.2
1991	8,015.1	5,764.3	5,707.0	56.9	1,038.5	572.0	467.4	1,279.4	486.7	799.4	754.6
1992	8,287.1	5,991.8	5,921.3	66.2	1,071.4	589.0	483.5	1,283.7	476.5	813.0	776.7
1993	8,523.4	6,185.0	6,128.2	57.8	1,106.9	603.5	504.9	1,286.5	467.4	824.2	789.1
1994	8,870.7	6,488.2	6,414.2	70.5	1,140.0	631.9	508.7	1,286.8	452.2	838.5	821.7
1995	9,093.7	6,670.8	6,617.8	56.4	1,175.5	651.3	524.8	1,287.7	435.1	855.1	846.9
1996	9,433.9	6,974.6	6,909.4	65.3	1,199.8	665.4	535.0	1,289.8	423.2	868.4	860.4
1997	9,854.3	7,335.7	7,261.4	72.5	1,240.5	687.6	553.5	1,299.6	415.2	885.6	885.6
1998	10,283.5	7,702.4	7,633.5	69.4	1,280.2	703.7	577.8	1,314.3	410.4	904.6	900.9
1999	10,779.8	8,132.8	8,060.6	72.8	1,325.5	740.3	585.3	1,326.3	407.1	919.5	942.3
2000	11,226.0	8,500.9	8,417.8	83.5	1,376.2	774.1	601.8	1,349.4	410.5	939.0	977.8
2001	11,347.2	8,569.1	8,491.9	77.7	1,407.0	793.1	613.4	1,373.7	412.1	961.3	997.8
2002	11,553.0	8,736.6	8,655.9	81.2	1,417.3	789.9	627.7	1,401.4	420.2	980.9	988.5
2003	11,840.7	9,005.9	8,914.8	91.6	1,417.8	787.1	631.1	1,418.2	431.5	986.7	969.3
2004	12,263.8	9,379.9	9,282.0	97.9	1,457.4	821.7	635.9	1,426.8	435.8	991.0	1,008.4
2005	12,638.4	9,695.5	9,593.5	102.0	1,506.4	864.4	642.0	1,436.5	438.7	997.7	1,054.0
2006	12,976.2	9,991.7	9,892.3	99.1	1,539.8	898.0	642.0	1,445.0	438.4	1,006.5	1,098.6
2007	13,228.9	10,195.0	10,104.6	90.3	1,571.9	914.2	657.8	1,462.5	441.8	1,020.8	1,132.4
2008	13,228.8	10,099.6	9,994.8	102.3	1,630.1	959.3	671.2	1,496.8	459.0	1,037.8	1,185.2
2009	12,880.6	9,730.8	9,619.8	108.5	1,621.7	952.4	669.7	1,520.5	485.6	1,035.3	1,190.3
2010 ᴾ	13,248.7	10,091.0	9,977.0	111.6	1,624.9	942.7	682.0	1,529.2	502.9	1,027.1	1,188.2
2007: I	13,089.3	10,074.9	9,980.7	93.7	1,559.8	901.6	658.2	1,454.7	439.5	1,015.1	1,113.0
II	13,194.1	10,173.2	10,083.4	89.8	1,563.5	905.0	658.5	1,458.0	439.0	1,019.0	1,122.1
III	13,268.5	10,229.6	10,145.6	85.1	1,574.9	917.9	657.2	1,464.5	443.3	1,021.3	1,139.1
IV	13,363.5	10,302.1	10,208.7	92.9	1,589.5	932.4	657.5	1,472.8	445.1	1,027.6	1,155.5
2008: I	13,339.2	10,250.2	10,143.3	103.7	1,606.1	942.1	664.4	1,482.7	449.6	1,033.2	1,164.1
II	13,359.0	10,236.1	10,134.7	99.7	1,630.6	960.6	670.5	1,491.4	454.5	1,036.9	1,183.5
III	13,223.5	10,077.6	9,974.1	101.3	1,639.8	966.2	674.1	1,503.2	462.2	1,041.1	1,193.5
IV	12,993.7	9,834.3	9,727.1	104.7	1,643.9	968.5	675.9	1,509.8	469.8	1,040.1	1,199.7
2009: I	12,832.6	9,678.5	9,567.6	108.7	1,633.2	959.6	674.0	1,513.1	475.0	1,038.3	1,193.6
II	12,810.0	9,671.5	9,562.2	106.6	1,608.7	945.2	663.9	1,521.8	485.3	1,036.9	1,182.0
III	12,860.8	9,709.4	9,596.0	111.5	1,620.9	952.1	669.2	1,522.2	489.5	1,033.2	1,191.7
IV	13,019.0	9,863.6	9,753.5	107.4	1,624.0	952.7	671.7	1,525.0	492.8	1,032.7	1,193.8
2010: I	13,138.8	9,984.1	9,874.1	107.2	1,623.0	947.3	675.8	1,527.0	497.5	1,030.1	1,190.6
II	13,194.9	10,028.7	9,913.0	113.2	1,628.1	946.8	681.2	1,533.3	504.8	1,029.3	1,191.4
III	13,278.5	10,122.7	10,005.3	114.8	1,624.7	940.8	683.6	1,528.0	503.6	1,025.3	1,187.3
IV ᴾ	13,382.6	10,228.7	10,115.3	111.3	1,623.6	935.8	687.3	1,528.5	505.6	1,023.8	1,183.5

[1] Gross domestic business value added equals gross domestic product excluding gross value added of households and institutions and of general government. Nonfarm value added equals gross domestic business value added excluding gross farm value added.
[2] Equals compensation of employees of nonprofit institutions, the rental value of nonresidential fixed assets owned and used by nonprofit institutions serving households, and rental income of persons for tenant-occupied housing owned by nonprofit institutions.
[3] Equals compensation of general government employees plus general government consumption of fixed capital.

Source: Department of Commerce (Bureau of Economic Analysis).

TABLE B–12. Gross domestic product (GDP) by industry, value added, in current dollars and as a percentage of GDP, 1979–2009

[Billions of dollars; except as noted]

Year	Gross domestic product	Total private industries	Agriculture, forestry, fishing, and hunting	Mining	Construction	Manufacturing			Utilities	Wholesale trade	Retail trade
						Total manufacturing	Durable goods	Non-durable goods			
					Private industries						
					Value added						
1979	2,562.2	2,216.8	70.2	59.1	124.8	544.9	334.6	210.3	53.8	174.4	193.0
1980	2,788.1	2,404.8	62.1	90.8	131.5	558.3	339.2	219.2	61.0	186.3	198.3
1981	3,126.8	2,701.6	75.6	121.5	133.1	619.6	376.2	243.4	72.0	206.2	218.0
1982	3,253.2	2,791.4	71.6	118.5	131.0	606.5	359.2	247.3	83.2	206.6	226.9
1983	3,534.6	3,041.7	57.2	102.8	139.6	657.5	385.5	272.0	94.4	222.4	255.3
1984	3,930.9	3,393.0	77.0	107.2	160.7	731.8	451.0	280.7	105.7	249.8	286.8
1985	4,217.5	3,634.6	76.6	106.2	177.0	751.4	458.6	292.8	113.0	269.2	309.1
1986	4,460.1	3,840.4	73.7	70.3	197.2	777.4	468.4	308.9	117.5	279.3	331.4
1987	4,736.4	4,077.9	78.8	73.1	210.1	823.1	492.5	330.6	125.8	285.6	345.7
1988	5,100.4	4,395.3	78.1	74.1	226.5	900.2	537.9	362.2	125.1	314.3	366.8
1989	5,482.1	4,729.7	91.6	78.6	238.6	950.2	562.4	387.7	138.2	335.7	390.7
1990	5,800.5	4,994.3	95.7	88.4	243.6	968.9	558.9	410.1	145.5	347.7	400.4
1991	5,992.1	5,133.2	88.3	79.5	228.8	976.7	554.2	422.5	153.8	362.6	407.9
1992	6,342.3	5,442.0	99.3	73.6	233.2	1,016.7	574.5	442.2	159.7	380.1	430.0
1993	6,667.4	5,735.9	90.6	74.4	250.4	1,058.9	603.0	456.0	164.3	402.5	462.9
1994	7,085.2	6,119.9	105.6	75.9	277.2	1,127.3	650.2	477.1	171.2	444.5	500.5
1995	7,414.7	6,420.0	91.3	76.7	294.2	1,180.9	675.4	505.5	175.3	460.2	525.0
1996	7,838.5	6,812.6	114.2	90.0	320.9	1,208.5	705.0	503.5	173.4	492.5	556.8
1997	8,332.4	7,271.0	108.4	94.8	346.7	1,277.3	748.9	528.3	169.9	524.9	589.9
1998	8,793.5	7,694.4	100.3	81.0	383.7	1,326.7	781.2	545.6	165.1	557.3	626.9
1999	9,353.5	8,199.6	92.8	82.0	428.4	1,368.1	802.4	565.6	172.7	579.1	653.4
2000	9,951.5	8,736.1	95.6	108.9	467.3	1,415.6	839.1	576.5	173.9	617.7	686.2
2001	10,286.2	9,010.8	98.6	119.3	490.5	1,343.9	758.8	585.2	177.6	613.3	703.9
2002	10,642.3	9,289.3	94.4	109.5	494.3	1,355.5	767.8	587.8	181.0	614.9	731.2
2003	11,142.1	9,706.8	115.6	134.8	515.9	1,374.0	766.2	607.9	191.9	638.1	768.9
2004	11,867.8	10,360.1	142.7	159.3	554.4	1,482.7	822.0	660.6	208.0	684.5	794.7
2005	12,638.4	11,052.5	127.1	192.0	611.7	1,568.0	877.6	690.4	205.7	725.3	838.8
2006	13,398.9	11,731.1	122.5	229.0	651.1	1,651.5	923.1	728.4	236.2	769.6	875.0
2007	14,061.8	12,301.9	144.7	254.2	657.2	1,698.9	942.8	756.1	248.8	813.3	886.1
2008	14,369.1	12,514.0	160.1	317.1	623.4	1,647.6	927.3	720.3	262.6	822.9	840.2
2009	14,119.0	12,196.5	133.1	240.8	537.5	1,584.8	867.2	717.6	268.1	780.8	819.6
	Percent					Industry value added as a percentage of GDP (percent)					
1979	100.0	86.5	2.7	2.3	4.9	21.3	13.1	8.2	2.1	6.8	7.5
1980	100.0	86.3	2.2	3.3	4.7	20.0	12.2	7.9	2.2	6.7	7.1
1981	100.0	86.4	2.4	3.9	4.3	19.8	12.0	7.8	2.3	6.6	7.0
1982	100.0	85.8	2.2	3.6	4.0	18.6	11.0	7.6	2.6	6.4	7.0
1983	100.0	86.1	1.6	2.9	3.9	18.6	10.9	7.7	2.7	6.3	7.2
1984	100.0	86.3	2.0	2.7	4.1	18.6	11.5	7.1	2.7	6.4	7.3
1985	100.0	86.2	1.8	2.5	4.2	17.8	10.9	6.9	2.7	6.4	7.3
1986	100.0	86.1	1.7	1.6	4.4	17.4	10.5	6.9	2.6	6.3	7.4
1987	100.0	86.1	1.7	1.5	4.4	17.4	10.4	7.0	2.7	6.0	7.3
1988	100.0	86.2	1.5	1.5	4.4	17.6	10.5	7.1	2.5	6.2	7.2
1989	100.0	86.3	1.7	1.4	4.4	17.3	10.3	7.1	2.5	6.1	7.1
1990	100.0	86.1	1.6	1.5	4.2	16.7	9.6	7.1	2.5	6.0	6.9
1991	100.0	85.7	1.5	1.3	3.8	16.3	9.2	7.1	2.6	6.1	6.8
1992	100.0	85.8	1.6	1.2	3.7	16.0	9.1	7.0	2.5	6.0	6.8
1993	100.0	86.0	1.4	1.1	3.8	15.9	9.0	6.8	2.5	6.0	6.9
1994	100.0	86.4	1.5	1.1	3.9	15.9	9.2	6.7	2.4	6.3	7.1
1995	100.0	86.6	1.2	1.0	4.0	15.9	9.1	6.8	2.4	6.2	7.1
1996	100.0	86.9	1.5	1.1	4.1	15.4	9.0	6.4	2.2	6.3	7.1
1997	100.0	87.3	1.3	1.1	4.2	15.3	9.0	6.3	2.0	6.3	7.1
1998	100.0	87.5	1.1	.9	4.4	15.1	8.9	6.2	1.9	6.3	7.1
1999	100.0	87.7	1.0	.9	4.6	14.6	8.6	6.0	1.8	6.2	7.0
2000	100.0	87.8	1.0	1.1	4.7	14.2	8.4	5.8	1.7	6.2	6.9
2001	100.0	87.6	1.0	1.2	4.8	13.1	7.4	5.7	1.7	6.0	6.8
2002	100.0	87.3	.9	1.0	4.6	12.7	7.2	5.5	1.7	5.8	6.9
2003	100.0	87.1	1.0	1.2	4.6	12.3	6.9	5.5	1.7	5.7	6.9
2004	100.0	87.3	1.2	1.3	4.7	12.5	6.9	5.6	1.8	5.8	6.7
2005	100.0	87.5	1.0	1.5	4.8	12.4	6.9	5.5	1.6	5.7	6.6
2006	100.0	87.6	.9	1.7	4.9	12.3	6.9	5.4	1.8	5.7	6.5
2007	100.0	87.5	1.0	1.8	4.7	12.1	6.7	5.4	1.8	5.8	6.3
2008	100.0	87.1	1.1	2.2	4.3	11.5	6.5	5.0	1.8	5.7	5.8
2009	100.0	86.4	.9	1.7	3.8	11.2	6.1	5.1	1.9	5.5	5.8

[1] Consists of agriculture, forestry, fishing, and hunting; mining; construction; and manufacturing.

[2] Consists of utilities; wholesale trade; retail trade; transportation and warehousing; information; finance, insurance, real estate, rental, and leasing; professional and business services; educational services, health care, and social assistance; arts, entertainment, recreation, accommodation, and food services; and other services, except government.

Note: Data shown in Tables B–12 and B–13 are consistent with the 2010 comprehensive revision of the annual industry accounts released in May 2010, and with the annual revision of the industry accounts released in December 2010. For details see *Survey of Current Business*, January 2011.

See next page for continuation of table.

[Billions of dollars; except as noted]

Year	Private industries—Continued							Government	Private goods-producing industries [1]	Private services-producing industries [2]
	Transportation and warehousing	Information	Finance, insurance, real estate, rental, and leasing	Professional and business services	Educational services, health care, and social assistance	Arts, entertainment, recreation, accommodation, and food services	Other services, except government			
	Value added									
1979	97.5	96.9	393.5	152.1	118.2	77.9	60.6	345.4	799.0	1,417.8
1980	102.6	108.3	446.8	173.1	134.1	83.0	68.5	383.3	842.8	1,562.0
1981	110.1	123.5	502.8	197.3	152.9	92.9	76.0	425.2	949.9	1,751.7
1982	106.3	135.3	544.7	213.2	169.2	100.0	78.3	461.8	927.7	1,863.7
1983	118.0	152.5	611.6	242.4	189.7	111.5	86.8	492.9	957.1	2,084.6
1984	131.4	160.0	677.5	280.9	207.1	120.8	96.3	537.9	1,076.7	2,316.3
1985	137.1	176.4	739.4	316.3	225.4	132.0	105.3	582.9	1,111.2	2,523.4
1986	147.0	185.6	804.0	352.4	245.2	144.0	115.3	619.7	1,118.6	2,721.8
1987	152.6	197.4	850.3	384.5	277.7	152.3	121.1	658.4	1,185.0	2,892.9
1988	161.4	205.4	915.7	424.3	301.5	168.8	133.0	705.1	1,278.8	3,116.5
1989	166.3	222.4	981.0	470.4	337.4	184.0	144.8	752.4	1,358.9	3,370.8
1990	172.8	235.6	1,049.2	516.5	376.7	199.6	153.9	806.2	1,396.5	3,597.7
1991	182.3	244.3	1,109.8	524.0	413.4	205.9	155.9	858.9	1,373.2	3,760.0
1992	192.0	260.5	1,192.1	566.6	452.9	219.0	166.3	900.3	1,422.8	4,019.2
1993	206.4	279.6	1,259.3	600.9	476.4	230.9	178.3	931.4	1,474.3	4,261.6
1994	223.7	299.4	1,321.6	639.7	500.2	242.3	190.7	965.3	1,586.1	4,533.8
1995	231.7	311.5	1,405.7	687.3	523.9	255.3	200.7	994.6	1,643.1	4,776.9
1996	241.3	338.6	1,490.3	756.5	545.4	272.8	211.2	1,025.9	1,733.6	5,079.0
1997	261.8	349.4	1,610.6	842.1	571.4	300.3	223.8	1,061.3	1,827.2	5,443.8
1998	275.6	386.1	1,696.8	927.0	601.2	321.1	245.6	1,099.1	1,891.7	5,802.7
1999	287.1	438.5	1,834.0	1,010.2	638.5	355.4	259.3	1,153.9	1,971.3	6,228.3
2000	301.4	417.8	1,997.7	1,116.8	678.0	381.6	277.6	1,215.4	2,087.4	6,648.7
2001	302.6	451.1	2,154.8	1,170.7	729.2	391.2	264.2	1,275.4	2,052.3	6,958.5
2002	302.4	499.7	2,222.3	1,198.3	789.8	411.1	285.0	1,353.0	2,053.7	7,235.6
2003	319.8	508.6	2,316.1	1,259.4	847.3	426.9	289.7	1,435.3	2,140.3	7,566.6
2004	347.0	564.1	2,409.7	1,346.8	906.4	456.7	303.0	1,507.7	2,339.2	8,020.9
2005	369.7	592.6	2,606.5	1,461.8	953.4	481.6	318.5	1,585.9	2,498.8	8,553.7
2006	395.5	593.3	2,777.6	1,571.4	1,015.2	511.3	332.0	1,667.8	2,654.1	9,077.0
2007	405.4	633.3	2,891.3	1,700.5	1,078.3	545.2	344.6	1,759.9	2,755.0	9,546.9
2008	418.7	652.5	2,974.9	1,768.8	1,148.9	535.4	340.9	1,855.1	2,748.2	9,765.8
2009	389.5	639.3	3,040.3	1,701.3	1,212.9	513.1	335.4	1,922.5	2,496.3	9,700.3
	Industry value added as a percentage of GDP (percent)									
1979	3.8	3.8	15.4	5.9	4.6	3.0	2.4	13.5	31.2	55.3
1980	3.7	3.9	16.0	6.2	4.8	3.0	2.5	13.7	30.2	56.0
1981	3.5	4.0	16.1	6.3	4.9	3.0	2.4	13.6	30.4	56.0
1982	3.3	4.2	16.7	6.6	5.2	3.1	2.4	14.2	28.5	57.3
1983	3.3	4.3	17.3	6.9	5.4	3.2	2.5	13.9	27.1	59.0
1984	3.3	4.1	17.2	7.1	5.3	3.1	2.4	13.7	27.4	58.9
1985	3.3	4.2	17.5	7.5	5.3	3.1	2.5	13.8	26.3	59.8
1986	3.3	4.2	18.0	7.9	5.5	3.2	2.6	13.9	25.1	61.0
1987	3.2	4.2	18.0	8.1	5.9	3.2	2.6	13.9	25.0	61.1
1988	3.2	4.0	18.0	8.3	5.9	3.3	2.6	13.8	25.1	61.1
1989	3.0	4.1	17.9	8.6	6.2	3.4	2.6	13.7	24.8	61.5
1990	3.0	4.1	18.1	8.9	6.5	3.4	2.7	13.9	24.1	62.0
1991	3.0	4.1	18.5	8.7	6.9	3.4	2.6	14.3	22.9	62.8
1992	3.0	4.1	18.8	8.9	7.1	3.5	2.6	14.2	22.4	63.4
1993	3.1	4.2	18.9	9.0	7.1	3.5	2.7	14.0	22.1	63.9
1994	3.2	4.2	18.7	9.0	7.1	3.4	2.7	13.6	22.4	64.0
1995	3.1	4.2	19.0	9.3	7.1	3.4	2.7	13.4	22.2	64.4
1996	3.1	4.3	19.0	9.7	7.0	3.5	2.7	13.1	22.1	64.8
1997	3.1	4.2	19.3	10.1	6.9	3.6	2.7	12.7	21.9	65.3
1998	3.1	4.4	19.3	10.5	6.8	3.7	2.8	12.5	21.5	66.0
1999	3.1	4.7	19.6	10.8	6.8	3.8	2.8	12.3	21.1	66.6
2000	3.0	4.2	20.1	11.2	6.8	3.8	2.8	12.2	21.0	66.8
2001	2.9	4.4	20.9	11.4	7.1	3.8	2.6	12.4	20.0	67.6
2002	2.8	4.7	20.9	11.3	7.4	3.9	2.7	12.7	19.3	68.0
2003	2.9	4.6	20.8	11.3	7.6	3.8	2.6	12.9	19.2	67.9
2004	2.9	4.8	20.3	11.3	7.6	3.8	2.6	12.7	19.7	67.6
2005	2.9	4.7	20.6	11.6	7.5	3.8	2.5	12.5	19.8	67.7
2006	3.0	4.4	20.7	11.7	7.6	3.8	2.5	12.4	19.8	67.7
2007	2.9	4.5	20.6	12.1	7.7	3.9	2.5	12.5	19.6	67.9
2008	2.9	4.5	20.7	12.3	8.0	3.7	2.4	12.9	19.1	68.0
2009	2.8	4.5	21.5	12.0	8.6	3.6	2.4	13.6	17.7	68.7

Note (cont'd): Value added is the contribution of each private industry and of government to GDP. Value added is equal to an industry's gross output minus its intermediate inputs. Current-dollar value added is calculated as the sum of distributions by an industry to its labor and capital, which are derived from the components of gross domestic income.

Value added industry data shown in Tables B–12 and B–13 are based on the 2002 North American Industry Classification System (NAICS).

Source: Department of Commerce (Bureau of Economic Analysis).

TABLE B–13. Real gross domestic product by industry, value added, and percent changes, 1979–2009

Year	Gross domestic product	Private industries									
		Total private industries	Agriculture, forestry, fishing, and hunting	Mining	Construction	Manufacturing			Utilities	Wholesale trade	Retail trade
						Total manufacturing	Durable goods	Non-durable goods			
					Chain-type quantity indexes for value added (2005=100)						
1979	46.328	44.422	38.902	104.743	79.704	45.755	35.703	64.781	63.354	29.180	36.155
1980	46.200	44.148	38.454	115.624	75.211	43.375	33.804	61.531	59.106	28.966	34.138
1981	47.373	45.306	48.390	114.903	68.588	45.443	34.733	66.409	59.011	30.729	35.128
1982	46.453	44.203	51.018	109.777	60.598	42.139	31.312	64.239	57.783	30.875	35.081
1983	48.552	46.243	36.393	104.272	62.839	45.469	33.348	70.630	60.847	32.228	38.330
1984	52.041	49.664	47.093	114.566	70.715	49.812	38.718	70.877	66.315	34.849	41.993
1985	54.194	51.868	55.760	121.159	75.914	51.384	39.879	73.291	70.594	36.661	44.267
1986	56.071	53.375	54.888	116.832	77.566	51.353	40.178	72.348	74.085	40.328	47.562
1987	57.866	55.367	56.757	122.387	79.216	55.139	43.002	78.055	82.798	39.197	45.892
1988	60.244	57.994	50.682	136.936	83.047	58.999	47.272	80.230	82.088	41.311	50.498
1989	62.397	60.136	56.749	132.300	85.400	59.678	48.018	80.652	90.510	43.312	52.734
1990	63.568	61.155	60.082	130.811	84.852	58.890	47.127	80.201	95.653	42.697	53.582
1991	63.419	61.051	60.764	133.137	78.684	57.985	45.631	80.759	96.912	44.443	53.419
1992	65.571	63.424	67.973	129.046	80.472	59.918	46.583	84.786	97.768	48.496	56.212
1993	67.441	65.180	58.991	131.186	82.720	62.321	48.542	87.971	96.511	49.963	58.957
1994	70.188	68.252	70.457	142.454	87.368	66.434	52.274	92.504	99.477	53.141	63.237
1995	71.953	69.987	59.562	143.501	88.299	69.169	56.311	91.928	102.702	52.908	66.413
1996	74.645	73.015	66.294	133.707	93.062	71.380	59.761	91.280	101.797	57.790	72.553
1997	77.971	76.703	71.600	138.123	95.251	75.667	64.745	93.825	97.186	64.076	78.828
1998	81.367	80.397	69.846	148.876	98.361	79.448	71.155	92.244	95.083	74.166	83.815
1999	85.295	84.641	73.042	137.872	103.712	83.717	76.614	94.228	104.776	78.084	86.228
2000	88.825	88.538	81.616	121.050	107.083	89.061	85.168	94.085	108.396	83.555	89.582
2001	89.783	89.675	78.875	136.811	104.669	84.955	79.979	91.695	93.929	87.739	92.379
2002	91.412	91.193	82.096	138.440	101.024	87.073	82.953	92.545	97.457	88.572	95.428
2003	93.688	93.334	90.690	120.419	101.265	89.592	85.395	95.160	100.942	93.923	97.588
2004	97.036	96.936	96.562	119.398	101.341	96.800	93.168	101.568	104.921	98.968	97.623
2005	100.000	100.000	100.000	100.000	100.000	100.000	100.000	100.000	100.000	100.000	100.000
2006	102.673	103.013	100.784	108.114	97.084	104.372	106.821	101.349	100.686	103.057	101.833
2007	104.672	105.167	93.306	111.347	91.930	107.804	110.781	104.154	104.154	108.789	103.176
2008	104.672	104.468	101.803	107.584	86.669	102.589	111.935	91.910	110.368	108.671	96.007
2009	101.917	101.313	107.165	137.088	73.150	93.729	97.689	88.811	100.447	111.743	94.153
					Percent change from year earlier						
1979	3.1	3.8	8.3	−10.8	3.4	3.5	1.8	6.4	−8.1	7.6	0.2
1980	−.3	−.6	−1.2	10.4	−5.6	−5.2	−5.3	−5.0	−6.7	−.7	−5.6
1981	2.5	2.6	25.8	−.6	−8.8	4.8	2.7	7.9	−.2	6.1	2.9
1982	−1.9	−2.4	5.4	−4.5	−11.6	−7.3	−9.8	−3.3	−2.1	.5	−.1
1983	4.5	4.6	−28.7	−5.0	3.7	7.9	6.5	9.9	5.3	4.4	9.3
1984	7.2	7.4	29.4	9.9	12.5	9.6	16.1	.3	9.0	8.1	9.6
1985	4.1	4.4	18.4	5.8	7.4	3.2	3.0	3.4	6.5	5.2	5.4
1986	3.5	2.9	−1.6	−3.6	2.2	−.1	.7	−1.3	4.9	10.0	7.4
1987	3.2	3.7	3.4	4.8	2.1	7.4	7.0	7.9	11.8	−2.8	−3.5
1988	4.1	4.7	−10.7	11.9	4.8	7.0	9.9	2.8	−.9	5.4	10.0
1989	3.6	3.7	12.0	−3.4	2.8	1.2	1.6	.5	10.3	4.8	4.4
1990	1.9	1.7	5.9	−1.1	−.6	−1.3	−1.9	−.6	5.7	−1.4	1.6
1991	−.2	−.2	1.1	1.8	−7.3	−1.5	−3.2	.7	1.3	4.1	−.3
1992	3.4	3.9	11.9	−3.1	2.3	3.3	2.1	5.0	.9	9.1	5.2
1993	2.9	2.8	−13.2	1.7	2.8	4.0	4.2	3.8	−1.3	3.0	4.9
1994	4.1	4.7	19.4	8.6	5.6	6.6	7.7	5.2	3.1	6.4	7.3
1995	2.5	2.5	−15.5	.7	1.1	4.1	7.7	−.6	3.2	−.4	5.0
1996	3.7	4.3	11.3	−6.8	5.4	3.2	6.1	−.7	−.9	9.2	9.2
1997	4.5	5.1	8.0	3.3	2.4	6.0	8.3	2.8	−4.5	10.9	8.6
1998	4.4	4.8	−2.4	7.8	3.3	5.0	9.9	−1.7	−2.2	15.7	6.3
1999	4.8	5.3	4.6	−7.4	5.4	5.4	7.7	2.2	10.2	5.3	2.9
2000	4.1	4.6	11.7	−12.2	3.3	6.4	11.2	−.2	3.5	7.0	3.9
2001	1.1	1.3	−3.4	13.0	−2.3	−4.6	−6.1	−2.5	−13.3	5.0	3.1
2002	1.8	1.7	4.1	1.2	−3.5	2.5	3.7	.9	3.8	.9	3.3
2003	2.5	2.3	10.5	−13.0	.2	2.9	2.9	2.8	3.6	6.0	2.3
2004	3.6	3.9	6.5	−.8	.1	8.0	9.1	6.7	3.9	5.4	.0
2005	3.1	3.2	3.6	−16.2	−1.3	3.3	7.3	−1.5	−4.7	1.0	2.4
2006	2.7	3.0	.8	8.1	−2.9	4.4	6.8	1.3	.7	3.1	1.8
2007	1.9	2.1	−7.4	3.0	−5.3	3.3	3.7	2.8	3.4	5.6	1.3
2008	.0	−.7	9.1	−3.4	−5.7	−4.8	1.0	−11.8	6.0	−.1	−6.9
2009	−2.6	−3.0	5.3	27.4	−15.6	−8.6	−12.7	−3.4	−9.0	2.8	−1.9

[1] Consists of agriculture, forestry, fishing, and hunting; mining; construction; and manufacturing.
[2] Consists of utilities; wholesale trade; retail trade; transportation and warehousing; information; finance, insurance, real estate, rental, and leasing; professional and business services; educational services, health care, and social assistance; arts, entertainment, recreation, accommodation, and food services; and other services, except government.

See next page for continuation of table.

Year	Transportation and warehousing	Information	Finance, insurance, real estate, rental, and leasing	Professional and business services	Educational services, health care, and social assistance	Arts, entertainment, recreation, accommodation, and food services	Other services, except government	Government	Private goods-producing industries [1]	Private services-producing industries [2]
	Private industries—Continued									
	Chain-type quantity indexes for value added (2005=100)									
1979	42.732	27.664	45.825	33.769	53.945	46.689	73.815	73.550	52.713	41.446
1980	41.760	29.988	48.114	34.655	55.860	45.007	74.448	74.782	50.798	41.897
1981	40.733	31.637	48.773	35.514	56.944	46.590	72.192	75.075	52.554	42.807
1982	38.778	31.546	49.227	35.392	56.779	47.792	69.475	75.210	49.081	42.725
1983	43.771	33.759	50.412	37.884	58.963	51.486	72.679	75.888	50.425	45.085
1984	45.875	33.440	52.274	41.968	60.646	53.681	76.528	76.705	56.085	47.643
1985	46.555	34.374	53.665	45.319	62.143	56.334	79.030	78.727	58.924	49.622
1986	46.631	34.534	54.463	48.867	63.312	60.001	80.813	80.557	58.880	51.707
1987	48.921	36.877	56.369	51.486	67.335	59.596	82.204	82.121	62.412	53.162
1988	50.362	38.084	58.409	54.083	67.932	62.997	86.216	84.242	65.943	55.487
1989	52.324	40.758	59.885	57.577	70.548	65.264	90.151	86.297	67.156	57.960
1990	55.071	42.101	61.289	60.081	73.134	67.251	92.110	88.409	66.675	59.504
1991	57.584	42.504	62.227	57.987	74.836	65.377	89.427	88.888	65.228	59.859
1992	61.240	44.846	64.170	59.726	77.106	67.676	91.483	89.409	67.410	62.301
1993	63.953	47.224	66.045	61.221	77.380	69.768	94.651	89.409	69.070	64.093
1994	69.084	49.639	67.622	63.354	77.702	71.854	99.123	89.676	74.113	66.546
1995	71.137	51.366	69.380	65.589	78.938	74.270	100.970	89.615	75.677	68.336
1996	75.034	54.612	71.010	70.109	79.845	77.410	101.882	90.016	78.365	71.476
1997	78.897	55.678	74.167	74.976	81.193	80.923	100.641	90.996	82.512	75.030
1998	77.955	61.310	76.408	79.247	82.287	83.221	106.252	92.177	86.102	78.758
1999	80.694	69.628	81.416	82.750	84.471	88.358	107.176	93.287	90.214	83.043
2000	86.090	66.972	86.781	86.863	86.443	91.942	108.829	95.033	94.722	86.764
2001	82.988	71.966	92.055	88.985	88.631	90.534	97.457	95.831	91.775	89.072
2002	81.854	79.941	91.863	89.646	92.344	92.187	100.527	97.690	92.720	90.752
2003	85.983	81.989	93.228	92.136	95.383	94.290	98.899	98.672	94.225	93.069
2004	93.805	92.731	94.593	95.298	98.309	98.107	99.641	99.394	99.314	96.253
2005	100.000	100.000	100.000	100.000	100.000	100.000	100.000	100.000	100.000	100.000
2006	104.458	100.965	104.212	103.363	103.332	103.007	100.109	100.463	102.662	103.115
2007	105.368	109.556	106.029	105.978	105.150	104.566	100.313	101.236	103.260	105.728
2008	106.244	114.033	106.034	109.243	109.327	99.731	95.527	103.390	98.943	106.108
2009	92.405	111.185	107.234	103.760	110.544	91.067	89.033	104.208	92.611	103.891
	Percent change from year earlier									
1979	5.7	8.4	5.8	6.8	4.2	2.8	0.8	1.3	2.8	4.4
1980	−2.3	8.4	5.0	2.6	3.5	−3.6	.9	1.7	−3.6	1.1
1981	−2.5	5.5	1.4	2.5	1.9	3.5	−3.0	.4	3.5	2.2
1982	−4.8	−.3	.9	−.3	−.3	2.6	−3.8	.2	−6.6	−.2
1983	12.9	7.0	2.4	7.0	3.8	7.7	4.6	.9	2.7	5.5
1984	4.8	−.9	3.7	10.8	2.9	4.3	5.3	1.1	11.2	5.7
1985	1.5	2.8	2.7	8.0	2.5	4.9	3.3	2.6	5.1	4.2
1986	.2	.5	1.5	7.8	1.9	6.5	2.3	2.3	−.1	4.2
1987	4.9	6.8	3.5	5.4	6.4	−.7	1.7	1.9	6.0	2.8
1988	2.9	3.3	3.6	5.0	.9	5.7	4.9	2.6	5.7	4.4
1989	3.9	7.0	2.5	6.5	3.9	3.6	4.6	2.4	1.8	4.5
1990	5.2	3.3	2.3	4.3	3.7	3.0	2.2	2.4	−.7	2.7
1991	4.6	1.0	1.5	−3.5	2.3	−2.8	−2.9	.5	−2.2	.6
1992	6.3	5.5	3.1	3.0	3.0	3.5	2.3	.6	3.3	4.1
1993	4.4	5.3	2.9	2.5	.4	3.1	3.5	.0	2.5	2.9
1994	8.0	5.1	2.4	3.5	.4	3.0	4.7	.3	7.3	3.8
1995	3.0	3.5	2.6	3.5	1.6	3.4	1.9	−.1	2.1	2.7
1996	5.5	6.3	2.3	6.9	1.1	4.2	.9	.4	3.6	4.6
1997	5.1	2.0	4.4	6.9	1.7	4.5	−1.2	1.1	5.3	5.0
1998	−1.2	10.1	3.0	5.7	1.3	2.8	5.6	1.3	4.4	5.0
1999	3.5	13.6	6.6	4.4	2.7	6.2	.9	1.2	4.8	5.4
2000	6.7	−3.8	6.6	5.0	2.3	4.1	1.5	1.9	5.0	4.5
2001	−3.6	7.5	6.1	2.4	2.5	−1.5	−10.4	.8	−3.1	2.7
2002	−1.4	11.1	−.2	.7	4.2	1.8	3.2	1.9	1.0	1.9
2003	5.0	2.6	1.5	2.8	3.3	2.3	−1.6	1.0	1.6	2.6
2004	9.1	13.1	1.5	3.4	3.1	4.0	.8	.7	5.4	3.4
2005	6.6	7.8	5.7	4.9	1.7	1.9	.4	.6	.7	3.9
2006	4.5	1.0	4.2	3.4	3.3	3.0	.1	.5	2.7	3.1
2007	.9	8.5	1.7	2.5	1.8	1.5	.2	.8	.6	2.5
2008	.8	4.1	.0	3.1	4.0	−4.6	−4.8	2.1	−4.2	.4
2009	−13.0	−2.5	1.1	−5.0	1.1	−8.7	−6.8	.8	−6.4	−2.1

Note: Data are based on the 2002 North American Industry Classification System (NAICS).
See Note, Table B–12.

Source: Department of Commerce (Bureau of Economic Analysis).

TABLE B–14. Gross value added of nonfinancial corporate business, 1962–2010

[Billions of dollars; quarterly data at seasonally adjusted annual rates]

Year or quarter	Gross value added of non-financial corporate business [1]	Con-sumption of fixed capital	Net value added Total	Com-pensa-tion of employ-ees	Taxes on produc-tion and imports less sub-sidies	Net operating surplus Total	Net interest and miscel-laneous pay-ments	Busi-ness current transfer pay-ments	Corporate profits with inven-tory valuation and capital consumption adjustments Total	Taxes on corpo-rate income	Profits after tax [2]	Profits before tax	Inven-tory valua-tion adjust-ment	Capital con-sumption adjust-ment
1962	309.8	24.5	285.2	199.3	29.9	56.1	4.3	1.7	50.1	20.6	29.5	44.6	0.0	5.4
1963	329.9	25.6	304.3	210.1	31.7	62.5	4.7	1.7	56.1	22.8	33.4	49.7	.1	6.4
1964	356.1	27.0	329.0	225.7	33.9	69.5	5.2	2.0	62.4	23.9	38.5	55.9	–.5	7.0
1965	391.2	29.1	362.1	245.4	36.0	80.7	5.8	2.2	72.7	27.1	45.5	66.1	–1.2	7.8
1966	429.0	31.9	397.1	272.9	37.0	87.2	7.0	2.7	77.5	29.5	48.0	71.4	–2.1	8.1
1967	451.2	35.2	416.0	291.1	39.3	85.6	8.4	2.8	74.4	27.8	46.5	67.6	–1.6	8.3
1968	497.8	38.7	459.1	321.9	45.5	91.7	9.7	3.1	78.9	33.5	45.4	74.0	–3.7	8.6
1969	540.5	42.9	497.5	357.1	50.2	90.3	12.7	3.2	74.4	33.3	41.0	71.2	–5.9	9.1
1970	558.3	47.5	510.8	376.5	54.2	80.1	16.6	3.3	60.2	27.3	32.9	58.5	–6.6	8.3
1971	603.0	52.0	551.1	399.4	59.5	92.1	17.6	3.7	70.8	30.0	40.8	67.4	–4.6	8.0
1972	669.4	56.5	613.0	443.9	63.7	105.4	18.6	4.0	82.8	33.8	49.0	79.5	–6.6	9.9
1973	750.8	63.1	687.6	502.2	70.1	115.4	21.8	4.7	88.9	40.4	48.5	99.5	–19.6	9.0
1974	809.8	74.2	735.7	552.2	74.4	109.1	27.5	4.1	77.5	42.8	34.6	110.2	–38.2	5.5
1975	876.7	88.6	788.0	575.5	80.2	132.4	28.4	5.0	98.9	41.9	57.0	110.7	–10.5	–1.2
1976	989.7	97.8	892.0	651.4	86.7	153.9	26.0	7.0	121.0	53.5	67.5	138.2	–14.1	–3.2
1977	1,119.4	110.1	1,009.2	735.3	94.6	179.3	28.5	9.0	141.9	60.6	81.3	159.5	–15.7	–1.9
1978	1,272.7	125.1	1,147.5	845.1	102.7	199.7	33.4	9.5	156.8	67.6	89.2	183.7	–23.7	–3.2
1979	1,414.4	144.3	1,270.2	958.4	108.8	203.0	41.8	9.5	151.8	70.6	81.2	197.2	–40.1	–5.3
1980	1,534.5	166.7	1,367.8	1,047.2	121.5	199.1	54.2	10.2	134.7	68.2	66.5	184.1	–42.1	–7.2
1981	1,742.2	192.4	1,549.8	1,157.6	146.7	245.5	67.2	11.4	166.8	66.0	100.8	185.0	–24.6	6.5
1982	1,802.6	212.8	1,589.8	1,200.4	152.9	236.5	77.4	8.8	150.2	48.8	101.5	140.0	–7.5	17.8
1983	1,929.1	219.3	1,709.8	1,263.1	168.0	278.7	77.0	10.5	191.2	61.7	129.5	163.4	–7.4	35.2
1984	2,161.4	228.8	1,932.6	1,400.0	185.0	347.5	86.0	11.7	249.8	75.9	173.9	197.6	–4.0	56.2
1985	2,293.9	244.0	2,049.9	1,496.1	196.6	357.2	91.5	16.1	249.6	71.1	178.6	173.5	.0	76.2
1986	2,383.2	258.0	2,125.2	1,575.4	204.6	345.2	98.5	27.3	219.5	76.2	143.2	149.7	7.1	62.7
1987	2,551.0	270.0	2,280.9	1,678.4	216.8	385.6	95.9	29.9	259.9	94.2	165.7	213.5	–16.2	62.6
1988	2,765.4	287.3	2,478.1	1,804.7	233.8	439.6	107.9	27.4	304.3	104.0	200.3	264.1	–22.2	62.3
1989	2,899.2	303.9	2,595.3	1,905.7	248.2	441.5	133.9	24.0	283.5	101.2	182.3	243.1	–16.3	56.7
1990	3,035.2	321.0	2,714.2	2,005.5	263.5	445.2	143.1	25.4	276.7	98.5	178.3	243.3	–12.9	46.3
1991	3,104.1	336.1	2,768.0	2,044.8	285.7	437.5	139.6	26.6	271.3	88.6	182.7	226.8	4.9	39.6
1992	3,241.1	344.1	2,897.0	2,152.9	302.5	441.6	114.2	31.3	296.1	94.4	201.7	258.6	–2.8	40.3
1993	3,398.4	359.0	3,039.3	2,244.0	318.0	477.3	99.8	30.1	347.5	108.0	239.5	308.7	–4.0	42.9
1994	3,677.6	380.1	3,297.5	2,382.1	347.8	567.5	98.8	35.3	433.5	132.4	301.1	391.9	–12.4	54.0
1995	3,888.0	408.3	3,479.7	2,511.5	354.2	614.0	112.7	30.7	470.6	140.3	330.3	431.2	–18.3	57.6
1996	4,119.4	435.1	3,684.4	2,631.3	365.6	687.5	112.1	38.0	537.4	152.9	384.5	471.3	3.1	63.0
1997	4,412.5	466.9	3,945.6	2,814.6	381.0	750.0	124.7	39.2	586.2	161.4	424.8	506.8	14.1	65.3
1998	4,668.3	499.9	4,168.5	3,049.7	393.1	725.7	146.8	35.2	543.7	158.7	385.1	460.5	15.7	67.5
1999	4,955.5	539.3	4,416.3	3,256.5	414.6	745.1	164.5	47.1	533.5	171.4	362.1	468.6	–4.0	68.9
2000	5,279.4	590.1	4,689.4	3,541.8	439.4	708.2	192.8	47.9	467.5	170.2	297.3	432.5	–16.8	51.8
2001	5,252.5	632.0	4,620.5	3,559.4	434.5	626.7	197.7	58.9	370.1	111.2	258.8	315.1	8.0	47.0
2002	5,307.7	654.5	4,653.1	3,544.2	461.9	647.1	163.7	56.3	427.2	97.1	330.1	342.3	–2.6	87.5
2003	5,503.7	669.0	4,834.7	3,651.3	484.2	699.2	147.9	65.2	486.1	132.9	353.2	425.9	–11.3	71.5
2004	5,877.5	695.6	5,181.9	3,786.7	517.7	877.5	134.4	65.5	677.5	187.0	490.6	662.1	–34.3	49.7
2005	6,302.8	743.0	5,559.8	3,976.3	558.4	1,025.1	148.2	79.3	797.6	271.9	525.8	957.1	–30.7	–128.8
2006	6,740.3	800.9	5,939.4	4,182.3	593.3	1,163.7	164.0	75.8	923.9	307.6	616.2	1,117.9	–38.0	–156.0
2007	6,946.0	840.1	6,106.0	4,361.0	607.7	1,137.4	232.3	69.1	835.9	293.8	542.2	1,042.0	–47.2	–158.8
2008	6,990.5	878.8	6,111.7	4,435.3	615.3	1,061.1	271.3	66.2	723.5	226.4	497.1	782.0	–44.1	–14.4
2009	6,625.2	879.0	5,746.3	4,193.6	590.2	962.5	220.1	79.1	663.3	170.3	492.9	706.4	11.9	–55.1
2010 [p]	....	876.1	....	4,289.8	611.9	....	....	78.8	....	....	....	....	....	–110.3
2007: I	6,896.9	829.3	6,067.6	4,309.2	599.6	1,158.8	204.5	71.9	882.4	311.2	571.2	1,086.5	–50.3	–153.9
II	6,965.5	836.4	6,129.0	4,340.0	605.6	1,183.4	219.8	69.8	893.9	302.4	591.5	1,091.1	–34.8	–162.4
III	6,908.6	842.9	6,065.7	4,361.9	610.1	1,093.7	242.6	67.8	783.3	278.9	504.5	974.9	–29.1	–162.5
IV	7,013.2	851.6	6,161.6	4,432.8	615.3	1,113.5	262.4	66.9	784.2	282.6	501.5	1,015.4	–74.8	–156.4
2008: I	6,971.4	859.5	6,111.8	4,459.5	613.8	1,038.5	269.9	65.0	703.6	250.6	453.0	851.2	–128.7	–18.9
II	6,971.5	872.5	6,099.0	4,456.8	619.5	1,022.7	273.0	63.5	686.2	252.0	434.2	838.6	–140.0	–12.4
III	7,087.3	887.2	6,200.1	4,444.5	619.5	1,136.0	270.3	63.1	802.7	247.1	555.6	882.0	–66.7	–12.6
IV	6,932.0	896.1	6,035.9	4,380.5	608.2	1,047.1	272.1	73.4	701.6	156.0	545.6	556.1	159.1	–13.6
2009: I	6,694.3	894.0	5,800.3	4,217.2	588.5	994.5	250.1	78.6	665.4	160.8	504.6	639.3	93.0	–66.9
II	6,580.4	880.1	5,700.3	4,189.6	589.4	921.3	219.0	84.9	617.4	155.1	462.3	642.6	30.6	–55.9
III	6,558.4	871.0	5,687.4	4,175.0	584.5	927.9	205.5	75.2	647.1	163.7	483.5	704.8	–8.7	–48.9
IV	6,667.8	870.7	5,797.1	4,192.4	598.3	1,006.4	205.3	77.8	723.2	201.8	521.4	839.1	–67.2	–48.7
2010: I	6,804.4	868.2	5,936.2	4,205.1	604.8	1,126.3	208.3	77.5	840.4	265.2	575.3	1,021.8	–36.4	–144.9
II	6,923.0	872.9	6,050.0	4,271.7	609.0	1,169.3	202.3	78.3	888.6	287.4	601.1	1,037.5	–3.5	–145.4
III	6,978.3	877.5	6,100.7	4,319.4	613.4	1,167.9	199.2	79.8	888.9	293.6	595.3	1,069.7	–36.4	–144.4
IV [p]	....	885.9	....	4,363.0	620.5	....	....	79.4	....	....	....	....	....	–6.4

[1] Estimates for nonfinancial corporate business for 2000 and earlier periods are based on the Standard Industrial Classification (SIC); later estimates are based on the North American Industry Classification System (NAICS).
[2] With inventory valuation and capital consumption adjustments.

Source: Department of Commerce (Bureau of Economic Analysis).

TABLE B–15. Gross value added and price, costs, and profits of nonfinancial corporate business, 1962–2010

[Quarterly data at seasonally adjusted annual rates]

Year or quarter	Gross value added of nonfinancial corporate business (billions of dollars)[1]		Price per unit of real gross value added of nonfinancial corporate business (dollars)[1,2]									
	Current dollars	Chained (2005) dollars	Total	Compensation of employees (unit labor cost)	Unit nonlabor cost				Corporate profits with inventory valuation and capital consumption adjustments[4]		
					Total	Consumption of fixed capital	Taxes on production and imports[3]	Net interest and miscellaneous payments	Total	Taxes on corporate income	Profits after tax[5]
1962	309.8	1,206.3	0.257	0.165	0.050	0.020	0.026	0.004	0.042	0.017	0.024
1963	329.9	1,278.7	.258	.164	.050	.020	.026	.004	.044	.018	.026
1964	356.1	1,369.0	.260	.165	.050	.020	.026	.004	.046	.017	.028
1965	391.2	1,482.8	.264	.165	.050	.020	.026	.004	.049	.018	.031
1966	429.0	1,589.1	.270	.172	.049	.020	.025	.004	.049	.019	.030
1967	451.2	1,632.0	.276	.178	.053	.022	.026	.005	.046	.017	.029
1968	497.8	1,737.9	.286	.185	.056	.022	.028	.006	.045	.019	.026
1969	540.5	1,808.1	.299	.197	.061	.024	.030	.007	.041	.018	.023
1970	558.3	1,793.6	.311	.210	.067	.026	.032	.009	.034	.015	.018
1971	603.0	1,867.6	.323	.214	.071	.028	.034	.009	.038	.016	.022
1972	669.4	2,010.3	.333	.221	.071	.028	.034	.009	.041	.017	.024
1973	750.8	2,134.2	.352	.235	.075	.030	.035	.010	.042	.019	.023
1974	809.8	2,100.4	.386	.263	.085	.035	.037	.013	.037	.020	.016
1975	876.7	2,069.5	.424	.278	.098	.043	.041	.014	.048	.020	.028
1976	989.7	2,238.7	.442	.291	.098	.044	.042	.012	.054	.024	.030
1977	1,119.4	2,404.6	.466	.306	.101	.046	.043	.012	.059	.025	.034
1978	1,272.7	2,561.9	.497	.330	.106	.049	.044	.013	.061	.026	.035
1979	1,414.4	2,642.1	.535	.363	.116	.055	.045	.016	.057	.027	.031
1980	1,534.5	2,615.1	.587	.400	.135	.064	.050	.021	.052	.026	.025
1981	1,742.2	2,719.6	.641	.426	.154	.071	.058	.025	.061	.024	.037
1982	1,802.6	2,654.7	.679	.452	.170	.080	.061	.029	.057	.018	.038
1983	1,929.1	2,783.0	.693	.454	.171	.079	.064	.028	.069	.022	.047
1984	2,161.4	3,029.7	.713	.462	.169	.076	.065	.028	.082	.025	.057
1985	2,293.9	3,160.0	.726	.473	.173	.077	.067	.029	.079	.022	.057
1986	2,383.2	3,237.7	.736	.487	.182	.080	.072	.030	.068	.024	.044
1987	2,551.0	3,404.8	.749	.493	.179	.079	.072	.028	.076	.028	.049
1988	2,765.4	3,601.5	.768	.501	.183	.080	.073	.030	.084	.029	.056
1989	2,899.2	3,661.2	.792	.521	.194	.083	.074	.037	.077	.028	.050
1990	3,035.2	3,715.6	.817	.540	.203	.086	.078	.039	.074	.026	.048
1991	3,104.1	3,697.9	.839	.553	.213	.091	.084	.038	.073	.024	.049
1992	3,241.1	3,807.5	.851	.565	.208	.090	.088	.030	.078	.025	.053
1993	3,398.4	3,907.7	.870	.574	.207	.092	.089	.026	.089	.028	.061
1994	3,677.6	4,158.1	.884	.573	.207	.091	.092	.024	.104	.032	.072
1995	3,888.0	4,351.9	.893	.577	.208	.094	.088	.026	.108	.032	.076
1996	4,119.4	4,591.7	.897	.573	.207	.095	.088	.024	.117	.033	.084
1997	4,412.5	4,891.1	.902	.575	.206	.095	.086	.025	.120	.033	.087
1998	4,668.3	5,170.8	.903	.590	.208	.097	.083	.028	.105	.031	.074
1999	4,955.5	5,456.0	.908	.597	.214	.099	.085	.030	.098	.031	.066
2000	5,279.4	5,749.6	.918	.616	.222	.103	.085	.034	.081	.030	.052
2001	5,252.5	5,641.5	.931	.631	.234	.112	.087	.035	.066	.020	.046
2002	5,307.7	5,679.3	.935	.624	.235	.115	.091	.029	.075	.017	.058
2003	5,503.7	5,819.6	.946	.627	.234	.115	.094	.025	.084	.023	.061
2004	5,877.5	6,085.2	.966	.622	.232	.114	.096	.022	.111	.031	.081
2005	6,302.8	6,302.8	1.000	.631	.243	.118	.101	.024	.127	.043	.083
2006	6,740.3	6,542.2	1.030	.639	.249	.122	.102	.025	.141	.047	.094
2007	6,946.0	6,616.1	1.050	.659	.264	.127	.102	.035	.126	.044	.082
2008	6,990.5	6,520.3	1.072	.680	.282	.135	.105	.042	.111	.035	.076
2009	6,625.2	6,141.7	1.079	.683	.288	.143	.109	.036	.108	.028	.080
2007: I	6,896.9	6,622.4	1.041	.651	.257	.125	.101	.031	.133	.047	.086
II	6,965.5	6,633.0	1.050	.654	.261	.126	.102	.033	.135	.046	.089
III	6,908.6	6,543.2	1.056	.667	.270	.129	.104	.037	.120	.043	.077
IV	7,013.2	6,665.8	1.052	.665	.269	.128	.102	.039	.118	.042	.075
2008: I	6,971.4	6,607.8	1.055	.675	.274	.130	.103	.041	.106	.038	.069
II	6,971.5	6,547.4	1.065	.681	.279	.133	.104	.042	.105	.038	.066
III	7,087.3	6,525.7	1.086	.681	.282	.136	.105	.041	.123	.038	.085
IV	6,932.0	6,400.6	1.083	.684	.289	.140	.106	.043	.110	.024	.085
2009: I	6,694.3	6,151.5	1.088	.686	.294	.145	.108	.041	.108	.026	.082
II	6,580.4	6,073.3	1.084	.690	.292	.145	.111	.036	.102	.026	.076
III	6,558.4	6,075.5	1.079	.687	.286	.143	.109	.034	.107	.027	.080
IV	6,667.8	6,266.5	1.064	.669	.280	.139	.108	.033	.115	.032	.083
2010: I	6,804.4	6,431.3	1.058	.654	.273	.135	.106	.032	.131	.041	.089
II	6,923.0	6,501.5	1.065	.657	.271	.134	.106	.031	.137	.044	.092
III	6,978.3	6,478.7	1.077	.667	.273	.135	.107	.031	.137	.045	.092

[1] Estimates for nonfinancial corporate business for 2000 and earlier periods are based on the Standard Industrial Classification (SIC); later estimates are based on the North American Industry Classification System (NAICS).
[2] The implicit price deflator for gross value added of nonfinancial corporate business divided by 100.
[3] Less subsidies plus business current transfer payments.
[4] Unit profits from current production.
[5] With inventory valuation and capital consumption adjustments.

Source: Department of Commerce (Bureau of Economic Analysis).

[Billions of dollars; quarterly data at seasonally adjusted annual rates]

Year or quarter	Personal consumption expenditures	Goods						Services					Addendum: Personal consumption expenditures excluding food and energy²
		Total	Durable		Nondurable			Total	Household consumption expenditures				
			Total¹	Motor vehicles and parts	Total¹	Food and beverages purchased for off-premises consumption	Gasoline and other energy goods		Total¹	Housing and utilities	Health care	Financial services and insurance	
1962	363.3	189.0	49.5	21.4	139.5	64.7	16.3	174.4	168.7	64.5	19.1	15.4	272.9
1963	382.7	198.2	54.2	24.2	143.9	65.9	16.9	184.6	178.6	68.2	21.0	15.9	290.0
1964	411.5	212.3	59.6	25.8	152.7	69.5	17.7	199.2	192.5	72.1	24.2	17.7	313.8
1965	443.8	229.7	66.4	29.6	163.3	74.4	19.1	214.1	206.9	76.6	26.0	19.4	339.3
1966	480.9	249.6	71.7	29.9	177.9	80.6	20.7	231.3	223.5	81.2	28.7	21.3	368.1
1967	507.8	259.0	74.0	29.6	185.0	82.6	21.9	248.8	240.4	86.3	31.9	22.8	391.1
1968	558.0	284.6	84.8	35.4	199.8	88.8	23.2	273.4	264.0	92.7	36.6	25.8	432.9
1969	605.1	304.7	90.5	37.4	214.2	95.4	25.0	300.4	290.4	101.0	42.1	28.5	470.8
1970	648.3	318.8	90.0	34.5	228.8	103.5	26.3	329.5	318.4	109.4	47.7	31.1	503.3
1971	701.6	342.1	102.4	43.2	239.7	107.1	27.6	359.5	347.2	120.0	53.7	34.1	550.1
1972	770.2	373.8	116.4	49.4	257.4	114.5	29.4	396.4	382.8	131.2	59.8	38.3	607.9
1973	852.0	416.6	130.5	54.4	286.1	126.7	34.3	435.4	420.7	143.5	67.2	41.5	670.9
1974	932.9	451.5	130.2	48.2	321.4	143.0	43.8	481.4	465.0	158.6	76.1	45.9	722.4
1975	1,033.8	491.3	142.2	52.6	349.2	156.6	48.0	542.5	524.4	176.5	89.0	54.0	800.6
1976	1,151.3	546.3	168.6	68.2	377.7	167.3	53.0	604.9	584.9	194.7	101.8	59.3	898.3
1977	1,277.8	600.4	192.0	79.8	408.4	179.8	57.8	677.4	655.6	217.8	115.7	67.8	1,002.5
1978	1,427.6	663.6	213.3	89.2	450.2	196.1	61.5	764.1	739.6	244.3	131.2	80.6	1,127.8
1979	1,591.2	737.9	226.3	90.2	511.6	218.4	80.4	853.2	825.4	273.4	148.8	87.6	1,245.4
1980	1,755.8	799.8	226.4	84.4	573.4	239.2	101.9	956.0	924.1	311.8	171.7	95.6	1,358.3
1981	1,939.5	869.4	243.9	93.0	625.4	255.3	113.4	1,070.1	1,033.9	352.0	201.9	102.0	1,507.1
1982	2,075.5	899.3	253.0	100.0	646.3	267.1	108.4	1,176.2	1,136.1	387.0	225.2	116.3	1,627.2
1983	2,288.6	973.8	295.0	122.9	678.8	277.0	106.5	1,314.8	1,271.9	421.2	253.1	145.9	1,824.2
1984	2,501.1	1,063.7	342.2	147.2	721.5	291.1	108.2	1,437.4	1,389.8	458.3	276.5	156.6	2,016.9
1985	2,717.6	1,137.6	380.4	170.1	757.2	303.0	110.5	1,580.0	1,529.7	500.7	302.2	180.5	2,215.1
1986	2,896.7	1,195.6	421.4	187.5	774.2	316.4	91.2	1,701.1	1,645.8	535.7	330.2	196.7	2,401.8
1987	3,097.0	1,256.3	442.0	188.2	814.3	324.3	96.4	1,840.7	1,782.1	571.8	366.0	207.1	2,587.3
1988	3,350.1	1,337.3	475.1	202.2	862.3	342.8	99.9	2,012.7	1,946.0	614.5	410.1	219.4	2,813.2
1989	3,594.5	1,423.8	494.3	207.8	929.5	365.4	110.4	2,170.7	2,099.0	655.6	451.2	235.7	3,019.8
1990	3,835.5	1,491.3	497.1	205.1	994.2	391.2	124.2	2,344.2	2,264.5	696.4	506.2	253.2	3,221.3
1991	3,980.1	1,497.4	477.2	185.7	1,020.3	403.0	121.1	2,482.6	2,398.4	735.5	555.8	282.0	3,351.1
1992	4,236.9	1,563.3	508.1	204.8	1,055.2	404.5	125.0	2,673.6	2,581.3	771.2	612.8	311.8	3,601.1
1993	4,483.6	1,642.3	551.5	224.7	1,090.8	413.5	126.9	2,841.2	2,746.6	814.5	648.8	341.0	3,828.2
1994	4,750.8	1,746.6	607.2	249.8	1,139.4	432.1	129.2	3,004.3	2,901.9	866.5	680.5	349.0	4,072.3
1995	4,987.3	1,815.5	635.7	255.7	1,179.8	443.7	133.4	3,171.7	3,064.6	913.8	719.9	364.7	4,291.9
1996	5,273.6	1,917.7	676.3	273.5	1,241.4	461.9	144.7	3,355.9	3,240.2	961.2	752.1	393.6	4,542.0
1997	5,570.6	2,006.8	715.5	293.1	1,291.2	474.8	147.7	3,563.9	3,451.6	1,009.9	790.9	431.3	4,821.6
1998	5,918.5	2,110.0	780.0	320.2	1,330.0	486.5	133.4	3,808.5	3,677.5	1,065.2	832.0	469.6	5,173.5
1999	6,342.8	2,290.0	857.4	350.7	1,432.6	513.6	148.8	4,052.8	3,907.4	1,125.0	863.6	514.2	5,554.6
2000	6,830.4	2,459.1	915.8	363.2	1,543.4	537.5	188.8	4,371.2	4,205.9	1,198.6	918.4	570.0	5,966.4
2001	7,148.8	2,534.0	946.3	383.3	1,587.7	559.7	183.6	4,614.8	4,428.6	1,287.7	996.6	562.8	6,255.9
2002	7,439.2	2,610.0	992.1	401.3	1,617.9	569.6	174.6	4,829.2	4,624.2	1,334.8	1,082.9	576.2	6,549.4
2003	7,804.0	2,727.4	1,014.8	401.5	1,712.6	593.1	209.6	5,076.6	4,864.8	1,393.8	1,149.3	601.8	6,840.9
2004	8,285.1	2,892.3	1,061.6	404.7	1,830.7	628.2	249.9	5,392.8	5,182.8	1,462.2	1,229.7	667.5	7,238.8
2005	8,819.0	3,073.9	1,105.5	409.6	1,968.4	665.0	304.8	5,745.1	5,531.0	1,582.8	1,316.0	712.6	7,658.8
2006	9,322.7	3,221.7	1,133.0	397.1	2,088.7	698.0	336.9	6,100.9	5,860.6	1,686.0	1,380.7	752.4	8,086.9
2007	9,806.3	3,357.7	1,159.4	402.5	2,198.2	737.4	366.6	6,448.6	6,194.5	1,755.8	1,465.4	818.9	8,491.9
2008	10,104.5	3,379.5	1,083.5	343.2	2,296.0	775.2	411.4	6,725.0	6,446.1	1,833.1	1,547.2	848.1	8,694.4
2009	10,001.3	3,230.7	1,026.5	319.7	2,204.2	777.9	303.7	6,770.6	6,511.8	1,876.3	1,623.2	813.8	8,705.0
2010 ᵖ	10,351.9	3,427.6	1,089.6	345.2	2,338.0	801.9	358.3	6,924.3	6,658.2	1,901.9	1,686.5	820.7	8,966.7
2007: I	9,632.8	3,293.8	1,149.8	399.1	2,143.9	724.0	332.6	6,339.0	6,089.8	1,737.3	1,441.0	795.6	8,367.8
II	9,753.2	3,343.4	1,158.7	405.3	2,184.7	730.2	365.1	6,409.8	6,164.2	1,748.8	1,455.0	811.5	8,446.4
III	9,850.8	3,369.8	1,163.2	403.4	2,206.6	740.6	369.5	6,481.1	6,224.3	1,762.0	1,470.3	826.1	8,527.9
IV	9,988.4	3,423.8	1,166.0	402.2	2,257.8	755.0	399.1	6,564.6	6,299.5	1,775.0	1,495.3	842.3	8,625.6
2008: I	10,065.7	3,415.4	1,131.0	381.5	2,284.3	762.6	419.7	6,650.3	6,378.9	1,802.1	1,524.0	848.3	8,665.8
II	10,183.0	3,458.7	1,117.1	358.4	2,341.6	777.6	444.4	6,724.3	6,449.8	1,827.0	1,543.5	856.3	8,734.3
III	10,202.0	3,450.0	1,080.2	334.9	2,369.9	785.2	467.0	6,751.9	6,469.3	1,839.7	1,552.8	850.5	8,728.2
IV	9,967.2	3,194.0	1,005.6	298.1	2,188.4	775.4	314.4	6,773.3	6,486.5	1,863.8	1,568.5	837.5	8,649.5
2009: I	9,913.0	3,158.4	1,012.2	306.2	2,146.2	773.8	264.8	6,754.6	6,489.6	1,870.2	1,594.4	816.5	8,654.4
II	9,920.1	3,175.4	1,004.7	306.5	2,170.7	774.2	279.9	6,744.7	6,493.8	1,870.0	1,618.9	813.3	8,658.1
III	10,040.7	3,276.1	1,045.2	339.1	2,231.0	777.0	326.2	6,764.6	6,507.5	1,877.5	1,629.5	809.3	8,726.9
IV	10,131.5	3,312.9	1,043.9	327.0	2,269.0	786.5	344.1	6,818.6	6,556.2	1,887.6	1,650.1	816.3	8,780.9
2010: I	10,230.8	3,380.0	1,060.7	328.3	2,319.3	797.4	364.1	6,850.9	6,589.6	1,887.1	1,657.5	824.9	8,851.5
II	10,285.4	3,377.5	1,074.1	335.9	2,303.4	794.6	340.0	6,907.9	6,643.2	1,892.5	1,680.4	829.9	8,931.3
III	10,366.3	3,419.6	1,087.8	342.2	2,331.8	801.4	348.2	6,946.7	6,679.2	1,910.9	1,694.3	812.2	8,984.9
IV ᵖ	10,525.2	3,533.3	1,135.7	374.5	2,397.7	814.0	381.1	6,991.8	6,720.7	1,916.9	1,713.8	815.6	9,099.2

¹ Includes other items not shown separately.
² Food consists of food and beverages purchased for off-premises consumption; food services, which include purchased meals and beverages, are not classified as food.

Source: Department of Commerce (Bureau of Economic Analysis).

TABLE B–17. Real personal consumption expenditures, 1995–2010

[Billions of chained (2005) dollars; quarterly data at seasonally adjusted annual rates]

| Year or quarter | Personal consumption expenditures | Goods | | | | | | Services | | | | | Addendum: Personal consumption expenditures excluding food and energy[2] |
| | | Total | Durable | | Nondurable | | | Total | Household consumption expenditures | | | | |
			Total[1]	Motor vehicles and parts	Total[1]	Food and beverages purchased for off-premises consumption	Gasoline and other energy goods		Total[1]	Housing and utilities	Health care	Financial services and insurance	
1995	6,079.0	1,898.6	511.6	255.6	1,437.8	548.5	264.3	4,208.2	4,068.6	1,234.9	947.5	489.4	5,126.4
1996	6,291.2	1,983.6	549.8	268.0	1,479.4	554.0	268.5	4,331.4	4,183.3	1,261.7	967.1	507.8	5,321.9
1997	6,523.4	2,078.2	594.7	286.1	1,522.9	558.9	273.9	4,465.0	4,327.2	1,290.4	997.1	525.2	5,543.3
1998	6,865.5	2,218.6	667.2	316.1	1,580.3	565.5	283.8	4,661.8	4,510.6	1,329.8	1,029.5	558.6	5,862.9
1999	7,240.9	2,395.3	753.8	345.1	1,660.9	587.4	292.5	4,852.8	4,690.4	1,371.8	1,045.6	605.6	6,202.5
2000	7,608.1	2,521.7	819.9	356.1	1,714.7	600.6	287.1	5,093.3	4,917.8	1,413.7	1,081.5	665.4	6,548.6
2001	7,813.9	2,600.9	864.4	374.3	1,745.6	607.6	289.2	5,218.7	5,028.8	1,451.5	1,135.4	660.7	6,745.7
2002	8,021.9	2,706.6	930.0	394.0	1,780.2	609.0	294.0	5,318.1	5,109.3	1,462.0	1,202.3	658.3	6,941.9
2003	8,247.6	2,829.9	986.1	405.3	1,845.6	622.4	302.2	5,418.4	5,199.0	1,480.2	1,229.4	657.8	7,142.0
2004	8,532.7	2,955.3	1,051.0	411.3	1,904.6	639.2	306.5	5,577.6	5,359.3	1,512.8	1,268.6	691.8	7,402.6
2005	8,819.0	3,073.9	1,105.5	409.6	1,968.4	665.0	304.8	5,745.1	5,531.0	1,582.8	1,316.0	712.6	7,658.8
2006	9,073.5	3,173.9	1,150.4	396.6	2,023.6	686.2	298.4	5,899.7	5,664.4	1,616.7	1,340.0	735.4	7,905.7
2007	9,209.5	3,261.6	1,198.6	403.9	2,064.3	697.5	295.9	6,028.3	5,783.2	1,626.4	1,371.6	766.4	8,111.1
2008	9,265.0	3,180.3	1,136.4	348.2	2,041.2	691.6	282.0	6,082.3	5,816.1	1,638.6	1,410.0	770.9	8,114.2
2009	9,153.9	3,117.4	1,094.6	324.0	2,017.4	685.1	285.5	6,032.7	5,777.0	1,656.9	1,440.4	743.0	8,002.9
2010 ᵖ	9,315.7	3,251.8	1,178.6	334.8	2,073.7	703.7	285.0	6,065.4	5,803.7	1,675.4	1,459.6	725.9	8,136.5
2007: I	9,235.2	3,241.1	1,181.2	401.6	2,060.2	697.3	298.4	5,994.4	5,753.7	1,625.8	1,362.9	755.9	8,053.7
II	9,270.5	3,252.4	1,194.5	407.4	2,059.0	693.5	296.4	6,018.3	5,780.8	1,624.8	1,368.2	765.7	8,095.1
III	9,310.0	3,271.9	1,205.7	404.4	2,067.7	696.4	296.1	6,038.7	5,792.4	1,628.6	1,372.9	769.8	8,129.8
IV	9,342.3	3,281.0	1,212.9	402.0	2,070.3	702.7	292.8	6,061.7	5,805.9	1,626.2	1,382.3	774.2	8,165.7
2008: I	9,324.1	3,232.6	1,178.6	383.0	2,054.5	700.3	287.2	6,090.6	5,830.2	1,636.3	1,401.5	774.9	8,152.0
II	9,326.2	3,235.2	1,170.0	362.1	2,064.6	699.8	284.0	6,090.2	5,828.5	1,637.6	1,411.0	772.1	8,162.9
III	9,243.5	3,171.4	1,133.2	339.8	2,035.6	691.2	274.7	6,070.0	5,802.1	1,630.9	1,410.1	772.8	8,113.7
IV	9,166.3	3,082.3	1,063.9	307.9	2,010.1	675.1	282.2	6,078.5	5,803.6	1,649.7	1,417.4	763.9	8,028.2
2009: I	9,154.1	3,095.7	1,076.6	317.1	2,012.0	675.2	287.0	6,053.6	5,793.5	1,650.1	1,430.0	753.9	8,015.2
II	9,117.0	3,084.0	1,068.2	313.5	2,008.3	681.2	286.5	6,027.7	5,778.4	1,652.0	1,442.1	746.2	7,973.7
III	9,161.6	3,138.2	1,118.3	342.7	2,016.9	687.8	285.1	6,020.7	5,766.5	1,659.4	1,441.6	739.4	8,007.1
IV	9,182.9	3,151.8	1,115.1	322.7	2,032.3	696.3	283.5	6,028.7	5,769.7	1,666.3	1,447.9	732.5	8,015.4
2010: I	9,225.4	3,195.4	1,138.9	320.6	2,053.5	702.7	284.0	6,029.6	5,769.9	1,664.3	1,446.7	727.4	8,055.2
II	9,275.7	3,222.6	1,157.8	326.0	2,063.4	697.6	286.1	6,053.4	5,791.7	1,668.9	1,457.6	729.5	8,106.8
III	9,330.6	3,255.2	1,179.3	330.1	2,076.2	703.0	286.1	6,076.9	5,814.4	1,683.0	1,461.9	720.7	8,144.6
IV ᵖ	9,431.2	3,334.1	1,238.5	362.3	2,101.7	711.4	283.9	6,101.9	5,838.6	1,685.6	1,472.4	725.8	8,239.4

[1] Includes other items not shown separately.

[2] Food consists of food and beverages purchased for off-premises consumption; food services, which include purchased meals and beverages, are not classified as food.

Note: See Table B–2 for data for total personal consumption expenditures for 1962–94.

Source: Department of Commerce (Bureau of Economic Analysis).

[Billions of dollars; quarterly data at seasonally adjusted annual rates]

Year or quarter	Private fixed invest-ment	Total non-resi-den-tial	Struc-tures	Equipment and software Total	Information processing equipment and software Total	Com-puters and periph-eral equip-ment	Soft-ware	Other	Indus-trial equip-ment	Trans-por-tation equip-ment	Other equip-ment	Total resi-den-tial [1]	Structures Total [1]	Single family
1962	82.0	53.1	20.8	32.3	5.7	0.3	0.2	5.1	9.3	9.8	7.5	29.0	28.4	15.1
1963	88.1	56.0	21.2	34.8	6.5	.7	.4	5.4	10.0	9.4	8.8	32.1	31.5	16.0
1964	97.2	63.0	23.7	39.2	7.4	.9	.5	5.9	11.4	10.6	9.9	34.3	33.6	17.6
1965	109.0	74.8	28.3	46.5	8.5	1.2	.7	6.7	13.7	13.2	11.0	34.2	33.5	17.8
1966	117.7	85.4	31.3	54.0	10.7	1.7	1.0	8.0	16.2	14.5	12.7	32.3	31.6	16.6
1967	118.7	86.4	31.5	54.9	11.3	1.9	1.2	8.2	16.9	14.3	12.4	32.4	31.6	16.8
1968	132.1	93.4	33.6	59.9	11.9	1.9	1.3	8.7	17.3	17.6	13.0	38.7	37.9	19.5
1969	147.3	104.7	37.7	67.0	14.6	2.4	1.8	10.4	19.1	18.9	14.4	42.6	41.6	19.7
1970	150.4	109.0	40.3	68.7	16.6	2.7	2.3	11.6	20.3	16.2	15.6	41.4	40.2	17.5
1971	169.9	114.1	42.7	71.5	17.3	2.8	2.4	12.2	19.5	18.4	16.3	55.8	54.5	25.8
1972	198.5	128.8	47.2	81.7	19.5	3.5	2.8	13.2	21.4	21.8	19.0	69.7	68.1	32.8
1973	228.6	153.3	55.0	98.3	23.1	3.5	3.2	16.3	26.0	26.6	22.6	75.3	73.6	35.2
1974	235.4	169.5	61.2	108.2	27.0	3.9	3.9	19.2	30.7	26.3	24.3	66.0	64.1	29.7
1975	236.5	173.7	61.4	112.4	28.5	3.6	4.8	20.2	31.3	25.2	27.4	62.7	60.8	29.6
1976	274.8	192.4	65.9	126.4	32.7	4.4	5.2	23.1	34.1	30.0	29.6	82.5	80.4	43.9
1977	339.0	228.7	74.6	154.1	39.2	5.7	5.5	28.0	39.4	39.3	36.3	110.3	107.9	62.2
1978	412.2	280.6	93.6	187.0	48.7	7.6	6.3	34.8	47.7	47.3	43.2	131.6	128.9	72.8
1979	474.9	333.9	117.7	216.2	58.5	10.2	8.1	40.2	56.2	53.6	47.9	141.0	137.8	72.3
1980	485.6	362.4	136.2	226.2	68.8	12.5	9.8	46.4	60.7	48.4	48.3	123.2	119.8	52.9
1981	542.6	420.0	167.3	252.7	81.5	17.1	11.8	52.5	65.5	50.6	55.2	122.6	118.9	52.0
1982	532.1	426.5	177.6	248.9	88.3	18.9	14.0	55.3	62.7	46.8	51.2	105.7	102.0	41.5
1983	570.1	417.2	154.3	262.9	100.1	23.9	16.4	59.8	58.9	53.5	50.4	152.9	148.6	72.5
1984	670.2	489.6	177.4	312.2	121.5	31.6	20.4	69.6	68.1	64.4	58.1	180.6	175.9	86.4
1985	714.4	526.2	194.5	331.7	130.3	33.7	23.8	72.9	72.5	69.0	59.9	188.2	183.1	87.4
1986	739.9	519.8	176.5	343.3	136.8	33.4	25.6	77.7	75.4	70.5	60.7	220.1	214.6	104.1
1987	757.8	524.1	174.2	349.9	141.2	35.8	29.0	76.4	76.7	68.1	63.9	233.7	227.9	117.2
1988	803.1	563.8	182.8	381.0	154.9	38.0	34.2	82.8	84.2	72.9	69.0	239.3	233.2	120.1
1989	847.3	607.7	193.7	414.0	172.6	43.1	41.9	87.6	93.3	67.9	80.2	239.5	233.4	120.9
1990	846.4	622.4	202.9	419.5	177.2	38.6	47.6	90.9	92.1	70.0	80.2	224.0	218.0	112.9
1991	803.3	598.2	183.6	414.6	182.9	37.7	53.7	91.5	89.3	71.5	70.8	205.1	199.4	99.4
1992	848.5	612.1	172.6	439.6	199.9	44.0	57.9	98.1	93.0	74.7	72.0	236.3	230.4	122.0
1993	932.5	666.6	177.2	489.4	217.6	47.9	64.3	105.4	102.2	89.4	80.2	266.0	259.9	140.1
1994	1,033.5	731.4	186.8	544.6	235.2	52.4	68.3	114.6	113.6	107.7	88.1	302.1	295.9	162.3
1995	1,112.9	810.0	207.3	602.8	263.0	66.1	74.6	122.3	129.0	116.1	94.7	302.9	296.5	153.5
1996	1,209.4	875.4	224.6	650.8	290.1	72.8	85.5	131.9	136.5	123.2	101.0	334.1	327.7	170.8
1997	1,317.7	968.6	250.3	718.3	330.3	81.4	107.5	141.4	140.4	135.5	112.1	349.1	342.8	175.2
1998	1,447.1	1,061.1	275.1	786.0	366.1	87.9	126.0	152.2	147.4	147.1	125.4	385.9	379.2	199.4
1999	1,580.7	1,154.9	283.9	871.0	417.1	97.2	157.3	162.5	149.1	174.4	130.4	425.8	418.5	223.8
2000	1,717.7	1,268.7	318.1	950.5	478.2	103.2	184.5	190.6	162.9	170.8	138.6	449.0	441.2	236.8
2001	1,700.2	1,227.8	329.7	898.1	452.5	87.6	186.6	178.4	151.9	154.2	139.5	472.4	464.4	249.1
2002	1,634.9	1,125.4	282.8	842.7	419.8	79.7	183.0	157.0	141.7	141.6	139.6	509.5	501.3	265.9
2003	1,713.3	1,135.7	281.9	853.8	430.9	77.6	191.3	162.0	142.6	132.9	147.5	577.6	569.1	310.6
2004	1,903.6	1,223.0	306.7	916.4	455.3	80.2	205.7	169.4	142.0	161.1	157.9	680.6	671.4	377.6
2005	2,122.3	1,347.3	351.8	995.6	475.3	78.9	218.0	178.4	159.6	181.7	178.9	775.0	765.2	433.5
2006	2,267.2	1,505.3	433.7	1,071.7	505.2	84.9	229.8	190.6	178.4	198.2	189.8	761.9	751.6	416.0
2007	2,266.1	1,637.5	524.9	1,112.6	536.6	87.0	245.0	204.6	193.0	190.2	192.8	628.6	618.4	305.2
2008	2,137.8	1,665.3	582.4	1,082.9	549.9	88.6	259.7	201.6	193.7	147.2	192.1	472.5	462.7	185.8
2009	1,716.5	1,364.4	451.6	912.8	530.7	80.0	260.2	190.4	150.4	76.4	155.4	352.1	343.1	105.3
2010 p	1,752.8	1,412.5	381.8	1,030.7	590.2	97.6	282.7	210.0	160.9	112.6	166.9	340.4	331.2	112.6
2007: I	2,260.4	1,579.6	479.5	1,100.1	531.4	88.1	242.8	200.6	182.7	199.0	187.0	680.7	670.4	339.8
II	2,282.1	1,624.9	512.3	1,112.6	532.1	84.7	243.3	204.2	197.8	188.8	193.9	657.2	646.9	324.1
III	2,274.0	1,660.7	545.5	1,115.1	534.9	86.1	245.3	203.5	199.7	186.2	194.4	613.3	603.1	298.0
IV	2,247.9	1,684.6	562.2	1,122.4	548.0	89.3	248.7	210.0	191.9	186.6	195.8	563.3	553.1	258.8
2008: I	2,212.5	1,695.4	567.1	1,128.3	556.9	92.6	257.2	206.6	195.3	184.9	191.3	517.1	507.2	221.3
II	2,194.1	1,697.5	584.4	1,113.2	562.8	94.4	260.2	208.1	197.2	161.3	191.8	496.6	486.6	202.1
III	2,140.8	1,678.2	590.4	1,087.9	552.2	88.1	261.9	202.1	196.5	141.6	197.6	462.5	452.7	174.0
IV	2,003.8	1,590.1	587.9	1,002.2	527.9	79.4	259.1	189.4	185.7	100.9	187.7	413.7	404.3	145.7
2009: I	1,782.3	1,415.2	507.5	907.8	511.5	75.0	253.6	182.8	157.1	70.9	168.3	367.0	357.9	112.4
II	1,709.8	1,367.5	464.0	903.5	518.6	76.0	257.7	184.8	150.8	79.8	154.4	342.2	333.3	94.5
III	1,691.8	1,343.8	436.6	907.2	533.7	78.9	260.0	194.7	147.1	76.0	150.5	348.0	339.1	104.4
IV	1,681.9	1,330.9	398.2	932.7	559.0	90.1	269.4	199.5	146.4	78.8	148.6	351.0	342.1	110.1
2010: I	1,689.8	1,349.6	380.1	969.5	568.0	90.5	274.7	202.8	146.8	97.0	157.7	340.2	331.1	114.8
II	1,761.4	1,404.2	381.5	1,022.7	586.2	98.4	279.6	208.3	161.6	110.9	163.9	357.2	348.1	118.9
III	1,768.6	1,438.8	380.9	1,057.9	595.5	97.8	285.3	212.4	164.7	125.4	172.3	329.8	320.7	110.5
IV p	1,791.5	1,457.2	384.7	1,072.5	611.2	103.6	291.2	216.4	170.4	117.1	173.8	334.3	325.1	106.2

[1] Includes other items not shown separately.

Source: Department of Commerce (Bureau of Economic Analysis).

Table B–19. Real private fixed investment by type, 1995–2010

[Billions of chained (2005) dollars; quarterly data at seasonally adjusted annual rates]

Year or quarter	Private fixed investment	Total nonresidential	Nonresidential — Structures	Equipment and software — Total	Information processing equipment and software — Total	Computers and peripheral equipment[1]	Software	Other	Industrial equipment	Transportation equipment	Other equipment	Residential — Total residential[2]	Structures — Total[2]	Structures — Single family
1995	1,235.7	792.2	342.0	493.0	149.5	....	66.9	93.7	145.5	131.5	110.6	456.1	450.1	240.2
1996	1,346.5	866.2	361.4	545.4	179.1	....	78.5	102.7	150.9	136.8	114.8	492.5	486.8	262.4
1997	1,470.8	970.8	387.9	620.4	220.8	....	101.7	111.5	154.1	148.2	125.9	501.8	496.3	261.6
1998	1,630.4	1,087.4	407.7	710.4	271.1	....	122.8	125.5	160.8	162.0	138.8	540.4	534.5	290.1
1999	1,782.1	1,200.9	408.2	810.9	332.0	....	151.5	139.9	161.8	190.3	142.4	574.2	567.5	311.5
2000	1,913.8	1,318.5	440.0	895.8	391.9	....	172.4	168.4	175.8	186.2	150.4	580.0	572.6	315.0
2001	1,877.6	1,281.8	433.3	866.9	390.2	....	173.7	163.2	162.8	169.6	149.3	583.3	575.6	315.4
2002	1,798.1	1,180.2	356.6	830.3	379.3	....	173.4	148.4	151.9	154.2	148.2	613.8	605.9	327.7
2003	1,856.2	1,191.0	343.0	851.4	405.0	....	185.6	156.4	151.6	140.4	155.0	664.3	655.9	362.6
2004	1,992.5	1,263.0	346.7	917.3	443.1	....	204.6	168.1	147.4	162.3	164.4	729.5	720.1	406.1
2005	2,122.3	1,347.3	351.8	995.6	475.3	....	218.0	178.4	159.6	181.7	178.9	775.0	785.2	433.5
2006	2,171.3	1,453.9	384.0	1,069.6	514.8	....	227.1	191.2	172.9	196.5	185.5	718.2	708.1	391.1
2007	2,132.7	1,552.0	438.2	1,109.0	560.5	....	240.9	210.6	179.9	185.8	184.2	584.2	574.2	284.0
2008	1,997.0	1,556.6	464.2	1,082.0	594.7	....	254.9	217.9	172.2	143.0	177.5	444.2	434.7	178.2
2009	1,630.7	1,290.8	369.6	916.3	595.8	....	259.3	215.5	132.2	69.4	137.8	342.7	333.9	105.4
2010 p	1,692.1	1,362.2	317.7	1,054.8	675.5	....	284.3	242.5	139.8	111.6	150.2	332.5	323.1	114.6
2007: I	2,127.7	1,499.0	404.8	1,093.0	546.5	....	238.9	201.4	172.6	195.1	179.9	631.3	621.3	314.0
II	2,147.2	1,539.1	430.6	1,104.6	550.2	....	239.2	205.8	185.0	184.1	185.8	611.4	601.5	301.8
III	2,140.8	1,574.1	454.6	1,112.6	561.5	....	241.1	210.9	185.4	181.3	185.6	570.6	560.7	278.0
IV	2,114.9	1,595.9	462.9	1,125.7	583.8	....	244.2	224.5	176.5	182.6	185.6	523.3	513.5	242.1
2008: I	2,081.6	1,603.7	462.7	1,134.0	597.4	....	253.4	221.0	177.6	182.1	180.8	482.2	472.6	209.5
II	2,057.3	1,597.0	471.2	1,116.5	606.2	....	254.8	224.1	176.2	158.1	181.1	464.4	454.6	193.0
III	1,993.8	1,561.5	466.9	1,084.1	598.1	....	256.3	219.3	172.4	136.5	182.3	435.6	426.1	168.2
IV	1,855.6	1,464.2	456.1	993.3	577.2	....	255.0	207.4	162.8	95.3	165.7	394.7	385.7	142.3
2009: I	1,663.4	1,313.7	399.7	903.4	567.3	....	250.7	204.8	138.2	64.2	148.1	352.7	344.0	110.0
II	1,619.6	1,288.3	377.8	903.8	581.4	....	256.2	209.5	132.8	70.5	136.4	333.9	325.4	94.7
III	1,622.4	1,282.9	365.5	913.1	601.8	....	260.7	220.3	129.3	68.5	134.1	342.4	333.6	106.2
IV	1,617.1	1,278.3	335.3	944.7	632.9	....	269.5	227.4	128.3	74.5	132.7	341.7	332.7	110.9
2010: I	1,630.5	1,302.6	319.3	989.7	645.7	....	275.4	232.3	128.4	95.8	142.4	330.7	321.4	115.9
II	1,702.5	1,355.3	318.9	1,046.0	669.1	....	280.9	239.5	140.7	110.2	147.8	350.1	340.7	121.9
III	1,708.8	1,388.0	316.0	1,084.2	683.3	....	287.5	245.9	143.0	124.8	154.5	323.3	313.8	112.9
IV p	1,726.6	1,403.1	316.7	1,099.5	704.0	....	293.5	252.4	147.2	115.5	155.8	326.0	316.3	107.8

[1] Because computers exhibit rapid changes in prices relative to other prices in the economy, the chained-dollar estimates should not be used to measure the component's relative importance or its contribution to the growth rate of more aggregate series. The quantity index for computers can be used to accurately measure the real growth rate of this series. For information on this component, see *Survey of Current Business* Table 5.3.1 (for growth rates), Table 5.3.2 (for contributions), and Table 5.3.3 (for quantity indexes).

[2] Includes other items not shown separately.

Source: Department of Commerce (Bureau of Economic Analysis).

TABLE B–20. Government consumption expenditures and gross investment by type, 1962–2010

[Billions of dollars; quarterly data at seasonally adjusted annual rates]

Year or quarter	Total	Government consumption expenditures and gross investment												
		Federal									State and local			
		Total	National defense				Nondefense				Total	Consumption expenditures	Gross investment	
			Total	Consumption expenditures	Gross investment		Total	Consumption expenditures	Gross investment				Structures	Equipment and software
					Structures	Equipment and software			Structures	Equipment and software				
1962	130.1	75.2	61.1	46.6	2.0	12.5	14.1	11.3	2.1	0.8	54.9	39.0	14.5	1.3
1963	136.4	76.9	61.0	48.3	1.6	11.0	15.9	12.4	2.3	1.2	59.5	41.9	16.0	1.5
1964	143.2	78.4	60.2	48.8	1.3	10.2	18.2	14.0	2.5	1.6	64.8	45.8	17.2	1.8
1965	151.4	80.4	60.6	50.6	1.1	8.9	19.8	15.1	2.8	1.9	71.0	50.2	19.0	1.9
1966	171.6	92.4	71.7	59.9	1.3	10.5	20.8	15.9	2.8	2.1	79.2	56.1	21.0	2.1
1967	192.5	104.6	83.4	69.9	1.2	12.3	21.2	17.0	2.2	1.9	87.9	62.6	23.0	2.3
1968	209.3	111.3	89.2	77.1	1.2	10.9	22.0	18.2	2.1	1.7	98.0	70.4	25.2	2.4
1969	221.4	113.3	89.5	78.1	1.5	9.9	23.8	20.2	1.9	1.7	108.2	79.8	25.6	2.7
1970	233.7	113.4	87.6	76.5	1.3	9.8	25.8	22.1	2.1	1.7	120.3	91.5	25.8	3.0
1971	246.4	113.6	84.6	77.1	1.8	5.7	29.1	24.9	2.5	1.7	132.8	102.7	27.0	3.1
1972	263.4	119.6	86.9	79.5	1.8	5.7	32.7	28.2	2.7	1.8	143.8	113.2	27.1	3.5
1973	281.7	122.5	88.1	79.4	2.1	6.6	34.3	29.4	3.1	1.8	159.2	126.0	29.1	4.1
1974	317.9	134.5	95.6	84.5	2.2	8.9	39.0	33.4	3.4	2.2	183.4	143.7	34.7	4.9
1975	357.7	149.0	103.9	90.9	2.3	10.7	45.1	38.7	4.1	2.4	208.7	165.1	38.1	5.5
1976	383.0	159.7	111.1	95.8	2.1	13.2	48.6	41.4	4.6	2.7	223.3	179.5	38.1	5.7
1977	414.1	175.4	120.9	104.2	2.4	14.4	54.5	46.5	5.0	3.0	238.7	195.9	36.9	5.9
1978	453.6	190.9	130.5	112.7	2.5	15.3	60.4	50.6	6.1	3.7	262.7	213.2	42.8	6.6
1979	500.7	210.6	145.2	123.8	2.5	18.9	65.4	55.1	6.3	4.0	290.2	233.3	49.0	7.8
1980	566.1	243.7	168.0	143.7	3.2	21.1	75.8	63.8	7.1	4.9	322.4	258.4	55.1	8.9
1981	627.5	280.2	196.2	167.3	3.2	25.7	83.9	71.0	7.7	5.3	347.3	282.3	55.4	9.5
1982	680.4	310.8	225.9	191.1	4.0	30.8	84.9	72.1	6.8	6.0	369.7	304.9	54.2	10.6
1983	733.4	342.9	250.6	208.7	4.8	37.1	92.3	77.7	6.7	7.8	390.5	324.1	54.2	12.2
1984	796.9	374.3	281.5	232.8	4.9	43.8	92.7	77.1	7.0	8.7	422.6	347.7	60.5	14.4
1985	878.9	412.8	311.2	253.7	6.2	51.3	101.6	84.7	7.3	9.6	466.1	381.8	67.6	16.8
1986	949.3	438.4	330.8	267.9	6.8	56.1	107.6	90.1	8.0	9.5	510.9	418.1	74.2	18.6
1987	999.4	459.5	350.0	283.6	7.7	58.8	109.6	90.1	9.0	10.4	539.9	441.4	78.8	19.6
1988	1,038.9	461.6	354.7	293.5	7.4	53.9	106.8	88.3	6.8	11.7	577.3	471.0	84.8	21.5
1989	1,100.6	481.4	362.1	299.4	6.4	56.3	119.3	99.1	6.9	13.4	619.2	504.5	88.7	26.0
1990	1,181.7	507.5	373.9	308.0	6.1	59.8	133.6	111.0	8.0	14.6	674.2	547.0	98.5	28.7
1991	1,236.1	526.6	383.1	319.7	4.6	58.8	143.4	118.6	9.2	15.7	709.5	577.5	103.2	28.9
1992	1,273.5	532.9	376.8	315.2	5.2	56.3	156.1	128.9	10.3	16.9	740.6	606.2	104.2	30.1
1993	1,294.8	525.0	363.0	307.5	5.3	50.1	162.0	133.7	11.2	17.0	769.8	634.2	104.5	31.2
1994	1,329.8	518.6	353.8	300.8	5.8	47.2	164.8	139.9	10.2	14.7	811.2	668.2	108.7	34.3
1995	1,374.0	518.8	348.8	297.0	6.7	45.1	170.0	143.2	10.8	16.0	855.3	701.3	117.3	36.7
1996	1,421.0	527.0	354.8	303.2	6.3	45.4	172.2	143.4	11.3	17.5	894.0	730.2	126.8	36.9
1997	1,474.4	531.0	349.8	304.5	6.1	39.2	181.1	153.0	9.9	18.2	943.5	764.5	139.5	39.4
1998	1,526.1	531.0	346.1	300.3	5.8	39.9	184.9	154.3	10.8	19.9	995.0	808.6	143.6	42.9
1999	1,631.3	554.9	361.1	313.0	5.4	42.8	193.8	160.3	10.7	22.7	1,076.3	870.6	159.7	46.1
2000	1,731.0	576.1	371.0	321.8	5.4	43.8	205.0	174.2	8.3	22.5	1,154.9	930.6	176.0	48.3
2001	1,846.4	611.7	393.0	342.0	5.3	45.6	218.7	188.1	8.1	22.5	1,234.7	994.2	192.3	48.2
2002	1,983.3	680.6	437.7	380.7	5.8	51.2	242.9	209.8	9.9	23.2	1,302.7	1,049.4	205.8	47.5
2003	2,112.6	756.5	497.9	435.2	7.3	55.4	258.5	225.1	10.3	23.1	1,356.1	1,096.5	211.8	47.8
2004	2,232.8	824.6	550.8	481.2	7.1	62.4	273.9	240.2	9.1	24.6	1,408.2	1,139.1	220.2	48.9
2005	2,369.9	876.3	589.0	514.8	7.5	66.8	287.3	251.0	8.3	28.0	1,493.6	1,212.0	230.8	50.8
2006	2,518.4	931.7	624.9	543.9	8.1	72.9	306.8	267.1	9.5	30.2	1,586.7	1,282.3	249.9	54.5
2007	2,674.2	976.3	662.3	575.4	10.1	76.9	314.0	273.5	11.1	29.4	1,697.9	1,368.9	268.4	60.7
2008	2,878.3	1,079.9	737.3	635.7	11.3	90.3	342.5	299.0	11.3	32.2	1,798.5	1,448.2	286.7	63.6
2009	2,914.9	1,139.6	771.6	664.1	15.9	91.5	368.0	323.0	12.1	32.9	1,775.3	1,424.4	288.5	62.4
2010 p	3,002.3	1,214.4	817.8	698.3	19.0	100.4	396.6	345.0	15.4	36.2	1,788.0	1,447.5	276.7	63.8
2007: I	2,604.4	944.0	637.6	555.8	9.0	72.9	306.4	267.0	10.4	29.0	1,660.3	1,337.8	264.1	58.5
II	2,656.0	968.7	657.0	569.0	11.5	76.5	311.7	271.4	10.9	29.4	1,687.3	1,360.6	266.6	60.1
III	2,698.4	992.1	674.7	585.8	10.3	78.5	317.4	276.2	11.7	29.5	1,706.4	1,376.2	268.7	61.5
IV	2,738.2	1,000.6	679.9	590.9	9.5	79.6	320.7	279.6	11.3	29.7	1,737.6	1,401.0	274.0	62.6
2008: I	2,802.3	1,033.4	702.1	612.2	8.7	81.1	331.3	289.7	10.4	31.3	1,768.9	1,427.8	277.7	63.4
II	2,869.8	1,065.2	724.9	622.8	11.6	90.5	340.3	297.3	10.8	32.2	1,804.6	1,455.0	285.7	63.9
III	2,934.7	1,105.5	762.1	655.1	12.5	94.5	343.4	299.2	11.7	32.6	1,829.2	1,474.2	291.2	63.7
IV	2,906.5	1,115.4	760.2	652.5	12.5	95.1	355.1	309.8	12.6	32.8	1,791.2	1,435.7	292.2	63.3
2009: I	2,872.0	1,103.2	743.9	642.8	14.2	86.8	359.4	315.3	11.7	32.4	1,768.8	1,415.7	290.9	62.1
II	2,919.3	1,139.8	769.9	663.4	13.8	92.8	369.8	325.6	11.7	32.5	1,779.5	1,424.0	293.2	62.3
III	2,933.8	1,155.4	787.3	676.9	17.7	92.7	368.1	322.8	12.4	32.9	1,778.4	1,425.6	290.6	62.3
IV	2,934.5	1,159.9	785.4	673.5	18.1	93.8	374.5	328.3	12.5	33.6	1,774.7	1,432.2	279.5	63.0
2010: I	2,955.7	1,178.1	796.3	684.0	18.3	94.1	381.8	333.3	13.7	34.7	1,777.6	1,447.4	267.0	63.2
II	2,990.8	1,206.7	813.0	695.2	18.2	99.7	393.7	343.3	15.0	35.4	1,784.1	1,446.7	273.5	63.9
III	3,022.2	1,233.9	830.8	711.2	19.1	100.5	403.1	350.4	15.6	37.1	1,788.2	1,441.3	283.0	64.0
IV p	3,040.7	1,238.7	831.0	703.0	20.6	107.4	407.7	352.8	17.4	37.5	1,802.0	1,454.7	283.3	64.0

Source: Department of Commerce (Bureau of Economic Analysis).

TABLE B–21. Real government consumption expenditures and gross investment by type, 1995–2010

[Billions of chained (2005) dollars; quarterly data at seasonally adjusted annual rates]

		Government consumption expenditures and gross investment											
		Federal									State and local			
			National defense				Nondefense						Gross investment	
Year or quarter	Total	Total	Total	Consumption expenditures	Gross investment		Total	Consumption expenditures	Gross investment		Total	Consumption expenditures		Equipment and software
					Structures	Equipment and software			Structures	Equipment and software			Structures	
1995	1,888.9	704.1	476.8	424.5	10.1	43.7	227.5	201.2	15.7	13.7	1,183.6	983.0	175.4	29.1
1996	1,907.9	696.0	470.4	418.5	9.2	43.8	225.7	196.2	15.9	15.5	1,211.1	1,001.0	184.3	29.9
1997	1,943.8	689.1	457.2	412.2	8.7	38.9	231.9	203.2	13.8	16.6	1,254.3	1,027.7	196.7	33.1
1998	1,985.0	681.4	447.5	401.2	8.1	40.1	233.7	201.2	14.5	18.7	1,303.8	1,070.8	196.5	37.7
1999	2,056.1	694.6	455.8	407.6	7.2	42.4	238.7	202.9	14.0	21.7	1,361.8	1,109.5	210.9	41.8
2000	2,097.8	698.1	453.5	403.9	6.9	43.6	244.4	212.4	10.4	21.5	1,400.1	1,133.7	222.2	44.3
2001	2,178.3	726.5	470.7	418.5	6.5	46.3	255.5	224.2	9.8	21.6	1,452.3	1,172.6	234.8	45.3
2002	2,279.6	779.5	505.3	445.8	7.0	52.7	273.9	239.7	11.8	22.7	1,500.6	1,211.3	244.2	45.8
2003	2,330.5	831.1	549.2	484.1	8.5	57.0	281.7	247.1	11.9	23.0	1,499.7	1,207.5	245.5	47.2
2004	2,362.0	865.0	580.4	509.4	7.8	63.3	284.6	250.2	9.9	24.6	1,497.1	1,207.4	241.3	48.6
2005	2,369.9	876.3	589.0	514.8	7.5	66.8	287.3	251.0	8.3	28.0	1,493.6	1,212.0	230.8	50.8
2006	2,402.1	894.9	598.4	519.1	7.5	71.9	296.6	257.5	8.8	30.3	1,507.2	1,220.7	231.4	55.2
2007	2,434.2	906.1	611.8	528.0	8.8	75.1	294.2	254 7	9.8	29.7	1,528.1	1,239.8	227.6	61.6
2008	2,502.7	971.8	657.7	562.1	9.6	86.5	314.0	271.8	9.5	32.9	1,532.6	1,240.2	229.3	64.2
2009	2,542.6	1,027.6	693.0	591.7	13.5	87.9	334.6	290.6	10.1	33.9	1,518.8	1,232.1	225.4	62.5
2010 ᵖ	2,570.1	1,077.0	720.3	608.8	16.2	95.7	356.8	306.4	13.1	37.2	1,499.0	1,220.1	216.6	64.4
2007: I	2,406.7	883.6	595.3	515.9	8.0	71.5	288.2	249.7	9.4	29.1	1,522.9	1,235.5	228.8	59.3
II	2,426.8	898.9	607.3	522.3	10.1	75.0	291.5	252.2	9.7	29.6	1,527.8	1,239.8	227.8	60.9
III	2,447.9	919.7	622.3	536.8	9.0	76.6	297.3	257.1	10.2	29.8	1,528.4	1,240.6	226.4	62.6
IV	2,455.3	922.2	622.4	537.0	8.1	77.4	299.8	259.8	9.8	30.2	1,533.3	1,243.4	227.4	63.8
2008: I	2,469.2	937.6	632.7	547.0	7.5	78.5	304.8	264.3	8.9	31.8	1,532.2	1,241.6	227.3	64.6
II	2,489.4	955.3	643.4	547.4	9.8	86.9	311.9	270.1	9.2	32.8	1,535.1	1,240.2	231.3	64.8
III	2,521.5	987.5	673.0	573.0	10.5	90.1	314.2	271.4	9.7	33.2	1,536.2	1,241.3	231.7	64.2
IV	2,530.7	1,006.9	681.6	581.0	10.6	90.5	325.2	281.4	10.3	33.6	1,526.8	1,237.8	227.0	63.3
2009: I	2,511.5	994.1	666.7	571.7	11.8	83.4	327.3	284.5	9.6	33.4	1,520.1	1,235.7	223.8	62.1
II	2,549.3	1,029.2	693.2	592.6	11.6	89.3	335.9	292.7	9.7	33.5	1,523.8	1,234.7	227.9	62.2
III	2,559.3	1,043.5	708.3	604.0	15.0	89.2	335.2	290.7	10.5	34.0	1,520.0	1,229.5	228.9	62.4
IV	2,550.3	1,043.6	703.8	598.5	15.4	89.9	339.8	294.5	10.7	34.6	1,511.2	1,228.4	220.9	63.5
2010: I	2,540.2	1,048.4	704.4	598.9	15.6	89.9	344.0	296.6	11.7	35.7	1,496.8	1,225.1	210.5	63.6
II	2,564.9	1,071.5	717.1	606.8	15.6	95.0	354.5	305.3	12.8	36.4	1,499.1	1,222.3	214.6	64.4
III	2,589.6	1,094.3	731.8	619.8	16.3	96.0	362.6	311.3	13.2	38.2	1,501.7	1,217.9	221.1	64.4
IV ᵖ	2,585.8	1,093.9	728.1	609.6	17.4	101.9	365.9	312.6	14.7	38.7	1,498.4	1,215.3	220.1	64.9

Note: See Table B–2 for data for total government consumption expenditures and gross investment for 1962–94.

Source: Department of Commerce (Bureau of Economic Analysis).

TABLE B–22. Private inventories and domestic final sales by industry, 1962–2010

[Billions of dollars, except as noted; seasonally adjusted]

Quarter	Private inventories [1]								Final sales of domestic business [3]	Ratio of private inventories to final sales of domestic business	
	Total [2]	Farm	Mining, utilities, and construction [2]	Manufac- turing	Wholesale trade	Retail trade	Other indus- tries [2]	Non- farm [2]		Total	Non- farm
Fourth quarter:											
1962	147.4	47.0		53.2	18.0	22.7	6.6	100.5	35.6	4.14	2.82
1963	149.9	44.4		55.1	19.5	23.9	7.1	105.5	37.9	3.95	2.78
1964	154.5	42.2		58.6	20.8	25.2	7.7	112.2	40.8	3.79	2.75
1965	169.4	47.2		63.4	22.5	28.0	8.3	122.2	44.9	3.77	2.72
1966	185.6	47.3		73.0	25.8	30.6	8.9	138.3	47.4	3.92	2.92
1967	194.8	45.7		79.9	28.1	30.9	10.1	149.1	49.9	3.90	2.99
1968	208.1	48.8		85.1	29.3	34.2	10.6	159.3	55.0	3.79	2.90
1969	227.4	52.8		92.6	32.5	37.5	12.0	174.6	58.7	3.88	2.98
1970	235.7	52.4		95.5	36.4	38.5	12.9	183.3	61.9	3.81	2.96
1971	253.7	59.3		96.6	39.4	44.7	13.7	194.4	67.5	3.76	2.88
1972	283.6	73.7		102.1	43.1	49.8	14.8	209.9	75.7	3.74	2.77
1973	351.5	102.2		121.5	51.7	58.4	17.7	249.4	83.7	4.20	2.98
1974	405.6	87.6		162.6	66.9	63.9	24.7	318.1	89.8	4.52	3.54
1975	408.5	89.5		162.2	66.5	64.4	25.9	319.0	101.1	4.04	3.16
1976	439.6	85.3		178.7	74.1	73.0	28.5	354.2	111.2	3.95	3.19
1977	482.0	90.6		193.2	84.0	80.9	33.3	391.4	124.0	3.89	3.16
1978	570.9	119.3		219.8	99.0	94.1	38.8	451.7	143.6	3.98	3.15
1979	667.6	134.9		261.8	119.5	104.7	46.6	532.6	159.4	4.19	3.34
1980	739.0	140.3		293.4	139.4	111.7	54.1	598.7	174.1	4.24	3.44
1981	779.1	127.4		313.1	148.8	123.2	66.6	651.7	186.7	4.17	3.49
1982	773.9	131.3		304.6	147.9	123.2	66.8	642.6	194.8	3.97	3.30
1983	796.9	131.7		308.9	153.4	137.6	65.2	665.1	215.7	3.69	3.08
1984	869.0	131.4		344.5	169.1	157.0	66.9	737.6	233.6	3.72	3.16
1985	875.9	125.8		333.3	175.9	171.4	69.5	750.2	249.5	3.51	3.01
1986	858.0	113.0		320.6	182.0	176.2	66.3	745.1	264.2	3.25	2.82
1987	924.2	119.9		339.6	195.8	199.1	69.9	804.4	277.7	3.33	2.90
1988	999.7	130.7		372.4	213.9	213.2	69.5	869.1	304.1	3.29	2.86
1989	1,044.3	129.6		390.5	222.8	231.4	70.1	914.7	322.8	3.23	2.83
1990	1,082.0	133.1		404.5	236.8	236.6	71.0	948.9	335.9	3.22	2.82
1991	1,057.2	123.2		384.1	239.2	240.2	70.5	934.0	345.7	3.06	2.70
1992	1,082.6	133.1		377.6	248.3	249.4	74.3	949.5	370.9	2.92	2.56
1993	1,116.0	132.3		380.1	258.6	268.6	76.5	983.7	391.4	2.85	2.51
1994	1,194.5	134.5		404.3	281.5	293.6	80.6	1,060.0	413.9	2.89	2.56
1995	1,257.2	131.1		424.5	303.7	312.2	85.6	1,126.1	436.0	2.88	2.58
NAICS:											
1996	1,284.7	136.6	31.1	421.0	285.1	328.7	82.1	1,148.1	465.6	2.76	2.47
1997	1,327.3	136.9	33.0	432.0	302.5	335.9	87.1	1,190.4	492.2	2.70	2.42
1998	1,341.6	120.5	36.6	432.3	312.0	349.2	91.1	1,221.1	525.8	2.55	2.32
1999	1,432.7	124.3	38.5	457.6	334.8	377.7	99.8	1,308.4	557.2	2.57	2.35
2000	1,524.0	132.1	42.3	476.5	357.7	400.8	114.6	1,391.8	588.3	2.59	2.37
2001	1,447.3	126.2	45.3	440.9	335.8	386.0	113.0	1,321.1	603.0	2.40	2.19
2002	1,489.1	135.9	46.5	443.7	343.2	408.0	111.8	1,353.2	608.5	2.45	2.22
2003	1,545.7	151.0	54.7	447.6	352.6	425.5	114.3	1,394.7	646.3	2.39	2.16
2004	1,681.5	157.2	64.1	487.2	388.9	460.9	123.2	1,524.3	685.2	2.45	2.22
2005	1,804.6	165.2	81.7	531.5	422.8	473.7	129.8	1,639.4	728.7	2.48	2.25
2006	1,917.1	165.1	90.7	575.7	456.4	491.6	137.7	1,752.0	771.9	2.48	2.27
2007: I	1,952.5	177.2	93.8	583.2	464.3	493.4	140.7	1,775.3	782.9	2.49	2.27
II	1,976.8	174.7	98.1	594.7	468.7	497.5	143.2	1,802.2	793.9	2.49	2.27
III	2,008.4	182.7	94.3	603.7	479.1	504.1	144.5	1,825.7	802.3	2.50	2.28
IV	2,077.5	188.3	95.6	635.6	497.2	511.8	148.9	1,889.2	810.2	2.56	2.33
2008: I	2,147.8	197.0	101.3	670.9	515.7	509.4	153.4	1,950.8	807.6	2.66	2.42
II	2,223.4	212.6	111.0	697.2	536.1	509.7	156.8	2,010.8	814.5	2.73	2.47
III	2,202.2	205.5	108.9	682.0	535.9	509.6	160.4	1,996.7	809.1	2.72	2.47
IV	2,022.6	185.4	91.8	607.7	489.2	490.3	158.2	1,837.2	791.1	2.56	2.32
2009: I	1,952.5	180.8	87.8	586.2	468.6	476.4	152.8	1,771.7	784.5	2.49	2.26
II	1,906.3	177.5	85.4	576.7	451.4	465.2	150.0	1,728.8	781.2	2.44	2.21
III	1,886.7	174.6	85.8	576.1	440.1	461.4	148.7	1,712.1	782.9	2.41	2.19
IV	1,922.8	178.8	85.7	593.7	449.5	465.9	149.1	1,744.0	786.6	2.44	2.22
2010: I	1,954.7	188.8	86.8	597.5	458.0	472.8	150.9	1,766.0	790.1	2.47	2.23
II	1,952.6	186.1	86.3	588.4	461.1	479.0	151.7	1,766.5	795.9	2.45	2.22
III	2,038.1	211.1	86.4	606.5	492.0	490.0	152.1	1,827.0	802.2	2.54	2.28
IV *p*	2,118.5	231.4	86.2	639.2	520.1	485.7	155.9	1,887.1	821.8	2.58	2.30

[1] Inventories at end of quarter. Quarter-to-quarter change calculated from this table is not the current-dollar change in private inventories component of gross domestic product (GDP). The former is the difference between two inventory stocks, each valued at its respective end-of-quarter prices. The latter is the change in the physical volume of inventories valued at average prices of the quarter. In addition, changes calculated from this table are at quarterly rates, whereas change in private inventories is stated at annual rates.

[2] Inventories of construction, mining, and utilities establishments are included in other industries through 1995.

[3] Quarterly totals at monthly rates. Final sales of domestic business equals final sales of domestic product less gross output of general government, gross value added of nonprofit institutions, compensation paid to domestic workers, and imputed rental of owner-occupied nonfarm housing. Includes a small amount of final sales by farm and by government enterprises.

Note: The industry classification of inventories is on an establishment basis. Estimates through 1995 are based on the Standard Industrial Classification (SIC). Beginning with 1996, estimates are based on the North American Industry Classification System (NAICS).

Source: Department of Commerce (Bureau of Economic Analysis).

TABLE B–23. Real private inventories and domestic final sales by industry, 1962–2010

[Billions of chained (2005) dollars, except as noted; seasonally adjusted]

Quarter	Private inventories [1]								Final sales of domestic business [3]	Ratio of private inventories to final sales of domestic business	
	Total [2]	Farm	Mining, utilities, and construction [2]	Manufacturing	Wholesale trade	Retail trade	Other industries [2]	Nonfarm [2]		Total	Nonfarm
Fourth quarter:											
1962	520.4	137.6		180.9	71.6	73.0	39.4	366.5	157.0	3.31	2.33
1963	540.6	139.0		187.8	77.5	77.0	42.1	385.5	166.3	3.25	2.32
1964	557.9	135.1		198.2	82.2	81.1	44.7	407.3	176.4	3.16	2.31
1965	590.8	137.7		212.2	87.8	89.3	46.6	437.8	191.6	3.08	2.29
1966	637.9	136.3		240.6	99.5	96.6	47.9	487.9	195.7	3.26	2.49
1967	671.8	138.8		259.6	107.7	96.6	53.5	519.5	200.6	3.35	2.59
1968	702.6	142.9		271.5	111.5	104.8	55.1	545.9	211.5	3.32	2.58
1969	732.9	142.9		284.1	119.7	112.1	57.9	576.8	215.8	3.40	2.67
1970	738.5	140.5		284.0	128.7	112.2	58.6	585.5	218.4	3.38	2.68
1971	763.5	144.6		280.6	135.5	127.4	60.7	606.1	229.6	3.33	2.64
1972	789.1	145.0		288.3	141.6	137.3	63.7	632.8	248.7	3.17	2.54
1973	828.1	146.8		309.6	145.4	148.4	67.0	673.3	257.4	3.22	2.62
1974	857.2	142.4		333.0	158.9	146.2	71.4	712.3	247.8	3.46	2.87
1975	844.4	148.2		324.6	152.1	138.8	73.3	690.9	259.6	3.25	2.66
1976	878.7	146.6		340.1	162.2	149.5	74.0	728.5	272.4	3.23	2.67
1977	921.8	153.9		349.6	175.3	158.1	79.6	764.2	286.7	3.21	2.67
1978	967.4	155.9		365.6	189.3	168.7	84.4	809.1	308.2	3.14	2.63
1979	995.4	160.2		379.7	198.7	168.6	84.3	832.8	315.4	3.16	2.64
1980	986.0	153.0		380.1	204.0	163.8	82.9	832.4	315.1	3.13	2.64
1981	1,025.0	163.1		305.2	209.8	172.0	92.3	060.6	312.8	3.20	2.75
1982	1,005.3	170.6		367.9	207.2	168.9	89.4	833.3	311.6	3.23	2.67
1983	997.7	153.1		367.5	206.3	182.7	88.3	844.0	335.2	2.98	2.52
1984	1,075.9	159.4		399.4	222.8	205.0	89.7	916.3	353.5	3.04	2.59
1985	1,101.3	166.5		392.4	229.2	220.8	94.8	934.7	369.9	2.98	2.53
1986	1,109.8	164.2		388.3	237.7	224.3	98.3	945.1	383.8	2.89	2.46
1987	1,143.0	155.1		397.6	245.4	246.1	100.8	986.2	394.3	2.90	2.50
1988	1,164.9	142.0		416.2	254.9	253.9	99.3	1,021.6	414.7	2.81	2.46
1989	1,195.6	142.0		431.8	258.5	268.8	94.8	1,052.4	426.9	2.80	2.47
1990	1,212.1	148.6		441.6	267.2	267.2	91.2	1,066.4	428.2	2.83	2.49
1991	1,210.7	146.7		434.2	271.5	267.7	94.8	1,066.8	428.0	2.83	2.49
1992	1,228.6	153.8		429.0	280.3	272.5	97.7	1,077.7	451.1	2.72	2.39
1993	1,250.8	146.3		432.9	286.5	288.3	101.2	1,107.6	466.9	2.68	2.37
1994	1,320.1	160.0		446.3	302.7	309.4	106.1	1,163.4	485.5	2.72	2.40
1995	1,352.2	147.0		461.7	316.2	321.9	108.6	1,207.7	503.4	2.69	2.40
NAICS:											
1996	1,383.4	155.3	47.6	465.7	298.0	335.3	87.6	1,230.9	529.2	2.61	2.33
1997	1,460.8	159.0	50.1	490.0	324.9	349.5	93.2	1,304.4	551.4	2.65	2.37
1998	1,532.4	160.6	59.1	507.6	348.6	364.7	99.0	1,373.9	586.2	2.61	2.34
1999	1,600.9	156.9	57.1	523.8	369.7	390.5	106.6	1,444.7	616.4	2.60	2.34
2000	1,661.1	155.2	54.3	531.9	390.4	411.1	119.3	1,505.9	638.7	2.60	2.36
2001	1,619.4	155.3	65.1	505.7	376.8	400.5	119.1	1,464.4	645.1	2.51	2.27
2002	1,632.1	152.2	61.0	500.5	376.7	424.2	118.0	1,480.0	645.5	2.53	2.29
2003	1,649.5	152.4	68.2	492.0	376.3	441.5	119.6	1,497.2	676.7	2.44	2.21
2004	1,715.8	160.3	69.6	498.0	396.8	465.2	126.0	1,555.6	698.6	2.46	2.23
2005	1,765.8	160.4	73.4	519.0	415.0	469.8	128.3	1,605.4	719.8	2.45	2.23
2006	1,825.2	156.7	90.3	536.0	428.3	480.6	132.9	1,668.6	746.3	2.45	2.24
2007: I	1,829.5	158.0	91.7	537.9	428.7	478.5	134.3	1,671.6	749.2	2.44	2.23
II	1,840.7	156.7	93.5	543.3	430.2	480.9	135.7	1,684.2	754.6	2.44	2.23
III	1,849.8	156.1	91.7	546.4	434.5	484.2	136.4	1,693.9	759.9	2.43	2.23
IV	1,852.9	155.9	90.3	551.4	432.8	484.8	137.2	1,697.3	769.3	2.41	2.21
2008: I	1,850.9	154.0	88.7	558.6	433.4	476.7	138.2	1,697.3	766.3	2.42	2.21
II	1,845.7	155.1	87.1	552.9	438.1	471.9	139.0	1,690.9	767.9	2.40	2.20
III	1,838.9	155.5	84.9	547.0	440.9	469.0	140.0	1,683.6	753.0	2.44	2.24
IV	1,815.3	156.9	80.7	539.1	434.8	459.6	142.4	1,658.3	738.2	2.46	2.25
2009: I	1,783.8	157.4	81.7	531.4	421.6	449.0	140.8	1,626.2	727.8	2.45	2.23
II	1,743.4	158.9	82.2	521.8	402.9	436.8	138.8	1,584.0	726.6	2.40	2.18
III	1,711.3	158.7	81.8	513.7	388.0	430.4	137.0	1,552.1	726.6	2.36	2.14
IV	1,702.2	160.3	77.9	512.5	385.9	428.2	135.5	1,541.4	732.2	2.32	2.11
2010: I	1,713.2	162.2	75.2	517.8	389.2	431.4	135.5	1,550.5	734.7	2.33	2.11
II	1,730.4	164.1	76.3	517.0	397.0	437.6	136.5	1,565.8	735.1	2.35	2.13
III	1,760.8	165.4	75.7	524.4	411.3	444.8	137.0	1,594.9	736.0	2.39	2.17
IV p	1,762.5	166.4	75.3	529.5	414.8	436.1	137.3	1,595.6	756.0	2.33	2.11

[1] Inventories at end of quarter. Quarter-to-quarter changes calculated from this table are at quarterly rates, whereas the change in private inventories component of gross domestic product (GDP) is stated at annual rates.

[2] Inventories of construction, mining, and utilities establishments are included in other industries through 1995.

[3] Quarterly totals at monthly rates. Final sales of domestic business equals final sales of domestic product less gross output of general government, gross value added of nonprofit institutions, compensation paid to domestic workers, and imputed rental of owner-occupied nonfarm housing. Includes a small amount of final sales by farm and by government enterprises.

Note: The industry classification of inventories is on an establishment basis. Estimates through 1995 are based on the Standard Industrial Classification (SIC). Beginning with 1996, estimates are based on the North American Industry Classification System (NAICS).

See *Survey of Current Business*, Tables 5.7.6A and 5.7.6B, for detailed information on calculation of the chained (2005) dollar inventory series.

Source: Department of Commerce (Bureau of Economic Analysis).

TABLE B–24. Foreign transactions in the national income and product accounts, 1962–2010

[Billions of dollars; quarterly data at seasonally adjusted annual rates]

Year or quarter	Current receipts from rest of the world					Current payments to rest of the world									Balance on current account, NIPA[2]
	Total	Exports of goods and services			In-come re-ceipts	Total	Imports of goods and services			In-come pay-ments	Current taxes and transfer payments to rest of the world (net)				
		Total	Goods[1]	Services[1]			Total	Goods[1]	Services[1]		Total	From persons (net)	From government (net)	From business (net)	
1962	35.0	29.1	21.7	7.4	5.9	31.2	25.0	16.9	8.1	1.8	4.4	0.6	3.7	0.1	3.8
1963	37.6	31.1	23.3	7.7	6.5	32.7	26.1	17.7	8.4	2.1	4.5	.7	3.7	.1	4.9
1964	42.3	35.0	26.7	8.3	7.2	34.8	28.1	19.4	8.7	2.3	4.4	.7	3.5	.2	7.5
1965	45.0	37.1	27.8	9.4	7.9	38.9	31.5	22.2	9.3	2.6	4.7	.8	3.8	.2	6.2
1966	49.0	40.9	30.7	10.2	8.1	45.2	37.1	26.3	10.7	3.0	5.1	.8	4.1	.2	3.8
1967	52.1	43.5	32.2	11.3	8.7	48.7	39.9	27.8	12.2	3.3	5.5	1.0	4.2	.2	3.5
1968	58.0	47.9	35.3	12.6	10.1	56.5	46.6	33.9	12.6	4.0	5.9	1.0	4.6	.3	1.5
1969	63.7	51.9	38.3	13.7	11.8	62.1	50.5	36.8	13.7	5.7	5.9	1.1	4.5	.3	1.6
1970	72.5	59.7	44.5	15.2	12.8	68.8	55.8	40.9	14.9	6.4	6.6	1.3	4.9	.4	3.7
1971	77.0	63.0	45.6	17.4	14.0	76.7	62.3	46.6	15.8	6.4	7.9	1.4	6.1	.4	.3
1972	87.1	70.8	51.8	19.0	16.3	91.2	74.2	56.9	17.3	7.7	9.2	1.4	7.4	.5	−4.0
1973	118.8	95.3	73.9	21.3	23.5	109.9	91.2	71.8	19.3	10.9	7.9	1.6	5.6	.7	8.9
1974	156.5	126.7	101.0	25.7	29.8	150.5	127.5	104.5	22.9	14.3	8.7	1.4	6.4	1.0	6.0
1975	166.7	138.7	109.6	29.1	28.0	146.9	122.7	99.0	23.7	15.0	9.1	1.3	7.1	.7	19.8
1976	181.9	149.5	117.8	31.7	32.4	174.8	151.1	124.6	26.5	15.5	8.1	1.4	5.7	1.1	7.1
1977	196.6	159.4	123.7	35.7	37.2	207.5	182.4	152.6	29.8	16.9	8.1	1.4	5.3	1.4	−10.9
1978	233.1	186.9	145.4	41.5	46.3	245.8	212.3	177.4	34.8	24.7	8.8	1.6	5.9	1.4	−12.6
1979	298.5	230.1	184.0	46.1	68.3	299.6	252.7	212.8	39.9	36.4	10.6	1.7	6.8	2.0	−1.2
1980	359.9	280.8	225.8	55.0	79.1	351.4	293.8	248.6	45.3	44.9	12.6	2.0	8.3	2.4	8.5
1981	397.3	305.2	239.1	66.1	92.0	393.9	317.8	267.8	49.9	59.1	17.0	5.6	8.3	3.2	3.4
1982	384.2	283.2	215.0	68.2	101.0	387.5	303.2	250.5	52.6	64.5	19.8	6.7	9.7	3.4	−3.3
1983	378.9	277.0	207.3	69.7	101.9	413.9	328.6	272.7	56.0	64.8	20.5	7.0	10.1	3.4	−35.1
1984	424.2	302.4	225.6	76.7	121.9	514.3	405.1	336.3	68.8	85.6	23.8	7.9	12.2	3.5	−90.1
1985	414.5	302.0	222.2	79.8	112.4	528.8	417.2	343.3	73.9	85.9	25.7	8.3	14.4	2.9	−114.3
1986	431.3	320.3	226.0	94.3	111.0	574.0	452.9	370.0	82.9	93.4	27.8	9.1	15.4	3.2	−142.7
1987	486.6	363.8	257.5	106.2	122.8	640.7	508.7	414.8	93.9	105.2	26.8	10.0	13.4	3.4	−154.1
1988	595.5	443.9	325.8	118.1	151.6	711.2	554.0	452.1	101.9	128.3	29.0	10.8	13.7	4.5	−115.7
1989	680.3	503.1	369.4	133.8	177.2	772.7	591.0	484.8	106.2	151.2	30.4	11.6	14.2	4.6	−92.4
1990	740.6	552.1	396.6	155.5	188.5	815.6	629.7	508.1	121.7	154.1	31.7	12.2	14.7	4.8	−74.9
1991	764.7	596.6	423.6	173.0	168.1	756.9	623.5	500.7	122.8	138.2	−4.9	14.1	−24.0	5.0	7.9
1992	786.8	635.0	448.0	187.0	151.8	832.4	667.8	544.9	122.9	122.7	41.9	14.5	22.0	5.4	−45.6
1993	810.8	655.6	459.9	195.7	155.2	889.4	720.0	592.8	127.2	124.0	45.4	17.1	22.9	5.4	−78.6
1994	904.8	720.7	510.1	210.6	184.1	1,019.5	813.4	676.8	136.6	160.0	46.1	18.9	21.1	6.0	−114.7
1995	1,041.1	811.9	583.3	228.6	229.3	1,146.2	902.6	757.4	145.1	199.6	44.1	20.3	15.6	8.2	−105.1
1996	1,113.5	867.7	618.3	249.3	245.8	1,227.6	964.0	807.4	156.5	214.2	49.5	22.6	20.0	6.9	−114.1
1997	1,233.9	954.4	687.7	266.7	279.5	1,363.3	1,055.8	885.7	170.1	256.1	51.4	25.7	16.7	9.1	−129.3
1998	1,240.1	953.9	680.9	273.0	286.2	1,444.6	1,115.7	930.8	184.9	268.9	60.0	29.7	17.4	13.0	−204.5
1999	1,308.8	989.3	697.2	292.1	319.5	1,600.7	1,251.4	1,047.7	203.7	291.7	57.6	32.2	18.0	7.4	−291.9
2000	1,473.7	1,093.2	784.3	308.9	380.5	1,884.1	1,475.3	1,246.5	228.8	342.8	66.1	34.6	20.0	11.4	−410.4
2001	1,350.8	1,027.7	731.2	296.5	323.0	1,742.4	1,398.7	1,171.7	227.0	271.1	72.6	38.1	16.2	18.3	−391.6
2002	1,316.5	1,003.0	700.3	302.7	313.5	1,768.1	1,430.2	1,193.9	236.3	264.4	73.5	40.6	21.6	11.3	−451.6
2003	1,394.4	1,041.0	726.8	314.2	353.3	1,910.5	1,545.1	1,289.3	255.9	284.6	80.7	41.2	25.8	13.7	−516.1
2004	1,628.8	1,180.2	817.0	363.2	448.6	2,253.4	1,798.9	1,501.7	297.3	357.4	97.1	43.6	27.2	26.3	−624.6
2005	1,878.1	1,305.1	906.1	399.0	573.0	2,618.6	2,027.8	1,708.0	319.8	475.9	115.0	48.4	35.3	31.3	−740.5
2006	2,192.1	1,471.0	1,024.4	446.6	721.1	2,990.5	2,240.3	1,884.9	355.4	648.6	101.5	51.6	28.8	21.1	−798.4
2007	2,532.7	1,661.7	1,162.0	499.7	871.0	3,249.6	2,375.7	2,001.6	374.0	747.7	126.2	59.3	36.1	30.8	−716.9
2008	2,682.6	1,843.4	1,295.1	548.3	839.2	3,353.0	2,553.8	2,148.8	405.0	664.7	134.5	64.6	38.4	31.5	−670.4
2009	2,208.2	1,578.4	1,063.1	515.3	629.8	2,587.9	1,964.7	1,587.8	376.9	483.6	139.5	66.5	50.2	22.9	−379.7
2010 ᵖ	....	1,837.1	1,276.4	560.7	....	....	2,352.6	1,948.0	404.6		158.2	71.7	62.0	24.5	....
2007: I	2,373.2	1,575.5	1,105.4	470.2	797.6	3,167.3	2,300.6	1,939.0	361.6	727.4	139.4	57.6	45.4	36.4	−794.2
II	2,481.7	1,619.1	1,138.3	480.8	862.6	3,249.5	2,349.8	1,978.9	370.9	783.1	116.6	58.6	25.1	32.8	−767.8
III	2,595.9	1,690.3	1,179.3	511.0	905.6	3,278.9	2,394.7	2,013.7	381.0	760.8	123.3	60.0	31.9	31.5	−683.0
IV	2,679.9	1,761.8	1,225.1	536.7	918.0	3,302.5	2,457.5	2,074.9	382.6	719.4	125.6	61.2	41.9	22.6	−622.7
2008: I	2,709.9	1,819.9	1,279.4	540.5	890.0	3,398.4	2,558.4	2,161.1	397.3	697.6	142.4	63.2	43.5	35.7	−688.5
II	2,806.3	1,925.3	1,364.9	560.4	881.0	3,518.1	2,677.2	2,273.4	403.7	705.5	135.4	66.9	39.1	29.4	−711.8
III	2,783.1	1,927.3	1,367.6	559.6	855.8	3,473.8	2,690.4	2,276.9	413.5	651.5	131.9	67.3	35.9	28.7	−690.7
IV	2,430.9	1,700.9	1,168.3	532.6	730.0	3,021.6	2,289.3	1,883.8	405.5	604.0	128.3	61.1	35.0	32.3	−590.7
2009: I	2,136.8	1,521.2	1,014.5	506.7	615.6	2,521.6	1,896.9	1,519.9	377.0	493.1	131.6	65.4	39.9	26.2	−384.8
II	2,131.9	1,520.2	1,011.7	508.5	611.7	2,475.1	1,855.3	1,485.7	369.7	482.0	137.8	64.6	54.5	18.7	−343.3
III	2,209.5	1,582.1	1,068.6	513.6	627.4	2,599.6	1,990.5	1,613.8	376.6	460.1	149.0	66.3	61.1	21.7	−390.1
IV	2,354.6	1,689.9	1,157.6	532.3	664.7	2,755.2	2,116.3	1,731.8	384.5	499.1	139.7	69.5	45.3	24.9	−400.6
2010: I	2,451.5	1,757.8	1,213.0	544.8	693.7	2,896.5	2,237.6	1,843.5	394.1	502.6	156.3	70.7	60.6	25.0	−445.0
II	2,514.0	1,817.9	1,262.8	555.1	696.1	3,006.4	2,357.1	1,957.2	400.0	500.8	148.5	72.2	51.9	24.4	−492.5
III	2,552.8	1,848.9	1,282.0	566.9	704.0	3,066.8	2,399.4	1,988.2	411.2	515.5	151.9	71.1	56.3	24.5	−514.0
IV ᵖ	....	1,923.9	1,347.7	576.1	....	....	2,416.0	2,002.9	413.1	....	155.4	72.8	58.4	24.1	....

[1] Certain goods, primarily military equipment purchased and sold by the Federal Government, are included in services. Beginning with 1986, repairs and alterations of equipment were reclassified from goods to services.

[2] National income and product accounts (NIPA).

Source: Department of Commerce (Bureau of Economic Analysis).

TABLE B–25. Real exports and imports of goods and services, 1995–2010

[Billions of chained (2005) dollars; quarterly data at seasonally adjusted annual rates]

Year or quarter	Exports of goods and services					Imports of goods and services				
	Total	Goods [1]			Services [1]	Total	Goods [1]			Services [1]
		Total	Durable goods	Non-durable goods			Total	Durable goods	Non-durable goods	
1995	845.7	575.4	363.6	216.2	272.6	944.5	766.1	422.9	360.0	180.9
1996	916.0	626.2	405.4	223.4	291.7	1,026.7	837.9	468.1	384.1	190.3
1997	1,025.1	716.2	478.7	237.9	308.9	1,165.0	958.7	545.4	424.1	206.9
1998	1,048.5	732.2	494.2	237.6	316.4	1,301.1	1,072.3	617.2	462.9	229.4
1999	1,094.3	760.0	517.8	240.8	334.6	1,450.9	1,206.0	707.1	500.2	244.9
2000	1,188.3	844.3	584.6	256.5	343.5	1,639.9	1,367.9	814.8	549.2	271.7
2001	1,121.6	792.0	535.9	255.2	329.3	1,593.8	1,324.2	764.5	564.2	269.6
2002	1,099.2	763.5	505.6	259.1	335.6	1,648.0	1,373.4	796.5	580.2	274.5
2003	1,116.8	777.2	514.5	263.8	339.6	1,720.7	1,440.9	830.6	615.2	279.8
2004	1,222.8	842.9	571.0	272.2	380.0	1,910.8	1,599.7	945.0	655.8	311.0
2005	1,305.1	906.1	624.9	281.2	399.0	2,027.8	1,708.0	1,025.4	682.6	319.8
2006	1,422.0	991.4	691.9	299.6	430.6	2,151.2	1,808.8	1,115.3	694.5	342.4
2007	1,554.4	1,088.1	756.1	331.9	466.3	2,209.3	1,862.2	1,141.0	721.6	347.1
2008	1,647.7	1,156.6	796.0	359.3	491.1	2,151.7	1,796.6	1,096.8	699.4	355.5
2009	1,490.7	1,018.2	660.2	350.9	472.0	1,853.8	1,513.5	870.6	633.7	340.5
2010 [P]	1,665.4	1,166.8	773.8	386.8	499.3	2,086.6	1,735.2	1,067.1	667.4	352.4
2007: I	1,496.4	1,050.5	727.7	322.7	445.9	2,192.7	1,848.9	1,139.0	710.2	343.8
II	1,521.3	1,070.0	744.2	325.8	451.3	2,217.5	1,870.5	1,138.1	731.7	346.9
III	1,578.0	1,102.7	767.3	335.4	475.3	2,244.6	1,893.9	1,151.7	741.7	350.6
IV	1,622.0	1,129.1	785.3	343.7	492.9	2,182.4	1,835.4	1,135.3	702.7	347.1
2008: I	1,644.7	1,155.3	795.4	358.6	489.4	2,174.6	1,820.1	1,136.7	689.3	355.0
II	1,696.6	1,195.1	828.0	367.0	501.5	2,190.4	1,840.9	1,146.3	700.1	349.6
III	1,675.0	1,181.9	820.4	361.7	493.1	2,189.8	1,836.1	1,110.8	721.8	353.8
IV	1,574.5	1,094.1	740.2	350.1	480.5	2,052.2	1,689.3	993.4	686.6	363.7
2009: I	1,451.6	985.8	645.6	334.2	465.0	1,840.8	1,493.3	844.4	638.0	347.4
II	1,447.8	976.4	627.0	342.1	470.4	1,789.9	1,452.0	818.3	623.2	337.5
III	1,490.0	1,019.1	659.4	352.4	470.5	1,880.8	1,542.7	879.3	652.8	338.7
IV	1,573.5	1,091.7	708.9	375.0	482.0	1,903.6	1,566.1	940.2	620.7	338.3
2010: I	1,616.4	1,128.0	735.4	385.0	488.9	1,954.8	1,611.0	982.3	626.3	344.6
II	1,652.1	1,159.2	775.4	378.7	493.6	2,101.1	1,753.9	1,074.5	677.8	348.3
III	1,679.3	1,175.8	787.2	383.4	504.2	2,184.3	1,825.5	1,108.2	714.1	360.1
IV [P]	1,713.9	1,204.1	797.2	400.0	510.5	2,106.1	1,750.4	1,103.4	651.2	356.7

[1] Certain goods, primarily military equipment purchased and sold by the Federal Government, are included in services. Beginning with 1986, repairs and alterations of equipment were reclassified from goods to services.

Note: See Table B–2 for data for total exports of goods and services and total imports of goods and services for 1962–94.

Source: Department of Commerce (Bureau of Economic Analysis).

TABLE B–26. Relation of gross domestic product, gross national product, net national product, and national income, 1962–2010

[Billions of dollars; quarterly data at seasonally adjusted annual rates]

Year or quarter	Gross domestic product	Plus: Income receipts from rest of the world	Less: Income payments to rest of the world	Equals: Gross national product	Less: Consumption of fixed capital			Equals: Net national product	Less: Statistical discrepancy	Equals: National income
					Total	Private	Government			
1962	585.7	5.9	1.8	589.7	60.6	44.1	16.5	529.2	0.3	528.9
1963	617.8	6.5	2.1	622.2	63.3	45.9	17.5	558.9	−.8	559.7
1964	663.6	7.2	2.3	668.6	66.4	48.3	18.1	602.2	.8	601.4
1965	719.1	7.9	2.6	724.4	70.7	51.9	18.9	653.7	1.5	652.2
1966	787.7	8.1	3.0	792.8	76.5	56.5	20.0	716.3	6.2	710.1
1967	832.4	8.7	3.3	837.8	82.9	61.6	21.4	754.9	4.5	750.4
1968	909.8	10.1	4.0	915.9	90.4	67.4	23.0	825.5	4.3	821.2
1969	984.4	11.8	5.7	990.5	99.2	74.5	24.7	891.4	2.9	888.5
1970	1,038.3	12.8	6.4	1,044.7	108.3	81.7	26.6	936.4	6.9	929.5
1971	1,126.8	14.0	6.4	1,134.4	117.8	89.5	28.2	1,016.6	11.0	1,005.6
1972	1,237.9	16.3	7.7	1,246.4	127.2	97.7	29.4	1,119.3	8.9	1,110.3
1973	1,382.3	23.5	10.9	1,394.9	140.8	109.5	31.3	1,254.1	8.0	1,246.1
1974	1,499.5	29.8	14.3	1,515.0	163.7	127.8	35.9	1,351.3	9.8	1,341.5
1975	1,637.7	28.0	15.0	1,650.7	190.4	150.4	39.9	1,460.3	16.3	1,444.0
1976	1,824.6	32.4	15.5	1,841.4	208.2	165.5	42.6	1,633.3	23.5	1,609.8
1977	2,030.1	37.2	16.9	2,050.4	231.8	186.1	45.6	1,818.6	21.2	1,797.4
1978	2,293.8	46.3	24.7	2,315.3	261.4	212.0	49.5	2,053.9	26.1	2,027.9
1979	2,562.2	68.3	36.4	2,594.2	298.9	244.5	54.4	2,295.3	47.0	2,248.3
1980	2,788.1	79.1	44.9	2,822.3	344.1	282.3	61.8	2,478.2	45.3	2,433.0
1981	3,126.8	92.0	59.1	3,159.8	393.3	323.2	70.1	2,766.4	36.6	2,729.8
1982	3,253.2	101.0	64.5	3,289.7	433.5	356.4	77.1	2,856.2	4.8	2,851.4
1983	3,534.6	101.9	64.8	3,571.7	451.1	369.5	81.6	3,120.6	49.7	3,070.9
1984	3,930.9	121.9	85.6	3,967.2	474.3	387.5	86.9	3,492.8	31.5	3,461.3
1985	4,217.5	112.4	85.9	4,244.0	505.4	412.8	92.7	3,738.6	42.3	3,696.3
1986	4,460.1	111.0	93.4	4,477.7	538.5	439.1	99.4	3,939.2	67.7	3,871.5
1987	4,736.4	122.8	105.2	4,754.0	571.1	464.5	106.6	4,182.9	32.9	4,150.0
1988	5,100.4	151.6	128.3	5,123.8	611.0	497.1	113.9	4,512.8	−9.5	4,522.3
1989	5,482.1	177.2	151.2	5,508.1	651.5	529.6	121.8	4,856.6	56.1	4,800.5
1990	5,800.5	188.5	154.1	5,835.0	691.2	560.4	130.8	5,143.7	84.2	5,059.5
1991	5,992.1	168.1	138.2	6,022.0	724.4	585.4	138.9	5,297.6	79.7	5,217.9
1992	6,342.3	151.8	122.7	6,371.4	744.4	599.9	144.5	5,627.1	110.0	5,517.1
1993	6,667.4	155.2	124.0	6,698.5	778.0	626.4	151.6	5,920.5	135.8	5,784.7
1994	7,085.2	184.1	160.0	7,109.2	819.2	661.0	158.2	6,290.1	108.8	6,181.3
1995	7,414.7	229.3	199.6	7,444.3	869.5	704.6	164.8	6,574.9	52.5	6,522.3
1996	7,838.5	245.8	214.2	7,870.1	912.5	743.4	169.2	6,957.6	25.9	6,931.7
1997	8,332.4	279.5	256.1	8,355.8	963.8	789.7	174.1	7,392.0	−14.0	7,406.0
1998	8,793.5	286.2	268.9	8,810.8	1,020.5	841.6	179.0	7,790.3	−85.3	7,875.6
1999	9,353.5	319.5	291.7	9,381.3	1,094.4	907.2	187.2	8,286.9	−71.1	8,358.0
2000	9,951.5	380.5	342.8	9,989.2	1,184.3	986.8	197.5	8,804.9	−134.0	8,938.9
2001	10,286.2	323.0	271.1	10,338.1	1,256.2	1,051.6	204.6	9,081.9	−103.4	9,185.2
2002	10,642.3	313.5	264.4	10,691.4	1,305.0	1,094.0	210.9	9,386.4	−22.1	9,408.5
2003	11,142.1	353.3	284.6	11,210.8	1,354.1	1,135.9	218.1	9,856.8	16.6	9,840.2
2004	11,867.8	448.6	357.4	11,959.0	1,432.8	1,200.9	231.9	10,526.2	−7.8	10,534.0
2005	12,638.4	573.0	475.9	12,735.5	1,541.4	1,290.8	250.6	11,194.2	−79.7	11,273.8
2006	13,398.9	721.1	648.6	13,471.3	1,660.7	1,391.4	269.3	11,810.7	−220.6	12,031.2
2007	14,061.8	871.0	747.7	14,185.1	1,767.5	1,476.2	291.3	12,417.6	21.1	12,396.4
2008	14,369.1	839.2	664.7	14,543.6	1,849.2	1,536.9	312.3	12,694.4	136.6	12,557.8
2009	14,119.0	629.8	483.6	14,265.3	1,861.1	1,535.8	325.3	12,404.2	179.1	12,225.0
2010 ᵖ	14,660.2	....	....	....	1,868.7	1,533.8	334.8	....	....	....
2007: I	13,789.5	797.6	727.4	13,859.8	1,733.9	1,449.6	284.3	12,125.9	−135.6	12,261.4
II	14,008.2	862.6	783.1	14,087.6	1,757.6	1,468.6	289.0	12,330.0	−30.9	12,360.9
III	14,158.2	905.6	760.8	14,302.9	1,778.2	1,484.8	293.4	12,524.7	117.6	12,407.1
IV	14,291.3	918.0	719.4	14,489.9	1,800.3	1,501.8	298.5	12,689.7	133.4	12,556.3
2008: I	14,328.4	890.0	697.6	14,520.7	1,814.8	1,511.2	303.6	12,705.9	77.9	12,628.0
II	14,471.8	881.0	705.5	14,647.3	1,838.4	1,529.2	309.2	12,808.9	189.0	12,619.9
III	14,484.9	855.8	651.5	14,689.2	1,864.0	1,548.8	315.2	12,825.2	138.7	12,686.4
IV	14,191.2	730.0	604.0	14,317.2	1,879.6	1,558.3	321.3	12,437.6	140.7	12,296.9
2009: I	14,049.7	615.6	493.1	14,172.2	1,881.6	1,557.2	324.3	12,290.7	140.4	12,150.3
II	14,034.5	611.7	482.0	14,164.2	1,862.3	1,537.5	324.9	12,301.8	172.2	12,129.7
III	14,114.7	627.4	460.1	14,281.9	1,848.3	1,523.1	325.1	12,433.6	228.9	12,204.8
IV	14,277.3	664.7	499.1	14,442.8	1,852.2	1,525.5	326.8	12,590.6	175.2	12,415.5
2010: I	14,446.4	693.7	502.6	14,637.6	1,852.4	1,522.8	329.6	12,785.2	164.2	12,621.0
II	14,578.7	696.1	500.8	14,774.0	1,860.4	1,527.4	333.0	12,913.7	131.1	12,782.6
III	14,745.1	704.0	515.5	14,933.6	1,871.9	1,535.5	336.4	13,061.7	184.1	12,877.5
IV ᵖ	14,870.4	....	....	....	1,890.0	1,549.7	340.3	....	....	....

Source: Department of Commerce (Bureau of Economic Analysis).

TABLE B–27. Relation of national income and personal income, 1962–2010

[Billions of dollars; quarterly data at seasonally adjusted annual rates]

Year or quarter	National income	Less: Corporate profits with inventory valuation and capital consumption adjustments	Less: Taxes on production and imports less subsidies	Less: Contributions for government social insurance, domestic	Less: Net interest and miscellaneous payments on assets	Less: Business current transfer payments (net)	Less: Current surplus of government enterprises	Plus: Wage accruals less disbursements	Plus: Personal income receipts on assets	Plus: Personal current transfer receipts	Equals: Personal income
1962	528.9	62.3	48.1	19.1	14.2	2.2	0.9	0.0	44.1	30.4	456.4
1963	559.7	68.3	51.2	21.7	15.2	2.7	1.4	.0	47.9	32.2	479.5
1964	601.4	75.5	54.5	22.4	17.4	3.1	1.3	.0	53.8	33.5	514.3
1965	652.2	86.5	57.7	23.4	19.6	3.6	1.3	.0	59.4	36.2	555.5
1966	710.1	92.5	59.3	31.3	22.4	3.5	1.0	.0	64.1	39.6	603.8
1967	750.4	90.2	64.1	34.9	25.5	3.8	.9	.0	69.0	48.0	648.1
1968	821.2	97.3	72.2	38.7	27.1	4.3	1.2	.0	75.2	56.1	711.7
1969	888.5	94.5	79.3	44.1	32.7	4.9	1.0	.0	84.1	62.3	778.3
1970	929.5	82.5	86.6	46.4	39.1	4.5	.0	.0	93.5	74.7	838.6
1971	1,005.6	96.1	95.8	51.2	43.9	4.3	−.2	.6	101.0	88.1	903.1
1972	1,110.3	111.4	101.3	59.2	47.9	4.9	.5	.0	109.6	97.9	992.6
1973	1,246.1	124.5	112.0	75.5	55.2	6.0	−.4	−.1	124.7	112.6	1,110.5
1974	1,341.5	115.1	121.6	85.2	70.8	7.1	−.9	−.5	146.4	133.3	1,222.7
1975	1,444.0	133.3	130.8	89.3	81.6	9.4	−3.2	.1	162.2	170.0	1,334.9
1976	1,609.8	161.6	141.3	101.3	85.5	9.5	−1.8	.1	178.4	184.0	1,474.7
1977	1,797.4	191.8	152.6	113.1	101.1	8.5	−2.7	.1	205.3	194.2	1,632.5
1978	2,027.9	218.4	162.0	131.3	115.0	10.8	−2.2	.3	234.8	209.6	1,836.7
1979	2,248.3	225.4	171.6	152.7	138.9	13.3	−2.9	−.2	274.7	235.3	2,059.5
1980	2,433.0	201.4	190.5	166.2	181.8	14.7	−5.1	.0	338.7	279.5	2,301.5
1981	2,729.8	223.3	224.2	195.7	232.3	17.9	−5.6	.1	421.9	318.4	2,582.3
1982	2,851.4	205.7	225.9	208.9	271.1	20.6	−4.5	.0	488.4	354.8	2,766.8
1983	3,070.9	259.8	242.0	226.0	285.3	22.6	−3.2	−.4	529.6	383.7	2,952.2
1984	3,461.3	318.6	268.7	257.5	327.1	30.3	−1.9	.2	607.9	400.1	3,268.9
1985	3,696.3	332.5	286.8	281.4	341.5	35.2	.6	−.2	653.2	424.9	3,496.7
1986	3,871.5	314.1	298.5	303.4	367.1	36.9	.9	.0	694.5	451.0	3,696.0
1987	4,150.0	367.8	317.3	323.1	366.7	34.1	.2	.0	715.8	467.6	3,924.4
1988	4,522.3	426.6	345.0	361.5	385.3	33.6	2.6	.0	767.0	496.5	4,231.2
1989	4,800.5	425.6	371.4	385.2	434.1	39.2	4.9	.0	874.8	542.6	4,557.5
1990	5,059.5	434.4	398.0	410.1	444.2	40.1	1.6	.1	920.8	594.9	4,846.7
1991	5,217.9	457.3	429.6	430.2	418.2	39.9	5.7	−.1	928.6	665.9	5,031.5
1992	5,517.1	496.2	453.3	455.0	387.7	40.7	8.2	−15.8	909.7	745.8	5,347.3
1993	5,784.7	543.7	466.4	477.4	364.6	40.5	8.7	6.4	900.5	790.8	5,568.1
1994	6,181.3	628.2	512.7	508.2	362.2	41.9	9.6	17.6	947.7	826.4	5,874.8
1995	6,522.3	716.2	523.1	532.8	358.3	45.8	13.1	16.4	1,005.4	878.9	6,200.9
1996	6,931.7	801.5	545.5	555.1	371.1	53.8	14.4	3.6	1,080.7	924.1	6,591.6
1997	7,406.0	884.8	577.8	587.2	407.6	51.3	14.1	−2.9	1,165.5	949.2	7,000.7
1998	7,875.6	812.4	603.1	624.7	479.3	65.2	13.3	−.7	1,269.2	977.9	7,525.4
1999	8,358.0	856.3	628.4	661.3	481.4	69.0	14.1	5.2	1,246.8	1,021.6	7,910.8
2000	8,938.9	819.2	662.7	705.8	539.3	87.0	9.1	.0	1,360.7	1,083.0	8,559.4
2001	9,185.2	784.2	669.0	733.2	544.4	101.3	4.0	.0	1,346.0	1,188.1	8,883.3
2002	9,408.5	872.2	721.4	751.5	506.4	82.4	6.3	.0	1,309.6	1,282.1	9,060.1
2003	9,840.2	977.8	757.7	778.9	504.1	76.1	7.0	15.0	1,312.9	1,341.7	9,378.1
2004	10,534.0	1,246.9	817.0	827.3	461.6	81.7	1.2	−15.0	1,408.5	1,415.5	9,937.2
2005	11,273.8	1,456.1	869.3	872.7	543.0	95.9	−3.5	5.0	1,542.0	1,508.6	10,485.9
2006	12,031.2	1,608.3	935.5	921.8	652.2	83.0	−4.2	1.3	1,829.7	1,605.0	11,268.1
2007	12,396.4	1,510.6	972.6	959.5	731.6	103.3	−11.8	−6.3	2,057.0	1,718.5	11,912.3
2008	12,557.8	1,262.8	992.3	987.2	812.8	121.7	−16.7	−5.0	2,109.3	1,879.2	12,391.1
2009	12,225.0	1,258.0	964.4	970.3	784.3	134.0	−13.2	5.0	1,919.7	2,132.8	12,174.9
2010 ᵖ	....	....	999.9	1,004.3	737.6	131.8	−13.6	.0	1,906.4	2,295.2	12,545.3
2007: I	12,261.4	1,515.5	964.7	953.4	703.9	105.6	−10.1	−25.0	1,959.2	1,701.6	11,714.3
II	12,360.9	1,565.3	965.8	954.2	693.7	102.9	−11.0	.0	2,050.4	1,698.6	11,839.0
III	12,407.1	1,501.0	975.1	958.7	743.3	104.4	−11.2	.0	2,098.7	1,719.8	11,954.4
IV	12,556.3	1,460.8	984.9	971.6	785.6	100.4	−14.8	.0	2,119.8	1,753.8	12,141.4
2008: I	12,628.0	1,376.3	990.0	988.3	787.4	118.4	−16.0	.0	2,123.6	1,793.2	12,300.4
II	12,619.9	1,329.0	1,000.1	987.7	794.3	114.0	−17.0	.0	2,114.7	1,934.4	12,460.9
III	12,686.4	1,350.8	1,000.1	989.5	804.7	115.7	−16.5	.0	2,129.8	1,875.2	12,447.0
IV	12,296.9	995.0	979.1	983.4	864.9	138.8	−17.3	−20.0	2,069.1	1,914.2	12,356.3
2009: I	12,150.3	1,138.2	959.9	964.2	847.4	139.7	−15.8	20.0	1,972.7	2,023.7	12,093.2
II	12,129.7	1,178.0	961.6	971.6	773.4	141.8	−14.2	.0	1,925.9	2,160.2	12,203.4
III	12,204.8	1,297.5	959.2	970.6	750.7	124.9	−11.7	.0	1,891.1	2,159.3	12,164.0
IV	12,415.5	1,418.2	976.8	974.8	765.6	129.8	−11.3	.0	1,889.2	2,188.2	12,239.0
2010: I	12,621.0	1,566.6	988.5	987.8	765.9	130.5	−12.1	.0	1,911.1	2,245.5	12,350.3
II	12,782.6	1,614.1	996.1	1,001.9	736.2	130.8	−13.1	.0	1,914.4	2,286.1	12,517.1
III	12,877.5	1,640.1	1,002.2	1,009.8	719.6	133.4	−14.2	.0	1,889.7	2,316.4	12,592.8
IV ᵖ	....	....	1,012.7	1,017.7	728.8	132.5	−14.9	.0	1,910.5	2,333.0	12,721.1

Source: Department of Commerce (Bureau of Economic Analysis).

[Billions of dollars; quarterly data at seasonally adjusted annual rates]

Year or quarter	National income	Compensation of employees							Proprietors' income with inventory valuation and capital consumption adjustments			Rental income of persons with capital consumption adjustment
		Total	Wage and salary accruals			Supplements to wages and salaries			Total	Farm	Nonfarm	
			Total	Government	Other	Total	Employer contributions for employee pension and insurance funds	Employer contributions for government social insurance				
1962	528.9	327.1	299.4	56.3	243.0	27.8	16.6	11.2	55.3	11.2	44.1	18.6
1963	559.7	345.2	314.9	60.0	254.8	30.4	18.0	12.4	56.5	11.0	45.5	19.3
1964	601.4	370.7	337.8	64.9	272.9	32.9	20.3	12.6	59.4	9.8	49.6	19.4
1965	652.2	399.5	363.8	69.9	293.8	35.7	22.7	13.1	63.9	12.0	51.9	19.9
1966	710.1	442.7	400.3	78.4	321.9	42.3	25.5	16.8	68.2	13.0	55.2	20.5
1967	750.4	475.1	429.0	86.5	342.5	46.1	28.1	18.0	69.8	11.6	58.2	20.9
1968	821.2	524.3	472.0	96.7	375.3	52.3	32.4	20.0	74.2	11.7	62.5	20.6
1969	888.5	577.6	518.3	105.6	412.7	59.3	36.5	22.8	77.5	12.8	64.7	20.9
1970	929.5	617.2	551.6	117.2	434.3	65.7	41.8	23.8	78.5	12.9	65.6	21.1
1971	1,005.6	658.9	584.5	126.8	457.8	74.4	47.9	26.4	84.7	13.4	71.3	22.2
1972	1,110.3	725.1	638.8	137.9	500.9	86.4	55.2	31.2	96.0	17.0	79.0	23.1
1973	1,246.1	811.2	708.8	148.8	560.0	102.5	62.7	39.8	113.6	29.1	84.6	23.9
1974	1,341.5	890.2	772.3	160.5	611.8	118.0	73.3	44.7	113.5	23.5	90.0	24.0
1975	1,444.0	949.1	814.8	176.2	638.6	134.3	87.6	46.7	119.6	22.0	97.6	23.4
1976	1,609.8	1,059.3	899.7	188.9	710.8	159.6	105.2	54.4	132.2	17.2	115.0	22.1
1977	1,797.4	1,180.5	994.2	202.6	791.6	186.4	125.3	61.1	146.0	16.0	130.1	19.6
1978	2,027.9	1,335.5	1,120.6	220.0	900.6	214.9	143.4	71.5	167.5	19.9	147.6	20.9
1979	2,248.3	1,498.3	1,253.3	237.1	1,016.2	245.0	162.4	82.6	181.1	22.2	159.0	22.6
1980	2,433.0	1,647.6	1,373.4	261.5	1,112.0	274.2	185.2	88.9	173.5	11.7	161.8	28.5
1981	2,729.8	1,819.7	1,511.4	285.8	1,225.5	308.3	204.7	103.6	181.6	19.0	162.6	36.5
1982	2,851.4	1,919.6	1,587.5	307.5	1,280.0	332.1	222.4	109.8	174.8	13.3	161.5	38.1
1983	3,070.9	2,035.5	1,677.5	324.8	1,352.7	358.0	238.1	119.9	190.7	6.2	184.5	38.2
1984	3,461.3	2,245.4	1,844.9	348.1	1,496.8	400.5	261.5	139.0	233.1	20.9	212.1	40.0
1985	3,696.3	2,411.7	1,982.6	373.9	1,608.7	429.2	281.5	147.7	246.1	21.0	225.1	41.9
1986	3,871.5	2,557.7	2,102.3	397.2	1,705.1	455.3	297.5	157.9	262.6	22.8	239.7	33.8
1987	4,150.0	2,735.6	2,256.3	423.1	1,833.1	479.4	313.1	166.3	294.2	28.9	265.3	34.2
1988	4,522.3	2,954.2	2,439.8	452.0	1,987.7	514.4	329.7	184.6	334.8	26.8	308.0	40.2
1989	4,800.5	3,131.3	2,583.1	481.1	2,101.9	548.3	354.6	193.7	351.6	33.0	318.6	42.4
1990	5,059.5	3,326.3	2,741.2	519.0	2,222.2	585.1	378.6	206.5	365.1	32.2	333.0	49.8
1991	5,217.9	3,438.3	2,814.5	548.8	2,265.7	623.9	408.7	215.1	367.3	27.5	339.8	61.6
1992	5,517.1	3,631.4	2,957.8	572.0	2,385.8	673.6	445.2	228.4	414.9	35.8	379.1	84.6
1993	5,784.7	3,797.1	3,083.0	589.0	2,494.0	714.1	474.4	239.7	449.6	32.0	417.6	114.1
1994	6,181.3	3,998.5	3,248.5	609.5	2,639.0	750.1	495.9	254.1	485.1	35.6	449.5	142.9
1995	6,522.3	4,195.2	3,434.4	629.0	2,805.4	760.8	496.7	264.1	516.0	23.4	492.6	154.6
1996	6,931.7	4,391.4	3,620.0	648.1	2,971.9	771.4	496.6	274.8	583.7	38.4	545.2	170.4
1997	7,406.0	4,665.6	3,873.6	671.8	3,201.8	792.0	502.4	289.6	628.2	32.6	595.6	176.5
1998	7,875.6	5,023.2	4,180.9	701.2	3,479.7	842.3	535.1	307.2	687.5	28.9	658.7	191.5
1999	8,358.0	5,353.9	4,465.2	733.7	3,731.5	888.8	565.4	323.3	746.8	28.5	718.3	208.2
2000	8,938.9	5,788.8	4,827.7	779.7	4,048.0	961.2	615.9	345.2	817.5	29.6	787.8	215.3
2001	9,185.2	5,979.3	4,952.2	821.9	4,130.3	1,027.1	669.1	358.0	870.7	30.5	840.2	232.4
2002	9,408.5	6,110.8	4,997.3	873.1	4,124.2	1,113.5	747.4	366.1	890.3	18.5	871.8	218.7
2003	9,840.2	6,382.6	5,154.6	913.3	4,241.3	1,228.0	845.6	382.4	930.6	36.5	894.1	204.2
2004	10,534.0	6,693.4	5,410.7	952.8	4,457.9	1,282.7	874.6	408.1	1,033.8	49.7	984.1	198.4
2005	11,273.8	7,065.0	5,706.0	991.5	4,714.5	1,359.1	931.6	427.5	1,069.8	43.9	1,025.9	178.2
2006	12,031.2	7,477.0	6,070.1	1,035.2	5,035.0	1,406.9	960.1	446.7	1,133.0	29.3	1,103.6	146.5
2007	12,396.4	7,855.9	6,415.5	1,089.0	5,326.4	1,440.4	980.5	459.9	1,090.4	37.8	1,052.6	143.7
2008	12,557.8	8,060.8	6,554.0	1,144.0	5,410.1	1,506.8	1,036.6	470.1	1,102.0	50.8	1,051.2	222.0
2009	12,225.0	7,811.7	6,279.1	1,173.6	5,105.5	1,532.6	1,072.0	460.6	1,011.9	30.5	981.5	274.0
2010 ᵖ		7,990.8	6,404.7	1,187.2	5,217.5	1,586.1	1,106.9	479.2	1,055.8	45.6	1,010.2	301.3
2007: I	12,261.4	7,756.4	6,328.1	1,076.4	5,251.8	1,428.3	970.2	458.0	1,103.0	36.2	1,066.8	122.4
II	12,360.9	7,814.4	6,382.8	1,082.7	5,300.1	1,431.6	974.2	457.4	1,090.0	34.1	1,056.0	139.8
III	12,407.1	7,868.5	6,427.6	1,092.6	5,335.0	1,441.0	982.0	459.0	1,079.3	35.0	1,044.3	146.8
IV	12,556.3	7,984.3	6,523.4	1,104.5	5,418.9	1,460.9	995.6	465.2	1,089.1	45.9	1,043.3	165.9
2008: I	12,628.0	8,082.2	6,595.9	1,127.0	5,468.9	1,486.2	1,015.3	471.0	1,107.3	60.7	1,046.6	182.4
II	12,619.9	8,077.3	6,575.1	1,138.2	5,436.9	1,502.2	1,031.9	470.4	1,116.1	52.7	1,063.4	206.0
III	12,686.4	8,082.9	6,567.9	1,150.9	5,417.0	1,515.1	1,043.9	471.2	1,111.5	50.5	1,061.1	237.1
IV	12,296.9	8,000.7	6,477.3	1,159.7	5,317.5	1,523.5	1,055.5	468.0	1,073.0	39.5	1,033.5	262.6
2009: I	12,150.3	7,797.7	6,280.0	1,167.6	5,112.5	1,517.7	1,060.2	457.4	1,018.7	29.6	989.0	264.7
II	12,129.7	7,819.0	6,287.7	1,176.2	5,111.4	1,531.4	1,069.9	461.5	1,000.5	28.0	972.5	269.4
III	12,204.8	7,798.7	6,263.9	1,175.6	5,088.3	1,534.8	1,074.0	460.8	1,006.4	28.0	978.4	279.1
IV	12,415.5	7,831.4	6,284.9	1,174.9	5,110.0	1,546.5	1,084.0	462.5	1,022.1	36.2	985.9	282.8
2010: I	12,621.0	7,858.1	6,291.4	1,185.5	5,105.9	1,566.7	1,095.8	470.9	1,030.7	36.8	994.0	292.7
II	12,782.6	7,969.9	6,388.8	1,193.1	5,195.7	1,581.1	1,103.1	478.0	1,049.7	38.9	1,010.8	298.8
III	12,877.5	8,033.0	6,440.8	1,185.3	5,255.5	1,592.2	1,110.3	482.0	1,059.5	48.5	1,011.0	303.8
IV ᵖ		8,102.1	6,497.9	1,185.0	5,312.9	1,604.2	1,118.2	486.0	1,083.3	58.1	1,025.1	309.9

See next page for continuation of table.

TABLE B–28. National income by type of income, 1962–2010—*Continued*

[Billions of dollars; quarterly data at seasonally adjusted annual rates]

Year or quarter	Corporate profits with inventory valuation and capital consumption adjustments								Capital consumption adjustment	Net interest and miscellaneous payments	Taxes on production and imports	Less: Subsidies	Business current transfer payments (net)	Current surplus of government enterprises
	Total	Profits with inventory valuation adjustment and without capital consumption adjustment												
		Total	Profits		Profits after tax			Inventory valuation adjustment						
			Profits before tax	Taxes on corporate income	Total	Net dividends	Undistributed profits							
1962	62.3	57.0	57.0	24.1	32.9	15.0	17.9	0.0	5.3	14.2	50.4	2.3	2.2	0.9
1963	68.3	62.1	62.1	26.4	35.7	16.2	19.5	.1	6.2	15.2	53.4	2.2	2.7	1.4
1964	75.5	68.6	69.1	28.2	40.9	18.2	22.7	-.5	6.9	17.4	57.3	2.7	3.1	1.3
1965	86.5	78.9	80.2	31.1	49.1	20.2	28.9	-1.2	7.6	19.6	60.7	3.0	3.6	1.3
1966	92.5	84.6	86.7	33.9	52.8	20.7	32.1	-2.1	8.0	22.4	63.2	3.9	3.5	1.0
1967	90.2	82.0	83.5	32.9	50.6	21.5	29.1	-1.6	8.2	25.5	67.9	3.8	3.8	.9
1968	97.3	88.8	92.4	39.6	52.8	23.5	29.3	-3.7	8.5	27.1	76.4	4.2	4.3	1.2
1969	94.5	85.5	91.4	40.0	51.4	24.2	27.2	-5.9	9.0	32.7	83.9	4.5	4.9	1.0
1970	82.5	74.4	81.0	34.8	46.2	24.3	21.9	-6.6	8.1	39.1	91.4	4.8	4.5	.0
1971	96.1	88.3	92.9	38.2	54.7	25.0	29.7	-4.6	7.8	43.9	100.5	4.7	4.3	-.2
1972	111.4	101.6	108.2	42.3	65.9	26.8	39.0	-6.6	9.8	47.9	107.9	6.6	4.9	.5
1973	124.5	115.4	135.0	50.0	85.0	29.9	55.1	-19.6	9.1	55.2	117.2	5.2	6.0	-.4
1974	115.1	109.6	147.8	52.8	95.0	33.2	61.8	-38.2	5.6	70.8	124.9	3.3	7.1	-.9
1975	133.3	135.0	145.5	51.6	93.9	33.0	60.9	-10.5	-1.7	81.6	135.3	4.5	9.4	-3.2
1976	161.6	165.6	179.7	65.3	114.5	39.0	75.4	-14.1	-4.0	85.5	146.4	5.1	9.5	-1.8
1977	191.8	194.8	210.5	74.4	136.1	44.8	91.3	-15.7	-3.0	101.1	159.7	7.1	8.5	2.7
1978	218.4	222.4	246.1	84.9	161.3	50.8	110.5	-23.7	-4.0	115.0	170.9	8.9	10.8	-2.2
1979	225.4	232.0	272.1	90.0	182.1	57.5	124.6	-40.1	-6.6	138.9	180.1	8.5	13.3	-2.9
1980	201.4	211.4	253.5	87.2	166.4	64.1	102.3	-42.1	-10.0	181.8	200.3	9.8	14.7	-5.1
1981	223.3	219.1	243.7	84.3	159.4	73.8	85.6	-24.6	4.2	232.3	235.6	11.5	17.9	-5.6
1982	205.7	191.1	198.6	66.5	132.1	77.7	54.4	-7.5	14.6	271.1	240.9	15.0	20.6	-4.5
1983	259.8	226.6	234.0	80.6	153.4	83.5	69.9	-7.4	33.3	285.3	263.3	21.3	22.6	-3.2
1984	318.6	264.6	268.6	97.5	171.1	90.8	80.3	-4.0	54.0	327.1	289.8	21.1	30.3	-1.9
1985	332.5	257.5	257.5	99.4	158.1	97.6	60.5	.0	75.1	341.5	308.1	21.4	35.2	.6
1986	314.1	253.0	246.0	109.7	136.3	106.2	30.1	7.1	61.1	367.1	323.4	24.9	36.9	.9
1987	367.8	306.9	323.1	130.4	192.7	112.3	80.3	-16.2	61.0	366.7	347.5	30.3	34.1	.2
1988	426.6	367.7	389.9	141.6	248.3	129.9	118.4	-22.2	58.9	385.3	374.5	29.5	33.6	2.6
1989	425.6	374.1	390.5	146.1	244.4	158.0	86.4	-16.3	51.5	434.1	398.9	27.4	39.2	4.9
1990	434.4	398.8	411.7	145.4	266.3	169.1	97.2	-12.9	35.7	444.2	425.0	27.0	40.1	1.6
1991	457.3	430.3	425.4	138.6	286.8	180.7	106.1	4.9	27.0	418.2	457.1	27.5	39.9	5.7
1992	496.2	471.6	474.4	148.7	325.7	188.0	137.7	-2.8	24.6	387.7	483.4	30.1	40.7	8.2
1993	543.7	515.0	519.0	171.0	348.0	202.9	145.1	-4.0	28.7	364.6	503.1	36.7	40.5	8.7
1994	628.2	586.6	599.0	193.1	405.9	235.7	170.2	-12.4	41.6	362.2	545.2	32.5	41.9	9.6
1995	716.2	666.0	684.3	217.8	466.5	254.4	212.1	-18.3	50.2	358.3	557.9	34.8	45.8	13.1
1996	801.5	743.8	740.7	231.5	509.3	297.7	211.5	3.1	57.7	371.1	580.8	35.2	53.8	14.4
1997	884.8	815.9	801.8	245.4	556.3	331.2	225.1	14.1	69.0	407.6	611.6	33.8	51.3	14.1
1998	812.4	738.6	722.9	248.4	474.5	351.5	123.1	15.7	73.8	479.3	639.5	36.4	65.2	13.3
1999	856.3	776.6	780.5	258.8	521.7	337.4	184.3	-4.0	79.7	481.4	673.6	45.2	69.0	14.1
2000	819.2	755.7	772.5	265.1	507.4	377.9	129.5	-16.8	63.6	539.3	708.6	45.8	87.0	9.1
2001	784.2	720.8	712.7	203.3	509.4	370.9	138.5	8.0	63.4	544.4	727.7	58.7	101.3	4.0
2002	872.2	762.8	765.3	192.3	573.0	399.3	173.8	-2.6	109.4	506.4	762.8	41.4	82.4	6.3
2003	977.8	892.2	903.5	243.8	659.7	424.9	234.8	-11.3	85.6	504.1	806.8	49.1	76.1	7.0
2004	1,246.9	1,195.1	1,229.4	306.1	923.3	550.3	373.0	-34.3	51.8	461.6	863.4	46.4	81.7	1.2
2005	1,456.1	1,609.5	1,640.2	412.4	1,227.8	557.3	670.5	-30.7	-153.4	543.0	930.2	60.9	95.9	-3.5
2006	1,608.3	1,784.7	1,822.7	473.3	1,349.5	704.8	644.7	-38.0	-176.4	652.2	986.8	51.4	83.0	-4.2
2007	1,510.6	1,691.1	1,738.4	445.5	1,292.9	794.5	498.4	-47.2	-180.5	731.6	1,027.2	54.6	103.3	-11.8
2008	1,262.8	1,289.1	1,333.2	308.4	1,024.8	797.7	227.2	-44.1	-26.3	812.8	1,045.1	52.8	121.7	-16.7
2009	1,258.0	1,328.6	1,316.7	254.9	1,061.8	718.9	342.9	11.9	-70.6	784.3	1,024.7	60.3	134.0	-13.2
2010 ᵖ	....	....	....	....	....	732.6	....	....	-131.4	737.6	1,058.8	59.0	131.8	-13.6
2007: I	1,515.5	1,688.3	1,738.6	474.1	1,264.4	756.5	508.0	-50.3	-172.8	703.9	1,014.7	50.0	105.6	-10.1
II	1,565.3	1,748.7	1,783.5	467.9	1,315.6	804.4	511.2	-34.8	-183.3	693.7	1,023.9	58.1	102.9	-11.0
III	1,501.0	1,686.0	1,715.1	431.0	1,284.1	809.7	474.3	-29.1	-185.1	743.3	1,030.7	55.7	104.4	-11.2
IV	1,460.8	1,641.5	1,716.3	408.8	1,307.5	807.4	500.1	-74.8	-180.7	785.6	1,039.4	54.5	100.4	-14.8
2008: I	1,376.3	1,406.1	1,534.8	356.7	1,178.1	812.7	365.4	-128.7	-29.8	787.4	1,041.7	51.7	118.4	-16.0
II	1,329.0	1,353.3	1,493.3	343.0	1,150.4	802.1	348.3	-140.0	-24.3	794.3	1,051.9	51.8	114.0	-17.0
III	1,350.8	1,376.0	1,442.7	313.3	1,129.4	798.4	331.0	-66.7	-25.2	804.7	1,052.6	52.4	115.7	-16.5
IV	995.0	1,021.0	861.9	220.4	641.5	777.5	-135.9	159.1	-26.1	864.9	1,034.3	55.2	138.8	-17.3
2009: I	1,138.2	1,223.0	1,130.0	222.0	908.0	747.8	160.2	93.0	-84.8	847.4	1,016.7	56.8	139.7	-15.8
II	1,178.0	1,249.8	1,219.2	222.8	996.5	719.7	276.7	30.6	-71.8	773.4	1,018.7	57.2	141.8	-14.2
III	1,297.5	1,360.5	1,369.2	255.7	1,113.5	699.6	413.9	-8.7	-63.0	750.7	1,028.2	69.1	124.9	-11.7
IV	1,418.2	1,481.2	1,548.4	319.1	1,229.3	708.5	520.8	-67.2	-63.0	765.6	1,035.2	58.4	129.8	-11.3
2010: I	1,566.6	1,736.5	1,772.9	403.2	1,369.7	720.3	649.4	-36.4	-169.9	765.9	1,045.9	57.4	130.5	-12.1
II	1,614.1	1,784.7	1,788.2	405.6	1,382.6	728.4	654.2	-3.5	-170.7	736.2	1,054.6	58.5	130.8	-13.1
III	1,640.1	1,809.3	1,845.7	429.4	1,416.3	736.5	679.9	-36.4	-169.3	719.6	1,060.8	58.6	133.4	-14.2
IV ᵖ	....	....	....	....	....	745.3	....	....	-15.8	728.8	1,074.0	61.4	132.5	-14.9

Source: Department of Commerce (Bureau of Economic Analysis).

TABLE B–29. Sources of personal income, 1962–2010

[Billions of dollars; quarterly data at seasonally adjusted annual rates]

Year or quarter	Personal income	Compensation of employees, received							Proprietors' income with inventory valuation and capital consumption adjustments			Rental income of persons with capital consumption adjustment
		Total	Wage and salary disbursements			Supplements to wages and salaries			Total	Farm	Non-farm	
			Total	Private industries	Government	Total	Employer contributions for employee pension and insurance funds	Employer contributions for government social insurance				
1962	456.4	327.1	299.4	243.0	56.3	27.8	16.6	11.2	55.3	11.2	44.1	18.6
1963	479.5	345.2	314.9	254.8	60.0	30.4	18.0	12.4	56.5	11.0	45.5	19.3
1964	514.3	370.7	337.8	272.9	64.9	32.9	20.3	12.6	59.4	9.8	49.6	19.4
1965	555.5	399.5	363.8	293.8	69.9	35.7	22.7	13.1	63.9	12.0	51.9	19.9
1966	603.8	442.7	400.3	321.9	78.4	42.3	25.5	16.8	68.2	13.0	55.2	20.5
1967	648.1	475.1	429.0	342.5	86.5	46.1	28.1	18.0	69.8	11.6	58.2	20.9
1968	711.7	524.3	472.0	375.3	96.7	52.3	32.4	20.0	74.2	11.7	62.5	20.6
1969	778.3	577.6	518.3	412.7	105.6	59.3	36.5	22.8	77.5	12.8	64.7	20.9
1970	838.6	617.2	551.6	434.3	117.2	65.7	41.8	23.8	78.5	12.9	65.6	21.1
1971	903.1	658.3	584.0	457.4	126.6	74.4	47.9	26.4	84.7	13.4	71.3	22.2
1972	992.6	725.1	638.8	501.2	137.6	86.4	55.2	31.2	96.0	17.0	79.0	23.1
1973	1,110.5	811.3	708.8	560.0	148.8	102.5	62.7	39.8	113.6	29.1	84.6	23.9
1974	1,222.7	890.7	772.8	611.8	161.0	118.0	73.3	44.7	113.5	23.5	90.0	24.0
1975	1,334.9	949.0	814.7	638.6	176.1	134.3	87.6	46.7	119.6	22.0	97.6	23.4
1976	1,474.7	1,059.2	899.6	710.8	188.8	159.6	105.2	54.4	132.2	17.2	115.0	22.1
1977	1,632.5	1,180.4	994.1	791.6	202.5	186.4	125.3	61.1	146.0	16.0	130.1	19.6
1978	1,836.7	1,335.2	1,120.3	900.6	219.7	214.9	143.4	71.5	167.5	19.9	147.6	20.9
1979	2,059.5	1,498.5	1,253.5	1,016.2	237.3	245.0	162.4	82.6	181.1	22.2	159.0	22.6
1980	2,301.5	1,647.6	1,373.5	1,112.0	261.5	274.2	185.2	88.9	173.5	11.7	161.8	28.5
1981	2,582.3	1,819.6	1,511.3	1,225.5	285.8	308.3	204.7	103.6	181.6	19.0	162.6	36.5
1982	2,766.8	1,919.6	1,587.5	1,280.0	307.5	332.1	222.4	109.8	174.8	13.3	161.5	38.1
1983	2,952.2	2,036.0	1,678.0	1,352.7	325.2	358.0	238.1	119.9	190.7	6.2	184.5	38.2
1984	3,268.9	2,245.2	1,844.7	1,496.8	347.9	400.5	261.5	139.0	233.1	20.9	212.1	40.0
1985	3,496.7	2,412.0	1,982.8	1,608.7	374.1	429.2	281.5	147.7	246.1	21.0	225.1	41.9
1986	3,696.0	2,557.7	2,102.3	1,705.1	397.2	455.3	297.5	157.9	262.6	22.8	239.7	33.8
1987	3,924.4	2,735.6	2,256.3	1,833.1	423.1	479.4	313.1	166.3	294.2	28.9	265.3	34.2
1988	4,231.2	2,954.2	2,439.8	1,987.7	452.0	514.4	329.7	184.6	334.8	26.8	308.0	40.2
1989	4,557.5	3,131.3	2,583.1	2,101.9	481.1	548.3	354.6	193.7	351.6	33.0	318.6	42.4
1990	4,846.7	3,326.2	2,741.1	2,222.2	519.0	585.1	378.6	206.5	365.1	32.2	333.0	49.8
1991	5,031.5	3,438.4	2,814.5	2,265.7	548.8	623.9	408.7	215.1	367.3	27.5	339.8	61.6
1992	5,347.3	3,647.2	2,973.5	2,401.5	572.0	673.6	445.2	228.4	414.9	35.8	379.1	84.6
1993	5,568.1	3,790.6	3,076.6	2,487.6	589.0	714.1	474.4	239.7	449.6	32.0	417.6	114.1
1994	5,874.8	3,980.9	3,230.8	2,621.3	609.5	750.1	495.9	254.1	485.1	35.6	449.5	142.9
1995	6,200.9	4,178.8	3,418.0	2,789.0	629.0	760.8	496.7	264.1	516.0	23.4	492.6	154.6
1996	6,591.6	4,387.7	3,616.3	2,968.3	648.1	771.4	496.6	274.8	583.7	38.4	545.2	170.4
1997	7,000.7	4,668.6	3,876.6	3,204.8	671.8	792.0	502.4	289.6	628.2	32.6	595.6	176.5
1998	7,525.4	5,023.9	4,181.6	3,480.4	701.2	842.3	535.1	307.2	687.5	28.9	658.7	191.5
1999	7,910.8	5,348.8	4,460.0	3,726.3	733.7	888.8	565.4	323.3	746.8	28.5	718.3	208.2
2000	8,559.4	5,788.8	4,827.7	4,048.0	779.7	961.2	615.9	345.2	817.5	29.6	787.8	215.3
2001	8,883.3	5,979.3	4,952.2	4,130.3	821.9	1,027.1	669.1	358.0	870.7	30.5	840.2	232.4
2002	9,060.1	6,110.8	4,997.3	4,124.2	873.1	1,113.5	747.4	366.1	890.3	18.5	871.8	218.7
2003	9,378.1	6,367.6	5,139.6	4,226.3	913.3	1,228.0	845.6	382.4	930.6	36.5	894.1	204.2
2004	9,937.2	6,708.4	5,425.7	4,472.9	952.8	1,282.7	874.6	408.1	1,033.8	49.7	984.1	198.4
2005	10,485.9	7,060.0	5,701.0	4,709.5	991.5	1,359.1	931.6	427.5	1,069.8	43.9	1,025.9	178.2
2006	11,268.1	7,475.7	6,068.9	5,033.7	1,035.2	1,406.9	960.1	446.7	1,133.0	29.3	1,103.6	146.5
2007	11,912.3	7,862.2	6,421.7	5,332.7	1,089.0	1,440.4	980.5	459.9	1,090.4	37.8	1,052.6	143.7
2008	12,391.1	8,065.8	6,559.0	5,415.1	1,144.0	1,506.8	1,036.6	470.1	1,102.0	50.8	1,051.2	222.0
2009	12,174.9	7,806.7	6,274.1	5,100.5	1,173.6	1,532.6	1,072.0	460.6	1,011.9	30.5	981.5	274.0
2010 ᵖ	12,545.3	7,990.8	6,404.7	5,217.5	1,187.2	1,586.1	1,106.9	479.2	1,055.8	45.6	1,010.2	301.3
2007: I	11,714.3	7,781.4	6,353.1	5,276.8	1,076.4	1,428.3	970.2	458.0	1,103.0	36.2	1,066.8	122.4
II	11,839.0	7,814.4	6,382.8	5,300.1	1,082.7	1,431.6	974.2	457.4	1,090.0	34.1	1,056.0	139.8
III	11,954.4	7,868.5	6,427.6	5,335.0	1,092.6	1,441.0	982.0	459.0	1,079.3	35.0	1,044.3	146.8
IV	12,141.4	7,984.3	6,523.4	5,418.9	1,104.5	1,460.9	995.6	465.2	1,089.1	45.9	1,043.3	165.9
2008: I	12,300.4	8,082.2	6,595.9	5,468.9	1,127.0	1,486.2	1,015.3	471.0	1,107.3	60.7	1,046.6	182.4
II	12,460.9	8,077.3	6,575.1	5,436.9	1,138.2	1,502.2	1,031.9	470.4	1,116.1	52.7	1,063.4	206.0
III	12,447.0	8,082.9	6,567.9	5,417.0	1,150.9	1,515.1	1,043.9	471.2	1,111.5	50.5	1,061.1	237.1
IV	12,356.3	8,020.7	6,497.3	5,337.5	1,159.7	1,523.5	1,055.5	468.0	1,073.0	39.5	1,033.5	262.6
2009: I	12,093.2	7,777.7	6,260.0	5,092.5	1,167.6	1,517.7	1,060.2	457.4	1,018.7	29.6	989.0	264.7
II	12,203.4	7,819.0	6,287.7	5,111.4	1,176.2	1,531.4	1,069.9	461.5	1,000.5	28.0	972.5	269.4
III	12,164.0	7,798.7	6,263.9	5,088.3	1,175.6	1,534.8	1,074.0	460.8	1,006.4	28.0	978.4	279.1
IV	12,239.0	7,831.4	6,284.9	5,110.0	1,174.9	1,546.5	1,084.0	462.5	1,022.1	36.2	985.9	282.8
2010: I	12,350.3	7,858.1	6,291.4	5,105.9	1,185.5	1,566.7	1,095.8	470.9	1,030.7	36.8	994.0	292.7
II	12,517.1	7,969.9	6,388.8	5,195.7	1,193.1	1,581.1	1,103.1	478.0	1,049.7	38.9	1,010.8	298.8
III	12,592.8	8,033.0	6,440.8	5,255.5	1,185.3	1,592.2	1,110.3	482.0	1,059.5	48.5	1,011.0	303.8
IV ᵖ	12,721.1	8,102.1	6,497.9	5,312.9	1,185.0	1,604.2	1,118.2	486.0	1,083.3	58.1	1,025.1	309.9

See next page for continuation of table.

TABLE B–29. Sources of personal income, 1962–2010—*Continued*

[Billions of dollars; quarterly data at seasonally adjusted annual rates]

Year or quarter	Personal income receipts on assets			Personal current transfer receipts								Less: Contributions for government social insurance, domestic
					Government social benefits to persons						Other current transfer receipts, from business (net)	
	Total	Personal interest income	Personal dividend income	Total	Total	Old-age, survivors, disability, and health insurance benefits	Government unemployment insurance benefits	Veterans benefits	Family assistance [1]	Other		
1962	44.1	29.1	15.0	30.4	28.8	14.3	3.1	4.7	1.3	5.5	1.5	19.1
1963	47.9	31.7	16.2	32.2	30.3	15.2	3.0	4.8	1.4	5.9	1.9	21.7
1964	53.8	35.6	18.2	33.5	31.3	16.0	2.7	4.7	1.5	6.4	2.2	22.4
1965	59.4	39.2	20.2	36.2	33.9	18.1	2.3	4.9	1.7	7.0	2.3	23.4
1966	64.1	43.4	20.7	39.6	37.5	20.8	1.9	4.9	1.9	8.1	2.1	31.3
1967	69.0	47.5	21.5	48.0	45.8	25.8	2.2	5.6	2.3	9.9	2.3	34.9
1968	75.2	51.6	23.5	56.1	53.3	30.5	2.1	5.9	2.8	11.9	2.8	38.7
1969	84.1	59.9	24.2	62.3	59.0	33.1	2.2	6.7	3.5	13.4	3.3	44.1
1970	93.5	69.2	24.3	74.7	71.7	38.6	4.0	7.7	4.8	16.6	2.9	46.4
1971	101.0	75.9	25.0	88.1	85.4	44.7	5.8	8.8	6.2	20.0	2.7	51.2
1972	109.6	82.8	26.8	97.9	94.8	49.8	5.7	9.7	6.9	22.7	3.1	59.2
1973	124.7	94.8	29.9	112.6	108.6	60.9	4.4	10.4	7.2	25.7	3.9	75.5
1974	146.4	113.2	33.2	133.3	128.6	70.3	6.8	11.8	8.0	31.7	4.7	85.2
1975	162.2	129.3	32.9	170.0	163.1	81.5	17.6	14.5	9.3	40.2	6.8	89.3
1976	178.4	139.5	39.0	184.0	177.3	93.3	15.8	14.4	10.1	43.7	6.7	101.3
1977	205.3	160.6	44.7	194.2	189.1	105.3	12.7	13.8	10.6	46.7	5.1	113.1
1978	234.8	184.0	50.7	209.6	203.2	116.9	9.1	13.9	10.8	52.5	6.5	131.3
1979	274.7	217.3	57.4	235.3	227.1	132.5	9.4	14.4	11.1	59.6	8.2	152.7
1980	338.7	274.7	64.0	279.5	270.8	154.8	15.7	15.0	12.5	72.8	8.6	166.2
1981	421.9	348.3	73.6	318.4	307.2	182.1	15.6	16.1	13.1	80.2	11.2	195.7
1982	488.4	410.8	77.6	354.8	342.4	204.6	25.1	16.4	12.9	83.4	12.4	208.9
1983	529.6	446.3	83.3	383.7	369.9	222.2	26.2	16.6	13.8	91.0	13.8	226.0
1984	607.9	517.2	90.6	400.1	380.4	237.8	15.9	16.4	14.5	95.9	19.7	257.5
1985	653.2	555.8	97.4	424.9	402.6	253.0	15.7	16.7	15.2	102.0	22.3	281.4
1986	694.5	588.4	106.0	451.0	428.0	268.9	16.3	16.7	16.1	109.9	22.9	303.4
1987	715.8	603.6	112.2	467.6	447.4	282.6	14.5	16.6	16.4	117.3	20.2	323.1
1988	767.0	637.3	129.7	496.5	475.9	300.2	13.2	16.9	16.9	128.7	20.6	361.5
1989	874.8	717.0	157.8	542.6	519.4	325.6	14.3	17.3	17.5	144.8	23.2	385.2
1990	920.8	751.9	168.8	594.9	572.7	351.8	18.0	17.8	19.2	165.9	22.2	410.1
1991	928.6	748.2	180.3	665.9	648.2	381.7	26.6	18.3	21.1	200.5	17.6	430.2
1992	909.7	722.2	187.6	745.8	729.5	414.4	38.9	19.3	22.2	234.6	16.3	455.0
1993	900.5	698.1	202.3	790.8	776.7	444.7	34.1	20.0	22.8	255.0	14.1	477.4
1994	947.7	712.7	235.0	826.4	813.1	476.6	23.5	20.1	23.2	269.7	13.3	508.2
1995	1,005.4	751.9	253.4	878.9	860.2	508.9	21.4	20.9	22.6	286.4	18.7	532.8
1996	1,080.7	784.4	296.4	924.1	901.2	536.9	22.0	21.7	20.3	300.3	22.9	555.1
1997	1,165.5	835.8	329.7	949.2	929.8	563.5	19.9	22.6	17.9	306.0	19.4	587.2
1998	1,269.2	919.3	349.8	977.9	951.9	574.7	19.5	23.5	17.4	316.8	26.0	624.7
1999	1,246.8	910.9	335.9	1,021.6	987.6	588.6	20.3	24.3	17.9	336.4	34.0	661.3
2000	1,360.7	984.2	376.5	1,083.0	1,040.6	620.5	20.6	25.2	18.4	355.9	42.4	705.8
2001	1,346.0	976.5	369.5	1,188.1	1,141.3	667.7	31.7	26.8	18.1	397.1	46.8	733.2
2002	1,309.6	911.9	397.7	1,282.1	1,247.9	706.1	53.2	29.8	17.7	441.1	34.2	751.5
2003	1,312.9	889.8	423.1	1,341.7	1,316.0	740.4	52.8	32.2	18.4	472.3	25.7	778.9
2004	1,408.5	860.2	548.3	1,415.5	1,398.6	790.2	36.0	34.5	18.4	519.6	16.9	827.3
2005	1,542.0	987.0	555.0	1,508.6	1,482.7	844.7	31.3	36.8	18.2	551.7	25.8	872.7
2006	1,829.7	1,127.5	702.2	1,605.0	1,583.6	943.3	29.9	39.3	18.2	552.9	21.4	921.8
2007	2,057.0	1,265.1	791.9	1,718.5	1,687.9	1,003.2	32.3	42.1	18.3	592.0	30.5	959.5
2008	2,109.3	1,314.7	794.6	1,879.2	1,842.6	1,068.3	50.7	45.6	19.3	658.7	36.7	987.2
2009	1,919.7	1,222.3	697.4	2,132.8	2,096.8	1,164.5	128.6	52.3	20.1	731.3	36.0	970.3
2010 ᵖ	1,906.4	1,193.8	712.7	2,295.2	2,257.8	1,213.9	136.7	61.8	19.8	825.6	37.4	1,004.3
2007: I	1,959.2	1,205.4	753.8	1,701.6	1,674.9	989.1	31.3	41.0	18.2	595.3	26.7	953.4
II	2,050.4	1,248.5	801.8	1,698.6	1,669.0	998.5	30.6	42.1	18.2	579.6	29.6	954.2
III	2,098.7	1,291.6	807.1	1,719.8	1,687.8	1,007.1	32.8	42.3	18.4	587.3	32.0	958.7
IV	2,119.8	1,315.0	804.8	1,753.8	1,719.9	1,018.1	34.7	43.0	18.5	605.7	33.9	971.6
2008: I	2,123.6	1,313.7	809.9	1,793.2	1,757.5	1,044.7	35.6	44.7	18.8	613.6	35.7	988.3
II	2,114.7	1,315.3	799.4	1,934.4	1,897.7	1,060.8	37.6	45.1	19.1	735.1	36.7	987.7
III	2,129.8	1,334.0	795.7	1,875.2	1,838.0	1,076.9	58.1	46.0	19.4	637.6	37.2	989.5
IV	2,069.1	1,295.9	773.2	1,914.2	1,877.1	1,090.9	71.5	46.5	19.7	648.6	37.1	983.4
2009: I	1,972.7	1,240.5	732.2	2,023.7	1,987.2	1,138.6	98.2	50.2	19.9	680.3	36.5	964.2
II	1,925.9	1,229.5	696.4	2,160.2	2,124.1	1,158.2	127.7	51.0	20.1	767.0	36.1	971.6
III	1,891.1	1,213.3	677.8	2,159.3	2,123.4	1,172.6	145.0	52.8	20.2	732.9	35.8	970.6
IV	1,889.2	1,205.8	683.4	2,188.2	2,152.5	1,188.8	143.4	55.1	20.1	745.0	35.8	974.8
2010: I	1,911.1	1,208.7	702.4	2,245.5	2,208.9	1,191.3	146.1	57.8	19.9	793.8	36.6	987.8
II	1,914.4	1,205.3	709.2	2,286.1	2,249.1	1,208.1	136.8	60.4	19.4	824.4	37.0	1,001.9
III	1,889.7	1,174.7	715.0	2,316.4	2,279.2	1,223.5	135.7	63.3	19.9	836.8	37.2	1,009.8
IV ᵖ	1,910.5	1,186.5	724.1	2,333.0	2,294.2	1,232.6	128.3	65.9	19.9	847.5	38.8	1,017.7

[1] Consists of aid to families with dependent children and, beginning in 1996, assistance programs operating under the Personal Responsibility and Work Opportunity Reconciliation Act of 1996.

Source: Department of Commerce (Bureau of Economic Analysis).

TABLE B–30. Disposition of personal income, 1962–2010

[Billions of dollars, except as noted; quarterly data at seasonally adjusted annual rates]

Year or quarter	Personal income	Less: Personal current taxes	Equals: Disposable personal income	Less: Personal outlays — Total	Personal consumption expenditures	Personal interest payments[1]	Personal current transfer payments	Equals: Personal saving	Percent of disposable personal income[2] — Personal outlays — Total	Personal consumption expenditures	Personal saving
1962	456.4	51.6	404.9	371.4	363.3	7.0	1.1	33.5	91.7	89.7	8.3
1963	479.5	54.6	425.0	391.8	382.7	7.9	1.2	33.1	92.2	90.0	7.8
1964	514.3	52.1	462.3	421.7	411.5	8.9	1.3	40.5	91.2	89.0	8.8
1965	555.5	57.7	497.8	455.1	443.8	9.9	1.4	42.7	91.4	89.2	8.6
1966	603.8	66.4	537.4	493.1	480.9	10.7	1.6	44.3	91.8	89.5	8.2
1967	648.1	73.0	575.1	520.9	507.8	11.1	2.0	54.2	90.6	88.3	9.4
1968	711.7	87.0	624.7	572.2	558.0	12.2	2.0	52.5	91.6	89.3	8.4
1969	778.3	104.5	673.8	621.4	605.1	14.0	2.2	52.5	92.2	89.8	7.8
1970	838.6	103.1	735.5	666.1	648.3	15.2	2.6	69.4	90.6	88.1	9.4
1971	903.1	101.7	801.4	721.0	701.6	16.6	2.8	80.4	90.0	87.5	10.0
1972	992.6	123.6	869.0	791.5	770.2	18.1	3.2	77.5	91.1	88.6	8.9
1973	1,110.5	132.4	978.1	875.2	852.0	19.8	3.4	102.9	89.5	87.1	10.5
1974	1,222.7	151.0	1,071.7	957.5	932.9	21.2	3.4	114.2	89.3	87.0	10.7
1975	1,334.9	147.6	1,187.3	1,061.3	1,033.8	23.7	3.8	125.9	89.4	87.1	10.6
1976	1,474.7	172.3	1,302.3	1,179.6	1,151.3	23.9	4.4	122.8	90.6	88.4	9.4
1977	1,632.5	197.5	1,435.0	1,309.7	1,277.8	27.0	4.8	125.3	91.3	89.0	8.7
1978	1,836.7	229.4	1,607.3	1,465.0	1,427.6	31.9	5.4	142.4	91.1	88.8	8.9
1979	2,059.5	268.7	1,790.9	1,633.4	1,591.2	36.2	6.0	157.5	91.2	88.8	8.8
1980	2,301.5	298.9	2,002.7	1,806.4	1,755.8	43.6	6.9	196.3	90.2	87.7	9.8
1981	2,582.3	345.2	2,237.1	2,000.4	1,939.5	49.3	11.5	236.7	89.4	86.7	10.6
1982	2,766.8	354.1	2,412.7	2,148.8	2,075.5	59.5	13.8	263.9	89.1	86.0	10.9
1983	2,952.2	352.3	2,599.8	2,372.9	2,288.6	69.2	15.1	226.9	91.3	88.0	8.7
1984	3,268.9	377.4	2,891.5	2,595.2	2,501.1	77.0	17.1	296.3	89.8	86.5	10.2
1985	3,496.7	417.3	3,079.3	2,825.7	2,717.6	89.4	18.8	253.6	91.8	88.3	8.2
1986	3,696.0	437.2	3,258.8	3,012.4	2,896.7	94.5	21.1	246.5	92.4	88.9	7.6
1987	3,924.4	489.1	3,435.3	3,211.9	3,097.0	91.7	23.2	223.4	93.5	90.2	6.5
1988	4,231.2	504.9	3,726.3	3,469.7	3,350.1	94.0	25.6	256.6	93.1	89.9	6.9
1989	4,557.5	566.1	3,991.4	3,726.4	3,594.5	103.9	28.0	265.0	93.4	90.1	6.6
1990	4,846.7	592.7	4,254.0	3,977.3	3,835.5	111.3	30.6	276.7	93.5	90.2	6.5
1991	5,031.5	586.6	4,444.9	4,131.7	3,980.1	115.0	36.7	313.2	93.0	89.5	7.0
1992	5,347.3	610.5	4,736.7	4,388.7	4,236.9	111.3	40.5	348.1	92.7	89.4	7.3
1993	5,568.1	646.5	4,921.6	4,636.2	4,483.6	107.0	45.6	285.4	94.2	91.1	5.8
1994	5,874.8	690.5	5,184.3	4,913.6	4,750.8	113.0	49.8	270.7	94.8	91.6	5.2
1995	6,200.9	743.9	5,457.0	5,170.8	4,987.3	130.6	52.9	286.3	94.8	91.4	5.2
1996	6,591.6	832.0	5,759.6	5,478.5	5,273.6	147.3	57.6	281.1	95.1	91.6	4.9
1997	7,000.7	926.2	6,074.6	5,794.2	5,570.6	159.7	63.9	280.4	95.4	91.7	4.6
1998	7,525.4	1,026.4	6,498.9	6,157.5	5,918.5	169.5	69.5	341.5	94.7	91.1	5.3
1999	7,910.8	1,107.5	6,803.3	6,595.5	6,342.8	176.5	76.2	207.8	96.9	93.2	3.1
2000	8,559.4	1,232.3	7,327.2	7,114.1	6,830.4	200.3	83.4	213.1	97.1	93.2	2.9
2001	8,883.3	1,234.8	7,648.5	7,443.5	7,148.8	203.7	91.0	204.9	97.3	93.5	2.7
2002	9,060.1	1,050.4	8,009.7	7,727.5	7,439.2	191.3	97.0	282.2	96.5	92.9	3.5
2003	9,378.1	1,000.3	8,377.8	8,088.0	7,804.0	182.7	101.3	289.8	96.5	93.2	3.5
2004	9,937.2	1,047.8	8,889.4	8,585.7	8,285.1	190.3	110.3	303.7	96.6	93.2	3.4
2005	10,485.9	1,208.6	9,277.3	9,149.6	8,819.0	210.8	119.8	127.7	98.6	95.1	1.4
2006	11,268.1	1,352.4	9,915.7	9,680.7	9,322.7	230.1	128.0	235.0	97.6	94.0	2.4
2007	11,912.3	1,488.7	10,423.6	10,208.9	9,806.3	260.9	141.7	214.7	97.9	94.1	2.1
2008	12,391.1	1,438.2	10,952.9	10,505.0	10,104.5	246.2	154.3	447.9	95.9	92.3	4.1
2009	12,174.9	1,140.0	11,034.9	10,379.6	10,001.3	216.8	161.4	655.3	94.1	90.6	5.9
2010 ᵖ	12,545.3	1,167.0	11,378.3	10,723.2	10,351.9	198.6	172.7	655.1	94.2	91.0	5.8
2007: I	11,714.3	1,458.7	10,255.5	10,014.9	9,632.8	244.4	137.7	240.6	97.7	93.9	2.3
II	11,839.0	1,480.4	10,358.6	10,153.8	9,753.2	260.6	140.0	204.8	98.0	94.2	2.0
III	11,954.4	1,497.5	10,456.9	10,267.2	9,850.8	273.4	143.0	189.7	98.2	94.2	1.8
IV	12,141.4	1,518.0	10,623.4	10,399.7	9,988.4	265.2	146.1	223.7	97.9	94.0	2.1
2008: I	12,300.4	1,535.8	10,764.6	10,475.2	10,065.7	259.2	150.3	289.3	97.3	93.5	2.7
II	12,460.9	1,331.6	11,129.2	10,591.6	10,183.0	252.6	155.9	537.7	95.2	91.5	4.8
III	12,447.0	1,442.4	11,004.7	10,608.0	10,202.0	248.0	158.0	396.7	96.4	92.7	3.6
IV	12,356.3	1,443.0	10,913.3	10,345.3	9,967.2	225.0	153.1	568.0	94.8	91.3	5.2
2009: I	12,093.2	1,213.4	10,879.8	10,291.6	9,913.0	220.1	158.5	588.2	94.6	91.1	5.4
II	12,203.4	1,112.5	11,090.9	10,297.4	9,920.1	218.4	158.9	793.5	92.8	89.4	7.2
III	12,164.0	1,117.0	11,047.0	10,423.6	10,040.7	220.9	161.9	623.4	94.4	90.9	5.6
IV	12,239.0	1,117.2	11,121.7	10,505.7	10,131.5	207.8	166.4	616.0	94.5	91.1	5.5
2010: I	12,350.3	1,134.7	11,215.6	10,603.9	10,230.8	203.8	169.2	611.8	94.5	91.2	5.5
II	12,517.1	1,149.1	11,368.0	10,663.7	10,285.4	206.0	172.3	704.3	93.8	90.5	6.2
III	12,592.8	1,177.7	11,415.1	10,736.3	10,366.3	197.1	172.9	678.7	94.1	90.8	5.9
IV ᵖ	12,721.1	1,206.4	11,514.7	10,888.9	10,525.2	187.3	176.4	625.8	94.6	91.4	5.4

[1] Consists of nonmortgage interest paid by households.
[2] Percents based on data in millions of dollars.

Source: Department of Commerce (Bureau of Economic Analysis).

TABLE B–31. Total and per capita disposable personal income and personal consumption expenditures, and per capita gross domestic product, in current and real dollars, 1962–2010

[Quarterly data at seasonally adjusted annual rates, except as noted]

| Year or quarter | Disposable personal income | | | | Personal consumption expenditures | | | | Gross domestic product per capita (dollars) | | Population (thousands) [1] |
| | Total (billions of dollars) | | Per capita (dollars) | | Total (billions of dollars) | | Per capita (dollars) | | | | |
	Current dollars	Chained (2005) dollars	Current dollars	Chained (2005) dollars	Current dollars	Chained (2005) dollars	Current dollars	Chained (2005) dollars	Current dollars	Chained (2005) dollars	
1962	404.9	2,129.6	2,170	11,413	363.3	1,911.2	1,947	10,243	3,139	16,466	186,590
1963	425.0	2,209.5	2,245	11,672	382.7	1,989.9	2,022	10,512	3,263	16,940	189,300
1964	462.3	2,368.7	2,408	12,342	411.5	2,108.4	2,144	10,985	3,458	17,675	191,927
1965	497.8	2,514.7	2,562	12,939	443.8	2,241.8	2,284	11,535	3,700	18,576	194,347
1966	537.4	2,647.3	2,733	13,465	480.9	2,369.0	2,446	12,050	4,007	19,559	196,599
1967	575.1	2,763.5	2,894	13,904	507.8	2,440.0	2,555	12,276	4,188	19,836	198,752
1968	624.7	2,889.2	3,112	14,392	558.0	2,580.7	2,780	12,856	4,532	20,590	200,745
1969	673.8	2,981.4	3,324	14,706	605.1	2,677.4	2,985	13,206	4,856	21,021	202,736
1970	735.5	3,108.8	3,586	15,158	648.3	2,740.2	3,161	13,361	5,063	20,820	205,089
1971	801.4	3,249.1	3,859	15,644	701.6	2,844.6	3,378	13,696	5,425	21,249	207,692
1972	869.0	3,406.6	4,140	16,228	770.2	3,019.5	3,669	14,384	5,897	22,140	209,924
1973	978.1	3,638.2	4,615	17,166	852.0	3,169.1	4,020	14,953	6,522	23,200	211,939
1974	1,071.7	3,610.2	5,010	16,878	932.9	3,142.8	4,362	14,693	7,010	22,861	213,898
1975	1,187.3	3,691.3	5,497	17,091	1,033.8	3,214.1	4,786	14,881	7,583	22,592	215,981
1976	1,302.3	3,838.3	5,972	17,600	1,151.3	3,393.1	5,279	15,558	8,366	23,575	218,086
1977	1,435.0	3,970.7	6,514	18,025	1,277.8	3,535.9	5,801	16,051	9,216	24,412	220,289
1978	1,607.3	4,156.5	7,220	18,670	1,427.6	3,691.8	6,413	16,583	10,303	25,503	222,629
1979	1,790.9	4,253.8	7,956	18,897	1,591.2	3,779.5	7,069	16,790	11,382	26,010	225,106
1980	2,002.7	4,295.6	8,794	18,863	1,755.8	3,766.2	7,710	16,538	12,243	25,640	227,726
1981	2,237.1	4,410.0	9,726	19,173	1,939.5	3,823.3	8,432	16,623	13,594	26,030	230,008
1982	2,412.7	4,506.5	10,390	19,406	2,075.5	3,876.7	8,938	16,694	14,009	25,282	232,218
1983	2,599.8	4,655.7	11,095	19,868	2,288.6	4,098.3	9,766	17,489	15,084	26,186	234,333
1984	2,891.5	4,989.1	12,232	21,105	2,501.1	4,315.6	10,580	18,256	16,629	27,823	236,394
1985	3,079.3	5,144.8	12,911	21,571	2,717.6	4,540.4	11,394	19,037	17,683	28,717	238,506
1986	3,258.8	5,315.0	13,540	22,083	2,896.7	4,724.5	12,036	19,630	18,531	29,443	240,683
1987	3,435.3	5,402.4	14,146	22,246	3,097.0	4,870.3	12,753	20,055	19,504	30,115	242,843
1988	3,726.3	5,635.6	15,206	22,997	3,350.1	5,066.6	13,670	20,675	20,813	31,069	245,061
1989	3,991.4	5,785.1	16,134	23,385	3,594.5	5,209.9	14,530	21,060	22,160	31,877	247,387
1990	4,254.0	5,896.3	17,004	23,568	3,835.5	5,316.2	15,331	21,249	23,185	32,112	250,181
1991	4,444.9	5,945.9	17,532	23,453	3,980.1	5,324.2	15,699	21,000	23,635	31,614	253,530
1992	4,736.7	6,155.3	18,436	23,958	4,236.9	5,505.7	16,491	21,430	24,686	32,255	256,922
1993	4,921.6	6,258.2	18,909	24,044	4,483.6	5,701.2	17,226	21,904	25,616	32,747	260,282
1994	5,184.3	6,459.0	19,678	24,517	4,750.8	5,918.9	18,033	22,466	26,893	33,671	263,455
1995	5,457.0	6,651.6	20,470	24,951	4,987.3	6,079.0	18,708	22,803	27,813	34,112	266,588
1996	5,759.6	6,870.9	21,355	25,475	5,273.6	6,291.2	19,553	23,325	29,062	34,977	269,714
1997	6,074.6	7,113.5	22,255	26,061	5,570.6	6,523.4	20,408	23,899	30,526	36,102	272,958
1998	6,498.9	7,538.8	23,534	27,299	5,918.5	6,865.5	21,432	24,861	31,843	37,238	276,154
1999	6,803.3	7,766.7	24,356	27,805	6,342.8	7,240.9	22,707	25,923	33,486	38,592	279,328
2000	7,327.2	8,161.5	25,944	28,899	6,830.4	7,608.1	24,185	26,939	35,237	39,750	282,418
2001	7,648.5	8,360.1	26,805	29,299	7,148.8	7,813.9	25,054	27,385	36,049	39,768	285,335
2002	8,009.7	8,637.1	27,799	29,976	7,439.2	8,021.9	25,819	27,841	36,935	40,096	288,133
2003	8,377.8	8,853.9	28,805	30,442	7,804.0	8,247.6	26,832	28,357	38,310	40,711	290,845
2004	8,889.4	9,155.1	30,287	31,193	8,285.1	8,532.7	28,228	29,072	40,435	41,784	293,502
2005	9,277.3	9,277.3	31,318	31,318	8,819.0	8,819.0	29,771	29,771	42,664	42,664	296,229
2006	9,915.7	9,650.7	33,157	32,271	9,322.7	9,073.5	31,174	30,341	44,805	43,391	299,052
2007	10,423.6	9,874.2	34,512	32,693	9,806.3	9,289.5	32,469	30,757	46,558	43,801	302,025
2008	10,952.9	10,042.9	35,931	32,946	10,104.5	9,265.0	33,148	30,394	47,138	43,397	304,831
2009	11,034.9	10,099.8	35,888	32,847	10,001.3	9,153.9	32,526	29,770	45,918	41,890	307,483
2010 ᴾ	11,378.3	10,239.4	36,691	33,019	10,351.9	9,315.7	33,382	30,040	47,274	42,723	310,109
2007: I	10,255.5	9,832.1	34,081	32,674	9,632.8	9,235.2	32,012	30,691	45,826	43,499	300,913
II	10,358.6	9,845.9	34,344	32,644	9,753.2	9,270.5	32,336	30,736	46,444	43,745	301,617
III	10,456.9	9,882.8	34,579	32,681	9,850.8	9,310.0	32,575	30,786	46,818	43,876	302,406
IV	10,623.4	9,936.1	35,042	32,775	9,988.4	9,342.3	32,947	30,816	47,140	44,080	303,166
2008: I	10,764.6	9,971.4	35,432	32,821	10,065.7	9,324.1	33,132	30,690	47,162	43,906	303,810
II	11,129.2	10,192.8	36,556	33,480	10,183.0	9,326.2	33,448	30,634	47,535	43,880	304,445
III	11,004.7	9,970.8	36,060	32,672	10,202.0	9,243.5	33,430	30,289	47,464	43,331	305,177
IV	10,913.9	10,036.3	35,677	32,810	9,967.2	9,166.3	32,584	29,966	46,393	42,478	305,890
2009: I	10,879.8	10,046.9	35,497	32,780	9,913.0	9,154.1	32,343	29,867	45,840	41,869	306,496
II	11,090.9	10,193.0	36,115	33,191	9,920.1	9,117.0	32,302	29,687	45,700	41,713	307,101
III	11,047.0	10,079.7	35,888	32,746	10,040.7	9,161.6	32,619	29,763	45,855	41,781	307,815
IV	11,121.7	10,080.4	36,049	32,673	10,131.5	9,182.9	32,839	29,764	46,277	42,198	308,521
2010: I	11,215.6	10,113.3	36,282	32,717	10,230.8	9,225.4	33,097	29,844	46,734	42,504	309,120
II	11,368.0	10,251.9	36,704	33,100	10,285.4	9,275.7	33,208	29,948	47,070	42,602	309,724
III	11,415.1	10,274.6	36,771	33,097	10,366.3	9,330.6	33,392	30,056	47,498	42,773	310,438
IV ᴾ	11,514.7	10,317.8	37,006	33,160	10,525.2	9,431.2	33,826	30,310	47,791	43,009	311,155

[1] Population of the United States including Armed Forces overseas. Annual data are averages of quarterly data. Quarterly data are averages for the period.

Source: Department of Commerce (Bureau of Economic Analysis and Bureau of the Census).

TABLE B–32. Gross saving and investment, 1962–2010

[Billions of dollars, except as noted; quarterly data at seasonally adjusted annual rates]

Year or quarter	Total gross saving	Gross saving									Consumption of fixed capital		
		Net saving											
		Total net saving	Net private saving				Net government saving			Total	Private	Government
			Total	Personal saving	Undistributed corporate profits[1]	Wage accruals less disbursements	Total	Federal	State and local			
1962	124.9	64.3	56.7	33.5	23.2	0.0	7.7	2.4	5.2	60.6	44.1	16.5
1963	133.2	69.8	58.8	33.1	25.7	.0	11.0	5.3	5.7	63.3	45.9	17.5
1964	143.4	77.0	69.7	40.5	29.2	.0	7.3	.9	6.4	66.4	48.3	18.1
1965	158.5	87.7	78.0	42.7	35.3	.0	9.8	3.2	6.5	70.7	51.9	18.9
1966	168.7	92.3	82.3	44.3	38.0	.0	10.0	2.3	7.8	76.5	56.5	20.0
1967	170.6	87.6	89.9	54.2	35.8	.0	-2.3	-9.3	7.0	82.9	61.6	21.4
1968	182.0	91.6	86.6	52.5	34.1	.0	5.1	-2.4	7.5	90.4	67.4	23.0
1969	198.4	99.3	82.7	52.5	30.3	.0	16.5	8.6	8.0	99.2	74.5	24.7
1970	192.8	84.5	92.9	69.4	23.4	.0	-8.4	-15.5	7.1	108.3	81.7	26.6
1971	209.2	91.5	113.7	80.4	32.9	.4	-22.2	-28.7	6.5	117.8	89.5	28.2
1972	237.3	110.1	119.4	77.5	42.2	-.3	-9.3	-24.9	15.6	127.2	97.7	29.4
1973	292.2	151.4	147.5	102.9	44.6	.0	3.9	-11.8	15.7	140.8	109.5	31.3
1974	301.8	138.1	143.3	114.2	29.1	.0	-5.2	-14.5	9.3	163.7	127.8	35.9
1975	296.9	106.5	174.6	125.9	48.7	.0	-68.2	-70.6	2.5	190.4	150.4	39.9
1976	342.0	133.8	180.1	122.8	57.3	.0	-46.3	-53.7	7.4	208.2	165.5	42.6
1977	396.7	164.9	197.9	125.3	72.6	.0	-33.0	-46.1	13.1	231.8	186.1	45.6
1978	476.3	214.9	225.2	142.4	82.8	.0	-10.2	-28.9	18.7	261.4	212.0	49.5
1979	533.2	234.3	235.3	157.5	77.8	.0	-1.0	-14.0	13.0	298.9	244.5	54.4
1980	542.7	198.6	246.5	196.3	50.2	.0	-47.8	-56.6	8.8	344.1	282.3	61.8
1981	646.1	252.7	301.9	236.7	65.2	.0	-49.2	-56.8	7.6	393.3	323.2	70.1
1982	621.5	187.9	325.4	263.9	61.5	.0	-137.5	-135.3	-2.2	433.5	356.4	77.1
1983	602.4	151.3	322.6	226.9	95.7	.0	-171.4	-176.2	4.9	451.1	369.5	81.6
1984	753.4	279.0	426.5	296.3	130.3	.0	-147.5	-171.5	23.9	474.3	387.5	86.9
1985	738.4	232.9	389.2	253.6	135.6	.0	-156.3	-178.6	22.4	505.4	412.8	92.7
1986	709.3	170.8	344.7	246.5	98.3	.0	-173.9	-194.6	20.7	538.5	439.1	99.4
1987	782.3	211.2	348.5	223.4	125.1	.0	-137.4	-149.3	12.0	571.1	464.5	106.6
1988	901.5	290.5	411.7	256.6	155.1	.0	-121.2	-138.4	17.2	611.0	497.1	113.9
1989	924.1	272.7	386.5	265.0	121.5	.0	-113.8	-133.9	20.1	651.5	529.6	121.8
1990	917.6	226.4	396.7	276.7	120.0	.0	-170.3	-176.4	6.2	691.2	560.4	130.8
1991	951.3	227.0	451.2	313.2	138.0	.0	-224.2	-218.4	-5.8	724.4	585.4	138.9
1992	932.3	187.9	491.8	348.1	159.5	-15.8	-303.9	-302.5	-1.4	744.4	599.9	144.5
1993	958.4	180.4	461.6	285.4	169.7	6.4	-281.2	-280.2	-.9	778.0	626.4	151.6
1994	1,094.7	275.5	487.7	270.7	199.4	17.6	-212.2	-220.4	8.2	819.2	661.0	158.2
1995	1,219.0	349.6	546.6	286.3	243.9	16.4	-197.0	-206.2	9.2	869.5	704.6	164.8
1996	1,344.4	431.8	557.1	281.1	272.3	3.6	-125.3	-148.2	23.0	912.5	743.4	169.2
1997	1,525.7	561.9	585.7	280.4	308.2	-2.9	-23.8	-60.1	36.3	963.8	789.7	174.1
1998	1,654.4	633.9	553.4	341.5	212.6	-.7	80.5	33.6	46.9	1,020.5	841.6	179.0
1999	1,708.0	613.6	473.0	207.8	260.1	5.2	140.6	98.8	41.8	1,094.4	907.2	187.2
2000	1,800.1	615.8	389.4	213.1	176.3	.0	226.5	185.2	41.3	1,184.3	986.8	197.5
2001	1,695.7	439.4	414.9	204.9	210.0	.0	24.6	40.5	-15.9	1,256.2	1,051.6	204.6
2002	1,560.9	255.9	562.8	282.2	280.6	.0	-306.9	-252.8	-54.1	1,305.0	1,094.0	210.9
2003	1,552.8	198.7	613.9	289.8	309.2	15.0	-415.2	-376.4	-38.8	1,354.1	1,135.9	218.1
2004	1,724.2	291.4	679.2	303.7	390.5	-15.0	-387.8	-379.5	-8.4	1,432.8	1,200.9	231.9
2005	1,903.4	362.0	619.1	127.7	486.4	5.0	-257.1	-283.0	25.9	1,541.4	1,290.8	250.6
2006	2,174.4	513.7	666.5	235.0	430.3	1.3	-152.7	-203.8	51.0	1,660.7	1,391.4	269.3
2007	2,013.6	246.1	479.1	214.7	270.7	-6.3	-233.0	-245.2	12.2	1,767.5	1,476.2	291.3
2008	1,785.2	-64.0	599.6	447.9	156.7	-5.0	-663.6	-616.2	-47.4	1,849.2	1,536.9	312.3
2009	1,533.8	-327.4	944.5	655.3	284.2	5.0	-1,271.9	-1,251.7	-20.1	1,861.1	1,535.8	325.3
2010 p	....	....	....	655.1	....	.0	....	....	....	1,868.7	1,533.8	334.8
2007: I	2,062.6	328.7	500.5	240.6	284.9	-25.0	-171.8	-201.6	29.8	1,733.9	1,449.6	284.3
II	2,047.8	290.2	497.8	204.8	293.0	.0	-207.7	-237.4	29.8	1,757.6	1,468.6	289.0
III	1,972.9	194.7	449.9	189.7	260.2	.0	-255.2	-265.2	10.0	1,778.2	1,484.8	293.4
IV	1,971.1	170.8	468.2	223.7	244.6	.0	-297.4	-276.7	-20.7	1,800.3	1,501.8	298.5
2008: I	1,905.1	90.2	496.2	289.3	206.9	.0	-406.0	-376.7	-29.3	1,814.8	1,511.2	303.6
II	1,764.8	-73.6	721.6	537.7	183.9	.0	-795.2	-761.6	-33.6	1,838.4	1,529.2	309.2
III	1,788.1	-75.9	635.7	396.7	239.0	.0	-711.6	-646.7	-64.9	1,864.0	1,548.8	315.2
IV	1,682.9	-196.7	545.0	568.0	-2.9	-20.0	-741.7	-680.0	-61.8	1,879.6	1,558.3	321.3
2009: I	1,613.5	-268.1	776.7	588.2	168.5	20.0	-1,044.8	-1,003.2	-41.6	1,881.6	1,557.2	324.3
II	1,521.1	-341.3	1,029.0	793.5	235.5	.0	-1,370.3	-1,336.8	-33.6	1,862.3	1,537.5	324.9
III	1,438.0	-410.3	965.6	623.4	342.2	.0	-1,375.9	-1,356.7	-19.2	1,848.3	1,523.1	325.1
IV	1,562.5	-289.8	1,006.7	616.0	390.6	.0	-1,296.4	-1,310.3	13.9	1,852.2	1,525.5	326.8
2010: I	1,621.5	-230.9	1,054.8	611.8	443.0	.0	-1,285.7	-1,314.2	28.6	1,852.4	1,522.8	329.6
II	1,723.9	-136.5	1,184.3	704.3	480.1	.0	-1,320.8	-1,336.5	15.8	1,860.4	1,527.4	333.0
III	1,728.3	-143.6	1,152.9	678.7	474.2	.0	-1,296.5	-1,344.3	47.7	1,871.9	1,535.5	336.4
IV p	....	....	....	625.8	....	.0	....	....	....	1,890.0	1,549.7	340.3

[1] With inventory valuation and capital consumption adjustments.

See next page for continuation of table.

TABLE B–32. Gross saving and investment, 1962–2010—*Continued*

[Billions of dollars, except as noted; quarterly data at seasonally adjusted annual rates]

Year or quarter	Gross domestic investment, capital account transactions, and net lending, NIPA [2]							Addenda:						
		Gross domestic investment			Capital account transactions (net) [4]	Net lending or net borrowing (−), NIPA [2,5]	Statistical discrepancy	Gross private saving	Gross government saving			Net domestic investment	Gross saving as a percent of gross national income	Net saving as a percent of gross national income
	Total	Total	Gross private domestic investment [3]	Gross government investment [3]					Total	Federal	State and local			
1962	125.2	121.4	88.1	33.3	....	3.8	0.3	100.8	24.1	13.9	10.3	60.9	21.2	10.9
1963	132.3	127.4	93.8	33.6	....	4.9	−.8	104.7	28.4	17.4	11.1	64.1	21.4	11.2
1964	144.2	136.7	102.1	34.6	....	7.5	.8	118.0	25.4	13.2	12.1	70.3	21.5	11.5
1965	160.0	153.8	118.2	35.6	....	6.2	1.5	129.8	28.6	15.9	12.8	83.1	21.9	12.1
1966	174.9	171.1	131.3	39.8	....	3.8	6.2	138.7	30.0	15.3	14.6	94.6	21.5	11.7
1967	175.1	171.6	128.6	43.0	....	3.5	4.5	151.5	19.1	4.5	14.5	88.6	20.5	10.5
1968	186.4	184.8	141.2	43.6	....	1.5	4.3	154.0	28.0	12.2	15.8	94.4	20.0	10.1
1969	201.3	199.7	156.4	43.3	0.0	1.6	2.9	157.2	41.2	23.9	17.3	100.5	20.1	10.0
1970	199.7	196.0	152.4	43.6	.0	3.7	6.9	174.6	18.2	.6	17.7	87.6	18.6	8.1
1971	220.2	219.9	178.2	41.8	.0	.3	11.0	203.2	6.0	−12.2	18.3	102.2	18.6	8.1
1972	246.2	250.2	207.6	42.6	.0	−4.1	8.9	217.1	20.2	−8.3	28.5	123.1	19.2	8.9
1973	300.2	291.3	244.5	46.8	.0	8.8	8.0	257.0	35.2	5.2	30.0	150.6	21.1	10.9
1974	311.6	305.7	249.4	56.3	.0	5.9	9.8	271.1	30.7	3.7	27.0	142.0	20.1	9.2
1975	313.2	293.3	230.2	63.1	.1	19.8	16.3	325.1	−28.2	−50.9	22.7	102.9	18.2	6.5
1976	365.4	358.4	292.0	66.4	.1	7.0	23.5	345.6	−3.7	−32.3	28.6	150.2	18.8	7.4
1977	417.9	428.8	361.3	67.5	.1	−11.0	21.2	384.1	12.6	−23.1	35.7	197.1	19.6	8.1
1978	502.4	515.0	438.0	77.1	.1	−12.7	26.1	437.1	39.2	−3.9	43.2	253.6	20.8	9.4
1979	580.2	581.4	492.9	88.5	.1	−1.3	47.0	479.7	53.5	13.0	40.5	282.4	20.9	9.2
1980	588.0	579.5	479.3	100.3	.1	8.4	45.3	528.8	14.0	−26.6	40.6	235.4	19.5	7.2
1981	682.6	679.3	572.4	106.9	.1	3.2	36.6	625.2	20.9	−23.0	43.8	285.9	20.7	8.1
1982	626.2	629.5	517.2	112.3	.1	−3.4	4.8	681.9	−60.4	−97.7	37.3	196.0	18.9	5.7
1983	652.1	687.2	564.3	122.9	.1	−35.2	49.7	692.2	−89.8	−135.6	45.8	236.0	17.1	4.3
1984	784.9	875.0	735.6	139.4	.1	−90.2	31.5	814.0	−60.6	−126.9	66.3	400.6	19.1	7.1
1985	780.7	895.0	736.2	158.8	.1	−114.5	42.3	802.0	−63.6	−130.6	67.0	389.5	17.6	5.5
1986	777.1	919.7	746.5	173.2	.1	−142.8	67.7	783.8	−74.5	−143.0	68.6	381.3	16.1	3.9
1987	815.1	969.2	785.0	184.3	.1	−154.2	32.9	813.0	−30.8	−94.2	63.4	398.1	16.6	4.5
1988	892.0	1,007.7	821.6	186.1	.1	−115.9	−9.5	908.8	−7.3	−79.3	72.0	396.7	17.6	5.7
1989	980.3	1,072.6	874.9	197.7	.3	−92.7	56.1	916.1	8.0	−70.6	78.7	421.2	17.0	5.0
1990	1,001.8	1,076.7	861.0	215.7	7.4	−82.3	84.2	957.1	−39.5	−108.7	69.2	385.5	16.0	3.9
1991	1,031.0	1,023.2	802.9	220.3	5.3	2.6	79.7	1,036.6	−85.3	−146.4	61.1	298.8	16.0	3.8
1992	1,042.3	1,087.9	864.8	223.1	−1.3	−44.3	110.0	1,091.7	−159.4	−227.9	68.5	343.5	14.9	3.0
1993	1,094.2	1,172.8	953.3	219.4	.9	−79.4	135.8	1,088.0	−129.5	−202.4	72.9	394.8	14.6	2.7
1994	1,203.5	1,318.2	1,097.3	220.9	1.3	−116.0	108.8	1,148.6	−53.9	−140.3	86.4	499.0	15.6	3.9
1995	1,271.6	1,376.6	1,144.0	232.6	.4	−105.5	52.5	1,251.2	−32.2	−124.5	92.3	507.2	16.5	4.7
1996	1,370.3	1,484.4	1,240.2	244.2	.2	−114.4	25.9	1,300.5	43.9	−66.3	110.2	571.9	17.1	5.5
1997	1,511.7	1,641.0	1,388.7	252.4	.5	−129.8	−14.0	1,375.4	150.3	22.4	127.9	677.2	18.2	6.7
1998	1,569.1	1,773.6	1,510.8	262.9	.2	−204.8	−85.3	1,394.9	259.5	116.4	143.1	753.1	18.6	7.1
1999	1,637.0	1,928.9	1,641.5	287.4	4.5	−296.4	−71.1	1,380.3	327.8	183.9	143.9	834.5	18.1	6.5
2000	1,666.2	2,076.5	1,772.2	304.3	.3	−410.7	−134.0	1,376.2	424.0	273.0	151.0	892.2	17.8	6.1
2001	1,592.3	1,984.0	1,661.9	322.0	−12.9	−378.7	−103.4	1,466.5	229.2	129.1	100.1	727.7	16.2	4.2
2002	1,538.9	1,990.4	1,647.0	343.5	.5	−452.1	−22.1	1,656.8	−95.9	−163.6	67.7	685.4	14.6	2.4
2003	1,569.4	2,085.5	1,729.7	355.8	2.1	−518.2	16.6	1,749.8	−197.1	−285.5	88.4	731.4	13.9	1.8
2004	1,716.3	2,340.9	1,968.6	372.4	−2.8	−621.8	−7.8	1,880.1	−155.9	−284.6	128.7	908.2	14.4	2.4
2005	1,823.7	2,564.2	2,172.2	392.0	−12.9	−727.7	−79.7	1,909.9	−6.5	−182.6	176.1	1,022.9	14.9	2.8
2006	1,953.8	2,752.2	2,327.2	425.1	2.1	−800.5	−220.6	2,057.9	116.5	−97.2	213.8	1,091.6	15.9	3.8
2007	2,034.8	2,751.7	2,295.2	456.5	−.1	−716.8	21.1	1,955.3	58.3	−132.6	190.9	984.2	14.2	1.7
2008	1,921.8	2,592.2	2,096.7	495.5	−5.4	−665.0	136.6	2,136.5	−351.3	−496.5	145.1	743.0	12.4	−.4
2009	1,712.9	2,092.6	1,589.2	503.4	.6	−380.3	179.1	2,480.3	−946.6	−1,127.4	180.8	231.5	10.9	−2.3
2010 *p*	....	2,332.9	1,821.4	511.5	....	....	....	....	....	....	....	464.2	....	....
2007: I	1,927.0	2,721.2	2,277.4	443.8	.3	−794.4	−135.6	1,950.1	112.6	−91.1	203.7	987.3	14.7	2.3
II	2,016.9	2,784.7	2,329.6	455.0	−1.5	−766.3	−30.9	1,966.4	81.4	−125.4	206.8	1,027.0	14.5	2.1
III	2,090.6	2,773.6	2,313.4	460.2	.5	−683.5	117.6	1,934.7	38.2	−152.0	190.2	995.4	13.9	1.4
IV	2,104.5	2,727.2	2,260.4	466.8	.4	−623.0	133.4	1,970.0	1.1	−161.8	162.9	926.9	13.7	1.2
2008: I	1,982.9	2,671.4	2,198.8	472.6	.4	−688.9	77.9	2,007.5	−102.4	−260.1	157.8	856.6	13.2	.6
II	1,953.8	2,665.6	2,170.9	494.7	.4	−712.2	189.0	2,250.8	−486.0	−642.6	156.6	827.2	12.2	−.5
III	1,926.8	2,617.6	2,111.3	506.2	−23.8	−666.9	138.7	2,184.5	−396.5	−525.7	129.2	753.5	12.3	−.5
IV	1,823.6	2,414.3	1,905.8	508.5	1.4	−592.0	140.7	2,103.4	−420.5	−557.5	137.1	534.7	11.9	−1.4
2009: I	1,753.8	2,138.6	1,640.4	498.2	.5	−385.2	140.4	2,333.9	−720.4	−880.1	159.7	257.0	11.5	−1.9
II	1,693.3	2,036.5	1,530.2	506.3	.5	−343.8	172.2	2,566.5	−1,045.4	−1,213.0	167.6	174.2	10.9	−2.4
III	1,666.9	2,057.0	1,548.5	508.5	.6	−390.7	228.9	2,488.7	−1,050.7	−1,232.0	181.3	208.7	10.2	−2.9
IV	1,737.6	2,138.2	1,637.7	500.5	.7	−401.3	175.2	2,532.1	−969.7	−1,184.4	214.7	286.0	11.0	−2.0
2010: I	1,785.7	2,230.7	1,739.7	491.0	.4	−445.4	164.2	2,577.5	−956.0	−1,186.9	230.9	378.3	11.2	−1.6
II	1,855.0	2,347.4	1,841.8	505.6	.5	−493.0	131.1	2,711.7	−987.8	−1,207.8	220.0	487.1	11.8	−.9
III	1,912.4	2,426.4	1,907.2	519.3	.6	−514.6	184.1	2,688.5	−960.2	−1,214.0	253.9	554.5	11.7	−1.0
IV *p*	....	2,326.9	1,796.7	530.2	....	....	....	....	....	....	....	437.0	....	....

[2] National income and product accounts (NIPA).
[3] For details on government investment, see Table B–20.
[4] Consists of capital transfers and the acquisition and disposal of nonproduced nonfinancial assets.
[5] Prior to 1982, equals the balance on current account, NIPA (see Table B–24).

Source: Department of Commerce (Bureau of Economic Analysis).

TABLE B–33. Median money income (in 2009 dollars) and poverty status of families and people, by race, selected years, 1998–2009

Race and year	Families [1] Number (millions)	Median money income (in 2009 dollars) [2]	Below poverty level Total Number (millions)	Below poverty level Total Percent	Below poverty level Female householder Number (millions)	Below poverty level Female householder Percent	People below poverty level Number (millions)	People below poverty level Percent	Median money income — Males All people	Median money income — Males Year-round full-time workers	Median money income — Females All people	Median money income — Females Year-round full-time workers
ALL RACES												
1998	71.6	$61,419	7.2	10.0	3.8	29.9	34.5	12.7	$34,814	$47,640	$18,963	$35,291
1999 [3]	73.2	62,860	6.8	9.3	3.6	27.8	32.8	11.9	35,134	48,209	19,701	35,228
2000 [4]	73.8	63,189	6.4	8.7	3.3	25.4	31.6	11.3	35,303	48,441	20,007	36,274
2001	74.3	62,282	6.8	9.2	3.5	26.4	32.9	11.7	35,257	48,626	20,129	36,855
2002	75.6	61,617	7.2	9.6	3.6	26.5	34.6	12.1	34,860	48,296	20,045	36,925
2003	76.2	61,437	7.6	10.0	3.9	28.0	35.9	12.5	34,907	48,402	20,128	36,915
2004 [5]	76.9	61,389	7.8	10.2	4.0	28.3	37.0	12.7	34,652	47,315	20,062	36,469
2005	77.4	61,741	7.7	9.9	4.0	28.7	37.0	12.6	34,362	46,352	20,410	36,539
2006	78.5	62,135	7.7	9.8	4.1	28.3	36.5	12.3	34,324	47,828	21,291	37,222
2007	77.9	63,471	7.6	9.8	4.1	28.3	37.3	12.5	34,341	47,818	21,643	37,414
2008	78.9	61,288	8.1	10.3	4.2	28.7	39.8	13.2	33,035	47,598	20,788	36,549
2009	78.9	60,088	8.8	11.1	4.4	29.9	43.6	14.3	32,184	49,164	20,957	37,234
WHITE												
1998	60.1	64,423	4.8	8.0	2.1	24.9	23.5	10.5	36,331	48,881	19,209	35,881
1999 [3]	61.1	65,754	4.4	7.3	1.9	22.5	22.2	9.8	36,899	50,477	19,762	36,044
2000 [4]	61.3	66,050	4.3	7.1	1.8	21.2	21.6	9.5	37,114	50,137	20,027	37,306
2001	61.6	65,504	4.6	7.4	1.9	22.4	22.7	9.9	36,637	49,419	20,175	37,375
Alone [6]												
2002	62.3	65,138	4.9	7.8	2.0	22.6	23.5	10.2	36,225	49,331	20,076	37,438
2003	62.6	65,039	5.1	8.1	2.2	24.0	24.3	10.5	35,841	49,147	20,318	37,543
2004 [5]	63.1	64,411	5.3	8.4	2.3	24.7	25.3	10.8	35,594	48,370	20,098	37,168
2005	63.4	65,172	5.1	8.0	2.3	25.3	24.9	10.6	35,355	48,009	20,512	37,466
2006	64.1	65,191	5.1	8.0	2.4	25.1	24.4	10.3	36,003	48,865	21,364	37,793
2007	63.6	66,649	5.0	7.9	2.3	24.7	25.1	10.5	36,353	48,864	21,796	37,994
2008	64.2	64,753	5.4	8.4	2.4	25.2	27.0	11.2	34,987	49,735	20,870	37,069
2009	64.1	62,545	6.0	9.3	2.7	27.3	29.8	12.3	33,748	50,361	21,118	37,951
Alone or in combination [6]												
2002	63.0	64,918	5.0	7.9	2.1	22.6	24.1	10.3	36,145	49,260	20,036	37,423
2003	63.5	64,847	5.2	8.1	2.2	24.2	25.0	10.6	35,754	49,074	20,282	37,529
2004 [5]	64.0	64,255	5.4	8.5	2.3	24.8	26.1	10.9	35,515	48,245	20,064	37,124
2005	64.3	64,960	5.2	8.1	2.4	25.5	25.6	10.7	35,272	47,839	20,457	37,388
2006	65.0	65,104	5.2	8.0	2.4	25.0	25.2	10.4	35,822	48,796	21,318	37,755
2007	64.4	66,449	5.2	8.0	2.4	24.8	25.9	10.6	36,239	48,794	21,736	37,959
2008	65.0	64,558	5.5	8.5	2.4	25.4	27.9	11.3	34,880	49,566	20,842	37,036
2009	65.0	62,432	6.1	9.4	2.8	27.5	30.9	12.5	33,565	50,316	21,080	37,912
BLACK												
1998	8.5	38,641	2.0	23.4	1.6	40.8	9.1	26.1	25,391	36,102	17,264	31,361
1999 [3]	8.7	41,000	1.9	21.8	1.5	39.2	8.4	23.6	26,314	38,817	19,021	32,364
2000 [4]	8.7	41,945	1.7	19.3	1.3	34.3	8.0	22.5	26,584	37,976	19,781	32,073
2001	8.8	40,705	1.8	20.7	1.4	35.2	8.1	22.7	26,007	38,674	19,726	33,071
Alone [6]												
2002	8.9	39,971	1.9	21.5	1.4	35.8	8.6	24.1	25,707	38,072	19,946	32,937
2003	8.9	40,082	2.0	22.3	1.5	36.9	8.8	24.4	25,641	38,986	19,337	32,214
2004 [5]	8.9	39,912	2.0	22.8	1.5	37.6	9.0	24.7	25,766	36,019	19,712	33,095
2005	9.1	38,965	2.0	22.1	1.5	36.1	9.2	24.9	24,889	37,612	19,371	33,360
2006	9.3	40,712	2.0	21.6	1.5	36.6	9.0	24.3	26,664	37,741	20,322	32,911
2007	9.3	41,527	2.0	22.1	1.5	37.3	9.2	24.5	26,712	38,003	20,433	32,680
2008	9.4	39,728	2.1	22.0	1.5	37.2	9.4	24.7	25,158	38,465	20,120	32,064
2009	9.4	38,409	2.1	22.7	1.5	36.7	9.9	25.8	23,738	39,362	19,470	32,470
Alone or in combination [6]												
2002	9.1	40,101	2.0	21.4	1.5	35.7	8.9	23.9	25,645	38,112	19,876	33,030
2003	9.1	40,360	2.0	22.1	1.5	36.8	9.1	24.3	25,581	39,027	19,290	32,276
2004 [5]	9.1	40,109	2.1	22.8	1.5	37.6	9.4	24.7	25,792	36,009	19,698	33,150
2005	9.3	39,107	2.1	22.0	1.5	36.2	9.5	24.7	24,841	37,514	19,332	33,363
2006	9.5	40,979	2.0	21.5	1.5	36.4	9.4	24.2	26,676	37,777	20,282	32,962
2007	9.5	41,609	2.1	22.0	1.6	37.2	9.7	24.4	26,681	38,048	20,392	32,764
2008	9.6	39,784	2.1	21.9	1.6	37.1	9.9	24.6	25,023	38,219	20,126	32,082
2009	9.7	38,493	2.2	22.7	1.6	36.8	10.6	25.9	23,674	39,280	19,413	32,723

[1] The term "family" refers to a group of two or more persons related by birth, marriage, or adoption and residing together. Every family must include a reference person.

[2] Current dollar median money income adjusted by consumer price index research series (CPI-U-RS).

[3] Reflects implementation of Census 2000–based population controls comparable with succeeding years.

[4] Reflects household sample expansion.

[5] For 2004, figures are revised to reflect a correction to the weights in the 2005 Annual Social and Economic Supplement.

[6] Data are for "white alone," for "white alone or in combination," for "black alone," and for "black alone or in combination." ("Black" is also "black or African American.") Beginning with data for 2002 the Current Population Survey allowed respondents to choose more than one race; for earlier years respondents could report only one race group.

Note: Poverty thresholds are updated each year to reflect changes in the consumer price index (CPI-U).
For details see publication Series P–60 on the Current Population Survey and Annual Social and Economic Supplements.

Source: Department of Commerce (Bureau of the Census).

TABLE B–34. Population by age group, 1933–2010

[Thousands of persons]

July 1 [1]	Total	Age (years)						
		Under 5	5–15	16–19	20–24	25–44	45–64	65 and over
1933	125,579	10,612	26,897	9,302	11,152	37,319	22,933	7,363
1939	130,880	10,418	25,179	9,822	11,519	39,354	25,823	8,764
1940	132,122	10,579	24,811	9,895	11,690	39,868	26,249	9,031
1941	133,402	10,850	24,516	9,840	11,807	40,383	26,718	9,288
1942	134,860	11,301	24,231	9,730	11,955	40,861	27,196	9,584
1943	136,739	12,016	24,093	9,607	12,064	41,420	27,671	9,867
1944	138,397	12,524	23,949	9,561	12,062	42,016	28,138	10,147
1945	139,928	12,979	23,907	9,361	12,036	42,521	28,630	10,494
1946	141,389	13,244	24,103	9,119	12,004	43,027	29,064	10,828
1947	144,126	14,406	24,468	9,097	11,814	43,657	29,498	11,185
1948	146,631	14,919	25,209	8,952	11,794	44,288	29,931	11,538
1949	149,188	15,607	25,852	8,788	11,700	44,916	30,405	11,921
1950	152,271	16,410	26,721	8,542	11,680	45,672	30,849	12,397
1951	154,878	17,333	27,279	8,446	11,552	46,103	31,362	12,803
1952	157,553	17,312	28,894	8,414	11,350	46,495	31,884	13,203
1953	160,184	17,638	30,227	8,460	11,062	46,786	32,394	13,617
1954	163,026	18,057	31,480	8,637	10,832	47,001	32,942	14,076
1955	165,931	18,566	32,682	8,744	10,714	47,194	33,506	14,525
1956	168,903	19,003	33,994	8,916	10,616	47,379	34,057	14,938
1957	171,984	19,494	35,272	9,195	10,603	47,440	34,591	15,388
1958	174,882	19,887	36,445	9,543	10,756	47,337	35,109	15,806
1959	177,830	20,175	37,368	10,215	10,969	47,192	35,663	16,248
1960	180,671	20,341	38,494	10,683	11,134	47,140	36,203	16,675
1961	183,691	20,522	39,765	11,025	11,483	47,084	36,722	17,089
1962	186,538	20,469	41,205	11,180	11,959	47,013	37,255	17,457
1963	189,242	20,342	41,626	12,007	12,714	46,994	37,782	17,778
1964	191,889	20,165	42,297	12,736	13,269	46,958	38,338	18,127
1965	194,303	19,824	42,938	13,516	13,746	46,912	38,916	18,451
1966	196,560	19,208	43,702	14,311	14,050	47,001	39,534	18,755
1967	198,712	18,563	44,244	14,200	15,248	47,194	40,193	19,071
1968	200,706	17,913	44,622	14,452	15,786	47,721	40,846	19,365
1969	202,677	17,376	44,840	14,800	16,480	48,064	41,437	19,680
1970	205,052	17,166	44,816	15,289	17,202	48,473	41,999	20,107
1971	207,661	17,244	44,591	15,688	18,159	48,936	42,482	20,561
1972	209,896	17,101	44,203	16,039	18,153	50,482	42,898	21,020
1973	211,909	16,851	43,582	16,446	18,521	51,749	43,235	21,525
1974	213,854	16,487	42,989	16,769	18,975	53,051	43,522	22,061
1975	215,973	16,121	42,508	17,017	19,527	54,302	43,801	22,696
1976	218,035	15,617	42,099	17,194	19,986	55,852	44,008	23,278
1977	220,239	15,564	41,298	17,276	20,499	57,561	44,150	23,892
1978	222,585	15,735	40,428	17,288	20,946	59,400	44,286	24,502
1979	225,055	16,063	39,552	17,242	21,297	61,379	44,390	25,134
1980	227,726	16,451	38,838	17,167	21,590	63,470	44,504	25,707
1981	229,966	16,893	38,144	16,812	21,869	65,528	44,500	26,221
1982	232,188	17,228	37,784	16,332	21,902	67,692	44,462	26,787
1983	234,307	17,547	37,526	15,823	21,844	69,733	44,474	27,361
1984	236,348	17,695	37,461	15,295	21,737	71,735	44,547	27,878
1985	238,466	17,842	37,450	15,005	21,478	73,673	44,602	28,416
1986	240,651	17,963	37,404	15,024	20,942	75,651	44,660	29,008
1987	242,804	18,052	37,333	15,215	20,385	77,338	44,854	29,626
1988	245,021	18,195	37,593	15,198	19,846	78,595	45,471	30,124
1989	247,342	18,508	37,972	14,913	19,442	79,943	45,882	30,682
1990	250,132	18,856	38,632	14,466	19,323	81,291	46,316	31,247
1991	253,493	19,208	39,349	13,992	19,414	82,844	46,874	31,812
1992	256,894	19,528	40,161	13,781	19,314	83,201	48,553	32,356
1993	260,255	19,729	40,904	13,953	19,101	83,766	49,899	32,902
1994	263,436	19,777	41,689	14,228	18,758	84,334	51,318	33,331
1995	266,557	19,627	42,510	14,522	18,391	84,933	52,806	33,769
1996	269,667	19,408	43,172	15,057	17,965	85,527	54,396	34,143
1997	272,912	19,233	43,833	15,433	17,992	85,737	56,283	34,402
1998	276,115	19,145	44,332	15,856	18,250	85,663	58,249	34,619
1999	279,295	19,136	44,755	16,164	18,672	85,408	60,362	34,798
2000 [2]	282,385	19,204	45,158	16,227	19,188	85,126	62,408	35,074
2001 [2]	285,309	19,430	45,204	16,316	19,875	84,781	64,381	35,320
2002 [2]	288,105	19,668	45,168	16,402	20,418	84,383	66,496	35,571
2003 [2]	290,820	19,940	45,105	16,467	20,863	83,979	68,543	35,923
2004 [2]	293,463	20,243	44,981	16,618	21,109	83,698	70,551	36,263
2005 [2]	296,186	20,484	44,858	16,749	21,231	83,503	72,659	36,704
2006 [2]	298,996	20,613	44,734	17,057	21,302	83,452	74,632	37,206
2007 [2]	302,004	20,921	44,642	17,309	21,367	83,462	76,435	37,867
2008 [2]	304,798	21,153	44,625	17,435	21,468	83,441	77,876	38,800
2009 [2]	307,439	21,300	44,717	17,418	21,682	83,350	79,402	39,571
2010 [1]	308,746							

[1] Data for 2010 are as of April 1, 2010, reflect the results of the 2010 Census, and do not include Armed Forces overseas.
[2] Data are based on Census 2000 and do not reflect the results of the 2010 Census.

Note: Includes Armed Forces overseas beginning with 1940. Includes Alaska and Hawaii beginning with 1950.
All estimates are consistent with decennial census enumerations.

Source: Department of Commerce (Bureau of the Census).

Table B-35. Civilian population and labor force, 1929-2010

[Monthly data seasonally adjusted, except as noted]

Year or month	Civilian noninstitutional population [1]	Civilian labor force — Total	Employment — Total	Employment — Agricultural	Employment — Nonagricultural	Unemployment	Not in labor force	Civilian labor force participation rate [2]	Civilian employment/population ratio [3]	Unemployment rate, civilian workers [4]
								Percent		
			Thousands of persons 14 years of age and over						Percent	
1929	....	49,180	47,630	10,450	37,180	1,550	....	....	....	3.2
1933	....	51,590	38,760	10,090	28,670	12,830	....	....	....	24.9
1939	....	55,230	45,750	9,610	36,140	9,480	....	....	....	17.2
1940	99,840	55,640	47,520	9,540	37,980	8,120	44,200	55.7	47.6	14.6
1941	99,900	55,910	50,350	9,100	41,250	5,560	43,990	56.0	50.4	9.9
1942	98,640	56,410	53,750	9,250	44,500	2,660	42,230	57.2	54.5	4.7
1943	94,640	55,540	54,470	9,080	45,390	1,070	39,100	58.7	57.6	1.9
1944	93,220	54,630	53,960	8,950	45,010	670	38,590	58.6	57.9	1.2
1945	94,090	53,860	52,820	8,580	44,240	1,040	40,230	57.2	56.1	1.9
1946	103,070	57,520	55,250	8,320	46,930	2,270	45,550	55.8	53.6	3.9
1947	106,018	60,168	57,812	8,256	49,557	2,356	45,850	56.8	54.5	3.9
			Thousands of persons 16 years of age and over							
1947	101,827	59,350	57,038	7,890	49,148	2,311	42,477	58.3	56.0	3.9
1948	103,068	60,621	58,343	7,629	50,714	2,276	42,447	58.8	56.6	3.8
1949	103,994	61,286	57,651	7,658	49,993	3,637	42,708	58.9	55.4	5.9
1950	104,995	62,208	58,918	7,160	51,758	3,288	42,787	59.2	56.1	5.3
1951	104,621	62,017	59,961	6,726	53,235	2,055	42,604	59.2	57.3	3.3
1952	105,231	62,138	60,250	6,500	53,749	1,883	43,093	59.0	57.3	3.0
1953 [5]	107,056	63,015	61,179	6,260	54,919	1,834	44,041	58.9	57.1	2.9
1954	108,321	63,643	60,109	6,205	53,904	3,532	44,678	58.8	55.5	5.5
1955	109,683	65,023	62,170	6,450	55,722	2,852	44,660	59.3	56.7	4.4
1956	110,954	66,552	63,799	6,283	57,514	2,750	44,402	60.0	57.5	4.1
1957	112,265	66,929	64,071	5,947	58,123	2,859	45,336	59.6	57.1	4.3
1958	113,727	67,639	63,036	5,586	57,450	4,602	46,088	59.5	55.4	6.8
1959	115,329	68,369	64,630	5,565	59,065	3,740	46,960	59.3	56.0	5.5
1960 [5]	117,245	69,628	65,778	5,458	60,318	3,852	47,617	59.4	56.1	5.5
1961	118,771	70,459	65,746	5,200	60,546	4,714	48,312	59.3	55.4	6.7
1962 [5]	120,153	70,614	66,702	4,944	61,759	3,911	49,539	58.8	55.5	5.5
1963	122,416	71,833	67,762	4,687	63,076	4,070	50,583	58.7	55.4	5.7
1964	124,485	73,091	69,305	4,523	64,782	3,786	51,394	58.7	55.7	5.2
1965	126,513	74,455	71,088	4,361	66,726	3,366	52,058	58.9	56.2	4.5
1966	128,058	75,770	72,895	3,979	68,915	2,875	52,288	59.2	56.9	3.8
1967	129,874	77,347	74,372	3,844	70,527	2,975	52,527	59.6	57.3	3.8
1968	132,028	78,737	75,920	3,817	72,103	2,817	53,291	59.6	57.5	3.6
1969	134,335	80,734	77,902	3,606	74,296	2,832	53,602	60.1	58.0	3.5
1970	137,085	82,771	78,678	3,463	75,215	4,093	54,315	60.4	57.4	4.9
1971	140,216	84,382	79,367	3,394	75,972	5,016	55,834	60.2	56.6	5.9
1972 [5]	144,126	87,034	82,153	3,484	78,669	4,882	57,091	60.4	57.0	5.6
1973 [5]	147,096	89,429	85,064	3,470	81,594	4,365	57,667	60.8	57.8	4.9
1974	150,120	91,949	86,794	3,515	83,279	5,156	58,171	61.3	57.8	5.6
1975	153,153	93,775	85,846	3,408	82,438	7,929	59,377	61.2	56.1	8.5
1976	156,150	96,158	88,752	3,331	85,421	7,406	59,991	61.6	56.8	7.7
1977	159,033	99,009	92,017	3,283	88,734	6,991	60,025	62.3	57.9	7.1
1978 [5]	161,910	102,251	96,048	3,387	92,661	6,202	59,659	63.2	59.3	6.1
1979	164,863	104,962	98,824	3,347	95,477	6,137	59,900	63.7	59.9	5.8
1980	167,745	106,940	99,303	3,364	95,938	7,637	60,806	63.8	59.2	7.1
1981	170,130	108,670	100,397	3,368	97,030	8,273	61,460	63.9	59.0	7.6
1982	172,271	110,204	99,526	3,401	96,125	10,678	62,067	64.0	57.8	9.7
1983	174,215	111,550	100,834	3,383	97,450	10,717	62,665	64.0	57.9	9.6
1984	176,383	113,544	105,005	3,321	101,685	8,539	62,839	64.4	59.5	7.5
1985	178,206	115,461	107,150	3,179	103,971	8,312	62,744	64.8	60.1	7.2
1986 [5]	180,587	117,834	109,597	3,163	106,434	8,237	62,752	65.3	60.7	7.0
1987	182,753	119,865	112,440	3,208	109,232	7,425	62,888	65.6	61.5	6.2
1988	184,613	121,669	114,968	3,169	111,800	6,701	62,944	65.9	62.3	5.5
1989	186,393	123,869	117,342	3,199	114,142	6,528	62,523	66.5	63.0	5.3
1990 [5]	189,164	125,840	118,793	3,223	115,570	7,047	63,324	66.5	62.8	5.6
1991	190,925	126,346	117,718	3,269	114,449	8,628	64,578	66.2	61.7	6.8
1992	192,805	128,105	118,492	3,247	115,245	9,613	64,700	66.4	61.5	7.5
1993	194,838	129,200	120,259	3,115	117,144	8,940	65,638	66.3	61.7	6.9
1994 [5]	196,814	131,056	123,060	3,409	119,651	7,996	65,758	66.6	62.5	6.1
1995	198,584	132,304	124,900	3,440	121,460	7,404	66,280	66.6	62.9	5.6
1996	200,591	133,943	126,708	3,443	123,264	7,236	66,647	66.8	63.2	5.4
1997 [5]	203,133	136,297	129,558	3,399	126,159	6,739	66,837	67.1	63.8	4.9
1998 [5]	205,220	137,673	131,463	3,378	128,085	6,210	67,547	67.1	64.1	4.5
1999 [5]	207,753	139,368	133,488	3,281	130,207	5,880	68,385	67.1	64.3	4.2

[1] Not seasonally adjusted.
[2] Civilian labor force as percent of civilian noninstitutional population.
[3] Civilian employment as percent of civilian noninstitutional population.
[4] Unemployed as percent of civilian labor force.

See next page for continuation of table.

TABLE B–35. Civilian population and labor force, 1929–2010—*Continued*

[Monthly data seasonally adjusted, except as noted]

Year or month	Civilian noninsti-tutional population [1]	Civilian labor force					Not in labor force	Civilian labor force participa-tion rate [2]	Civilian employ-ment/ population ratio [3]	Unemploy-ment rate, civilian workers [4]
		Total	Employment			Un-employ-ment				
			Total	Agricultural	Non-agricultural					
	Thousands of persons 16 years of age and over							Percent		
2000 [5,6]	212,577	142,583	136,891	2,464	134,427	5,692	69,994	67.1	64.4	4.0
2001	215,092	143,734	136,933	2,299	134,635	6,801	71,359	66.8	63.7	4.7
2002	217,570	144,863	136,485	2,311	134,174	8,378	72,707	66.6	62.7	5.8
2003 [5]	221,168	146,510	137,736	2,275	135,461	8,774	74,658	66.2	62.3	6.0
2004 [5]	223,357	147,401	139,252	2,232	137,020	8,149	75,956	66.0	62.3	5.5
2005 [5]	226,082	149,320	141,730	2,197	139,532	7,591	76,762	66.0	62.7	5.1
2006 [5]	228,815	151,428	144,427	2,206	142,221	7,001	77,387	66.2	63.1	4.6
2007 [5]	231,867	153,124	146,047	2,095	143,952	7,078	78,743	66.0	63.0	4.6
2008 [5]	233,788	154,287	145,362	2,168	143,194	8,924	79,501	66.0	62.2	5.8
2009 [5]	235,801	154,142	139,877	2,103	137,775	14,265	81,659	65.4	59.3	9.3
2010 [5]	237,830	153,889	139,064	2,206	136,858	14,825	83,941	64.7	58.5	9.6
2007: Jan [5]	230,650	153,133	146,033	2,215	143,750	7,100	77,516	66.4	63.3	4.6
Feb	230,834	152,966	146,066	2,298	143,755	6,900	77,868	66.3	63.3	4.5
Mar	231,034	153,054	146,334	2,179	144,190	6,721	77,979	66.2	63.3	4.4
Apr	231,253	152,446	145,610	2,069	143,423	6,836	78,807	65.9	63.0	4.5
May	231,480	152,666	145,901	2,082	143,774	6,766	78,814	66.0	63.0	4.4
June	231,713	153,038	146,058	1,947	144,087	6,980	78,674	66.0	63.0	4.6
July	231,958	153,035	145,886	2,014	144,005	7,149	78,923	66.0	62.9	4.7
Aug	232,211	152,756	145,670	1,865	143,841	7,085	79,455	65.8	62.7	4.6
Sept	232,461	153,422	146,231	2,091	144,142	7,191	79,039	66.0	62.9	4.7
Oct	232,715	153,209	145,937	2,118	143,908	7,272	79,506	65.8	62.7	4.7
Nov	232,939	153,845	146,584	2,145	144,463	7,261	79,094	66.0	62.9	4.7
Dec	233,156	153,936	146,272	2,218	144,013	7,664	79,220	66.0	62.7	5.0
2008: Jan [5]	232,616	154,060	146,407	2,208	144,136	7,653	78,556	66.2	62.9	5.0
Feb	232,809	153,624	146,183	2,193	143,995	7,441	79,185	66.0	62.8	4.8
Mar	232,995	153,924	146,143	2,176	144,014	7,781	79,071	66.1	62.7	5.1
Apr	233,198	153,779	146,173	2,108	143,965	7,606	79,420	65.9	62.7	4.9
May	233,405	154,322	145,925	2,116	143,767	8,398	79,083	66.1	62.5	5.4
June	233,627	154,315	145,725	2,122	143,582	8,590	79,312	66.1	62.4	5.6
July	233,864	154,432	145,479	2,138	143,387	8,953	79,432	66.0	62.2	5.8
Aug	234,107	154,656	145,167	2,152	143,011	9,489	79,450	66.1	62.0	6.1
Sept	234,360	154,613	145,056	2,232	142,816	9,557	79,746	66.0	61.9	6.2
Oct	234,612	154,953	144,778	2,196	142,669	10,176	79,659	66.0	61.7	6.6
Nov	234,828	154,621	144,068	2,205	141,902	10,552	80,207	65.8	61.4	6.8
Dec	235,035	154,669	143,324	2,203	141,091	11,344	80,366	65.8	61.0	7.3
2009: Jan [5]	234,739	154,185	142,201	2,151	140,010	11,984	80,554	65.7	60.6	7.8
Feb	234,913	154,424	141,687	2,134	139,606	12,737	80,489	65.7	60.3	8.2
Mar	235,086	154,100	140,822	2,034	138,859	13,278	80,985	65.6	59.9	8.6
Apr	235,271	154,453	140,720	2,121	138,568	13,734	80,818	65.6	59.8	8.9
May	235,452	154,805	140,292	2,154	138,121	14,512	80,647	65.7	59.6	9.4
June	235,655	154,754	139,978	2,149	137,772	14,776	80,900	65.7	59.4	9.5
July	235,870	154,457	139,794	2,136	137,590	14,663	81,413	65.5	59.3	9.5
Aug	236,087	154,362	139,409	2,102	137,229	14,953	81,725	65.4	59.0	9.7
Sept	236,322	153,940	138,791	2,038	136,772	15,149	82,382	65.1	58.7	9.8
Oct	236,550	154,022	138,393	2,042	136,424	15,628	82,528	65.1	58.5	10.1
Nov	236,743	153,795	138,590	2,097	136,550	15,206	82,947	65.0	58.5	9.9
Dec	236,924	153,172	137,960	2,079	135,854	15,212	83,752	64.7	58.2	9.9
2010: Jan [5]	236,832	153,353	138,511	2,134	136,391	14,842	83,479	64.8	58.5	9.7
Feb	236,998	153,558	138,698	2,311	136,527	14,860	83,440	64.8	58.5	9.7
Mar	237,159	153,895	138,952	2,212	136,842	14,943	83,264	64.9	58.6	9.7
Apr	237,329	154,520	139,382	2,242	137,134	15,138	82,809	65.1	58.7	9.8
May	237,499	154,237	139,353	2,214	137,152	14,884	83,262	64.9	58.7	9.6
June	237,690	153,684	139,092	2,118	136,876	14,593	84,006	64.7	58.5	9.5
July	237,890	153,628	138,991	2,189	136,599	14,637	84,262	64.6	58.4	9.5
Aug	238,099	154,117	139,267	2,187	136,957	14,849	83,983	64.7	58.5	9.6
Sept	238,322	154,124	139,378	2,172	137,266	14,746	84,198	64.7	58.5	9.6
Oct	238,530	153,960	139,084	2,348	136,797	14,876	84,570	64.5	58.3	9.7
Nov	238,715	153,950	138,909	2,185	136,752	15,041	84,765	64.5	58.2	9.8
Dec	238,889	153,690	139,206	2,176	137,001	14,485	85,199	64.3	58.3	9.4

[5] Not strictly comparable with earlier data due to population adjustments or other changes. See *Employment and Earnings* or population control adjustments to the Current Population Survey (CPS) at http://www.bls.gov/cps/documentation.htm#concepts for details on breaks in series.

[6] Beginning in 2000, data for agricultural employment are for agricultural and related industries; data for this series and for nonagricultural employment are not strictly comparable with data for earlier years. Because of independent seasonal adjustment for these two series, monthly data will not add to total civilian employment.

Note: Labor force data in Tables B–35 through B–44 are based on household interviews and relate to the calendar week including the 12th of the month. For definitions of terms, area samples used, historical comparability of the data, comparability with other series, etc., see *Employment and Earnings* or population control adjustments to the CPS at http://www.bls.gov/cps/documentation.htm#concepts.

Source: Department of Labor (Bureau of Labor Statistics).

Population, Employment, Wages, and Productivity | 233

TABLE B–36. Civilian employment and unemployment by sex and age, 1964–2010

[Thousands of persons 16 years of age and over; monthly data seasonally adjusted]

Year or month	Civilian employment Total	Males Total	Males 16–19 years	Males 20 years and over	Females Total	Females 16–19 years	Females 20 years and over	Unemployment Total	Males Total	Males 16–19 years	Males 20 years and over	Females Total	Females 16–19 years	Females 20 years and over
1964	69,305	45,474	2,587	42,886	23,831	1,929	21,903	3,786	2,205	487	1,718	1,581	385	1,195
1965	71,088	46,340	2,918	43,422	24,748	2,118	22,630	3,366	1,914	479	1,435	1,452	395	1,056
1966	72,895	46,919	3,253	43,668	25,976	2,468	23,510	2,875	1,551	432	1,120	1,324	405	921
1967	74,372	47,479	3,186	44,294	26,893	2,496	24,397	2,975	1,508	448	1,060	1,468	391	1,078
1968	75,920	48,114	3,255	44,859	27,807	2,526	25,281	2,817	1,419	426	993	1,397	412	985
1969	77,902	48,818	3,430	45,388	29,084	2,687	26,397	2,832	1,403	440	963	1,429	413	1,015
1970	78,678	48,990	3,409	45,581	29,688	2,735	26,952	4,093	2,238	599	1,638	1,855	506	1,349
1971	79,367	49,390	3,478	45,912	29,976	2,730	27,246	5,016	2,789	693	2,097	2,227	568	1,658
1972	82,153	50,896	3,765	47,130	31,257	2,980	28,276	4,882	2,659	711	1,948	2,222	598	1,625
1973	85,064	52,349	4,039	48,310	32,715	3,231	29,484	4,365	2,275	653	1,624	2,089	583	1,507
1974	86,794	53,024	4,103	48,922	33,769	3,345	30,424	5,156	2,714	757	1,957	2,441	665	1,777
1975	85,846	51,857	3,839	48,018	33,989	3,263	30,726	7,929	4,442	966	3,476	3,486	802	2,684
1976	88,752	53,138	3,947	49,190	35,615	3,389	32,226	7,406	4,036	939	3,098	3,369	780	2,588
1977	92,017	54,728	4,174	50,555	37,289	3,514	33,775	6,991	3,667	874	2,794	3,324	789	2,535
1978	96,048	56,479	4,336	52,143	39,569	3,734	35,836	6,202	3,142	813	2,328	3,061	769	2,292
1979	98,824	57,607	4,300	53,308	41,217	3,783	37,434	6,137	3,120	811	2,308	3,018	743	2,276
1980	99,303	57,186	4,085	53,101	42,117	3,625	38,492	7,637	4,267	913	3,353	3,370	755	2,615
1981	100,397	57,397	3,815	53,582	43,000	3,411	39,590	8,273	4,577	962	3,615	3,696	800	2,895
1982	99,526	56,271	3,379	52,891	43,256	3,170	40,086	10,678	6,179	1,090	5,089	4,499	886	3,613
1983	100,834	56,787	3,300	53,487	44,047	3,043	41,004	10,717	6,260	1,003	5,257	4,457	825	3,632
1984	105,005	59,091	3,322	55,769	45,915	3,122	42,793	8,539	4,744	812	3,932	3,794	687	3,107
1985	107,150	59,891	3,328	56,562	47,259	3,105	44,154	8,312	4,521	806	3,715	3,791	661	3,129
1986	109,597	60,892	3,323	57,569	48,706	3,149	45,556	8,237	4,530	779	3,751	3,707	675	3,032
1987	112,440	62,107	3,381	58,726	50,334	3,260	47,074	7,425	4,101	732	3,369	3,324	616	2,709
1988	114,968	63,273	3,492	59,781	51,696	3,313	48,383	6,701	3,655	667	2,987	3,046	558	2,487
1989	117,342	64,315	3,477	60,837	53,027	3,282	49,745	6,528	3,525	658	2,867	3,003	536	2,467
1990	118,793	65,104	3,427	61,678	53,689	3,154	50,535	7,047	3,906	667	3,239	3,140	544	2,596
1991	117,718	64,223	3,044	61,178	53,496	2,862	50,634	8,628	4,946	751	4,195	3,683	608	3,074
1992	118,492	64,440	2,944	61,496	54,052	2,724	51,328	9,613	5,523	806	4,717	4,090	621	3,469
1993	120,259	65,349	2,994	62,355	54,910	2,811	52,099	8,940	5,055	768	4,287	3,885	597	3,288
1994	123,060	66,450	3,156	63,294	56,610	3,005	53,606	7,996	4,367	740	3,627	3,629	580	3,049
1995	124,900	67,377	3,292	64,085	57,523	3,127	54,396	7,404	3,983	744	3,239	3,421	602	2,819
1996	126,708	68,207	3,310	64,897	58,501	3,190	55,311	7,236	3,880	733	3,146	3,356	573	2,783
1997	129,558	69,685	3,401	66,284	59,873	3,260	56,613	6,739	3,577	694	2,882	3,162	577	2,585
1998	131,463	70,693	3,558	67,135	60,771	3,493	57,278	6,210	3,266	686	2,580	2,944	519	2,424
1999	133,488	71,446	3,685	67,761	62,042	3,487	58,555	5,880	3,066	633	2,433	2,814	529	2,285
2000	136,891	73,305	3,671	69,634	63,586	3,519	60,067	5,692	2,975	599	2,376	2,717	483	2,235
2001	136,933	73,196	3,420	69,776	63,737	3,320	60,417	6,801	3,690	650	3,040	3,111	512	2,599
2002	136,485	72,903	3,169	69,734	63,582	3,162	60,420	8,378	4,597	700	3,896	3,781	553	3,228
2003	137,736	73,332	2,917	70,415	64,404	3,002	61,402	8,774	4,906	697	4,209	3,868	554	3,314
2004	139,252	74,524	2,952	71,572	64,728	2,955	61,773	8,149	4,456	664	3,791	3,694	543	3,150
2005	141,730	75,973	2,923	73,050	65,757	3,055	62,702	7,591	4,059	667	3,392	3,531	519	3,013
2006	144,427	77,502	3,071	74,431	66,925	3,091	63,834	7,001	3,753	622	3,131	3,247	496	2,751
2007	146,047	78,254	2,917	75,337	67,792	2,994	64,799	7,078	3,882	623	3,259	3,196	478	2,718
2008	145,362	77,486	2,736	74,750	67,876	2,837	65,039	8,924	5,033	736	4,297	3,891	549	3,342
2009	139,877	73,670	2,328	71,341	66,208	2,509	63,699	14,265	8,453	898	7,555	5,811	654	5,157
2010	139,064	73,359	2,129	71,230	65,705	2,249	63,456	14,825	8,626	863	7,763	6,199	665	5,534
2009: Jan	142,201	75,239	2,504	72,735	66,961	2,717	64,244	11,984	6,991	799	6,192	4,993	576	4,418
Feb	141,687	74,798	2,475	72,324	66,889	2,698	64,191	12,737	7,456	835	6,621	5,280	616	4,664
Mar	140,822	74,092	2,396	71,695	66,731	2,658	64,074	13,278	7,841	835	7,006	5,438	596	4,841
Apr	140,720	74,002	2,411	71,590	66,718	2,631	64,087	13,734	8,251	852	7,399	5,483	579	4,904
May	140,292	73,870	2,412	71,457	66,423	2,606	63,816	14,512	8,729	913	7,816	5,783	612	5,171
June	139,978	73,689	2,383	71,306	66,289	2,579	63,710	14,776	8,755	879	7,875	6,021	738	5,284
July	139,794	73,540	2,346	71,193	66,254	2,521	63,733	14,663	8,689	912	7,776	5,975	663	5,312
Aug	139,409	73,356	2,302	71,054	66,053	2,438	63,615	14,953	8,968	958	8,010	5,985	655	5,329
Sept	138,791	73,099	2,271	70,828	65,692	2,369	63,323	15,149	9,044	963	8,081	6,105	672	5,433
Oct	138,393	72,864	2,197	70,667	65,529	2,265	63,264	15,628	9,381	954	8,427	6,247	703	5,544
Nov	138,590	72,897	2,125	70,772	65,693	2,330	63,363	15,206	9,091	940	8,150	6,115	696	5,419
Dec	137,960	72,609	2,129	70,479	65,351	2,315	63,037	15,212	8,925	941	7,983	6,287	689	5,598
2010: Jan	138,511	72,667	2,143	70,525	65,844	2,295	63,549	14,842	8,789	928	7,861	6,053	644	5,409
Feb	138,698	72,884	2,177	70,707	65,813	2,297	63,516	14,860	8,696	835	7,861	6,164	655	5,509
Mar	138,952	73,163	2,187	70,977	65,789	2,310	63,479	14,943	8,778	914	7,864	6,165	668	5,497
Apr	139,382	73,526	2,177	71,348	65,856	2,355	63,501	15,138	8,829	898	7,931	6,309	643	5,665
May	139,353	73,603	2,153	71,451	65,750	2,263	63,487	14,884	8,572	845	7,728	6,312	741	5,570
June	139,092	73,385	2,056	71,329	65,706	2,223	63,483	14,593	8,614	850	7,765	5,978	635	5,343
July	138,991	73,466	2,126	71,340	65,526	2,186	63,340	14,637	8,520	867	7,653	6,117	659	5,458
Aug	139,267	73,600	2,095	71,505	65,667	2,288	63,379	14,849	8,666	876	7,789	6,183	680	5,504
Sept	139,378	73,594	2,035	71,559	65,784	2,221	63,562	14,746	8,571	841	7,729	6,175	656	5,520
Oct	139,084	73,470	2,106	71,365	65,613	2,214	63,400	14,876	8,530	879	7,651	6,346	728	5,618
Nov	138,909	73,337	2,206	71,130	65,572	2,187	63,385	15,041	8,649	800	7,849	6,392	626	5,766
Dec	139,206	73,600	2,121	71,480	65,605	2,177	63,428	14,485	8,245	818	7,426	6,240	641	5,599

Note: See footnote 5 and Note, Table B–35.

Source: Department of Labor (Bureau of Labor Statistics).

[Thousands of persons 16 years of age and over; monthly data seasonally adjusted]

Year or month	All civilian workers	White[1] Total	White[1] Males	White[1] Females	White[1] Both sexes 16–19	Black and other[1] Total	Black and other[1] Males	Black and other[1] Females	Black and other[1] Both sexes 16–19	Black or African American[1] Total	Black or African American[1] Males	Black or African American[1] Females	Black or African American[1] Both sexes 16–19
1964	69,305	61,922	41,115	20,807	4,076	7,383	4,359	3,024	440	....	....	....	....
1965	71,088	63,446	41,844	21,602	4,562	7,643	4,496	3,147	474	....	....	....	....
1966	72,895	65,021	42,331	22,690	5,176	7,877	4,588	3,289	545	....	....	....	....
1967	74,372	66,361	42,833	23,528	5,114	8,011	4,646	3,365	568	....	....	....	....
1968	75,920	67,750	43,411	24,339	5,195	8,169	4,702	3,467	584	....	....	....	....
1969	77,902	69,518	44,048	25,470	5,508	8,384	4,770	3,614	609	....	....	....	....
1970	78,678	70,217	44,178	26,039	5,571	8,464	4,813	3,650	574	....	....	....	....
1971	79,367	70,878	44,595	26,283	5,670	8,488	4,796	3,692	538	....	....	....	....
1972	82,153	73,370	45,944	27,426	6,173	8,783	4,952	3,832	573	7,802	4,368	3,433	509
1973	85,064	75,708	47,085	28,623	6,623	9,356	5,265	4,092	647	8,128	4,527	3,601	570
1974	86,794	77,184	47,674	29,511	6,796	9,610	5,352	4,258	652	8,203	4,527	3,677	554
1975	85,846	76,411	46,697	29,714	6,487	9,435	5,161	4,275	615	7,894	4,275	3,618	507
1976	88,752	78,853	47,775	31,078	6,724	9,899	5,363	4,536	611	8,227	4,404	3,823	508
1977	92,017	81,700	49,150	32,550	7,068	10,317	5,579	4,739	619	8,540	4,565	3,975	508
1978	96,048	84,936	50,544	34,392	7,367	11,112	5,936	5,177	703	9,102	4,796	4,307	571
1979	98,824	87,259	51,452	35,807	7,356	11,565	6,156	5,409	727	9,359	4,923	4,436	579
1980	99,303	87,715	51,127	36,587	7,021	11,588	6,059	5,529	689	9,313	4,798	4,515	547
1981	100,397	88,709	51,315	37,394	6,588	11,688	6,083	5,606	637	9,355	4,794	4,561	505
1982	99,526	87,903	50,287	37,615	5,984	11,624	5,983	5,641	565	9,189	4,637	4,552	428
1983	100,834	88,893	50,621	38,272	5,799	11,941	6,166	5,775	543	9,375	4,753	4,622	416
1984	105,005	92,120	52,462	39,659	5,836	12,885	6,629	6,256	607	10,119	5,124	4,995	474
1985	107,150	93,738	53,046	40,690	5,768	13,414	6,845	6,569	666	10,501	5,270	5,231	532
1986	109,597	95,660	53,785	41,876	5,792	13,937	7,107	6,830	681	10,814	5,420	5,386	536
1987	112,440	97,789	54,647	43,142	5,898	14,652	7,459	7,192	742	11,309	5,661	5,648	587
1988	114,968	99,812	55,550	44,262	6,030	15,156	7,722	7,434	774	11,658	5,824	5,834	601
1989	117,342	101,584	56,352	45,232	5,946	15,757	7,963	7,795	813	11,953	5,928	6,025	625
1990	118,793	102,261	56,703	45,558	5,779	16,533	8,401	8,131	801	12,175	5,995	6,180	598
1991	117,718	101,182	55,797	45,385	5,216	16,536	8,426	8,110	690	12,074	5,961	6,113	494
1992	118,492	101,669	55,959	45,710	4,985	16,823	8,482	8,342	684	12,151	5,930	6,221	492
1993	120,259	103,045	56,656	46,390	5,113	17,214	8,693	8,521	691	12,382	6,047	6,334	494
1994	123,060	105,190	57,452	47,738	5,398	17,870	8,998	8,872	763	12,835	6,241	6,595	552
1995	124,900	106,490	58,146	48,344	5,593	18,409	9,231	9,179	826	13,279	6,422	6,857	586
1996	126,708	107,808	58,888	48,920	5,667	18,900	9,319	9,580	832	13,542	6,456	7,086	613
1997	129,558	109,856	59,998	49,859	5,807	19,701	9,687	10,014	853	13,969	6,607	7,362	631
1998	131,463	110,931	60,604	50,327	6,089	20,532	10,089	10,443	962	14,556	6,871	7,685	736
1999	133,488	112,235	61,139	51,096	6,204	21,253	10,307	10,945	968	15,056	7,027	8,029	691
2000	136,891	114,424	62,289	52,136	6,160	....	....	....	....	15,156	7,082	8,073	711
2001	136,933	114,430	62,212	52,218	5,817	....	....	....	....	15,006	6,938	8,068	637
2002	136,485	114,013	61,849	52,164	5,441	....	....	....	....	14,872	6,959	7,914	611
2003	137,736	114,235	61,866	52,369	5,064	....	....	....	....	14,739	6,820	7,919	516
2004	139,252	115,239	62,712	52,527	5,039	....	....	....	....	14,909	6,912	7,997	520
2005	141,730	116,949	63,763	53,186	5,105	....	....	....	....	15,313	7,155	8,158	536
2006	144,427	118,833	64,883	53,950	5,215	....	....	....	....	15,765	7,354	8,410	618
2007	146,047	119,792	65,289	54,503	4,990	....	....	....	....	16,051	7,500	8,551	566
2008	145,362	119,126	64,624	54,501	4,697	....	....	....	....	15,953	7,398	8,554	541
2009	139,877	114,996	61,630	53,366	4,138	....	....	....	....	15,025	6,817	8,208	442
2010	139,064	114,168	61,252	52,916	3,733	....	....	....	....	15,010	6,865	8,145	386
2009: Jan	142,201	116,782	62,947	53,835	4,450	....	....	....	....	15,481	7,023	8,458	497
Feb	141,687	116,478	62,538	53,940	4,489	....	....	....	....	15,312	6,952	8,360	459
Mar	140,822	115,673	61,932	53,741	4,334	....	....	....	....	15,176	6,876	8,300	455
Apr	140,720	115,783	61,958	53,825	4,254	....	....	....	....	15,098	6,817	8,281	486
May	140,292	115,392	61,816	53,576	4,307	....	....	....	....	15,040	6,815	8,225	434
June	139,978	115,085	61,629	53,456	4,218	....	....	....	....	15,036	6,795	8,242	452
July	139,794	114,921	61,554	53,367	4,145	....	....	....	....	15,052	6,828	8,224	476
Aug	139,409	114,699	61,429	53,271	4,054	....	....	....	....	14,919	6,736	8,182	452
Sept	138,791	114,051	61,210	52,841	3,976	....	....	....	....	14,798	6,713	8,085	411
Oct	138,393	113,854	60,993	52,861	3,814	....	....	....	....	14,749	6,736	8,013	408
Nov	138,590	113,854	60,911	52,943	3,831	....	....	....	....	14,883	6,753	8,131	374
Dec	137,960	113,439	60,670	52,769	3,822	....	....	....	....	14,760	6,764	7,995	389
2010: Jan	138,511	113,940	60,735	53,206	3,758	....	....	....	....	14,843	6,764	8,079	428
Feb	138,698	113,958	60,946	53,012	3,802	....	....	....	....	14,952	6,768	8,184	403
Mar	138,952	114,165	61,127	53,037	3,794	....	....	....	....	14,939	6,799	8,140	421
Apr	139,382	114,465	61,371	53,094	3,846	....	....	....	....	14,996	6,884	8,112	420
May	139,353	114,350	61,461	52,889	3,728	....	....	....	....	15,175	6,972	8,203	428
June	139,092	114,176	61,305	52,872	3,626	....	....	....	....	15,020	6,838	8,182	379
July	138,991	114,312	61,472	52,840	3,706	....	....	....	....	14,908	6,854	8,054	376
Aug	139,267	114,457	61,509	52,947	3,747	....	....	....	....	14,972	6,868	8,104	370
Sept	139,378	114,433	61,507	52,927	3,674	....	....	....	....	14,920	6,825	8,094	310
Oct	139,084	113,975	61,235	52,739	3,715	....	....	....	....	15,127	6,934	8,193	366
Nov	138,990	113,728	61,052	52,676	3,775	....	....	....	....	15,142	6,926	8,216	372
Dec	139,206	114,079	61,307	52,773	3,676	....	....	....	....	15,119	6,941	8,178	361

[1] Beginning in 2003, persons who selected this race group only. Prior to 2003, persons who selected more than one race were included in the group they identified as the main race. Data for "black or African American" were for "black" prior to 2003. Data discontinued for "black and other" series. See *Employment and Earnings* or concepts and methodology of the Current Population Survey (CPS) at http://www.bls.gov/cps/documentation.htm#concepts for details.

Note: Beginning with data for 2000, detail will not sum to total because data for all race groups are not shown here.
See footnote 5 and Note, Table B–35.

Source: Department of Labor (Bureau of Labor Statistics).

TABLE B–38. Unemployment by demographic characteristic, 1964–2010

[Thousands of persons 16 years of age and over; monthly data seasonally adjusted]

Year or month	All civilian workers	White [1]				Black and other [1]				Black or African American [1]			
		Total	Males	Females	Both sexes 16–19	Total	Males	Females	Both sexes 16–19	Total	Males	Females	Both sexes 16–19
1964	3,786	2,999	1,779	1,220	708	787	426	361	165	....	....	....	....
1965	3,366	2,691	1,556	1,135	705	678	360	318	171	....	....	....	....
1966	2,875	2,255	1,241	1,014	651	622	310	312	186	....	....	....	....
1967	2,975	2,338	1,208	1,130	635	638	300	338	203	....	....	....	....
1968	2,817	2,226	1,142	1,084	644	590	277	313	194	....	....	....	....
1969	2,832	2,260	1,137	1,123	660	571	267	304	193	....	....	....	....
1970	4,093	3,339	1,857	1,482	871	754	380	374	235	....	....	....	....
1971	5,016	4,085	2,309	1,777	1,011	930	481	450	249	....	....	....	....
1972	4,882	3,906	2,173	1,733	1,021	977	486	491	288	906	448	458	279
1973	4,365	3,442	1,836	1,606	955	924	440	484	280	846	395	451	262
1974	5,156	4,097	2,169	1,927	1,104	1,058	544	514	318	965	494	470	297
1975	7,929	6,421	3,627	2,794	1,413	1,507	815	692	355	1,369	741	629	330
1976	7,406	5,914	3,258	2,656	1,364	1,492	779	713	355	1,334	698	637	330
1977	6,991	5,441	2,883	2,558	1,284	1,550	784	766	379	1,393	698	695	354
1978	6,202	4,698	2,411	2,287	1,189	1,505	731	774	394	1,330	641	690	360
1979	6,137	4,664	2,405	2,260	1,193	1,473	714	759	362	1,319	636	683	333
1980	7,637	5,884	3,345	2,540	1,291	1,752	922	830	377	1,553	815	738	343
1981	8,273	6,343	3,580	2,762	1,374	1,930	997	933	388	1,731	891	840	357
1982	10,678	8,241	4,846	3,395	1,534	2,437	1,334	1,104	443	2,142	1,167	975	396
1983	10,717	8,128	4,859	3,270	1,387	2,588	1,401	1,187	441	2,272	1,213	1,059	392
1984	8,539	6,372	3,600	2,772	1,116	2,167	1,144	1,022	384	1,914	1,003	911	353
1985	8,312	6,191	3,426	2,765	1,074	2,121	1,095	1,026	394	1,864	951	913	357
1986	8,237	6,140	3,433	2,708	1,070	2,097	1,097	999	383	1,840	946	894	347
1987	7,425	5,501	3,132	2,369	995	1,924	969	955	353	1,684	826	858	312
1988	6,701	4,944	2,766	2,177	910	1,757	888	869	316	1,547	771	776	288
1989	6,528	4,770	2,636	2,135	863	1,757	889	868	331	1,544	773	772	300
1990	7,047	5,186	2,935	2,251	903	1,860	971	889	308	1,565	806	758	268
1991	8,628	6,560	3,859	2,701	1,029	2,068	1,087	981	330	1,723	890	833	280
1992	9,613	7,169	4,209	2,959	1,037	2,444	1,314	1,130	390	2,011	1,067	944	324
1993	8,940	6,655	3,828	2,827	992	2,285	1,227	1,058	373	1,844	971	872	313
1994	7,996	5,892	3,275	2,617	960	2,104	1,092	1,011	360	1,666	848	818	300
1995	7,404	5,459	2,999	2,460	952	1,945	984	961	394	1,538	762	777	325
1996	7,236	5,300	2,896	2,404	939	1,936	984	952	367	1,592	808	784	310
1997	6,739	4,836	2,641	2,195	912	1,903	935	967	359	1,560	747	813	302
1998	6,210	4,484	2,431	2,053	876	1,726	835	891	329	1,426	671	756	281
1999	5,880	4,273	2,274	1,999	844	1,606	792	814	318	1,309	626	684	268
2000	5,692	4,121	2,177	1,944	795	....	....	....	....	1,241	620	621	230
2001	6,801	4,969	2,754	2,215	845	....	....	....	....	1,416	709	706	260
2002	8,378	6,137	3,459	2,678	925	....	....	....	....	1,693	835	858	260
2003	8,774	6,311	3,643	2,668	909	....	....	....	....	1,787	891	895	255
2004	8,149	5,847	3,282	2,565	890	....	....	....	....	1,729	860	868	241
2005	7,591	5,350	2,931	2,419	845	....	....	....	....	1,700	844	856	267
2006	7,001	5,002	2,730	2,271	794	....	....	....	....	1,549	774	775	253
2007	7,078	5,143	2,869	2,274	805	....	....	....	....	1,445	752	693	235
2008	8,924	6,509	3,727	2,782	947	....	....	....	....	1,788	949	839	246
2009	14,265	10,648	6,421	4,227	1,157	....	....	....	....	2,606	1,448	1,159	288
2010	14,825	10,916	6,476	4,440	1,128	....	....	....	....	2,852	1,550	1,302	291
2009: Jan	11,984	8,861	5,209	3,652	1,017	....	....	....	....	2,253	1,297	956	283
Feb	12,737	9,425	5,593	3,832	1,089	....	....	....	....	2,404	1,358	1,046	292
Mar	13,278	10,005	5,960	4,045	1,103	....	....	....	....	2,364	1,349	1,015	229
Apr	13,734	10,196	6,199	3,998	1,072	....	....	....	....	2,663	1,533	1,130	277
May	14,512	10,827	6,637	4,190	1,106	....	....	....	....	2,651	1,491	1,160	292
June	14,776	11,024	6,714	4,310	1,177	....	....	....	....	2,641	1,444	1,197	289
July	14,663	10,986	6,687	4,299	1,199	....	....	....	....	2,618	1,416	1,202	276
Aug	14,953	11,266	6,873	4,392	1,286	....	....	....	....	2,643	1,492	1,151	244
Sept	15,149	11,352	6,948	4,404	1,210	....	....	....	....	2,694	1,458	1,236	285
Oct	15,628	11,771	7,191	4,580	1,263	....	....	....	....	2,774	1,513	1,261	286
Nov	15,206	11,438	6,927	4,510	1,165	....	....	....	....	2,765	1,565	1,201	358
Dec	15,212	11,264	6,719	4,544	1,180	....	....	....	....	2,856	1,527	1,329	355
2010: Jan	14,842	10,795	6,591	4,203	1,146	....	....	....	....	2,922	1,585	1,337	323
Feb	14,860	10,999	6,502	4,497	1,108	....	....	....	....	2,811	1,575	1,236	290
Mar	14,943	10,939	6,466	4,473	1,180	....	....	....	....	2,962	1,722	1,239	294
Apr	15,138	11,275	6,762	4,513	1,178	....	....	....	....	2,971	1,564	1,407	261
May	14,884	10,977	6,403	4,574	1,193	....	....	....	....	2,785	1,507	1,279	268
June	14,593	10,788	6,435	4,353	1,095	....	....	....	....	2,725	1,543	1,182	258
July	14,637	10,782	6,415	4,366	1,131	....	....	....	....	2,767	1,488	1,279	265
Aug	14,849	10,901	6,511	4,391	1,162	....	....	....	....	2,904	1,575	1,329	312
Sept	14,746	10,899	6,459	4,440	1,119	....	....	....	....	2,857	1,559	1,298	300
Oct	14,876	10,940	6,427	4,513	1,138	....	....	....	....	2,818	1,489	1,330	334
Nov	15,041	11,096	6,533	4,563	1,008	....	....	....	....	2,878	1,516	1,362	321
Dec	14,485	10,620	6,188	4,433	1,070	....	....	....	....	2,839	1,471	1,367	287

[1] See footnote 1 and Note, Table B–37.

Note: See footnote 5 and Note, Table B–35.

Source: Department of Labor (Bureau of Labor Statistics).

[Percent [1]; monthly data seasonally adjusted]

Year or month	Labor force participation rate							Employment/population ratio						
	All civilian workers	Males	Females	Both sexes 16–19 years	White [2]	Black and other [2]	Black or African American [2]	All civilian workers	Males	Females	Both sexes 16–19 years	White [2]	Black and other [2]	Black or African American [2]
1964	58.7	81.0	38.7	44.5	58.2	63.1	....	55.7	77.3	36.3	37.3	55.5	57.0	....
1965	58.9	80.7	39.3	45.7	58.4	62.9	....	56.2	77.5	37.1	38.9	56.0	57.8	....
1966	59.2	80.4	40.3	48.2	58.7	63.0	....	56.9	77.9	38.3	42.1	56.8	58.4	....
1967	59.6	80.4	41.1	48.4	59.2	62.8	....	57.3	78.0	39.0	42.2	57.2	58.2	....
1968	59.6	80.1	41.6	48.3	59.3	62.2	....	57.5	77.8	39.6	42.2	57.4	58.0	....
1969	60.1	79.8	42.7	49.4	59.9	62.1	....	58.0	77.6	40.7	43.4	58.0	58.1	....
1970	60.4	79.7	43.3	49.9	60.2	61.8	....	57.4	76.2	40.8	42.3	57.5	56.8	....
1971	60.2	79.1	43.4	49.7	60.1	60.9	....	56.6	74.9	40.4	41.3	56.8	54.9	....
1972	60.4	78.9	43.9	51.9	60.4	60.2	59.9	57.0	75.0	41.0	43.5	57.4	54.1	53.7
1973	60.8	78.8	44.7	53.7	60.8	60.5	60.2	57.8	75.5	42.0	45.9	58.2	55.0	54.5
1974	61.3	78.7	45.7	54.8	61.4	60.3	59.8	57.8	74.9	42.6	46.0	58.3	54.3	53.5
1975	61.2	77.9	46.3	54.0	61.5	59.6	58.8	56.1	71.7	42.0	43.3	56.7	51.4	50.1
1976	61.6	77.5	47.3	54.5	61.8	59.8	59.0	56.8	72.0	43.2	44.2	57.5	52.0	50.8
1977	62.3	77.7	48.4	56.0	62.5	60.4	59.8	57.9	72.8	44.5	46.1	58.6	52.5	51.4
1978	63.2	77.9	50.0	57.8	63.3	62.2	61.5	59.3	73.8	46.4	48.3	60.0	54.7	53.6
1979	63.7	77.8	50.9	57.9	63.9	62.2	61.4	59.9	73.8	47.5	48.5	60.6	55.2	53.8
1980	63.8	77.4	51.5	56.7	64.1	61.7	61.0	59.2	72.0	47.7	46.6	60.0	53.6	52.3
1981	63.9	77.0	52.1	55.4	64.3	61.3	60.8	59.0	71.3	48.0	44.6	60.0	52.6	51.3
1982	64.0	76.6	52.6	54.1	64.3	61.6	61.0	57.8	69.0	47.7	41.5	58.8	50.9	49.4
1983	64.0	76.4	52.9	53.5	64.3	62.1	61.5	57.9	68.8	48.0	41.5	58.9	51.0	49.5
1984	64.4	76.4	53.6	53.9	64.6	62.6	62.2	59.5	70.7	49.5	43.7	60.5	53.6	52.3
1985	64.8	76.3	54.5	54.5	65.0	63.3	62.9	60.1	70.9	50.4	44.4	61.0	54.7	53.4
1986	65.3	76.3	55.3	54.7	65.5	63.7	63.3	60.7	71.0	51.4	44.6	61.5	55.4	54.1
1987	65.6	76.2	56.0	54.7	65.8	64.3	63.8	61.5	71.5	52.5	45.5	62.3	56.8	55.6
1988	65.9	76.2	56.6	55.3	66.2	64.0	63.8	62.3	72.0	53.4	46.8	63.1	57.4	56.3
1989	66.5	76.4	57.4	55.9	66.7	64.7	64.2	63.0	72.5	54.3	47.5	63.8	58.2	56.9
1990	66.5	76.4	57.5	53.7	66.9	64.4	64.0	62.8	72.0	54.3	45.3	63.7	57.9	56.7
1991	66.2	75.8	57.4	51.6	66.6	63.8	63.3	61.7	70.4	53.7	42.0	62.6	56.7	55.4
1992	66.4	75.8	57.8	51.3	66.8	64.6	63.9	61.5	69.8	53.8	41.0	62.4	56.4	54.9
1993	66.3	75.4	57.9	51.5	66.8	63.8	63.2	61.7	70.0	54.1	41.7	62.7	56.3	55.0
1994	66.6	75.1	58.8	52.7	67.1	63.9	63.4	62.5	70.4	55.3	43.4	63.5	57.2	56.1
1995	66.6	75.0	58.9	53.5	67.1	64.3	63.7	62.9	70.8	55.6	44.2	63.8	58.1	57.1
1996	66.8	74.9	59.3	52.3	67.2	64.6	64.1	63.2	70.9	56.0	43.5	64.1	58.6	57.4
1997	67.1	75.0	59.8	51.6	67.5	65.2	64.7	63.8	71.3	56.8	43.4	64.6	59.4	58.2
1998	67.1	74.9	59.8	52.8	67.3	66.0	65.6	64.1	71.6	57.1	45.1	64.7	60.9	59.7
1999	67.1	74.7	60.0	52.0	67.3	65.9	65.8	64.3	71.6	57.4	44.7	64.8	61.3	60.6
2000	67.1	74.8	59.9	52.0	67.3	....	65.8	64.4	71.9	57.5	45.2	64.9	....	60.9
2001	66.8	74.4	59.8	49.6	67.0	....	65.3	63.7	70.9	57.0	42.3	64.2	....	59.7
2002	66.6	74.1	59.6	47.4	66.8	....	64.8	62.7	69.7	56.3	39.6	63.4	....	58.1
2003	66.2	73.5	59.5	44.5	66.5	....	64.3	62.3	68.9	56.1	36.8	63.0	....	57.4
2004	66.0	73.3	59.2	43.9	66.3	....	63.8	62.3	69.2	56.0	36.4	63.1	....	57.2
2005	66.0	73.3	59.3	43.7	66.3	....	64.2	62.7	69.6	56.2	36.5	63.4	....	57.7
2006	66.2	73.5	59.4	43.7	66.5	....	64.1	63.1	70.1	56.6	36.9	63.8	....	58.4
2007	66.0	73.2	59.3	41.3	66.4	....	63.7	63.0	69.8	56.6	34.8	63.6	....	58.4
2008	66.0	73.0	59.5	40.2	66.3	....	63.7	62.2	68.5	56.2	32.6	62.8	....	57.3
2009	65.4	72.0	59.2	37.5	65.8	....	62.4	59.3	64.5	54.4	28.4	60.2	....	53.2
2010	64.7	71.2	58.6	34.9	65.1	....	62.2	58.5	63.7	53.6	25.9	59.4	....	52.3
2009: Jan	65.7	72.4	59.4	38.6	66.0	....	63.2	60.6	66.2	55.3	30.5	61.4	....	55.2
Feb	65.7	72.4	59.5	38.8	66.1	....	63.1	60.3	65.8	55.2	30.3	61.2	....	54.5
Mar	65.6	72.0	59.5	38.0	66.0	....	62.4	59.9	65.1	55.0	29.6	60.7	....	54.0
Apr	65.6	72.2	59.5	37.9	66.1	....	63.1	59.8	65.0	55.0	29.5	60.8	....	53.6
May	65.7	72.5	59.4	38.4	66.2	....	62.8	59.6	64.8	54.7	29.4	60.5	....	53.4
June	65.7	72.3	59.5	38.6	66.1	....	62.6	59.4	64.6	54.5	29.1	60.3	....	53.3
July	65.5	72.0	59.4	37.8	65.9	....	62.5	59.3	64.4	54.4	28.6	60.2	....	53.3
Aug	65.4	72.0	59.1	37.3	65.9	....	62.1	59.0	64.2	54.2	27.8	60.0	....	52.7
Sept	65.1	71.8	58.9	36.9	65.6	....	61.7	58.7	63.9	53.9	27.3	59.6	....	52.2
Oct	65.1	71.8	58.8	36.0	65.6	....	61.8	58.5	63.6	53.7	26.2	59.5	....	52.0
Nov	65.0	71.5	58.8	35.9	65.4	....	62.1	58.5	63.6	53.8	26.2	59.4	....	52.4
Dec	64.7	71.1	58.6	35.8	65.1	....	61.9	58.2	63.3	53.5	26.2	59.2	....	51.9
2010: Jan	64.8	71.0	58.8	35.3	65.2	....	62.3	58.5	63.4	53.9	26.0	59.5	....	52.0
Feb	64.8	71.1	58.9	35.1	65.2	....	62.2	58.5	63.5	53.8	26.3	59.5	....	52.4
Mar	64.9	71.4	58.8	35.8	65.3	....	62.6	58.6	63.7	53.8	26.5	59.6	....	52.3
Apr	65.1	71.7	58.9	35.8	65.6	....	62.8	58.7	64.0	53.8	26.7	59.7	....	52.4
May	64.9	71.5	58.8	35.4	65.3	....	62.7	58.7	64.0	53.7	26.1	59.6	....	53.0
June	64.7	71.2	58.5	34.1	65.1	....	61.9	58.5	63.8	53.6	25.3	59.5	....	52.4
July	64.6	71.2	58.4	34.6	65.1	....	61.5	58.4	63.8	53.4	25.5	59.5	....	51.9
Aug	64.7	71.3	58.5	35.2	65.2	....	62.2	58.5	63.8	53.5	26.0	59.5	....	52.1
Sept	64.7	71.2	58.6	34.2	65.1	....	61.7	58.5	63.8	53.5	25.3	59.5	....	51.8
Oct	64.5	71.0	58.5	35.2	64.9	....	62.2	58.3	63.6	53.3	25.7	59.2	....	52.5
Nov	64.5	70.9	58.5	34.6	64.8	....	62.4	58.2	63.4	53.3	26.2	59.0	....	52.5
Dec	64.3	70.7	58.3	34.3	64.7	....	62.1	58.3	63.6	53.3	25.6	59.2	....	52.3

[1] Civilian labor force or civilian employment as percent of civilian noninstitutional population in group specified.
[2] See footnote 1, Table B–37.

Note: Data relate to persons 16 years of age and over.
See footnote 5 and Note, Table B–35.

Source: Department of Labor (Bureau of Labor Statistics).

TABLE B–40. Civilian labor force participation rate by demographic characteristic, 1970–2010

[Percent [1]; monthly data seasonally adjusted]

Year or month	All civilian workers	White [2] Total	White Males Total	White Males 16–19 years	White Males 20 years and over	White Females Total	White Females 16–19 years	White Females 20 years and over	Black and other or black or African American [2] Total	Males Total	Males 16–19 years	Males 20 years and over	Females Total	Females 16–19 years	Females 20 years and over
									Black and other [2]						
1970	60.4	60.2	80.0	57.5	82.8	42.6	45.6	42.2	61.8	76.5	47.4	81.4	49.5	34.1	51.8
1971	60.2	60.1	79.6	57.9	82.3	42.6	45.4	42.3	60.9	74.9	44.7	80.0	49.2	31.2	51.8
1972	60.4	60.4	79.6	60.1	82.0	43.2	48.1	42.7	60.2	73.9	46.0	78.6	48.8	32.3	51.2
									Black or African American [2]						
1972	60.4	60.4	79.6	60.1	82.0	43.2	48.1	42.7	59.9	73.6	46.3	78.5	48.7	32.2	51.2
1973	60.8	60.8	79.4	62.0	81.6	44.1	50.1	43.5	60.2	73.4	45.7	78.4	49.3	34.2	51.6
1974	61.3	61.4	79.4	62.9	81.4	45.2	51.7	44.4	59.8	72.9	46.7	77.6	49.0	33.4	51.4
1975	61.2	61.5	78.7	61.9	80.7	45.9	51.5	45.3	58.8	70.9	42.6	76.0	48.8	34.2	51.1
1976	61.6	61.8	78.4	62.3	80.3	46.9	52.8	46.2	59.0	70.0	41.3	75.4	49.8	32.9	52.5
1977	62.3	62.5	78.5	64.0	80.2	48.0	54.5	47.3	59.8	70.6	43.2	75.6	50.8	32.9	53.6
1978	63.2	63.3	78.6	65.0	80.1	49.4	56.7	48.7	61.5	71.5	44.9	76.2	53.1	37.3	55.5
1979	63.7	63.9	78.6	64.8	80.1	50.5	57.4	49.8	61.4	71.3	43.6	76.3	53.1	36.8	55.4
1980	63.8	64.1	78.2	63.7	79.8	51.2	56.2	50.6	61.0	70.3	43.2	75.1	53.1	34.9	55.6
1981	63.9	64.3	77.9	62.4	79.5	51.9	55.4	51.5	60.8	70.0	41.6	74.5	53.5	34.0	56.0
1982	64.0	64.3	77.4	60.0	79.2	52.4	55.0	52.2	61.0	70.1	39.8	74.7	53.7	33.5	56.2
1983	64.0	64.3	77.1	59.4	78.9	52.7	54.5	52.5	61.5	70.6	39.9	75.2	54.2	33.0	56.8
1984	64.4	64.6	77.1	59.0	78.7	53.3	55.4	53.1	62.2	70.8	41.7	74.8	55.2	35.0	57.6
1985	64.8	65.0	77.0	59.7	78.5	54.1	55.2	54.0	62.9	70.8	44.6	74.4	56.5	37.9	58.6
1986	65.3	65.5	76.9	59.3	78.5	55.0	56.3	54.9	63.3	71.2	43.7	74.8	56.9	39.1	58.9
1987	65.6	65.8	76.8	59.0	78.4	55.7	56.5	55.6	63.8	71.1	43.6	74.7	58.0	39.6	60.0
1988	65.9	66.2	76.9	60.0	78.3	56.4	57.2	56.3	63.8	71.0	43.8	74.6	58.0	37.9	60.1
1989	66.5	66.7	77.1	61.0	78.5	57.2	57.1	57.2	64.2	71.0	44.6	74.4	58.7	40.4	60.6
1990	66.5	66.9	77.1	59.6	78.5	57.4	55.3	57.6	64.0	71.0	40.7	75.0	58.3	36.8	60.6
1991	66.2	66.6	76.5	57.3	78.0	57.4	54.1	57.6	63.3	70.4	37.3	74.6	57.5	33.5	60.0
1992	66.4	66.8	76.5	56.9	78.0	57.7	52.5	58.1	63.9	70.7	40.6	74.3	58.5	35.2	60.8
1993	66.3	66.8	76.2	56.6	77.7	58.0	53.5	58.3	63.2	69.6	39.5	73.2	57.9	34.6	60.2
1994	66.6	67.1	75.9	57.7	77.3	58.9	55.1	59.2	63.4	69.1	40.8	72.5	58.7	36.3	60.9
1995	66.6	67.1	75.7	58.5	77.1	59.0	55.5	59.2	63.7	69.0	40.1	72.5	59.5	39.8	61.4
1996	66.8	67.2	75.8	57.1	77.3	59.1	54.7	59.4	64.1	68.7	39.5	72.3	60.4	38.9	62.6
1997	67.1	67.5	75.9	56.1	77.5	59.5	54.1	59.9	64.7	68.3	37.4	72.2	61.7	39.9	64.0
1998	67.1	67.3	75.6	56.6	77.2	59.4	55.4	59.7	65.6	69.0	40.7	72.5	62.8	42.5	64.8
1999	67.1	67.3	75.6	56.4	77.2	59.6	54.5	59.9	65.8	68.7	38.6	72.4	63.5	38.8	66.1
2000	67.1	67.3	75.5	56.5	77.1	59.5	54.5	59.9	65.8	69.2	39.2	72.8	63.1	39.6	65.4
2001	66.8	67.0	75.1	53.7	76.9	59.4	52.4	59.9	65.3	68.4	37.9	72.1	62.8	37.3	65.2
2002	66.6	66.8	74.8	50.3	76.7	59.3	50.8	60.0	64.8	68.4	37.3	72.1	61.8	34.7	64.4
2003	66.2	66.5	74.2	47.5	76.3	59.2	47.9	59.9	64.3	67.3	31.1	71.5	61.9	33.7	64.6
2004	66.0	66.3	74.1	47.4	76.2	58.9	46.7	59.7	63.8	66.7	30.0	70.9	61.5	32.8	64.2
2005	66.0	66.3	74.1	46.2	76.2	58.9	47.6	59.7	64.2	67.3	32.6	71.3	61.6	32.2	64.4
2006	66.2	66.5	74.3	46.9	76.4	59.0	46.6	59.9	64.1	67.0	32.3	71.1	61.7	35.6	64.2
2007	66.0	66.4	74.0	44.3	76.3	59.0	44.6	60.1	63.7	66.8	29.4	71.2	61.1	31.2	64.0
2008	66.0	66.3	73.7	43.0	76.1	59.2	43.3	60.3	63.7	66.7	29.1	71.1	61.3	29.7	64.3
2009	65.4	65.8	72.8	40.3	75.3	59.1	40.9	60.4	62.4	65.0	26.4	69.6	60.3	27.9	63.4
2010	64.7	65.1	72.0	37.4	74.6	58.5	38.0	59.9	62.2	65.0	25.8	69.5	59.9	25.1	63.2
2009: Jan	65.7	66.0	73.2	41.7	75.7	59.2	41.9	60.4	63.2	66.0	27.2	70.6	61.0	30.7	63.9
Feb	65.7	66.1	73.2	41.6	75.6	59.4	43.8	60.5	63.1	65.8	27.3	70.4	60.8	28.5	64.0
Mar	65.6	66.0	72.9	40.6	75.3	59.4	42.6	60.6	62.4	65.1	23.5	69.9	60.2	27.3	63.4
Apr	65.6	66.1	73.1	39.8	75.7	59.4	41.7	60.7	63.1	66.0	29.1	70.3	60.7	27.6	63.9
May	65.7	66.2	73.4	41.6	75.8	59.3	41.3	60.6	62.8	65.5	25.1	70.3	60.5	28.9	63.6
June	65.7	66.1	73.2	40.4	75.7	59.3	42.3	60.5	62.6	64.9	25.5	69.5	60.8	29.6	63.8
July	65.5	65.9	73.0	40.8	75.5	59.2	41.2	60.4	62.5	64.9	26.6	69.3	60.6	29.4	63.6
Aug	65.4	65.9	73.0	41.8	75.4	59.1	40.1	60.4	62.1	64.6	24.6	69.3	60.0	27.2	63.1
Sept	65.1	65.6	72.8	40.4	75.3	58.6	39.3	60.0	61.7	64.1	26.1	68.5	59.8	25.9	63.1
Oct	65.1	65.6	72.8	39.7	75.3	58.8	38.4	60.2	61.8	64.6	25.7	69.1	59.5	26.2	62.6
Nov	65.0	65.4	72.3	37.7	75.0	58.8	39.2	60.1	62.1	65.0	29.5	69.1	59.8	25.3	63.0
Dec	64.7	65.1	71.8	37.9	74.4	58.6	39.3	59.9	61.9	64.8	28.3	68.9	59.6	27.5	62.7
2010: Jan	64.8	65.2	71.8	37.8	74.4	58.8	37.6	60.2	62.3	65.0	27.9	69.3	60.1	28.0	63.1
Feb	64.8	65.2	71.9	37.0	74.6	58.8	38.6	60.2	62.2	64.9	26.4	69.3	60.0	25.4	63.3
Mar	64.9	65.3	72.0	38.2	74.6	58.8	38.5	60.2	62.6	66.2	27.6	70.6	59.7	25.9	62.9
Apr	65.1	65.6	72.6	38.3	75.1	58.9	39.3	60.2	62.8	65.5	25.5	70.1	60.5	25.5	63.8
May	64.9	65.3	72.2	37.7	74.8	58.7	38.5	60.1	62.7	65.7	23.9	70.4	60.2	28.2	63.2
June	64.7	65.1	72.0	36.1	74.7	58.4	37.2	59.9	61.9	64.8	24.9	69.4	59.4	23.0	62.8
July	64.6	65.1	72.1	37.6	74.7	58.4	37.6	59.8	61.5	64.4	25.5	68.8	59.2	22.9	62.5
Aug	64.7	65.2	72.2	37.3	74.8	58.5	39.1	59.8	62.2	65.1	27.7	69.3	59.7	23.8	63.1
Sept	64.7	65.1	72.1	36.4	74.8	58.5	38.3	59.8	61.7	64.6	24.3	69.1	59.4	21.9	62.9
Oct	64.5	64.9	71.7	37.4	74.3	58.3	38.3	59.7	62.2	64.8	26.9	69.0	60.2	26.2	63.3
Nov	64.5	64.8	71.6	38.2	74.1	58.3	36.5	59.7	62.4	64.9	26.4	69.1	60.4	26.3	63.6
Dec	64.3	64.7	71.5	37.6	74.0	58.2	36.6	59.7	62.1	64.5	23.6	69.1	60.2	25.6	63.3

[1] Civilian labor force as percent of civilian noninstitutional population in group specified.
[2] See footnote 1, Table B–37.

Note: Data relate to persons 16 years of age and over.
See footnote 5 and Note, Table B–35.

Source: Department of Labor (Bureau of Labor Statistics).

TABLE B–41. Civilian employment/population ratio by demographic characteristic, 1970–2010

[Percent [1]; monthly data seasonally adjusted]

Year or month	All civilian work-ers	White [2]						Black and other or black or African American [2]						
		Total	Males			Females		Total	Males			Females		
			Total	16–19 years	20 years and over	Total	16–19 years	20 years and over		Total	16–19 years	20 years and over	Total	16–19 years	20 years and over
									Black and other [2]						
1970	57.4	57.5	76.8	49.6	80.1	40.3	39.5	40.4	56.8	70.9	35.5	76.8	44.9	22.4	48.2
1971	56.6	56.8	75.7	49.2	79.0	39.9	38.6	40.1	54.9	68.1	31.8	74.2	43.9	20.2	47.3
1972	57.0	57.4	76.0	51.5	79.0	40.7	41.3	40.6	54.1	67.3	32.4	73.2	43.3	19.9	46.7
									Black or African American [2]						
1972	57.0	57.4	76.0	51.5	79.0	40.7	41.3	40.6	53.7	66.8	31.6	73.0	43.0	19.2	46.5
1973	57.8	58.2	76.5	54.3	79.2	41.8	43.6	41.6	54.5	67.5	32.8	73.7	43.8	22.0	47.2
1974	57.8	58.3	75.9	54.4	78.6	42.4	44.3	42.2	53.5	65.8	31.4	71.9	43.5	20.9	46.9
1975	56.1	56.7	73.0	50.6	75.7	42.0	42.5	41.9	50.1	60.6	26.3	66.5	41.6	20.2	44.9
1976	56.8	57.5	73.4	51.5	76.0	43.2	44.2	43.1	50.8	60.6	25.8	66.8	42.8	19.2	46.4
1977	57.9	58.6	74.1	54.4	76.5	44.5	45.9	44.4	51.4	61.4	26.4	67.5	43.3	18.5	47.0
1978	59.3	60.0	75.0	56.3	77.2	46.3	48.5	46.1	53.6	63.3	28.5	69.1	45.8	22.1	49.3
1979	59.9	60.6	75.1	55.7	77.3	47.5	49.4	47.3	53.8	63.4	28.7	69.1	46.0	22.4	49.3
1980	59.2	60.0	73.4	53.4	75.6	47.8	47.9	47.8	52.3	60.4	27.0	65.8	45.7	21.0	49.1
1981	59.0	60.0	72.8	51.3	75.1	48.3	46.2	48.5	51.3	59.1	24.6	64.5	45.1	19.7	48.5
1982	57.8	58.8	70.6	47.0	73.0	48.1	44.6	48.4	49.4	56.0	20.3	61.4	44.2	17.7	47.5
1983	57.9	58.9	70.4	47.4	72.6	48.5	44.5	48.9	49.5	56.3	20.4	61.6	44.1	17.0	47.4
1984	59.5	60.5	72.1	49.1	74.3	49.8	47.0	50.0	52.3	59.2	23.9	64.1	46.7	20.1	49.8
1985	60.1	61.0	72.3	49.9	74.3	50.7	47.1	51.0	53.4	60.0	26.3	64.6	48.1	23.1	50.9
1986	60.7	61.5	72.3	49.6	74.3	51.7	47.9	52.0	54.1	60.6	26.5	65.1	48.8	23.8	51.6
1987	61.5	62.3	72.7	49.9	74.7	52.8	49.0	53.1	55.6	62.0	28.5	66.4	50.3	25.8	53.0
1988	62.3	63.1	73.2	51.7	75.1	53.8	50.2	54.0	56.3	62.7	29.4	67.1	51.2	25.8	53.9
1989	63.0	63.8	73.7	52.6	75.4	54.6	50.5	54.9	56.9	62.8	30.4	67.0	52.0	27.1	54.6
1990	62.8	63.7	73.3	51.0	75.1	54.7	48.3	55.2	56.7	62.6	27.7	67.1	51.9	25.8	54.7
1991	61.7	62.6	71.6	47.2	73.5	54.2	45.9	54.8	55.4	61.3	23.8	65.9	50.6	21.5	53.6
1992	61.5	62.4	71.1	46.4	73.1	54.2	44.2	54.9	54.9	59.9	23.6	64.3	50.8	22.1	53.6
1993	61.7	62.7	71.4	46.6	73.3	54.6	45.7	55.2	55.0	60.0	23.6	64.3	50.9	21.6	53.8
1994	62.5	63.5	71.8	48.3	73.6	55.8	47.5	56.4	56.1	60.8	25.4	65.0	52.3	24.5	55.0
1995	62.9	63.8	72.0	49.4	73.8	56.1	48.1	56.7	57.1	61.7	25.2	66.1	53.4	26.1	56.1
1996	63.2	64.1	72.3	48.2	74.2	56.3	47.6	57.0	57.4	61.1	24.9	65.5	54.4	27.1	57.1
1997	63.8	64.6	72.7	48.1	74.7	57.0	47.2	57.8	58.2	61.4	23.7	66.1	55.6	28.5	58.4
1998	64.1	64.7	72.7	48.6	74.7	57.1	49.3	57.7	59.7	62.9	28.4	67.1	57.2	31.8	59.7
1999	64.3	64.8	72.8	49.3	74.8	57.3	48.3	58.0	60.6	63.1	26.7	67.5	58.6	29.0	61.5
2000	64.4	64.9	73.0	49.5	74.9	57.4	48.8	58.0	60.9	63.6	28.9	67.7	58.6	30.6	61.3
2001	63.7	64.2	72.0	46.2	74.0	57.0	46.5	57.7	59.7	62.1	26.4	66.3	57.8	27.0	60.7
2002	62.7	63.4	70.8	42.3	73.1	56.4	44.1	57.3	58.1	61.1	25.6	65.2	55.8	24.9	58.7
2003	62.3	63.0	70.1	39.4	72.5	56.3	41.5	57.3	57.4	59.5	19.9	64.1	55.6	23.4	58.6
2004	62.3	63.1	70.4	39.7	72.8	56.1	40.3	57.2	57.2	59.3	19.3	63.9	55.5	23.6	58.5
2005	62.7	63.4	70.8	38.8	73.3	56.3	41.8	57.4	57.7	60.2	20.8	64.7	55.7	22.4	58.9
2006	63.1	63.8	71.3	40.0	73.7	56.6	41.1	57.7	58.4	60.6	21.7	65.2	56.5	26.4	59.4
2007	63.0	63.6	70.9	37.3	73.5	56.7	39.2	57.9	58.4	60.7	19.5	65.5	56.5	23.3	59.8
2008	62.2	62.8	69.7	34.8	72.4	56.3	37.1	57.7	57.3	59.1	18.7	63.9	55.8	21.7	59.1
2009	59.3	60.2	66.0	30.2	68.7	54.8	33.4	56.3	53.2	53.7	14.3	58.2	52.8	18.6	56.1
2010	58.5	59.4	65.1	27.6	67.9	54.0	30.4	55.6	52.3	53.1	14.1	57.5	51.7	14.9	55.1
2009: Jan	60.6	61.4	67.6	32.6	70.3	55.4	35.4	56.8	55.2	55.7	15.2	60.5	54.8	21.6	58.0
Feb	60.3	61.2	67.2	32.2	69.9	55.5	36.5	56.8	54.5	55.1	14.6	59.8	54.1	19.4	57.4
Mar	59.9	60.7	66.5	31.1	69.2	55.3	35.3	56.7	54.0	54.4	13.8	59.2	53.6	19.9	56.9
Apr	59.8	60.8	66.4	30.7	69.2	55.3	34.5	56.8	53.6	53.8	16.2	58.3	53.5	19.9	56.7
May	59.6	60.5	66.3	31.3	68.9	55.0	34.7	56.5	53.4	53.8	13.2	58.5	53.0	19.0	56.3
June	59.4	60.3	66.0	30.5	68.7	54.9	34.2	56.3	53.3	53.5	14.0	58.2	53.1	19.6	56.3
July	59.3	60.2	65.9	30.1	68.6	54.7	33.5	56.2	53.3	53.7	16.0	58.1	52.9	19.4	56.1
Aug	59.0	60.0	65.7	30.1	68.4	54.6	32.2	56.2	52.7	52.9	13.3	57.5	52.6	20.4	55.7
Sept	58.7	59.6	65.4	29.6	68.1	54.1	31.5	55.7	52.2	52.7	13.1	57.2	51.9	17.6	55.2
Oct	58.5	59.5	65.1	28.4	67.9	54.1	30.3	55.8	52.0	52.8	15.0	57.1	51.4	15.5	54.8
Nov	58.5	59.4	65.0	27.7	67.8	54.2	31.3	55.8	52.4	52.8	13.2	57.4	52.1	14.8	55.6
Dec	58.2	59.2	64.7	27.6	67.5	54.0	31.4	55.5	51.9	52.8	13.4	57.4	51.1	15.7	54.5
2010: Jan	58.5	59.5	64.8	27.4	67.6	54.5	30.5	56.1	52.0	52.6	14.7	57.0	51.5	17.2	54.8
Feb	58.5	59.5	65.0	27.8	67.8	54.2	30.8	55.9	52.4	52.6	14.6	57.0	52.1	15.4	55.6
Mar	58.6	59.6	65.1	27.9	68.0	54.2	30.7	55.9	52.3	52.8	14.7	57.2	51.8	16.8	55.1
Apr	58.7	59.7	65.4	27.9	68.2	54.3	31.6	55.8	52.4	53.4	16.1	57.6	51.6	15.4	55.0
May	58.7	59.6	65.4	27.7	68.3	54.0	30.1	55.7	53.0	54.0	15.2	58.4	52.1	16.9	55.4
June	58.5	59.5	65.2	26.3	68.1	54.0	30.0	55.6	52.4	52.9	14.0	57.3	51.9	14.5	55.4
July	58.4	59.5	65.3	27.7	68.1	53.9	29.9	55.6	51.9	53.0	14.1	57.3	51.1	14.3	54.5
Aug	58.5	59.5	65.3	27.3	68.2	54.0	31.1	55.6	52.1	53.0	13.5	57.4	51.3	14.4	54.7
Sept	58.5	59.5	65.3	26.7	68.1	53.9	30.6	55.5	51.8	52.6	12.6	57.1	51.2	10.9	54.9
Oct	58.3	59.2	64.9	27.7	67.7	53.7	30.3	55.3	52.5	53.3	13.1	57.8	51.8	14.6	55.2
Nov	58.2	59.0	64.7	29.3	67.3	53.6	29.7	55.2	52.5	53.2	13.3	57.6	51.8	14.9	55.2
Dec	58.3	59.2	64.9	27.9	67.7	53.7	29.6	55.3	52.3	53.3	13.6	57.6	51.6	13.9	55.0

[1] Civilian employment as percent of civilian noninstitutional population in group specified.
[2] See footnote 1, Table B–37.

Note: Data relate to persons 16 years of age and over.
See footnote 5 and Note, Table B–35.

Source: Department of Labor (Bureau of Labor Statistics).

TABLE B–42. Civilian unemployment rate, 1964–2010

[Percent [1]; monthly data seasonally adjusted, except as noted]

Year or month	All civilian workers	Males			Females			Both sexes 16–19 years	By race				Hispanic or Latino ethnicity [4]	Married men, spouse present	Women who maintain families (NSA) [3]
		Total	16–19 years	20 years and over	Total	16–19 years	20 years and over		White [2]	Black and other [2]	Black or African American [2]	Asian (NSA) [2,3]			
1964	5.2	4.6	15.8	3.9	6.2	16.6	5.2	16.2	4.6	9.6	....	....	....	2.8	....
1965	4.5	4.0	14.1	3.2	5.5	15.7	4.5	14.8	4.1	8.1	....	....	....	2.4	....
1966	3.8	3.2	11.7	2.5	4.8	14.1	3.8	12.8	3.4	7.3	....	....	....	1.9	....
1967	3.8	3.1	12.3	2.3	5.2	13.5	4.2	12.9	3.4	7.4	....	....	....	1.8	4.9
1968	3.6	2.9	11.6	2.2	4.8	14.0	3.8	12.7	3.2	6.7	....	....	....	1.6	4.4
1969	3.5	2.8	11.4	2.1	4.7	13.3	3.7	12.2	3.1	6.4	....	....	....	1.5	4.4
1970	4.9	4.4	15.0	3.5	5.9	15.6	4.8	15.3	4.5	8.2	....	....	....	2.6	5.4
1971	5.9	5.3	16.6	4.4	6.9	17.2	5.7	16.9	5.4	9.9	....	....	....	3.2	7.3
1972	5.6	5.0	15.9	4.0	6.6	16.7	5.4	16.2	5.1	10.0	10.4	....	....	2.8	7.2
1973	4.9	4.2	13.9	3.3	6.0	15.3	4.9	14.5	4.3	9.0	9.4	....	7.5	2.3	7.1
1974	5.6	4.9	15.6	3.8	6.7	16.6	5.5	16.0	5.0	9.9	10.5	....	8.1	2.7	7.0
1975	8.5	7.9	20.1	6.8	9.3	19.7	8.0	19.9	7.8	13.8	14.8	....	12.2	5.1	10.0
1976	7.7	7.1	19.2	5.9	8.6	18.7	7.4	19.0	7.0	13.1	14.0	....	11.5	4.2	10.1
1977	7.1	6.3	17.3	5.2	8.2	18.3	7.0	17.8	6.2	13.1	14.0	....	10.1	3.6	9.4
1978	6.1	5.3	15.8	4.3	7.2	17.1	6.0	16.4	5.2	11.9	12.8	....	9.1	2.8	8.5
1979	5.8	5.1	15.9	4.2	6.8	16.4	5.7	16.1	5.1	11.3	12.3	....	8.3	2.8	8.3
1980	7.1	6.9	18.3	5.9	7.4	17.2	6.4	17.8	6.3	13.1	14.3	....	10.1	4.2	9.2
1981	7.6	7.4	20.1	6.3	7.9	19.0	6.8	19.6	6.7	14.2	15.6	....	10.4	4.3	10.4
1982	9.7	9.9	24.4	8.8	9.4	21.9	8.3	23.2	8.6	17.3	18.9	....	13.8	6.5	11.7
1983	9.6	9.9	23.3	8.9	9.2	21.3	8.1	22.4	8.4	17.8	19.5	....	13.7	6.5	12.2
1984	7.5	7.4	19.6	6.6	7.6	18.0	6.8	18.9	6.5	14.4	15.9	....	10.7	4.6	10.3
1985	7.2	7.0	19.5	6.2	7.4	17.6	6.6	18.6	6.2	13.7	15.1	....	10.5	4.3	10.4
1986	7.0	6.9	19.0	6.1	7.1	17.6	6.2	18.3	6.0	13.1	14.5	....	10.6	4.4	9.8
1987	6.2	6.2	17.8	5.4	6.2	15.9	5.4	16.9	5.3	11.6	13.0	....	8.8	3.9	9.2
1988	5.5	5.5	16.0	4.8	5.6	14.4	4.9	15.3	4.7	10.4	11.7	....	8.2	3.3	8.1
1989	5.3	5.2	15.9	4.5	5.4	14.0	4.7	15.0	4.5	10.0	11.4	....	8.0	3.0	8.1
1990	5.6	5.7	16.3	5.0	5.5	14.7	4.9	15.5	4.8	10.1	11.4	....	8.2	3.4	8.3
1991	6.8	7.2	19.8	6.4	6.4	17.5	5.7	18.7	6.1	11.1	12.5	....	10.0	4.4	9.3
1992	7.5	7.9	21.5	7.1	7.0	18.6	6.3	20.1	6.6	12.7	14.2	....	11.6	5.1	10.0
1993	6.9	7.2	20.4	6.4	6.6	17.5	5.9	19.0	6.1	11.7	13.0	....	10.8	4.4	9.7
1994	6.1	6.2	19.0	5.4	6.0	16.2	5.4	17.6	5.3	10.5	11.5	....	9.9	3.7	8.9
1995	5.6	5.6	18.4	4.8	5.6	16.1	4.9	17.3	4.9	9.6	10.4	....	9.3	3.3	8.0
1996	5.4	5.4	18.1	4.6	5.4	15.2	4.8	16.7	4.7	9.3	10.5	....	8.9	3.0	8.2
1997	4.9	4.9	16.9	4.2	5.0	15.0	4.4	16.0	4.2	8.8	10.0	....	7.7	2.7	8.1
1998	4.5	4.4	16.2	3.7	4.6	12.9	4.1	14.6	3.9	7.8	8.9	....	7.2	2.4	7.2
1999	4.2	4.1	14.7	3.5	4.3	13.2	3.8	13.9	3.7	7.0	8.0	....	6.4	2.2	6.4
2000	4.0	3.9	14.0	3.3	4.1	12.1	3.6	13.1	3.5	....	7.6	3.6	5.7	2.0	5.9
2001	4.7	4.8	16.0	4.2	4.7	13.4	4.1	14.7	4.2	....	8.6	4.5	6.6	2.7	6.6
2002	5.8	5.9	18.1	5.3	5.6	14.9	5.1	16.5	5.1	....	10.2	5.9	7.5	3.6	8.0
2003	6.0	6.3	19.3	5.6	5.7	15.6	5.1	17.5	5.2	....	10.8	6.0	7.7	3.8	8.5
2004	5.5	5.6	18.4	5.0	5.4	15.5	4.9	17.0	4.8	....	10.4	4.4	7.0	3.1	8.0
2005	5.1	5.1	18.6	4.4	5.1	14.5	4.6	16.6	4.4	....	10.0	4.0	6.0	2.8	7.8
2006	4.6	4.6	16.9	4.0	4.6	13.8	4.1	15.4	4.0	....	8.9	3.0	5.2	2.4	7.1
2007	4.6	4.7	17.6	4.1	4.5	13.8	4.0	15.7	4.1	....	8.3	3.2	5.6	2.5	6.5
2008	5.8	6.1	21.2	5.4	5.4	16.2	4.9	18.7	5.2	....	10.1	4.0	7.6	3.4	8.0
2009	9.3	10.3	27.8	9.6	8.1	20.7	7.5	24.3	8.5	....	14.8	7.3	12.1	6.6	11.5
2010	9.6	10.5	28.8	9.8	8.6	22.8	8.0	25.9	8.7	....	16.0	7.5	12.5	6.8	12.3
2009: Jan	7.8	8.5	24.2	7.8	6.9	17.5	6.4	20.8	7.1	....	12.7	6.2	9.9	5.2	10.3
Feb	8.2	9.1	25.2	8.4	7.3	18.6	6.8	21.9	7.5	....	13.6	6.9	11.1	5.7	10.3
Mar	8.6	9.6	25.8	8.9	7.5	18.3	7.0	22.1	8.0	....	13.5	6.4	11.5	6.0	10.8
Apr	8.9	10.0	26.1	9.4	7.6	18.0	7.1	22.1	8.1	....	15.0	6.6	11.4	6.4	10.0
May	9.4	10.6	27.5	9.9	8.0	19.0	7.5	23.3	8.6	....	15.0	6.7	12.8	6.8	11.0
June	9.5	10.6	26.9	9.9	8.3	22.2	7.7	24.6	8.7	....	14.9	8.2	12.2	6.9	11.7
July	9.5	10.6	28.0	9.8	8.3	20.8	7.7	24.4	8.7	....	14.8	8.3	12.5	7.0	12.6
Aug	9.7	10.9	29.4	10.1	8.3	21.2	7.7	25.4	8.9	....	15.0	7.5	13.1	7.0	12.2
Sept	9.8	11.0	29.8	10.2	8.5	22.1	7.9	26.1	9.1	....	15.4	7.4	12.7	7.2	11.6
Oct	10.1	11.4	30.3	10.7	8.7	23.7	8.1	27.1	9.4	....	15.8	7.5	13.1	7.3	12.9
Nov	9.9	11.1	30.7	10.3	8.5	23.0	7.9	26.9	9.1	....	15.7	7.3	12.6	7.3	11.4
Dec	9.9	10.9	30.7	10.2	8.8	22.9	8.2	26.8	9.0	....	16.2	8.4	12.8	7.2	13.0
2010: Jan	9.7	10.8	30.2	10.0	8.4	21.9	7.8	26.2	8.7	....	16.4	8.4	12.5	6.6	12.3
Feb	9.7	10.7	27.7	10.0	8.6	22.2	8.0	25.0	8.8	....	15.8	8.4	12.3	6.8	11.6
Mar	9.7	10.7	29.5	10.0	8.6	22.4	8.0	26.0	8.7	....	16.5	7.5	12.5	6.8	11.3
Apr	9.8	10.7	29.2	10.0	8.7	21.5	8.2	25.4	9.0	....	16.5	6.8	12.4	6.7	11.0
May	9.6	10.4	28.2	9.8	8.8	24.7	8.1	26.4	8.8	....	15.5	7.5	12.4	6.7	11.6
June	9.5	10.5	29.2	9.8	8.3	22.2	7.8	25.8	8.6	....	15.4	7.7	12.4	6.8	12.1
July	9.5	10.4	29.0	9.7	8.5	23.2	7.9	26.1	8.6	....	15.7	8.2	12.1	6.6	13.4
Aug	9.6	10.5	29.5	9.8	8.6	22.9	8.0	26.2	8.7	....	16.2	7.2	12.1	6.8	13.4
Sept	9.6	10.4	29.3	9.7	8.6	22.8	8.0	26.0	8.7	....	16.1	6.4	12.5	6.8	12.9
Oct	9.7	10.4	29.4	9.7	8.8	24.8	8.1	27.1	8.8	....	15.7	7.1	12.6	6.9	12.4
Nov	9.8	10.5	26.6	9.9	8.9	22.3	8.3	24.5	8.9	....	16.0	7.6	13.2	6.9	13.0
Dec	9.4	10.1	27.8	9.4	8.7	22.8	8.1	25.4	8.5	....	15.8	7.2	13.0	6.6	12.0

[1] Unemployed as percent of civilian labor force in group specified.
[2] See footnote 1, Table B–37.
[3] Not seasonally adjusted (NSA).
[4] Persons whose ethnicity is identified as Hispanic or Latino may be of any race.

Note: Data relate to persons 16 years of age and over.
See footnote 5 and Note, Table B–35.

Source: Department of Labor (Bureau of Labor Statistics).

TABLE B–43. Civilian unemployment rate by demographic characteristic, 1970–2010

[Percent [1]; monthly data seasonally adjusted]

Year or month	All civilian workers	White [2] Total	Males Total	Males 16–19 years	Males 20 years and over	Females Total	Females 16–19 years	Females 20 years and over	Black and other or black or African American [2] Total	Males Total	Males 16–19 years	Males 20 years and over	Females Total	Females 16–19 years	Females 20 years and over
									Black and other [2]						
1970	4.9	4.5	4.0	13.7	3.2	5.4	13.4	4.4	8.2	7.3	25.0	5.6	9.3	34.5	6.9
1971	5.9	5.4	4.9	15.1	4.0	6.3	15.1	5.3	9.9	9.1	28.8	7.3	10.9	35.4	8.7
1972	5.6	5.1	4.5	14.2	3.6	5.9	14.2	4.9	10.0	8.9	29.7	6.9	11.4	38.4	8.8
									Black or African American [2]						
1972	5.6	5.1	4.5	14.2	3.6	5.9	14.2	4.9	10.4	9.3	31.7	7.0	11.8	40.5	9.0
1973	4.9	4.3	3.8	12.3	3.0	5.3	13.0	4.3	9.4	8.0	27.8	6.0	11.1	36.1	8.6
1974	5.6	5.0	4.4	13.5	3.5	6.1	14.5	5.1	10.5	9.8	33.1	7.4	11.3	37.4	8.8
1975	8.5	7.8	7.2	18.3	6.2	8.6	17.4	7.5	14.8	14.8	38.1	12.5	14.8	41.0	12.2
1976	7.7	7.0	6.4	17.3	5.4	7.9	16.4	6.8	14.0	13.7	37.5	11.4	14.3	41.6	11.7
1977	7.1	6.2	5.5	15.0	4.7	7.3	15.9	6.2	14.0	13.3	39.2	10.7	14.9	43.4	12.3
1978	6.1	5.2	4.6	13.5	3.7	6.2	14.4	5.2	12.8	11.8	36.7	9.3	13.8	40.8	11.2
1979	5.8	5.1	4.5	13.9	3.6	5.9	14.0	5.0	12.3	11.4	34.2	9.3	13.3	39.1	10.9
1980	7.1	6.3	6.1	16.2	5.3	6.5	14.8	5.6	14.3	14.5	37.5	12.4	14.0	39.8	11.9
1981	7.6	6.7	6.5	17.9	5.6	6.9	16.6	5.9	15.6	15.7	40.7	13.5	15.6	42.2	13.4
1982	9.7	8.6	8.8	21.7	7.8	8.3	19.0	7.3	18.9	20.1	48.9	17.8	17.6	47.1	15.4
1983	9.6	8.4	8.8	20.2	7.9	7.9	18.3	6.9	19.5	20.3	48.8	18.1	18.6	48.2	16.5
1984	7.5	6.5	6.4	16.8	5.7	6.5	15.2	5.8	15.9	16.4	42.7	14.3	15.4	42.6	13.5
1985	7.2	6.2	6.1	16.5	5.4	6.4	14.8	5.7	15.1	15.3	41.0	13.2	14.9	39.2	13.1
1986	7.0	6.0	6.0	16.3	5.3	6.1	14.9	5.4	14.5	14.8	39.3	12.9	14.2	39.2	12.4
1987	6.2	5.3	5.4	15.5	4.8	5.2	13.4	4.6	13.0	12.7	34.4	11.1	13.2	34.9	11.6
1988	5.5	4.7	4.7	13.9	4.1	4.7	12.3	4.1	11.7	11.7	32.7	10.1	11.7	32.0	10.4
1989	5.3	4.5	4.5	13.7	3.9	4.5	11.5	4.0	11.4	11.5	31.9	10.0	11.4	33.0	9.8
1990	5.6	4.8	4.9	14.3	4.3	4.7	12.6	4.1	11.4	11.9	31.9	10.4	10.9	29.9	9.7
1991	6.8	6.1	6.5	17.6	5.8	5.6	15.2	5.0	12.5	13.0	36.3	11.5	12.0	36.0	10.6
1992	7.5	6.6	7.0	18.5	6.4	6.1	15.8	5.5	14.2	15.2	42.0	13.5	13.2	37.2	11.8
1993	6.9	6.1	6.3	17.7	5.7	5.7	14.7	5.2	13.0	13.8	40.1	12.1	12.1	37.4	10.7
1994	6.1	5.3	5.4	16.3	4.8	5.2	13.8	4.6	11.5	12.0	37.6	10.3	11.0	32.6	9.8
1995	5.6	4.9	4.9	15.6	4.3	4.8	13.4	4.3	10.4	10.6	37.1	8.8	10.2	34.3	8.6
1996	5.4	4.7	4.7	15.5	4.1	4.7	12.9	4.1	10.5	11.1	36.9	9.4	10.0	30.3	8.7
1997	4.9	4.2	4.2	14.3	3.6	4.2	12.8	3.7	10.0	10.2	36.5	8.5	9.9	28.7	8.8
1998	4.5	3.9	3.9	14.1	3.2	3.9	10.9	3.4	8.9	8.9	30.1	7.4	9.0	25.3	7.9
1999	4.2	3.7	3.6	12.6	3.0	3.8	11.3	3.3	8.0	8.2	30.9	6.7	7.8	25.1	6.8
2000	4.0	3.5	3.4	12.3	2.8	3.6	10.4	3.1	7.6	8.0	26.2	6.9	7.1	22.8	6.2
2001	4.7	4.2	4.2	13.9	3.7	4.1	11.4	3.6	8.6	9.3	30.4	8.0	8.1	27.5	7.0
2002	5.8	5.1	5.3	15.9	4.7	4.9	13.1	4.4	10.2	10.7	31.3	9.5	9.8	28.3	8.8
2003	6.0	5.2	5.6	17.1	5.0	4.8	13.3	4.4	10.8	11.6	36.0	10.3	10.2	30.3	9.2
2004	5.5	4.8	5.0	16.3	4.4	4.7	13.6	4.2	10.4	11.1	35.6	9.9	9.8	28.2	8.9
2005	5.1	4.4	4.4	16.1	3.8	4.4	12.3	3.9	10.0	10.5	36.3	9.2	9.5	30.3	8.5
2006	4.6	4.0	4.0	14.6	3.5	4.0	11.7	3.6	8.9	9.5	32.7	8.3	8.4	25.9	7.5
2007	4.6	4.1	4.2	15.7	3.7	4.0	12.1	3.6	8.3	9.1	33.8	7.9	7.5	25.3	6.7
2008	5.8	5.2	5.5	19.1	4.9	4.9	14.4	4.4	10.1	11.4	35.9	10.2	8.9	26.8	8.1
2009	9.3	8.5	9.4	25.2	8.8	7.3	18.4	6.8	14.8	17.5	46.0	16.3	12.4	33.4	11.5
2010	9.6	8.7	9.6	26.3	8.9	7.7	20.0	7.2	16.0	18.4	45.4	17.3	13.8	40.5	12.8
2009: Jan	7.8	7.1	7.6	21.7	7.0	6.4	15.4	5.9	12.7	15.6	44.0	14.3	10.2	29.5	9.3
Feb	8.2	7.5	8.2	22.5	7.6	6.6	16.6	6.1	13.6	16.3	46.3	15.0	11.1	31.9	10.2
Mar	8.6	8.0	8.8	23.5	8.2	7.0	17.1	6.5	13.5	16.4	41.4	15.4	10.9	26.9	10.2
Apr	8.9	8.1	9.1	22.8	8.5	6.9	17.4	6.4	15.0	18.4	44.2	17.1	12.0	28.1	11.3
May	9.4	8.6	9.7	24.8	9.1	7.3	15.9	6.8	15.0	18.0	47.2	16.7	12.4	34.3	11.4
June	9.5	8.7	9.8	24.5	9.2	7.5	19.2	6.9	14.9	17.5	45.1	16.3	12.7	33.8	11.7
July	9.5	8.7	9.8	26.2	9.1	7.5	18.6	6.9	14.8	17.2	39.7	16.2	12.8	34.0	11.8
Aug	9.7	8.9	10.1	27.9	9.3	7.6	19.9	7.0	15.0	18.1	46.1	17.0	12.3	25.2	11.8
Sept	9.8	9.1	10.2	26.7	9.5	7.7	19.7	7.1	15.4	17.8	49.9	16.4	13.3	32.1	12.5
Oct	10.1	9.4	10.5	28.4	9.8	8.0	21.1	7.4	15.8	18.3	41.7	17.3	13.6	40.7	12.5
Nov	9.9	9.1	10.2	26.5	9.6	7.9	20.1	7.3	15.7	18.8	55.5	17.0	12.9	41.5	11.8
Dec	9.9	9.0	10.0	27.2	9.3	7.9	20.0	7.4	16.2	18.4	52.6	16.8	14.3	42.7	13.1
2010: Jan	9.7	8.7	9.8	27.6	9.1	7.3	18.9	6.8	16.4	19.0	47.4	17.7	14.2	38.7	13.2
Feb	9.7	8.8	9.6	24.9	9.1	7.8	20.2	7.3	15.8	18.9	44.4	17.8	13.1	39.2	12.1
Mar	9.7	8.7	9.6	27.0	8.9	7.8	20.4	7.2	16.5	20.2	46.8	19.0	13.2	35.1	12.4
Apr	9.8	9.0	9.9	27.2	9.3	7.8	19.6	7.3	16.5	18.5	37.0	17.7	14.8	39.7	13.8
May	9.6	8.8	9.4	26.6	8.8	8.0	21.8	7.3	15.5	17.8	36.4	17.1	13.5	40.2	12.4
June	9.5	8.6	9.5	27.1	8.9	7.6	19.3	7.1	15.4	18.4	43.7	17.4	12.6	37.0	11.8
July	9.5	8.6	9.4	26.2	8.8	7.6	20.4	7.1	15.7	17.8	44.6	16.7	13.7	37.7	12.9
Aug	9.6	8.7	9.6	27.0	8.9	7.7	20.4	7.1	16.2	18.6	51.2	17.2	14.1	39.5	13.2
Sept	9.6	8.7	9.5	26.8	8.9	7.7	19.9	7.2	16.1	18.6	48.3	17.4	13.8	50.1	12.7
Oct	9.7	8.8	9.5	26.0	8.9	7.9	20.8	7.3	15.7	17.7	51.3	16.2	14.0	44.0	12.8
Nov	9.8	8.9	9.7	23.3	9.1	8.0	18.7	7.5	16.0	18.0	49.5	16.6	14.2	43.1	13.1
Dec	9.4	8.5	9.2	25.7	8.5	7.7	19.1	7.3	15.8	17.5	42.5	16.5	14.3	45.8	13.2

[1] Unemployed as percent of civilian labor force in group specified.
[2] See footnote 1, Table B–37.

Note: Data relate to persons 16 years of age and over.
See footnote 5 and Note, Table B–35.

Source: Department of Labor (Bureau of Labor Statistics).

TABLE B–44. Unemployment by duration and reason, 1964–2010

[Thousands of persons, except as noted; monthly data seasonally adjusted [1]]

Year or month	Un-employ-ment	Duration of unemployment						Reason for unemployment					
		Less than 5 weeks	5–14 weeks	15–26 weeks	27 weeks and over	Average (mean) duration (weeks)	Median duration (weeks)	Job losers [3]			Job leavers	Re-entrants	New entrants
								Total	On layoff	Other			
1964	3,786	1,697	1,117	491	482	13.3	....	....	....	....	....	....	....
1965	3,366	1,628	983	404	351	11.8	....	....	....	....	....	....	....
1966	2,875	1,573	779	287	239	10.4	....	....	....	....	....	....	....
1967 [2]	2,975	1,634	893	271	177	8.7	2.3	1,229	394	836	438	945	396
1968	2,817	1,594	810	256	156	8.4	4.5	1,070	334	736	431	909	407
1969	2,832	1,629	827	242	133	7.8	4.4	1,017	339	678	436	965	413
1970	4,093	2,139	1,290	428	235	8.6	4.9	1,811	675	1,137	550	1,228	504
1971	5,016	2,245	1,585	668	519	11.3	6.3	2,323	735	1,588	590	1,472	630
1972	4,882	2,242	1,472	601	566	12.0	6.2	2,108	582	1,526	641	1,456	677
1973	4,365	2,224	1,314	483	343	10.0	5.2	1,694	472	1,221	683	1,340	649
1974	5,156	2,604	1,597	574	381	9.8	5.2	2,242	746	1,495	768	1,463	681
1975	7,929	2,940	2,484	1,303	1,203	14.2	8.4	4,386	1,671	2,714	827	1,892	823
1976	7,406	2,844	2,196	1,018	1,348	15.8	8.2	3,679	1,050	2,628	903	1,928	895
1977	6,991	2,919	2,132	913	1,028	14.3	7.0	3,166	865	2,300	909	1,963	953
1978	6,202	2,865	1,923	766	648	11.9	5.9	2,585	712	1,873	874	1,857	885
1979	6,137	2,950	1,946	706	535	10.8	5.4	2,635	851	1,784	880	1,806	817
1980	7,637	3,295	2,470	1,052	820	11.9	6.5	3,947	1,488	2,459	891	1,927	872
1981	8,273	3,449	2,539	1,122	1,162	13.7	6.9	4,267	1,430	2,837	923	2,102	981
1982	10,678	3,883	3,311	1,708	1,776	15.6	8.7	6,268	2,127	4,141	840	2,384	1,185
1983	10,717	3,570	2,937	1,652	2,559	20.0	10.1	6,258	1,780	4,478	830	2,412	1,216
1984	8,539	3,350	2,451	1,104	1,634	18.2	7.9	4,421	1,171	3,250	823	2,184	1,110
1985	8,312	3,498	2,509	1,025	1,280	15.6	6.8	4,139	1,157	2,982	877	2,256	1,039
1986	8,237	3,448	2,557	1,045	1,187	15.0	6.9	4,033	1,090	2,943	1,015	2,160	1,029
1987	7,425	3,246	2,196	943	1,040	14.5	6.5	3,566	943	2,623	965	1,974	920
1988	6,701	3,084	2,007	801	809	13.5	5.9	3,092	851	2,241	983	1,809	816
1989	6,528	3,174	1,978	730	646	11.9	4.8	2,983	850	2,133	1,024	1,843	677
1990	7,047	3,265	2,257	822	703	12.0	5.3	3,387	1,028	2,359	1,041	1,930	688
1991	8,628	3,480	2,791	1,246	1,111	13.7	6.8	4,694	1,292	3,402	1,004	2,139	792
1992	9,613	3,376	2,830	1,453	1,954	17.7	8.7	5,389	1,260	4,129	1,002	2,285	937
1993	8,940	3,262	2,584	1,297	1,798	18.0	8.3	4,848	1,115	3,733	976	2,198	919
1994	7,996	2,728	2,408	1,237	1,623	18.8	9.2	3,815	977	2,838	791	2,786	604
1995	7,404	2,700	2,342	1,085	1,278	16.6	8.3	3,476	1,030	2,446	824	2,525	579
1996	7,236	2,633	2,287	1,053	1,262	16.7	8.3	3,370	1,021	2,349	774	2,512	580
1997	6,739	2,538	2,138	995	1,067	15.8	8.0	3,037	931	2,106	795	2,338	569
1998	6,210	2,622	1,950	763	875	14.5	6.7	2,822	866	1,957	734	2,132	520
1999	5,880	2,568	1,832	755	725	13.4	6.4	2,622	848	1,774	783	2,005	469
2000	5,692	2,558	1,815	669	649	12.6	5.9	2,517	852	1,664	780	1,961	434
2001	6,801	2,853	2,196	951	801	13.1	6.8	3,476	1,067	2,409	835	2,031	459
2002	8,378	2,893	2,580	1,369	1,535	16.6	9.1	4,607	1,124	3,483	866	2,368	536
2003	8,774	2,785	2,612	1,442	1,936	19.2	10.1	4,838	1,121	3,717	818	2,477	641
2004	8,149	2,696	2,382	1,293	1,779	19.6	9.8	4,197	998	3,199	858	2,408	686
2005	7,591	2,667	2,304	1,130	1,490	18.4	8.9	3,667	933	2,734	872	2,386	666
2006	7,001	2,614	2,121	1,031	1,235	16.8	8.3	3,321	921	2,400	827	2,237	616
2007	7,078	2,542	2,232	1,061	1,243	16.8	8.5	3,515	976	2,539	793	2,142	627
2008	8,924	2,932	2,804	1,427	1,761	17.9	9.4	4,789	1,176	3,614	896	2,472	766
2009	14,265	3,165	3,828	2,775	4,496	24.4	15.1	9,160	1,630	7,530	882	3,187	1,035
2010	14,825	2,771	3,267	2,371	6,415	33.0	21.4	9,250	1,431	7,819	889	3,466	1,220
2009: Jan	11,984	3,522	3,638	2,080	2,689	19.9	10.7	7,420	1,486	5,935	905	2,776	783
Feb	12,737	3,399	3,931	2,425	2,982	20.1	11.6	8,032	1,504	6,528	840	2,917	1,013
Mar	13,278	3,377	4,056	2,594	3,233	20.9	12.2	8,432	1,552	6,880	884	2,991	888
Apr	13,734	3,325	4,066	2,597	3,702	21.6	12.9	8,869	1,657	7,212	878	3,097	916
May	14,512	3,230	4,387	3,003	4,005	22.6	14.4	9,396	1,790	7,607	893	3,214	963
June	14,776	3,164	4,030	3,429	4,397	24.1	17.4	9,551	1,740	7,811	822	3,343	989
July	14,663	3,150	3,587	2,895	4,951	25.2	15.8	9,524	1,767	7,757	882	3,301	998
Aug	14,953	3,000	3,975	2,822	5,051	25.3	16.1	9,729	1,696	8,033	836	3,310	1,074
Sept	15,149	2,887	3,797	2,958	5,497	26.6	18.0	10,056	1,906	8,150	881	3,283	1,139
Oct	15,628	3,225	3,607	3,098	5,649	27.3	18.9	10,076	1,701	8,375	915	3,420	1,099
Nov	15,206	2,767	3,475	2,955	5,919	28.8	20.2	9,763	1,518	8,245	933	3,218	1,319
Dec	15,212	2,908	3,483	2,781	6,133	29.3	20.4	9,688	1,530	8,158	916	3,385	1,244
2010: Jan	14,842	2,915	3,346	2,614	6,302	30.5	20.0	9,287	1,452	7,835	908	3,603	1,210
Feb	14,860	2,729	3,380	2,703	6,131	29.8	19.6	9,493	1,541	7,953	878	3,444	1,220
Mar	14,943	2,654	3,210	2,449	6,517	31.7	20.3	9,368	1,570	7,798	893	3,523	1,185
Apr	15,138	2,695	3,000	2,274	6,659	33.1	21.6	9,237	1,356	7,881	933	3,749	1,217
May	14,884	2,763	3,060	2,174	6,710	34.3	22.8	9,194	1,448	7,746	966	3,430	1,192
June	14,593	2,779	3,138	2,209	6,691	34.8	25.5	9,097	1,403	7,694	897	3,272	1,147
July	14,637	2,833	3,098	2,171	6,539	33.9	21.7	9,090	1,268	7,822	896	3,417	1,197
Aug	14,849	2,756	3,604	2,210	6,261	33.5	20.6	9,285	1,505	7,780	868	3,418	1,260
Sept	14,746	2,872	3,329	2,364	6,153	33.4	20.5	9,286	1,340	7,947	809	3,441	1,193
Oct	14,876	2,659	3,427	2,500	6,234	33.9	21.3	9,070	1,293	7,777	854	3,498	1,278
Nov	15,041	2,824	3,336	2,515	6,328	33.9	21.7	9,471	1,430	8,042	864	3,427	1,269
Dec	14,485	2,725	3,184	2,205	6,441	34.2	22.4	8,923	1,402	7,521	914	3,408	1,311

[1] Because of independent seasonal adjustment of the various series, detail will not sum to totals.
[2] For 1967, the sum of the unemployed categorized by reason for unemployment does not equal total unemployment.
[3] Beginning with January 1994, job losers and persons who completed temporary jobs.

Note: Data relate to persons 16 years of age and over.
See footnote 5 and Note, Table B–35.

Source: Department of Labor (Bureau of Labor Statistics).

TABLE B–45. Unemployment insurance programs, selected data, 1980–2010

[Thousands of persons, except as noted]

Year or month	All programs [1]		Regular State programs						
	Insured unemployment (weekly average) [2]	Total benefits paid (millions of dollars)	Covered employment [3]	Insured unemployment (weekly average) [2]	Initial claims (weekly average)	Exhaustions (weekly average) [4]	Insured unemployment as percent of covered employment	Benefits paid	
								Total (millions of dollars)	Average weekly check (dollars) [5]
1980	3,521	16,668	86,918	3,356	488	59	3.9	14,887	99.06
1981	3,248	15,910	87,783	3,045	460	57	3.5	14,568	106.61
1982	4,836	26,649	86,148	4,059	583	80	4.7	21,769	119.34
1983	5,216	31,615	86,867	3,395	438	80	3.9	19,025	123.59
1984	3,160	18,201	91,378	2,475	377	50	2.7	13,642	123.47
1985	2,751	16,444	94,027	2,617	397	49	2.8	14,941	128.09
1986	2,667	16,325	95,946	2,621	378	52	2.7	16,188	135.65
1987	2,349	14,632	98,760	2,300	328	46	2.3	14,561	140.39
1988	2,122	13,500	101,987	2,081	310	38	2.0	13,483	144.74
1989	2,158	14,618	104,750	2,156	330	37	2.1	14,603	151.43
1990	2,527	18,452	106,325	2,522	388	45	2.4	18,413	161.20
1991	3,514	27,004	104,642	3,342	447	67	3.2	25,924	169.56
1992	4,906	39,669	105,187	3,245	408	74	3.1	26,048	173.38
1993	4,188	34,649	107,263	2,751	341	62	2.6	22,599	179.41
1994	2,941	24,261	110,526	2,670	340	57	2.4	22,338	181.91
1995	2,648	22,026	113,504	2,572	357	51	2.3	21,925	187.04
1996	2,656	22,397	116,078	2,595	356	53	2.2	22,349	189.27
1997	2,372	20,333	119,159	2,323	323	48	1.9	20,287	192.84
1998	2,264	20,091	122,427	2,222	321	44	1.8	20,017	200.58
1999	2,223	21,037	125,280	2,188	298	44	1.7	21,001	212.10
2000	2,143	21,005	128,054	2,110	301	41	1.6	20,983	221.01
2001	3,012	32,227	127,923	2,974	404	54	2.3	32,135	238.07
2002	4,453	53,350	126,545	3,585	407	85	2.8	42,266	256.79
2003	4,400	53,352	126,084	3,531	404	85	2.8	41,896	261.67
2004	3,103	36,495	127,618	2,950	345	68	2.3	35,034	262.50
2005	2,709	32,154	129,929	2,661	328	55	2.0	32,098	266.63
2006	2,521	30,917	132,177	2,476	313	51	1.9	30,852	277.20
2007	2,612	33,212	133,688	2,572	324	51	1.9	33,156	287.73
2008	3,898	51,798	133,076	3,306	424	66	2.5	43,764	297.10
2009	9,121	141,404	126,763	5,724	568	145	4.5	80,584	309.49
2010 ᵖ	9,718	149,718	125,077	4,486	454	123	3.6	59,835	301.43
2009: Jan	7,902	8,445.8	127,626	5,870	804	98	4.6	6,211.3	306.17
Feb	8,085	8,824.5	127,220	6,050	644	98	4.8	6,533.2	308.36
Mar	10,305	11,948.1	127,142	7,550	679	128	5.9	8,223.3	305.03
Apr	9,249	11,286.1	127,187	6,634	641	139	5.2	7,402.7	312.11
May	9,411	11,286.4	127,915	6,497	567	156	5.1	7,024.1	314.16
June	10,394	12,892.4	127,805	6,833	640	181	5.3	7,681.1	312.39
July	10,165	12,592.2	125,010	6,444	632	195	5.2	7,104.9	311.21
Aug	10,948	12,858.7	125,251	6,450	504	198	5.2	6,758.0	308.38
Sept	9,998	12,614.3	126,275	5,557	483	188	4.4	6,221.8	310.93
Oct	9,428	11,403.7	126,581	5,077	537	167	4.0	5,382.8	309.53
Nov	10,902	12,492.4	126,639	5,638	553	166	4.5	5,701.8	306.69
Dec	11,790	14,759.6	126,502	5,810	701	169	4.6	6,338.6	308.41
2010: Jan	12,375	14,455.9	123,206	6,114	640	157	5.0	6,230.0	307.63
Feb	11,389	13,886.7	123,394	5,530	484	137	4.5	5,963.6	307.40
Mar	12,804	16,198.5	124,351	6,050	496	159	4.9	6,739.1	306.24
Apr	10,593	12,777.7	125,714	4,949	482	141	3.9	5,207.6	305.29
May	10,739	12,274.0	126,685	4,782	421	137	3.8	4,754.0	303.55
June	10,308	12,508.8	127,112	4,758	497	141	3.7	5,038.8	299.86
July	9,194	10,755.4	....	4,551	502	133	....	4,507.7	296.77
Aug	11,325	13,576.2	....	4,936	440	135	....	4,796.8	293.54
Sept	9,360	11,118.1	....	4,046	402	114	....	4,070.5	297.99
Oct	9,215	10,384.4	....	3,944	442	111	....	3,763.2	297.23
Nov	9,632	11,229.9	....	4,254	498	117	....	4,262.6	295.10
Dec ᵖ	9,402	10,552.5	....	4,411	596	112	....	4,501.3	299.05

[1] Includes State Unemployment Insurance (State), Unemployment Compensation for Federal Employees (UCFE), Unemployment Compensation for Ex-service members (UCX), and Federal and State extended benefit programs. Also includes temporary Federal emergency programs: Federal Supplemental Compensation (1982–1985), Emergency Unemployment Compensation (EUC, 1991–1994), Temporary Extended Unemployment Compensation (2002–2004), EUC 2008 (2008–2010), and Federal Additional Compensation (2009–2010).

[2] The number of people continuing to receive benefits.

[3] Workers covered by regular State Unemployment Insurance programs.

[4] Individuals receiving final payments in benefit year.

[5] For total unemployment only. Excludes partial payments.

Note: Includes data for the District of Columbia, Puerto Rico, and the Virgin Islands.

Source: Department of Labor (Employment and Training Administration).

[Thousands of persons; monthly data seasonally adjusted]

Year or month	Total non-agricultural employment	Private industries										
		Total private	Goods-producing industries						Private service-providing industries			
			Total	Mining and logging	Construction	Manufacturing			Total	Trade, transportation, and utilities [1]		
						Total	Durable goods	Non-durable goods		Total	Retail trade
1965	60,874	50,683	20,595	694	3,284	16,617	9,973	6,644	30,089	12,139	6,262
1966	64,020	53,110	21,740	690	3,371	17,680	10,803	6,878	31,370	12,611	6,530
1967	65,931	54,406	21,882	679	3,305	17,897	10,952	6,945	32,524	12,950	6,711
1968	68,023	56,050	22,292	671	3,410	18,211	11,137	7,074	33,759	13,334	6,977
1969	70,512	58,181	22,893	683	3,637	18,573	11,396	7,177	35,288	13,853	7,295
1970	71,006	58,318	22,179	677	3,654	17,848	10,762	7,086	36,139	14,144	7,463
1971	71,335	58,323	21,602	658	3,770	17,174	10,229	6,944	36,721	14,318	7,657
1972	73,798	60,333	22,299	672	3,957	17,669	10,630	7,039	38,034	14,788	8,038
1973	76,912	63,050	23,450	693	4,167	18,589	11,414	7,176	39,600	15,349	8,371
1974	78,389	64,086	23,364	755	4,095	18,514	11,432	7,082	40,721	15,693	8,536
1975	77,069	62,250	21,318	802	3,608	16,909	10,266	6,643	40,932	15,606	8,600
1976	79,502	64,501	22,025	832	3,662	17,531	10,640	6,891	42,476	16,128	8,966
1977	82,593	67,334	22,972	865	3,940	18,167	11,132	7,035	44,362	16,765	9,359
1978	86,826	71,014	24,156	902	4,322	18,932	11,770	7,162	46,858	17,658	9,879
1979	89,932	73,864	24,997	1,008	4,562	19,426	12,220	7,206	48,868	18,303	10,180
1980	90,528	74,154	24,263	1,077	4,454	18,733	11,679	7,054	49,891	18,413	10,244
1981	91,289	75,109	24,118	1,180	4,304	18,634	11,611	7,023	50,991	18,604	10,364
1982	89,677	73,695	22,550	1,163	4,024	17,363	10,610	6,753	51,145	18,457	10,372
1983	90,280	74,269	22,110	997	4,065	17,048	10,326	6,722	52,160	18,668	10,635
1984	94,530	78,371	23,435	1,014	4,501	17,920	11,050	6,870	54,936	19,653	11,223
1985	97,511	80,978	23,585	974	4,793	17,819	11,034	6,784	57,393	20,379	11,733
1986	99,474	82,636	23,318	829	4,937	17,552	10,795	6,757	59,318	20,795	12,078
1987	102,088	84,932	23,470	771	5,090	17,609	10,767	6,842	61,462	21,302	12,419
1988	105,345	87,806	23,909	770	5,233	17,906	10,969	6,938	63,897	21,974	12,808
1989	108,014	90,087	24,045	750	5,309	17,985	11,004	6,981	66,042	22,510	13,108
1990	109,487	91,072	23,723	765	5,263	17,695	10,737	6,958	67,349	22,666	13,182
1991	108,375	89,829	22,588	739	4,780	17,068	10,220	6,848	67,241	22,281	12,896
1992	108,726	89,940	22,095	689	4,608	16,799	9,946	6,853	67,845	22,125	12,828
1993	110,844	91,855	22,219	666	4,779	16,774	9,901	6,872	69,636	22,378	13,021
1994	114,291	95,016	22,774	659	5,095	17,020	10,132	6,889	72,242	23,128	13,491
1995	117,298	97,865	23,156	641	5,274	17,241	10,373	6,868	74,710	23,834	13,897
1996	119,708	100,169	23,409	637	5,536	17,237	10,486	6,751	76,760	24,239	14,143
1997	122,776	103,113	23,886	654	5,813	17,419	10,705	6,714	79,227	24,700	14,389
1998	125,930	106,021	24,354	645	6,149	17,560	10,911	6,649	81,667	25,186	14,609
1999	128,993	108,686	24,465	598	6,545	17,322	10,831	6,491	84,221	25,771	14,970
2000	131,785	110,995	24,649	599	6,787	17,263	10,877	6,386	86,346	26,225	15,280
2001	131,826	110,708	23,873	606	6,826	16,441	10,336	6,105	86,834	25,983	15,239
2002	130,341	108,828	22,557	583	6,716	15,259	9,485	5,774	86,271	25,497	15,025
2003	129,999	108,416	21,816	572	6,735	14,510	8,964	5,546	86,600	25,287	14,917
2004	131,435	109,814	21,882	591	6,976	14,315	8,925	5,390	87,932	25,533	15,058
2005	133,703	111,899	22,190	628	7,336	14,226	8,956	5,271	89,709	25,959	15,280
2006	136,086	114,113	22,531	684	7,691	14,155	8,981	5,174	91,582	26,276	15,353
2007	137,598	115,380	22,233	724	7,630	13,879	8,808	5,071	93,147	26,630	15,520
2008	136,790	114,281	21,334	767	7,162	13,406	8,463	4,943	92,947	26,293	15,283
2009	130,920	108,371	18,620	700	6,037	11,883	7,309	4,574	89,751	24,949	14,528
2010 ᵖ	130,262	107,791	17,987	729	5,614	11,644	7,151	4,493	89,804	24,763	14,444
2009: Jan	133,549	110,961	19,855	761	6,551	12,543	7,820	4,723	91,106	25,475	14,792
Feb	132,823	110,254	19,559	747	6,435	12,377	7,702	4,675	90,695	25,330	14,723
Mar	132,070	109,510	19,233	728	6,293	12,212	7,580	4,632	90,277	25,174	14,635
Apr	131,542	108,861	18,956	714	6,179	12,063	7,450	4,613	89,905	25,052	14,592
May	131,155	108,527	18,731	700	6,120	11,911	7,326	4,585	89,796	24,997	14,570
June	130,640	108,075	18,503	692	6,029	11,782	7,222	4,560	89,572	24,943	14,546
July	130,294	107,778	18,375	687	5,949	11,739	7,197	4,542	89,403	24,845	14,492
Aug	130,082	107,563	18,245	678	5,885	11,682	7,151	4,531	89,318	24,819	14,477
Sept	129,857	107,377	18,124	676	5,814	11,634	7,112	4,522	89,253	24,754	14,429
Oct	129,633	107,115	17,993	669	5,747	11,577	7,070	4,507	89,122	24,670	14,366
Nov	129,697	107,190	17,960	676	5,732	11,552	7,047	4,505	89,230	24,678	14,375
Dec	129,588	107,107	17,906	676	5,696	11,534	7,036	4,498	89,201	24,653	14,360
2010: Jan	129,602	107,123	17,876	684	5,636	11,556	7,062	4,494	89,247	24,666	14,409
Feb	129,641	107,185	17,848	691	5,585	11,572	7,071	4,501	89,337	24,667	14,416
Mar	129,849	107,343	17,905	702	5,612	11,591	7,095	4,496	89,438	24,714	14,439
Apr	130,162	107,584	17,972	709	5,634	11,629	7,123	4,506	89,612	24,741	14,453
May	130,594	107,635	17,993	720	5,605	11,668	7,159	4,509	89,642	24,742	14,448
June	130,419	107,696	17,994	726	5,596	11,672	7,166	4,506	89,702	24,741	14,431
July	130,353	107,813	18,031	733	5,594	11,704	7,201	4,503	89,782	24,771	14,442
Aug	130,352	107,956	18,048	742	5,628	11,678	7,180	4,498	89,908	24,779	14,449
Sept	130,328	108,068	18,038	749	5,617	11,672	7,185	4,487	90,030	24,795	14,445
Oct	130,538	108,261	18,048	759	5,621	11,668	7,186	4,482	90,213	24,849	14,483
Nov ᵖ	130,609	108,340	18,043	764	5,619	11,660	7,184	4,476	90,297	24,849	14,464
Dec ᵖ	130,712	108,453	18,041	768	5,603	11,670	7,194	4,476	90,412	24,880	14,476

[1] Includes wholesale trade, transportation and warehousing, and utilities, not shown separately.

Note: Data in Tables B–46 and B–47 are based on reports from employing establishments and relate to full- and part-time wage and salary workers in nonagricultural establishments who received pay for any part of the pay period that includes the 12th of the month. Not comparable with labor force data (Tables B–35 through B–44), which include proprietors, self-employed persons, unpaid family workers, and private household workers; which count persons as employed when they are not at work because of industrial disputes, bad weather, etc., even if they are not paid for the time off; which are based on a sample of the

See next page for continuation of table.

[Thousands of persons; monthly data seasonally adjusted]

Year or month	Private industries—Continued						Government			
	Private service-providing industries—Continued									
	Information	Financial activities	Professional and business services	Education and health services	Leisure and hospitality	Other services	Total	Federal	State	Local
1965	1,824	2,878	4,306	3,587	3,951	1,404	10,191	2,495	1,996	5,700
1966	1,908	2,961	4,517	3,770	4,127	1,475	10,910	2,690	2,141	6,080
1967	1,955	3,087	4,720	3,986	4,269	1,558	11,525	2,852	2,302	6,371
1968	1,991	3,234	4,918	4,191	4,453	1,638	11,972	2,871	2,442	6,660
1969	2,048	3,404	5,156	4,428	4,670	1,731	12,330	2,893	2,533	6,904
1970	2,041	3,532	5,267	4,577	4,789	1,789	12,687	2,865	2,664	7,158
1971	2,009	3,651	5,328	4,675	4,914	1,827	13,012	2,828	2,747	7,437
1972	2,056	3,784	5,523	4,863	5,121	1,900	13,465	2,815	2,859	7,790
1973	2,135	3,920	5,774	5,092	5,341	1,990	13,862	2,794	2,923	8,146
1974	2,160	4,023	5,974	5,322	5,471	2,078	14,303	2,858	3,039	8,407
1975	2,061	4,047	6,034	5,497	5,544	2,144	14,820	2,882	3,179	8,758
1976	2,111	4,155	6,287	5,756	5,794	2,244	15,001	2,863	3,273	8,865
1977	2,185	4,348	6,587	6,052	6,065	2,359	15,258	2,859	3,377	9,023
1978	2,287	4,599	6,972	6,427	6,411	2,505	15,812	2,893	3,474	9,446
1979	2,375	4,843	7,312	6,767	6,631	2,637	16,068	2,894	3,541	9,633
1980	2,361	5,025	7,544	7,072	6,721	2,755	16,375	3,000	3,610	9,765
1981	2,382	5,163	7,782	7,357	6,840	2,865	16,180	2,922	3,640	9,619
1982	2,317	5,209	7,848	7,515	6,874	2,924	15,982	2,884	3,640	9,458
1983	2,253	5,334	8,039	7,766	7,078	3,021	16,011	2,915	3,662	9,434
1984	2,398	5,553	8,464	8,193	7,489	3,186	16,159	2,943	3,734	9,482
1985	2,437	5,815	8,871	8,657	7,869	3,366	16,533	3,014	3,832	9,687
1986	2,445	6,128	9,211	9,061	8,156	3,523	16,838	3,044	3,893	9,901
1987	2,507	6,385	9,608	9,515	8,446	3,699	17,156	3,089	3,967	10,100
1988	2,585	6,500	10,090	10,063	8,778	3,907	17,540	3,124	4,076	10,339
1989	2,622	6,562	10,555	10,616	9,062	4,116	17,927	3,136	4,182	10,609
1990	2,688	6,614	10,848	10,984	9,288	4,261	18,415	3,196	4,305	10,914
1991	2,677	6,558	10,714	11,506	9,256	4,249	18,545	3,110	4,355	11,081
1992	2,641	6,540	10,970	11,891	9,437	4,240	18,787	3,111	4,408	11,267
1993	2,668	6,709	11,495	12,303	9,732	4,350	18,989	3,063	4,488	11,438
1994	2,738	6,867	12,174	12,807	10,100	4,428	19,275	3,018	4,576	11,682
1995	2,843	6,827	12,844	13,289	10,501	4,572	19,432	2,949	4,635	11,849
1996	2,940	6,969	13,462	13,683	10,777	4,690	19,539	2,877	4,606	12,056
1997	3,084	7,178	14,335	14,087	11,018	4,825	19,664	2,806	4,582	12,276
1998	3,218	7,462	15,147	14,446	11,232	4,976	19,909	2,772	4,612	12,525
1999	3,419	7,648	15,957	14,798	11,543	5,087	20,307	2,769	4,709	12,829
2000	3,630	7,687	16,666	15,109	11,862	5,168	20,790	2,865	4,786	13,139
2001	3,629	7,808	16,476	15,645	12,036	5,258	21,118	2,764	4,905	13,449
2002	3,395	7,847	15,976	16,199	11,986	5,372	21,513	2,766	5,029	13,718
2003	3,188	7,977	15,987	16,588	12,173	5,401	21,583	2,761	5,002	13,820
2004	3,118	8,031	16,394	16,953	12,493	5,409	21,621	2,730	4,982	13,909
2005	3,061	8,153	16,954	17,372	12,816	5,395	21,804	2,732	5,032	14,041
2006	3,038	8,328	17,566	17,826	13,110	5,438	21,974	2,732	5,075	14,167
2007	3,032	8,301	17,942	18,322	13,427	5,494	22,218	2,734	5,122	14,362
2008	2,984	8,145	17,735	18,838	13,436	5,515	22,509	2,762	5,177	14,571
2009	2,807	7,758	16,580	19,191	13,102	5,364	22,549	2,828	5,180	14,542
2010 *p*	2,723	7,597	16,697	19,560	13,112	5,353	22,471	2,959	5,175	14,338
2009: Jan	2,888	7,945	17,091	19,069	13,209	5,429	22,588	2,803	5,197	14,588
Feb	2,873	7,894	16,920	19,085	13,183	5,410	22,569	2,792	5,188	14,589
Mar	2,861	7,852	16,774	19,095	13,137	5,384	22,560	2,797	5,183	14,580
Apr	2,837	7,805	16,636	19,099	13,103	5,373	22,681	2,919	5,184	14,578
May	2,812	7,773	16,585	19,137	13,126	5,366	22,628	2,865	5,189	14,574
June	2,797	7,742	16,453	19,165	13,105	5,367	22,565	2,810	5,177	14,578
July	2,785	7,719	16,405	19,186	13,101	5,362	22,516	2,816	5,154	14,546
Aug	2,776	7,695	16,371	19,221	13,083	5,353	22,519	2,815	5,172	14,532
Sept	2,777	7,683	16,349	19,247	13,099	5,344	22,480	2,818	5,173	14,489
Oct	2,774	7,664	16,360	19,282	13,045	5,327	22,518	2,836	5,182	14,500
Nov	2,762	7,666	16,466	19,313	13,024	5,321	22,507	2,833	5,172	14,502
Dec	2,748	7,657	16,488	19,350	12,991	5,314	22,481	2,824	5,178	14,479
2010: Jan	2,745	7,635	16,511	19,370	13,003	5,317	22,479	2,857	5,169	14,453
Feb	2,739	7,628	16,567	19,400	13,026	5,310	22,456	2,860	5,175	14,421
Mar	2,728	7,609	16,568	19,449	13,049	5,321	22,506	2,910	5,174	14,422
Apr	2,727	7,611	16,638	19,477	13,085	5,333	22,578	2,988	5,169	14,421
May	2,725	7,602	16,664	19,502	13,070	5,337	22,959	3,396	5,157	14,406
June	2,711	7,591	16,697	19,532	13,100	5,330	22,723	3,173	5,159	14,391
July	2,717	7,581	16,692	19,558	13,111	5,352	22,540	3,030	5,175	14,335
Aug	2,724	7,578	16,730	19,599	13,135	5,363	22,396	2,919	5,158	14,319
Sept	2,717	7,582	16,758	19,625	13,173	5,380	22,260	2,843	5,170	14,247
Oct	2,713	7,585	16,798	19,691	13,172	5,405	22,277	2,838	5,182	14,257
Nov *p*	2,715	7,581	16,847	19,728	13,184	5,393	22,269	2,842	5,184	14,243
Dec *p*	2,711	7,585	16,854	19,772	13,231	5,379	22,259	2,852	5,184	14,223

Note (cont'd): working-age population; and which count persons only once—as employed, unemployed, or not in the labor force. In the data shown here, persons who work at more than one job are counted each time they appear on a payroll.

Establishment data for employment, hours, and earnings are classified based on the 2007 North American Industry Classification System (NAICS). For further description and details see *Employment and Earnings.*

Source: Department of Labor (Bureau of Labor Statistics).

TABLE B–47. Hours and earnings in private nonagricultural industries, 1964–2010 [1]

[Monthly data seasonally adjusted]

Year or month	Average weekly hours			Average hourly earnings			Average weekly earnings, total private			
	Total private	Manufacturing		Total private		Manufacturing (current dollars)	Level		Percent change from year earlier	
		Total	Overtime	Current dollars	1982–84 dollars[2]		Current dollars	1982–84 dollars[2]	Current dollars	1982–84 dollars[2]
1964	38.5	40.8	3.1	$2.53	$8.11	$2.41	$97.41	$312.21	....	....
1965	38.6	41.2	3.6	2.63	8.30	2.49	101.52	320.25	4.2	2.6
1966	38.5	41.4	3.9	2.73	8.37	2.60	105.11	322.42	3.5	.7
1967	37.9	40.6	3.3	2.85	8.48	2.71	108.02	321.49	2.8	-.3
1968	37.7	40.7	3.5	3.02	8.63	2.89	113.85	325.29	5.4	1.2
1969	37.5	40.6	3.6	3.22	8.73	3.07	120.75	327.24	6.1	.6
1970	37.0	39.8	2.9	3.40	8.72	3.23	125.80	322.56	4.2	-1.4
1971	36.8	39.9	2.9	3.63	8.92	3.45	133.58	327.32	6.2	1.5
1972	36.9	40.6	3.4	3.90	9.26	3.70	143.91	341.83	7.7	4.4
1973	36.9	40.7	3.8	4.14	9.26	3.97	152.77	341.77	6.2	.0
1974	36.4	40.0	3.2	4.43	8.93	4.31	161.25	325.10	5.6	-4.9
1975	36.0	39.5	2.6	4.73	8.74	4.71	170.28	314.75	5.6	-3.2
1976	36.1	40.1	3.1	5.06	8.85	5.09	182.67	319.35	7.3	1.5
1977	35.9	40.3	3.4	5.44	8.93	5.55	195.30	320.69	6.9	.4
1978	35.8	40.4	3.6	5.88	8.96	6.05	210.50	320.88	7.8	.1
1979	35.6	40.2	3.3	6.34	8.67	6.57	225.70	308.76	7.2	-3.8
1980	35.2	39.7	2.8	6.85	8.26	7.15	241.12	290.86	6.8	-5.8
1981	35.2	39.8	2.8	7.44	8.14	7.86	261.89	286.53	8.6	-1.5
1982	34.7	38.9	2.3	7.87	8.12	8.36	273.09	281.83	4.3	-1.6
1983	34.9	40.1	2.9	8.20	8.22	8.70	286.18	286.75	4.8	1.7
1984	35.1	40.7	3.4	8.49	8.22	9.05	298.00	288.48	4.1	.6
1985	34.9	40.5	3.3	8.74	8.18	9.40	305.03	285.34	2.4	-1.1
1986	34.7	40.7	3.4	8.93	8.22	9.59	309.87	285.33	1.6	.0
1987	34.7	40.9	3.7	9.14	8.12	9.77	317.16	281.92	2.4	-1.2
1988	34.6	41.0	3.8	9.44	8.07	10.05	326.62	279.16	3.0	-1.0
1989	34.5	40.9	3.8	9.80	7.99	10.35	338.10	275.77	3.5	-1.2
1990	34.3	40.5	3.9	10.20	7.91	10.78	349.75	271.12	3.4	-1.7
1991	34.1	40.4	3.8	10.52	7.83	11.13	358.51	266.95	2.5	-1.5
1992	34.2	40.7	4.0	10.77	7.79	11.40	368.25	266.46	2.7	-.2
1993	34.3	41.1	4.4	11.05	7.78	11.70	378.91	266.65	2.9	.1
1994	34.5	41.7	5.0	11.34	7.79	12.04	391.22	268.70	3.2	.8
1995	34.3	41.3	4.7	11.65	7.78	12.34	400.07	267.07	2.3	-.6
1996	34.3	41.3	4.8	12.04	7.81	12.75	413.28	268.19	3.3	.4
1997	34.5	41.7	5.1	12.51	7.94	13.14	431.86	274.02	4.5	2.2
1998	34.5	41.4	4.9	13.01	8.15	13.45	448.56	280.88	3.9	2.5
1999	34.3	41.4	4.9	13.49	8.27	13.85	463.15	283.79	3.3	1.0
2000	34.3	41.3	4.7	14.02	8.30	14.32	481.01	284.79	3.9	.4
2001	34.0	40.3	4.0	14.54	8.38	14.76	493.79	284.61	2.7	-.1
2002	33.9	40.5	4.2	14.97	8.51	15.29	506.75	288.09	2.6	1.2
2003	33.7	40.4	4.2	15.37	8.55	15.74	518.06	288.13	2.2	.0
2004	33.7	40.8	4.6	15.69	8.50	16.14	529.09	286.77	2.1	-.5
2005	33.8	40.7	4.6	16.13	8.45	16.56	544.33	284.99	2.9	-.6
2006	33.9	41.1	4.4	16.76	8.50	16.81	567.87	288.11	4.3	1.1
2007	33.9	41.2	4.2	17.43	8.60	17.26	590.04	290.99	3.9	1.0
2008	33.6	40.8	3.7	18.08	8.57	17.75	607.95	288.06	3.0	-1.0
2009	33.1	39.8	2.9	18.62	8.88	18.23	617.11	294.38	1.5	2.2
2010 P	33.4	41.1	3.8	19.04	8.90	18.57	636.15	297.31	3.1	1.0
2009: Jan	33.3	39.8	2.8	18.43	8.92	18.01	613.72	297.11	2.5	3.3
Feb	33.2	39.5	2.7	18.47	8.90	18.09	613.20	295.41	2.1	2.6
Mar	33.1	39.4	2.6	18.52	8.93	18.14	613.01	295.66	1.4	2.4
Apr	33.1	39.6	2.8	18.53	8.93	18.15	613.34	295.56	1.2	2.4
May	33.1	39.5	2.8	18.55	8.93	18.15	614.01	295.53	1.2	2.9
June	33.0	39.5	2.8	18.57	8.86	18.17	612.81	292.37	.7	2.5
July	33.1	39.9	3.0	18.62	8.87	18.26	616.32	293.67	1.2	3.9
Aug	33.1	40.0	3.0	18.69	8.86	18.31	618.64	293.28	.9	2.9
Sept	33.1	39.9	3.0	18.71	8.85	18.39	619.30	293.02	1.5	3.3
Oct	33.0	40.0	3.2	18.78	8.86	18.41	619.74	292.47	1.2	1.5
Nov	33.2	40.5	3.4	18.80	8.85	18.38	624.16	293.84	2.0	-.3
Dec	33.2	40.5	3.4	18.85	8.85	18.38	625.82	293.92	2.2	-1.2
2010: Jan	33.3	40.9	3.6	18.90	8.85	18.42	629.37	294.60	2.6	-.8
Feb	33.2	40.5	3.5	18.92	8.86	18.47	628.14	294.01	2.4	-.5
Mar	33.3	41.0	3.7	18.90	8.84	18.47	629.37	294.41	2.7	-.4
Apr	33.4	41.2	3.8	18.95	8.88	18.48	632.93	296.49	3.2	.3
May	33.5	41.5	3.9	19.00	8.93	18.56	636.50	298.99	3.7	1.2
June	33.4	41.0	3.9	19.02	8.95	18.54	635.27	298.97	3.7	2.3
July	33.4	41.1	3.8	19.04	8.93	18.57	635.94	298.18	3.2	1.5
Aug	33.5	41.1	3.8	19.09	8.92	18.59	639.52	298.81	3.4	1.9
Sept	33.5	41.2	3.9	19.11	8.92	18.64	640.19	298.67	3.4	1.9
Oct	33.6	41.2	3.9	19.18	8.92	18.66	644.45	299.74	4.0	2.5
Nov P	33.5	41.2	4.0	19.19	8.92	18.66	642.87	298.87	3.0	1.7
Dec P	33.6	41.2	4.0	19.21	8.87	18.66	645.46	298.19	3.1	1.5

[1] For production or nonsupervisory workers; total includes private industry groups shown in Table B–46.
[2] Current dollars divided by the consumer price index for urban wage earners and clerical workers on a 1982–84=100 base.

Note: See Note, Table B–46.

Source: Department of Labor (Bureau of Labor Statistics).

TABLE B–48. Employment cost index, private industry, 1997–2010

Year and month	Total private			Goods-producing			Service-providing [1]			Manufacturing		
	Total compensation	Wages and salaries	Benefits [2]	Total compensation	Wages and salaries	Benefits [2]	Total compensation	Wages and salaries	Benefits [2]	Total compensation	Wages and salaries	Benefits [2]
	Indexes on SIC basis, December 2005=100; not seasonally adjusted											
December:												
1997	74.9	77.6	68.5	74.5	78.3	67.3	75.1	77.4	69.2	74.6	78.6	67.4
1998	77.5	80.6	70.2	76.5	81.1	68.1	78.0	80.5	71.4	76.6	81.3	67.9
1999	80.2	83.5	72.6	79.1	83.8	70.5	80.6	83.4	73.8	79.2	84.1	70.3
2000	83.6	86.7	76.7	82.6	87.1	74.3	84.2	86.6	78.1	82.3	87.1	73.6
2001	87.1	90.0	80.6	85.7	90.2	77.3	87.8	89.9	82.5	85.3	90.2	76.3
	Indexes on NAICS basis, December 2005=100; not seasonally adjusted											
2001 [3]	87.3	89.9	81.3	86.0	90.0	78.5	87.8	89.8	82.4	85.5	90.2	77.2
2002	90.0	92.2	84.7	89.0	92.6	82.3	90.4	92.1	85.8	88.7	92.8	81.3
2003	93.6	95.1	90.2	92.6	94.9	88.2	94.0	95.2	91.0	92.4	95.1	87.3
2004	97.2	97.6	96.2	96.9	97.2	96.3	97.3	97.7	96.1	96.9	97.4	96.0
2005	100.0	100.0	100.0	100.0	100.0	100.0	100.0	100.0	100.0	100.0	100.0	100.0
2006	103.2	103.2	103.1	102.5	102.9	101.7	103.4	103.3	103.7	101.8	102.3	100.8
2007	106.3	106.6	105.6	105.0	106.0	103.2	106.7	106.8	106.6	103.8	104.9	101.7
2008	108.9	109.4	107.7	107.5	109.0	104.7	109.4	109.6	108.9	105.9	107.7	102.5
2009	110.2	110.8	108.7	108.6	110.0	105.8	110.8	111.1	109.9	107.0	108.9	103.6
2010	112.5	112.8	111.9	111.1	111.6	110.1	113.0	113.1	112.6	110.0	110.7	108.8
2010: Mar	111.1	111.4	110.4	109.7	110.5	108.4	111.6	111.7	111.3	108.4	109.4	106.6
June	111.7	111.9	111.0	110.3	110.9	109.0	112.1	112.3	111.9	109.1	110.0	107.4
Sept	112.2	112.4	111.7	111.0	111.5	110.0	112.6	112.7	112.3	109.9	110.6	108.7
Dec	112.5	112.8	111.9	111.1	111.6	110.1	113.0	113.1	112.6	110.0	110.7	100.0
	Indexes on NAICS basis, December 2005=100; seasonally adjusted											
2009: Mar	109.3	109.8	108.1	107.9	109.2	105.4	109.7	110.0	109.2	106.4	108.0	103.4
June	109.6	110.1	108.3	108.1	109.4	105.6	110.0	110.3	109.4	106.7	108.3	103.6
Sept	110.0	110.5	108.6	108.3	109.8	105.6	110.5	110.7	109.8	106.8	108.6	103.4
Dec	110.4	111.0	108.9	108.7	110.2	106.0	110.9	111.2	110.1	107.2	109.1	103.7
2010: Mar	111.1	111.3	110.4	109.7	110.5	108.4	111.5	111.6	111.2	108.3	109.3	106.6
June	111.6	111.9	111.0	110.2	110.8	108.9	112.1	112.2	111.8	109.0	109.9	107.4
Sept	112.1	112.4	111.6	110.9	111.5	109.9	112.5	112.6	112.3	109.9	110.5	108.7
Dec	112.6	112.9	112.1	111.2	111.8	110.2	113.1	113.2	112.8	110.2	111.0	108.9
	Percent change from 12 months earlier, not seasonally adjusted											
December:												
SIC:												
1997	3.5	3.9	2.2	2.5	3.0	1.4	3.9	4.3	2.8	2.3	3.0	1.4
1998	3.5	3.9	2.5	2.7	3.6	1.2	3.9	4.0	3.2	2.7	3.4	.7
1999	3.5	3.6	3.4	3.4	3.3	3.5	3.3	3.6	3.4	3.4	3.4	3.5
2000	4.2	3.8	5.6	4.4	3.9	5.4	4.5	3.8	5.8	3.9	3.6	4.7
2001	4.2	3.8	5.1	3.8	3.6	4.0	4.3	3.8	5.6	3.6	3.6	3.7
NAICS:												
2001 [3]	4.1	3.8	5.2	3.6	3.6	3.7	4.4	3.8	5.6	3.4	3.6	3.5
2002	3.1	2.6	4.2	3.5	2.9	4.8	3.0	2.6	4.1	3.7	2.9	5.3
2003	4.0	3.1	6.5	4.0	2.5	7.2	4.0	3.4	6.1	4.2	2.5	7.4
2004	3.8	2.6	6.7	4.6	2.4	9.2	3.5	2.6	5.6	4.9	2.4	10.0
2005	2.9	2.5	4.0	3.2	2.9	3.8	2.8	2.4	4.1	3.2	2.7	4.2
2006	3.2	3.2	3.1	2.5	2.9	1.7	3.4	3.3	3.7	1.8	2.3	.8
2007	3.0	3.3	2.4	2.4	3.0	1.5	3.2	3.4	2.8	2.0	2.5	.9
2008	2.4	2.6	2.0	2.4	2.8	1.5	2.5	2.6	2.2	2.0	2.7	.8
2009	1.2	1.3	.9	1.0	.9	1.1	1.3	1.4	.9	1.0	1.1	1.1
2010	2.1	1.8	2.9	2.3	1.5	4.1	2.0	1.8	2.5	2.8	1.7	5.0
2010: Mar	1.6	1.5	2.0	1.7	1.2	2.8	1.6	1.5	1.8	1.8	1.2	3.0
June	1.9	1.6	2.4	1.9	1.3	3.1	1.8	1.8	2.2	2.2	1.5	3.7
Sept	2.0	1.6	2.8	2.4	1.5	4.1	1.9	1.7	2.2	2.9	1.8	5.1
Dec	2.1	1.8	2.9	2.3	1.5	4.1	2.0	1.8	2.5	2.8	1.7	5.0
	Percent change from 3 months earlier, seasonally adjusted											
2009: Mar	0.2	0.2	0.2	0.3	0.1	0.6	0.2	0.3	0.1	0.4	0.1	0.8
June	.3	.3	.2	.2	.2	.2	.3	.3	.2	.3	.3	.2
Sept	.4	.4	.3	.2	.4	.0	.5	.4	.4	.1	.3	−.2
Dec	.4	.5	.3	.4	.4	.4	.4	.5	.3	.4	.5	.3
2010: Mar	.6	.3	1.4	.9	.3	2.3	.5	.4	1.0	1.0	.2	2.8
June	.5	.5	.5	.5	.3	.5	.5	.5	.5	.6	.5	.8
Sept	.4	.4	.5	.6	.6	.9	.4	.4	.4	.8	.5	1.2
Dec	.4	.4	.4	.3	.3	.3	.5	.5	.4	.3	.5	.2

[1] On Standard Industrial Classification (SIC) basis, data are for service-producing industries.
[2] Employer costs for employee benefits.
[3] Data on North American Industry Classification System (NAICS) basis available beginning with 2001; not strictly comparable with earlier data shown on SIC basis.

Note: Changes effective with the release of March 2006 data (in April 2006) include changing industry classification to NAICS from SIC and rebasing data to December 2005=100. Historical SIC data are available through December 2005.
Data exclude farm and household workers.

Source: Department of Labor (Bureau of Labor Statistics).

Population, Employment, Wages, and Productivity | 247

TABLE B–49. Productivity and related data, business and nonfarm business sectors, 1960–2010

[Index numbers, 2005=100; quarterly data seasonally adjusted]

Year or quarter	Output per hour of all persons		Output [1]		Hours of all persons [2]		Compensation per hour [3]		Real compensation per hour [4]		Unit labor costs		Implicit price deflator [5]	
	Business sector	Nonfarm business sector	Business sector	Nonfarm business sector	Business sector	Nonfarm business sector	Business sector	Nonfarm business sector	Business sector	Nonfarm business sector	Business sector	Nonfarm business sector	Business sector	Nonfarm business sector
1960	35.8	38.3	19.9	19.7	55.5	51.4	8.5	8.9	51.2	53.7	23.8	23.3	21.8	21.3
1961	37.1	39.5	20.3	20.1	54.7	50.9	8.8	9.2	52.6	54.9	23.8	23.3	21.9	21.4
1962	38.8	41.3	21.6	21.5	55.7	52.0	9.2	9.6	54.4	56.5	23.8	23.2	22.2	21.6
1963	40.3	42.7	22.6	22.5	56.1	52.6	9.6	9.9	55.6	57.7	23.7	23.2	22.3	21.8
1964	41.6	44.0	24.0	24.0	57.7	54.5	9.9	10.2	57.0	58.7	23.8	23.3	22.5	22.1
1965	43.1	45.3	25.7	25.7	59.6	56.6	10.3	10.6	58.2	59.7	23.9	23.3	22.9	22.4
1966	44.9	46.9	27.4	27.5	61.2	58.6	11.0	11.2	60.3	61.5	24.5	23.8	23.5	22.9
1967	45.8	47.8	28.0	28.0	61.0	58.6	11.6	11.8	61.9	63.1	25.3	24.8	24.1	23.6
1968	47.4	49.4	29.4	29.4	61.9	59.6	12.5	12.8	64.2	65.3	26.5	25.8	25.1	24.5
1969	47.7	49.5	30.3	30.3	63.5	61.3	13.4	13.6	65.1	66.2	28.2	27.6	26.2	25.6
1970	48.6	50.2	30.3	30.3	62.2	60.4	14.4	14.6	66.3	67.1	29.7	29.1	27.3	26.8
1971	50.6	52.2	31.4	31.5	62.1	60.2	15.4	15.5	67.5	68.3	30.3	29.8	28.5	27.9
1972	52.2	54.0	33.4	33.6	64.0	62.2	16.3	16.6	69.6	70.5	31.3	30.7	29.5	28.8
1973	53.8	55.7	35.8	36.0	66.5	64.7	17.7	17.9	71.0	71.8	32.9	32.2	31.1	29.8
1974	52.9	54.8	35.2	35.5	66.6	64.8	19.4	19.7	70.1	71.0	36.7	35.9	34.1	32.9
1975	54.8	56.3	34.9	34.9	63.7	62.0	21.4	21.6	70.8	71.6	39.0	38.4	37.4	36.4
1976	56.6	58.1	37.2	37.4	65.8	64.2	23.2	23.5	72.7	73.4	41.1	40.3	39.4	38.4
1977	57.5	59.1	39.3	39.4	68.3	66.8	25.1	25.4	73.7	74.5	43.6	42.9	41.7	40.9
1978	58.1	59.8	41.8	42.0	71.8	70.3	27.3	27.6	74.9	75.8	46.9	46.1	44.7	43.6
1979	58.1	59.6	43.2	43.4	74.3	72.8	29.9	30.2	74.9	75.7	51.4	50.7	48.5	47.3
1980	58.0	59.4	42.7	42.9	73.6	72.2	33.1	33.4	74.6	75.4	57.0	56.2	52.8	51.9
1981	59.2	60.3	43.9	43.8	74.1	72.7	36.2	36.7	74.5	75.5	61.2	60.8	57.7	56.8
1982	58.7	59.6	42.5	42.4	72.5	71.1	38.8	39.3	75.4	76.3	66.1	65.8	61.0	60.4
1983	60.8	62.2	44.8	45.1	73.7	72.5	40.4	40.9	75.3	76.2	66.5	65.7	63.1	62.3
1984	62.4	63.5	48.7	48.8	78.0	76.9	42.1	42.6	75.4	76.2	67.5	67.0	64.9	64.1
1985	63.8	64.5	51.0	50.9	79.9	78.9	44.1	44.5	76.3	76.9	69.1	68.9	66.4	65.9
1986	65.7	66.5	52.9	52.9	80.5	79.5	46.4	46.8	78.8	79.5	70.6	70.4	67.5	67.0
1987	65.9	66.7	54.6	54.7	82.9	81.9	48.0	48.5	79.0	79.7	72.9	72.7	69.2	68.6
1988	66.9	67.8	57.0	57.2	85.2	84.3	50.5	50.9	80.1	80.8	75.6	75.1	71.3	70.7
1989	67.6	68.3	59.1	59.2	87.4	86.6	51.9	52.2	78.9	79.4	76.8	76.4	74.0	73.3
1990	69.0	69.6	60.0	60.0	86.9	86.3	55.2	55.5	80.0	80.3	80.0	79.7	76.6	76.0
1991	70.1	70.7	59.5	59.5	84.9	84.2	58.0	58.4	81.1	81.6	82.8	82.6	79.1	78.6
1992	73.0	73.5	61.8	61.7	84.7	84.0	61.1	61.5	83.3	83.9	83.7	83.7	80.6	80.2
1993	73.4	73.9	63.8	63.9	86.9	86.4	62.5	62.7	83.1	83.5	85.2	84.9	82.2	81.8
1994	74.0	74.7	66.9	66.9	90.4	89.6	63.4	63.9	82.6	83.2	85.7	85.6	83.6	83.3
1995	74.1	75.0	68.8	69.0	92.9	92.0	64.7	65.2	82.3	82.9	87.4	87.0	85.1	84.8
1996	76.2	76.9	71.9	72.0	94.4	93.7	66.9	67.3	82.9	83.4	87.8	87.6	86.5	85.9
1997	77.6	78.1	75.7	75.7	97.5	96.9	69.1	69.4	83.8	84.2	89.1	88.9	87.7	87.5
1998	79.9	80.4	79.4	79.6	99.4	99.0	73.3	73.6	87.7	88.0	91.8	91.6	88.4	88.2
1999	82.7	83.0	83.9	84.0	101.4	101.2	76.6	76.8	89.8	89.9	92.7	92.4	89.1	89.0
2000	85.6	85.9	87.7	87.7	102.4	102.2	82.3	82.5	93.3	93.5	96.1	96.1	90.8	90.8
2001	88.1	88.4	88.4	88.5	100.3	100.2	86.1	86.2	95.0	95.0	97.7	97.5	92.4	92.3
2002	92.1	92.4	90.1	90.2	97.8	97.7	88.8	88.9	96.3	96.5	96.4	96.2	93.1	93.1
2003	95.6	95.7	92.9	92.9	97.2	97.1	93.0	93.1	98.7	98.8	97.3	97.2	94.4	94.3
2004	98.4	98.4	96.7	96.8	98.3	98.3	96.2	96.2	99.5	99.4	97.8	97.8	96.9	96.6
2005	100.0	100.0	100.0	100.0	100.0	100.0	100.0	100.0	100.0	100.0	100.0	100.0	100.0	100.0
2006	100.9	100.9	103.1	103.1	102.1	102.2	103.8	103.8	100.5	100.5	102.8	102.8	102.9	103.0
2007	102.5	102.5	105.2	105.3	102.6	102.7	108.1	107.9	101.8	101.6	105.4	105.3	105.7	105.5
2008	103.6	103.6	104.2	104.2	100.5	100.6	111.5	111.5	101.1	101.1	107.6	107.6	107.6	107.4
2009	107.3	107.2	100.4	100.3	93.6	93.5	113.6	113.5	103.4	103.3	105.9	105.9	108.1	108.3
2007: I	101.1	101.3	103.9	104.0	102.7	102.7	106.8	106.9	102.1	102.1	105.6	105.5	104.8	104.7
II	102.0	101.9	104.9	105.1	102.9	103.1	107.4	107.2	101.5	101.2	105.3	105.1	105.7	105.5
III	103.0	103.0	105.5	105.8	102.4	102.7	108.3	108.0	101.7	101.4	105.1	104.9	106.1	105.8
IV	103.8	103.9	106.3	106.4	102.4	102.4	109.8	109.7	101.9	101.8	105.7	105.6	106.1	105.8
2008: I	103.6	103.5	105.7	105.7	102.1	102.1	111.0	111.0	101.8	101.8	107.1	107.2	106.3	106.0
II	103.9	103.8	105.6	105.6	101.6	101.7	111.0	110.9	100.6	100.5	106.8	106.8	107.3	107.1
III	103.6	103.5	103.9	104.0	100.3	100.5	112.0	111.9	99.9	99.8	108.1	108.1	108.7	108.5
IV	103.5	103.5	101.4	101.4	98.0	98.0	112.2	112.2	102.5	102.5	108.4	108.4	108.0	108.0
2009: I	104.4	104.3	99.8	99.7	95.6	95.6	111.2	111.1	102.1	102.1	106.5	106.5	108.2	108.4
II	106.5	106.5	99.8	99.7	93.7	93.6	113.6	113.6	103.9	103.9	106.6	106.7	108.0	108.2
III	108.4	108.3	100.1	100.0	92.4	92.4	114.6	114.5	103.9	103.8	105.8	105.8	108.2	108.5
IV	110.0	109.9	101.7	101.7	92.5	92.5	115.1	115.0	103.6	103.5	104.6	104.7	108.1	108.2
2010: I	111.0	110.9	103.0	102.9	92.8	92.8	114.7	114.7	102.9	102.9	103.4	103.4	108.4	108.5
II	110.4	110.4	103.4	103.3	93.7	93.6	115.5	115.5	103.8	103.8	104.6	104.7	109.1	109.2
III	111.1	111.0	104.4	104.3	93.9	93.9	116.2	116.2	104.1	104.0	104.6	104.6	109.8	109.7

[1] Output refers to real gross domestic product in the sector.

[2] Hours at work of all persons engaged in sector, including hours of proprietors and unpaid family workers. Estimates based primarily on establishment data.

[3] Wages and salaries of employees plus employers' contributions for social insurance and private benefit plans. Also includes an estimate of wages, salaries, and supplemental payments for the self-employed.

[4] Hourly compensation divided by the consumer price index for all urban consumers for recent quarters. The trend from 1978–2009 is based on the consumer price index research series (CPI-U-RS).

[5] Current dollar output divided by the output index.

Source: Department of Labor (Bureau of Labor Statistics).

TABLE B–50. Changes in productivity and related data, business and nonfarm business sectors, 1960–2010

[Percent change from preceding period; quarterly data at seasonally adjusted annual rates]

Year or quarter	Output per hour of all persons Business sector	Output per hour of all persons Nonfarm business sector	Output [1] Business sector	Output [1] Nonfarm business sector	Hours of all persons [2] Business sector	Hours of all persons [2] Nonfarm business sector	Compensation per hour [3] Business sector	Compensation per hour [3] Nonfarm business sector	Real compensation per hour [4] Business sector	Real compensation per hour [4] Nonfarm business sector	Unit labor costs Business sector	Unit labor costs Nonfarm business sector	Implicit price deflator [5] Business sector	Implicit price deflator [5] Nonfarm business sector
1960	1.7	1.2	1.9	1.8	0.2	0.6	4.2	4.3	2.4	2.5	2.4	3.1	1.1	1.1
1961	3.5	3.1	2.0	2.0	-1.5	-1.1	3.9	3.3	2.8	2.3	.4	.2	.8	.8
1962	4.6	4.5	6.5	6.8	1.8	2.2	4.4	4.0	3.4	3.0	-.2	-.5	1.0	1.0
1963	3.9	3.5	4.6	4.7	.7	1.1	3.6	3.4	2.2	2.1	-.3	-.1	.5	.7
1964	3.4	2.9	6.3	6.7	2.9	3.7	3.8	3.1	2.4	1.8	.4	.2	1.1	1.3
1965	3.5	3.1	7.1	7.1	3.4	3.9	3.7	3.3	2.1	1.7	.2	.2	1.6	1.3
1966	4.1	3.6	6.8	7.1	2.6	3.5	6.7	5.9	3.8	3.0	2.6	2.3	2.5	2.3
1967	2.2	1.7	1.9	1.7	-.3	.0	5.7	5.8	2.5	2.7	3.4	4.0	2.7	3.2
1968	3.4	3.4	5.0	5.2	1.5	1.8	8.1	7.8	3.7	3.5	4.5	4.3	4.0	3.9
1969	.5	.2	3.1	3.0	2.5	2.9	7.0	6.8	1.4	1.3	6.5	6.6	4.6	4.5
1970	2.0	1.5	.0	-.1	-2.0	-1.6	7.7	7.2	1.9	1.4	5.6	5.6	4.3	4.4
1971	4.1	4.0	3.8	3.8	-.3	-.2	6.3	6.4	1.8	1.9	2.1	2.3	4.2	4.3
1972	3.2	3.3	6.4	6.6	3.1	3.2	6.3	6.5	3.0	3.2	3.0	3.1	3.6	3.2
1973	3.1	3.1	7.0	7.3	3.8	4.1	8.4	8.1	2.1	1.8	5.2	4.9	5.2	3.5
1974	-1.7	-1.6	-1.5	-1.5	.2	.1	9.6	9.8	-1.3	-1.2	11.5	11.6	9.7	10.3
1975	3.5	2.8	-.9	-1.6	-4.3	-4.3	10.2	10.1	1.0	.9	6.5	7.1	9.7	10.7
1976	3.2	3.3	6.6	7.0	3.3	3.6	8.6	8.4	2.7	2.5	5.3	4.9	5.3	5.5
1977	1.7	1.6	5.6	5.6	3.8	3.9	8.0	8.1	1.4	1.5	6.2	6.5	6.0	6.3
1978	1.1	1.3	6.3	6.6	5.1	5.2	8.7	8.8	1.5	1.7	7.5	7.4	7.1	6.7
1979	-.1	-.4	3.3	3.2	3.4	3.6	9.6	9.4	.0	-.1	9.6	9.9	8.5	8.5
1980	-.2	-.3	-1.1	-1.1	-.9	-.8	10.7	10.7	-.4	-.4	10.9	11.0	9.0	9.6
1981	2.1	1.4	2.8	2.1	.7	.7	9.5	9.7	.0	.1	7.3	8.1	9.2	9.6
1982	-.8	-1.1	-3.0	-3.2	-2.3	-2.2	7.2	7.1	1.1	1.0	8.1	8.3	5.7	6.2
1983	3.6	4.4	5.4	6.4	1.8	1.9	4.1	4.2	-.1	-.1	.5	-.7	3.4	3.2
1984	2.7	2.0	8.7	8.2	5.8	6.1	4.2	4.1	.1	.0	1.5	2.0	2.9	2.9
1985	2.3	1.6	4.6	4.3	2.3	2.6	4.7	4.4	1.2	1.0	2.4	2.8	2.4	2.9
1986	2.9	3.1	3.7	3.9	.8	.8	5.1	5.2	3.3	3.4	2.2	2.1	1.6	1.7
1987	.3	.3	3.3	3.3	3.0	3.0	3.6	3.6	.2	.2	3.3	3.3	2.4	2.4
1988	1.5	1.6	4.3	4.6	2.7	2.9	5.2	5.0	1.5	1.3	3.7	3.3	3.2	3.0
1989	1.0	.8	3.7	3.5	2.6	2.7	2.7	2.6	-1.6	-1.7	1.6	1.8	3.7	3.6
1990	2.1	1.8	1.5	1.4	-.6	-.4	6.4	6.2	1.4	1.1	4.2	4.3	3.6	3.7
1991	1.5	1.5	-.9	-.9	-2.4	-2.4	5.1	5.3	1.5	1.6	3.5	3.7	3.3	3.5
1992	4.2	4.0	3.9	3.8	-.2	-.2	5.3	5.4	2.7	2.8	1.1	1.3	1.9	2.0
1993	.5	.6	3.2	3.5	2.7	2.9	2.2	2.0	-.2	-.4	1.7	1.4	2.0	2.0
1994	.9	1.0	4.9	4.7	4.0	3.6	1.5	1.8	-.6	-.3	.6	.8	1.7	1.8
1995	.0	.4	2.8	3.2	2.8	2.8	2.1	2.1	-.3	-.3	2.0	1.7	1.8	1.8
1996	2.9	2.6	4.6	4.4	1.6	1.8	3.4	3.3	.7	.6	.5	.7	1.6	1.4
1997	1.8	1.5	5.2	5.1	3.4	3.5	3.2	3.1	1.1	.9	1.5	1.6	1.6	1.9
1998	3.0	2.9	5.0	5.1	2.0	2.1	6.1	6.0	4.6	4.5	3.0	3.0	.7	.8
1999	3.5	3.3	5.6	5.6	2.0	2.2	4.5	4.3	2.4	2.2	.9	.9	.8	1.0
2000	3.5	3.4	4.5	4.4	1.0	1.0	7.4	7.4	3.9	4.0	3.7	3.9	1.8	1.9
2001	3.0	2.9	.8	.9	-2.1	-2.0	4.7	4.5	1.8	1.6	1.7	1.5	1.8	1.7
2002	4.5	4.6	2.0	1.9	-2.4	-2.5	3.1	3.2	1.5	1.5	-1.3	-1.3	.8	.9
2003	3.8	3.6	3.1	3.0	-.7	-.6	4.8	4.7	2.5	2.4	.9	1.1	1.4	1.3
2004	2.9	2.8	4.2	4.1	1.2	1.3	3.5	3.3	.7	.6	.5	.5	2.6	2.4
2005	1.7	1.6	3.4	3.4	1.7	1.7	3.9	3.9	.5	.6	2.2	2.3	3.3	3.5
2006	.9	.9	3.1	3.1	2.1	2.2	3.8	3.8	.5	.5	2.8	2.8	2.9	3.0
2007	1.5	1.6	2.0	2.1	.5	.5	4.1	4.0	1.2	1.1	2.5	2.4	2.6	2.4
2008	1.1	1.0	-.9	-1.1	-2.0	-2.1	3.2	3.3	-.6	-.5	2.1	2.2	1.8	1.8
2009	3.5	3.5	-3.7	-3.8	-6.9	-7.0	1.8	1.9	2.2	2.2	-1.6	-1.6	.5	.8
2007: I	.0	.2	.2	.3	.2	.0	3.8	3.8	-.2	-.2	3.8	3.5	4.2	3.8
II	3.4	2.6	4.0	4.2	.6	1.5	2.4	1.2	-2.2	-3.4	-.9	-1.4	3.3	3.1
III	4.1	4.1	2.2	2.5	-1.8	-1.6	3.4	3.1	.9	.6	-.8	-1.0	1.6	1.3
IV	3.1	3.6	2.9	2.5	-.2	-1.0	5.5	6.4	.6	1.5	2.3	2.7	-.1	-.3
2008: I	-.9	-1.4	-2.0	-2.5	-1.1	-1.2	4.5	4.7	-.3	.0	5.4	6.2	.9	.8
II	1.2	1.2	-.6	-.3	-1.8	-1.5	.1	-.2	-4.8	-5.1	-1.1	-1.4	4.0	4.2
III	-1.1	-1.3	-6.1	-6.2	-5.0	-4.9	3.6	3.7	-2.6	-2.6	4.8	5.0	5.1	5.4
IV	-.3	-.1	-9.3	-9.5	-9.0	-9.5	.8	1.1	11.0	11.3	1.1	1.2	-2.6	-1.9
2009: I	3.5	3.4	-6.2	-6.4	-9.4	-9.5	-3.6	-3.7	-1.5	-1.6	-6.9	-6.9	.8	1.4
II	8.3	8.4	-.3	-.2	-7.9	-7.9	9.0	9.1	7.1	7.2	.6	.6	-.8	-.8
III	7.2	7.0	1.6	1.4	-5.3	-5.2	3.8	3.4	.0	-.3	-3.2	-3.3	.9	1.1
IV	6.1	6.0	6.5	6.7	.3	.7	1.5	1.5	-1.2	-1.1	-4.4	-4.2	-.5	-1.1
2010: I	3.5	3.9	5.0	5.0	1.4	1.1	-1.1	-.9	-2.6	-2.4	-4.5	-4.6	1.2	1.2
II	-1.8	-1.8	1.8	1.6	3.7	3.5	2.7	2.9	3.5	3.7	4.6	4.9	2.5	2.6
III	2.5	2.3	3.7	3.7	1.2	1.4	2.5	2.2	1.0	.8	.0	-.1	2.5	2.1

[1] Output refers to real gross domestic product in the sector.
[2] Hours at work of all persons engaged in the sector. See footnote 2, Table B–49.
[3] Wages and salaries of employees plus employers' contributions for social insurance and private benefit plans. Also includes an estimate of wages, salaries, and supplemental payments for the self-employed.
[4] Hourly compensation divided by a consumer price index. See footnote 4, Table B–49.
[5] Current dollar output divided by the output index.

Note: Percent changes are based on original data and may differ slightly from percent changes based on indexes in Table B–49.

Source: Department of Labor (Bureau of Labor Statistics).

Table B–51. Industrial production indexes, major industry divisions, 1962–2010

[2007=100; monthly data seasonally adjusted]

| Year or month | Total industrial production [1] | Manufacturing | | | | Mining | Utilities |
		Total [1]	Durable	Nondurable	Other (non-NAICS) [1]		
1962	25.2	22.6	....	....	....	....	....
1963	26.7	23.9	....	....	....	....	....
1964	28.5	25.6	....	....	....	....	....
1965	31.4	28.3	....	....	....	....	....
1966	34.2	30.9	....	....	....	....	....
1967	34.9	31.5	....	....	....	....	....
1968	36.8	33.3	....	....	....	....	....
1969	38.5	34.8	....	....	....	....	....
1970	37.3	33.2	....	....	....	....	....
1971	37.8	33.7	....	....	....	....	....
1972	41.4	37.2	25.3	57.3	71.9	106.4	46.4
1973	44.8	40.6	28.5	59.9	74.1	106.9	49.1
1974	44.7	40.5	28.3	60.2	74.6	105.4	48.9
1975	40.7	36.3	24.6	55.9	71.0	102.9	49.8
1976	43.9	39.5	26.9	61.0	73.2	103.6	52.1
1977	47.3	42.9	29.5	65.1	80.2	106.0	54.2
1978	49.9	45.5	31.9	67.4	83.0	109.3	55.6
1979	51.4	47.0	33.4	67.8	84.8	112.6	56.8
1980	50.1	45.3	32.0	65.8	87.7	114.7	57.3
1981	50.7	45.8	32.3	66.4	89.9	117.6	58.1
1982	48.1	43.3	29.6	65.4	90.7	111.8	56.2
1983	49.4	45.4	31.1	68.4	93.4	105.9	56.7
1984	53.9	49.8	35.4	71.6	97.6	112.8	60.0
1985	54.5	50.6	36.2	72.0	101.5	110.6	61.3
1986	55.0	51.7	36.8	74.1	103.5	102.6	61.8
1987	57.9	54.7	39.0	78.0	109.5	103.4	64.7
1988	60.9	57.6	41.9	80.6	109.0	106.1	68.4
1989	61.4	58.0	42.4	81.1	107.4	104.8	70.6
1990	62.0	58.5	42.5	82.4	106.1	106.4	71.9
1991	61.1	57.4	41.2	82.1	101.8	104.0	73.7
1992	62.8	59.5	43.4	84.2	99.7	101.7	73.6
1993	64.9	61.5	45.7	85.4	100.5	101.7	76.2
1994	68.3	65.2	49.6	88.4	99.6	104.1	77.7
1995	71.5	68.6	53.9	89.9	99.6	103.9	80.5
1996	74.7	71.9	58.7	90.2	98.7	105.7	82.8
1997	80.1	77.9	65.7	93.5	107.0	107.5	82.8
1998	84.8	83.1	72.7	94.9	113.4	105.8	84.9
1999	88.4	87.3	78.8	95.5	116.7	100.2	87.4
2000	92.0	90.9	84.6	95.9	116.4	102.9	89.9
2001	88.9	87.3	80.8	93.0	108.8	103.4	89.5
2002	89.1	87.6	80.7	94.3	105.2	98.7	92.3
2003	90.2	88.7	82.9	94.5	102.1	98.9	94.1
2004	92.3	91.2	86.2	95.9	102.9	98.1	95.3
2005	95.3	94.8	91.1	98.3	102.6	96.6	97.3
2006	97.4	97.1	95.3	98.9	101.4	99.5	96.7
2007	100.0	100.0	100.0	100.0	100.0	100.0	100.0
2008	96.7	95.5	96.4	94.7	93.5	100.8	99.9
2009	87.7	85.0	82.1	89.0	79.9	95.8	97.3
2010 [p]	92.8	90.2	89.4	92.8	76.3	101.2	100.4
2009: Jan	89.1	85.7	83.5	88.3	85.8	99.9	100.5
Feb	88.5	85.5	82.8	88.9	84.6	98.3	97.1
Mar	87.2	84.1	81.0	88.1	81.0	96.4	98.0
Apr	86.5	83.5	80.3	87.9	78.5	94.8	97.3
May	85.7	82.9	79.0	88.1	77.9	93.7	96.1
June	85.5	82.7	78.6	88.3	78.3	93.0	95.8
July	86.7	84.1	81.3	88.3	77.9	94.1	95.4
Aug	87.8	85.3	82.6	89.3	78.4	95.8	95.5
Sept	88.4	85.9	83.6	89.5	78.6	96.0	96.6
Oct	88.6	86.0	83.5	89.8	78.2	96.0	98.4
Nov	89.1	86.8	84.3	90.7	79.7	96.7	95.8
Dec	89.6	86.9	84.5	90.8	79.7	94.9	101.2
2010: Jan	90.5	87.8	85.7	91.3	78.1	96.5	102.1
Feb	90.5	87.5	85.5	91.2	76.4	97.5	102.6
Mar	91.0	88.5	86.7	91.9	76.8	98.9	99.0
Apr	91.5	89.3	88.2	92.1	76.3	100.8	95.3
May	92.6	90.3	89.5	92.7	78.1	100.0	99.2
June	92.6	90.1	89.6	92.3	76.9	99.8	101.6
July	93.5	90.8	90.8	92.6	76.7	101.1	102.6
Aug [p]	93.7	90.9	90.4	93.3	76.4	103.2	101.4
Sept [p]	94.0	91.0	90.6	93.4	74.9	104.5	101.9
Oct [p]	93.8	91.4	91.2	93.5	74.9	104.8	97.5
Nov [p]	94.1	91.6	91.5	93.7	75.5	104.1	99.0
Dec [p]	94.9	92.0	91.8	94.2	75.5	104.5	103.2

[1] Total industry and total manufacturing series include manufacturing as defined in the North American Industry Classification System (NAICS) plus those industries—logging and newspaper, periodical, book, and directory publishing—that have traditionally been considered to be manufacturing and included in the industrial sector.

Note: Data based on NAICS; see footnote 1.

Source: Board of Governors of the Federal Reserve System.

[2007=100; monthly data seasonally adjusted]

Year or month	Total indus-trial pro-duc-tion	Final products Total	Consumer goods Total	Auto-motive prod-ucts	Other dur-able goods	Non-dur-able goods	Equipment Total [1]	Busi-ness	De-fense and space	Nonindustrial supplies Total	Con-struc-tion	Busi-ness	Materials Total	Non-energy	Energy
1962	25.2	24.4	32.6	21.8	20.8	38.9	14.4	10.0	43.0	26.2	36.3	22.1	25.0	....	53.2
1963	26.7	25.8	34.4	23.9	22.5	40.7	15.2	10.5	46.4	27.7	38.0	23.6	26.6	....	56.4
1964	28.5	27.3	36.3	25.1	24.5	42.7	16.1	11.8	44.9	29.5	40.3	25.2	28.8	....	58.7
1965	31.4	30.0	39.2	30.9	27.8	44.5	18.2	13.5	49.7	31.4	42.8	26.9	32.1	....	61.3
1966	34.2	32.8	41.2	30.7	30.6	46.6	21.2	15.6	58.4	33.3	44.6	29.0	34.9	....	65.2
1967	34.9	34.1	42.2	27.0	31.0	49.1	22.6	15.9	66.6	34.7	45.7	30.5	34.6	27.3	67.5
1968	36.8	35.8	44.7	32.2	33.2	51.0	23.2	16.6	66.7	36.7	48.1	32.4	36.9	29.3	70.6
1969	38.5	36.9	46.4	32.3	35.4	52.7	23.8	17.7	63.5	38.7	50.2	34.4	39.1	31.1	74.2
1970	37.3	35.6	45.9	27.2	34.3	53.6	22.1	17.0	53.8	38.1	48.4	34.6	37.7	29.3	77.8
1971	37.8	35.9	48.5	34.7	36.4	55.1	20.7	16.2	48.3	39.3	50.0	35.6	38.3	29.8	78.5
1972	41.4	39.0	52.4	37.4	41.6	58.7	22.7	18.5	47.0	43.8	56.7	39.2	42.1	33.4	81.5
1973	44.8	42.0	54.8	40.6	44.5	60.5	25.9	21.4	51.5	46.9	61.5	41.6	45.9	37.0	83.5
1974	44.7	41.9	53.2	35.1	41.8	60.5	27.2	22.6	53.2	46.5	60.1	41.6	45.8	36.9	83.1
1975	40.7	39.6	51.1	33.8	36.6	59.4	24.8	20.2	53.7	41.7	50.9	38.4	40.8	31.7	82.4
1976	43.9	42.4	53.3	38.5	41.1	63.1	26.1	21.5	52.1	44.6	54.8	40.9	44.4	35.3	84.2
1977	47.3	45.8	58.7	43.6	45.9	65.5	29.2	24.9	46.7	48.4	59.7	44.3	47.5	38.2	86.9
1978	49.9	48.6	60.5	43.3	48.0	67.8	32.5	28.1	47.5	51.0	63.1	46.7	49.8	40.7	87.9
1979	51.4	50.2	59.6	39.0	48.3	67.4	36.2	31.6	50.9	52.6	64.7	48.3	51.2	41.8	90.3
1980	50.1	50.0	57.4	30.0	44.8	67.4	38.0	32.4	60.4	50.5	59.8	47.2	49.2	39.3	91.0
1981	50.7	51.2	57.8	30.9	45.2	67.8	39.8	33.4	65.5	51.1	50.8	48.3	49.5	39.5	91.9
1982	48.1	50.1	57.6	30.0	41.9	68.9	37.9	30.5	78.3	49.2	53.4	47.7	45.7	35.5	87.9
1983	49.4	51.1	59.8	34.9	45.4	69.7	37.6	30.7	78.8	51.9	57.2	50.0	46.9	38.0	85.2
1984	53.9	55.3	62.5	39.0	50.6	71.1	43.0	35.3	90.3	56.4	62.2	54.3	51.4	42.3	90.6
1985	54.5	56.7	63.1	39.0	50.7	72.0	45.1	36.6	101.0	57.9	63.7	55.7	51.3	42.4	90.0
1986	55.0	57.5	65.3	41.9	53.6	73.7	44.4	36.0	107.3	59.8	65.9	57.6	51.2	43.2	86.5
1987	57.9	60.2	68.0	44.7	56.5	76.3	46.9	38.5	109.6	63.4	70.1	61.0	54.0	46.0	88.5
1988	60.9	63.5	70.6	47.1	59.5	78.8	50.7	42.4	110.6	65.6	71.8	63.3	57.0	49.0	91.6
1989	61.4	64.2	70.9	48.9	60.2	78.6	51.9	43.8	110.8	66.2	71.5	64.2	57.4	49.3	92.5
1990	62.0	64.8	71.2	45.9	60.1	79.9	53.0	45.5	106.8	67.2	70.9	65.7	57.8	49.4	94.3
1991	61.1	64.1	71.1	42.9	58.4	81.0	51.2	44.7	98.9	65.5	67.0	64.8	56.9	48.3	94.4
1992	62.8	65.6	73.3	50.2	61.0	81.7	51.8	46.5	91.8	67.3	69.8	66.3	58.8	50.7	93.6
1993	64.9	67.6	75.6	55.4	65.2	82.8	53.4	48.6	86.7	69.7	72.9	68.4	60.7	52.9	93.8
1994	68.3	70.5	79.0	62.1	70.7	84.8	55.4	51.4	81.4	73.0	78.2	71.1	64.7	57.2	95.3
1995	71.5	73.4	81.4	64.0	74.9	86.9	59.1	55.9	78.9	75.7	80.0	74.0	68.3	61.1	96.7
1996	74.7	76.2	83.0	66.0	78.4	88.0	63.5	61.2	76.5	78.7	83.6	76.9	71.9	65.0	98.2
1997	80.1	81.2	86.0	70.9	83.4	90.1	71.4	70.4	75.3	83.9	87.6	82.3	77.7	71.8	98.1
1998	84.8	85.9	89.2	75.7	90.1	92.0	78.5	78.3	78.6	88.6	92.3	87.0	82.4	77.3	98.4
1999	88.4	88.3	91.0	82.9	94.7	92.0	81.7	82.8	76.2	91.9	94.7	90.7	87.3	83.2	98.0
2000	92.0	90.9	92.8	84.7	98.4	93.4	86.0	89.0	67.8	95.1	96.8	94.4	91.8	88.3	99.5
2001	88.9	89.2	91.8	82.0	93.0	93.6	82.7	83.7	74.3	91.4	92.4	91.0	87.7	83.4	98.3
2002	89.1	88.7	93.3	90.7	94.6	94.2	77.1	77.8	75.0	91.5	92.4	91.1	88.6	84.7	98.0
2003	90.2	89.8	95.1	95.7	95.5	94.9	77.7	77.6	79.7	92.5	92.2	92.7	89.8	86.2	98.1
2004	92.3	91.5	96.1	95.6	98.6	95.7	81.0	81.7	77.7	94.4	94.4	94.4	92.3	89.8	97.7
2005	95.3	95.2	98.7	94.0	101.7	99.0	87.3	87.6	85.8	97.8	98.9	97.3	94.4	93.3	96.5
2006	97.4	97.7	99.2	93.4	103.0	99.6	94.2	95.7	84.5	99.3	101.2	98.4	96.5	95.6	98.1
2007	100.0	100.0	100.0	100.0	100.0	100.0	100.0	100.0	100.0	100.0	100.0	100.0	100.0	100.0	100.0
2008	96.7	96.9	95.8	85.5	93.8	97.9	99.3	98.5	102.5	94.3	90.5	96.2	97.3	95.3	100.7
2009 p	87.7	89.4	90.2	69.8	79.1	95.6	87.4	86.5	103.6	82.8	75.4	86.5	87.9	81.6	98.6
2010 p	92.8	94.5	94.4	84.8	81.9	98.2	94.6	93.6	107.6	84.9	78.6	87.9	94.0	88.7	102.9
2009: Jan	89.1	90.6	89.7	57.5	82.9	96.3	92.5	91.2	102.4	85.5	78.1	89.1	89.0	82.1	100.8
Feb	88.5	90.2	90.0	63.7	80.5	96.0	90.7	89.9	102.6	84.3	77.0	87.8	88.3	81.7	99.4
Mar	87.2	89.1	89.7	65.2	78.5	95.7	87.8	87.2	102.2	83.0	75.4	86.7	86.8	79.9	98.7
Apr	86.5	88.2	89.1	65.4	78.6	94.9	86.1	85.5	101.8	82.3	74.8	86.0	86.3	79.7	97.7
May	85.7	87.1	88.2	60.4	77.7	94.6	84.8	83.9	102.5	82.0	75.1	85.3	85.6	79.2	96.7
June	85.5	86.8	87.9	58.8	77.3	94.6	84.5	83.6	102.5	82.1	75.2	85.5	85.4	79.1	96.4
July	86.7	88.1	89.3	71.6	78.3	94.1	85.6	84.6	104.4	82.1	75.4	85.4	86.9	80.8	97.3
Aug	87.8	89.3	90.5	75.6	77.9	95.1	86.7	85.9	105.1	82.6	75.9	85.8	88.1	82.2	98.2
Sept	88.4	90.1	91.5	80.2	78.7	95.6	87.1	86.1	106.5	82.3	75.1	85.8	88.9	82.9	99.1
Oct	88.6	90.8	92.2	78.5	79.1	96.7	87.6	86.8	105.5	82.0	73.8	86.1	88.9	82.9	99.2
Nov	89.1	90.6	92.1	80.5	80.0	96.1	87.3	86.4	104.4	82.7	75.3	86.3	89.9	84.4	99.1
Dec	89.6	91.2	92.6	80.1	79.1	97.0	88.2	87.4	103.3	83.1	73.6	87.8	90.3	84.4	100.2
2010: Jan	90.5	92.4	93.7	83.1	79.0	98.0	89.6	88.6	104.7	83.4	74.8	87.6	91.2	85.7	100.2
Feb	90.5	92.0	93.0	81.7	78.9	97.3	89.8	88.4	105.1	82.8	74.4	86.9	91.7	85.8	101.6
Mar	91.0	92.7	93.4	82.7	80.1	97.5	91.2	89.3	107.8	83.4	76.1	87.0	92.1	86.6	101.1
Apr	91.5	92.5	92.3	81.4	82.0	95.9	93.0	91.2	108.3	84.7	79.4	87.3	92.9	87.8	101.4
May	92.6	94.4	94.4	84.7	83.0	98.0	94.4	93.0	107.9	85.2	79.3	88.1	93.5	88.4	102.0
June	92.6	94.4	94.4	84.2	82.5	98.1	94.5	93.7	106.4	85.4	79.6	88.2	93.6	88.5	102.0
July	93.5	95.5	95.7	92.1	83.5	98.4	95.3	94.4	108.4	85.4	78.9	88.5	94.4	89.1	103.1
Aug p	93.7	95.5	95.4	86.8	82.5	99.1	95.8	94.8	108.6	85.5	79.3	88.5	94.9	89.3	104.1
Sept p	94.0	95.5	95.1	86.6	82.1	98.8	96.3	95.4	108.4	85.2	79.0	88.2	95.6	89.7	105.4
Oct p	93.8	95.7	95.0	87.7	82.3	98.4	97.4	96.7	108.2	84.7	79.3	87.3	95.3	89.9	104.3
Nov p	94.1	95.4	94.5	82.8	83.4	98.4	97.5	97.1	107.3	85.8	80.6	88.3	95.8	90.6	104.2
Dec p	94.9	96.3	95.5	82.4	82.9	99.8	98.1	97.7	107.3	85.9	80.0	88.8	96.7	91.4	105.6

[1] Includes other items not shown separately.

Note: See footnote 1 and Note, Table B–51.

Source: Board of Governors of the Federal Reserve System.

TABLE B–53. Industrial production indexes, selected manufacturing industries, 1967–2010

[2007=100; monthly data seasonally adjusted]

	Durable manufacturing								Nondurable manufacturing					
	Primary metal		Fabricated metal products	Machinery	Computer and electronic products		Transportation equipment		Apparel	Paper	Printing and support	Chemical	Plastics and rubber products	Food
Year or month	Total	Iron and steel products			Total	Selected high-technology[1]	Total	Motor vehicles and parts						
1967	....	....	....	....	....	0.1	....	....	....	....	....	....	....	....
1968	....	....	....	....	....	.1	....	....	....	....	....	....	....	....
1969	....	....	....	....	....	.1	....	....	....	....	....	....	....	....
1970	....	....	....	....	....	.1	....	....	....	....	....	....	....	....
1971	....	....	....	....	....	.1	....	....	....	....	....	....	....	....
1972	109.5	113.1	60.4	56.8	0.7	.1	47.1	43.2	286.3	68.2	49.7	41.0	34.7	55.8
1973	127.5	135.6	66.8	65.7	.9	.2	53.8	49.4	295.0	73.8	52.3	44.9	39.0	55.9
1974	130.6	144.9	65.7	68.9	1.0	.2	49.6	42.5	274.6	76.9	50.7	46.6	38.0	56.5
1975	101.4	107.5	56.7	60.0	.9	.2	45.0	37.0	268.7	66.5	47.4	41.0	32.5	55.4
1976	107.7	111.5	60.7	62.6	1.0	.2	50.3	47.3	283.8	73.5	50.8	45.9	36.0	59.9
1977	108.8	109.0	65.9	68.4	1.3	.3	54.7	53.7	301.7	76.7	55.0	49.9	42.4	61.0
1978	115.8	117.0	69.1	73.7	1.6	.4	58.2	56.0	310.4	80.2	58.2	52.4	43.8	62.8
1979	118.6	121.2	72.2	77.8	2.0	.5	58.8	51.3	294.2	81.4	60.0	53.6	43.2	62.2
1980	104.2	102.7	68.1	74.0	2.4	.7	52.2	37.9	298.6	81.1	60.4	50.7	38.4	63.3
1981	104.3	106.5	67.6	73.3	2.8	.8	50.2	36.9	296.8	82.3	62.0	51.5	40.7	64.2
1982	73.7	65.5	60.6	61.3	3.1	.9	46.2	33.3	300.7	80.9	66.7	48.2	39.9	66.6
1983	75.6	66.0	61.0	55.3	3.6	1.1	51.0	42.5	309.5	86.2	71.6	51.5	43.5	67.4
1984	82.8	72.7	66.4	64.5	4.5	1.4	57.9	50.9	313.8	90.5	78.0	54.6	50.2	68.7
1985	76.5	67.5	67.4	64.7	4.7	1.5	60.9	52.8	301.7	88.8	81.1	54.1	52.2	71.2
1986	74.7	65.9	66.9	63.7	4.9	1.5	62.4	52.8	305.2	92.4	85.2	56.6	54.4	72.3
1987	80.5	75.1	68.2	65.0	5.6	1.9	64.6	54.7	307.2	95.5	91.5	60.9	60.2	73.8
1988	89.9	87.4	71.7	71.6	6.3	2.2	68.6	58.5	301.7	99.2	94.4	64.4	62.9	75.7
1989	87.9	84.3	71.1	74.3	6.5	2.3	70.0	57.9	286.8	100.3	94.8	65.6	65.0	75.9
1990	86.8	83.3	70.3	72.5	7.1	2.6	67.8	54.4	281.0	100.3	98.4	67.1	66.8	78.2
1991	81.5	76.1	67.1	68.0	7.3	2.8	65.1	52.0	282.5	100.5	95.3	66.9	66.1	79.6
1992	83.5	79.7	69.1	67.8	8.2	3.4	67.5	59.2	287.9	102.9	100.5	67.9	71.2	81.1
1993	87.5	84.4	71.7	72.9	9.1	4.0	69.5	65.4	294.7	104.1	100.8	68.7	76.2	83.3
1994	94.1	91.1	78.0	79.8	10.7	5.1	72.7	75.1	300.6	108.6	101.9	70.5	82.5	83.8
1995	95.2	92.5	82.8	85.5	13.8	7.2	72.8	77.3	301.0	110.2	103.4	71.6	84.6	85.9
1996	97.5	94.7	85.8	88.5	17.9	10.3	74.1	77.9	292.5	106.8	104.1	73.1	87.4	84.2
1997	101.7	97.6	89.6	93.3	24.0	15.2	80.8	84.0	289.2	109.0	106.2	77.4	92.8	86.5
1998	103.4	97.4	92.6	95.7	30.9	21.3	87.9	88.4	273.8	109.9	107.5	78.7	96.2	90.3
1999	103.4	97.8	93.2	93.7	40.4	30.6	92.7	98.1	261.6	110.7	107.5	80.2	101.3	91.3
2000	99.9	96.5	96.9	98.5	52.9	42.9	88.3	97.4	249.6	107.8	108.4	81.4	102.3	92.9
2001	91.0	87.6	89.9	87.1	54.0	44.2	84.9	88.8	215.0	101.7	104.8	79.9	96.4	93.0
2002	91.0	88.7	87.6	83.7	52.7	44.0	88.6	97.6	170.1	102.9	102.1	85.3	99.8	95.0
2003	89.4	89.3	86.6	83.3	60.2	53.1	89.5	101.1	156.7	100.4	98.1	86.7	99.9	95.6
2004	97.3	101.1	86.9	86.8	68.4	60.6	89.3	101.6	134.6	101.2	98.5	90.1	101.1	95.6
2005	94.9	93.8	91.0	92.1	76.9	70.9	93.1	102.3	129.1	100.8	98.6	93.1	102.2	98.6
2006	97.6	97.8	95.9	96.5	87.1	84.3	94.2	100.7	125.8	99.6	97.8	95.4	102.8	99.4
2007	100.0	100.0	100.0	100.0	100.0	100.0	100.0	100.0	100.0	100.0	100.0	100.0	100.0	100.0
2008	98.3	103.5	96.4	97.7	109.4	113.5	87.8	80.7	79.7	95.3	94.3	94.1	91.1	98.6
2009	67.3	61.8	82.4	76.4	100.4	100.0	76.0	60.6	65.3	85.2	79.7	90.9	75.6	97.6
2010 p	84.8	91.2	88.6	83.8	113.9	115.9	83.0	75.8	65.7	88.3	76.8	94.4	82.1	103.3
2009: Jan	66.8	51.5	88.1	85.6	97.3	93.8	71.6	49.8	69.8	84.5	85.5	87.5	79.3	95.8
Feb	62.8	48.6	86.2	83.7	96.1	92.2	74.7	55.7	68.1	86.9	82.5	88.9	77.1	96.6
Mar	60.1	46.9	82.8	79.1	96.4	93.1	74.5	56.7	67.5	83.1	81.1	89.0	74.6	96.2
Apr	59.3	45.4	81.2	77.0	97.7	95.9	73.5	56.9	66.6	81.4	79.6	89.8	73.9	96.6
May	58.4	47.2	80.1	74.8	98.1	96.5	70.0	51.1	66.3	83.6	79.0	89.6	73.5	97.3
June	60.0	53.3	80.3	72.8	99.2	97.7	69.0	49.1	62.3	85.2	79.3	90.3	73.6	97.3
July	66.1	62.7	80.5	72.8	100.6	100.9	76.6	61.7	64.4	84.9	78.8	91.1	74.4	96.4
Aug	70.0	68.7	81.1	74.0	102.1	103.0	78.4	64.8	64.4	86.5	79.0	91.6	74.8	98.2
Sept	72.6	73.5	81.6	72.7	103.6	105.4	81.8	70.4	63.9	86.0	78.1	92.3	75.4	98.5
Oct	73.3	78.0	81.6	74.5	104.1	106.9	80.5	69.3	62.5	85.4	78.2	92.1	76.1	99.4
Nov	77.5	79.9	82.4	73.5	105.2	107.4	80.7	71.0	63.0	88.2	77.5	93.8	76.7	99.5
Dec	80.7	85.8	82.6	76.5	105.6	107.8	80.3	71.2	64.2	86.9	77.4	94.3	77.6	99.2
2010: Jan	81.8	89.9	83.3	78.2	107.0	109.1	81.6	73.5	67.1	87.2	77.1	95.4	78.6	100.0
Feb	82.5	89.5	83.3	78.4	108.5	111.2	80.4	71.7	66.4	88.3	76.0	94.2	79.1	101.0
Mar	84.5	93.5	84.3	78.7	110.3	112.4	81.7	73.2	65.9	89.3	75.6	94.2	80.1	101.7
Apr	86.3	95.8	85.9	81.9	112.4	115.1	80.9	72.0	66.8	88.7	76.6	94.1	82.3	101.6
May	86.5	96.1	87.3	83.9	114.3	116.5	82.7	76.0	66.3	88.8	78.1	93.4	83.1	102.5
June	87.0	94.6	88.4	84.9	114.3	116.7	82.2	75.3	65.6	89.2	77.4	93.0	81.9	102.5
July	82.1	85.3	89.7	84.8	115.9	117.7	86.6	82.6	63.9	88.9	76.6	93.1	82.8	102.8
Aug p	81.7	84.6	90.8	84.7	116.5	118.6	84.2	77.4	65.5	88.1	77.8	93.6	82.8	104.9
Sept p	83.3	87.8	91.2	84.9	116.6	118.8	84.4	77.7	63.7	88.3	76.4	94.8	81.9	105.9
Oct p	82.4	83.8	90.8	87.0	117.0	118.7	84.9	78.9	65.2	87.4	76.0	94.4	82.6	105.5
Nov p	86.4	91.1	92.2	88.1	117.2	119.5	82.5	74.7	65.1	88.1	76.7	95.2	83.5	105.7
Dec p	89.6	97.7	92.2	88.3	119.2	120.8	82.1	74.6	66.0	87.5	75.2	96.2	84.7	105.9

[1] Computers and peripheral equipment, communications equipment, and semiconductors and related electronic components.

Note: See footnote 1 and Note, Table B–51.

Source: Board of Governors of the Federal Reserve System.

TABLE B–54. Capacity utilization rates, 1962–2010

[Percent [1]; monthly data seasonally adjusted]

Year or month	Total industry [2]	Manufacturing				Mining	Utilities	Stage-of-process		
		Total [2]	Durable goods	Nondurable goods	Other (non-NAICS) [2]			Crude	Primary and semi-finished	Finished
1962	....	81.4	....	....	....	....	....	....	81.5	81.6
1963	....	83.5	....	....	....	....	....	....	83.8	83.4
1964	....	85.6	....	....	....	....	....	....	87.8	84.6
1965	....	89.5	....	....	....	....	....	....	91.0	88.8
1966	....	91.1	....	....	....	....	....	....	91.4	91.1
1967	87.0	87.2	87.5	86.3	....	81.2	94.5	81.1	85.0	88.2
1968	87.3	87.1	87.4	86.5	....	83.6	95.1	83.4	86.8	87.1
1969	87.4	86.7	87.2	86.1	....	86.7	96.8	85.6	88.1	85.6
1970	81.3	79.5	77.8	82.1	....	89.1	96.3	85.0	81.5	78.2
1971	79.6	78.0	75.6	81.8	....	87.8	94.7	84.2	81.7	75.8
1972	84.7	83.4	82.1	85.2	85.6	90.6	95.3	88.2	88.2	79.6
1973	88.3	87.6	88.5	86.6	84.7	91.6	93.3	90.0	92.1	83.1
1974	85.0	84.4	84.6	84.1	82.7	90.9	86.9	90.8	87.3	80.2
1975	75.7	73.6	71.6	76.0	77.2	89.0	85.1	83.7	75.2	73.6
1976	79.7	78.2	76.3	81.1	77.6	89.4	85.5	86.9	80.1	76.7
1977	83.3	82.4	81.1	84.3	83.1	89.5	86.6	89.0	84.5	79.7
1978	85.0	84.3	83.7	85.1	85.0	89.6	86.9	88.6	86.2	82.0
1979	85.0	84.1	84.1	83.8	85.7	91.0	87.0	89.8	86.0	81.7
1980	80.8	78.7	77.6	79.6	87.0	91.1	85.5	89.2	78.8	79.4
1981	79.6	77.0	75.2	78.8	87.5	90.9	84.4	89.3	77.3	77.4
1982	73.1	70.9	66.6	76.3	87.2	84.2	80.2	82.3	70.7	73.0
1983	74.9	73.4	68.7	79.5	88.0	80.0	79.6	80.0	74.5	73.1
1984	80.5	79.3	76.8	82.2	89.6	85.9	82.2	85.8	81.2	77.3
1985	79.2	78.1	75.6	80.6	90.2	84.4	81.9	83.8	79.8	76.7
1986	78.7	78.4	75.4	81.8	88.8	77.6	81.1	79.1	79.7	77.2
1987	81.2	81.0	77.7	84.7	90.7	80.3	83.6	82.8	82.8	78.8
1988	84.3	84.0	82.1	86.0	88.5	84.3	86.7	86.3	85.9	81.7
1989	83.8	83.3	81.9	84.9	85.4	85.2	86.9	86.8	84.7	81.8
1990	82.6	81.7	79.6	84.2	83.7	86.8	86.5	87.8	82.7	80.8
1991	79.8	78.5	75.3	82.3	80.7	84.9	87.9	85.1	79.9	78.2
1992	80.5	79.6	77.2	82.7	79.9	84.4	86.4	85.3	81.6	78.1
1993	81.4	80.3	78.5	82.7	81.1	85.7	88.3	85.7	83.4	78.1
1994	83.6	82.8	81.6	84.6	81.3	87.5	88.4	88.3	86.5	79.1
1995	84.1	83.3	82.3	84.6	82.1	88.0	89.4	89.1	86.5	79.9
1996	83.4	82.2	81.7	83.2	80.5	90.4	90.9	88.9	85.8	79.2
1997	84.2	83.2	82.4	83.9	85.5	91.4	90.4	90.5	86.2	80.3
1998	82.9	81.7	80.8	82.4	86.8	89.2	92.7	87.4	84.3	80.2
1999	81.8	80.5	80.0	80.3	87.2	86.1	94.2	86.4	84.2	78.0
2000	81.5	79.7	79.5	79.1	87.4	90.7	93.9	88.7	84.0	76.8
2001	76.0	73.7	71.2	75.9	82.8	90.3	89.6	85.6	77.3	72.4
2002	74.7	72.8	69.4	76.3	81.7	86.0	87.5	82.8	76.8	70.7
2003	75.9	73.8	70.7	77.0	81.8	87.9	85.7	84.6	77.9	71.5
2004	77.9	76.2	73.5	78.8	83.3	88.2	84.5	86.2	79.9	73.3
2005	80.1	78.5	76.1	80.8	83.1	88.5	85.1	86.3	81.9	75.8
2006	80.7	79.1	77.5	80.7	81.7	90.4	83.3	88.0	81.7	76.7
2007	81.3	79.6	78.5	80.8	80.7	89.1	85.7	88.5	81.7	78.0
2008	77.9	75.0	74.2	75.7	78.2	89.5	84.2	87.2	76.8	74.7
2009	70.0	67.2	63.7	71.2	69.9	82.2	79.7	80.4	67.4	69.5
2010 [P]	74.2	71.7	69.5	75.0	67.7	86.4	80.5	86.0	71.3	73.4
2009: Jan	71.3	67.4	64.4	70.4	73.9	86.9	83.5	82.2	69.2	69.3
Feb	70.7	67.3	63.9	70.9	73.1	85.2	80.5	81.6	67.9	69.6
Mar	69.6	66.2	62.6	70.2	70.3	83.3	81.0	79.6	66.9	69.0
Apr	69.0	65.9	62.2	70.1	68.3	81.5	80.3	79.0	66.4	68.4
May	68.3	65.4	61.2	70.3	68.0	80.3	79.1	78.5	65.8	67.8
June	68.2	65.4	61.0	70.5	68.6	79.6	78.6	78.3	65.7	67.5
July	69.1	66.6	63.2	70.6	68.4	80.4	78.0	79.5	66.5	68.7
Aug	70.0	67.6	64.3	71.5	69.0	81.7	77.9	80.6	67.1	69.8
Sept	70.5	68.1	65.1	71.8	69.4	81.8	78.6	81.1	67.6	70.4
Oct	70.7	68.2	65.1	72.1	69.1	81.8	79.9	81.2	67.9	70.7
Nov	71.1	69.0	65.8	72.8	70.5	82.4	77.6	81.7	68.2	71.1
Dec	71.6	69.1	65.9	73.0	70.7	80.9	81.8	81.4	69.1	71.2
2010: Jan	72.3	69.8	66.9	73.5	69.3	82.2	82.4	82.6	69.7	72.0
Feb	72.4	69.7	66.7	73.5	67.8	83.2	82.6	83.2	69.9	71.6
Mar	72.8	70.4	67.6	74.2	68.2	84.3	79.7	84.2	69.9	72.3
Apr	73.2	71.1	68.8	74.4	67.7	86.0	76.6	85.4	70.2	72.5
May	74.2	72.0	69.8	74.9	69.3	85.4	79.6	84.6	71.6	73.5
June	74.2	71.8	69.8	74.7	68.2	85.2	81.5	84.6	72.0	73.2
July	74.9	72.3	70.6	74.9	68.0	86.3	82.2	85.7	72.3	74.0
Aug [P]	75.1	72.4	70.3	75.6	67.7	88.1	81.2	87.1	72.0	74.1
Sept [P]	75.3	72.5	70.4	75.7	66.3	89.1	81.5	88.3	72.0	74.2
Oct [P]	75.2	72.8	70.8	75.9	66.3	89.3	77.9	88.5	71.3	74.7
Nov [P]	75.4	72.9	71.0	76.0	66.8	88.7	79.0	88.5	72.1	74.2
Dec [P]	76.0	73.2	71.2	76.5	66.7	88.9	82.3	89.0	73.2	74.3

[1] Output as percent of capacity.
[2] See footnote 1 and Note, Table B–51.

Source: Board of Governors of the Federal Reserve System.

TABLE B–55. New construction activity, 1965–2010

[Value put in place, billions of dollars; monthly data at seasonally adjusted annual rates]

Year or month	Total new construction	Private construction Total	Residential buildings [1] Total [2]	Residential buildings New housing units [3]	Nonresidential buildings and other construction Total	Lodging	Office	Commercial [4]	Manufacturing	Other [5]	Public construction Total	Federal	State and local
1965	81.9	60.0	30.2	23.8	29.7						21.9	3.9	18.0
1966	85.8	61.9	28.6	21.8	33.3						23.8	3.8	20.0
1967	87.2	61.8	28.7	21.5	33.1						25.4	3.3	22.1
1968	96.8	69.4	34.2	26.7	35.2						27.4	3.2	24.2
1969	104.9	77.2	37.2	29.2	39.9						27.8	3.2	24.6
1970	105.9	78.0	35.9	27.1	42.1						27.9	3.1	24.8
1971	122.4	92.7	48.5	38.7	44.2						29.7	3.8	25.9
1972	139.1	109.1	60.7	50.1	48.4						30.0	4.2	25.8
1973	153.8	121.4	65.1	54.6	56.3						32.3	4.7	27.6
1974	155.2	117.0	56.0	43.4	61.1						38.1	5.1	33.0
1975	152.6	109.3	51.6	36.3	57.8						43.3	6.1	37.2
1976	172.1	128.2	68.3	50.8	59.9						44.0	6.8	37.2
1977	200.5	157.4	92.0	72.2	65.4						43.1	7.1	36.0
1978	239.9	189.7	109.8	85.6	79.9						50.1	8.1	42.0
1979	272.9	216.2	116.4	89.3	99.8						56.6	8.6	48.1
1980	273.9	210.3	100.4	69.6	109.9						63.6	9.6	54.0
1981	289.1	224.4	99.2	69.4	125.1						64.7	10.4	54.3
1982	279.3	216.3	84.7	57.0	131.6						63.1	10.0	53.1
1983	311.9	248.4	125.8	95.0	122.6						63.5	10.6	52.9
1984	370.2	300.0	155.0	114.6	144.9						70.2	11.2	59.0
1985	403.4	325.6	160.5	115.9	165.1						77.8	12.0	65.8
1986	433.5	348.9	190.7	135.2	158.2						84.6	12.4	72.2
1987	446.6	356.0	199.7	142.7	156.3						90.6	14.1	76.6
1988	462.0	367.3	204.5	142.4	162.8						94.7	12.3	82.5
1989	477.5	379.3	204.3	143.2	175.1						98.2	12.2	86.0
1990	476.8	369.3	191.1	132.1	178.2						107.5	12.1	95.4
1991	432.6	322.5	166.3	114.6	156.2						110.1	12.8	97.3
1992	463.7	347.8	199.4	135.1	148.4						115.8	14.4	101.5
1993	485.5	358.2	208.2	150.9	150.0	4.6	20.0	34.4	23.4	67.7	127.4	14.4	112.9
1994	531.9	401.5	241.0	176.4	160.4	4.7	20.4	39.6	28.8	66.9	130.4	14.4	116.0
1995	548.7	408.7	228.1	171.4	180.5	7.1	23.0	44.1	35.4	70.9	140.0	15.8	124.3
1996	599.7	453.0	257.5	191.1	195.5	10.9	26.5	49.4	38.1	70.6	146.7	15.3	131.4
1997	631.9	478.4	264.7	198.1	213.7	12.9	32.8	53.1	37.6	77.3	153.4	14.1	139.4
1998	688.5	533.7	296.3	224.0	237.4	14.8	40.4	55.7	40.5	86.0	154.8	14.3	140.5
1999	744.6	575.5	326.3	251.3	249.2	16.0	45.1	59.4	35.1	93.7	169.1	14.0	155.1
2000	802.8	621.4	346.1	265.0	275.3	16.3	52.4	64.1	37.6	104.9	181.3	14.2	167.2
2001	840.2	638.3	364.4	279.4	273.9	14.5	49.7	63.6	37.8	108.2	201.9	15.1	186.8
2002	847.9	634.4	396.7	298.8	237.7	10.5	35.3	59.0	22.7	110.2	213.4	16.6	196.9
2003	891.5	675.4	446.0	345.7	229.3	9.9	30.6	57.5	21.4	109.9	216.1	17.9	198.2
2004	991.4	771.2	532.9	417.5	238.3	12.0	32.9	63.2	23.2	107.0	220.2	18.3	201.8
2005	1,104.1	870.0	611.9	480.8	258.1	12.7	37.3	66.6	28.4	113.1	234.2	17.3	216.9
2006	1,167.2	911.8	613.7	468.8	298.1	17.6	45.7	73.4	32.3	129.2	255.4	17.6	237.8
2007	1,152.4	863.3	493.2	354.1	370.0	27.5	53.8	85.9	40.2	162.7	289.1	20.6	268.5
2008	1,067.6	758.8	350.3	230.1	408.6	35.4	55.5	82.7	52.8	182.3	308.7	23.7	285.0
2009	907.8	592.3	245.6	133.6	346.7	25.4	37.9	51.3	58.0	174.2	315.5	28.3	287.1
2009: Jan	958.1	653.0	276.6	162.0	376.4	30.1	48.0	64.6	60.7	173.0	305.1	26.9	278.2
Feb	951.4	634.2	259.9	149.6	374.3	30.5	44.7	63.0	63.1	173.0	317.2	27.9	289.3
Mar	941.5	620.1	245.5	140.1	374.6	30.5	42.5	60.5	62.7	178.4	321.4	28.4	293.0
Apr	931.6	613.8	245.4	131.3	368.3	30.8	41.0	58.1	64.0	174.3	317.9	26.8	291.1
May	915.4	600.7	234.5	123.1	366.2	29.0	41.2	55.1	63.0	177.9	314.7	26.3	288.4
June	907.7	586.1	231.1	122.9	355.0	26.9	39.5	50.9	61.4	176.4	321.6	28.7	293.0
July	901.2	576.6	227.7	128.1	348.9	25.1	37.8	48.6	58.2	179.3	324.5	30.5	294.0
Aug	901.8	585.1	242.5	130.1	342.6	23.2	36.5	46.2	57.7	179.0	316.7	28.4	288.3
Sept	894.8	579.3	247.4	130.9	331.9	22.2	33.4	46.1	56.2	174.0	315.5	28.4	287.1
Oct	884.7	571.0	253.0	130.6	318.0	20.1	32.8	42.3	54.5	168.3	313.6	29.1	284.5
Nov	861.5	555.8	249.0	130.4	306.8	18.5	29.9	42.2	52.3	164.0	305.7	28.7	277.0
Dec	841.8	540.0	243.0	130.6	297.0	17.2	29.4	42.7	44.0	163.8	301.8	29.2	272.7
2010: Jan	841.0	547.6	266.2	129.9	281.5	14.1	28.0	41.6	42.6	155.3	293.4	28.4	265.0
Feb	815.8	524.6	248.7	130.5	275.9	13.0	27.7	40.1	42.7	152.4	291.2	29.8	261.3
Mar	824.0	524.4	249.3	131.2	275.1	12.0	26.0	39.0	45.0	153.1	299.6	30.0	269.6
Apr	843.1	538.4	264.2	134.0	274.1	11.3	25.2	39.5	44.1	154.1	304.8	30.9	273.9
May	819.7	519.1	251.8	132.8	267.3	11.2	24.3	39.5	40.2	152.0	300.6	29.8	270.8
June	820.2	510.7	247.7	130.9	263.0	10.9	23.6	38.6	38.7	151.2	309.5	32.9	276.7
July	798.8	489.9	237.6	128.9	252.3	10.8	22.5	38.0	36.8	144.2	308.8	29.9	278.9
Aug	791.5	476.1	222.8	123.3	253.3	10.8	23.3	37.4	36.0	145.7	315.4	30.3	285.0
Sept	801.0	483.7	225.4	121.1	258.3	10.1	24.3	37.2	36.9	149.8	317.3	32.3	285.0
Oct [p]	806.7	490.5	234.1	120.0	256.3	9.3	23.0	36.0	34.6	153.5	316.2	32.7	283.5
Nov [p]	810.2	491.8	235.7	121.1	256.1	9.1	22.6	35.9	33.8	154.7	318.5	35.3	283.1

[1] Includes farm residential buildings.
[2] Includes residential improvements, not shown separately.
[3] New single- and multi-family units.
[4] Including farm.
[5] Health care, educational, religious, public safety, amusement and recreation, transportation, communication, power, highway and street, sewage and waste disposal, water supply, and conservation and development.

Note: Data beginning with 1993 reflect reclassification.

Source: Department of Commerce (Bureau of the Census).

TABLE B-56. New private housing units started, authorized, and completed and houses sold, 1964-2010

[Thousands; monthly data at seasonally adjusted annual rates]

Year or month	New housing units started				New housing units authorized [1]				New housing units completed	New houses sold
		Type of structure				Type of structure				
	Total	1 unit	2 to 4 units [2]	5 units or more	Total	1 unit	2 to 4 units	5 units or more		
1964	1,528.8	970.5	108.3	450.0	1,285.8	720.1	100.8	464.9	....	565
1965	1,472.8	963.7	86.7	422.5	1,240.6	709.9	84.7	445.9	....	575
1966	1,164.9	778.6	61.2	325.1	971.9	563.2	61.0	347.7	....	461
1967	1,291.6	843.9	71.7	376.1	1,141.0	650.6	73.0	417.5	....	487
1968	1,507.6	899.4	80.7	527.3	1,353.4	694.7	84.3	574.4	1,319.8	490
1969	1,466.8	810.6	85.1	571.2	1,322.3	624.8	85.2	612.4	1,399.0	448
1970	1,433.6	812.9	84.9	535.9	1,351.5	646.8	88.1	616.7	1,418.4	485
1971	2,052.2	1,151.0	120.5	780.9	1,924.6	906.1	132.9	885.7	1,706.1	656
1972	2,356.6	1,309.2	141.2	906.2	2,218.9	1,033.1	148.6	1,037.2	2,003.9	718
1973	2,045.3	1,132.0	118.2	795.0	1,819.5	882.1	117.0	820.5	2,100.5	634
1974	1,337.7	888.1	68.0	381.6	1,074.4	643.8	64.4	366.2	1,728.5	519
1975	1,160.4	892.2	64.0	204.3	939.2	675.5	63.8	199.8	1,317.2	549
1976	1,537.5	1,162.4	85.8	289.2	1,296.2	893.6	93.1	309.5	1,377.2	646
1977	1,987.1	1,450.9	121.7	414.4	1,690.0	1,126.1	121.3	442.7	1,657.1	819
1978	2,020.3	1,433.3	125.1	462.0	1,800.5	1,182.6	130.6	487.3	1,867.5	817
1979	1,745.1	1,194.1	122.0	429.0	1,551.8	981.5	125.4	444.8	1,870.8	709
1980	1,292.2	852.2	109.5	330.5	1,190.6	710.4	114.5	365.7	1,501.6	545
1981	1,084.2	705.4	91.2	287.7	985.5	564.3	101.8	319.4	1,265.7	436
1982	1,062.2	662.6	80.1	319.6	1,000.5	546.4	88.3	365.8	1,005.5	412
1983	1,703.0	1,067.6	113.5	522.0	1,605.2	901.5	133.7	570.1	1,390.3	623
1984	1,749.5	1,084.2	121.4	543.9	1,681.8	922.4	142.6	616.8	1,652.2	639
1985	1,741.8	1,072.4	93.5	576.0	1,733.3	956.6	120.1	656.6	1,703.3	688
1986	1,805.4	1,179.4	84.0	542.0	1,769.4	1,077.6	108.4	583.5	1,756.4	750
1987	1,620.5	1,146.4	65.1	408.7	1,534.8	1,024.4	89.3	421.1	1,668.8	671
1988	1,488.1	1,081.3	58.7	348.0	1,455.6	993.8	75.7	386.1	1,529.8	676
1989	1,376.1	1,003.3	55.3	317.6	1,338.4	931.7	66.9	339.8	1,422.8	650
1990	1,192.7	894.8	37.6	260.4	1,110.8	793.9	54.3	262.6	1,308.0	534
1991	1,013.9	840.4	35.6	137.9	948.8	753.5	43.1	152.1	1,090.8	509
1992	1,199.7	1,029.9	30.9	139.0	1,094.9	910.7	45.8	138.4	1,157.5	610
1993	1,287.6	1,125.7	29.4	132.6	1,199.1	986.5	52.4	160.2	1,192.7	666
1994	1,457.0	1,198.4	35.2	223.5	1,371.6	1,068.5	62.2	241.0	1,346.9	670
1995	1,354.1	1,076.2	33.8	244.1	1,332.5	997.3	63.8	271.5	1,312.6	667
1996	1,476.8	1,160.9	45.3	270.8	1,425.6	1,069.5	65.8	290.3	1,412.9	757
1997	1,474.0	1,133.7	44.5	295.8	1,441.1	1,062.4	68.4	310.3	1,400.5	804
1998	1,616.9	1,271.4	42.6	302.9	1,612.3	1,187.6	69.2	355.5	1,474.2	886
1999	1,640.9	1,302.4	31.9	306.6	1,663.5	1,246.7	65.8	351.1	1,604.9	880
2000	1,568.7	1,230.9	38.7	299.1	1,592.3	1,198.1	64.9	329.3	1,573.7	877
2001	1,602.7	1,273.3	36.6	292.8	1,636.7	1,235.6	66.0	335.2	1,570.8	908
2002	1,704.9	1,358.6	38.5	307.9	1,747.7	1,332.6	73.7	341.4	1,648.4	973
2003	1,847.7	1,499.0	33.5	315.2	1,889.2	1,460.9	82.5	345.8	1,678.7	1,086
2004	1,955.8	1,610.5	42.3	303.0	2,070.1	1,613.4	90.4	366.2	1,841.9	1,203
2005	2,068.3	1,715.8	41.1	311.4	2,155.3	1,682.0	84.0	389.3	1,931.4	1,283
2006	1,800.9	1,465.4	42.7	292.8	1,838.9	1,378.2	76.6	384.1	1,979.4	1,051
2007	1,355.0	1,046.0	31.7	277.3	1,398.4	979.9	59.6	359.0	1,502.8	776
2008	905.5	622.0	17.5	266.0	905.4	575.6	34.4	295.4	1,119.7	485
2009	554.0	445.1	11.6	97.3	583.0	441.1	20.7	121.1	794.4	375
2010 [p]	587.6	470.9	11.5	105.2	598.0	446.6	20.8	130.6	653.5	321
2009: Jan	488	360	13	115	549	343	22	184	775	339
Feb	581	362	14	205	566	386	21	159	829	370
Mar	520	363	31	126	522	371	21	130	830	350
Apr	477	386	11	80	523	395	20	108	842	341
May	550	406	9	135	550	425	22	103	812	367
June	583	476	11	96	600	451	25	124	798	396
July	587	500	15	72	587	479	19	89	787	408
Aug	585	482	7	96	610	482	20	108	790	405
Sept	586	507	9	70	605	473	20	112	721	391
Oct	529	475	5	49	576	468	16	92	751	396
Nov	589	504	9	76	621	489	26	106	850	368
Dec	576	486	12	78	681	517	19	145	752	356
2010: Jan	612	511	7	94	629	509	19	101	662	349
Feb	605	527	16	62	650	523	20	107	668	347
Mar	634	535	8	91	685	542	22	121	643	384
Apr	679	563	12	104	610	486	17	107	747	414
May	588	459	12	117	574	436	18	120	705	282
June	539	450	5	84	583	421	20	142	879	310
July	550	427	20	103	559	406	19	134	576	283
Aug	614	432	14	168	571	403	18	150	606	274
Sept	601	447	6	148	547	402	25	120	631	317
Oct	533	433	12	88	552	404	24	124	602	280
Nov [p]	553	458	14	81	544	417	20	107	562	280
Dec [p]	529	417	10	102	627	442	24	161	585	329

[1] Authorized by issuance of local building permits in permit-issuing places: 20,000 places beginning with 2004; 19,000 for 1994–2003; 17,000 for 1984–93; 16,000 for 1978–83; 14,000 for 1972–77; 13,000 for 1967–71; and 12,000 for 1964–66.
[2] Monthly data do not meet reliability standards for stable seasonality.

Note: One unit estimates prior to 1999, for new housing units started and completed and for new houses sold, include an upward adjustment of 3.3 percent to account for structures in permit-issuing areas that did not have permit authorization.

Source: Department of Commerce (Bureau of the Census).

[Amounts in millions of dollars; monthly data seasonally adjusted]

Year or month	Total manufacturing and trade			Manufacturing			Merchant wholesalers[1]			Retail trade			Retail and food services sales
	Sales[2]	Inventories[3]	Ratio[4]	Sales[2]	Inventories[3]	Ratio[4]	Sales[2]	Inventories[3]	Ratio[4]	Sales[2,5]	Inventories[3]	Ratio[4]	
SIC:[6]													
1969	105,690	170,400	1.61	53,501	98,145	1.83	22,818	29,800	1.31	29,371	42,455	1.45	
1970	108,221	178,594	1.65	52,805	101,599	1.92	24,167	33,354	1.38	31,249	43,641	1.40	
1971	116,895	188,991	1.62	55,906	102,567	1.83	26,492	36,568	1.38	34,497	49,856	1.45	
1972	131,081	203,227	1.55	63,027	108,121	1.72	29,866	40,297	1.35	38,189	54,809	1.44	
1973	153,677	234,406	1.53	72,931	124,499	1.71	38,115	46,918	1.23	42,631	62,989	1.48	
1974	177,912	287,144	1.61	84,790	157,625	1.86	47,982	58,667	1.22	45,141	70,852	1.57	
1975	182,198	288,992	1.59	86,589	159,708	1.84	46,634	57,774	1.24	48,975	71,510	1.46	
1976	204,150	318,345	1.56	98,797	174,636	1.77	50,698	64,622	1.27	54,655	79,087	1.45	
1977	229,513	350,706	1.53	113,201	188,378	1.66	56,136	73,179	1.30	60,176	89,149	1.48	
1978	260,320	400,931	1.54	126,905	211,691	1.67	66,413	86,934	1.31	67,002	102,306	1.53	
1979	297,701	452,640	1.52	143,936	242,157	1.68	79,051	99,679	1.26	74,713	110,804	1.48	
1980	327,233	508,924	1.56	154,391	265,215	1.72	93,099	122,631	1.32	79,743	121,078	1.52	
1981	355,822	545,786	1.53	168,129	283,413	1.69	101,180	129,654	1.28	86,514	132,719	1.53	
1982	347,625	573,908	1.67	163,351	311,852	1.95	95,211	127,428	1.36	89,062	134,628	1.49	
1983	369,286	590,287	1.56	172,547	312,379	1.78	99,225	130,075	1.28	97,514	147,833	1.44	
1984	410,124	649,780	1.53	190,682	339,516	1.73	112,199	142,452	1.23	107,243	167,812	1.49	
1985	422,583	664,039	1.56	194,538	334,749	1.73	113,459	147,409	1.28	114,586	181,881	1.52	
1986	430,419	662,738	1.55	194,657	322,654	1.68	114,960	153,574	1.32	120,803	186,510	1.56	
1987	457,735	709,848	1.50	206,326	338,109	1.59	122,968	163,903	1.29	128,442	207,836	1.55	
1988	497,157	767,222	1.49	224,619	369,374	1.57	134,521	178,801	1.30	138,017	219,047	1.54	
1989	527,039	815,455	1.52	236,698	391,212	1.63	143,760	187,009	1.28	146,581	237,234	1.58	
1990	545,909	840,594	1.52	242,686	405,073	1.65	149,506	195,833	1.29	153,718	239,688	1.56	
1991	542,815	834,609	1.53	239,847	390,950	1.65	148,306	200,448	1.33	154,661	243,211	1.54	
1992	567,176	842,809	1.48	250,394	382,510	1.54	154,150	208,302	1.32	162,632	251,997	1.52	
NAICS:[6]													
1992	540,573	836,902	1.53	242,002	378,619	1.57	147,261	196,914	1.31	151,310	261,369	1.67	168,261
1993	567,580	864,022	1.50	251,708	379,654	1.50	154,018	204,842	1.30	161,854	279,526	1.68	179,858
1994	610,253	927,253	1.46	269,843	399,833	1.44	164,575	221,978	1.29	175,835	305,442	1.66	194,638
1995	655,097	986,069	1.48	289,973	424,752	1.44	179,915	238,392	1.29	185,209	322,925	1.72	204,677
1996	687,350	1,005,417	1.46	299,766	430,441	1.43	190,362	241,050	1.27	197,222	333,926	1.67	217,463
1997	723,879	1,046,749	1.42	319,558	443,565	1.37	198,154	258,575	1.26	206,167	344,609	1.64	227,670
1998	742,837	1,078,652	1.43	324,984	448,934	1.39	202,260	272,449	1.31	215,592	357,269	1.62	238,278
1999	786,634	1,138,547	1.40	335,991	463,507	1.35	216,597	290,077	1.30	234,046	384,963	1.59	257,797
2000	834,325	1,196,993	1.41	350,715	481,951	1.35	234,546	308,906	1.29	249,063	406,730	1.59	274,518
2001	818,615	1,119,541	1.42	330,875	427,852	1.38	232,096	297,135	1.32	255,644	394,554	1.58	282,131
2002	823,714	1,139,673	1.36	326,227	422,883	1.28	236,294	300,813	1.25	261,194	415,977	1.55	288,845
2003	854,559	1,147,796	1.34	334,616	408,162	1.24	247,624	307,550	1.22	272,319	432,084	1.56	301,572
2004	925,277	1,240,354	1.30	359,081	440,559	1.19	276,213	338,542	1.17	289,983	461,253	1.56	321,217
2005	1,002,939	1,310,916	1.27	395,173	473,841	1.17	299,630	365,037	1.18	308,136	472,038	1.51	341,289
2006	1,065,569	1,405,709	1.28	417,963	523,573	1.20	324,142	395,634	1.18	323,464	486,502	1.49	358,818
2007	1,124,749	1,482,537	1.29	444,859	563,456	1.22	346,119	420,779	1.18	333,771	498,302	1.48	370,960
2008	1,154,682	1,474,215	1.32	457,189	558,969	1.28	367,564	436,423	1.21	329,930	478,823	1.51	368,110
2009	1,003,274	1,329,337	1.36	384,168	509,938	1.36	313,174	390,453	1.29	305,932	428,946	1.45	344,223
2009: Jan	987,107	1,456,120	1.48	378,408	553,700	1.46	305,636	432,529	1.42	303,063	469,891	1.55	341,617
Feb	992,262	1,432,637	1.44	381,006	544,227	1.43	308,505	425,041	1.38	302,751	463,369	1.53	341,390
Mar	971,434	1,411,982	1.45	373,041	536,541	1.44	300,489	416,943	1.39	297,904	458,498	1.54	336,207
Apr	973,357	1,393,526	1.43	373,090	530,312	1.42	301,970	411,072	1.36	298,297	452,142	1.52	336,671
May	975,508	1,376,902	1.41	370,431	525,392	1.42	304,669	407,175	1.34	300,408	444,335	1.48	338,785
June	989,712	1,357,275	1.37	376,929	517,394	1.37	307,704	400,173	1.30	305,079	439,708	1.44	343,411
July	997,809	1,343,452	1.35	381,862	513,340	1.34	310,693	395,259	1.27	305,254	434,853	1.42	343,518
Aug	1,010,215	1,324,053	1.31	383,721	509,353	1.33	313,554	389,962	1.24	312,940	424,738	1.36	351,128
Sept	1,011,367	1,319,439	1.30	390,032	506,088	1.30	316,318	386,281	1.22	305,017	427,070	1.40	343,179
Oct	1,023,258	1,325,619	1.30	394,253	508,967	1.29	319,244	388,562	1.22	309,761	428,090	1.38	347,880
Nov	1,044,587	1,330,575	1.27	400,731	510,192	1.27	330,005	392,549	1.19	313,851	427,834	1.36	352,231
Dec	1,056,059	1,329,337	1.26	408,429	509,938	1.25	332,897	390,453	1.17	314,733	428,946	1.36	352,888
2010: Jan	1,063,822	1,331,665	1.25	410,972	511,430	1.24	335,870	391,038	1.16	316,980	429,197	1.35	355,197
Feb	1,066,760	1,340,176	1.26	408,967	516,707	1.26	339,739	393,220	1.16	318,054	430,249	1.35	357,272
Mar	1,093,913	1,349,012	1.23	419,787	519,045	1.24	348,691	396,057	1.14	325,435	433,910	1.33	364,836
Apr	1,100,530	1,354,192	1.23	422,133	522,387	1.24	351,783	396,876	1.13	326,614	434,929	1.33	365,997
May	1,087,459	1,356,256	1.25	414,648	520,464	1.26	349,899	398,732	1.14	322,912	437,060	1.35	362,219
June	1,082,515	1,362,503	1.26	412,660	520,897	1.26	347,997	399,807	1.15	321,858	441,699	1.37	361,170
July	1,091,658	1,377,960	1.26	417,504	525,722	1.26	350,681	406,035	1.16	323,473	446,203	1.38	362,829
Aug	1,095,236	1,389,687	1.27	416,480	527,696	1.27	352,417	410,732	1.17	326,339	451,259	1.38	365,992
Sept	1,103,464	1,407,883	1.28	419,568	533,549	1.27	354,136	419,298	1.18	329,760	455,036	1.38	369,440
Oct	1,119,910	1,418,527	1.27	421,092	539,681	1.28	363,247	426,407	1.17	335,571	452,439	1.35	375,460
Nov[p]	1,133,114	1,421,557	1.25	424,518	543,771	1.28	370,124	425,538	1.15	338,472	452,248	1.34	378,578

[1] Excludes manufacturers' sales branches and offices.

[2] Annual data are averages of monthly not seasonally adjusted figures.

[3] Seasonally adjusted, end of period. Inventories beginning with January 1982 for manufacturing and December 1980 for wholesale and retail trade are not comparable with earlier periods.

[4] Inventory/sales ratio. Monthly inventories are inventories at the end of the month to sales for the month. Annual data beginning with 1982 are the average of monthly ratios for the year. Annual data for 1969–81 are the ratio of December inventories to monthly average sales for the year.

[5] Food services included on Standard Industrial Classification (SIC) basis and excluded on North American Industry Classification System (NAICS) basis. See last column for retail and food services sales.

[6] Effective in 2001, data classified based on NAICS. Data on NAICS basis available beginning with 1992. Earlier data based on SIC. Data on both NAICS and SIC basis include semiconductors.

Source: Department of Commerce (Bureau of the Census).

Table B–58. Manufacturers' shipments and inventories, 1969–2010

[Millions of dollars; monthly data seasonally adjusted]

Year or month	Shipments [1]			Inventories [2]								
					Durable goods industries				Nondurable goods industries			
	Total	Durable goods industries	Non-durable goods industries	Total	Total	Materials and supplies	Work in process	Finished goods	Total	Materials and supplies	Work in process	Finished goods
SIC: [3]												
1969	53,501	29,403	24,098	98,145	64,598	18,636	30,282	15,680	33,547	12,753	5,120	15,674
1970	52,805	28,156	24,649	101,599	66,651	19,149	29,745	17,757	34,948	13,168	5,271	16,509
1971	55,906	29,924	25,982	102,567	66,136	19,679	28,550	17,907	36,431	13,686	5,678	17,067
1972	63,027	33,987	29,040	108,121	70,067	20,807	30,713	18,547	38,054	14,677	5,998	17,379
1973	72,931	39,635	33,296	124,499	81,192	25,944	35,490	19,758	43,307	18,147	6,729	18,431
1974	84,790	44,173	40,617	157,625	101,493	35,070	42,530	23,893	56,132	23,744	8,189	24,199
1975	86,589	43,598	42,991	159,708	102,590	33,903	43,227	25,460	57,118	23,565	8,834	24,719
1976	98,797	50,623	48,174	174,636	111,988	37,457	46,074	28,457	62,648	25,847	9,929	26,872
1977	113,201	59,168	54,033	188,378	120,877	40,186	50,226	30,465	67,501	27,387	10,961	29,153
1978	126,905	67,731	59,174	211,691	138,181	45,198	58,848	34,135	73,510	29,619	12,085	31,806
1979	143,936	75,927	68,009	242,157	160,734	52,670	69,325	38,739	81,423	32,814	13,910	34,699
1980	154,391	77,419	76,972	265,215	174,788	55,113	76,945	42,670	90,427	36,606	15,884	37,937
1981	168,129	83,727	84,402	283,413	186,443	57,998	80,998	47,447	96,970	38,165	16,194	42,611
1982	163,351	79,212	84,139	311,852	200,444	59,136	86,707	54,601	111,408	44,039	18,612	48,757
1983	172,547	85,481	87,066	312,379	199,854	60,325	86,899	52,630	112,525	44,816	18,691	49,018
1984	190,682	97,940	92,742	339,516	221,330	66,031	98,251	57,048	118,186	45,692	19,328	53,166
1985	194,538	101,279	93,259	334,749	218,193	63,904	98,162	56,127	116,556	44,106	19,442	53,008
1986	194,657	103,238	91,419	322,654	211,997	61,331	97,000	53,666	110,657	42,335	18,124	50,198
1987	200,320	100,120	90,198	338,109	220,799	63,562	102,393	54,844	117,310	45,319	19,270	52,721
1988	224,619	118,458	106,161	369,374	242,468	69,611	112,958	59,899	126,906	46,394	20,559	56,951
1989	236,698	123,158	113,540	391,212	257,513	72,435	122,251	62,827	133,699	50,674	21,653	61,372
1990	242,686	123,776	118,910	405,073	263,209	73,559	124,130	65,520	141,864	52,645	22,817	66,402
1991	239,847	121,000	118,847	390,950	250,019	70,834	114,960	64,225	140,931	53,011	22,815	65,105
1992	250,394	128,489	121,905	382,510	238,105	69,459	104,424	64,222	144,405	54,007	23,532	66,866
NAICS: [3]												
1992	242,002	126,572	115,430	378,619	238,000	69,671	104,231	64,098	140,619	53,064	23,413	64,142
1993	251,708	133,712	117,996	379,654	238,716	72,632	102,031	64,053	140,938	54,192	23,399	63,347
1994	269,843	147,005	122,838	399,833	253,044	78,568	106,528	67,948	146,789	57,108	24,437	65,244
1995	289,973	158,568	131,405	424,752	267,315	85,521	106,620	75,174	157,437	60,751	25,781	70,905
1996	299,766	164,883	134,883	430,441	272,448	86,307	110,575	75,566	157,993	59,181	26,465	72,347
1997	319,558	178,949	140,610	443,565	281,042	92,312	109,908	78,822	162,523	60,231	28,505	73,787
1998	324,984	185,966	139,019	448,934	290,567	93,581	115,129	81,857	158,367	58,250	27,072	73,045
1999	335,991	193,895	142,096	463,507	296,456	97,873	113,991	84,592	167,051	61,106	28,770	77,175
2000	350,715	197,807	152,908	481,357	306,472	106,057	110,990	89,425	174,885	61,539	30,016	83,330
2001	330,875	181,201	149,674	427,852	267,628	91,200	93,814	82,614	160,224	55,821	27,052	77,351
2002	326,227	176,968	149,259	422,883	260,366	88,493	92,302	79,571	162,517	56,664	27,787	78,066
2003	334,616	178,549	156,067	408,162	246,823	82,277	88,615	75,931	161,339	56,996	26,960	77,383
2004	359,081	188,722	170,359	440,559	264,895	92,088	91,082	81,725	175,664	61,867	29,823	83,974
2005	395,173	202,070	193,103	473,841	283,756	98,500	98,743	86,513	190,085	67,022	32,764	90,299
2006	417,963	213,516	204,447	523,573	317,786	111,375	107,239	99,172	205,787	70,565	37,016	98,186
2007	444,859	224,653	220,206	563,456	335,615	116,487	118,366	100,762	227,841	75,513	45,064	107,264
2008	457,189	218,725	238,464	558,969	338,808	119,602	115,586	103,620	220,161	72,679	41,765	105,717
2009	384,168	183,154	201,014	509,938	295,335	101,878	106,969	86,488	214,603	71,790	45,580	97,233
2009: Jan	378,408	183,552	194,856	553,700	335,428	119,650	114,627	101,151	218,272	71,512	43,143	103,617
Feb	381,006	183,930	197,076	544,227	330,106	118,241	112,959	98,906	214,121	69,960	42,479	101,682
Mar	373,041	180,693	192,348	536,541	322,476	115,046	111,077	96,353	214,065	69,335	43,338	101,392
Apr	373,090	180,149	192,941	530,312	318,548	113,409	110,231	94,908	211,764	68,033	43,499	100,232
May	370,431	176,178	194,253	525,392	314,153	111,213	109,751	93,189	211,239	68,225	43,366	99,648
June	376,929	175,996	200,933	517,394	307,985	107,771	109,047	91,167	209,409	67,833	42,875	98,701
July	381,862	183,564	198,298	513,340	304,403	105,481	108,911	90,011	208,937	68,481	42,656	97,800
Aug	383,721	182,319	201,402	509,353	300,186	104,001	107,019	89,166	209,167	68,089	43,172	97,906
Sept	390,032	185,857	204,175	506,088	297,925	103,667	106,318	87,940	208,163	67,819	43,564	96,780
Oct	394,253	185,949	208,304	508,967	296,632	102,539	106,785	87,308	212,335	68,828	44,721	98,786
Nov	400,731	187,705	213,026	510,192	295,936	101,751	107,144	87,041	214,256	70,361	45,145	98,750
Dec	408,429	192,426	216,003	509,938	295,335	101,878	106,969	86,488	214,603	71,790	45,580	97,233
2010: Jan	410,972	192,141	218,831	511,430	295,440	101,416	107,365	86,659	215,990	71,656	45,083	99,251
Feb	408,967	189,328	219,639	516,707	297,545	102,277	108,468	86,800	219,162	73,418	46,132	99,612
Mar	419,787	193,305	226,482	519,565	299,463	102,888	109,211	87,364	219,582	73,497	46,474	99,611
Apr	422,133	197,099	225,034	522,387	301,985	103,354	110,727	87,904	220,402	72,568	46,740	101,094
May	414,648	195,799	218,849	520,464	305,591	104,821	111,791	88,979	214,873	70,359	44,792	99,722
June	412,660	196,120	216,540	520,897	309,396	106,228	113,114	90,054	211,501	69,609	43,760	98,132
July	417,504	201,103	216,401	525,722	311,100	105,914	113,995	91,191	214,622	71,174	44,083	99,365
Aug	416,480	198,420	218,060	527,696	313,187	106,014	115,068	92,105	214,509	70,549	44,337	99,623
Sept	419,568	198,431	221,137	533,549	315,405	106,184	116,435	92,786	218,144	72,120	44,941	101,083
Oct	421,092	196,626	224,466	539,681	317,215	106,634	117,102	93,479	222,466	73,183	46,437	102,846
Nov [p]	424,518	196,332	228,186	543,771	319,201	107,113	118,128	93,960	224,570	74,344	46,577	103,649

[1] Annual data are averages of monthly not seasonally adjusted figures.
[2] Seasonally adjusted, end of period. Data beginning with 1982 are not comparable with earlier data.
[3] Effective in 2001, data classified based on North American Industry Classification System (NAICS). Data on NAICS basis available beginning with 1992. Earlier data based on Standard Industrial Classification (SIC). Data on both NAICS and SIC basis include semiconductors.

Source: Department of Commerce (Bureau of the Census).

TABLE B–59. Manufacturers' new and unfilled orders, 1969–2010

[Amounts in millions of dollars; monthly data seasonally adjusted]

Year or month	New orders [1]				Unfilled orders [2]			Unfilled orders to shipments ratio [2]		
	Total	Durable goods industries		Nondurable goods industries	Total	Durable goods industries	Nondurable goods industries	Total	Durable goods industries	Nondurable goods industries
		Total	Capital goods, nondefense							
SIC: [3]										
1969	53,990	29,876	7,046	24,114	114,341	110,161	4,180	3.71	4.45	0.69
1970	52,022	27,340	6,072	24,682	105,008	100,412	4,596	3.61	4.36	.76
1971	55,921	29,905	6,682	26,016	105,247	100,225	5,022	3.32	4.00	.76
1972	64,182	35,038	7,745	29,144	119,349	113,034	6,315	3.26	3.85	.86
1973	76,003	42,627	9,926	33,376	156,561	149,204	7,357	3.80	4.51	.91
1974	87,327	46,862	11,594	40,465	187,043	181,519	5,524	4.09	4.93	.62
1975	85,139	41,957	9,886	43,181	169,546	161,664	7,882	3.69	4.45	.82
1976	99,513	51,307	11,490	48,206	178,128	169,857	8,271	3.24	3.88	.74
1977	115,109	61,035	13,681	54,073	202,024	193,323	8,701	3.24	3.85	.71
1978	131,629	72,278	17,588	59,351	259,169	248,281	10,888	3.57	4.20	.81
1979	147,604	79,483	21,154	68,121	303,593	291,321	12,272	3.89	4.62	.82
1980	156,359	79,392	21,135	76,967	327,416	315,202	12,214	3.85	4.58	.75
1981	168,025	83,654	21,806	84,371	326,547	314,707	11,840	3.87	4.68	.69
1982	162,140	78,064	19,213	84,077	311,887	300,798	11,089	3.84	4.74	.62
1983	175,451	88,140	19,624	87,311	347,273	333,114	14,159	3.53	4.29	.69
1984	192,879	100,164	23,669	92,715	373,529	359,651	13,878	3.60	4.37	.64
1985	195,706	102,356	24,545	93,351	387,196	372,097	15,099	3.67	4.47	.68
1986	195,204	103,647	23,982	91,557	393,515	376,699	16,816	3.59	4.41	.70
1987	209,389	110,809	26,094	98,579	430,426	408,688	21,738	3.63	4.43	.83
1988	228,270	122,076	31,108	106,194	474,154	452,150	22,004	3.64	4.46	.76
1989	239,572	126,055	32,988	113,516	508,849	487,098	21,751	3.96	4.85	.77
1990	244,507	125,583	33,331	118,924	531,131	509,124	22,007	4.15	5.15	.76
1991	238,805	119,849	30,471	118,957	519,199	495,802	23,397	4.08	5.07	.79
1992	248,212	126,308	31,524	121,905	492,893	469,381	23,512	3.51	4.30	.75
NAICS: [3]										
1992	....	....	....	....	451,163	....	....	5.14	....	....
1993	246,668	128,672	40,681	....	425,824	....	....	4.66	....	....
1994	266,641	143,803	45,175	....	434,707	....	....	4.21	....	....
1995	285,542	154,137	51,011	....	447,041	....	....	3.97	....	....
1996	297,282	162,399	54,066	....	488,282	....	....	4.14	....	....
1997	314,986	174,377	60,697	....	512,591	....	....	4.04	....	....
1998	317,345	178,327	62,133	....	495,861	....	....	3.97	....	....
1999	329,770	187,674	64,392	....	505,300	....	....	3.76	....	....
2000	346,789	193,881	69,278	....	549,193	....	....	3.87	....	....
2001	322,736	173,062	58,240	....	514,132	....	....	4.21	....	....
2002	316,835	167,577	51,858	....	462,279	....	....	4.05	....	....
2003	330,432	174,366	53,086	....	478,545	....	....	3.92	....	....
2004	354,655	184,296	56,179	....	497,801	....	....	3.89	....	....
2005	395,383	202,280	65,849	....	574,104	....	....	3.85	....	....
2006	419,417	214,970	71,713	....	661,749	....	....	4.18	....	....
2007	456,124	235,918	84,340	....	868,116	....	....	4.80	....	....
2008	453,583	215,118	73,685	....	892,699	....	....	5.73	....	....
2009	371,038	170,024	53,799	....	793,288	....	....	6.20	....	....
2009: Jan	357,692	162,836	51,431	....	876,377	....	....	6.54	....	....
Feb	362,261	165,185	51,066	....	861,357	....	....	6.39	....	....
Mar	352,850	160,502	49,918	....	845,062	....	....	6.39	....	....
Apr	356,003	163,062	48,316	....	833,134	....	....	6.41	....	....
May	361,322	167,069	53,791	....	828,981	....	....	6.49	....	....
June	365,278	164,345	53,264	....	820,690	....	....	6.33	....	....
July	374,824	176,526	59,075	....	819,234	....	....	6.18	....	....
Aug	373,332	171,930	53,579	....	814,274	....	....	6.19	....	....
Sept	381,676	177,501	56,574	....	810,520	....	....	5.97	....	....
Oct	385,773	177,469	57,481	....	807,298	....	....	5.99	....	....
Nov	390,090	177,064	56,072	....	801,847	....	....	5.87	....	....
Dec	394,645	178,642	55,795	....	793,288	....	....	5.63	....	....
2010: Jan	406,306	187,475	59,563	....	794,513	....	....	5.72	....	....
Feb	407,985	188,346	64,937	....	798,552	....	....	5.76	....	....
Mar	415,012	188,530	60,600	....	797,869	....	....	5.60	....	....
Apr	419,055	194,021	65,483	....	800,948	....	....	5.59	....	....
May	411,469	192,620	65,218	....	803,078	....	....	5.61	....	....
June	408,867	192,327	65,965	....	803,897	....	....	5.59	....	....
July	411,101	194,700	65,505	....	804,173	....	....	5.53	....	....
Aug	411,259	193,199	66,371	....	805,524	....	....	5.61	....	....
Sept	423,713	202,576	74,093	....	816,371	....	....	5.67	....	....
Oct	420,691	196,225	71,307	....	822,064	....	....	5.75	....	....
Nov [p]	423,845	195,659	66,465	....	826,863	....	....	5.75	....	....

[1] Annual data are averages of monthly not seasonally adjusted figures.

[2] Unfilled orders are seasonally adjusted, end of period. Ratios are unfilled orders at end of period to shipments for period (excludes industries with no unfilled orders). Annual ratios relate to seasonally adjusted data for December.

[3] Effective in 2001, data classified based on North American Industry Classification System (NAICS). Data on NAICS basis available beginning with 1992. Earlier data based on the Standard Industrial Classification (SIC). Data on SIC basis include semiconductors. Data on NAICS basis do not include semiconductors.

Note: For NAICS basis data beginning with 1992, because there are no unfilled orders for manufacturers' nondurable goods, manufacturers' nondurable new orders and nondurable shipments are the same (see Table B–58).

Source: Department of Commerce (Bureau of the Census).

PRICES

TABLE B-60. Consumer price indexes for major expenditure classes, 1967–2010

[For all urban consumers; 1982–84=100, except as noted]

Year or month	All items	Food and beverages		Apparel	Housing	Transportation	Medical care	Recreation[2]	Education and communication[2]	Other goods and services	Energy[3]
		Total[1]	Food								
1967	33.4	35.0	34.1	51.0	30.8	33.3	28.2	....	....	35.1	23.8
1968	34.8	36.2	35.3	53.7	32.0	34.3	29.9	....	....	36.9	24.2
1969	36.7	38.1	37.1	56.8	34.0	35.7	31.9	....	....	38.7	24.8
1970	38.8	40.1	39.2	59.2	36.4	37.5	34.0	....	....	40.9	25.5
1971	40.5	41.4	40.4	61.1	38.0	39.5	36.1	....	....	42.9	26.5
1972	41.8	43.1	42.1	62.3	39.4	39.9	37.3	....	....	44.7	27.2
1973	44.4	48.8	48.2	64.6	41.2	41.2	38.8	....	....	46.4	29.4
1974	49.3	55.5	55.1	69.4	45.8	45.8	42.4	....	....	49.8	38.1
1975	53.8	60.2	59.8	72.5	50.7	50.1	47.5	....	....	53.9	42.1
1976	56.9	62.1	61.6	75.2	53.8	55.1	52.0	....	....	57.0	45.1
1977	60.6	65.8	65.5	78.6	57.4	59.0	57.0	....	....	60.4	49.4
1978	65.2	72.2	72.0	81.4	62.4	61.7	61.8	....	....	64.3	52.5
1979	72.6	79.9	79.9	84.9	70.1	70.5	67.5	....	....	68.9	65.7
1980	82.4	86.7	86.8	90.9	81.1	83.1	74.9	....	....	75.2	86.0
1981	90.9	93.5	93.6	95.3	90.4	93.2	82.9	....	....	82.6	97.7
1982	96.5	97.3	97.4	97.8	96.9	97.0	92.5	....	....	91.1	99.2
1983	99.6	99.5	99.4	100.2	99.5	99.3	100.6	....	....	101.1	99.9
1984	103.9	103.2	103.2	102.1	103.6	103.7	106.8	....	....	107.9	100.9
1985	107.6	105.6	105.6	105.0	107.7	106.4	113.5	....	....	114.5	101.6
1986	109.6	109.1	109.0	105.9	110.9	102.3	122.0	....	....	121.4	88.2
1987	113.6	113.5	113.5	110.6	114.2	105.4	130.1	....	....	128.5	88.6
1988	118.3	118.2	118.2	115.4	118.5	108.7	138.6	....	....	137.0	89.3
1989	124.0	124.9	125.1	118.6	123.0	114.1	149.3	....	....	147.7	94.3
1990	130.7	132.1	132.4	124.1	128.5	120.5	162.8	....	....	159.0	102.1
1991	136.2	136.8	136.3	128.7	133.6	123.8	177.0	....	....	171.6	102.5
1992	140.3	138.7	137.9	131.9	137.5	126.5	190.1	....	....	183.3	103.0
1993	144.5	141.6	140.9	133.7	141.2	130.4	201.4	90.7	85.5	192.9	104.2
1994	148.2	144.9	144.3	133.4	144.8	134.3	211.0	92.7	88.8	198.5	104.6
1995	152.4	148.9	148.4	132.0	148.5	139.1	220.5	94.5	92.2	206.9	105.2
1996	156.9	153.7	153.3	131.7	152.8	143.0	228.2	97.4	95.3	215.4	110.1
1997	160.5	157.7	157.3	132.9	156.8	144.3	234.6	99.6	98.4	224.8	111.5
1998	163.0	161.1	160.7	133.0	160.4	141.6	242.1	101.1	100.3	237.7	102.9
1999	166.6	164.6	164.1	131.3	163.9	144.4	250.6	102.0	101.2	258.3	106.6
2000	172.2	168.4	167.8	129.6	169.6	153.3	260.8	103.3	102.5	271.1	124.6
2001	177.1	173.6	173.1	127.3	176.4	154.3	272.8	104.9	105.2	282.6	129.3
2002	179.9	176.8	176.2	124.0	180.3	152.9	285.6	106.2	107.9	293.2	121.7
2003	184.0	180.5	180.0	120.9	184.8	157.6	297.1	107.5	109.8	298.7	136.5
2004	188.9	186.6	186.2	120.4	189.5	163.1	310.1	108.6	111.6	304.7	151.4
2005	195.3	191.2	190.7	119.5	195.7	173.9	323.2	109.4	113.7	313.4	177.1
2006	201.6	195.7	195.2	119.5	203.2	180.9	336.2	110.9	116.8	321.7	196.9
2007	207.342	203.300	202.916	118.998	209.586	184.682	351.054	111.443	119.577	333.328	207.723
2008	215.303	214.225	214.106	118.907	216.264	195.549	364.065	113.254	123.631	345.381	236.666
2009	214.537	218.249	217.955	120.078	217.057	179.252	375.613	114.272	127.393	368.586	193.126
2010	218.056	219.984	219.625	119.503	216.256	193.396	388.436	113.313	129.919	381.291	211.449
2009: Jan	211.143	219.729	219.675	114.764	216.928	166.738	369.830	113.822	126.151	350.259	174.622
Feb	212.193	219.333	219.205	118.825	217.180	169.542	372.405	114.461	126.190	351.223	178.741
Mar	212.709	218.794	218.600	122.545	217.374	169.647	373.189	114.625	126.187	361.156	177.454
Apr	213.240	218.364	218.162	123.208	217.126	171.987	374.170	114.261	126.273	370.606	179.704
May	213.856	218.076	217.826	121.751	216.971	175.997	375.026	114.264	126.467	369.901	186.909
June	215.693	218.030	217.740	118.799	218.071	183.735	375.093	114.643	126.519	370.595	205.408
July	215.351	217.608	217.257	115.620	218.085	182.798	375.739	114.619	126.914	372.894	201.938
Aug	215.834	217.701	217.350	117.130	217.827	184.386	376.537	114.755	128.128	372.699	204.971
Sept	215.969	217.617	217.218	122.476	217.718	183.932	377.727	114.629	129.035	374.219	202.243
Oct	216.177	217.957	217.526	123.998	216.612	185.362	378.552	114.157	129.128	375.444	199.198
Nov	216.330	217.733	217.265	122.465	215.808	188.587	379.575	113.820	128.845	376.702	204.026
Dec	215.949	218.049	217.637	119.357	215.523	188.318	379.516	113.212	128.883	377.330	202.301
2010: Jan	216.687	219.223	218.874	116.678	215.925	190.512	382.688	113.310	129.072	377.652	208.026
Feb	216.741	219.140	218.778	118.869	215.841	189.577	385.907	113.345	129.105	377.992	204.455
Mar	217.631	219.378	219.032	122.073	216.023	192.130	387.142	113.339	129.236	378.808	209.999
Apr	218.009	219.536	219.218	122.143	215.798	193.994	387.703	113.781	129.344	378.911	212.977
May	218.178	219.693	219.374	121.006	215.981	194.761	387.762	113.684	129.270	379.714	214.363
June	217.965	219.562	219.218	118.319	216.778	192.651	388.199	113.802	129.263	380.926	211.660
July	218.011	219.539	219.121	115.248	217.076	193.038	387.898	113.689	129.586	383.247	212.372
Aug	218.312	219.877	219.491	116.667	216.976	193.454	388.467	113.521	130.599	383.685	212.663
Sept	218.439	220.586	220.216	121.011	216.602	192.412	390.616	113.120	131.154	383.663	210.003
Oct	218.711	221.005	220.616	122.454	216.100	194.283	391.240	112.984	130.959	382.764	210.947
Nov	218.803	220.991	220.617	121.498	215.830	195.659	391.660	112.839	130.894	383.633	211.970
Dec	219.179	221.278	220.946	118.071	216.142	198.280	391.946	112.345	130.548	384.502	217.953

[1] Includes alcoholic beverages, not shown separately.
[2] December 1997=100.
[3] Household energy—gas (piped), electricity, fuel oil, etc.—and motor fuel. Motor oil, coolant, etc. also included through 1982.

Note: Data beginning with 1983 incorporate a rental equivalence measure for homeowners' costs.
Series reflect changes in composition and renaming beginning in 1998, and formula and methodology changes beginning in 1999.

Source: Department of Labor (Bureau of Labor Statistics).

Table B-61. Consumer price indexes for selected expenditure classes, 1967–2010

[For all urban consumers; 1982–84=100, except as noted]

Year or month	Food and beverages Total[1]	Food Total	Food At home	Food Away from home	Housing Total[2]	Shelter Total[2]	Shelter Rent of primary residence	Shelter Owners' equivalent rent of residences[3,4]	Fuels and utilities Total[2]	Household energy Total[2]	Household energy Gas (piped) and electricity
1967	35.0	34.1	35.1	31.3	30.8	28.8	42.2	....	27.1	21.4	23.7
1968	36.2	35.3	36.3	32.9	32.0	30.1	43.3	....	27.4	21.7	23.9
1969	38.1	37.1	38.0	34.9	34.0	32.6	44.7	....	28.0	22.1	24.3
1970	40.1	39.2	39.9	37.5	36.4	35.5	46.5	....	29.1	23.1	25.4
1971	41.4	40.4	40.9	39.4	38.0	37.0	48.7	....	31.1	24.7	27.1
1972	43.1	42.1	42.7	41.0	39.4	38.7	50.4	....	32.5	25.7	28.5
1973	48.8	48.2	49.7	44.2	41.2	40.5	52.5	....	34.3	27.5	29.9
1974	55.5	55.1	57.1	49.8	45.8	44.4	55.2	....	40.7	34.4	34.5
1975	60.2	59.8	61.8	54.5	50.7	48.8	58.0	....	45.4	39.4	40.1
1976	62.1	61.6	63.1	58.2	53.8	51.5	61.1	....	49.4	43.3	44.7
1977	65.8	65.5	66.8	62.6	57.4	54.9	64.8	....	54.7	49.0	50.5
1978	72.2	72.0	73.8	68.3	62.4	60.5	69.3	....	58.5	53.0	55.0
1979	79.9	79.9	81.8	75.9	70.1	68.9	74.3	....	64.8	61.3	61.0
1980	86.7	86.8	88.4	83.4	81.1	81.0	80.9	....	75.4	74.8	71.4
1981	93.5	93.6	94.8	90.9	90.4	90.5	87.9	....	86.4	87.2	81.9
1982	97.3	97.4	98.1	95.8	96.9	96.9	94.6	....	94.9	95.6	93.2
1983	99.5	99.4	99.1	100.0	99.5	99.1	100.1	102.5	100.2	100.5	101.5
1984	103.2	103.2	102.8	104.2	103.6	104.0	105.3	107.3	104.8	104.0	105.4
1985	105.6	105.6	104.3	108.3	107.7	109.8	111.8	113.2	106.5	104.5	107.1
1986	109.1	109.0	107.3	112.5	110.9	115.8	118.3	119.4	104.1	99.2	105.7
1987	113.5	113.5	111.9	117.0	114.2	121.3	123.1	124.8	103.0	97.3	103.8
1988	118.2	118.2	116.6	121.8	118.5	127.1	127.8	131.1	104.4	98.0	104.6
1989	124.9	125.1	124.2	127.4	123.0	132.8	132.8	137.4	107.8	100.9	107.5
1990	132.1	132.4	132.3	133.4	128.5	140.0	138.4	144.8	111.6	104.5	109.3
1991	136.8	136.3	135.8	137.9	133.6	146.3	143.3	150.4	115.3	106.7	112.6
1992	138.7	137.9	136.8	140.7	137.5	151.2	146.9	155.5	117.8	108.1	114.8
1993	141.6	140.9	140.1	143.2	141.2	155.7	150.3	160.5	121.3	111.2	118.5
1994	144.9	144.3	144.1	145.7	144.8	160.5	154.0	165.8	122.8	111.7	119.2
1995	148.9	148.4	148.8	149.0	148.5	165.7	157.8	171.3	123.7	111.5	119.2
1996	153.7	153.3	154.3	152.7	152.8	171.0	162.0	176.8	127.5	115.2	122.1
1997	157.7	157.3	158.1	157.0	156.8	176.3	166.7	181.9	130.8	117.9	125.1
1998	161.1	160.7	161.1	161.1	160.4	182.1	172.1	187.8	128.5	113.7	121.2
1999	164.6	164.1	164.2	165.1	163.9	187.3	177.5	192.9	128.8	113.5	120.9
2000	168.4	167.8	167.9	169.0	169.6	193.4	183.9	198.7	137.9	122.8	128.0
2001	173.6	173.1	173.4	173.9	176.4	200.6	192.1	206.3	150.2	135.4	142.4
2002	176.8	176.2	175.6	178.3	180.3	208.1	199.7	214.7	143.6	127.2	134.4
2003	180.5	180.0	179.4	182.1	184.8	213.1	205.5	219.9	154.5	138.2	145.0
2004	186.6	186.2	186.2	187.5	189.5	218.8	211.0	224.9	161.9	144.4	150.6
2005	191.2	190.7	189.8	193.4	195.7	224.4	217.3	230.2	179.0	161.6	166.5
2006	195.7	195.2	193.1	199.4	203.2	232.1	225.1	238.2	194.7	177.1	182.1
2007	203.300	202.916	201.245	206.659	209.586	240.611	234.679	246.235	200.632	181.744	186.262
2008	214.225	214.106	214.125	215.769	216.264	246.666	243.271	252.426	220.018	200.808	202.212
2009	218.249	217.955	215.124	223.272	217.057	249.354	248.812	256.610	210.696	188.113	193.563
2010	219.984	219.625	215.836	226.114	216.256	248.396	249.385	256.584	214.187	189.286	192.886
2009: Jan	219.729	219.675	219.744	221.319	216.928	248.292	247.974	255.500	215.232	194.149	199.791
Feb	219.333	219.205	218.389	221.968	217.180	248.878	248.305	255.779	213.520	192.168	197.886
Mar	218.794	218.600	217.110	222.216	217.374	249.597	248.639	256.321	210.501	188.736	194.752
Apr	218.364	218.162	215.783	222.905	217.126	249.855	248.899	256.622	207.175	184.903	190.686
May	218.076	217.826	215.088	223.023	216.971	249.779	249.069	256.875	206.358	183.783	189.619
June	218.030	217.740	214.824	223.163	218.071	250.243	249.092	256.981	212.677	190.647	196.754
July	217.608	217.257	213.815	223.345	218.085	250.310	248.994	256.872	212.961	190.534	196.767
Aug	217.701	217.350	213.722	223.675	217.827	250.248	249.029	257.155	212.661	189.735	195.475
Sept	217.617	217.218	213.227	224.003	217.178	249.501	248.965	256.865	211.618	188.509	194.176
Oct	217.957	217.526	213.605	224.224	216.612	249.474	248.888	256.890	207.937	184.146	188.963
Nov	217.733	217.265	212.816	224.633	215.808	248.211	248.886	256.731	208.955	185.165	189.166
Dec	218.049	217.637	213.359	224.789	215.523	247.863	248.999	256.727	208.760	184.886	188.724
2010: Jan	219.223	218.874	215.404	224.916	215.925	247.950	249.144	256.591	211.381	187.330	190.439
Feb	219.140	218.778	215.118	225.081	215.841	248.001	249.017	256.483	210.819	186.345	189.549
Mar	219.378	219.032	215.623	224.991	216.023	248.052	249.089	256.272	212.295	187.864	191.280
Apr	219.536	219.218	215.737	225.276	215.798	248.031	249.012	256.170	211.726	187.054	190.284
May	219.693	219.374	215.793	225.573	215.981	248.100	248.925	256.163	212.773	188.017	191.628
June	219.562	219.218	215.361	225.797	216.778	248.470	248.999	256.352	217.820	193.678	198.207
July	219.539	219.121	215.256	225.710	217.076	248.677	249.126	256.395	219.614	195.268	200.177
Aug	219.877	219.491	215.382	226.422	216.976	248.595	249.024	256.509	219.602	194.865	199.632
Sept	220.586	220.216	216.161	227.075	216.602	248.522	249.368	256.590	217.695	192.635	197.049
Oct	221.005	220.616	216.698	227.287	216.100	248.646	249.618	256.823	213.031	187.271	190.603
Nov	220.991	220.617	216.538	227.512	215.830	248.738	250.317	257.202	210.978	184.764	187.335
Dec	221.278	220.946	216.955	227.722	216.142	248.972	250.986	257.452	212.505	186.338	188.443

[1] Includes alcoholic beverages, not shown separately.
[2] Includes other items not shown separately.
[3] December 1982=100.
[4] Beginning January 2010, includes expenditure weight for second homes. Prior data are for primary residence only.

See next page for continuation of table.

[For all urban consumers; 1982-84=100, except as noted]

Year or month	Transportation							Medical care		
	Total	Private transportation					Public trans-porta-tion	Total	Medical care com-modities	Medical care services
		Total [2]	New vehicles		Used cars and trucks	Motor fuel				
			Total [2]	New cars						
1967	33.3	33.8	49.3	49.3	29.9	26.4	27.4	28.2	44.9	26.0
1968	34.3	34.8	50.7	50.7	....	26.8	28.7	29.9	45.0	27.9
1969	35.7	36.0	51.5	51.5	30.9	27.6	30.9	31.9	45.4	30.2
1970	37.5	37.5	53.1	53.0	31.2	27.9	35.2	34.0	46.5	32.3
1971	39.5	39.4	55.3	55.2	33.0	28.1	37.8	36.1	47.3	34.7
1972	39.9	39.7	54.8	54.7	33.1	28.4	39.3	37.3	47.4	35.9
1973	41.2	41.0	54.8	54.8	35.2	31.2	39.7	38.8	47.5	37.5
1974	45.8	46.2	58.0	57.9	36.7	42.2	40.6	42.4	49.2	41.4
1975	50.1	50.6	63.0	62.9	43.8	45.1	43.5	47.5	53.3	46.6
1976	55.1	55.6	67.0	66.9	50.3	47.0	47.8	52.0	56.5	51.3
1977	59.0	59.7	70.5	70.4	54.7	49.7	50.0	57.0	60.2	56.4
1978	61.7	62.5	75.9	75.8	55.8	51.8	51.5	61.8	64.4	61.2
1979	70.5	71.7	81.9	81.8	60.2	70.1	54.9	67.5	69.0	67.2
1980	83.1	84.2	88.5	88.4	62.3	97.4	69.0	74.9	75.4	74.8
1981	93.2	93.8	93.9	93.7	76.9	108.5	85.6	82.9	83.7	82.8
1982	97.0	97.1	97.5	97.4	88.8	102.8	94.9	92.5	92.3	92.6
1983	99.3	99.3	99.9	99.9	98.7	99.4	99.5	100.6	100.2	100.7
1984	103.7	103.6	102.6	102.8	112.5	97.9	105.7	106.8	107.5	106.7
1985	106.4	106.2	106.1	106.1	113.7	98.7	110.5	113.5	115.2	113.2
1986	102.3	101.2	110.6	110.6	108.8	77.1	117.0	122.0	122.8	121.9
1987	105.4	104.2	114.4	114.6	113.1	80.2	121.1	130.1	131.0	130.0
1988	108.7	107.6	116.5	116.9	118.0	80.9	123.3	138.6	139.9	138.3
1989	114.1	112.9	119.2	119.2	120.4	88.5	129.5	149.3	150.8	148.9
1990	120.5	118.8	121.4	121.0	117.6	101.2	142.6	162.8	163.4	162.7
1991	123.8	121.9	126.0	125.3	118.1	99.4	148.9	177.0	176.8	177.1
1992	126.5	124.6	129.2	128.4	123.2	99.0	151.4	190.1	188.1	190.5
1993	130.4	127.5	132.7	131.5	133.9	98.0	167.0	201.4	195.0	202.9
1994	134.3	131.4	137.6	136.0	141.7	98.5	172.0	211.0	200.7	213.4
1995	139.1	136.3	141.0	139.0	156.5	100.0	175.9	220.5	204.5	224.2
1996	143.0	140.0	143.7	141.4	157.0	106.3	181.9	228.2	210.4	232.4
1997	144.3	141.0	144.3	141.7	151.1	106.2	186.7	234.6	215.3	239.1
1998	141.6	137.9	143.4	140.7	150.6	92.2	190.3	242.1	221.8	246.8
1999	144.4	140.5	142.9	139.6	152.0	100.7	197.7	250.6	230.7	255.1
2000	153.3	149.1	142.8	139.6	155.8	129.3	209.6	260.8	238.1	266.0
2001	154.3	150.0	142.1	138.9	158.7	124.7	210.6	272.8	247.6	278.8
2002	152.9	148.8	140.0	137.3	152.0	116.6	207.4	285.6	256.4	292.9
2003	157.6	153.6	137.9	134.7	142.9	135.8	209.3	297.1	262.8	306.0
2004	163.1	159.4	137.1	133.9	133.3	160.4	209.1	310.1	269.3	321.3
2005	173.9	170.2	137.9	135.2	139.4	195.7	217.3	323.2	276.0	336.7
2006	180.9	177.0	137.6	136.4	140.0	221.0	226.6	336.2	285.9	350.6
2007	184.682	180.778	136.254	135.865	135.747	239.070	230.002	351.054	289.999	369.302
2008	195.549	191.039	134.194	135.401	133.951	279.652	250.549	364.065	296.045	384.943
2009	179.252	174.762	135.623	136.685	126.973	201.978	236.348	375.613	305.108	397.299
2010	193.396	188.747	138.005	138.094	143.128	239.178	251.351	388.436	314.717	411.208
2009: Jan	166.738	161.788	133.273	135.637	124.863	156.604	234.394	369.830	299.998	391.365
Feb	169.542	164.871	134.186	135.984	122.837	167.395	231.529	372.405	302.184	394.047
Mar	169.647	165.023	134.611	135.947	121.061	168.404	230.735	373.189	302.908	394.837
Apr	171.987	167.516	134.863	136.037	121.213	177.272	229.827	374.170	303.979	395.753
May	175.997	171.757	135.162	136.172	122.650	193.609	228.878	375.026	304.697	396.648
June	183.735	179.649	135.719	136.486	124.323	225.021	232.540	375.093	304.683	396.750
July	182.798	178.330	136.055	136.844	125.061	217.860	238.932	375.739	304.229	397.868
Aug	184.386	179.987	134.080	134.666	128.028	225.089	238.997	376.537	305.797	398.303
Sept	183.932	179.466	134.576	135.041	129.369	220.690	239.855	377.727	307.671	399.160
Oct	185.362	180.896	137.268	137.851	132.689	219.015	241.060	378.552	308.379	400.015
Nov	188.587	184.099	138.831	139.821	134.173	228.050	244.226	379.575	308.546	401.392
Dec	188.318	183.766	138.857	139.728	137.406	224.730	245.203	379.516	308.221	401.452
2010: Jan	190.512	186.308	138.743	139.290	139.174	234.106	241.058	382.688	310.494	404.937
Feb	189.577	185.274	138.851	139.198	140.218	227.674	241.967	385.907	312.864	408.447
Mar	192.130	187.796	138.600	138.712	140.797	237.671	244.766	387.142	314.023	409.687
Apr	193.994	189.503	138.174	138.170	141.315	244.801	249.135	387.703	314.535	410.256
May	194.761	190.071	137.750	137.896	142.537	246.671	253.275	387.762	314.923	410.173
June	192.651	187.593	137.503	137.759	144.399	234.868	257.825	388.199	314.888	410.802
July	193.038	188.028	137.323	137.462	146.379	234.642	257.337	387.898	314.113	410.710
Aug	193.454	188.616	137.119	137.180	147.909	235.690	254.717	388.467	314.881	411.182
Sept	192.412	187.646	137.365	137.423	146.065	232.518	252.525	390.616	315.804	413.807
Oct	194.283	189.674	137.849	137.880	144.040	240.303	251.435	391.240	316.082	414.564
Nov	195.659	190.915	138.222	138.015	142.250	245.165	254.995	391.660	316.794	414.850
Dec	198.280	193.545	138.567	138.147	142.454	256.025	257.172	391.946	317.199	415.079

Source: Department of Labor (Bureau of Labor Statistics).

TABLE B–62. Consumer price indexes for commodities, services, and special groups, 1967–2010

[For all urban consumers; 1982–84=100, except as noted]

Year or month	All items (CPI-U)[1]	Commodities		Services	Special indexes				All items		
		All commodities	Commodities less food		All items less food	All items less energy	All items less food and energy	All items less medical care	CPI-U-X1 (Dec. 1982 = 97.6)[2]	CPI-U-RS (Dec. 1977 = 100)[3]	C-CPI-U (Dec. 1999 = 100)[4]
1967	33.4	36.8	38.6	28.8	33.4	34.4	34.7	33.7	36.3		
1968	34.8	38.1	40.0	30.3	34.9	35.9	36.3	35.1	37.7		
1969	36.7	39.9	41.7	32.4	36.8	38.0	38.4	37.0	39.4		
1970	38.8	41.7	43.4	35.0	39.0	40.3	40.8	39.2	41.3		
1971	40.5	43.2	45.1	37.0	40.8	42.0	42.7	40.8	43.1		
1972	41.8	44.5	46.1	38.4	42.0	43.4	44.0	42.1	44.4		
1973	44.4	47.8	47.7	40.1	43.7	46.1	45.6	44.8	47.2		
1974	49.3	53.5	52.8	43.8	48.0	50.6	49.4	49.8	51.9		
1975	53.8	58.2	57.6	48.0	52.5	55.1	53.9	54.3	56.2		
1976	56.9	60.7	60.5	52.0	56.0	58.2	57.4	57.2	59.4		
1977	60.6	64.2	63.8	56.0	59.6	61.9	61.0	60.8	63.2		
1978	65.2	68.8	67.5	60.8	63.9	66.7	65.5	65.4	67.5	104.4	
1979	72.6	76.6	75.3	67.5	71.2	73.4	71.9	72.9	74.0	114.4	
1980	82.4	86.0	85.7	77.9	81.5	81.9	80.8	82.8	82.3	127.1	
1981	90.9	93.2	93.1	88.1	90.4	90.1	89.2	91.4	90.1	139.2	
1982	96.5	97.0	96.9	96.0	96.3	96.1	95.8	96.8	95.6	147.6	
1983	99.6	99.8	100.0	99.4	99.7	99.6	99.6	99.6	99.6	153.9	
1984	103.9	103.2	103.1	104.6	104.0	104.3	104.6	103.7	103.9	160.2	
1985	107.6	105.4	105.2	109.9	108.0	108.4	109.1	107.2	107.6	165.7	
1986	109.6	104.4	101.7	115.4	109.8	112.6	113.5	108.8	109.6	168.7	
1987	113.6	107.7	104.3	120.2	113.6	117.2	118.2	112.6	113.6	174.4	
1988	118.3	111.5	107.7	125.7	118.3	122.3	123.4	117.0	118.3	180.8	
1989	124.0	116.7	112.0	131.9	123.7	128.1	129.0	122.4	124.0	188.6	
1990	130.7	122.8	117.4	139.2	130.3	134.7	135.5	128.8	130.7	198.0	
1991	136.2	126.6	121.3	146.3	136.1	140.9	142.1	133.8	136.2	205.1	
1992	140.3	129.1	124.2	152.0	140.8	145.4	147.3	137.5	140.3	210.3	
1993	144.5	131.5	126.3	157.9	145.1	150.0	152.2	141.2	144.5	215.5	
1994	148.2	133.8	127.9	163.1	149.0	154.1	156.5	144.7	148.2	220.1	
1995	152.4	136.4	129.8	168.7	153.1	158.7	161.2	148.6	152.4	225.4	
1996	156.9	139.9	132.6	174.1	157.5	163.1	165.6	152.8	156.9	231.4	
1997	160.5	141.8	133.4	179.4	161.1	167.1	169.5	156.3	160.5	236.4	
1998	163.0	141.9	132.0	184.2	163.4	170.9	173.4	158.6	163.0	239.7	
1999	166.6	144.4	134.0	188.8	167.0	174.4	177.0	162.0	166.6	244.7	
2000	172.2	149.2	139.2	195.3	173.0	178.6	181.3	167.3	172.2	252.9	102.0
2001	177.1	150.7	138.9	203.4	177.8	183.5	186.1	171.9	177.1	260.0	104.3
2002	179.9	149.7	136.0	209.8	180.5	187.7	190.5	174.3	179.9	264.2	105.6
2003	184.0	151.2	136.5	216.5	184.7	190.6	193.2	178.1	184.0	270.1	107.8
2004	188.9	154.7	138.8	222.8	189.4	194.4	196.6	182.7	188.9	277.4	110.5
2005	195.3	160.2	144.5	230.1	196.0	198.7	200.9	188.7	195.3	286.7	113.7
2006	201.6	164.0	148.0	238.9	202.7	203.7	205.9	194.7	201.6	296.1	117.0
2007	207.342	167.509	149.720	246.848	208.098	208.925	210.729	200.080	207.342	304.5	119.957
2008	215.303	174.764	155.310	255.498	215.528	214.751	215.572	207.777	215.303	316.2	124.433
2009	214.537	169.698	147.071	259.154	214.008	218.433	219.235	206.555	214.537	315.0	124.353
2010	218.056	174.566	152.990	261.274	217.828	220.458	221.337	209.689	218.056	320.2	
2009: Jan	211.143	164.360	139.258	257.780	209.777	216.586	216.719	203.281	211.143	310.1	122.155
Feb	212.193	165.891	141.491	258.328	211.076	217.325	217.685	204.265	212.193	311.6	122.868
Mar	212.709	166.645	142.728	258.597	211.775	218.033	218.639	204.766	212.709	312.4	123.139
Apr	213.240	167.816	144.464	258.466	212.464	218.388	219.143	205.275	213.240	313.1	123.494
May	213.856	169.060	146.261	258.433	213.236	218.323	219.128	205.876	213.856	314.0	123.988
June	215.693	171.593	149.697	259.544	215.389	218.440	219.283	207.764	215.693	316.7	125.216
July	215.351	170.483	148.386	259.992	215.069	218.421	219.350	207.388	215.351	316.2	124.933
Aug	215.834	171.081	149.155	260.355	215.617	218.642	219.596	207.855	215.834	316.9	125.226
Sept	215.969	171.559	149.846	260.136	215.795	219.076	220.137	207.855	215.969	317.1	125.238
Oct	216.177	172.252	150.663	259.844	215.986	219.624	220.731	208.131	216.177	317.5	125.359
Nov	216.330	173.061	151.847	259.323	216.207	219.291	220.384	208.250	216.330	317.7	125.447
Dec	215.949	172.572	151.052	259.055	215.703	219.048	220.025	207.860	215.949	317.1	125.174
2010: Jan	216.687	173.240	152.035	259.459	216.362	219.287	220.086	208.499	216.687	318.2	125.628
Feb	216.741	173.419	151.767	259.792	216.440	219.708	220.602	208.432	216.741	318.3	125.604
Mar	217.631	174.798	153.516	260.196	217.430	220.133	221.059	209.301	217.631	319.6	126.162
Apr	218.009	175.333	154.163	260.420	217.839	220.252	221.166	209.669	218.009	320.1	126.375
May	218.178	175.333	154.106	260.756	218.010	220.298	221.193	209.841	218.178	320.4	126.451
June	217.965	173.899	152.247	261.756	217.788	220.336	221.265	209.605	217.965	320.1	126.247
July	218.011	173.503	151.754	262.241	217.857	220.316	221.258	209.662	218.011	320.1	126.203
Aug	218.312	173.925	152.182	262.421	218.147	220.619	221.551	209.952	218.312	320.6	126.353
Sept	218.439	174.282	152.395	262.320	218.179	221.030	221.907	210.001	218.439	320.8	126.418
Oct	218.711	175.225	153.508	261.927	218.431	221.236	222.079	210.257	218.711	321.2	126.614
Nov	218.803	175.415	153.761	261.921	218.538	221.235	222.077	210.336	218.803	321.3	126.650
Dec	219.179	176.015	154.443	262.074	218.921	221.045	221.795	210.712	219.179	321.9	126.866

[1] Consumer price index, all urban consumers.

[2] CPI-U-X1 reflects a rental equivalence approach to homeowners' costs for the CPI-U for years prior to 1983, the first year for which the official index incorporates such a measure. CPI-U-X1 is rebased to the December 1982 value of the CPI-U (1982–84=100) and is identical with CPI-U data from December 1982 forward. Data prior to 1967 estimated by moving the series at the same rate as the CPI-U for each year.

[3] Consumer price index research series (CPI-U-RS) using current methods introduced in June 1999. Data for 2010 are preliminary. All data are subject to revision annually.

[4] Chained consumer price index (C-CPI-U) introduced in August 2002. Data for 2009 and 2010 are subject to revision.

Source: Department of Labor (Bureau of Labor Statistics).

TABLE B-63. Changes in special consumer price indexes, 1967–2010

[For all urban consumers; percent change]

Year or month	All items		All items less food		All items less energy		All items less food and energy		All items less medical care	
	Dec. to Dec.[1]	Year to year	Dec. to Dec.[1]	Year to year	Dec. to Dec.[1]	Year to year	Dec. to Dec.[1]	Year to year	Dec. to Dec.[1]	Year to year
1967	3.0	3.1	3.3	3.4	3.2	2.7	3.8	3.6	2.7	2.1
1968	4.7	4.2	5.0	4.5	4.9	4.4	5.1	4.6	4.7	4.2
1969	6.2	5.5	5.6	5.4	6.5	5.8	6.2	5.8	6.1	5.4
1970	5.6	5.7	6.6	6.0	5.4	6.1	6.6	6.3	5.2	5.9
1971	3.3	4.4	3.0	4.6	3.4	4.2	3.1	4.7	3.2	4.1
1972	3.4	3.2	2.9	2.9	3.5	3.3	3.0	3.0	3.4	3.2
1973	8.7	6.2	5.6	4.0	8.2	6.2	4.7	3.6	9.1	6.4
1974	12.3	11.0	12.2	9.8	11.7	9.8	11.1	8.3	12.2	11.2
1975	6.9	9.1	7.3	9.4	6.6	8.9	6.7	9.1	6.7	9.0
1976	4.9	5.8	6.1	6.7	4.8	5.6	6.1	6.5	4.5	5.3
1977	6.7	6.5	6.4	6.4	6.7	6.4	6.5	6.3	6.7	6.3
1978	9.0	7.6	8.3	7.2	9.1	7.8	8.5	7.4	9.1	7.6
1979	13.3	11.3	14.0	11.4	11.1	10.0	11.3	9.8	13.4	11.5
1980	12.5	13.5	13.0	14.5	11.7	11.6	12.2	12.4	12.5	13.6
1981	8.9	10.3	9.8	10.9	8.5	10.0	9.5	10.4	8.8	10.4
1982	3.8	6.2	4.1	6.5	4.2	6.7	4.5	7.4	3.6	5.9
1983	3.8	3.2	4.1	3.5	4.5	3.6	4.8	4.0	3.6	2.9
1984	3.9	4.3	3.9	4.3	4.4	4.7	4.7	5.0	3.9	4.1
1985	3.8	3.6	4.1	3.8	4.0	3.9	4.3	4.3	3.5	3.4
1986	1.1	1.9	.5	1.7	3.8	3.9	3.8	4.0	.7	1.5
1987	4.4	3.6	4.6	3.5	4.1	4.1	4.2	4.1	4.3	3.5
1988	4.4	4.1	4.2	4.1	4.7	4.4	4.7	4.4	4.7	3.9
1989	4.6	4.8	4.5	4.6	4.6	4.7	4.4	4.5	4.5	4.6
1990	6.1	5.4	6.3	5.3	5.2	5.2	5.2	5.0	5.9	5.2
1991	3.1	4.2	3.3	4.5	3.9	4.6	4.4	4.9	2.7	3.9
1992	2.9	3.0	3.2	3.5	3.0	3.2	3.3	3.7	2.7	2.8
1993	2.7	3.0	2.7	3.1	3.1	3.2	3.2	3.3	2.6	2.7
1994	2.7	2.6	2.6	2.7	2.6	2.7	2.6	2.8	2.5	2.5
1995	2.5	2.8	2.7	2.8	2.9	3.0	3.0	3.0	2.5	2.7
1996	3.3	3.0	3.1	2.9	2.9	2.8	2.6	2.7	3.3	2.8
1997	1.7	2.3	1.8	2.3	2.1	2.5	2.2	2.4	1.6	2.3
1998	1.6	1.6	1.5	1.4	2.4	2.3	2.4	2.3	1.5	1.5
1999	2.7	2.2	2.8	2.2	2.0	2.0	1.9	2.1	2.6	2.1
2000	3.4	3.4	3.5	3.6	2.6	2.4	2.6	2.4	3.3	3.3
2001	1.6	2.8	1.3	2.8	2.8	2.7	2.7	2.6	1.4	2.7
2002	2.4	1.6	2.6	1.5	1.8	2.3	1.9	2.4	2.2	1.4
2003	1.9	2.3	1.5	2.3	1.5	1.5	1.1	1.4	1.8	2.2
2004	3.3	2.7	3.4	2.5	2.2	2.0	2.2	1.8	3.2	2.6
2005	3.4	3.4	3.6	3.5	2.2	2.2	2.2	2.2	3.3	3.3
2006	2.5	3.2	2.6	3.4	2.5	2.5	2.6	2.5	2.5	3.2
2007	4.1	2.8	4.0	2.7	2.8	2.6	2.4	2.3	4.0	2.8
2008	.1	3.8	−.8	3.6	2.4	2.8	1.8	2.3	−.1	3.8
2009	2.7	−.4	3.3	−.7	1.4	1.7	1.8	1.7	2.7	−.6
2010	1.5	1.6	1.5	1.8	.9	.9	.8	1.0	1.4	1.5

	Percent change from preceding month									
	Unadjusted	Seasonally adjusted	Unadjusted	Seasonally adjusted	Unadjusted	Seasonally adjusted	Unadjusted	Seasonally adjusted	Unadjusted	Seasonally adjusted
2009: Jan	0.4	0.3	0.4	0.3	0.3	0.2	0.3	0.2	0.4	0.3
Feb	.5	.4	.6	.5	.3	.1	.4	.2	.5	.4
Mar	.2	−.1	.3	−.1	.3	.1	.4	.2	.2	−.1
Apr	.2	.1	.3	.1	.2	.2	.2	.2	.2	.1
May	.3	.1	.4	.2	.0	.1	.0	.1	.3	.1
June	.9	.7	1.0	.8	.1	.1	.1	.2	.9	.7
July	−.2	.1	−.1	.2	.0	.1	.0	.1	−.2	.1
Aug	.2	.4	.3	.4	.1	.1	.1	.1	.2	.4
Sept	.1	.2	.1	.2	.1	.1	.1	.2	.0	.1
Oct	.1	.2	.1	.2	.3	.2	.3	.2	.1	.2
Nov	.1	.2	.1	.3	−.2	.0	−.2	.0	.1	.2
Dec	−.2	.2	−.2	.2	−.1	.1	−.2	.1	−.2	.2
2010: Jan	.3	.2	.3	.2	.1	−.1	.0	−.1	.3	.1
Feb	.0	.0	.0	.0	.2	.1	.2	.1	.0	.0
Mar	.4	.1	.5	.0	.2	.1	.0	.0	.4	.0
Apr	.2	−.1	.2	−.1	.1	.1	.0	.0	.2	−.1
May	.1	−.2	.1	−.2	.0	.1	.0	.1	.1	−.2
June	−.1	−.1	−.1	−.2	.0	.1	.0	.2	−.1	−.2
July	.0	.3	.0	.4	.0	.1	.0	.1	.0	.3
Aug	.1	.3	.1	.3	.1	.1	.1	.0	.1	.3
Sept	.1	.1	.0	.1	.2	.0	.2	.0	.0	.1
Oct	.1	.2	.1	.3	.1	.0	.1	.0	.1	.2
Nov	.0	.1	.0	.1	.0	.1	.0	.1	.0	.1
Dec	.2	.5	.2	.6	−.1	.1	−.1	.1	.2	.5

[1] Changes from December to December are based on unadjusted indexes.

Source: Department of Labor (Bureau of Labor Statistics).

TABLE B–64. Changes in consumer price indexes for commodities and services, 1939–2010

[For all urban consumers: percent change]

Year	All items		Commodities				Services				Medical care [2]		Energy [3]	
			Total		Food		Total		Medical care					
	Dec. to Dec. [1]	Year to year	Dec. to Dec. [1]	Year to year	Dec. to Dec. [1]	Year to year	Dec. to Dec. [1]	Year to year	Dec. to Dec. [1]	Year to year	Dec. to Dec. [1]	Year to year	Dec. to Dec. [1]	Year to year
1939	0.0	−1.4	−0.7	−2.0	−2.5	−2.5	0.0	0.0	1.2	1.2	1.0	0.0	....	....
1940	.7	.7	1.4	.7	2.5	1.7	.8	.8	.0	.0	.0	1.0	....	....
1941	9.9	5.0	13.3	6.7	15.7	9.2	2.4	.8	1.2	.0	1.0	.0	....	....
1942	9.0	10.9	12.9	14.5	17.9	17.6	2.3	3.1	3.5	3.5	3.8	2.9	....	....
1943	3.0	6.1	4.2	9.3	3.0	11.0	2.3	2.3	5.6	4.5	4.6	4.7	....	....
1944	2.3	1.7	2.0	1.0	.0	−1.2	2.2	2.2	3.2	4.3	2.6	3.6	....	....
1945	2.2	2.3	2.9	3.0	3.5	2.4	.7	1.5	3.1	3.1	2.6	2.6	....	....
1946	18.1	8.3	24.8	10.6	31.3	14.5	3.6	1.4	9.0	5.1	8.3	5.0	....	....
1947	8.8	14.4	10.3	20.5	11.3	21.7	5.6	4.3	6.4	8.7	6.9	8.0	....	....
1948	3.0	8.1	1.7	7.2	−.8	8.3	5.9	6.1	6.9	7.1	5.8	6.7	....	....
1949	−2.1	−1.2	−4.1	−2.7	−3.9	−4.2	3.7	5.1	1.6	3.3	1.4	2.8	....	....
1950	5.9	1.3	7.8	.7	9.8	1.6	3.6	3.0	4.0	2.4	3.4	2.0	....	....
1951	6.0	7.9	5.9	9.0	7.1	11.0	5.2	5.3	5.3	4.7	5.8	5.3	....	....
1952	.8	1.9	−.9	1.3	−1.0	1.8	4.4	4.5	5.8	6.7	4.3	5.0	....	....
1953	.7	.8	−.3	−.3	−1.1	−1.4	4.2	4.3	3.4	3.5	3.5	3.6	....	....
1954	−.7	.7	−1.6	−.9	−1.8	−.4	2.0	3.1	2.6	3.4	2.3	2.9	....	....
1955	.4	−.4	−.3	−.9	−.7	−1.4	2.0	2.0	3.2	2.6	3.3	2.2	....	....
1956	3.0	1.5	2.6	1.0	2.9	.7	3.4	2.5	3.8	3.8	3.2	3.8	....	....
1957	2.9	3.3	2.8	3.2	2.8	3.2	4.2	4.3	4.8	4.3	4.7	4.2	....	....
1958	1.8	2.8	1.2	2.1	2.4	4.5	2.7	3.7	4.6	5.3	4.5	4.6	−0.9	0.0
1959	1.7	.7	.6	.0	−1.0	−1.7	3.9	3.1	4.9	4.5	3.8	4.4	4.7	1.9
1960	1.4	1.7	1.2	.9	3.1	1.0	2.5	3.4	3.7	4.3	3.2	3.7	1.3	2.3
1961	.7	1.0	.0	.6	−.7	1.3	2.1	1.7	3.5	3.6	3.1	2.7	−1.3	.4
1962	1.3	1.0	.9	.9	1.3	.7	1.6	2.0	2.9	3.5	2.2	2.6	2.2	.4
1963	1.6	1.3	1.5	.9	2.0	1.6	2.4	2.0	2.8	2.9	2.5	2.6	−.9	.0
1964	1.0	1.3	.9	1.2	1.3	1.3	1.6	2.0	2.3	2.3	2.1	2.1	.0	−.4
1965	1.9	1.6	1.4	1.1	3.5	2.2	2.7	2.3	3.6	3.2	2.8	2.4	1.8	1.8
1966	3.5	2.9	2.5	2.6	4.0	5.0	4.8	3.8	8.3	5.3	6.7	4.4	1.7	1.7
1967	3.0	3.1	2.5	1.9	1.2	.9	4.3	4.3	8.0	8.8	6.3	7.2	1.7	2.1
1968	4.7	4.2	4.0	3.5	4.4	3.5	5.8	5.2	7.1	7.3	6.2	6.0	1.7	1.7
1969	6.2	5.5	5.4	4.7	7.0	5.1	7.7	6.9	7.3	8.2	6.2	6.7	2.9	2.5
1970	5.6	5.7	3.9	4.5	2.3	5.7	8.1	8.0	8.1	7.0	7.4	6.6	4.8	2.8
1971	3.3	4.4	2.8	3.6	4.3	3.1	4.1	5.7	5.4	7.4	4.6	6.2	3.1	3.9
1972	3.4	3.2	3.4	3.0	4.6	4.2	3.4	3.8	3.7	3.5	3.3	3.3	2.6	2.6
1973	8.7	6.2	10.4	7.4	20.3	14.5	6.2	4.4	6.0	4.5	5.3	4.0	17.0	8.1
1974	12.3	11.0	12.8	11.9	12.0	14.3	11.4	9.2	13.2	10.4	12.6	9.3	21.6	29.6
1975	6.9	9.1	6.2	8.8	6.6	8.5	8.2	9.6	10.3	12.6	9.8	12.0	11.4	10.5
1976	4.9	5.8	3.3	4.3	.5	3.0	7.2	8.3	10.8	10.1	10.0	9.5	7.1	7.1
1977	6.7	6.5	6.1	5.8	8.1	6.3	8.0	7.7	9.0	9.9	8.9	9.6	7.2	9.5
1978	9.0	7.6	8.8	7.2	11.8	9.9	9.3	8.6	9.3	8.5	8.8	8.4	7.9	6.3
1979	13.3	11.3	13.0	11.3	10.2	11.0	13.6	11.0	10.5	9.8	10.1	9.2	37.5	25.1
1980	12.5	13.5	11.0	12.3	10.2	8.6	14.2	15.4	10.1	11.3	9.9	11.0	18.0	30.9
1981	8.9	10.3	6.0	8.4	4.3	7.8	13.0	13.1	12.6	10.7	12.5	10.7	11.9	13.6
1982	3.8	6.2	3.6	4.1	3.1	4.1	4.3	9.0	11.2	11.8	11.0	11.6	1.3	1.5
1983	3.8	3.2	2.9	2.9	2.7	2.1	4.8	3.5	6.2	8.7	6.4	8.8	−.5	.7
1984	3.9	4.3	2.7	3.4	3.8	3.8	5.4	5.2	5.8	6.0	6.1	6.2	.2	1.0
1985	3.8	3.6	2.5	2.1	2.6	2.3	5.1	5.1	6.8	6.1	6.8	6.3	1.8	.7
1986	1.1	1.9	−2.0	−.9	3.8	3.2	4.5	5.0	7.9	7.7	7.7	7.5	−19.7	−13.2
1987	4.4	3.6	4.6	3.2	3.5	4.1	4.3	4.2	5.6	6.6	5.8	6.6	8.2	.5
1988	4.4	4.1	3.8	3.5	5.2	4.1	4.8	4.6	6.9	6.4	6.9	6.5	.5	.8
1989	4.6	4.8	4.1	4.7	5.6	5.8	5.1	4.9	8.6	7.7	8.5	7.7	5.1	5.6
1990	6.1	5.4	6.6	5.2	5.3	5.8	5.7	5.5	9.9	9.3	9.6	9.0	18.1	8.3
1991	3.1	4.2	1.2	3.1	1.9	2.9	4.6	5.1	8.0	8.9	7.9	8.7	−7.4	.4
1992	2.9	3.0	2.0	2.0	1.5	1.2	3.6	3.9	7.0	7.6	6.6	7.4	2.0	.5
1993	2.7	3.0	1.5	1.9	2.9	2.2	3.8	3.9	5.9	6.5	5.4	5.9	−1.4	1.2
1994	2.7	2.6	2.3	1.7	2.9	2.4	2.9	3.3	5.4	5.2	4.9	4.8	2.2	.4
1995	2.5	2.8	1.4	1.9	2.1	2.8	3.5	3.4	4.4	5.1	3.9	4.5	−1.3	.6
1996	3.3	3.0	3.2	2.6	4.3	3.3	3.3	3.2	3.2	3.7	3.0	3.5	8.6	4.7
1997	1.7	2.3	.2	1.4	1.5	2.6	2.8	3.0	2.9	2.9	2.8	2.8	−3.4	1.3
1998	1.6	1.6	.4	.1	2.3	2.2	2.6	2.7	3.2	3.2	3.4	3.2	−8.8	−7.7
1999	2.7	2.2	2.7	1.8	1.9	2.1	2.6	2.5	3.6	3.4	3.7	3.5	13.4	3.6
2000	3.4	3.4	2.7	3.3	2.8	2.3	3.9	3.4	4.6	4.3	4.2	4.1	14.2	16.9
2001	1.6	2.8	−1.4	1.0	2.8	3.2	3.7	4.1	4.8	4.8	4.7	4.6	−13.0	3.8
2002	2.4	1.6	1.2	−.7	1.5	1.8	3.2	3.1	5.6	5.1	5.0	4.7	10.7	−5.9
2003	1.9	2.3	.5	1.0	3.6	2.2	2.8	3.2	4.2	4.5	3.7	4.0	6.9	12.2
2004	3.3	2.7	3.6	2.3	2.7	3.4	3.1	2.9	4.9	5.0	4.2	4.4	16.6	10.9
2005	3.4	3.4	2.7	3.6	2.3	2.4	3.8	3.3	4.5	4.8	4.3	4.2	17.1	17.0
2006	2.5	3.2	1.3	2.4	2.1	2.4	3.4	3.8	4.1	4.1	3.6	4.0	2.9	11.2
2007	4.1	2.8	5.2	2.1	4.9	4.0	3.3	3.3	5.9	5.3	5.2	4.4	17.4	5.5
2008	.1	3.8	−4.1	4.3	5.9	5.5	3.0	3.5	3.0	4.2	2.6	3.7	−21.3	13.9
2009	2.7	−.4	5.5	−2.9	−.5	1.8	.9	1.4	3.4	3.2	3.4	3.2	18.2	−18.4
2010	1.5	1.6	2.0	2.9	1.5	.8	1.2	.8	3.4	3.5	3.3	3.4	7.7	9.5

[1] Changes from December to December are based on unadjusted indexes.
[2] Commodities and services.
[3] Household energy—gas (piped), electricity, fuel oil, etc.—and motor fuel. Motor oil, coolant, etc. also included through 1982.

Source: Department of Labor (Bureau of Labor Statistics).

Table B-65. Producer price indexes by stage of processing, 1965–2010

[1982=100]

Year or month	Total finished goods	Finished goods								Total finished consumer goods
		Consumer foods			Finished goods excluding consumer foods					
		Total	Crude	Processed	Total	Consumer goods			Capital equipment	
						Total	Durable	Nondurable		
1965	34.1	36.8	39.0	36.8	....	33.6	43.2	28.8	33.8	34.2
1966	35.2	39.2	41.5	39.2	....	34.1	43.4	29.3	34.6	35.4
1967	35.6	38.5	39.6	38.8	35.0	34.7	44.1	30.0	35.8	35.6
1968	36.6	40.0	42.5	40.0	35.9	35.5	45.1	30.6	37.0	36.5
1969	38.0	42.4	45.9	42.3	36.9	36.3	45.9	31.5	38.3	37.9
1970	39.3	43.8	46.0	43.9	38.2	37.4	47.2	32.5	40.1	39.1
1971	40.5	44.5	45.8	44.7	39.6	38.7	48.9	33.5	41.7	40.2
1972	41.8	46.9	48.0	47.2	40.4	39.4	50.0	34.1	42.8	41.5
1973	45.6	56.5	63.6	55.8	42.0	41.2	50.9	36.1	44.2	46.0
1974	52.6	64.4	71.6	63.9	48.8	48.2	55.5	44.0	50.5	53.1
1975	58.2	69.8	71.7	70.3	54.7	53.2	61.0	48.9	58.2	58.2
1976	60.8	69.6	76.7	69.0	58.1	56.5	63.7	52.4	62.1	60.4
1977	64.7	73.3	79.5	72.7	62.2	60.6	67.4	56.8	66.1	64.3
1978	69.8	79.9	85.8	79.4	66.7	64.9	73.6	60.0	71.3	69.4
1979	77.6	87.3	92.3	86.8	74.6	73.5	80.8	69.3	77.5	77.5
1980	88.0	92.4	93.9	92.3	86.7	87.1	91.0	85.1	85.8	88.6
1981	96.1	97.8	104.4	97.2	95.6	96.1	96.4	95.8	94.6	96.6
1982	100.0	100.0	100.0	100.0	100.0	100.0	100.0	100.0	100.0	100.0
1983	101.6	101.0	102.4	100.9	101.8	101.2	102.8	100.5	102.8	101.3
1984	103.7	105.4	111.4	104.9	103.2	102.2	104.5	101.1	105.2	103.3
1985	104.7	104.6	102.9	104.8	104.6	103.3	106.5	101.7	107.5	103.8
1986	103.2	107.3	105.6	107.4	101.9	98.5	108.9	93.3	109.7	101.4
1987	105.4	109.5	107.1	109.6	104.0	100.7	111.5	94.9	111.7	103.6
1988	108.0	112.6	109.8	112.7	106.5	103.1	113.8	97.3	114.3	106.2
1989	113.6	118.7	119.6	118.6	111.8	108.9	117.6	103.8	118.8	112.1
1990	119.2	124.4	123.0	124.4	117.4	115.3	120.4	111.5	122.9	118.2
1991	121.7	124.1	119.3	124.4	120.9	118.7	123.9	115.0	126.7	120.5
1992	123.2	123.3	107.6	124.4	123.1	120.8	125.7	117.3	129.1	121.7
1993	124.7	125.7	114.4	126.5	124.4	121.7	128.0	117.6	131.4	123.0
1994	125.5	126.8	111.3	127.9	125.1	121.6	130.9	116.2	134.1	123.3
1995	127.9	129.0	118.8	129.8	127.5	124.0	132.7	118.8	136.7	125.6
1996	131.3	133.6	129.2	133.8	130.5	127.6	134.2	123.3	138.3	129.5
1997	131.8	134.5	126.6	135.1	130.9	128.2	133.7	124.3	138.2	130.2
1998	130.7	134.3	127.2	134.8	129.5	126.4	132.9	122.2	137.6	128.9
1999	133.0	135.1	125.5	135.9	132.3	130.5	133.0	127.9	137.6	132.0
2000	138.0	137.2	123.5	138.3	138.1	138.4	133.9	138.7	138.8	138.2
2001	140.7	141.3	127.7	142.4	140.4	141.4	134.0	142.8	139.7	141.5
2002	138.9	140.1	128.5	141.0	138.3	138.8	133.0	139.8	139.1	139.4
2003	143.3	145.9	130.0	147.2	142.4	144.7	133.1	148.4	139.5	145.3
2004	148.5	152.7	138.2	153.9	147.2	150.9	135.0	156.6	141.4	151.7
2005	155.7	155.7	140.2	156.9	155.5	161.9	136.6	172.0	144.6	160.4
2006	160.4	156.7	151.3	157.1	161.0	169.2	136.9	182.6	146.9	166.0
2007	166.6	167.0	170.2	166.7	166.2	175.6	138.3	191.7	149.5	173.5
2008	177.1	178.3	175.5	178.6	176.6	189.1	141.2	210.5	153.8	186.3
2009	172.5	175.5	157.8	177.3	171.1	179.4	144.3	194.1	156.7	179.1
2010 p	179.9	182.5	172.6	183.4	178.4	190.5	144.9	210.3	157.3	189.2
2009: Jan	170.4	177.7	169.7	178.4	168.0	174.4	144.3	186.5	157.4	175.8
Feb	169.9	175.0	155.6	177.0	168.0	174.5	144.3	186.6	157.2	175.2
Mar	169.1	173.8	155.0	175.8	167.2	173.5	144.1	185.2	156.9	174.2
Apr	170.3	175.9	165.4	176.9	168.3	175.2	144.4	187.7	156.8	176.0
May	171.1	174.0	134.6	178.3	169.7	177.5	144.2	191.2	156.3	177.3
June	174.3	176.1	156.2	178.2	173.1	182.7	144.7	198.7	156.6	181.7
July	172.4	173.5	141.8	177.0	171.3	180.2	143.3	195.7	155.9	179.2
Aug	174.2	173.9	145.5	177.0	173.4	183.3	143.8	200.1	156.4	181.6
Sept	173.2	173.9	145.0	177.0	172.2	181.6	142.9	198.1	155.9	180.4
Oct	173.8	175.6	165.0	176.6	172.6	181.6	144.8	197.1	157.0	180.8
Nov	175.7	176.9	173.4	177.0	174.7	184.6	145.4	201.2	157.5	183.3
Dec	176.0	179.8	186.6	178.8	174.3	184.2	144.9	200.9	157.1	183.8
2010: Jan	178.0	180.1	178.3	180.1	176.7	187.7	145.4	205.9	157.5	186.5
Feb	177.0	180.9	180.7	180.7	175.3	185.6	145.2	202.8	157.3	185.1
Mar	179.1	185.6	223.6	181.0	176.9	188.2	145.0	206.8	157.1	188.3
Apr	179.5	184.2	196.8	182.6	177.6	189.4	144.8	208.7	157.1	188.8
May	179.8	184.1	176.0	184.8	178.1	190.0	145.0	209.6	157.2	189.2
June	179.0	179.5	146.0	183.2	178.1	190.1	144.3	210.1	157.0	188.2
July	179.5	180.5	157.8	182.9	178.5	190.8	144.2	211.2	156.9	188.9
Aug	179.9	180.1	151.9	183.2	179.1	191.6	144.3	212.3	157.1	189.4
Sept [1]	180.2	182.8	152.3	186.1	178.8	191.3	144.3	211.9	157.0	189.9
Oct [1]	181.2	182.0	150.0	185.5	180.2	193.0	145.5	213.8	157.8	191.0
Nov [1]	181.9	184.0	169.2	185.5	180.6	193.5	145.7	214.4	158.0	191.9
Dec [1]	183.0	186.1	188.9	185.6	181.4	194.9	145.3	216.7	157.8	193.4

[1] Data have been revised through August 2010; data are subject to revision four months after date of original publication.

See next page for continuation of table.

TABLE B–65. Producer price indexes by stage of processing, 1965–2010—*Continued*

[1982=100]

Year or month	Intermediate materials, supplies, and components								Crude materials for further processing				
	Total	Foods and feeds [2]	Other	Materials and components		Proc-essed fuels and lubri-cants	Con-tainers	Supplies	Total	Food-stuffs and feed-stuffs	Other		
				For manu-factur-ing	For con-struc-tion						Total	Fuel	Other
1965	31.2	....	30.7	33.6	32.8	16.5	33.5	35.0	31.1	39.2	....	10.6	27.7
1966	32.0	....	31.3	34.3	33.6	16.8	34.5	36.5	33.1	42.7	....	10.9	28.3
1967	32.2	41.8	31.7	34.5	34.0	16.9	35.0	36.8	31.3	40.3	21.1	11.3	26.5
1968	33.0	41.5	32.5	35.3	35.7	16.5	35.9	37.1	31.8	40.9	21.6	11.5	27.1
1969	34.1	42.9	33.6	36.5	37.7	16.6	37.2	37.8	33.9	44.1	22.5	12.0	28.4
1970	35.4	45.6	34.8	38.0	38.3	17.7	39.0	39.7	35.2	45.2	23.8	13.8	29.1
1971	36.8	46.7	36.2	38.9	40.8	19.5	40.8	40.8	36.0	46.1	24.7	15.7	29.4
1972	38.2	49.5	37.7	40.4	43.0	20.1	42.7	42.5	39.9	51.5	27.0	16.8	32.3
1973	42.4	70.3	40.6	44.1	46.5	22.2	45.2	51.7	54.5	72.6	34.3	18.6	42.9
1974	52.5	83.6	50.5	56.0	55.0	33.6	53.3	56.8	61.4	76.4	44.1	24.8	54.5
1975	58.0	81.6	56.6	61.7	60.1	39.4	60.0	61.8	61.6	77.4	43.7	30.6	50.0
1976	60.9	77.4	60.0	64.0	64.1	42.3	63.1	65.8	63.4	76.8	48.2	34.5	54.9
1977	64.9	79.6	64.1	67.4	69.3	47.7	65.9	69.3	65.5	77.5	51.7	42.0	56.3
1978	69.5	84.8	68.6	72.0	76.5	49.9	71.0	72.9	73.4	87.3	57.5	48.2	61.9
1979	78.4	94.5	77.4	80.9	84.2	61.6	79.4	80.2	85.9	100.0	69.6	57.3	75.5
1980	90.3	105.5	89.4	91.7	91.3	85.0	89.1	89.9	95.3	104.6	84.6	69.4	91.8
1981	98.6	104.6	98.2	98.7	97.9	100.6	96.7	96.9	103.0	103.9	101.8	84.8	109.8
1982	100.0	100.0	100.0	100.0	100.0	100.0	100.0	100.0	100.0	100.0	100.0	100.0	100.0
1983	100.6	103.6	100.5	101.2	102.8	95.4	100.4	101.8	101.3	101.8	100.7	105.1	98.8
1984	103.1	105.7	103.0	104.1	105.6	95.7	105.9	104.1	103.5	104.7	102.2	105.1	101.0
1985	102.7	97.3	103.0	103.3	107.3	92.8	109.0	104.4	95.8	94.8	96.9	102.7	94.3
1986	99.1	96.2	99.3	102.2	108.1	72.7	110.3	105.6	87.7	93.2	81.6	92.2	76.0
1987	101.5	99.2	101.7	105.3	109.8	73.3	114.5	107.7	93.7	96.2	87.9	84.1	88.5
1988	107.1	109.5	106.9	113.2	116.1	71.2	120.1	113.7	96.0	106.1	85.5	82.1	85.9
1989	112.0	113.8	111.9	118.1	121.3	76.4	125.4	118.1	103.1	111.2	93.4	85.3	95.8
1990	114.5	113.3	114.5	118.7	122.9	85.9	127.7	119.4	108.9	113.1	101.5	84.8	107.3
1991	114.4	111.1	114.6	118.1	124.5	85.3	128.1	121.4	101.2	105.5	94.6	82.9	97.5
1992	114.7	110.7	114.9	117.9	126.5	84.5	127.7	122.7	100.4	105.1	93.5	84.0	94.2
1993	116.2	112.7	116.4	118.9	132.0	84.7	126.4	125.0	102.4	108.4	94.7	87.1	94.1
1994	118.5	114.8	118.7	122.1	136.6	83.1	129.7	127.0	101.8	106.5	94.8	82.4	97.0
1995	124.9	114.8	125.5	130.4	142.1	84.2	148.8	132.1	102.7	105.8	96.8	72.1	105.8
1996	125.7	128.1	125.6	128.6	143.6	90.0	141.1	135.9	113.8	121.5	104.5	92.6	105.7
1997	125.6	125.4	125.7	128.3	146.5	89.3	136.0	135.9	111.1	112.2	106.4	101.3	103.5
1998	123.0	116.2	123.4	126.1	146.8	81.1	140.8	134.8	96.8	103.9	88.4	86.7	84.5
1999	123.2	111.1	123.9	124.6	148.9	84.6	142.5	134.2	98.2	98.7	94.3	91.2	91.1
2000	129.2	111.7	130.1	128.1	150.7	102.0	151.6	136.9	120.6	100.2	130.4	136.9	118.0
2001	129.7	115.9	130.5	127.4	150.6	104.5	153.1	138.7	121.0	106.1	126.8	151.4	101.5
2002	127.8	115.5	128.5	126.1	151.3	96.3	152.1	138.9	108.1	99.5	111.4	117.3	101.0
2003	133.7	125.9	134.2	129.7	153.6	112.6	153.7	141.5	135.3	113.5	148.2	185.7	116.9
2004	142.6	137.1	143.0	137.9	166.4	124.3	159.3	146.7	159.0	127.0	179.2	211.4	149.2
2005	154.0	133.8	155.1	146.0	176.6	150.0	167.1	151.9	182.2	122.7	223.4	279.7	176.7
2006	164.0	135.2	165.4	155.9	188.4	162.8	175.0	157.0	184.8	119.3	230.6	241.5	210.0
2007	170.7	154.4	171.5	162.4	192.5	173.9	180.3	161.7	207.1	146.7	246.3	236.8	238.7
2008	188.3	181.6	188.7	177.2	205.4	206.2	191.8	173.8	251.8	163.4	313.9	298.3	308.5
2009	172.5	166.0	173.0	162.7	202.9	161.9	195.8	172.2	175.2	134.5	197.5	166.3	211.1
2010 ᵖ	183.6	171.8	184.5	174.0	205.6	185.7	202.4	174.9	212.0	152.3	249.0	187.4	280.7
2009: Jan	171.4	165.8	171.8	162.7	207.0	153.4	200.8	172.9	170.2	136.1	186.5	217.1	160.3
Feb	169.7	164.6	170.1	161.0	204.8	150.7	199.5	172.3	160.7	133.3	171.5	178.9	160.9
Mar	168.0	163.5	168.4	159.5	204.2	146.5	198.4	171.9	160.1	131.0	172.6	158.3	176.2
Apr	168.6	164.5	168.9	158.9	203.2	151.4	197.6	172.0	163.9	136.5	174.6	152.8	182.9
May	170.2	167.3	170.4	160.1	202.8	156.5	196.1	172.3	171.5	140.5	184.7	147.7	202.6
June	172.7	169.3	172.9	160.9	202.0	167.0	195.4	172.8	179.8	141.0	199.8	150.6	225.1
July	172.3	166.5	172.7	161.6	201.9	164.1	194.3	172.2	172.9	133.2	194.5	159.8	210.2
Aug	174.8	166.1	175.5	163.8	201.5	172.2	193.5	171.9	178.4	130.2	207.5	156.0	234.1
Sept	174.7	165.8	175.4	164.9	202.0	169.0	193.7	172.0	173.5	127.6	201.0	137.8	235.8
Oct	174.5	164.5	175.3	165.2	201.9	167.9	193.3	171.7	184.0	132.0	216.2	161.2	244.9
Nov	176.0	165.7	176.8	166.1	201.7	172.6	193.2	172.0	192.1	134.0	229.4	182.2	252.3
Dec	176.6	168.0	177.2	167.5	202.0	171.4	193.2	171.5	195.5	138.9	231.2	193.2	247.7
2010: Jan	179.4	168.7	180.2	169.4	202.3	180.2	194.2	172.9	212.8	142.0	260.3	232.3	269.0
Feb	179.2	168.3	180.1	171.0	203.5	174.9	196.1	173.1	208.5	142.3	252.2	222.3	262.4
Mar	181.2	167.7	182.3	172.6	204.6	180.0	198.8	173.3	212.7	146.9	255.5	201.8	281.6
Apr	183.2	168.5	184.4	175.0	206.1	183.1	200.1	173.8	211.0	148.6	250.7	174.8	292.1
May	184.3	170.8	185.4	175.4	207.4	185.9	201.6	174.7	208.3	153.0	241.5	180.3	273.2
June	183.3	169.7	184.4	173.6	206.6	185.2	204.1	174.5	203.7	146.3	239.3	182.1	268.4
July	183.1	170.0	184.2	172.6	206.3	186.3	204.4	174.8	208.7	150.7	244.4	195.6	267.6
Aug	183.9	171.2	184.9	173.1	206.2	188.4	205.0	175.1	211.8	152.5	248.5	195.3	274.6
Sept ¹	184.4	174.5	185.2	174.1	205.7	188.2	206.2	175.6	208.7	157.9	237.5	166.0	276.3
Oct ¹	185.7	175.5	186.5	175.6	205.8	190.2	206.1	176.4	215.2	160.6	246.9	169.5	289.4
Nov ¹	187.1	178.1	187.8	177.2	206.1	192.4	205.8	177.3	216.7	162.3	248.2	151.8	303.4
Dec ¹	188.1	178.4	188.9	178.2	207.0	193.9	206.2	177.9	225.8	164.6	262.9	176.8	310.7

[2] Intermediate materials for food manufacturing and feeds.

Source: Department of Labor (Bureau of Labor Statistics).

TABLE B–66. Producer price indexes by stage of processing, special groups, 1974–2010

[1982=100]

Year or month	Finished goods						Intermediate materials, supplies, and components				Crude materials for further processing			
	Total	Foods	Energy	Excluding foods and energy			Total	Foods and feeds[1]	Energy	Other	Total	Food-stuffs and feed-stuffs	Energy	Other
				Total	Capital equip-ment	Con-sumer goods exclud-ing foods and energy								
1974	52.6	64.4	26.2	53.6	50.5	55.5	52.5	83.6	33.1	54.0	61.4	76.4	27.8	83.3
1975	58.2	69.8	30.7	59.7	58.2	60.6	58.0	81.6	38.7	60.2	61.6	77.4	33.3	69.3
1976	60.8	69.6	34.3	63.1	62.1	63.7	60.9	77.4	41.5	63.8	63.4	76.8	35.3	80.2
1977	64.7	73.3	39.7	66.9	66.1	67.3	64.9	79.6	46.8	67.6	65.5	77.5	40.4	79.8
1978	69.8	79.9	42.3	71.9	71.3	72.2	69.5	84.8	49.1	72.5	73.4	87.3	45.2	87.8
1979	77.6	87.3	57.1	78.3	77.5	78.8	78.4	94.5	61.1	80.7	85.9	100.0	54.9	106.2
1980	88.0	92.4	85.2	87.1	85.8	87.8	90.3	105.5	84.9	90.3	95.3	104.6	73.1	113.1
1981	96.1	97.8	101.5	94.6	94.6	94.6	98.6	104.6	100.5	97.7	103.0	103.9	97.7	111.7
1982	100.0	100.0	100.0	100.0	100.0	100.0	100.0	100.0	100.0	100.0	100.0	100.0	100.0	100.0
1983	101.6	101.0	95.2	103.0	102.8	103.1	100.6	103.6	95.3	101.6	101.3	101.8	98.7	105.3
1984	103.7	105.4	91.2	105.5	105.2	105.7	103.1	105.7	95.5	104.7	103.5	104.7	98.0	111.7
1985	104.7	104.6	87.6	108.1	107.5	108.4	102.7	97.3	92.6	105.2	95.8	94.8	93.3	104.9
1986	103.2	107.3	63.0	110.6	109.7	111.1	99.1	96.2	72.6	104.9	87.7	93.2	71.8	103.1
1987	105.4	109.5	61.8	113.3	111.7	114.2	101.5	99.2	73.0	107.8	93.7	96.2	75.0	115.7
1988	108.0	112.0	59.0	117.0	114.3	118.5	107.1	109.5	70.9	115.2	96.0	106.1	67.7	133.0
1989	113.6	118.7	65.7	122.1	118.8	124.0	112.0	113.8	76.1	120.2	103.1	111.2	75.9	137.9
1990	119.2	124.4	75.0	126.6	122.9	128.8	114.5	113.3	85.5	120.9	108.9	113.1	85.9	136.3
1991	121.7	124.1	78.1	131.1	126.7	133.7	114.4	111.1	85.1	121.4	101.2	105.5	80.4	128.2
1992	123.2	123.3	77.8	134.2	129.1	137.3	114.7	110.7	84.3	122.0	100.4	105.1	78.8	128.4
1993	124.7	125.7	78.0	135.8	131.4	138.5	116.2	112.7	84.6	123.8	102.4	108.4	76.7	140.2
1994	125.5	126.8	77.0	137.1	134.1	139.0	118.5	114.8	83.0	127.1	101.8	106.5	72.1	156.2
1995	127.9	129.0	78.1	140.0	136.7	141.9	124.9	114.8	84.1	135.2	102.7	105.8	69.4	173.6
1996	131.3	133.6	83.2	142.0	138.3	144.3	125.7	128.1	89.8	134.0	113.8	121.5	85.0	155.8
1997	131.8	134.5	83.4	142.4	138.2	145.1	125.6	125.4	89.0	134.2	111.1	112.2	87.3	156.5
1998	130.7	134.3	75.1	143.7	137.6	147.7	123.0	116.2	80.8	133.5	96.8	103.9	68.6	142.1
1999	133.0	135.1	78.8	146.1	137.6	151.7	123.2	111.1	84.3	133.1	98.2	98.7	78.5	135.2
2000	138.0	137.2	94.1	148.0	138.8	154.0	129.2	111.7	101.7	136.6	120.6	100.2	122.1	145.2
2001	140.7	141.3	96.7	150.0	139.7	156.9	129.7	115.9	104.1	136.4	121.0	106.1	122.3	130.7
2002	138.9	140.1	88.8	150.2	139.1	157.6	127.8	115.5	95.9	135.8	108.1	99.5	102.0	135.7
2003	143.3	145.9	102.0	150.5	139.5	157.9	133.7	125.9	111.9	138.5	135.3	113.5	147.2	152.5
2004	148.5	152.7	113.0	152.7	141.4	160.3	142.6	137.1	123.2	146.5	159.0	127.0	174.6	193.0
2005	155.7	155.7	132.6	156.4	144.6	164.3	154.0	133.8	149.2	154.6	182.2	122.7	234.0	202.4
2006	160.4	156.7	145.9	158.7	146.9	166.7	164.0	135.2	162.8	163.8	184.8	119.3	226.9	244.5
2007	166.6	167.0	156.3	161.7	149.5	170.0	170.7	154.4	174.6	168.4	207.1	146.7	232.8	282.6
2008	177.1	178.3	178.7	167.2	153.8	176.4	188.3	181.6	208.1	180.9	251.8	163.4	309.4	324.4
2009	172.5	175.5	146.9	171.5	156.7	181.6	172.5	166.0	162.5	173.4	175.2	134.5	176.8	248.4
2010 p	179.9	182.5	167.3	173.5	157.3	185.0	183.6	171.8	188.4	180.8	212.0	152.3	216.4	329.0
2009: Jan	170.4	177.7	136.4	171.3	157.4	180.7	171.4	165.8	152.2	174.6	170.2	136.1	173.0	225.2
Feb	169.9	175.0	136.3	171.3	157.2	181.0	169.7	164.6	149.3	173.4	160.7	133.3	152.1	224.9
Mar	169.1	173.8	133.2	171.4	156.9	181.4	168.0	163.5	144.1	172.6	160.1	131.0	153.3	222.9
Apr	170.3	175.9	137.2	171.4	156.8	181.5	168.6	164.5	149.5	171.8	163.9	136.5	155.0	224.4
May	171.1	174.0	142.9	171.1	156.3	181.3	170.2	167.3	157.2	171.6	171.5	140.5	164.2	234.9
June	174.3	176.1	154.4	171.4	156.6	181.7	172.7	169.3	167.8	171.9	179.8	141.0	181.2	242.6
July	172.4	173.5	149.6	170.8	155.9	181.1	172.3	166.5	165.3	172.3	172.9	133.2	173.0	247.1
Aug	174.2	173.9	156.1	171.2	156.4	181.5	174.8	166.1	174.5	173.3	178.4	130.2	184.1	263.6
Sept	173.2	173.9	152.8	170.8	155.9	181.2	174.7	165.8	171.0	174.2	173.5	127.6	173.5	267.9
Oct	173.8	175.6	151.2	172.0	157.0	182.3	174.5	164.5	169.8	174.4	184.0	132.0	193.1	270.9
Nov	175.7	176.9	156.8	172.6	157.5	183.1	176.0	165.7	175.2	174.8	192.1	134.0	211.0	270.9
Dec	176.0	179.8	156.0	172.4	157.1	183.0	176.6	168.0	173.8	175.7	195.5	138.9	208.6	285.3
2010: Jan	178.0	180.1	162.7	173.0	157.5	183.9	179.4	168.7	183.2	176.8	212.8	142.0	241.5	304.0
Feb	177.0	180.9	157.7	173.0	157.3	184.0	179.2	168.3	177.4	178.3	208.5	142.3	229.8	306.0
Mar	179.1	185.6	163.3	173.0	157.1	184.2	181.2	167.7	182.9	179.6	212.7	146.9	226.8	324.6
Apr	179.5	184.2	165.9	173.0	157.1	184.2	183.2	168.5	185.8	181.5	211.0	148.6	216.0	335.3
May	179.8	184.1	166.7	173.3	157.2	184.6	184.3	170.8	188.5	181.9	208.3	153.0	205.9	330.0
June	179.0	179.5	166.8	173.2	157.0	184.7	183.3	169.7	187.3	181.0	203.7	146.3	207.7	317.1
July	179.5	180.5	168.0	173.3	156.9	184.9	183.1	170.0	188.4	180.4	208.7	150.7	216.1	313.2
Aug	179.9	180.1	169.6	173.5	157.1	185.1	183.9	171.2	190.8	180.5	211.8	152.5	217.7	324.1
Sept [2]	180.2	182.8	168.8	173.5	157.0	185.2	184.4	174.5	190.5	181.1	208.7	157.9	198.4	335.5
Oct [2]	181.2	182.0	171.1	174.5	157.8	186.3	185.7	175.5	192.8	182.0	215.2	160.6	209.0	340.8
Nov [2]	181.9	184.0	171.8	174.7	158.0	186.6	187.1	178.1	195.2	183.0	216.7	162.3	205.9	352.6
Dec [2]	183.0	186.1	174.6	174.7	157.8	186.8	188.1	178.4	197.5	183.8	225.8	164.6	221.5	365.3

[1] Intermediate materials for food manufacturing and feeds.
[2] Data have been revised through August 2010; data are subject to revision four months after date of original publication.

Source: Department of Labor (Bureau of Labor Statistics).

TABLE B–67. Producer price indexes for major commodity groups, 1965–2010

[1982=100]

Year or month	Farm products and processed foods and feeds			Industrial commodities				
	Total	Farm products	Processed foods and feeds	Total	Textile products and apparel	Hides, skins, leather, and related products	Fuels and related products and power	Chemicals and allied products
1965	39.0	40.7	38.0	30.9	48.8	35.9	13.8	33.9
1966	41.6	43.7	40.2	31.5	48.9	39.4	14.1	34.0
1967	40.2	41.3	39.8	32.0	48.9	38.1	14.4	34.2
1968	41.1	42.3	40.6	32.8	50.7	39.3	14.3	34.1
1969	43.4	45.0	42.7	33.9	51.8	41.5	14.6	34.2
1970	44.9	45.8	44.6	35.2	52.4	42.0	15.3	35.0
1971	45.8	46.6	45.5	36.5	53.3	43.4	16.6	35.6
1972	49.2	51.6	48.0	37.8	55.5	50.0	17.1	35.6
1973	63.9	72.7	58.9	40.3	60.5	54.5	19.4	37.6
1974	71.3	77.4	68.0	49.2	68.0	55.2	30.1	50.2
1975	74.0	77.0	72.6	54.9	67.4	56.5	35.4	62.0
1976	73.6	78.8	70.8	58.4	72.4	63.9	38.3	64.0
1977	75.9	79.4	74.0	62.5	75.3	68.3	43.6	65.9
1978	83.0	87.7	80.6	67.0	78.1	76.1	46.5	68.0
1979	92.3	99.6	88.5	75.7	82.5	96.1	58.9	76.0
1980	98.3	102.9	95.9	88.0	89.7	94.7	82.8	89.0
1981	101.1	105.2	98.9	97.4	97.6	99.3	100.2	98.4
1982	100.0	100.0	100.0	100.0	100.0	100.0	100.0	100.0
1983	102.0	102.4	101.8	101.1	100.3	103.2	95.9	100.3
1984	105.5	105.5	105.4	103.3	102.7	109.0	94.8	102.9
1985	100.7	95.1	103.5	103.7	102.9	108.9	91.4	103.7
1986	101.2	92.9	105.4	100.0	103.2	113.0	69.8	102.6
1987	103.7	95.5	107.9	102.6	105.1	120.4	70.2	106.4
1988	110.0	104.9	112.7	106.3	109.2	131.4	66.7	116.3
1989	115.4	110.9	117.8	111.6	112.3	136.3	72.9	123.0
1990	118.6	112.2	121.9	115.8	115.0	141.7	82.3	123.6
1991	116.4	105.7	121.9	116.5	116.3	138.9	81.2	125.6
1992	115.9	103.6	122.1	117.4	117.8	140.4	80.4	125.9
1993	118.4	107.1	124.0	119.0	118.0	143.7	80.0	128.2
1994	119.1	106.3	125.5	120.7	118.3	148.5	77.8	132.1
1995	120.5	107.4	127.0	125.5	120.8	153.7	78.0	142.5
1996	129.7	122.4	133.3	127.3	122.4	150.5	85.8	142.1
1997	127.0	112.9	134.0	127.7	122.6	154.2	86.1	143.6
1998	122.7	104.6	131.6	124.8	122.9	148.0	75.3	143.9
1999	120.3	98.4	131.1	126.5	121.1	146.0	80.5	144.2
2000	122.0	99.5	133.1	134.8	121.4	151.5	103.5	151.0
2001	126.2	103.8	137.3	135.7	121.3	158.4	105.3	151.8
2002	123.9	99.0	136.2	132.4	119.9	157.6	93.2	151.9
2003	132.8	111.5	143.4	139.1	119.8	162.3	112.9	161.8
2004	142.0	123.3	151.2	147.6	121.0	164.5	126.9	174.4
2005	141.3	118.5	153.1	160.2	122.8	165.4	156.4	192.0
2006	141.2	117.0	153.8	168.8	124.5	168.4	166.7	205.8
2007	157.8	143.4	165.1	175.1	125.8	173.6	177.6	214.8
2008	173.8	161.3	180.5	192.3	128.9	173.1	214.6	245.5
2009	161.4	134.6	176.2	174.8	129.5	157.0	158.7	229.4
2010 *p*	171.2	150.9	182.3	187.1	131.4	181.1	186.2	246.6
2009: Jan	162.4	136.4	176.8	172.6	130.2	157.0	148.5	226.8
Feb	160.4	132.8	175.5	170.8	129.9	157.0	143.6	226.5
Mar	158.9	130.6	174.4	169.5	129.4	157.9	140.2	225.8
Apr	161.8	136.8	175.5	170.3	129.7	153.6	144.8	225.2
May	163.4	137.8	177.4	172.0	129.1	153.8	152.2	225.8
June	165.2	142.1	177.9	175.5	129.6	151.9	165.0	227.8
July	160.3	131.6	176.2	174.6	129.1	153.1	160.7	230.0
Aug	159.6	130.1	175.9	177.7	129.4	155.2	169.6	231.1
Sept	158.3	126.8	175.8	176.9	129.5	158.9	164.9	232.0
Oct	160.3	133.2	175.3	177.8	129.4	162.0	166.8	231.7
Nov	161.6	135.5	176.0	180.1	129.5	160.4	174.7	233.3
Dec	165.0	141.5	177.9	180.4	129.6	163.4	173.2	236.7
2010: Jan	166.0	142.5	178.9	184.6	130.1	165.9	185.6	239.9
Feb	166.2	142.3	179.3	183.6	130.3	173.3	178.9	244.2
Mar	169.2	150.3	179.5	185.6	131.0	176.1	183.4	246.1
Apr	169.3	149.1	180.4	187.0	131.1	176.3	184.4	248.9
May	171.2	150.0	182.8	187.2	131.5	182.7	184.6	246.9
June	167.1	141.6	181.1	186.4	131.5	182.9	184.1	244.1
July	169.0	146.8	181.2	186.7	131.5	184.2	186.3	243.3
Aug	170.0	148.4	181.8	187.5	131.8	185.1	188.4	244.3
Sept [1]	173.9	153.8	184.9	187.0	131.5	184.8	184.9	245.5
Oct [1]	175.3	157.2	185.2	188.7	132.1	187.0	188.7	248.7
Nov [1]	177.8	162.2	186.3	189.7	132.1	186.8	189.8	252.8
Dec [1]	179.8	167.0	186.6	191.5	132.5	188.6	194.7	254.4

[1] Data have been revised through August 2010; data are subject to revision four months after date of original publication.

See next page for continuation of table.

[1982=100]

Year or month	Rubber and plastic products	Lumber and wood products	Pulp, paper, and allied products	Metals and metal products	Machinery and equipment	Furniture and household durables	Non-metallic mineral products	Transportation equipment Total	Motor vehicles and equipment	Miscellaneous products
1965	39.7	33.7	33.3	32.0	33.7	46.8	30.4	....	39.2	34.7
1966	40.5	35.2	34.2	32.8	34.7	47.4	30.7	....	39.2	35.3
1967	41.4	35.1	34.6	33.2	35.9	48.3	31.2	....	39.8	36.2
1968	42.8	39.8	35.0	34.0	37.0	49.7	32.4	....	40.9	37.0
1969	43.6	44.0	36.0	36.0	38.2	50.7	33.6	40.4	41.7	38.1
1970	44.9	39.9	37.5	38.7	40.0	51.9	35.3	41.9	43.3	39.8
1971	45.2	44.7	38.1	39.4	41.4	53.1	38.2	44.2	45.7	40.8
1972	45.3	50.7	39.3	40.9	42.3	53.8	39.4	45.5	47.0	41.5
1973	46.6	62.2	42.3	44.0	43.7	55.7	40.7	46.1	47.4	43.3
1974	56.4	64.5	52.5	57.0	50.0	61.8	47.8	50.3	51.4	48.1
1975	62.2	62.1	59.0	61.5	57.9	67.5	54.4	56.7	57.6	53.4
1976	66.0	72.2	62.1	65.0	61.3	70.3	58.2	60.5	61.2	55.6
1977	69.4	83.0	64.6	69.3	65.2	73.2	62.6	64.6	65.2	59.4
1978	72.4	96.9	67.7	75.3	70.3	77.5	69.6	69.5	70.0	66.7
1979	80.5	105.5	75.9	86.0	76.7	82.8	77.6	75.3	75.8	75.5
1980	90.1	101.5	86.3	95.0	86.0	90.7	88.4	82.9	83.1	93.6
1981	96.4	102.8	94.8	99.6	94.4	95.9	96.7	94.3	94.6	96.1
1982	100.0	100.0	100.0	100.0	100.0	100.0	100.0	100.0	100.0	100.0
1983	100.8	107.9	103.3	101.8	102.7	103.4	101.6	102.8	102.2	104.8
1984	102.3	108.0	110.3	104.8	105.1	105.7	105.4	105.2	104.1	107.0
1985	101.9	106.6	113.3	104.4	107.2	107.1	108.6	107.9	106.4	109.4
1986	101.9	107.2	116.1	103.2	108.8	108.2	110.0	110.5	109.1	111.6
1987	103.0	112.8	121.8	107.1	110.4	109.9	110.0	112.5	111.7	114.9
1988	109.3	118.9	130.4	118.7	113.2	113.1	111.2	114.3	113.1	120.2
1989	112.6	126.7	137.8	124.1	117.4	116.9	112.6	117.7	116.2	126.5
1990	113.6	129.7	141.2	122.9	120.7	119.2	114.7	121.5	118.2	134.2
1991	115.1	132.1	142.9	120.2	123.0	121.2	117.2	126.4	122.1	140.8
1992	115.1	146.6	145.2	119.2	123.4	122.2	117.3	130.4	124.9	145.3
1993	116.0	174.0	147.3	119.2	124.0	123.7	120.0	133.7	128.0	145.4
1994	117.6	180.0	152.5	124.8	125.1	126.1	124.2	137.2	131.4	141.9
1995	124.3	178.1	172.2	134.5	126.6	128.2	129.0	139.7	133.0	145.4
1996	123.8	176.1	168.7	131.0	126.5	130.4	131.0	141.7	134.1	147.7
1997	123.2	183.8	167.9	131.8	125.9	130.8	133.2	141.6	132.7	150.9
1998	122.6	179.1	171.7	127.8	124.9	131.3	135.4	141.2	131.4	156.0
1999	122.5	183.6	174.1	124.6	124.3	131.7	138.9	141.8	131.7	166.6
2000	125.5	178.2	183.7	128.1	124.0	132.6	142.5	143.8	132.3	170.8
2001	127.2	174.4	184.8	125.4	123.7	133.2	144.3	145.2	131.5	181.3
2002	126.8	173.3	185.9	125.9	122.9	133.5	146.2	144.6	129.9	182.4
2003	130.1	177.4	190.0	129.2	121.9	133.9	148.2	145.7	129.6	179.6
2004	133.8	195.6	195.7	149.6	122.1	135.1	153.2	148.6	131.0	183.2
2005	143.8	196.5	202.6	160.8	123.7	139.4	164.2	151.0	131.5	195.1
2006	153.8	194.4	209.8	181.6	126.2	142.6	179.9	152.6	131.0	205.6
2007	155.0	192.4	216.9	193.5	127.3	144.7	186.2	155.0	132.2	210.3
2008	165.9	191.3	226.8	213.0	129.7	148.9	197.1	158.6	134.1	216.6
2009	165.2	182.8	225.6	186.8	131.3	153.1	202.4	162.2	137.0	217.5
2010 ^p	170.6	192.7	236.8	207.7	131.1	153.2	201.9	163.4	137.6	221.3
2009: Jan	167.5	185.3	228.0	187.0	131.4	152.9	205.8	162.8	137.2	218.0
Feb	165.3	183.5	227.0	183.9	131.3	153.3	203.8	162.7	137.0	219.0
Mar	164.9	181.7	226.7	181.7	131.5	153.3	203.9	162.2	136.6	220.0
Apr	164.5	181.2	225.8	179.9	131.3	153.4	203.7	162.3	136.9	217.9
May	163.9	180.9	224.8	180.5	131.3	153.3	203.4	161.8	136.8	216.6
June	163.7	180.8	224.5	181.7	131.1	153.1	202.5	162.3	137.5	216.4
July	163.9	182.8	224.0	183.5	131.2	153.1	202.1	160.9	135.7	216.2
Aug	164.5	183.0	224.4	189.1	131.2	152.6	201.2	161.6	136.4	215.9
Sept	165.5	183.7	224.9	192.1	131.2	153.1	201.4	160.7	135.2	216.8
Oct	165.8	182.7	224.9	193.3	131.2	153.1	200.6	162.9	137.9	216.9
Nov	166.2	183.3	225.7	193.0	131.3	153.0	200.5	163.5	138.6	218.0
Dec	166.3	184.6	226.2	196.0	131.1	153.1	200.4	163.0	137.8	218.3
2010: Jan	166.8	185.8	227.2	200.5	131.1	153.0	200.7	163.7	138.4	218.4
Feb	167.4	190.2	229.7	200.8	131.1	152.5	201.4	163.6	138.3	218.7
Mar	168.5	193.2	233.1	205.0	131.2	152.6	201.6	163.1	137.7	219.6
Apr	169.9	197.2	234.6	210.3	131.1	152.8	201.9	163.4	137.9	219.8
May	170.6	200.6	237.3	210.1	131.2	153.0	202.3	163.4	137.9	220.9
June	171.7	195.7	237.5	207.4	131.1	153.5	202.5	162.9	137.0	221.6
July	171.9	194.0	238.7	205.0	131.2	153.3	202.3	162.5	136.4	222.3
Aug	171.8	192.1	238.5	206.5	131.1	153.7	202.3	162.9	136.8	222.7
Sept ¹	171.7	191.5	240.5	208.5	131.1	153.4	202.3	162.9	136.7	222.0
Oct ¹	171.9	190.6	240.6	210.8	131.0	153.4	202.1	164.3	138.3	222.6
Nov ¹	172.5	190.3	241.6	212.9	130.8	153.6	201.7	164.5	138.4	223.1
Dec ¹	172.9	191.4	242.7	215.0	131.0	153.7	201.9	164.0	137.8	224.3

Source: Department of Labor (Bureau of Labor Statistics).

TABLE B–68. Changes in producer price indexes for finished goods, 1970–2010

[Percent change]

Year or month	Total finished goods		Finished consumer foods		Finished goods excluding consumer foods						Finished energy goods		Finished goods excluding foods and energy	
					Total		Consumer goods		Capital equipment					
	Dec. to Dec.[1]	Year to year	Dec. to Dec.[1]	Year to year	Dec. to Dec.[1]	Year to year	Dec. to Dec.[1]	Year to year	Dec. to Dec.[1]	Year to year	Dec. to Dec.[1]	Year to year	Dec. to Dec.[1]	Year to year
1970	2.1	3.4	−2.3	3.3	4.3	3.5	3.8	3.0	4.8	4.7	....	....	....	....
1971	3.3	3.1	5.8	1.6	2.0	3.7	2.1	3.5	2.4	4.0	....	....	....	....
1972	3.9	3.2	7.9	5.4	2.3	2.0	2.1	1.8	2.1	2.6	....	....	....	....
1973	11.7	9.1	22.7	20.5	6.6	4.0	7.5	4.6	5.1	3.3	....	....	....	....
1974	18.3	15.4	12.8	14.0	21.1	16.2	20.3	17.0	22.7	14.3	....	....	17.7	11.4
1975	6.6	10.6	5.6	8.4	7.2	12.1	6.8	10.4	8.1	15.2	16.3	17.2	6.0	11.4
1976	3.8	4.5	−2.5	−.3	6.2	6.2	6.0	6.2	6.5	6.7	11.6	11.7	5.7	5.7
1977	6.7	6.4	6.9	5.3	6.8	7.1	6.7	7.3	7.2	6.4	12.0	15.7	6.2	6.0
1978	9.3	7.9	11.7	9.0	8.3	7.2	8.5	7.1	8.0	7.9	8.5	6.5	8.4	7.5
1979	12.8	11.2	7.4	9.3	14.8	11.8	17.6	13.3	8.8	8.7	58.1	35.0	9.4	8.9
1980	11.8	13.4	7.5	5.8	13.4	16.2	14.1	18.5	11.4	10.7	27.9	49.2	10.8	11.2
1981	7.1	9.2	1.5	5.8	8.7	10.3	8.6	10.3	9.2	10.3	14.1	19.1	7.7	8.6
1982	3.6	4.1	2.0	2.2	4.2	4.6	4.2	4.1	3.9	5.7	−.1	−1.5	4.9	5.7
1983	.6	1.6	2.3	1.0	.0	1.8	−.9	1.2	2.0	2.8	−9.2	−4.8	1.9	3.0
1984	1.7	2.1	3.5	4.4	1.1	1.4	.8	1.0	1.8	2.3	−4.2	−4.2	2.0	2.4
1985	1.8	1.0	.6	−.8	2.2	1.4	2.1	1.1	2.7	2.2	−.2	−3.9	2.7	2.5
1986	−2.3	−1.4	2.8	2.6	−4.0	−2.6	−6.6	−4.6	2.1	2.0	−38.1	−28.1	2.7	2.3
1987	2.2	2.1	−.2	2.1	3.2	2.1	4.1	2.2	1.3	1.8	11.2	−1.9	2.1	2.4
1988	4.0	2.5	5.7	2.8	3.2	2.4	3.1	2.4	3.6	2.3	−3.6	−3.2	4.3	3.3
1989	4.9	5.2	5.2	5.4	4.8	5.0	5.3	5.6	3.8	3.9	9.5	9.9	4.2	4.4
1990	5.7	4.9	2.6	4.8	6.9	5.0	8.7	5.9	3.4	3.5	30.7	14.2	3.5	3.7
1991	−.1	2.1	−1.5	−.2	.3	3.0	−.7	2.9	2.5	3.1	−9.6	4.1	3.1	3.6
1992	1.6	1.2	1.6	−.6	1.6	1.8	1.6	1.8	1.7	1.9	−.3	−.4	2.0	2.4
1993	.2	1.2	2.4	1.9	−.4	1.1	−1.4	.7	1.8	1.8	−4.1	.3	.4	1.2
1994	1.7	.6	1.1	.9	1.9	.6	2.0	−.1	2.0	2.1	3.5	−1.3	1.6	1.0
1995	2.3	1.9	1.9	1.7	2.3	1.9	2.3	2.0	2.2	1.9	1.1	1.4	2.6	2.1
1996	2.8	2.7	3.4	3.6	2.6	2.4	3.7	2.9	.4	1.2	11.7	6.5	.6	1.4
1997	−1.2	.4	−.8	.7	−1.2	.3	−1.5	.5	−.6	−.1	−6.4	.2	.0	.3
1998	.0	−.8	.1	−.1	−.1	−1.1	−.1	−1.4	.0	−.4	−11.7	−10.0	2.5	.9
1999	2.9	1.8	.8	.6	3.5	2.2	5.1	3.2	.3	.0	18.1	4.9	.9	1.7
2000	3.6	3.8	1.7	1.6	4.1	4.4	5.5	6.1	1.2	.9	16.6	19.4	1.3	1.3
2001	−1.6	2.0	1.8	3.0	−2.6	1.7	−3.9	2.2	.0	.6	−17.1	2.8	.9	1.4
2002	1.2	−1.3	−.6	−.8	1.7	−1.5	2.9	−1.8	−.6	−.4	12.3	−8.2	−.5	.1
2003	4.0	3.2	7.7	4.1	3.0	3.0	4.1	4.3	.8	.3	11.4	14.9	1.0	.2
2004	4.2	3.6	3.1	4.7	4.5	3.4	5.5	4.3	2.4	1.4	13.4	10.8	2.3	1.5
2005	5.4	4.8	1.7	2.0	6.4	5.6	8.8	7.3	1.2	2.3	23.9	17.3	1.4	2.4
2006	1.1	3.0	1.7	.6	1.0	3.5	.4	4.5	2.3	1.6	−2.0	10.0	2.0	1.5
2007	6.2	3.9	7.6	6.6	5.8	3.2	7.7	3.8	1.4	1.8	17.8	7.1	2.0	1.9
2008	−.9	6.3	3.2	6.8	−2.1	6.3	−4.8	7.7	4.3	2.9	−20.3	14.3	4.5	3.4
2009	4.3	−2.6	1.2	−1.6	4.9	−3.1	7.4	−5.1	−.1	1.9	19.4	−17.8	.9	2.6
2010 ᵖ	4.0	4.3	3.5	4.0	4.1	4.2	5.8	6.2	.4	.4	11.9	13.9	1.3	1.2

Percent change from preceding month

	Unadjusted	Seasonally adjusted	Unadjusted	Seasonally adjusted	Unadjusted	Seasonally adjusted	Unadjusted	Seasonally adjusted	Unadjusted	Seasonally adjusted	Unadjusted	Seasonally adjusted	Unadjusted	Seasonally adjusted
2009: Jan	0.9	1.1	0.0	0.1	1.1	1.2	1.7	1.8	0.1	0.1	4.4	4.9	0.3	0.2
Feb	−.3	−.2	−1.5	−1.5	.0	.2	.1	.2	−.1	−.1	−.1	.2	.0	.1
Mar	−.5	−.8	−.7	−.8	−.5	−.8	−.6	−1.1	−.2	.0	−2.3	−3.8	.1	.2
Apr	.7	.6	1.2	1.6	.7	.4	1.0	.5	−.1	.0	3.0	1.4	.0	.1
May	.5	.0	−1.1	−1.4	.8	.4	1.3	.6	−.3	−.1	4.2	1.8	−.2	−.1
June	1.9	1.8	1.2	1.0	2.0	2.0	2.9	2.8	.2	.3	8.0	7.6	.2	.3
July	−1.1	−1.2	−1.5	−1.3	−1.0	−1.2	−1.4	−1.7	−.4	−.1	−3.1	−4.5	−.4	−.1
Aug	1.0	1.5	.2	.3	1.2	1.7	1.7	2.4	.3	.3	4.3	6.2	.2	.3
Sept	−.6	−.5	.0	.0	−.7	−.5	−.9	−.7	−.3	−.2	−2.1	−1.8	−.2	−.1
Oct	.3	.2	1.0	1.3	.2	−.1	.0	.2	.7	−.6	1.0	1.2	.7	−.5
Nov	1.1	1.5	.7	.7	1.2	1.6	1.7	2.3	.3	.4	3.7	5.2	.3	.4
Dec	.2	.5	1.6	1.4	−.2	.4	−.2	.5	−.3	.0	−.5	1.2	−.1	.1
2010: Jan	1.1	1.3	.2	.2	1.4	1.5	1.9	2.2	.3	.2	4.3	4.9	.3	.3
Feb	−.6	−.5	.4	.4	−.8	−.8	−1.1	−1.1	−.1	.0	−3.1	−2.9	.0	.1
Mar	1.2	.8	2.6	2.4	.9	.5	1.4	.6	−.1	.0	3.6	1.2	.0	.1
Apr	.2	−.1	−.8	−.3	.4	−.1	.6	−.2	.0	.1	1.6	−.5	.0	.1
May	.2	−.3	−.1	−.5	.3	−.3	.3	−.6	.1	.3	.5	−2.0	.2	.3
June	−.4	−.4	−2.5	−2.6	.0	.1	.1	.1	−.1	−.1	.1	.0	−.1	.1
July	.3	.1	.6	.7	.2	−.1	.4	−.2	−.1	.3	.7	−1.0	.1	.3
Aug	.2	.7	−.2	−.1	.3	.9	.4	1.2	−.1	.2	1.0	3.0	.1	.2
Sept ²	.2	.3	1.5	1.4	−.2	.0	−.2	.0	−.1	.0	−.5	−.2	.0	.1
Oct ²	.6	.4	−.4	−.1	.8	.6	.9	1.2	.5	−.8	1.4	3.7	.6	−.6
Nov ²	.4	.8	1.1	1.0	.2	.7	.3	1.0	.1	.2	.4	2.1	.1	.3
Dec ²	.6	1.1	1.1	.8	.4	1.2	.7	1.6	−.1	.1	1.6	3.7	.0	.2

[1] Changes from December to December are based on unadjusted indexes.
[2] Data have been revised through August 2010; data are subject to revision four months after date of original publication.

Source: Department of Labor (Bureau of Labor Statistics).

MONEY STOCK, CREDIT, AND FINANCE
TABLE B-69. Money stock and debt measures, 1970–2010

[Averages of daily figures, except debt end-of-period basis; billions of dollars, seasonally adjusted]

Year and month	M1 — Sum of currency, demand deposits, travelers checks, and other checkable deposits (OCDs)	M2 — M1 plus retail MMMF balances, savings deposits (including MMDAs), and small time deposits [2]	Debt [1] — Debt of domestic nonfinancial sectors	Percent change — From year or 6 months earlier [3] M1	Percent change — From year or 6 months earlier [3] M2	Percent change — From previous period [4] Debt
December:						
1970	214.4	626.5	1,420.2	....	....	....
1971	228.3	710.3	1,555.2	6.5	13.4	9.5
1972	249.2	802.3	1,711.2	9.2	13.0	10.0
1973	262.9	855.5	1,895.5	5.5	6.6	10.7
1974	274.2	902.1	2,069.9	4.3	5.4	9.2
1975	287.1	1,016.2	2,261.8	4.7	12.6	9.3
1976	306.2	1,152.0	2,505.3	6.7	13.4	10.8
1977	330.9	1,270.3	2,826.6	8.1	10.3	12.8
1978	357.3	1,366.0	3,211.2	8.0	7.5	13.8
1979	381.8	1,473.7	3,603.0	6.9	7.9	12.2
1980	408.5	1,599.8	3,953.5	7.0	8.6	9.5
1981	436.7	1,755.5	4,361.7	6.9	9.7	10.4
1982	474.8	1,909.3	4,783.4	8.7	8.8	10.4
1983	521.4	2,125.7	5,359.2	9.8	11.3	12.0
1984	551.6	2,308.8	6,146.2	5.8	8.6	14.8
1985	619.8	2,494.6	7,123.1	12.4	8.0	15.6
1986	724.7	2,731.6	7,966.3	16.9	9.5	11.9
1987	750.2	2,831.0	8,670.1	3.5	3.6	9.1
1988	786.7	2,993.9	9,450.7	4.9	5.8	9.0
1989	792.9	3,158.4	10,152.1	.8	5.5	7.2
1990	824.7	3,276.2	10,834.9	4.0	3.7	6.5
1991	897.0	3,376.3	11,301.4	8.8	3.1	4.3
1992	1,024.9	3,428.7	11,816.5	14.3	1.6	4.5
1993	1,129.6	3,479.1	12,391.4	10.2	1.5	4.7
1994	1,150.6	3,493.4	12,973.6	1.9	.4	4.6
1995	1,127.5	3,637.1	13,667.5	−2.0	4.1	5.2
1996	1,081.5	3,816.6	14,399.8	−4.1	4.9	5.4
1997	1,072.8	4,031.5	15,210.8	−.8	5.6	5.6
1998	1,095.8	4,373.4	16,216.4	2.1	8.5	6.6
1999	1,122.4	4,632.9	17,291.2	2.4	5.9	6.4
2000	1,087.2	4,913.2	18,165.3	−3.1	6.1	5.0
2001	1,182.1	5,428.6	19,297.4	8.7	10.5	6.3
2002	1,219.7	5,775.2	20,716.1	3.2	6.4	7.4
2003	1,306.5	6,064.1	22,443.6	7.1	5.0	8.1
2004	1,376.4	6,407.8	24,441.8	5.4	5.7	8.8
2005	1,374.9	6,673.4	26,766.6	−.1	4.1	9.5
2006	1,366.3	7,065.2	29,178.1	−.6	5.9	9.0
2007	1,373.6	7,493.8	31,707.7	.5	6.1	8.6
2008	1,602.7	8,245.1	33,613.9	16.7	10.0	6.0
2009	1,693.6	8,528.7	34,646.6	5.7	3.4	3.0
2010	1,832.2	8,816.4	....	8.2	3.4	....
2009: Jan	1,587.1	8,307.8	....	23.6	13.0	....
Feb	1,568.9	8,347.2	....	23.7	14.3	....
Mar	1,577.4	8,399.0	34,016.6	15.9	12.9	4.7
Apr	1,609.8	8,390.5	....	18.6	9.7	....
May	1,610.5	8,431.8	....	13.0	9.5	....
June	1,651.7	8,452.8	34,391.0	6.1	5.0	4.4
July	1,661.5	8,452.8	....	9.4	3.5	....
Aug	1,655.3	8,428.7	....	11.0	2.0	....
Sept	1,665.8	8,452.4	34,570.8	11.2	1.3	2.1
Oct	1,679.8	8,482.3	....	8.7	2.2	....
Nov	1,679.9	8,511.5	....	8.6	1.9	....
Dec	1,693.6	8,528.7	34,646.6	5.1	1.8	.9
2010: Jan	1,681.0	8,469.5	....	2.3	.4	....
Feb	1,703.2	8,537.1	....	5.8	2.6	....
Mar	1,712.0	8,515.2	35,075.2	5.5	1.5	4.3
Apr	1,700.2	8,527.2	....	2.4	1.1	....
May	1,707.1	8,568.3	....	3.2	1.3	....
June	1,727.4	8,599.1	35,491.0	4.0	1.7	4.7
July	1,731.0	8,615.3	....	5.9	3.4	....
Aug	1,751.6	8,660.8	....	5.7	2.9	....
Sept	1,774.6	8,708.5	35,859.3	7.3	4.5	4.2
Oct	1,784.2	8,748.4	....	9.9	5.2	....
Nov	1,821.5	8,785.8	....	13.4	5.1	....
Dec	1,832.2	8,816.4	....	12.1	5.1	....

[1] Consists of outstanding credit market debt of the U.S. Government, State and local governments, and private nonfinancial sectors.
[2] Money market mutual fund (MMMF). Money market deposit account (MMDA).
[3] Annual changes are from December to December; monthly changes are from six months earlier at a simple annual rate.
[4] Annual changes are from fourth quarter to fourth quarter. Quarterly changes are from previous quarter at annual rate.

Note: The Federal Reserve no longer publishes the M3 monetary aggregate and most of its components. Institutional money market mutual funds is published as a memorandum item in the H.6 release, and the component on large-denomination time deposits is published in other Federal Reserve Board releases. For details, see H.6 release of March 23, 2006.

Source: Board of Governors of the Federal Reserve System.

TABLE B–70. Components of money stock measures, 1970–2010

[Averages of daily figures; billions of dollars, seasonally adjusted]

Year and month	Currency	Nonbank travelers checks	Demand deposits	Other checkable deposits (OCDs)		
				Total	At commercial banks	At thrift institutions
December:						
1970	48.6	0.9	164.7	0.1	0.0	0.1
1971	52.0	1.0	175.1	.2	.0	.2
1972	56.2	1.2	191.6	.2	.0	.2
1973	60.8	1.4	200.3	.3	.0	.3
1974	67.0	1.7	205.1	.4	.2	.4
1975	72.8	2.1	211.3	.9	.4	.5
1976	79.5	2.6	221.5	2.7	1.3	1.4
1977	87.4	2.9	236.4	4.2	1.8	2.3
1978	96.0	3.3	249.5	8.5	5.3	3.1
1979	104.8	3.5	256.6	16.8	12.7	4.2
1980	115.3	3.9	261.2	28.1	20.8	7.3
1981	122.5	4.1	231.4	78.7	63.0	15.6
1982	132.5	4.1	234.1	104.1	80.5	23.6
1983	146.2	4.7	238.5	132.1	97.3	34.8
1984	156.1	5.0	243.4	147.1	104.7	42.4
1985	167.7	5.6	266.9	179.5	124.7	54.9
1986	180.4	6.1	302.9	235.2	161.0	74.2
1987	196.7	6.6	287.7	259.2	178.2	81.0
1988	212.0	7.0	287.1	280.6	192.5	88.1
1989	222.3	6.9	278.6	285.1	197.4	87.7
1990	246.5	7.7	276.8	293.7	208.7	85.0
1991	267.1	7.7	289.6	332.5	241.6	90.9
1992	292.1	8.2	340.0	384.6	280.8	103.8
1993	321.6	8.0	385.4	414.6	302.6	112.0
1994	354.5	8.6	383.6	404.0	297.4	106.6
1995	372.8	9.0	389.0	356.6	249.0	107.6
1996	394.7	8.8	402.2	275.8	172.1	103.7
1997	425.4	8.4	393.8	245.2	148.3	96.8
1998	460.5	8.5	376.9	249.9	143.9	106.0
1999	517.9	8.6	352.9	243.0	139.7	103.3
2000	531.2	8.3	309.8	237.9	133.2	104.7
2001	581.1	8.0	335.8	257.1	142.0	115.1
2002	626.2	7.8	306.7	279.0	154.3	124.7
2003	662.5	7.7	326.3	309.9	175.2	134.7
2004	697.7	7.6	343.2	327.9	186.9	141.0
2005	724.1	7.2	324.3	319.2	180.6	138.6
2006	749.6	6.7	304.1	305.9	176.4	129.4
2007	759.7	6.3	300.4	307.2	172.2	135.0
2008	815.0	5.5	468.6	313.5	177.4	136.0
2009	861.5	5.1	441.0	386.0	231.6	154.4
2010	915.7	4.7	509.7	402.0	235.3	166.8
2009: Jan	827.6	5.5	442.4	311.6	178.8	132.8
Feb	836.8	5.5	405.4	321.2	183.0	138.1
Mar	842.9	5.4	405.7	323.4	183.9	139.5
Apr	847.6	5.3	424.6	332.3	189.9	142.3
May	849.2	5.3	422.2	333.9	193.5	140.5
June	852.8	5.2	443.3	350.3	207.8	142.4
July	855.4	5.1	443.2	357.8	214.0	143.8
Aug	858.3	5.1	430.6	361.3	217.2	144.2
Sept	861.4	5.1	432.9	366.3	220.1	146.3
Oct	861.7	5.1	435.4	377.5	225.9	151.6
Nov	860.3	5.1	432.3	382.3	229.2	153.0
Dec	861.5	5.1	441.0	386.0	231.6	154.4
2010: Jan	861.8	5.1	439.6	374.4	227.0	147.5
Feb	867.4	5.0	447.9	382.9	232.1	150.8
Mar	871.7	5.0	448.4	386.9	236.9	150.1
Apr	876.9	4.9	452.1	366.3	214.3	152.1
May	881.1	4.9	451.7	369.3	216.6	152.7
June	884.0	4.8	462.8	375.8	221.6	154.2
July	888.0	4.8	462.9	375.4	221.3	154.1
Aug	893.5	4.7	473.5	379.8	224.3	155.5
Sept	899.6	4.7	484.7	385.5	227.7	157.8
Oct	906.3	4.7	484.1	389.0	228.1	160.9
Nov	912.8	4.7	502.0	401.9	234.2	167.7
Dec	915.7	4.7	509.7	402.0	235.3	166.8

See next page for continuation of table.

TABLE B–70. Components of money stock measures, 1970–2010—*Continued*

[Averages of daily figures; billions of dollars, seasonally adjusted]

Year and month	Savings deposits [1]			Small-denomination time deposits [2]			Retail money funds	Institutional money funds [3]
	Total	At commercial banks	At thrift institutions	Total	At commercial banks	At thrift institutions		
December:								
1970	261.0	98.6	162.3	151.2	79.3	71.9	0.0	0.0
1971	292.2	112.8	179.4	189.7	94.7	95.1	.0	.0
1972	321.4	124.8	196.6	231.6	108.2	123.5	.0	.0
1973	326.8	128.0	198.7	265.8	116.8	149.0	.1	.0
1974	338.6	136.8	201.8	287.9	123.1	164.8	1.4	.2
1975	388.9	161.2	227.6	337.9	142.3	195.5	2.4	.5
1976	453.2	201.8	251.4	390.7	155.5	235.2	1.8	.6
1977	492.2	218.8	273.4	445.5	167.5	278.0	1.8	1.0
1978	481.9	216.5	265.4	521.0	185.1	335.8	5.8	3.5
1979	423.8	195.0	228.8	634.3	235.5	398.7	33.9	10.4
1980	400.3	185.7	214.5	728.5	286.2	442.3	62.5	16.0
1981	343.9	159.0	184.9	823.1	347.7	475.4	151.7	38.2
1982	400.1	190.1	210.0	850.9	379.9	471.0	183.4	48.8
1983	684.9	363.2	321.7	784.1	350.9	433.1	135.3	40.9
1984	704.7	389.3	315.4	888.8	387.9	500.9	163.8	63.7
1985	815.3	456.6	358.6	885.7	386.4	499.3	173.8	66.7
1986	940.9	533.5	407.4	858.4	369.4	489.0	207.6	87.3
1987	937.4	534.8	402.6	921.0	391.7	529.3	222.3	94.4
1988	926.4	542.4	383.9	1,037.1	451.2	585.9	243.7	94.7
1989	893.7	541.1	352.6	1,151.3	533.8	617.6	320.4	112.4
1990	922.9	501.3	341.6	1,173.3	610.7	562.6	355.4	142.1
1991	1,044.5	664.8	379.6	1,065.3	602.2	463.1	369.6	191.5
1992	1,187.2	754.2	433.1	867.7	508.1	359.7	348.9	216.9
1993	1,219.3	785.3	434.0	781.5	467.9	313.6	348.7	221.5
1994	1,151.3	752.8	398.5	817.5	503.6	313.9	374.0	217.8
1995	1,135.9	774.8	361.0	932.4	575.8	356.5	441.4	271.2
1996	1,275.0	906.2	368.8	947.9	594.2	353.7	512.2	332.5
1997	1,402.1	1,023.1	378.9	967.6	625.5	342.2	589.0	405.5
1998	1,605.8	1,189.1	416.7	951.3	626.4	324.9	720.6	559.8
1999	1,740.4	1,289.1	451.3	955.2	636.9	318.3	814.9	664.7
2000	1,878.0	1,424.1	453.9	1,046.0	700.8	345.2	902.0	820.1
2001	2,309.5	1,738.7	570.8	974.5	636.0	338.5	962.5	1,223.9
2002	2,773.4	2,059.8	713.6	894.5	591.1	303.4	887.5	1,277.9
2003	3,162.8	2,338.0	824.8	817.8	541.7	276.0	777.0	1,137.8
2004	3,508.8	2,632.7	876.1	827.9	551.7	276.2	694.7	1,088.7
2005	3,606.0	2,776.7	829.4	993.1	646.4	346.7	699.4	1,157.8
2006	3,694.6	2,911.3	783.3	1,205.3	780.3	425.0	799.0	1,365.1
2007	3,872.6	3,044.6	828.0	1,275.0	858.1	416.9	972.7	1,919.0
2008	4,106.1	3,334.6	771.5	1,455.7	1,076.9	378.8	1,080.5	2,401.8
2009	4,836.9	3,997.4	839.5	1,177.4	858.0	319.4	820.8	2,212.0
2010	5,357.6	4,436.8	920.8	926.6	656.7	269.9	700.0	1,856.1
2009: Jan	4,198.4	3,422.9	775.5	1,447.9	1,067.6	380.2	1,074.4	2,459.0
Feb	4,285.8	3,497.3	788.6	1,438.1	1,056.1	381.9	1,054.5	2,490.4
Mar	4,350.2	3,548.7	801.5	1,424.9	1,042.3	382.5	1,046.5	2,509.3
Apr	4,351.6	3,542.9	808.7	1,404.7	1,027.6	377.1	1,024.3	2,534.3
May	4,435.0	3,620.0	815.1	1,383.9	1,020.9	363.0	1,002.3	2,554.1
June	4,468.2	3,643.6	824.7	1,360.3	1,002.1	358.2	972.6	2,540.5
July	4,514.7	3,679.4	835.3	1,331.5	978.6	352.9	945.1	2,515.7
Aug	4,556.8	3,725.0	831.8	1,301.7	960.0	341.6	914.9	2,459.3
Sept	4,628.8	3,787.5	841.3	1,268.1	935.6	332.5	889.7	2,405.2
Oct	4,705.8	3,853.4	852.4	1,233.2	904.9	328.3	863.5	2,333.2
Nov	4,784.3	3,949.3	835.0	1,203.3	881.1	322.2	844.0	2,271.3
Dec	4,836.9	3,997.4	839.5	1,177.4	858.0	319.4	820.8	2,212.0
2010: Jan	4,837.7	3,994.9	842.9	1,149.4	834.0	315.4	801.4	2,164.2
Feb	4,913.5	4,052.6	860.9	1,131.0	819.6	311.3	789.5	2,102.8
Mar	4,931.2	4,061.0	870.2	1,109.6	802.2	307.3	762.5	2,032.2
Apr	4,991.7	4,120.9	870.8	1,089.6	787.0	302.6	745.7	1,964.5
May	5,046.1	4,166.4	879.7	1,069.5	771.4	298.2	745.7	1,920.9
June	5,073.6	4,186.8	886.9	1,050.4	756.7	293.7	747.6	1,894.3
July	5,111.0	4,219.1	891.9	1,032.7	742.9	289.9	740.5	1,890.6
Aug	5,163.9	4,264.8	899.1	1,014.3	727.8	286.5	731.0	1,892.2
Sept	5,216.9	4,314.7	902.2	991.3	708.8	282.6	725.7	1,893.8
Oct	5,278.2	4,369.2	909.1	968.3	689.8	278.5	717.7	1,884.7
Nov	5,310.3	4,395.2	915.1	945.9	672.0	273.9	708.1	1,878.1
Dec	5,357.6	4,436.8	920.8	926.6	656.7	269.9	700.0	1,856.1

[1] Savings deposits including money market deposit accounts (MMDAs); data prior to 1982 are savings deposits only.

[2] Small-denomination deposits are those issued in amounts of less than $100,000.

[3] Institutional money funds are not part of non-M1 M2.

Note: See also Table B–69.

Source: Board of Governors of the Federal Reserve System.

TABLE B–71. Aggregate reserves of depository institutions and the monetary base, 1980–2010

[Averages of daily figures [1]; millions of dollars; seasonally adjusted, except as noted]

| Year and month | Adjusted for changes in reserve requirements [2] | | | | | Borrowings from the Federal Reserve (NSA) [3] | | | | | | |
| | Reserves of depository institutions | | | | Monetary base | Total [4] | Term auction credit | Other borrowings from the Federal Reserve [5] | | | | |
	Total	Non-borrowed	Required	Excess (NSA) [3]				Primary	Primary dealer and other broker-dealer credit [6]	Asset-backed commercial paper money market mutual fund liquidity facility	Credit extended to American International Group, Inc., net [7]	Term asset-backed securities loan facility, net [8]
December:												
1980	22,015	20,325	21,501	514	142,004	1,690						
1981	22,443	21,807	22,124	319	149,021	636						
1982	23,600	22,966	23,100	500	160,127	634						
1983	25,367	24,593	24,806	561	175,467	774						
1984	26,913	23,727	26,078	835	187,252	3,186						
1985	31,569	30,250	30,505	1,063	203,555	1,318						
1986	38,840	38,014	37,667	1,173	223,416	827						
1987	38,913	38,135	37,893	1,019	239,829	777						
1988	40,453	38,738	39,392	1,061	256,897	1,716						
1989	40,486	40,221	39,545	941	267,774	265						
1990	41,766	41,440	40,101	1,665	293,280	326						
1991	45,516	45,324	44,526	990	317,538	192						
1992	54,421	54,298	53,267	1,154	350,873	124						
1993	60,566	60,484	59,497	1,069	386,595	82						
1994	59,466	59,257	58,295	1,171	418,306	209						
1995	56,483	56,226	55,193	1,290	434,630	257						
1996	50,185	50,030	48,766	1,418	452,079	155						
1997	46,875	46,551	45,189	1,687	479,992	324						
1998	45,172	45,055	43,660	1,512	513,932	117						
1999	42,173	41,853	40,879	1,294	593,470	[9] 320						
2000	38,703	38,493	37,377	1,325	584,885	210						
2001	41,402	41,336	39,759	1,643	635,441	67						
2002	40,319	40,240	38,311	2,008	681,484	80						
2003	42,618	42,572	41,572	1,046	720,218	46		17				
2004	46,547	46,484	44,639	1,908	759,260	63		11				
2005	45,101	44,932	43,201	1,900	787,447	169		97				
2006	43,234	43,042	41,371	1,862	812,410	191		111				
2007	43,274	27,843	41,489	1,784	824,369	15,430	11,613	3,787				
2008	820,379	166,813	53,049	767,330	1,653,876	653,565	438,327	88,245	47,631	32,102	47,206	
2009	1,138,986	969,059	63,785	1,075,201	2,017,207	169,927	82,014	19,025	0	0	22,023	46,310
2010	1,077,808	1,032,320	70,637	1,007,172	2,008,527	45,488	0	41			20,394	25,025
2009: Jan	857,110	293,613	60,263	796,846	1,703,064	563,496	403,523	70,436	33,061	17,745	38,690	
Feb	700,348	117,851	58,264	642,085	1,555,360	582,497	438,822	65,463	26,250	13,533	38,414	
Mar	779,437	167,326	56,321	723,116	1,640,598	612,111	477,049	62,513	20,292	7,857	43,328	1,061
Apr	880,691	322,497	58,085	822,607	1,746,690	558,194	444,933	47,324	10,918	4,267	45,057	5,649
May	900,803	375,355	58,660	842,143	1,768,730	525,448	403,970	40,124	701	23,347	44,915	12,367
June	809,350	370,627	59,918	749,431	1,680,399	438,722	316,868	37,302	0	18,891	43,057	22,552
July	795,377	428,416	63,122	732,255	1,667,937	366,961	255,119	34,366	0	6,230	43,108	27,993
Aug	828,864	497,414	63,239	765,625	1,704,317	331,450	224,490	32,147	0	184	40,021	33,898
Sept	922,593	615,767	62,706	859,887	1,801,013	306,827	196,731	29,243	0	79	39,074	41,036
Oct	1,056,631	791,573	62,130	994,501	1,935,814	265,058	155,396	25,163	0	28	41,222	42,765
Nov	1,140,782	923,475	63,770	1,077,012	2,017,699	217,307	110,049	20,434	0	0	43,222	43,497
Dec	1,138,986	969,059	63,785	1,077,201	2,017,207	169,927	82,014	19,025	0	0	22,023	46,310
2010: Jan	1,108,984	966,842	63,183	1,045,801	1,987,415	142,142	54,209	16,407	0	0	23,213	47,342
Feb	1,224,796	1,113,569	62,943	1,161,852	2,109,363	111,227	23,677	14,258	0	0	25,544	46,874
Mar	1,185,967	1,094,323	65,596	1,120,371	2,074,803	91,644	7,286	11,136			25,252	47,306
Apr	1,116,371	1,036,147	66,145	1,050,227	2,009,880	80,225	796	6,468			25,739	46,617
May	1,109,378	1,033,753	64,592	1,044,787	2,007,137	75,626	0	4,198			26,397	44,565
June	1,099,260	1,029,363	64,331	1,034,929	1,999,809	69,897	0	288			25,937	43,401
July	1,087,205	1,021,358	65,555	1,021,649	1,991,566	65,847	0	39			24,185	41,548
Aug	1,085,632	1,025,548	66,065	1,019,567	1,994,969	60,083	0	22			22,064	37,913
Sept	1,048,373	995,853	67,529	980,844	1,963,262	52,521	0	32			19,791	32,620
Oct	1,040,230	991,658	66,689	973,541	1,962,121	48,573	0	37			19,478	29,012
Nov	1,038,712	992,023	66,693	972,019	1,967,310	46,689	0	89			19,912	26,665
Dec	1,077,808	1,032,320	70,637	1,007,172	2,008,527	45,488	0	41			20,394	25,025

[1] Data are prorated averages of biweekly (maintenance period) averages of daily figures.

[2] Aggregate reserves incorporate adjustments for discontinuities associated with regulatory changes to reserve requirements. For details on aggregate reserves series see *Federal Reserve Bulletin.*

[3] Not seasonally adjusted (NSA).

[4] Includes secondary, seasonal, other credit extensions, adjustment credit, and extended credit not shown separately.

[5] Does not include credit extensions made by the Federal Reserve Bank of New York to Maiden Lane LLC, Maiden Lane II LLC, Maiden Lane III LLC, and Commercial Paper Funding Facility LLC.

[6] Includes credit extended through the Primary Dealer Credit Facility and credit extended to certain other broker-dealers.

[7] Includes outstanding principal and capitalized interest net of unamortized deferred commitment fees and allowance for loan restructuring. Excludes credit extended to consolidated LLCs as described in footnote 5.

[8] Includes credit extended by Federal Reserve Bank of New York to eligible borrowers through the Term Asset-Backed Securities Loan Facility, net of unamortized deferred administrative fees.

[9] Total includes borrowing under the terms and conditions established for the Century Date Change Special Liquidity Facility in effect from October 1, 1999 through April 7, 2000.

Source: Board of Governors of the Federal Reserve System.

[Monthly average; billions of dollars, seasonally adjusted [1]]

Year and month	Total bank credit	Securities in bank credit [2]			Loans and leases in bank credit						
		Total securities	U.S. Treasury and agency securities	Other securities	Total loans and leases [3]	Commercial and industrial loans	Real estate loans			Consumer loans [6]	Other loans and leases [7]
							Total [4]	Revolving home equity loans	Commercial loans [5]		
December:											
1972	561.8	159.7	86.9	72.8	402.0	133.1	96.9	....	....	85.3	86.8
1973	643.1	166.9	90.1	76.8	476.2	161.2	117.0			98.4	99.7
1974	707.5	172.1	88.2	83.9	535.4	191.3	128.9			102.1	112.2
1975	737.8	204.9	118.1	86.8	532.9	183.4	134.1			104.3	111.1
1976	798.6	226.7	137.5	89.1	571.9	185.2	148.5			115.8	123.3
1977	885.6	234.3	137.5	96.8	651.3	204.7	175.1			138.0	133.5
1978	1,003.8	240.3	138.4	101.9	763.5	237.2	210.5			164.4	151.4
1979	1,118.8	258.6	146.7	111.9	860.2	279.7	241.6			183.8	155.1
1980	1,217.5	294.2	172.1	122.0	923.3	312.0	262.2			178.7	170.4
1981	1,298.1	307.4	180.4	127.0	990.7	350.3	283.5			182.1	174.7
1982	1,397.8	334.4	203.0	131.4	1,063.5	392.0	299.6			187.9	184.1
1983	1,549.5	398.6	260.9	137.8	1,150.9	413.8	330.2			212.9	194.0
1984	1,715.0	401.3	260.2	141.1	1,313.7	473.0	376.0			253.8	210.8
1985	1,876.4	440.2	263.8	176.4	1,436.2	498.8	421.8			291.0	224.7
1986	2,071.4	498.3	309.6	188.8	1,573.1	539.0	490.4			314.8	229.0
1987	2,220.8	525.2	335.3	189.9	1,695.6	564.8	585.4	30.1		327.3	218.1
1988	2,394.5	548.4	359.2	189.2	1,846.1	604.3	662.8	40.5		355.5	223.5
1989	2,558.5	569.7	400.3	169.4	1,988.8	636.4	760.2	50.4		373.8	210.4
1990	2,695.9	618.0	458.8	159.3	2,077.9	639.3	841.4	61.9		375.6	221.6
1991	2,805.7	726.8	559.6	167.2	2,078.9	617.2	868.4	70.2		363.7	229.7
1992	2,906.2	824.0	658.5	165.4	2,082.2	596.9	887.2	73.4		354.8	243.3
1993	3,062.4	896.3	724.0	172.3	2,166.1	584.1	928.9	72.7		386.2	267.0
1994	3,234.9	893.6	714.1	179.6	2,341.3	643.8	987.4	74.8		443.7	266.4
1995	3,463.6	895.7	694.2	201.4	2,568.0	715.4	1,061.5	78.8		484.4	306.7
1996	3,635.0	895.8	694.4	201.3	2,739.2	778.8	1,121.8	85.4		505.6	333.1
1997	3,958.0	988.3	747.2	241.1	2,969.7	845.8	1,220.0	98.1		498.8	405.1
1998	4,364.5	1,096.3	790.5	305.7	3,268.2	939.2	1,310.3	96.8		495.9	522.8
1999	4,624.7	1,163.9	805.4	358.4	3,460.8	1,001.8	1,459.8	101.1		485.7	513.5
2000	5,031.3	1,197.3	781.6	415.6	3,834.1	1,086.9	1,638.6	129.3		532.0	576.5
2001	5,215.8	1,330.7	839.7	491.0	3,885.1	1,023.7	1,759.0	153.7		550.0	552.5
2002	5,646.9	1,519.8	1,005.6	514.2	4,127.0	961.6	2,010.7	212.3		578.9	575.9
2003	6,008.1	1,649.3	1,089.5	559.8	4,358.8	888.7	2,208.9	278.4		635.4	625.7
2004	6,580.2	1,742.7	1,146.9	595.7	4,837.6	912.7	2,555.2	395.1	1,081.9	685.6	684.0
2005	7,298.6	1,853.0	1,136.0	717.0	5,445.6	1,043.3	2,926.0	443.1	1,272.1	697.0	779.3
2006	8,083.9	1,981.9	1,187.4	794.6	6,102.0	1,191.7	3,369.0	467.8	1,459.6	730.8	810.5
2007	8,887.2	2,099.1	1,108.1	991.0	6,788.1	1,429.9	3,596.2	484.4	1,583.4	792.1	969.8
2008	9,358.3	2,099.9	1,238.4	861.4	7,258.4	1,584.4	3,821.3	588.4	1,726.5	859.5	993.2
2009	9,003.0	2,330.4	1,440.1	890.3	6,672.7	1,290.6	3,781.7	601.8	1,641.7	830.7	769.7
2010	9,190.3	2,426.4	1,620.8	805.6	6,763.9	1,219.5	3,612.9	580.7	1,496.6	1,113.9	817.7
2009: Jan	9,330.9	2,150.2	1,269.5	880.6	7,180.7	1,569.3	3,802.6	593.4	1,720.2	869.7	939.1
Feb	9,345.0	2,164.4	1,259.6	904.9	7,180.5	1,554.5	3,826.4	596.3	1,721.0	881.8	917.9
Mar	9,303.0	2,182.5	1,271.4	911.1	7,120.5	1,534.3	3,827.9	600.1	1,720.0	873.0	885.3
Apr	9,259.1	2,180.0	1,259.2	920.8	7,079.1	1,517.1	3,831.8	604.6	1,714.8	861.6	868.6
May	9,317.9	2,202.8	1,262.5	940.2	7,115.2	1,495.4	3,873.0	612.4	1,712.4	859.4	887.3
June	9,292.2	2,246.3	1,302.9	943.4	7,045.9	1,463.2	3,855.8	610.5	1,703.9	856.9	870.0
July	9,209.1	2,271.5	1,346.7	924.8	6,937.6	1,426.7	3,834.7	607.4	1,696.1	852.9	823.3
Aug	9,153.8	2,297.3	1,378.3	919.0	6,856.5	1,392.8	3,811.6	605.9	1,687.9	850.5	801.6
Sept	9,066.7	2,306.6	1,395.7	911.0	6,760.0	1,361.3	3,764.3	604.0	1,677.9	847.2	787.2
Oct	8,979.2	2,296.3	1,387.3	909.0	6,682.9	1,328.7	3,741.5	601.9	1,666.0	843.2	769.4
Nov	9,044.2	2,309.2	1,406.3	902.8	6,735.0	1,312.3	3,806.4	605.0	1,657.9	838.9	777.5
Dec	9,003.0	2,330.4	1,440.1	890.3	6,672.7	1,290.6	3,781.7	601.8	1,641.7	830.7	769.7
2010: Jan	8,934.7	2,330.7	1,439.2	891.5	6,604.0	1,262.3	3,759.2	599.0	1,627.8	814.6	767.9
Feb	8,874.3	2,330.7	1,448.6	882.0	6,543.6	1,244.7	3,721.8	598.2	1,620.0	813.9	763.1
Mar	8,939.0	2,321.5	1,461.9	859.6	6,617.5	1,231.9	3,706.4	599.2	1,610.2	893.2	786.0
Apr	9,258.7	2,329.1	1,507.1	822.0	6,929.6	1,229.8	3,709.5	602.2	1,601.1	1,165.4	824.8
May	9,204.4	2,310.8	1,504.9	805.9	6,893.6	1,220.6	3,696.8	599.4	1,588.3	1,156.0	820.2
June	9,163.9	2,296.1	1,497.5	798.6	6,867.8	1,216.4	3,679.8	597.4	1,575.7	1,152.2	819.5
July	9,216.0	2,364.1	1,551.4	812.7	6,851.9	1,216.5	3,658.4	596.3	1,561.5	1,151.4	825.6
Aug	9,233.4	2,397.3	1,579.3	818.0	6,836.1	1,216.7	3,652.2	594.9	1,550.5	1,145.3	821.9
Sept	9,223.9	2,424.5	1,604.4	820.2	6,799.4	1,212.7	3,640.5	592.2	1,537.8	1,131.2	814.9
Oct	9,239.4	2,447.1	1,631.1	816.0	6,792.3	1,211.6	3,624.5	588.3	1,521.9	1,126.4	829.8
Nov	9,235.0	2,456.2	1,638.2	817.9	6,778.9	1,211.8	3,621.6	585.2	1,509.5	1,119.9	825.5
Dec	9,190.3	2,426.4	1,620.8	805.6	6,763.9	1,219.5	3,612.9	580.7	1,496.6	1,113.9	817.7

[1] Data are prorated averages of Wednesday values for domestically chartered commercial banks, branches and agencies of foreign banks, New York State investment companies (through September 1996), and Edge Act and agreement corporations.

[2] Includes securities held in trading accounts, held-to-maturity, and available for sale. Excludes all non-security trading assets, such as derivatives with a positive fair value or loans held in trading accounts.

[3] Excludes unearned income. Includes the allowance for loan and lease losses. Excludes Federal funds sold to, reverse repurchase agreements (RPs) with, and loans to commercial banks. Includes all loans held in trading accounts under a fair value option.

[4] Includes closed-end residential loans, not shown separately.

[5] Includes construction, land development, and other land loans, and loans secured by farmland, multifamily (5 or more) residential properties, and nonfarm nonresidential properties.

[6] Includes credit cards and other consumer loans.

[7] Includes other items, not shown separately.

Note: Data in this table are shown as of January 21, 2011.

Source: Board of Governors of the Federal Reserve System.

[Percent per annum]

| Year and month | U.S. Treasury securities | | | | | Corporate bonds (Moody's) | | High-grade municipal bonds (Standard & Poor's) | New-home mortgage yields[4] | Prime rate charged by banks[5] | Discount window (Federal Reserve Bank of New York)[5,6] | | Federal funds rate[7] |
| | Bills (at auction)[1] | | Constant maturities[2] | | | | | | | | | | |
	3-month	6-month	3-year	10-year	30-year	Aaa[3]	Baa				Primary credit	Adjustment credit	
1933	0.515	....	....	....	....	4.49	7.76	4.71	....	1.50–4.00	....	2.56	....
1939	.023	....	....	....	....	3.01	4.96	2.76	....	1.50	....	1.00	....
1940	.014	....	....	....	....	2.84	4.75	2.50	....	1.50	....	1.00	....
1941	.103	....	....	....	....	2.77	4.33	2.10	....	1.50	....	1.00	....
1942	.326	....	....	....	....	2.83	4.28	2.36	....	1.50	....	[8]1.00	....
1943	.373	....	....	....	....	2.73	3.91	2.06	....	1.50	....	[8]1.00	....
1944	.375	....	....	....	....	2.72	3.61	1.86	....	1.50	....	[8]1.00	....
1945	.375	....	....	....	....	2.62	3.29	1.67	....	1.50	....	[8]1.00	....
1946	.375	....	....	....	....	2.53	3.05	1.64	....	1.50	....	[8]1.00	....
1947	.594	....	....	....	....	2.61	3.24	2.01	....	1.50–1.75	....	1.00	....
1948	1.040	....	....	....	....	2.82	3.47	2.40	....	1.75–2.00	....	1.34	....
1949	1.102	....	....	....	....	2.66	3.42	2.21	....	2.00	....	1.50	....
1950	1.218	....	....	....	....	2.62	3.24	1.98	....	2.07	....	1.59	....
1951	1.552	....	....	....	....	2.86	3.41	2.00	....	2.56	....	1.75	....
1952	1.766	....	....	....	....	2.96	3.52	2.19	....	3.00	....	1.75	....
1953	1.931	....	2.47	2.85	....	3.20	3.74	2.72	....	3.17	....	1.99	....
1954	.953	....	1.63	2.40	....	2.90	3.51	2.37	....	3.05	....	1.60	....
1955	1.753	....	2.47	2.82	....	3.06	3.53	2.53	....	3.16	....	1.89	1.79
1956	2.658	....	3.19	3.18	....	3.36	3.88	2.93	....	3.77	....	2.77	2.73
1957	3.267	....	3.98	3.65	....	3.89	4.71	3.60	....	4.20	....	3.12	3.11
1958	1.839	....	2.84	3.32	....	3.79	4.73	3.56	....	3.83	....	2.15	1.57
1959	3.405	3.832	4.46	4.33	....	4.38	5.05	3.95	....	4.48	....	3.36	3.31
1960	2.93	3.25	3.98	4.12	....	4.41	5.19	3.73	....	4.82	....	3.53	3.21
1961	2.38	2.61	3.54	3.88	....	4.35	5.08	3.46	....	4.50	....	3.00	1.95
1962	2.78	2.91	3.47	3.95	....	4.33	5.02	3.18	....	4.50	....	3.00	2.71
1963	3.16	3.25	3.67	4.00	....	4.26	4.86	3.23	5.89	4.50	....	3.23	3.18
1964	3.56	3.69	4.03	4.19	....	4.40	4.83	3.22	5.83	4.50	....	3.55	3.50
1965	3.95	4.05	4.22	4.28	....	4.49	4.87	3.27	5.81	4.54	....	4.04	4.07
1966	4.88	5.08	5.23	4.93	....	5.13	5.67	3.82	6.25	5.63	....	4.50	5.11
1967	4.32	4.63	5.03	5.07	....	5.51	6.23	3.98	6.46	5.63	....	4.19	4.22
1968	5.34	5.47	5.68	5.64	....	6.18	6.94	4.51	6.97	6.31	....	5.17	5.66
1969	6.68	6.85	7.02	6.67	....	7.03	7.81	5.81	7.81	7.96	....	5.87	8.21
1970	6.43	6.53	7.29	7.35	....	8.04	9.11	6.51	8.45	7.91	....	5.95	7.17
1971	4.35	4.51	5.66	6.16	....	7.39	8.56	5.70	7.74	5.73	....	4.88	4.67
1972	4.07	4.47	5.72	6.21	....	7.21	8.16	5.27	7.60	5.25	....	4.50	4.44
1973	7.04	7.18	6.96	6.85	....	7.44	8.24	5.18	7.96	8.03	....	6.45	8.74
1974	7.89	7.93	7.84	7.56	....	8.57	9.50	6.09	8.92	10.81	....	7.83	10.51
1975	5.84	6.12	7.50	7.99	....	8.83	10.61	6.89	9.00	7.86	....	6.25	5.82
1976	4.99	5.27	6.77	7.61	....	8.43	9.75	6.49	9.00	6.84	....	5.50	5.05
1977	5.27	5.52	6.68	7.42	7.75	8.02	8.97	5.56	9.02	6.83	....	5.46	5.54
1978	7.22	7.58	8.29	8.41	8.49	8.73	9.49	5.90	9.56	9.06	....	7.46	7.94
1979	10.05	10.02	9.70	9.43	9.28	9.63	10.69	6.39	10.78	12.67	....	10.29	11.20
1980	11.51	11.37	11.51	11.43	11.27	11.94	13.67	8.51	12.66	15.26	....	11.77	13.35
1981	14.03	13.78	14.46	13.92	13.45	14.17	16.04	11.23	14.70	18.87	....	13.42	16.39
1982	10.69	11.08	12.93	13.01	12.76	13.79	16.11	11.57	15.14	14.85	....	11.01	12.24
1983	8.63	8.75	10.45	11.10	11.18	12.04	13.55	9.47	12.57	10.79	....	8.50	9.09
1984	9.53	9.77	11.92	12.46	12.41	12.71	14.19	10.15	12.38	12.04	....	8.80	10.23
1985	7.47	7.64	9.64	10.62	10.79	11.37	12.72	9.18	11.55	9.93	....	7.69	8.10
1986	5.98	6.03	7.06	7.67	7.78	9.02	10.39	7.38	10.17	8.33	....	6.32	6.80
1987	5.82	6.05	7.68	8.39	8.59	9.38	10.58	7.73	9.31	8.21	....	5.66	6.66
1988	6.69	6.92	8.26	8.85	8.96	9.71	10.83	7.76	9.19	9.32	....	6.20	7.57
1989	8.12	8.04	8.55	8.49	8.45	9.26	10.18	7.24	10.13	10.87	....	6.93	9.21
1990	7.51	7.47	8.26	8.55	8.61	9.32	10.36	7.25	10.05	10.01	....	6.98	8.10
1991	5.42	5.49	6.82	7.86	8.14	8.77	9.80	6.89	9.32	8.46	....	5.45	5.69
1992	3.45	3.57	5.30	7.01	7.67	8.14	8.98	6.41	8.24	6.25	....	3.25	3.52
1993	3.02	3.14	4.44	5.87	6.59	7.22	7.93	5.63	7.20	6.00	....	3.00	3.02
1994	4.29	4.66	6.27	7.09	7.37	7.96	8.62	6.19	7.49	7.15	....	3.60	4.21
1995	5.51	5.59	6.25	6.57	6.88	7.59	8.20	5.95	7.87	8.83	....	5.21	5.83
1996	5.02	5.09	5.99	6.44	6.71	7.37	8.05	5.75	7.80	8.27	....	5.02	5.30
1997	5.07	5.18	6.10	6.35	6.61	7.26	7.86	5.55	7.71	8.44	....	5.00	5.46
1998	4.81	4.85	5.14	5.26	5.58	6.53	7.22	5.12	7.07	8.35	....	4.92	5.35
1999	4.66	4.76	5.49	5.65	5.87	7.04	7.87	5.43	7.04	8.00	....	4.62	4.97
2000	5.85	5.92	6.22	6.03	5.94	7.62	8.36	5.77	7.52	9.23	....	5.73	6.24
2001	3.44	3.39	4.09	5.02	5.49	7.08	7.95	5.19	7.00	6.91	....	3.40	3.88
2002	1.62	1.69	3.10	4.61	5.43	6.49	7.80	5.05	6.43	4.67	....	1.17	1.67
2003	1.01	1.06	2.10	4.01	....	5.67	6.77	4.73	5.80	4.12	2.12	....	1.13
2004	1.38	1.57	2.78	4.27	....	5.63	6.39	4.63	5.77	4.34	2.34	....	1.35
2005	3.16	3.40	3.93	4.29	....	5.24	6.06	4.29	5.94	6.19	4.19	....	3.22
2006	4.73	4.80	4.77	4.80	4.91	5.59	6.48	4.42	6.63	7.96	5.96	....	4.97
2007	4.41	4.48	4.35	4.63	4.84	5.56	6.48	4.42	6.41	8.05	5.86	....	5.02
2008	1.48	1.71	2.24	3.66	4.28	5.63	7.45	4.80	6.05	5.09	2.39	....	1.92
2009	.16	.29	1.43	3.26	4.08	5.31	7.30	4.64	5.14	3.25	.50	....	.16
2010	.14	.20	1.11	3.22	4.25	4.94	6.04	4.16	4.80	3.25	.72	....	.18

[1] High bill rate at auction, issue date within period, bank-discount basis. On or after October 28, 1998, data are stop yields from uniform-price auctions. Before that date, they are weighted average yields from multiple-price auctions.

See next page for continuation of table.

[Percent per annum]

Year and month	U.S. Treasury securities					Corporate bonds (Moody's)		High-grade municipal bonds (Standard & Poor's)	New-home mortgage yields [4]	Prime rate charged by banks [5]	Discount window (Federal Reserve Bank of New York) [5,6]		Federal funds rate [7]
	Bills (at auction) [1]		Constant maturities [2]								Primary credit	Adjustment credit	
	3-month	6-month	3-year	10-year	30-year	Aaa [3]	Baa						
										High-low	High-low	High-low	
2006: Jan	4.20	4.29	4.35	4.42	....	5.29	6.24	4.31	6.12	7.50–7.25	5.50–5.25	....	4.29
Feb	4.41	4.51	4.64	4.57	4.54	5.35	6.27	4.41	6.40	7.50–7.50	5.50–5.50	....	4.49
Mar	4.51	4.61	4.74	4.72	4.73	5.53	6.41	4.44	6.53	7.75–7.50	5.75–5.50	....	4.59
Apr	4.59	4.71	4.89	4.99	5.06	5.84	6.68	4.60	6.64	7.75–7.75	5.75–5.75	....	4.79
May	4.72	4.81	4.97	5.11	5.20	5.95	6.75	4.61	6.69	8.00–7.75	6.00–5.75	....	4.94
June	4.79	4.95	5.09	5.11	5.15	5.89	6.78	4.64	6.79	8.25–8.00	6.25–6.00	....	4.99
July	4.96	5.09	5.07	5.09	5.13	5.85	6.76	4.64	6.81	8.25–8.25	6.25–6.25	....	5.24
Aug	4.98	4.99	4.85	4.88	5.00	5.68	6.59	4.43	6.87	8.25–8.25	6.25–6.25	....	5.25
Sept	4.82	4.90	4.69	4.72	4.85	5.51	6.43	4.30	6.72	8.25–8.25	6.25–6.25	....	5.25
Oct	4.89	4.91	4.72	4.73	4.85	5.51	6.42	4.32	6.69	8.25–8.25	6.25–6.25	....	5.25
Nov	4.95	4.95	4.64	4.60	4.69	5.33	6.20	4.17	6.55	8.25–8.25	6.25–6.25	....	5.25
Dec	4.84	4.87	4.58	4.56	4.68	5.32	6.22	4.17	6.37	8.25–8.25	6.25–6.25	....	5.24
2007: Jan	4.96	4.93	4.79	4.76	4.85	5.40	6.34	4.29	6.35	8.25–8.25	6.25–6.25	....	5.25
Feb	5.02	4.96	4.75	4.72	4.82	5.39	6.28	4.21	6.31	8.25–8.25	6.25–6.25	....	5.26
Mar	4.96	4.90	4.51	4.56	4.72	5.30	6.27	4.18	6.22	8.25–8.25	6.25–6.25	....	5.26
Apr	4.87	4.87	4.60	4.69	4.87	5.47	6.39	4.32	6.21	8.25–8.25	6.25–6.25	....	5.25
May	4.77	4.00	4.09	4.75	4.90	5.47	6.39	4.37	6.22	8.25–8.25	6.25–6.25	....	5.25
June	4.63	4.77	5.00	5.10	5.20	5.79	6.70	4.64	6.54	8.25–8.25	6.25–6.25	....	5.25
July	4.83	4.85	4.82	5.00	5.11	5.73	6.65	4.64	6.70	8.25–8.25	6.25–6.25	....	5.26
Aug	4.34	4.56	4.34	4.67	4.93	5.79	6.65	4.73	6.73	8.25–8.25	6.25–5.75	....	5.02
Sept	4.01	4.13	4.06	4.52	4.79	5.74	6.59	4.57	6.58	8.25–7.75	5.75–5.25	....	4.94
Oct	3.96	4.08	4.01	4.53	4.77	5.66	6.48	4.41	6.55	7.75–7.50	5.25–5.00	....	4.76
Nov	3.49	3.63	3.35	4.15	4.52	5.44	6.40	4.45	6.42	7.50–7.50	5.00–5.00	....	4.49
Dec	3.08	3.29	3.13	4.10	4.53	5.49	6.65	4.22	6.21	7.50–7.25	5.00–4.75	....	4.24
2008: Jan	2.86	2.84	2.51	3.74	4.33	5.33	6.54	4.00	6.02	7.25–6.00	4.75–3.50	....	3.94
Feb	2.21	2.09	2.19	3.74	4.52	5.53	6.82	4.35	5.96	6.00–6.00	3.50–3.50	....	2.98
Mar	1.38	1.53	1.80	3.51	4.39	5.51	6.89	4.67	5.92	6.00–5.25	3.50–2.50	....	2.61
Apr	1.32	1.54	2.23	3.68	4.44	5.55	6.97	4.43	5.98	5.25–5.00	2.50–2.25	....	2.28
May	1.71	1.82	2.69	3.88	4.60	5.57	6.93	4.34	6.01	5.00–5.00	2.25–2.25	....	1.98
June	1.89	2.15	3.08	4.10	4.69	5.68	7.07	4.48	6.13	5.00–5.00	2.25–2.25	....	2.00
July	1.72	1.99	2.87	4.01	4.57	5.67	7.16	4.88	6.29	5.00–5.00	2.25–2.25	....	2.01
Aug	1.79	1.96	2.70	3.89	4.50	5.64	7.15	4.90	6.33	5.00–5.00	2.25–2.25	....	2.00
Sept	1.46	1.78	2.32	3.69	4.27	5.65	7.31	5.03	6.09	5.00–5.00	2.25–2.25	....	1.81
Oct	.84	1.39	1.86	3.81	4.17	6.28	8.88	5.68	6.10	5.00–4.00	2.25–1.25	....	.97
Nov	.30	.86	1.51	3.53	4.00	6.12	9.21	5.28	6.16	4.00–4.00	1.25–1.25	....	.39
Dec	.04	.32	1.07	2.42	2.87	5.05	8.43	5.53	5.67	4.00–3.25	1.25–0.50	....	.16
2009: Jan	.12	.31	1.13	2.52	3.13	5.05	8.14	5.13	5.11	3.25–3.25	0.50–0.50	....	.15
Feb	.31	.46	1.37	2.87	3.59	5.27	8.08	5.00	5.09	3.25–3.25	0.50–0.50	....	.22
Mar	.25	.43	1.31	2.82	3.64	5.50	8.42	5.15	5.10	3.25–3.25	0.50–0.50	....	.18
Apr	.17	.37	1.32	2.93	3.76	5.39	8.39	4.88	4.96	3.25–3.25	0.50–0.50	....	.15
May	.19	.31	1.39	3.29	4.23	5.54	8.06	4.60	4.92	3.25–3.25	0.50–0.50	....	.18
June	.17	.32	1.76	3.72	4.52	5.61	7.50	4.84	5.17	3.25–3.25	0.50–0.50	....	.21
July	.19	.29	1.55	3.56	4.41	5.41	7.09	4.69	5.40	3.25–3.25	0.50–0.50	....	.16
Aug	.18	.27	1.65	3.59	4.37	5.26	6.58	4.58	5.32	3.25–3.25	0.50–0.50	....	.16
Sept	.13	.22	1.48	3.40	4.19	5.13	6.31	4.13	5.26	3.25–3.25	0.50–0.50	....	.15
Oct	.08	.17	1.46	3.39	4.19	5.15	6.29	4.20	5.14	3.25–3.25	0.50–0.50	....	.12
Nov	.06	.16	1.32	3.40	4.31	5.19	6.32	4.35	5.08	3.25–3.25	0.50–0.50	....	.12
Dec	.07	.17	1.38	3.59	4.49	5.26	6.37	4.16	5.01	3.25–3.25	0.50–0.50	....	.12
2010: Jan	.06	.15	1.49	3.73	4.60	5.26	6.25	4.22	5.04	3.25–3.25	0.50–0.50	....	.11
Feb	.10	.18	1.40	3.69	4.62	5.35	6.34	4.23	5.08	3.25–3.25	0.75–0.50	....	.13
Mar	.15	.22	1.51	3.73	4.64	5.27	6.27	4.22	5.09	3.25–3.25	0.75–0.75	....	.16
Apr	.15	.24	1.64	3.85	4.69	5.29	6.25	4.24	5.21	3.25–3.25	0.75–0.75	....	.20
May	.16	.23	1.32	3.42	4.29	4.96	6.05	4.15	5.12	3.25–3.25	0.75–0.75	....	.20
June	.12	.19	1.17	3.20	4.13	4.88	6.23	4.18	5.00	3.25–3.25	0.75–0.75	....	.18
July	.16	.20	.98	3.01	3.99	4.72	6.01	4.11	4.87	3.25–3.25	0.75–0.75	....	.18
Aug	.15	.19	.78	2.70	3.80	4.49	5.66	3.91	4.67	3.25–3.25	0.75–0.75	....	.19
Sept	.15	.19	.74	2.65	3.77	4.53	5.66	3.76	4.52	3.25–3.25	0.75–0.75	....	.19
Oct	.13	.17	.57	2.54	3.87	4.68	5.72	3.83	4.40	3.25–3.25	0.75–0.75	....	.19
Nov	.13	.17	.67	2.76	4.19	4.87	5.92	4.30	4.26	3.25–3.25	0.75–0.75	....	.19
Dec	.15	.20	.99	3.29	4.42	5.02	6.10	4.72	4.44	3.25–3.25	0.75–0.75	....	.18

[2] Yields on the more actively traded issues adjusted to constant maturities by the Department of the Treasury. The 30-year Treasury constant maturity series was discontinued on February 18, 2002, and reintroduced on February 9, 2006.

[3] Beginning with December 7, 2001, data for corporate Aaa series are industrial bonds only.

[4] Effective rate (in the primary market) on conventional mortgages, reflecting fees and charges as well as contract rate and assuming, on the average, repayment at end of 10 years. Rates beginning with January 1973 not strictly comparable with prior rates.

[5] For monthly data, high and low for the period. Prime rate for 1929–1933 and 1947–1948 are ranges of the rate in effect during the period.

[6] Primary credit replaced adjustment credit as the Federal Reserve's principal discount window lending program effective January 9, 2003.

[7] Since July 19, 1975, the daily effective rate is an average of the rates on a given day weighted by the volume of transactions at these rates. Prior to that date, the daily effective rate was the rate considered most representative of the day's transactions, usually the one at which most transactions occurred.

[8] From October 30, 1942 to April 24, 1946, a preferential rate of 0.50 percent was in effect for advances secured by Government securities maturing in one year or less.

Sources: Department of the Treasury, Board of Governors of the Federal Reserve System, Federal Housing Finance Agency, Moody's Investors Service, and Standard & Poor's.

TABLE B–74. Credit market borrowing, 2002–2010

[Billions of dollars; quarterly data at seasonally adjusted annual rates]

Item	2002	2003	2004	2005	2006	2007	2008	2009
NONFINANCIAL SECTORS								
Domestic	1,418.6	1,683.4	1,983.3	2,324.7	2,413.6	2,523.1	1,906.2	1,023.2
By instrument	1,418.6	1,683.4	1,983.3	2,324.7	2,413.6	2,523.1	1,906.2	1,023.2
Commercial paper	−57.9	−37.3	15.3	−7.7	22.4	11.3	7.7	−72.4
Treasury securities	257.1	398.4	362.5	307.3	183.7	237.5	1,239.0	1,443.7
Agency- and GSE-backed securities [1]	0.5	−2.4	−.6	−.4	−.3	−.4	.2	.1
Municipal securities	159.4	137.6	130.5	195.0	177.4	215.6	61.3	130.9
Corporate bonds	133.4	151.9	75.5	56.7	215.6	311.2	204.6	381.6
Bank loans n.e.c.	−108.2	−76.3	5.2	134.5	175.3	240.2	192.6	−295.7
Other loans and advances	39.7	10.3	58.6	119.3	159.8	311.0	74.9	−154.0
Mortgages	889.5	995.2	1,219.1	1,419.7	1,384.2	1,057.4	87.1	−295.9
Home	754.7	817.0	1,013.5	1,114.2	1,073.2	711.3	−103.7	−210.5
Multifamily residential	37.3	71.6	43.7	62.4	40.4	84.1	44.6	8.8
Commercial	90.7	118.8	149.5	234.0	267.4	257.4	125.4	−95.0
Farm	6.9	−12.2	12.5	9.1	3.3	4.6	20.9	.9
Consumer credit	105.2	105.9	117.2	100.4	95.4	139.3	38.8	−115.3
By sector	1,418.6	1,683.4	1,983.3	2,324.7	2,413.6	2,523.1	1,906.2	1,023.2
Household sector	825.0	1,000.8	1,049.7	1,173.3	1,186.6	873.4	35.9	−240.0
Nonfinancial business	191.5	166.0	457.6	672.6	889.9	1,221.7	579.6	−292.0
Corporate	33.6	87.0	196.6	323.7	467.1	752.3	364.2	.7
Nonfarm noncorporate	150.8	91.5	245.2	331.6	408.6	454.8	211.4	−290.7
Farm	7.1	−12.6	15.8	17.3	14.2	14.6	4.0	−2.0
State and local governments	144.6	120.5	114.1	172.0	153.7	191.0	51.5	111.3
Federal Government	257.6	396.0	361.9	306.9	183.4	237.1	1,239.2	1,443.9
Foreign borrowing in the United States	93.4	43.0	155.3	113.0	332.6	170.3	−226.3	191.8
Commercial paper	58.8	18.9	69.2	38.6	98.4	−69.3	−71.0	57.8
Bonds	31.6	28.7	85.8	64.5	227.8	218.7	−158.9	144.9
Bank loans n.e.c.	5.3	−2.5	3.8	14.5	13.8	24.1	5.1	−11.2
Other loans and advances	−2.3	−2.1	−3.6	−4.6	−7.4	−3.2	−1.5	.3
Nonfinancial domestic and foreign borrowing	1,512.0	1,726.3	2,138.6	2,437.8	2,746.2	2,693.5	1,679.9	1,215.0
FINANCIAL SECTORS								
By instrument	886.6	1,071.6	971.4	1,114.9	1,297.3	1,789.6	905.5	−1,858.9
Open market paper	−99.9	−63.5	21.7	214.2	196.3	−111.4	−125.6	−446.7
GSE issues [1]	219.8	250.9	75.0	−84.0	35.6	282.4	271.7	−475.3
Agency- and GSE-backed mortgage pool securities [1]	326.8	335.4	40.8	164.5	292.6	623.3	497.0	415.0
Corporate bonds	398.8	487.3	668.3	743.0	807.3	694.0	−273.8	−605.2
Bank loans n.e.c.	23.1	21.4	66.0	18.8	−62.3	70.9	496.1	−467.4
Other loans and advances	6.8	31.2	74.1	44.4	21.2	225.8	33.3	−282.6
Mortgages	11.2	8.9	25.5	14.1	6.6	4.7	6.8	3.4
By sector	886.6	1,071.6	971.4	1,114.9	1,297.3	1,789.6	905.5	−1,858.9
Commercial banking	49.7	48.5	78.4	85.1	177.4	263.2	161.1	−179.9
U.S.-chartered commercial banks	29.9	13.2	18.7	36.9	107.5	131.8	79.1	−152.6
Foreign banking offices in the United States	−0.4	−.1	.1	.0	−.3	.0	−.2	.0
Bank holding companies	20.3	35.4	59.5	48.2	70.2	131.3	82.3	−27.3
Savings institutions	−23.1	35.3	91.4	22.5	−108.2	104.1	−67.1	−169.6
Credit unions	2.0	2.2	2.3	3.3	4.2	13.4	8.3	−14.1
Life insurance companies	2.0	2.9	3.0	.4	2.7	14.5	26.2	−6.6
Government-sponsored enterprises	219.8	250.9	75.0	−84.0	35.6	282.4	271.7	−475.3
Agency- and GSE-backed mortgage pools [1]	326.8	335.4	40.8	164.5	292.6	623.3	497.0	415.0
Asset-backed securities issuers	228.5	249.8	439.3	729.4	807.8	336.0	−407.9	−755.9
Finance companies	66.2	111.1	134.3	33.5	34.8	34.9	−79.4	−156.2
REITs [2]	27.0	32.3	94.6	55.4	15.5	10.2	−48.6	−33.7
Brokers and dealers	−1.7	6.4	15.2	.1	6.4	−4.0	77.7	−49.7
Funding corporations	−10.7	−3.2	−2.9	104.7	28.3	111.6	466.4	−432.8
ALL SECTORS, BY INSTRUMENT								
Total	2,398.6	2,797.9	3,110.0	3,552.7	4,043.4	4,483.1	2,585.4	−643.9
Open market paper	−99.1	−82.0	106.2	245.1	317.1	−169.4	−189.0	−461.3
Treasury securities	257.1	398.4	362.5	307.3	183.7	237.5	1,239.0	1,443.7
Agency- and GSE-backed securities [1]	547.2	583.8	115.2	80.0	327.9	905.3	768.9	−60.2
Municipal securities	159.4	137.6	130.5	195.0	177.4	215.6	61.3	130.9
Corporate and foreign bonds	563.8	668.0	829.5	864.2	1,250.6	1,223.9	−228.1	−78.6
Bank loans n.e.c.	−79.8	−57.4	75.1	167.8	126.8	335.1	693.8	−774.3
Other loans and advances	44.2	39.4	129.2	159.1	173.6	533.6	106.7	−436.3
Mortgages	900.7	1,004.1	1,244.6	1,433.8	1,390.8	1,062.1	93.9	−292.5
Consumer credit	105.2	105.9	117.2	100.4	95.4	139.3	38.8	−115.3

[1] Government-sponsored enterprises (GSE).
[2] Real estate investment trusts (REITs).

See next page for continuation of table.

[Billions of dollars; quarterly data at seasonally adjusted annual rates]

Item	2009				2010		
	I	II	III	IV	I	II	III
NONFINANCIAL SECTORS							
Domestic	1,572.5	1,497.7	719.0	303.5	1,489.4	1,663.3	1,473.1
By instrument	1,572.5	1,497.7	719.0	303.5	1,489.4	1,663.3	1,473.1
Commercial paper	−138.4	−132.4	2.4	−21.2	54.6	67.1	47.6
Treasury securities	1,553.2	1,952.6	1,367.7	901.5	1,601.5	2,001.9	1,395.4
Agency- and GSE-backed securities [1]	−3.2	−1.1	3.7	1.2	.3	1.1	.5
Municipal securities	145.4	116.3	162.5	99.3	151.6	−43.6	140.4
Corporate bonds	579.2	396.5	270.0	280.7	432.4	229.0	486.8
Bank loans n.e.c.	−236.0	−240.0	−377.0	−329.7	−9.2	−52.1	−83.4
Other loans and advances	−195.3	−185.1	−156.7	−79.0	−21.6	47.7	−3.9
Mortgages	−35.5	−284.6	−454.9	−408.5	−624.0	−507.0	−473.3
Home	−64.1	−249.9	−354.5	−173.7	−506.5	−288.7	−289.6
Multifamily residential	28.1	22.5	11.0	−26.4	−4.8	−22.9	7.0
Commercial	−0.4	−58.1	−112.3	−209.3	−110.5	−193.1	−188.4
Farm	0.9	.9	.9	.9	−2.2	−2.2	−2.3
Consumer credit	−96.9	−124.4	−98.9	−140.8	−96.3	−80.7	−37.0
By sector	1,572.5	1,497.7	719.0	303.5	1,489.4	1,663.3	1,473.1
Household sector	−115.0	−264.7	−304.0	−276.4	−292.4	−293.4	−232.0
Nonfinancial business	11.8	−286.2	−482.5	−411.1	47.3	−9.4	185.2
Corporate	183.0	4.0	−117.9	−66.4	374.4	266.8	328.5
Nonfarm noncorporate	−173.6	−286.8	−360.8	−341.5	−320.6	−270.1	−162.7
Farm	2.4	−3.4	−3.8	−3.2	−6.5	−6.0	19.3
State and local governments	125.6	97.1	134.0	88.4	132.7	−36.9	124.1
Federal Government	1,550.0	1,951.5	1,371.5	902.6	1,601.9	2,003.0	1,395.9
Foreign borrowing in the United States	163.1	179.3	275.0	149.9	115.3	−34.7	174.0
Commercial paper	64.6	−22.0	201.9	−13.3	−27.1	−41.3	17.0
Bonds	119.4	206.3	82.9	170.9	141.4	−6.0	129.7
Bank loans n.e.c.	−19.4	−6.0	−9.8	−9.6	−.5	13.8	27.6
Other loans and advances	−1.5	.9	.0	1.8	1.5	−1.1	−.4
Nonfinancial domestic and foreign borrowing	1,735.6	1,677.0	994.0	453.4	1,604.7	1,628.7	1,647.1
FINANCIAL SECTORS							
By instrument	−1,891.3	−2,302.9	−1,808.4	−1,432.8	−1,249.9	−1,079.3	−584.9
Open market paper	−555.5	−568.2	−354.6	−308.7	−160.1	−276.8	273.1
GSE issues [1]	−254.5	−680.9	−590.3	−375.7	−155.5	−268.5	−347.0
Agency- and GSE-backed mortgage pool securities [1]	340.0	507.9	465.6	346.3	132.3	244.8	151.8
Corporate bonds	−590.8	−613.7	−484.7	−731.4	−826.1	−558.2	−254.0
Bank loans n.e.c.	−483.2	−648.7	−490.8	−246.9	−91.2	−82.2	−127.5
Other loans and advances	−353.0	−308.8	−352.2	−116.3	−150.2	−140.3	−283.7
Mortgages	5.6	9.5	−1.4	−.1	.8	1.9	2.4
By sector	−1,891.3	−2,302.9	−1,808.4	−1,432.8	−1,249.9	−1,079.3	−584.9
Commercial banking	−238.0	−27.7	−170.3	−283.5	−118.4	−227.2	−11.1
U.S.-chartered commercial banks	−247.0	−44.7	−249.1	−69.4	−114.9	−108.8	−211.6
Foreign banking offices in the United States	0.0	.0	.0	.0	.0	.0	.0
Bank holding companies	9.1	17.0	78.8	−214.1	−3.4	−118.3	200.5
Savings institutions	−148.6	−282.5	−178.3	−68.8	−68.2	−35.0	−91.9
Credit unions	−41.2	−7.2	−.8	−7.2	−4.4	−1.6	.8
Life insurance companies	−9.6	−8.0	−12.0	3.2	−10.8	.0	−1.2
Government-sponsored enterprises	−254.5	−680.9	−590.3	−375.7	−155.5	−268.5	−347.0
Agency- and GSE-backed mortgage pools [1]	340.0	507.9	465.6	346.3	132.3	244.8	151.8
Asset-backed securities issuers	−805.7	−735.8	−782.8	−699.4	−591.8	−482.9	−401.0
Finance companies	−159.5	−205.4	−112.0	−147.9	−301.3	−145.6	−153.8
REITs [2]	−34.3	−46.2	−18.9	−35.4	17.8	6.6	12.4
Brokers and dealers	−160.4	−1.0	7.4	−44.8	−2.4	34.6	20.4
Funding corporations	−379.5	−816.1	−415.9	−119.7	−147.2	−204.4	235.7
ALL SECTORS, BY INSTRUMENT							
Total	−155.7	−625.9	−814.4	−979.5	354.8	549.3	1,062.2
Open market paper	−629.2	−722.5	−150.3	−343.2	−132.7	−251.1	337.7
Treasury securities	1,553.2	1,952.6	1,367.7	901.5	1,601.5	2,001.9	1,395.4
Agency- and GSE-backed securities [1]	82.3	−174.1	−120.9	−28.2	−22.8	−22.6	−194.7
Municipal securities	145.4	116.3	162.5	99.3	151.6	−43.6	140.4
Corporate and foreign bonds	107.8	−10.8	−131.8	−279.7	−252.3	−335.2	362.5
Bank loans n.e.c.	−738.6	−894.7	−877.6	−586.2	−100.9	−120.5	−183.3
Other loans and advances	−549.8	−493.1	−508.9	−193.5	−170.3	−93.8	−288.0
Mortgages	−29.9	−275.1	−456.3	−408.6	−623.1	−505.1	−470.8
Consumer credit	−96.9	−124.4	−98.9	−140.8	−96.3	−80.7	−37.0

Source: Board of Governors of the Federal Reserve System.

[Billions of dollars]

End of year or quarter	All proper-ties	Farm proper-ties	Nonfarm properties				Nonfarm properties by type of mortgage					
							Government underwritten				Conventional [2]	
			Total	1- to 4-family houses	Multi-family proper-ties	Com-mercial proper-ties	Total [1]	1- to 4-family houses			Total	1- to 4-family houses
								Total	FHA-insured	VA-guar-anteed		
1952	91.3	7.2	84.1	58.4	12.3	13.4	29.3	25.4	10.8	14.6	54.8	33.1
1953	101.1	7.7	93.4	65.9	12.9	14.5	32.1	28.1	12.0	16.1	61.3	37.9
1954	113.6	8.2	105.4	75.7	13.5	16.3	36.2	32.1	12.8	19.3	69.3	43.6
1955	129.9	9.0	120.9	88.2	14.3	18.3	42.9	38.9	14.3	24.6	78.0	49.3
1956	144.5	9.8	134.6	99.0	14.9	20.7	47.8	43.9	15.5	28.4	86.8	55.1
1957	156.5	10.4	146.1	107.6	15.3	23.2	51.6	47.2	16.5	30.7	94.6	60.4
1958	171.8	11.1	160.7	117.7	16.8	26.1	55.2	50.1	19.7	30.4	105.5	67.6
1959	191.6	12.1	179.5	131.6	18.7	29.2	59.3	53.8	23.8	30.0	120.2	77.7
1960	208.3	12.8	195.4	142.7	20.3	32.4	62.3	56.4	26.7	29.7	133.1	86.3
1961	229.1	13.9	215.1	155.8	23.0	36.4	65.6	59.1	29.5	29.6	149.5	96.7
1962	252.7	15.2	237.5	170.5	25.8	41.1	69.4	62.2	32.3	29.9	168.1	108.3
1963	280.0	16.8	263.1	187.9	29.0	46.2	73.4	65.9	35.0	30.9	189.7	122.0
1964	307.4	18.9	288.4	204.8	33.6	50.0	77.2	69.2	38.3	30.9	211.3	135.6
1965	334.7	21.2	313.5	221.9	37.2	54.5	81.2	73.1	42.0	31.1	232.4	148.8
1966	357.9	23.1	334.8	234.4	40.3	60.1	84.1	76.1	44.8	31.3	250.7	158.3
1967	382.5	25.0	357.4	248.7	43.9	64.8	88.2	79.9	47.4	32.5	269.3	168.8
1968	412.1	27.3	384.8	266.1	47.3	71.4	93.4	84.4	50.6	33.8	291.4	181.6
1969	442.5	29.2	413.3	283.9	52.3	77.1	100.2	90.2	54.5	35.7	313.1	193.7
1970	474.5	30.5	444.0	298.0	60.1	85.8	109.2	97.3	59.9	37.3	334.7	200.8
1971	525.0	32.4	492.7	326.4	70.1	96.2	120.7	105.2	65.7	39.5	371.9	221.2
1972	598.2	35.4	562.9	367.0	82.8	113.1	131.1	113.0	68.2	44.7	431.7	254.1
1973	673.9	39.8	634.1	408.7	93.2	132.3	135.0	116.2	66.2	50.0	499.1	292.4
1974	734.0	44.9	689.1	441.5	100.0	147.5	140.2	121.3	65.1	56.2	548.8	320.2
1975	793.9	49.9	744.0	483.2	100.7	160.1	147.0	127.7	66.1	61.6	597.0	355.5
1976	881.1	55.4	825.7	546.4	105.9	173.4	154.0	133.5	66.5	67.0	671.6	412.9
1977	1,013.0	63.8	949.2	642.5	114.3	192.3	161.7	141.6	68.0	73.6	787.4	500.9
1978	1,165.5	72.8	1,092.8	753.7	125.2	213.9	176.4	153.4	71.4	82.0	916.4	600.3
1979	1,331.5	86.8	1,244.7	870.8	135.0	238.8	199.0	172.9	81.0	92.0	1,045.7	697.9
1980	1,467.6	97.5	1,370.1	969.7	141.1	259.3	225.1	195.2	93.6	101.6	1,145.1	774.5
1981	1,591.5	107.2	1,484.3	1,046.5	139.2	298.6	238.9	207.6	101.3	106.2	1,245.4	838.9
1982	1,676.1	111.3	1,564.8	1,091.1	141.1	332.6	248.9	217.9	108.0	109.9	1,315.9	873.3
1983	1,871.7	113.7	1,757.9	1,214.9	154.3	388.6	279.8	248.8	127.4	121.4	1,478.1	966.1
1984	2,120.6	112.4	2,008.2	1,358.9	177.4	471.9	294.8	265.9	136.7	129.1	1,713.4	1,093.0
1985	2,370.3	94.1	2,276.2	1,528.8	205.9	541.5	328.3	288.8	153.0	135.8	1,947.8	1,240.0
1986	2,657.9	84.0	2,573.9	1,732.8	239.3	601.7	370.5	328.6	185.5	143.1	2,203.4	1,404.2
1987	2,996.2	75.8	2,920.4	1,960.9	262.1	697.4	431.4	387.9	235.5	152.4	2,489.0	1,573.0
1988	3,313.1	70.8	3,242.3	2,194.7	279.0	768.6	459.7	414.2	258.8	155.4	2,782.6	1,780.5
1989	3,585.4	68.8	3,516.6	2,428.1	289.9	798.6	486.8	440.1	282.8	157.3	3,029.8	1,988.0
1990	3,788.2	67.6	3,720.6	2,613.6	288.3	818.8	517.9	470.9	310.9	160.0	3,202.7	2,142.7
1991	3,929.8	67.5	3,862.4	2,771.9	284.1	806.4	537.2	493.3	330.6	162.7	3,325.2	2,278.6
1992	4,043.4	67.9	3,975.5	2,942.0	270.9	762.6	533.3	489.8	326.0	163.8	3,442.2	2,452.2
1993	4,174.8	68.4	4,106.4	3,100.9	267.7	737.8	513.4	469.5	303.2	166.2	3,592.9	2,631.4
1994	4,339.2	69.9	4,269.3	3,278.2	268.2	722.9	559.3	514.2	336.8	177.3	3,710.0	2,764.0
1995	4,524.9	71.7	4,453.2	3,445.4	273.9	734.0	584.3	537.1	352.3	184.7	3,869.0	2,908.3
1996	4,792.5	74.4	4,718.1	3,668.4	286.1	763.6	620.3	571.2	379.2	192.0	4,097.8	3,097.3
1997	5,104.5	78.5	5,026.0	3,902.5	297.9	825.6	656.7	605.7	405.7	200.0	4,369.4	3,296.8
1998	5,589.6	83.1	5,506.5	4,259.0	332.0	915.5	674.1	623.8	417.9	205.9	4,832.4	3,635.2
1999	6,195.4	87.2	6,108.2	4,683.0	372.8	1,052.4	731.5	678.8	462.3	216.5	5,376.8	4,004.2
2000	6,753.0	84.7	6,668.2	5,106.5	402.1	1,159.6	773.1	720.0	499.9	220.1	5,895.1	4,386.6
2001	7,460.8	88.5	7,372.2	5,658.5	444.3	1,269.4	772.7	718.5	497.4	221.2	6,599.6	4,940.0
2002	8,361.5	95.4	8,266.1	6,413.2	483.3	1,369.6	759.3	704.0	486.2	217.7	7,506.8	5,709.2
2003	9,377.1	83.2	9,294.0	7,239.9	557.3	1,496.8	709.2	653.3	438.7	214.6	8,584.8	6,586.6
2004	10,636.6	95.7	10,541.0	8,268.2	604.5	1,668.2	661.5	605.4	398.1	207.3	9,879.5	7,662.9
2005	12,070.5	104.8	11,965.7	9,382.4	666.8	1,916.5	606.6	550.4	348.4	202.0	11,359.1	8,832.0
2006	13,462.5	108.0	13,354.4	10,455.6	707.5	2,191.3	600.2	543.5	336.9	206.6	12,754.3	9,912.1
2007	14,524.6	112.7	14,411.9	11,166.8	789.3	2,455.8	609.2	552.6	342.6	210.0	13,802.7	10,614.2
2008	14,618.5	132.2	14,486.2	11,072.9	840.6	2,572.7	807.2	750.7	534.0	216.7	13,679.0	10,322.2
2009	14,326.0	134.5	14,191.5	10,861.0	851.2	2,479.3	1,005.0	944.3	752.6	191.7	13,186.4	9,916.7
2009: I	14,615.0	132.8	14,482.2	11,066.8	848.2	2,567.1	863.6	806.7	577.8	228.9	13,618.6	10,260.2
II	14,558.1	134.0	14,424.0	11,013.6	855.4	2,554.8	921.5	863.1	628.0	235.2	13,502.5	10,150.7
III	14,447.0	134.3	14,312.8	10,926.3	858.2	2,528.3	940.9	881.0	697.3	183.7	13,371.9	10,045.3
IV	14,326.0	134.5	14,191.5	10,861.0	851.2	2,479.3	1,005.0	944.3	752.6	191.7	13,186.4	9,916.7
2010: I	14,178.3	134.0	14,044.4	10,747.9	850.4	2,446.1	1,069.5	1,006.1	806.9	199.1	12,974.8	9,741.8
II	14,062.4	133.4	13,929.0	10,684.8	844.6	2,399.6	1,129.9	1,063.0	856.7	206.3	12,799.1	9,621.8
III p	13,947.3	132.8	13,814.5	10,612.0	847.0	2,355.5	1,182.4	1,113.4	898.5	214.9	12,632.1	9,498.6

[1] Includes Federal Housing Administration (FHA)–insured multi-family properties, not shown separately.
[2] Derived figures. Total includes multi-family and commercial properties with conventional mortgages, not shown separately.

Source: Board of Governors of the Federal Reserve System, based on data from various Government and private organizations.

TABLE B–76. Mortgage debt outstanding by holder, 1952–2010

[Billions of dollars]

End of year or quarter	Total	Major financial institutions				Other holders	
		Total	Savings institutions [1]	Commercial banks [2]	Life insurance companies	Federal and related agencies [3]	Individuals and others [4]
1952	91.3	66.9	29.8	15.9	21.3	3.9	20.4
1953	101.1	75.0	34.8	16.9	23.3	4.4	21.7
1954	113.6	85.7	41.1	18.6	26.0	4.7	23.2
1955	129.9	99.3	48.9	21.0	29.4	5.3	25.3
1956	144.5	111.2	55.5	22.7	33.0	6.2	27.1
1957	156.5	119.7	61.2	23.3	35.2	7.7	29.1
1958	171.8	131.5	68.9	25.5	37.1	8.0	32.3
1959	191.6	145.5	78.1	28.1	39.2	10.2	35.9
1960	208.3	157.5	86.9	28.8	41.8	11.5	39.3
1961	229.1	172.6	98.0	30.4	44.2	12.2	44.2
1962	252.7	192.5	111.1	34.5	46.9	12.6	47.6
1963	280.0	217.1	127.2	39.4	50.5	11.8	51.0
1964	307.4	241.0	141.9	44.0	55.2	12.2	54.1
1965	334.7	264.6	154.9	49.7	60.0	13.5	56.6
1966	357.9	280.7	161.8	54.4	64.6	17.5	59.7
1967	382.5	298.7	172.3	58.9	67.5	20.9	62.8
1968	412.1	319.7	184.3	65.5	70.0	25.1	67.3
1969	442.5	338.9	196.4	70.5	72.0	31.1	72.4
1970	474.5	355.9	208.3	73.3	74.4	38.3	80.2
1971	525.0	394.2	236.2	82.5	75.5	46.3	84.5
1972	598.2	449.9	273.6	99.3	76.9	54.5	93.8
1973	673.9	505.4	305.0	119.1	81.4	64.7	103.9
1974	734.0	542.6	324.2	132.1	86.2	82.2	109.2
1975	793.9	581.2	355.8	136.2	89.2	101.1	111.5
1976	881.1	647.5	404.6	151.3	91.6	116.7	116.9
1977	1,013.0	745.2	469.4	179.0	96.8	140.5	127.3
1978	1,165.5	848.2	528.0	214.0	106.2	170.6	146.8
1979	1,331.5	938.2	574.6	245.2	118.4	216.0	177.3
1980	1,467.6	996.8	603.1	262.7	131.1	256.8	214.0
1981	1,591.5	1,040.5	618.5	284.2	137.7	289.4	261.6
1982	1,676.1	1,021.3	578.1	301.3	142.0	355.4	299.4
1983	1,871.7	1,108.1	626.6	330.5	151.0	433.3	330.2
1984	2,120.6	1,247.8	709.7	381.4	156.7	490.6	382.3
1985	2,370.3	1,363.5	760.5	431.2	171.8	580.9	425.8
1986	2,657.9	1,476.5	778.0	504.7	193.8	733.7	447.7
1987	2,996.2	1,667.6	860.5	594.8	212.4	857.9	470.7
1988	3,313.1	1,834.3	924.5	676.9	232.9	937.8	541.1
1989	3,585.4	1,935.2	910.3	770.7	254.2	1,067.3	582.9
1990	3,788.2	1,918.8	801.6	849.3	267.9	1,258.9	610.5
1991	3,929.8	1,846.2	705.4	881.3	259.5	1,422.5	661.2
1992	4,043.4	1,770.4	627.9	900.5	242.0	1,558.1	714.9
1993	4,174.8	1,770.1	598.4	947.8	223.9	1,682.8	721.8
1994	4,339.2	1,824.7	596.2	1,012.7	215.8	1,788.0	726.6
1995	4,524.9	1,900.1	596.8	1,090.2	213.1	1,878.7	746.2
1996	4,792.5	1,981.9	628.3	1,145.4	208.2	2,006.1	804.6
1997	5,104.5	2,084.0	631.8	1,245.3	206.8	2,111.4	909.1
1998	5,589.6	2,194.6	644.0	1,337.0	213.6	2,310.9	1,084.2
1999	6,195.4	2,394.3	668.1	1,495.4	230.8	2,613.3	1,187.9
2000	6,753.0	2,619.0	723.0	1,660.1	235.9	2,833.2	1,300.8
2001	7,460.8	2,790.9	758.0	1,789.8	243.0	3,203.8	1,466.1
2002	8,361.5	3,089.3	781.0	2,058.3	250.0	3,590.9	1,681.2
2003	9,377.1	3,387.3	870.6	2,255.8	260.9	4,037.4	1,952.5
2004	10,636.6	3,926.3	1,057.4	2,595.6	273.3	4,087.2	2,623.1
2005	12,070.5	4,396.2	1,152.7	2,958.0	285.5	4,213.9	3,460.3
2006	13,462.5	4,783.6	1,076.8	3,403.1	303.8	4,528.6	4,150.3
2007	14,524.6	5,064.6	1,094.0	3,644.4	326.2	5,189.9	4,270.1
2008	14,618.5	5,044.4	860.6	3,841.4	342.4	5,758.7	3,815.4
2009	14,326.0	4,778.1	633.3	3,818.7	326.1	6,192.5	3,355.4
2009: I	14,615.0	5,041.7	849.8	3,853.3	338.6	5,864.6	3,708.7
II	14,558.1	4,984.8	752.2	3,897.6	335.0	5,986.1	3,587.2
III	14,447.0	4,853.6	725.8	3,795.4	332.4	6,118.0	3,475.5
IV	14,326.0	4,778.1	633.3	3,818.7	326.1	6,192.5	3,355.4
2010: I	14,178.3	4,712.0	629.3	3,761.3	321.4	6,218.4	3,248.0
II	14,062.4	4,644.0	619.3	3,706.8	317.9	6,264.4	3,154.0
III _p_	13,947.3	4,610.3	617.9	3,674.4	318.0	6,263.1	3,073.9

[1] Includes savings banks and savings and loan associations. Data reported by Federal Savings and Loan Insurance Corporation–insured institutions include loans in process for 1987 and exclude loans in process beginning with 1988.

[2] Includes loans held by nondeposit trust companies but not loans held by bank trust departments.

[3] Includes Government National Mortgage Association (GNMA or Ginnie Mae), Federal Housing Administration, Veterans Administration, Farmers Home Administration (FmHA), Federal Deposit Insurance Corporation, Resolution Trust Corporation (through 1995), and in earlier years Reconstruction Finance Corporation, Homeowners Loan Corporation, Federal Farm Mortgage Corporation, and Public Housing Administration. Also includes U.S.-sponsored agencies such as Federal National Mortgage Association (FNMA or Fannie Mae), Federal Land Banks, Federal Home Loan Mortgage Corporation (FHLMC or Freddie Mac), Federal Agricultural Mortgage Corporation (Farmer Mac, beginning 1994), Federal Home Loan Banks (beginning 1997), and mortgage pass-through securities issued or guaranteed by GNMA, FHLMC, FNMA, FmHA, or Farmer Mac. Other U.S. agencies (amounts small or current separate data not readily available) included with "individuals and others."

[4] Includes private mortgage pools.

Source: Board of Governors of the Federal Reserve System, based on data from various Government and private organizations.

TABLE B–77. Consumer credit outstanding, 1959–2010

[Amount outstanding (end of month); millions of dollars, seasonally adjusted]

Year and month	Total consumer credit [1]	Revolving	Nonrevolving [2]
December:			
1959	56,010.68		56,010.68
1960	60,025.31		60,025.31
1961	62,248.53		62,248.53
1962	68,126.72		68,126.72
1963	76,581.45		76,581.45
1964	85,959.57		85,959.57
1965	95,954.72		95,954.72
1966	101,788.22		101,788.22
1967	106,842.64		106,842.64
1968	117,399.09	2,041.54	115,357.55
1969	127,156.18	3,604.84	123,551.35
1970	131,551.55	4,961.46	126,590.09
1971	146,930.18	8,245.33	138,684.84
1972	166,189.10	9,379.24	156,809.86
1973	190,086.31	11,342.22	178,744.09
1974	198,917.84	13,241.26	185,676.58
1975	204,002.00	14,495.27	189,506.73
1976	225,721.59	16,489.05	209,232.54
1977	260,562.70	37,414.82	223,147.88
1978	306,100.39	45,690.95	260,409.43
1979	348,589.11	53,596.43	294,992.67
1980	351,920.05	54,970.05	296,950.00
1981	371,301.44	60,928.00	310,373.44
1982	389,848.74	66,348.30	323,500.44
1983	437,068.86	79,027.25	358,041.61
1984	517,278.98	100,385.63	416,893.35
1985	599,711.23	124,465.80	475,245.43
1986	654,750.24	141,068.15	513,682.08
1987	686,318.77	160,853.91	525,464.86
1988 [3]	731,917.76	184,593.12	547,324.64
1989	794,612.18	211,229.83	583,382.34
1990	808,230.57	238,642.62	569,587.95
1991	798,028.97	263,768.55	534,260.42
1992	806,118.69	278,449.67	527,669.02
1993	865,650.58	309,908.02	555,742.56
1994	997,301.74	365,569.56	631,732.19
1995	1,140,744.36	443,920.09	696,824.27
1996	1,253,437.09	507,516.57	745,920.52
1997	1,324,757.33	540,005.56	784,751.77
1998	1,420,996.44	581,414.78	839,581.66
1999	1,531,105.96	610,696.47	920,409.49
2000	1,716,969.72	682,646.37	1,034,323.35
2001	1,866,496.25	714,608.44	1,151,887.80
2002	1,971,240.93	750,766.51	1,220,474.43
2003	2,076,894.89	768,156.14	1,308,738.75
2004	2,192,114.02	799,499.70	1,392,614.32
2005	2,291,027.40	829,575.97	1,461,451.43
2006	2,384,841.39	870,998.30	1,513,843.09
2007	2,522,187.04	941,825.28	1,580,361.76
2008	2,561,106.80	957,546.74	1,603,560.06
2009	2,449,375.16	865,847.75	1,583,527.41
2009: Jan	2,563,218.53	956,093.80	1,607,124.74
Feb	2,551,363.46	944,852.80	1,606,510.67
Mar	2,537,753.00	936,284.32	1,601,468.68
Apr	2,525,306.87	929,245.08	1,596,061.79
May	2,517,997.61	921,772.75	1,596,224.86
June	2,507,538.69	914,959.73	1,592,578.96
July	2,497,374.21	909,981.39	1,587,392.82
Aug	2,491,473.11	901,909.34	1,589,563.77
Sept	2,483,692.20	893,510.13	1,590,182.06
Oct	2,475,998.05	885,742.27	1,590,255.78
Nov	2,457,407.45	874,552.47	1,582,854.99
Dec	2,449,375.16	865,847.75	1,583,527.41
2010: Jan	2,447,314.97	856,762.95	1,590,552.02
Feb	2,435,435.03	846,734.66	1,588,700.37
Mar	2,425,292.42	840,702.37	1,584,590.05
Apr	2,413,939.47	830,262.64	1,583,676.83
May	2,407,162.84	828,350.32	1,578,812.51
June	2,405,119.22	825,399.45	1,579,719.77
July	2,399,592.94	820,168.56	1,579,424.38
Aug	2,394,641.84	814,908.33	1,579,733.51
Sept	2,394,633.27	806,089.28	1,588,543.99
Oct	2,401,633.73	800,669.75	1,600,963.98
Nov [p]	2,402,979.83	796,454.89	1,606,524.94

[1] Covers most short- and intermediate-term credit extended to individuals. Credit secured by real estate is excluded.

[2] Includes automobile loans and all other loans not included in revolving credit, such as loans for mobile homes, education, boats, trailers, or vacations. These loans may be secured or unsecured. Beginning with 1977, includes student loans extended by the Federal Government and by SLM Holding Corporation.

[3] Data newly available in January 1989 result in breaks in these series between December 1988 and subsequent months.

Source: Board of Governors of the Federal Reserve System.

TABLE B–78. Federal receipts, outlays, surplus or deficit, and debt, fiscal years, 1944–2012

[Billions of dollars; fiscal years]

Fiscal year or period	Total			On-budget			Off-budget			Federal debt (end of period)		Addendum: Gross domestic product
	Receipts	Outlays	Surplus or deficit (–)	Receipts	Outlays	Surplus or deficit (–)	Receipts	Outlays	Surplus or deficit (–)	Gross Federal	Held by the public	
1944	43.7	91.3	–47.6	42.5	91.2	–48.7	1.3	0.1	1.2	204.1	184.8	209.2
1945	45.2	92.7	–47.6	43.8	92.6	–48.7	1.3	.1	1.2	260.1	235.2	221.4
1946	39.3	55.2	–15.9	38.1	55.0	–17.0	1.2	.2	1.0	271.0	241.9	222.6
1947	38.5	34.5	4.0	37.1	34.2	2.9	1.5	.3	1.2	257.1	224.3	233.2
1948	41.6	29.8	11.8	39.9	29.4	10.5	1.6	.4	1.2	252.0	216.3	256.6
1949	39.4	38.8	.6	37.7	38.4	–.7	1.7	.4	1.3	252.6	214.3	271.3
1950	39.4	42.6	–3.1	37.3	42.0	–4.7	2.1	.5	1.6	256.9	219.0	273.1
1951	51.6	45.5	6.1	48.5	44.2	4.3	3.1	1.3	1.8	255.3	214.3	320.2
1952	66.2	67.7	–1.5	62.6	66.0	–3.4	3.6	1.7	1.9	259.1	214.8	348.7
1953	69.6	76.1	–6.5	65.5	73.8	–8.3	4.1	2.3	1.8	266.0	218.4	372.5
1954	69.7	70.9	–1.2	65.1	67.9	–2.8	4.6	2.9	1.7	270.8	224.5	377.0
1955	65.5	68.4	–3.0	60.4	64.5	–4.1	5.1	4.0	1.1	274.4	226.6	395.9
1956	74.6	70.6	3.9	68.2	65.7	2.5	6.4	5.0	1.5	272.7	222.2	427.0
1957	80.0	76.6	3.4	73.2	70.6	2.6	6.8	6.0	.8	272.3	219.3	450.9
1958	79.6	82.4	–2.8	71.6	74.9	–3.3	8.0	7.5	.5	279.7	226.3	460.0
1959	79.2	92.1	–12.8	71.0	83.1	–12.1	8.3	9.0	–.7	287.5	234.7	490.2
1960	92.5	92.2	.3	81.9	81.3	.5	10.6	10.9	–.2	290.5	236.8	518.9
1961	94.4	97.7	–3.3	82.3	86.0	–3.8	12.1	11.7	.4	292.6	238.4	529.9
1962	99.7	106.8	–7.1	87.4	93.3	–5.9	12.3	13.5	–1.3	302.9	248.0	567.8
1963	106.6	111.3	–4.8	92.4	96.4	–4.0	14.2	15.0	–.8	310.3	254.0	599.2
1964	112.6	118.5	–5.9	96.2	102.8	–6.5	16.4	15.7	.6	316.1	256.8	641.5
1965	116.8	118.2	–1.4	100.1	101.7	–1.6	16.7	16.5	.2	322.3	260.8	687.5
1966	130.8	134.5	–3.7	111.7	114.8	–3.1	19.1	19.7	–.6	328.5	263.7	755.8
1967	148.8	157.5	–8.6	124.4	137.0	–12.6	24.4	20.4	4.0	340.4	266.6	810.0
1968	153.0	178.1	–25.2	128.1	155.8	–27.7	24.9	22.3	2.6	368.7	289.5	868.4
1969	186.9	183.6	3.2	157.9	158.4	–.5	29.0	25.2	3.7	365.8	278.1	948.1
1970	192.8	195.6	–2.8	159.3	168.0	–8.7	33.5	27.6	5.9	380.9	283.2	1,012.7
1971	187.1	210.2	–23.0	151.3	177.3	–26.1	35.8	32.8	3.0	408.2	303.0	1,080.0
1972	207.3	230.7	–23.4	167.4	193.5	–26.1	39.9	37.2	2.7	435.9	322.4	1,176.5
1973	230.8	245.7	–14.9	184.7	200.0	–15.2	46.1	45.7	.3	466.3	340.9	1,310.6
1974	263.2	269.4	–6.1	209.3	216.5	–7.2	53.9	52.9	1.1	483.9	343.7	1,438.5
1975	279.1	332.3	–53.2	216.6	270.8	–54.1	62.5	61.6	.9	541.9	394.7	1,560.2
1976	298.1	371.8	–73.7	231.7	301.1	–69.4	66.4	70.7	–4.3	629.0	477.4	1,738.1
Transition quarter	81.2	96.0	–14.7	63.2	77.3	–14.1	18.0	18.7	–.7	643.6	495.5	459.4
1977	355.6	409.2	–53.7	278.7	328.7	–49.9	76.8	80.5	–3.7	706.4	549.1	1,973.5
1978	399.6	458.7	–59.2	314.2	369.6	–55.4	85.4	89.2	–3.8	776.6	607.1	2,217.5
1979	463.3	504.0	–40.7	365.3	404.9	–39.6	98.0	99.1	–1.1	829.5	640.3	2,501.4
1980	517.1	590.9	–73.8	403.9	477.0	–73.1	113.2	113.9	–.7	909.0	711.9	2,724.2
1981	599.3	678.2	–79.0	469.1	543.0	–73.9	130.2	135.3	–5.1	994.8	789.4	3,057.0
1982	617.8	745.7	–128.0	474.3	594.9	–120.6	143.5	150.9	–7.4	1,137.3	924.6	3,223.7
1983	600.6	808.4	–207.8	453.2	660.9	–207.7	147.3	147.4	–.1	1,371.7	1,137.3	3,440.7
1984	666.4	851.8	–185.4	500.4	685.6	–185.3	166.1	166.2	–.1	1,564.6	1,307.0	3,844.4
1985	734.0	946.3	–212.3	547.9	769.4	–221.5	186.2	176.9	9.2	1,817.4	1,507.3	4,146.3
1986	769.2	990.4	–221.2	568.9	806.8	–237.9	200.2	183.5	16.7	2,120.5	1,740.6	4,403.9
1987	854.3	1,004.0	–149.7	640.9	809.2	–168.4	213.4	194.8	18.6	2,346.0	1,889.8	4,651.4
1988	909.2	1,064.4	–155.2	667.7	860.0	–192.3	241.5	204.4	37.1	2,601.1	2,051.6	5,008.5
1989	991.1	1,143.7	–152.6	727.4	932.8	–205.4	263.7	210.9	52.8	2,867.8	2,190.7	5,399.5
1990	1,032.0	1,253.0	–221.0	750.3	1,027.9	–277.6	281.7	225.1	56.6	3,206.3	2,411.6	5,734.5
1991	1,055.0	1,324.2	–269.2	761.1	1,082.5	–321.4	293.9	241.7	52.2	3,598.2	2,689.0	5,930.5
1992	1,091.2	1,381.5	–290.3	788.8	1,129.2	–340.4	302.4	252.3	50.1	4,001.8	2,999.7	6,242.0
1993	1,154.3	1,409.4	–255.1	842.4	1,142.8	–300.4	311.9	266.6	45.3	4,351.0	3,248.4	6,587.3
1994	1,258.6	1,461.8	–203.2	923.5	1,182.4	–258.8	335.0	279.4	55.7	4,643.3	3,433.1	6,976.6
1995	1,351.8	1,515.7	–164.0	1,000.7	1,227.1	–226.4	351.1	288.7	62.4	4,920.6	3,604.4	7,341.1
1996	1,453.1	1,560.5	–107.4	1,085.6	1,259.6	–174.0	367.5	300.9	66.6	5,181.5	3,734.1	7,718.3
1997	1,579.2	1,601.1	–21.9	1,187.2	1,290.5	–103.2	392.0	310.6	81.4	5,369.2	3,772.3	8,211.7
1998	1,721.7	1,652.5	69.3	1,305.9	1,335.9	–29.9	415.8	316.6	99.2	5,478.2	3,721.1	8,663.0
1999	1,827.5	1,701.8	125.6	1,383.0	1,381.1	1.9	444.5	320.8	123.7	5,605.5	3,632.4	9,208.4
2000	2,025.2	1,789.0	236.2	1,544.6	1,458.2	86.4	480.6	330.8	149.8	5,628.7	3,409.8	9,821.0
2001	1,991.1	1,862.8	128.2	1,483.6	1,516.0	–32.4	507.5	346.8	160.7	5,769.9	3,319.6	10,225.3
2002	1,853.1	2,010.9	–157.8	1,337.8	1,655.2	–317.4	515.3	355.7	159.7	6,198.4	3,540.4	10,543.9
2003	1,782.3	2,159.9	–377.6	1,258.5	1,796.9	–538.4	523.8	363.0	160.8	6,760.0	3,913.4	10,979.8
2004	1,880.1	2,292.8	–412.7	1,345.4	1,913.3	–568.0	534.7	379.5	155.2	7,354.7	4,295.5	11,685.6
2005	2,153.6	2,472.0	–318.3	1,576.1	2,069.7	–493.6	577.5	402.2	175.3	7,905.3	4,592.2	12,445.7
2006	2,406.9	2,655.1	–248.2	1,798.5	2,233.0	–434.5	608.4	422.1	186.3	8,451.4	4,829.0	13,224.9
2007	2,568.0	2,728.7	–160.7	1,932.9	2,275.0	–342.2	635.1	453.6	181.5	8,950.7	5,035.1	13,891.8
2008	2,524.0	2,982.5	–458.6	1,865.9	2,507.8	–641.8	658.0	474.8	183.3	9,986.1	5,803.1	14,394.1
2009	2,105.0	3,517.7	–1,412.7	1,451.0	3,000.7	–1,549.7	654.0	517.0	137.0	11,875.9	7,544.7	14,097.5
2010	2,162.7	3,456.2	–1,293.5	1,531.0	2,901.5	–1,370.5	631.7	554.7	77.0	13,528.8	9,018.9	14,508.2
2011 (estimates)	2,173.7	3,818.8	–1,645.1	1,614.3	3,317.3	–1,703.0	559.4	501.5	57.9	15,476.2	10,856.5	15,079.6
2012 (estimates)	2,627.4	3,728.7	–1,101.2	1,968.7	3,145.9	–1,177.2	658.7	582.8	75.9	16,654.3	11,881.1	15,812.5

Note: Fiscal years through 1976 were on a July 1–June 30 basis; beginning with October 1976 (fiscal year 1977), the fiscal year is on an October 1–September 30 basis. The transition quarter is the three-month period from July 1, 1976 through September 30, 1976.

See Budget of the United States Government, Fiscal Year 2012, for additional information.

Sources: Department of Commerce (Bureau of Economic Analysis), Department of the Treasury, and Office of Management and Budget.

TABLE B–79. Federal receipts, outlays, surplus or deficit, and debt, as percent of gross domestic product, fiscal years 1938–2012

[Percent; fiscal years]

Fiscal year or period	Receipts	Outlays		Surplus or deficit (−)	Federal debt (end of period)	
		Total	National defense		Gross Federal	Held by public
1938	7.6	7.7		−0.1		
1939	7.1	10.3		−3.2	54.0	46.5
1940	6.8	9.8	1.7	−3.0	52.4	44.2
1941	7.6	12.0	5.6	−4.3	50.4	42.3
1942	10.1	24.3	17.8	−14.2	54.9	47.0
1943	13.3	43.6	37.0	−30.3	79.1	70.9
1944	20.9	43.6	37.8	−22.7	97.6	88.3
1945	20.4	41.9	37.5	−21.5	117.5	106.2
1946	17.7	24.8	19.2	−7.2	121.7	108.7
1947	16.5	14.8	5.5	1.7	110.3	96.2
1948	16.2	11.6	3.5	4.6	98.2	84.3
1949	14.5	14.3	4.8	.2	93.1	79.0
1950	14.4	15.6	5.0	−1.1	94.1	80.2
1951	16.1	14.2	7.4	1.9	79.7	66.9
1952	19.0	19.4	13.2	−.4	74.3	61.6
1953	18.7	20.4	14.2	−1.7	71.4	58.6
1954	18.5	18.8	13.1	−.3	71.8	59.5
1955	16.5	17.3	10.8	−.8	69.3	57.2
1956	17.5	16.5	10.0	.9	63.9	52.0
1957	17.7	17.0	10.1	.8	60.4	48.6
1958	17.3	17.9	10.2	−.6	60.8	49.2
1959	16.2	18.8	10.0	−2.6	58.6	47.9
1960	17.8	17.8	9.3	.1	56.0	45.6
1961	17.8	18.4	9.4	−.6	55.2	45.0
1962	17.6	18.8	9.2	−1.3	53.4	43.7
1963	17.8	18.6	8.9	−.8	51.8	42.4
1964	17.6	18.5	8.5	−.9	49.3	40.0
1965	17.0	17.2	7.4	−.2	46.9	37.9
1966	17.3	17.8	7.7	−.5	43.5	34.9
1967	18.4	19.4	8.8	−1.1	42.0	32.9
1968	17.6	20.5	9.4	−2.9	42.5	33.3
1969	19.7	19.4	8.7	.3	38.6	29.3
1970	19.0	19.3	8.1	−.3	37.6	28.0
1971	17.3	19.5	7.3	−2.1	37.8	28.1
1972	17.6	19.6	6.7	−2.0	37.1	27.4
1973	17.6	18.7	5.9	−1.1	35.6	26.0
1974	18.3	18.7	5.5	−.4	33.6	23.9
1975	17.9	21.3	5.5	−3.4	34.7	25.3
1976	17.1	21.4	5.2	−4.2	36.2	27.5
Transition quarter	17.7	20.9	4.8	−3.2	35.0	27.0
1977	18.0	20.7	4.9	−2.7	35.8	27.8
1978	18.0	20.7	4.7	−2.7	35.0	27.4
1979	18.5	20.1	4.7	−1.6	33.2	25.6
1980	19.0	21.7	4.9	−2.7	33.4	26.1
1981	19.6	22.2	5.2	−2.6	32.5	25.8
1982	19.2	23.1	5.7	−4.0	35.3	28.7
1983	17.5	23.5	6.1	−6.0	39.9	33.1
1984	17.3	22.2	5.9	−4.8	40.7	34.0
1985	17.7	22.8	6.1	−5.1	43.8	36.4
1986	17.5	22.5	6.2	−5.0	48.2	39.5
1987	18.4	21.6	6.1	−3.2	50.4	40.6
1988	18.2	21.3	5.8	−3.1	51.9	41.0
1989	18.4	21.2	5.6	−2.8	53.1	40.6
1990	18.0	21.9	5.2	−3.9	55.9	42.1
1991	17.8	22.3	4.6	−4.5	60.7	45.3
1992	17.5	22.1	4.8	−4.7	64.1	48.1
1993	17.5	21.4	4.4	−3.9	66.1	49.3
1994	18.0	21.0	4.0	−2.9	66.6	49.2
1995	18.4	20.6	3.7	−2.2	67.0	49.1
1996	18.8	20.2	3.4	−1.4	67.1	48.4
1997	19.2	19.5	3.3	−.3	65.4	45.9
1998	19.9	19.1	3.1	.8	63.2	43.0
1999	19.8	18.5	3.0	1.4	60.9	39.4
2000	20.6	18.2	3.0	2.4	57.3	34.7
2001	19.5	18.2	3.0	1.3	56.4	32.5
2002	17.6	19.1	3.3	−1.5	58.8	33.6
2003	16.2	19.7	3.7	−3.4	61.6	35.6
2004	16.1	19.6	3.9	−3.5	62.9	36.8
2005	17.3	19.9	4.0	−2.6	63.5	36.9
2006	18.2	20.1	3.9	−1.9	63.9	36.5
2007	18.5	19.6	4.0	−1.2	64.4	36.2
2008	17.5	20.7	4.3	−3.2	69.4	40.3
2009	14.9	25.0	4.7	−10.0	84.2	53.5
2010	14.9	23.8	4.8	−8.9	93.2	62.2
2011 (estimates)	14.4	25.3	5.1	−10.9	102.6	72.0
2012 (estimates)	16.6	23.6	4.7	−7.0	105.3	75.1

Note: See Note, Table B–78.

Sources: Department of the Treasury and Office of Management and Budget.

TABLE B–80. Federal receipts and outlays, by major category, and surplus or deficit, fiscal years 1944–2012

[Billions of dollars; fiscal years]

Fiscal year or period	Receipts (on-budget and off-budget)					Outlays (on-budget and off-budget)										Surplus or deficit (−) (on-budget and off-budget)
	Total	Individual income taxes	Corporation income taxes	Social insurance and retirement receipts	Other	Total	National defense		International affairs	Health	Medicare	Income security	Social security	Net interest	Other	
							Total	Department of Defense, military								
1944	43.7	19.7	14.8	3.5	5.7	91.3	79.1	....	1.4	0.2	....	1.5	0.2	2.2	6.6	−47.6
1945	45.2	18.4	16.0	3.5	7.3	92.7	83.0	....	1.9	.2	....	1.1	.3	3.1	3.1	−47.6
1946	39.3	16.1	11.9	3.1	8.2	55.2	42.7	....	1.9	.2	....	2.4	.4	4.1	3.6	−15.9
1947	38.5	17.9	8.6	3.4	8.5	34.5	12.8	....	5.8	.2	....	2.8	.5	4.2	8.2	4.0
1948	41.6	19.3	9.7	3.8	8.8	29.8	9.1	....	4.6	.2	....	2.5	.6	4.3	8.5	11.8
1949	39.4	15.6	11.2	3.8	8.9	38.8	13.2	....	6.1	.2	....	3.2	.7	4.5	11.1	.6
1950	39.4	15.8	10.4	4.3	8.9	42.6	13.7	....	4.7	.3	....	4.1	.8	4.8	14.2	−3.1
1951	51.6	21.6	14.1	5.7	10.2	45.5	23.6	....	3.6	.3	....	3.4	1.6	4.7	8.4	6.1
1952	66.2	27.9	21.2	6.4	10.6	67.7	46.1	....	2.7	.3	....	3.7	2.1	4.7	8.1	−1.5
1953	69.6	29.8	21.2	6.8	11.7	76.1	52.8	....	2.1	.3	....	3.8	2.7	5.2	9.1	−6.5
1954	69.7	29.5	21.1	7.2	11.9	70.9	49.3	....	1.6	.3	....	4.4	3.4	4.8	7.1	−1.2
1955	65.5	28.7	17.9	7.9	11.0	68.4	42.7	....	2.2	.3	....	5.1	4.4	4.9	8.9	−3.0
1956	74.6	32.2	20.9	9.3	12.2	70.6	42.5	....	2.4	.4	....	4.7	5.5	5.1	10.1	3.9
1957	80.0	35.6	21.2	10.0	13.2	76.6	45.4	....	3.1	.5	....	5.4	6.7	5.4	10.1	3.4
1958	79.6	34.7	20.1	11.2	13.6	82.4	46.8	....	3.4	.5	....	7.5	8.2	5.6	10.3	−2.8
1959	79.2	36.7	17.3	11.7	13.5	92.1	49.0	....	3.1	.7	....	8.2	9.7	5.8	15.5	−12.8
1960	92.5	40.7	21.5	14.7	15.6	92.2	48.1	....	3.0	.8	....	7.4	11.6	6.9	14.4	.3
1961	94.4	41.3	21.0	16.4	15.7	97.7	49.6	....	3.2	.9	....	9.7	12.5	6.7	15.2	−3.3
1962	99.7	45.6	20.5	17.0	16.5	106.8	52.3	50.1	5.6	1.2	....	9.2	14.4	6.9	17.2	−7.1
1963	106.6	47.6	21.6	19.8	17.6	111.3	53.4	51.1	5.3	1.5	....	9.3	15.8	7.7	18.3	−4.8
1964	112.6	48.7	23.5	22.0	18.5	118.5	54.8	52.6	4.9	1.8	....	9.7	16.6	8.2	22.6	−5.9
1965	116.8	48.8	25.5	22.2	20.3	118.2	50.6	48.8	5.3	1.8	....	9.5	17.5	8.6	25.0	−1.4
1966	130.8	55.4	30.1	25.5	19.8	134.5	58.1	56.6	5.6	2.5	0.1	9.7	20.7	9.4	28.5	−3.7
1967	148.8	61.5	34.0	32.6	20.7	157.5	71.4	70.1	5.6	3.4	2.7	10.3	21.7	10.3	32.1	−8.6
1968	153.0	68.7	28.7	33.9	21.7	178.1	81.9	80.4	5.3	4.4	4.6	11.8	23.9	11.1	35.1	−25.2
1969	186.9	87.2	36.7	39.0	23.9	183.6	82.5	80.8	4.6	5.2	5.7	13.1	27.3	12.7	32.6	3.2
1970	192.8	90.4	32.8	44.4	25.2	195.6	81.7	80.1	4.3	5.9	6.2	15.7	30.3	14.4	37.2	−2.8
1971	187.1	86.2	26.8	47.3	26.8	210.2	78.9	77.5	4.2	6.8	6.6	22.9	35.9	14.8	40.0	−23.0
1972	207.3	94.7	32.2	52.6	27.8	230.7	79.2	77.6	4.8	8.7	7.5	27.7	40.2	15.5	47.3	−23.4
1973	230.8	103.2	36.2	63.1	28.3	245.7	76.7	75.0	4.1	9.4	8.1	28.3	49.1	17.3	52.8	−14.9
1974	263.2	119.0	38.6	75.1	30.6	269.4	79.3	77.9	5.7	10.7	9.6	33.7	55.9	21.4	52.9	−6.1
1975	279.1	122.4	40.6	84.5	31.5	332.3	86.5	84.9	7.1	12.9	12.9	50.2	64.7	23.2	74.8	−53.2
1976	298.1	131.6	41.4	90.8	34.3	371.8	89.6	87.9	6.4	15.7	15.8	60.8	73.9	26.7	82.7	−73.7
Transition quarter	81.2	38.8	8.5	25.2	8.8	96.0	22.3	21.8	2.5	3.9	4.3	15.0	19.8	6.9	21.4	−14.7
1977	355.6	157.6	54.9	106.5	36.6	409.2	97.2	95.1	6.4	17.3	19.3	61.1	85.1	29.9	93.0	−53.7
1978	399.6	181.0	60.0	121.0	37.7	458.7	104.5	102.3	7.5	18.5	22.8	61.5	93.9	35.5	114.7	−59.2
1979	463.3	217.8	65.7	138.9	40.8	504.0	116.3	113.6	7.5	20.5	26.5	66.4	104.1	42.6	120.2	−40.7
1980	517.1	244.1	64.6	157.8	50.6	590.9	134.0	130.9	12.7	23.2	32.1	86.6	118.5	52.5	131.3	−73.8
1981	599.3	285.9	61.1	182.7	69.5	678.2	157.5	153.9	13.1	26.9	39.1	100.3	139.6	68.8	133.0	−79.0
1982	617.8	297.7	49.2	201.5	69.3	745.7	185.3	180.7	12.3	27.4	46.6	108.2	156.0	85.0	125.0	−128.0
1983	600.6	288.9	37.0	209.0	65.6	808.4	209.9	204.4	11.8	28.6	52.6	123.0	170.7	89.8	121.8	−207.8
1984	666.4	298.4	56.9	239.4	71.8	851.8	227.4	220.9	15.9	30.4	57.5	113.4	178.2	111.1	117.9	−185.4
1985	734.0	334.5	61.3	265.2	73.0	946.3	252.7	245.1	16.2	33.5	65.8	129.0	188.6	129.5	131.0	−212.3
1986	769.2	349.0	63.1	283.9	73.2	990.4	273.4	265.4	14.1	35.9	70.2	120.6	198.8	136.0	141.4	−221.2
1987	854.3	392.6	83.9	303.3	74.5	1,004.0	282.0	273.9	11.6	40.0	75.1	124.1	207.4	138.6	125.2	−149.7
1988	909.2	401.2	94.5	334.3	79.2	1,064.4	290.4	281.9	10.5	44.5	78.9	130.4	219.3	151.8	138.7	−155.2
1989	991.1	445.7	103.3	359.4	82.7	1,143.7	303.6	294.8	9.6	48.4	85.0	137.4	232.5	169.0	158.3	−152.6
1990	1,032.0	466.9	93.5	380.0	91.5	1,253.0	299.3	289.7	13.8	57.7	98.1	148.7	248.6	184.3	202.5	−221.0
1991	1,055.0	467.8	98.1	396.0	93.1	1,324.2	273.3	262.3	15.8	71.2	104.5	172.5	269.0	194.4	223.5	−269.2
1992	1,091.2	476.0	100.3	413.7	101.3	1,381.5	298.3	286.8	16.1	89.5	119.0	199.6	287.6	199.3	172.1	−290.3
1993	1,154.3	509.7	117.5	428.3	98.8	1,409.4	291.1	278.5	17.2	99.4	130.6	210.0	304.6	198.7	157.9	−255.1
1994	1,258.6	543.1	140.4	461.5	113.7	1,461.8	281.6	268.6	17.1	107.1	144.7	217.2	319.6	202.9	171.5	−203.2
1995	1,351.8	590.2	157.0	484.5	120.1	1,515.7	272.1	259.4	16.4	115.4	159.9	223.8	335.8	232.1	160.2	−164.0
1996	1,453.1	656.4	171.8	509.4	115.4	1,560.5	265.7	253.1	13.5	119.4	174.2	229.7	349.7	241.1	167.2	−107.4
1997	1,579.2	737.5	182.3	539.4	120.1	1,601.1	270.5	258.3	15.2	123.8	190.0	235.0	365.3	244.0	157.3	−21.9
1998	1,721.7	828.6	188.7	571.8	132.6	1,652.5	268.2	255.8	13.1	131.4	192.8	237.8	379.2	241.1	188.9	69.3
1999	1,827.5	879.5	184.7	611.8	151.5	1,701.8	274.8	261.2	15.2	141.0	190.4	242.5	390.0	229.8	218.1	125.6
2000	2,025.2	1,004.5	207.3	652.9	160.6	1,789.0	294.4	281.0	17.2	154.5	197.1	253.7	409.4	222.9	239.7	236.2
2001	1,991.1	994.3	151.1	694.0	151.7	1,862.8	304.7	290.2	16.5	172.2	217.4	269.8	433.0	206.2	243.1	128.2
2002	1,853.1	858.3	148.0	700.8	146.0	2,010.9	348.5	331.8	22.3	196.5	230.9	312.7	456.0	170.9	273.1	−157.8
2003	1,782.3	793.7	131.8	713.0	143.9	2,159.9	404.7	387.1	21.2	219.5	249.4	334.6	474.7	153.1	302.6	−377.6
2004	1,880.1	809.0	189.4	733.4	148.4	2,292.8	455.8	436.4	26.9	240.1	269.4	333.1	495.5	160.2	311.8	−412.7
2005	2,153.6	927.2	278.3	794.1	154.0	2,472.0	495.3	474.1	34.6	250.5	298.6	345.8	523.3	184.0	339.8	−318.3
2006	2,406.9	1,043.9	353.9	837.8	171.2	2,655.1	521.8	499.3	29.5	252.7	329.9	352.5	548.5	226.6	393.5	−248.2
2007	2,568.0	1,163.5	370.2	869.6	164.7	2,728.7	551.3	528.5	28.5	266.4	375.4	366.0	586.2	237.1	157.3	−160.7
2008	2,524.0	1,145.7	304.3	900.2	173.7	2,982.5	616.1	594.6	28.9	280.6	390.8	431.3	617.0	252.8	365.2	−458.6
2009	2,105.0	915.3	138.2	890.9	160.5	3,517.7	661.0	636.7	37.5	334.3	430.1	533.2	683.0	186.9	651.6	−1,412.7
2010	2,162.7	898.5	191.4	864.8	207.9	3,456.2	693.6	666.7	45.2	369.1	451.6	622.2	706.7	196.2	371.6	−1,293.5
2011 (estimates)	2,173.7	956.0	198.4	806.8	212.4	3,818.8	768.2	739.7	55.2	387.6	494.3	622.7	748.4	206.7	535.8	−1,645.1
2012 (estimates)	2,627.4	1,140.5	329.3	925.1	232.5	3,728.7	737.5	707.5	63.0	373.8	492.3	554.3	767.0	241.6	499.1	−1,101.2

Note: See Note, Table B–78.

Sources: Department of the Treasury and Office of Management and Budget.

TABLE B–81. Federal receipts, outlays, surplus or deficit, and debt, fiscal years 2007–2012

[Millions of dollars; fiscal years]

Description	Actual				Estimates	
	2007	2008	2009	2010	2011	2012
RECEIPTS, OUTLAYS, AND SURPLUS OR DEFICIT						
Total:						
Receipts	2,567,985	2,523,991	2,104,989	2,162,724	2,173,700	2,627,449
Outlays	2,728,686	2,982,544	3,517,677	3,456,213	3,818,819	3,728,686
Surplus or deficit (–)	–160,701	–458,553	–1,412,688	–1,293,489	–1,645,119	–1,101,237
On-budget:						
Receipts	1,932,896	1,865,945	1,450,980	1,531,037	1,614,278	1,968,719
Outlays	2,275,049	2,507,793	3,000,661	2,901,531	3,317,275	3,145,904
Surplus or deficit (–)	–342,153	–641,848	–1,549,681	–1,370,494	–1,702,997	–1,177,185
Off-budget:						
Receipts	635,089	658,046	654,009	631,687	559,422	658,730
Outlays	453,637	474,751	517,016	554,682	501,544	582,782
Surplus or deficit (–)	181,452	183,295	136,993	77,005	57,878	75,948
OUTSTANDING DEBT, END OF PERIOD						
Gross Federal debt	8,950,744	9,986,082	11,875,851	13,528,807	15,476,243	16,654,260
Held by Federal Government accounts	3,915,615	4,183,032	4,331,144	4,509,867	4,619,793	4,773,123
Held by the public	5,035,129	5,803,050	7,544,707	9,018,941	10,856,450	11,881,136
Federal Reserve System	779,632	491,127	769,160	811,669	....	....
Other	4,255,497	5,311,923	6,775,547	8,207,272	....	....
RECEIPTS BY SOURCE						
Total: On-budget and off-budget	2,567,985	2,523,991	2,104,989	2,162,724	2,173,700	2,627,449
Individual income taxes	1,163,472	1,145,747	915,308	898,549	956,033	1,140,504
Corporation income taxes	370,243	304,346	138,229	191,437	198,431	329,324
Social insurance and retirement receipts	869,607	900,155	890,917	864,814	806,801	925,081
On-budget	234,518	242,109	236,908	233,127	247,379	266,351
Off-budget	635,089	658,046	654,009	631,687	559,422	658,730
Excise taxes	65,069	67,334	62,483	66,909	74,079	103,069
Estate and gift taxes	26,044	28,844	23,482	18,885	12,227	13,600
Customs duties and fees	26,010	27,568	22,453	25,298	27,691	29,754
Miscellaneous receipts	47,540	49,997	52,117	96,832	98,438	86,117
Deposits of earnings by Federal Reserve System	32,043	33,598	34,318	75,845	79,511	65,803
All other	15,497	16,399	17,799	20,987	18,927	20,314
OUTLAYS BY FUNCTION						
Total: On-budget and off-budget	2,728,686	2,982,544	3,517,677	3,456,213	3,818,819	3,728,686
National defense	551,271	616,073	661,049	693,586	768,217	737,537
International affairs	28,482	28,857	37,529	45,195	55,172	63,001
General science, space and technology	25,525	27,731	29,449	31,047	33,356	32,284
Energy	–860	628	4,749	11,613	27,891	23,411
Natural resources and environment	31,716	31,817	35,568	43,662	49,002	42,703
Agriculture	17,662	18,387	22,237	21,356	25,087	18,929
Commerce and housing credit	487	27,870	291,535	–82,298	17,431	23,620
On-budget	–4,606	25,453	291,231	–86,998	15,899	23,895
Off-budget	5,093	2,417	304	4,700	1,532	–275
Transportation	72,905	77,616	84,289	91,972	94,511	104,854
Community and regional development	29,567	23,952	27,650	23,804	25,742	25,701
Education, training, employment, and social services	91,656	91,287	79,749	127,710	115,118	106,172
Health	266,382	280,599	334,335	369,054	387,617	373,774
Medicare	375,407	390,758	430,093	451,636	494,343	492,316
Income security	365,975	431,313	533,224	622,210	622,654	554,332
Social security	586,153	617,027	682,963	706,737	748,354	767,019
On-budget	19,307	17,830	34,071	23,317	117,465	55,417
Off-budget	566,846	599,197	648,892	683,420	630,889	711,602
Veterans benefits and services	72,818	84,653	95,429	108,384	141,409	124,659
Administration of justice	41,244	47,138	51,549	53,436	60,661	58,696
General government	17,425	20,323	22,017	23,031	32,075	31,149
Net interest	237,109	252,757	186,902	196,194	206,688	241,598
On-budget	343,112	366,475	304,856	314,696	322,427	354,938
Off-budget	–106,003	–113,718	–117,954	–118,502	–115,739	–113,340
Allowances	....	....	....	....	3,146	6,566
Undistributed offsetting receipts	–82,238	–86,242	–92,639	–82,116	–89,655	–99,635
On-budget	–69,939	–73,097	–78,413	–67,180	–74,517	–84,430
Off-budget	–12,299	–13,145	–14,226	–14,936	–15,138	–15,205

Note: See Note, Table B–78.

Sources: Department of the Treasury and Office of Management and Budget.

TABLE B–82. Federal and State and local government current receipts and expenditures, national income and product accounts (NIPA), 1962–2010

[Billions of dollars; quarterly data at seasonally adjusted annual rates]

Year or quarter	Total government			Federal Government			State and local government			Addendum: Grants-in-aid to State and local governments
	Current receipts	Current expenditures	Net government saving (NIPA)	Current receipts	Current expenditures	Net Federal Government saving (NIPA)	Current receipts	Current expenditures	Net State and local government saving (NIPA)	
1962	150.6	142.9	7.7	103.6	101.2	2.4	52.0	46.8	5.2	5.0
1963	162.2	151.2	11.0	111.8	106.5	5.3	56.0	50.3	5.7	5.6
1964	166.6	159.3	7.3	111.8	110.9	.9	61.3	54.9	6.4	6.5
1965	180.3	170.6	9.8	121.0	117.7	3.2	66.5	60.0	6.5	7.2
1966	202.8	192.8	10.0	138.0	135.7	2.3	74.9	67.2	7.8	10.1
1967	217.7	220.0	–2.3	146.9	156.2	–9.3	82.5	75.5	7.0	11.7
1968	252.1	247.0	5.1	171.3	173.7	–2.4	93.5	86.0	7.5	12.7
1969	283.5	267.0	16.5	192.7	184.1	8.6	105.5	97.5	8.0	14.6
1970	286.9	295.2	–8.4	186.1	201.6	–15.5	120.1	113.0	7.1	19.3
1971	303.6	325.8	–22.2	191.9	220.6	–28.7	134.9	128.5	6.5	23.2
1972	347.0	356.3	–9.3	220.3	245.2	–24.9	158.4	142.8	15.6	31.7
1973	390.4	386.5	3.9	250.8	262.6	–11.8	174.3	158.6	15.7	34.8
1974	431.8	436.9	–5.2	280.0	294.5	–14.5	188.1	178.7	9.3	36.3
1975	442.1	510.2	–68.2	277.6	348.3	–70.6	209.6	207.1	2.5	45.1
1976	505.9	552.2	–46.3	323.0	376.7	–53.7	233.7	226.3	7.4	50.7
1977	567.3	600.3	–33.0	364.0	410.1	–46.1	259.9	246.8	13.1	58.6
1978	646.1	656.3	–10.2	424.0	452.9	–28.9	287.6	268.9	18.7	65.5
1979	728.9	729.9	–1.0	486.9	500.9	–14.0	308.4	295.4	13.0	66.3
1980	798.7	846.5	–47.8	532.8	589.5	–56.6	338.2	329.4	8.8	72.3
1981	917.7	966.9	–49.2	619.9	676.7	–56.8	370.2	362.7	7.6	72.5
1982	939.3	1,076.8	–137.5	617.4	752.6	–135.3	391.4	393.6	–2.2	69.5
1983	1,000.3	1,171.7	–171.4	643.3	819.5	–176.2	428.6	423.7	4.9	71.6
1984	1,113.5	1,261.0	–147.5	710.0	881.5	–171.5	480.2	456.2	23.9	76.7
1985	1,214.6	1,370.9	–156.3	774.4	953.0	–178.6	521.1	498.7	22.4	80.9
1986	1,290.1	1,464.0	–173.9	816.0	1,010.7	–194.6	561.6	540.9	20.7	87.6
1987	1,403.2	1,540.5	–137.4	896.5	1,045.9	–149.3	590.6	578.6	12.0	83.9
1988	1,502.4	1,623.6	–121.2	958.5	1,096.9	–138.4	635.5	618.3	17.2	91.6
1989	1,627.2	1,741.0	–113.8	1,038.0	1,172.0	–133.9	687.5	667.4	20.1	98.3
1990	1,709.3	1,879.5	–170.3	1,082.8	1,259.2	–176.4	738.0	731.8	6.2	111.4
1991	1,759.7	1,984.0	–224.2	1,101.9	1,320.3	–218.4	789.4	795.2	–5.8	131.6
1992	1,845.1	2,149.0	–303.9	1,148.0	1,450.5	–302.5	846.2	847.6	–1.4	149.1
1993	1,948.2	2,229.4	–281.2	1,224.1	1,504.3	–280.2	888.2	889.1	–.9	164.0
1994	2,091.9	2,304.0	–212.2	1,322.1	1,542.5	–220.4	944.8	936.6	8.2	175.1
1995	2,215.5	2,412.5	–197.0	1,407.8	1,614.0	–206.2	991.9	982.7	9.2	184.2
1996	2,380.4	2,505.7	–125.3	1,526.4	1,674.7	–148.2	1,045.1	1,022.1	23.0	191.1
1997	2,557.2	2,581.1	–23.8	1,656.2	1,716.3	–60.1	1,099.5	1,063.2	36.3	198.4
1998	2,729.8	2,649.3	80.5	1,777.9	1,744.3	33.6	1,164.5	1,117.6	46.9	212.6
1999	2,902.5	2,761.9	140.6	1,895.0	1,796.2	98.8	1,240.4	1,198.6	41.8	232.9
2000	3,132.4	2,906.0	226.5	2,057.1	1,871.9	185.2	1,322.6	1,281.3	41.3	247.3
2001	3,118.2	3,093.6	24.6	2,020.3	1,979.8	40.5	1,374.0	1,389.9	–15.9	276.1
2002	2,967.9	3,274.7	–306.9	1,859.3	2,112.1	–252.8	1,412.7	1,466.8	–54.1	304.2
2003	3,043.4	3,458.6	–415.2	1,885.1	2,261.5	–376.4	1,496.3	1,535.1	–38.8	338.0
2004	3,265.7	3,653.5	–387.8	2,013.9	2,393.4	–379.5	1,601.0	1,609.3	–8.4	349.2
2005	3,659.3	3,916.4	–257.1	2,290.1	2,573.1	–283.0	1,730.4	1,704.5	25.9	361.2
2006	3,995.2	4,147.9	–152.7	2,524.5	2,728.3	–203.8	1,829.7	1,778.6	51.0	359.0
2007	4,197.0	4,430.0	–233.0	2,654.7	2,900.0	–245.2	1,923.1	1,910.8	12.2	380.8
2008	4,074.0	4,737.7	–663.6	2,503.1	3,119.3	–616.2	1,967.2	2,014.6	–47.4	396.2
2009	3,726.9	4,998.8	–1,271.9	2,205.8	3,457.5	–1,251.7	2,005.8	2,025.9	–20.1	484.6
2010 ᵖ	....	5,283.4	....	....	3,719.4	....	....	2,093.9	....	529.9
2007: I	4,172.2	4,344.0	–171.8	2,642.8	2,844.4	–201.6	1,906.7	1,876.9	29.8	377.3
II	4,200.3	4,407.9	–207.7	2,658.5	2,896.0	–237.4	1,923.4	1,893.6	29.8	381.6
III	4,195.5	4,450.7	–255.2	2,651.5	2,916.6	–265.2	1,926.2	1,916.2	10.0	382.1
IV	4,220.1	4,517.5	–297.4	2,666.1	2,942.8	–276.7	1,935.9	1,956.6	–20.7	381.9
2008: I	4,207.6	4,613.5	–406.0	2,640.7	3,017.4	–376.7	1,955.6	1,984.9	–29.3	388.8
II	4,003.3	4,798.5	–795.2	2,412.6	3,174.1	–761.6	1,985.9	2,019.6	–33.6	395.2
III	4,089.7	4,801.3	–711.6	2,506.1	3,152.8	–646.7	1,979.0	2,043.9	–64.9	395.4
IV	3,995.6	4,737.3	–741.7	2,452.9	3,132.9	–680.0	1,948.1	2,009.9	–61.8	405.5
2009: I	3,745.5	4,790.3	–1,044.8	2,223.9	3,227.1	–1,003.2	1,964.8	2,006.4	–41.6	443.2
II	3,674.6	5,045.0	–1,370.3	2,191.2	3,527.9	–1,336.8	1,986.6	2,020.2	–33.6	503.1
III	3,702.5	5,078.4	–1,375.9	2,176.3	3,532.9	–1,356.7	2,017.2	2,036.4	–19.2	490.9
IV	3,785.0	5,081.5	–1,296.4	2,231.7	3,542.0	–1,310.3	2,054.4	2,040.6	13.9	501.1
2010: I	3,904.0	5,189.6	–1,285.7	2,322.8	3,637.1	–1,314.2	2,095.7	2,067.2	28.6	514.6
II	3,947.8	5,268.6	–1,320.8	2,364.7	3,701.2	–1,336.5	2,108.1	2,092.4	15.8	525.0
III	4,019.9	5,316.4	–1,296.5	2,416.4	3,760.7	–1,344.3	2,142.7	2,095.0	47.7	539.3
IV ᵖ	....	5,358.8	....	....	3,778.8	....	....	2,120.9	....	540.9

Note: Federal grants-in-aid to State and local governments are reflected in Federal current expenditures and State and local current receipts. Total government current receipts and expenditures have been adjusted to eliminate this duplication.

Source: Department of Commerce (Bureau of Economic Analysis).

TABLE B–83. Federal and State and local government current receipts and expenditures, national income and product accounts (NIPA), by major type, 1962–2010

[Billions of dollars; quarterly data at seasonally adjusted annual rates]

Year or quarter	Current receipts									Current expenditures					Net government saving
	Total	Current tax receipts				Contributions for government social insurance	Income receipts on assets	Current transfer receipts	Current surplus of government enterprises	Total[2]	Consumption expenditures	Current transfer payments	Interest payments	Subsidies	
		Total[1]	Personal current taxes	Taxes on production and imports	Taxes on corporate income										
1962	150.6	126.1	51.6	50.4	24.0	19.2	3.2	1.2	0.9	142.9	96.8	32.8	11.1	2.3	7.7
1963	162.2	134.4	54.6	53.4	26.2	21.7	3.4	1.3	1.4	151.2	102.7	34.3	12.0	2.2	11.0
1964	166.6	137.5	52.1	57.3	28.0	22.5	3.7	1.6	1.3	159.3	108.6	35.1	12.9	2.7	7.3
1965	180.3	149.5	57.7	60.7	30.9	23.5	4.1	1.9	1.3	170.6	115.9	38.0	13.7	3.0	9.8
1966	202.8	163.5	66.4	63.2	33.7	31.4	4.7	2.2	1.0	192.8	131.8	42.0	15.1	3.9	10.0
1967	217.7	173.8	73.0	67.9	32.7	35.0	5.5	2.5	.9	220.0	149.5	50.3	16.4	3.8	−2.3
1968	252.1	203.1	87.0	76.4	39.4	38.8	6.4	2.6	1.2	247.0	165.7	58.4	18.8	4.2	5.1
1969	283.5	228.4	104.5	83.9	39.7	44.3	7.0	2.7	1.0	267.0	178.2	64.1	20.2	4.5	16.5
1970	286.9	229.2	103.1	91.4	34.4	46.6	8.2	2.9	.0	295.2	190.1	77.3	23.1	4.8	−8.4
1971	303.6	240.3	101.7	100.5	37.7	51.5	9.0	3.1	−.2	325.8	204.7	92.2	24.5	4.7	−22.2
1972	347.0	273.8	123.6	107.9	41.9	59.6	9.5	3.6	.5	356.3	220.8	103.0	26.3	6.6	−9.3
1973	390.4	299.3	132.4	117.2	49.3	76.0	11.6	3.9	−.4	386.5	234.8	115.2	31.3	5.2	3.9
1974	431.8	328.1	151.0	124.9	51.8	85.8	14.4	4.5	−.9	436.9	261.7	135.9	35.6	3.3	−5.2
1975	442.1	334.3	147.6	135.3	50.9	89.9	16.1	5.1	−3.2	510.2	294.6	171.3	40.0	4.5	−68.2
1976	505.9	383.6	172.3	146.4	64.2	102.0	16.3	5.8	−1.8	552.2	316.6	184.3	46.3	5.1	−46.3
1977	567.3	431.0	197.5	159.7	73.0	113.9	18.4	6.8	−2.7	600.3	346.6	195.9	50.8	7.1	−33.0
1978	646.1	484.8	229.4	170.9	83.5	132.1	23.2	8.2	−2.2	656.3	376.5	210.9	60.2	8.9	−10.2
1979	728.9	537.9	268.7	180.1	88.0	153.7	30.8	8.4	−2.9	729.9	412.3	236.0	72.9	8.5	−1.0
1980	798.7	585.6	298.9	200.3	84.8	167.2	39.9	11.1	−5.1	846.5	465.9	281.7	89.1	9.8	−47.8
1981	917.7	663.5	345.2	235.6	81.1	196.9	50.2	12.7	−5.6	966.9	520.6	318.1	116.7	11.5	−49.2
1982	939.3	659.5	354.1	240.9	63.1	210.1	58.9	15.3	−4.5	1,076.8	568.1	354.7	138.9	15.0	−137.5
1983	1,000.3	694.1	352.3	263.3	77.2	227.2	65.3	16.9	−3.2	1,171.7	610.5	382.5	156.9	21.3	−171.4
1984	1,113.5	762.5	377.4	289.8	94.0	258.8	74.3	19.7	−1.9	1,261.0	657.6	395.3	187.3	21.1	−147.5
1985	1,214.6	823.9	417.3	308.1	96.5	282.8	84.0	23.4	.6	1,370.9	720.1	420.4	208.8	21.4	−156.3
1986	1,290.1	868.8	437.2	323.4	106.5	304.9	89.7	25.9	.9	1,464.0	776.1	446.6	216.3	24.9	−173.9
1987	1,403.2	965.7	489.1	347.5	127.1	324.6	85.6	27.0	.2	1,540.5	815.1	464.4	230.8	30.3	−137.4
1988	1,502.4	1,018.9	504.9	374.5	137.2	363.2	89.9	27.9	2.6	1,623.6	852.8	493.6	247.7	29.5	−121.2
1989	1,627.2	1,109.2	566.1	398.9	141.5	386.9	93.7	32.5	4.9	1,741.0	902.9	538.1	272.5	27.4	−113.8
1990	1,709.3	1,161.3	592.7	425.0	140.6	412.1	98.0	36.3	1.6	1,879.5	966.0	592.4	294.2	27.0	−170.3
1991	1,759.7	1,179.9	586.6	457.1	133.6	432.2	97.0	44.9	5.7	1,984.0	1,015.8	628.9	311.7	27.5	−224.2
1992	1,845.1	1,239.7	610.5	483.4	143.1	457.1	89.6	50.5	8.2	2,149.0	1,050.4	756.3	312.3	30.1	−303.9
1993	1,948.2	1,317.8	646.5	503.1	165.4	479.6	86.8	55.3	8.7	2,229.4	1,075.4	804.6	312.7	36.7	−281.2
1994	2,091.9	1,425.6	690.5	545.2	186.7	510.7	86.0	60.0	9.6	2,304.0	1,108.9	839.9	322.7	32.5	−212.2
1995	2,215.5	1,516.7	743.9	557.9	211.0	535.5	91.8	58.4	13.1	2,412.5	1,141.4	882.4	353.9	34.8	−197.0
1996	2,380.4	1,641.5	832.0	580.8	223.6	557.9	99.9	66.8	14.4	2,505.7	1,176.7	929.2	364.6	35.2	−125.3
1997	2,557.2	1,780.0	926.2	611.6	237.1	590.3	103.6	69.3	14.1	2,581.1	1,222.1	954.6	370.6	33.8	−23.8
1998	2,729.8	1,910.8	1,026.4	639.5	239.2	627.8	102.7	75.3	13.3	2,649.3	1,263.2	978.1	371.6	36.4	80.5
1999	2,902.5	2,035.8	1,107.5	673.6	248.8	664.6	106.4	81.7	14.1	2,761.9	1,343.9	1,014.9	357.9	45.2	140.6
2000	3,132.4	2,202.8	1,232.3	708.6	254.7	709.4	118.8	92.3	9.1	2,906.0	1,426.6	1,071.5	362.0	45.8	226.5
2001	3,118.2	2,163.7	1,234.8	727.7	193.5	736.9	114.6	98.9	4.0	3,093.6	1,524.4	1,169.0	341.5	58.7	24.6
2002	2,967.9	2,002.1	1,050.4	762.8	181.3	755.2	99.9	104.3	6.3	3,274.7	1,639.9	1,280.9	312.6	41.4	−306.9
2003	3,043.4	2,047.9	1,000.3	806.8	231.8	782.8	96.8	108.9	7.0	3,458.6	1,756.8	1,354.8	298.0	49.1	−415.2
2004	3,265.7	2,213.2	1,047.8	863.4	292.0	831.7	100.3	119.3	1.2	3,653.5	1,860.4	1,440.1	306.6	46.4	−387.8
2005	3,659.3	2,546.8	1,208.6	930.2	395.9	877.4	111.9	126.7	−3.5	3,916.4	1,977.9	1,534.9	342.7	60.9	−257.1
2006	3,995.2	2,807.4	1,352.4	986.8	454.2	926.4	129.6	136.0	−4.2	4,147.9	2,093.3	1,631.0	372.2	51.4	−152.7
2007	4,197.0	2,951.2	1,488.7	1,027.2	420.6	964.2	144.2	149.2	−11.8	4,430.0	2,217.8	1,743.4	414.3	54.6	−233.0
2008	4,074.0	2,780.3	1,438.2	1,045.1	280.2	992.1	146.9	171.4	−16.7	4,737.7	2,382.8	1,902.7	399.4	52.8	−663.6
2009	3,726.9	2,409.3	1,140.0	1,024.7	231.4	975.1	162.2	193.5	−13.2	4,998.8	2,411.5	2,164.9	362.0	60.3	−1,271.9
2010 p	....	....	1,167.0	1,058.8	....	1,009.5	163.6	195.5	−13.6	5,283.4	2,490.8	2,332.4	401.2	59.0	....
2007: I	4,172.2	2,939.1	1,458.7	1,014.7	451.9	958.0	140.3	144.9	−10.1	4,344.0	2,160.6	1,738.7	394.8	50.0	−171.8
II	4,200.3	2,962.6	1,480.4	1,023.9	443.3	959.0	143.2	146.5	−11.0	4,407.9	2,201.0	1,714.0	434.9	58.1	−207.7
III	4,195.5	2,947.7	1,497.5	1,030.7	405.3	963.4	146.0	149.6	−11.2	4,450.7	2,238.2	1,738.5	418.3	55.7	−255.2
IV	4,220.1	2,955.3	1,518.0	1,039.4	381.9	976.4	147.5	155.7	−14.8	4,517.5	2,271.4	1,782.4	409.1	54.5	−297.4
2008: I	4,207.6	2,921.0	1,535.8	1,041.7	328.3	993.2	146.8	162.5	−16.0	4,613.5	2,329.7	1,821.1	411.1	51.7	−406.0
II	4,003.3	2,713.2	1,351.8	1,051.9	314.1	992.5	148.7	165.8	−17.0	4,798.5	2,375.1	1,957.3	414.4	51.8	−795.2
III	4,089.7	2,796.8	1,442.4	1,052.6	285.6	994.3	146.8	168.3	−16.5	4,801.3	2,428.5	1,895.1	425.3	52.4	−711.6
IV	3,995.6	2,690.2	1,443.0	1,034.3	192.7	988.3	145.2	189.1	−17.3	4,737.3	2,398.0	1,937.2	346.9	55.2	−741.7
2009: I	3,745.5	2,442.3	1,213.4	1,016.7	198.0	969.0	156.0	194.0	−15.8	4,790.3	2,373.8	2,046.2	313.5	56.8	−1,044.8
II	3,674.6	2,344.5	1,112.5	1,018.7	200.1	976.4	164.0	204.0	−14.2	5,045.0	2,413.0	2,196.5	378.3	57.2	−1,370.3
III	3,702.5	2,391.2	1,117.0	1,028.2	233.1	975.4	162.1	185.5	−11.7	5,078.4	2,425.3	2,202.1	382.0	69.1	−1,375.9
IV	3,785.0	2,459.4	1,117.2	1,035.2	294.6	979.5	166.8	190.5	−11.3	5,081.5	2,434.0	2,215.0	374.1	58.4	−1,296.4
2010: I	3,904.0	2,572.4	1,134.7	1,045.9	379.2	992.9	159.3	191.4	−12.1	5,189.6	2,464.7	2,287.2	380.3	57.4	−1,285.7
II	3,947.8	2,597.8	1,149.1	1,054.6	381.3	1,007.1	162.2	193.9	−13.1	5,268.6	2,485.2	2,319.0	405.9	58.5	−1,320.8
III	4,019.9	2,655.4	1,177.7	1,060.8	404.8	1,015.0	165.6	198.0	−14.2	5,316.4	2,502.9	2,352.9	402.1	58.6	−1,296.5
IV p	....	....	1,206.4	1,074.0	....	1,023.0	167.2	198.8	−14.9	5,358.8	2,510.5	2,370.6	416.4	61.4	....

1 Includes taxes from the rest of the world, not shown separately.
2 Includes an item for the difference between wage accruals and disbursements, not shown separately.

Source: Department of Commerce (Bureau of Economic Analysis).

TABLE B–84. Federal Government current receipts and expenditures, national income and product accounts (NIPA), 1962–2010

[Billions of dollars; quarterly data at seasonally adjusted annual rates]

Year or quarter	Current receipts									Current expenditures					Net Federal Government saving
	Total	Current tax receipts				Contributions for government social insurance	Income receipts on assets	Current transfer receipts	Current surplus of government enterprises	Total [2]	Consumption expenditures	Current transfer payments [3]	Interest payments	Subsidies	
		Total [1]	Personal current taxes	Taxes on production and imports	Taxes on corporate income										
1962	103.6	83.3	46.5	14.1	22.5	18.6	1.7	0.5	−0.5	101.2	57.8	32.5	8.6	2.3	2.4
1963	111.8	88.6	49.1	14.7	24.6	21.1	1.8	.6	−.3	106.5	60.8	34.2	9.3	2.2	5.3
1964	111.8	87.7	46.0	15.4	26.1	21.8	1.8	.7	−.3	110.9	62.8	35.4	10.0	2.7	.9
1965	121.0	95.6	51.1	15.4	28.9	22.7	1.9	1.1	−.3	117.7	65.7	38.5	10.6	3.0	3.2
1966	138.0	104.7	58.6	14.4	31.4	30.6	2.1	1.2	−.6	135.7	75.7	44.4	11.6	3.9	2.3
1967	146.9	109.8	64.4	15.2	30.0	34.1	2.5	1.1	−.6	156.2	87.0	52.8	12.7	3.8	−9.3
1968	171.3	129.7	76.4	16.9	36.1	37.9	2.9	1.1	−.3	173.7	95.3	59.7	14.6	4.1	−2.4
1969	192.7	146.0	91.7	17.8	36.1	43.3	2.7	1.1	−.4	184.1	98.3	65.5	15.8	4.5	8.6
1970	186.1	137.9	88.9	18.1	30.6	45.5	3.1	1.1	−1.5	201.6	98.6	80.5	17.7	4.8	−15.5
1971	191.9	138.6	85.8	19.0	33.5	50.3	3.5	1.1	−1.6	220.6	101.9	96.1	17.9	4.6	−28.7
1972	220.3	158.2	102.8	18.5	36.6	58.3	3.6	1.3	−1.1	245.2	107.6	112.7	18.8	6.6	−24.9
1973	250.8	173.0	109.6	19.8	43.3	74.5	3.8	1.3	−1.8	262.6	108.8	125.9	22.8	5.1	−11.8
1974	280.0	192.1	126.5	20.1	45.1	84.1	4.2	1.4	−1.8	294.5	117.9	146.9	26.0	3.2	−14.5
1975	277.6	186.8	120.7	22.1	43.6	88.1	4.9	1.5	−3.6	348.3	129.5	185.6	28.9	4.3	−70.6
1976	323.0	217.9	141.2	21.4	54.6	99.8	5.9	1.6	−2.2	376.7	137.1	200.9	33.8	4.9	−53.7
1977	364.0	247.2	162.2	22.7	61.6	111.1	6.7	2.0	−3.0	410.1	150.7	215.5	37.1	6.9	−46.1
1978	424.0	286.6	188.9	25.3	71.4	128.7	8.5	2.7	−2.5	452.9	163.3	235.7	45.3	8.7	−28.9
1979	486.9	325.9	224.6	25.7	74.4	149.8	10.7	3.1	−2.6	500.9	178.9	258.0	55.7	8.2	−14.0
1980	532.8	355.5	250.0	33.7	70.3	163.6	13.7	3.9	−3.9	589.5	207.4	302.9	69.7	9.4	−56.6
1981	619.9	407.7	290.6	49.9	65.7	193.0	18.3	4.1	−3.2	676.7	238.3	333.5	93.9	11.1	−56.8
1982	617.4	386.3	295.0	41.0	49.0	206.0	22.2	5.7	−2.9	752.6	263.3	363.0	111.8	14.6	−135.3
1983	643.3	393.2	286.2	44.4	61.3	223.1	23.8	6.1	−3.0	819.5	286.4	387.2	124.6	20.9	−176.2
1984	710.0	425.2	301.4	47.3	75.2	254.1	26.6	7.4	−3.4	881.5	309.9	400.8	150.3	20.7	−171.5
1985	774.4	460.2	336.0	46.1	76.3	277.9	29.1	9.7	−2.6	953.0	338.3	424.0	169.4	21.0	−178.6
1986	816.0	479.2	350.0	43.7	83.8	298.9	31.3	8.5	−1.9	1,010.7	358.0	449.9	178.2	24.6	−194.6
1987	896.5	543.6	392.5	45.9	103.2	317.4	27.5	11.0	−3.0	1,045.9	373.7	457.6	184.6	30.0	−149.3
1988	958.5	566.2	402.8	49.8	111.1	354.8	29.4	10.5	−2.3	1,096.9	381.7	486.8	199.3	29.2	−138.4
1989	1,038.0	621.2	451.5	49.7	117.2	378.0	28.0	12.7	−1.7	1,172.0	398.5	527.1	219.3	27.1	−133.9
1990	1,082.8	642.2	470.1	50.9	118.1	402.0	29.6	14.2	−5.3	1,259.2	419.0	576.2	237.5	26.6	−176.4
1991	1,101.9	635.6	461.3	61.8	109.9	420.6	29.1	18.2	−1.6	1,320.3	438.3	604.0	250.9	27.1	−218.4
1992	1,148.0	659.9	475.2	63.3	118.8	444.0	24.8	19.4	.0	1,450.5	444.1	725.4	251.3	29.7	−302.5
1993	1,224.1	713.0	505.5	66.4	138.5	465.5	25.5	21.3	−1.3	1,504.3	441.2	773.4	253.4	36.3	−280.2
1994	1,322.1	781.4	542.5	79.0	156.7	496.2	22.7	22.8	−.9	1,542.5	440.7	808.3	261.3	32.2	−220.4
1995	1,407.8	844.6	585.8	75.6	179.3	521.9	23.3	18.4	−.3	1,614.0	440.1	849.0	290.4	34.5	−206.2
1996	1,526.4	931.9	663.3	72.9	190.6	545.4	26.5	23.8	−1.2	1,674.7	446.5	896.0	297.3	34.9	−148.2
1997	1,656.2	1,030.1	744.2	77.8	203.0	579.4	25.4	21.3	−.1	1,716.3	457.5	925.4	300.0	33.4	−60.1
1998	1,777.9	1,115.8	825.2	80.7	204.2	617.4	21.2	22.6	.8	1,744.3	454.6	954.9	298.8	35.9	33.6
1999	1,895.0	1,195.4	893.0	83.4	213.0	654.8	20.6	23.4	.8	1,796.2	473.3	995.4	282.7	44.8	98.8
2000	2,057.1	1,309.6	995.6	87.3	219.4	698.6	24.5	25.7	−1.2	1,871.9	496.0	1,047.4	283.3	45.3	185.2
2001	2,020.3	1,249.4	991.8	85.3	164.7	723.3	24.5	27.0	−4.0	1,979.8	530.2	1,140.0	258.6	51.1	40.5
2002	1,859.3	1,073.5	828.6	86.8	150.5	739.3	20.3	26.1	.2	2,112.1	590.5	1,252.1	229.1	40.5	−252.8
2003	1,885.1	1,070.2	774.2	89.3	197.8	762.8	22.8	25.6	−.3	2,261.5	660.3	1,339.4	212.9	49.0	−376.4
2004	2,013.9	1,153.8	799.2	94.3	250.3	807.6	23.2	29.0	.3	2,393.4	721.4	1,405.0	221.0	46.0	−379.5
2005	2,290.1	1,383.7	931.9	98.8	341.0	852.6	23.7	33.6	−3.5	2,573.1	765.8	1,491.3	255.4	60.5	−283.0
2006	2,524.5	1,558.3	1,049.9	99.4	395.0	904.6	26.1	38.3	−2.9	2,728.3	811.0	1,587.1	279.2	51.0	−203.8
2007	2,654.7	1,637.6	1,165.6	94.5	362.8	945.3	29.8	44.8	−2.7	2,900.0	848.9	1,690.4	313.2	47.4	−245.2
2008	2,503.1	1,447.8	1,102.8	96.0	232.2	972.4	31.7	55.0	−3.7	3,119.3	934.6	1,843.7	291.2	49.8	−616.2
2009	2,205.8	1,142.4	852.7	94.4	182.1	953.5	46.2	67.9	−4.2	3,457.5	987.1	2,157.4	254.0	58.9	−1,251.7
2010 p		875.1	106.8		987.1	45.5	59.7	−4.5	3,719.4	1,043.3	2,329.2	289.6	57.4	
2007: I	2,642.8	1,637.2	1,136.5	94.1	392.8	938.4	28.2	43.5	−4.5	2,844.4	822.8	1,676.8	296.8	48.1	−201.6
II	2,658.5	1,648.6	1,155.1	94.5	384.0	940.1	29.0	43.6	−2.8	2,896.0	840.4	1,673.1	335.0	47.5	−237.4
III	2,651.5	1,632.6	1,174.2	95.2	349.1	944.9	30.3	44.5	−.8	2,916.6	862.0	1,691.5	316.2	46.9	−265.2
IV	2,666.1	1,632.0	1,196.4	94.2	325.4	957.8	31.5	47.6	−2.8	2,942.8	870.4	1,720.4	304.7	47.2	−276.7
2008: I	2,640.7	1,588.1	1,198.7	96.2	278.0	974.2	31.4	50.2	−3.1	3,017.4	901.9	1,763.3	304.5	47.7	−376.7
II	2,412.6	1,359.8	948.3	97.9	262.0	973.1	33.1	50.4	−3.8	3,174.1	920.1	1,899.7	305.6	48.8	−761.6
III	2,506.1	1,452.7	1,109.0	96.2	231.2	974.4	32.1	50.3	−4.4	3,152.8	954.2	1,831.7	316.6	50.3	−646.7
IV	2,452.9	1,390.5	1,119.1	93.6	157.4	967.8	30.1	68.9	−4.5	3,132.9	962.3	1,880.2	238.0	52.4	−680.0
2009: I	2,223.9	1,169.1	912.8	87.2	154.9	948.0	40.4	71.3	−4.9	3,227.1	958.1	2,009.8	204.4	54.8	−1,003.2
II	2,191.2	1,113.0	847.7	96.4	155.7	954.9	48.6	79.4	−4.8	3,527.9	989.0	2,211.8	271.3	56.0	−1,336.8
III	2,176.3	1,121.3	827.0	97.0	184.4	953.5	46.0	58.9	−3.5	3,532.9	999.7	2,191.5	273.8	67.9	−1,356.7
IV	2,231.7	1,166.2	823.4	97.1	233.2	957.4	50.0	61.8	−3.6	3,542.0	1,001.8	2,216.7	266.4	57.2	−1,310.3
2010: I	2,322.8	1,253.6	843.2	100.6	297.1	970.6	41.8	60.2	−3.4	3,637.1	1,017.3	2,292.3	271.6	55.8	−1,314.2
II	2,364.7	1,281.1	868.5	106.6	293.2	984.7	44.0	59.1	−4.2	3,701.2	1,038.5	2,311.4	294.9	56.4	−1,336.5
III	2,416.4	1,320.7	885.9	108.9	313.7	992.5	47.6	60.5	−4.9	3,760.7	1,061.6	2,352.3	289.8	57.0	−1,344.3
IV p			902.6	110.9		1,000.4	48.5	58.9	−5.6	3,778.8	1,055.8	2,360.7	301.9	60.4	

[1] Includes taxes from the rest of the world, not shown separately.
[2] Includes an item for the difference between wage accruals and disbursements, not shown separately.
[3] Includes Federal grants-in-aid to State and local governments. See Table B–82 for data on Federal grants-in-aid.

Source: Department of Commerce (Bureau of Economic Analysis)

TABLE B–85. State and local government current receipts and expenditures, national income and product accounts (NIPA), 1962–2010

[Billions of dollars; quarterly data at seasonally adjusted annual rates]

Year or quarter	Current receipts									Current expenditures					Net State and local government saving
	Total	Current tax receipts				Contributions for government social insurance	Income receipts on assets	Current transfer receipts [1]	Current surplus of government enterprises	Total [2]	Consumption expenditures	Government social benefit payments to persons	Interest payments	Subsidies	
		Total	Personal current taxes	Taxes on production and imports	Taxes on corporate income										
1962	52.0	42.8	5.0	36.3	1.5	0.5	1.5	5.8	1.4	46.8	39.0	5.3	2.4	0.0	5.2
1963	56.0	45.8	5.4	38.7	1.7	.6	1.6	6.4	1.6	50.3	41.9	5.7	2.7	.0	5.7
1964	61.3	49.8	6.1	41.8	1.8	.7	1.9	7.3	1.6	54.9	45.8	6.2	2.9	.0	6.4
1965	66.5	53.9	6.6	45.3	2.0	.8	2.2	8.0	1.7	60.0	50.2	6.7	3.1	.0	6.5
1966	74.9	58.8	7.8	48.8	2.2	.8	2.6	11.1	1.6	67.2	56.1	7.6	3.4	.0	7.8
1967	82.5	64.0	8.6	52.8	2.6	.9	3.0	13.1	1.5	75.5	62.6	9.2	3.7	.0	7.0
1968	93.5	73.4	10.6	59.5	3.3	.9	3.5	14.2	1.5	86.0	70.4	11.4	4.2	.0	7.5
1969	105.5	82.5	12.8	66.0	3.6	1.0	4.3	16.2	1.5	97.5	79.8	13.2	4.4	.0	8.0
1970	120.1	91.3	14.2	73.3	3.7	1.1	5.2	21.1	1.5	113.0	91.5	16.1	5.3	.0	7.1
1971	134.9	101.7	15.9	81.5	4.3	1.2	5.5	25.2	1.4	128.5	102.7	19.3	6.5	.0	6.5
1972	158.4	115.6	20.9	89.4	5.3	1.3	5.9	34.0	1.6	142.8	113.2	22.0	7.5	.1	15.6
1973	174.3	126.3	22.8	97.4	6.0	1.5	7.8	37.3	1.5	158.6	126.0	24.1	8.5	.1	15.7
1974	188.1	136.0	24.5	104.8	6.7	1.7	10.2	39.3	.9	178.7	143.7	25.3	9.6	.1	9.3
1975	209.6	147.4	26.9	113.2	7.3	1.8	11.2	48.7	.4	207.1	165.1	30.8	11.1	.2	2.5
1976	233.7	165.7	31.1	125.0	9.6	2.2	10.4	55.0	.4	226.3	179.5	34.1	12.5	.2	7.4
1977	259.9	183.7	35.4	136.9	11.4	2.8	11.7	61.4	.3	246.8	195.9	37.0	13.7	.2	13.1
1978	287.6	198.2	40.5	145.6	12.1	3.4	14.7	71.1	.3	268.9	213.2	40.8	14.9	.2	18.7
1979	308.4	212.0	44.0	154.4	13.6	3.9	20.1	72.7	−.3	295.4	233.3	44.3	17.2	.3	13.0
1980	338.2	230.0	48.9	166.7	14.5	3.6	26.3	79.5	−1.2	329.4	258.4	51.2	19.4	.4	8.8
1981	370.2	255.8	54.6	185.7	15.4	3.9	32.0	81.0	−2.4	362.7	282.3	57.1	22.8	.4	7.6
1982	391.4	273.2	59.1	200.0	14.0	4.0	36.7	79.1	−1.6	393.6	304.9	61.2	27.1	.5	−2.2
1983	428.6	300.9	66.1	218.9	15.9	4.1	41.4	82.4	−.2	423.7	324.1	66.9	32.3	.4	4.9
1984	480.2	337.3	76.0	242.5	18.8	4.7	47.7	89.0	1.5	456.2	347.7	71.2	37.0	.4	23.9
1985	521.1	363.7	81.4	262.1	20.2	4.9	54.8	94.5	3.2	498.7	381.8	77.3	39.4	.3	22.4
1986	561.6	389.5	87.2	279.7	22.7	6.0	58.4	105.0	2.8	540.9	418.1	84.3	38.2	.3	20.7
1987	590.6	422.1	96.6	301.6	23.9	7.2	58.2	100.0	3.1	578.6	441.4	90.7	46.2	.3	12.0
1988	635.5	452.8	102.1	324.6	26.0	8.4	60.5	109.0	4.8	618.3	471.0	98.5	48.4	.4	17.2
1989	687.5	488.0	114.6	349.1	24.2	9.0	65.7	118.1	6.7	667.4	504.5	109.3	53.2	.4	20.1
1990	738.0	519.1	122.6	374.1	22.5	10.0	68.5	133.5	6.9	731.8	547.0	127.7	56.8	.4	6.2
1991	789.4	544.3	125.3	395.3	23.6	11.6	68.0	158.2	7.3	795.2	577.5	156.5	60.8	.4	−5.8
1992	846.2	579.8	135.3	420.1	24.4	13.1	64.8	180.3	8.3	847.6	606.2	180.0	61.0	.4	−1.4
1993	888.2	604.7	141.1	436.8	26.9	14.1	61.3	198.1	9.9	889.1	634.2	195.2	59.4	.4	−.9
1994	944.8	644.2	148.0	466.3	30.0	14.5	63.3	212.3	10.5	936.6	668.2	206.7	61.4	.3	8.2
1995	991.9	672.1	158.1	482.4	31.7	13.6	68.5	224.2	13.5	982.7	701.3	217.6	63.5	.3	9.2
1996	1,045.1	709.6	168.7	507.9	33.0	12.5	73.4	234.0	15.6	1,022.1	730.2	224.3	67.3	.3	23.0
1997	1,099.5	749.9	182.0	533.8	34.1	10.8	78.2	246.4	14.2	1,063.2	764.5	227.6	70.6	.4	36.3
1998	1,164.5	794.9	201.2	558.8	34.9	10.4	81.5	265.3	12.5	1,117.6	808.6	235.8	72.8	.4	46.9
1999	1,240.4	840.4	214.5	590.2	35.8	9.8	85.8	291.1	13.3	1,198.6	870.6	252.3	75.2	.4	41.8
2000	1,322.6	893.2	236.7	621.3	35.2	10.8	94.3	313.9	10.4	1,281.3	930.6	271.4	78.8	.5	41.3
2001	1,374.0	914.3	243.0	642.4	28.9	13.7	90.0	348.0	8.0	1,389.9	994.2	305.1	83.0	7.7	−15.9
2002	1,412.7	928.7	221.8	676.0	30.9	15.9	79.6	382.3	6.1	1,466.8	1,049.4	333.0	83.5	.9	−54.1
2003	1,496.3	977.7	226.2	717.5	34.0	20.1	74.0	421.3	3.3	1,535.1	1,096.5	353.4	85.1	.1	−38.8
2004	1,601.0	1,059.4	248.6	769.1	41.7	24.1	77.1	439.4	1.0	1,609.3	1,139.1	384.3	85.6	.4	−8.4
2005	1,730.4	1,163.1	276.7	831.4	54.9	24.8	88.3	454.3	.1	1,704.5	1,212.0	404.8	87.3	.4	25.9
2006	1,829.7	1,249.0	302.5	887.4	59.2	21.8	103.5	456.7	−1.3	1,778.6	1,282.3	402.9	93.0	.4	51.0
2007	1,923.1	1,313.6	323.1	932.7	57.8	18.9	114.5	485.1	−9.1	1,910.8	1,368.9	433.7	101.1	7.1	12.2
2008	1,967.2	1,332.5	335.4	949.1	48.0	19.7	115.2	512.7	−13.0	2,014.6	1,448.2	455.2	108.2	3.0	−47.4
2009	2,005.8	1,267.0	287.3	930.3	49.4	21.6	116.0	610.2	−9.0	2,025.9	1,424.4	492.1	108.0	1.4	−20.1
2010 p	....	....	291.9	952.1	....	22.4	118.1	665.8	−9.1	2,093.9	1,447.5	533.1	111.6	1.6	....
2007: I	1,906.7	1,301.9	322.3	920.6	59.1	19.7	112.1	478.7	−5.6	1,876.9	1,337.8	439.3	98.0	1.9	29.8
II	1,923.4	1,314.0	325.3	929.4	59.3	18.9	114.2	484.6	−8.3	1,893.6	1,360.6	422.5	99.8	10.7	29.8
III	1,926.2	1,315.1	323.3	935.6	56.2	18.5	115.7	487.3	−10.4	1,916.2	1,376.2	429.1	102.1	8.8	10.0
IV	1,935.9	1,323.3	321.6	945.2	56.5	18.6	116.0	490.0	−11.9	1,956.6	1,401.0	444.0	104.4	7.2	−20.7
2008: I	1,955.6	1,332.9	337.1	945.5	50.3	19.0	115.5	501.1	−12.9	1,984.9	1,427.8	446.5	106.6	4.0	−29.3
II	1,985.9	1,353.4	347.4	954.0	52.1	19.4	115.6	510.6	−13.2	2,019.6	1,455.0	452.8	108.8	3.0	−33.6
III	1,979.0	1,344.1	333.4	956.4	54.3	19.9	114.7	513.4	−13.2	2,043.9	1,474.2	458.8	108.7	2.2	−64.9
IV	1,948.1	1,299.8	323.8	940.7	35.2	20.5	115.1	525.6	−12.8	2,009.9	1,435.7	462.5	108.9	2.8	−61.8
2009: I	1,964.8	1,273.2	300.6	929.5	43.1	21.0	115.6	565.9	−10.9	2,006.4	1,415.7	479.6	109.1	2.0	−41.6
II	1,986.6	1,231.5	264.7	922.3	44.4	21.5	115.3	627.7	−9.4	2,020.2	1,424.0	487.9	107.0	1.2	−33.6
III	2,017.2	1,270.0	290.0	931.3	48.7	21.8	116.1	617.5	−8.2	2,036.4	1,425.6	501.5	108.1	1.2	−19.2
IV	2,054.4	1,293.2	293.8	938.0	61.3	22.1	116.9	629.9	−7.7	2,040.6	1,432.2	499.4	107.7	1.2	13.9
2010: I	2,095.7	1,318.8	291.5	945.3	82.0	22.3	117.5	645.8	−8.7	2,067.2	1,447.4	509.4	108.7	1.6	28.6
II	2,108.1	1,316.7	280.6	948.1	88.1	22.4	118.1	659.8	−8.9	2,092.4	1,446.7	532.6	111.0	2.1	15.8
III	2,142.7	1,334.8	291.8	951.8	91.1	22.5	118.0	676.8	−9.2	2,095.0	1,441.3	539.8	112.3	1.6	47.7
IV p	....	....	303.8	963.1	....	22.5	118.7	680.8	−9.4	2,120.9	1,454.7	550.7	114.5	.9	....

[1] Includes Federal grants-in-aid. See Table B–82 for data on Federal grants-in-aid.
[2] Includes an item for the difference between wage accruals and disbursements, not shown separately.

Source: Department of Commerce (Bureau of Economic Analysis).

TABLE B–86. State and local government revenues and expenditures, selected fiscal years, 1944–2008

[Millions of dollars]

Fiscal year [1]	General revenues by source [2]							General expenditures by function [2]				
	Total	Property taxes	Sales and gross receipts taxes	Individual income taxes	Corpora-tion net income taxes	Revenue from Federal Govern-ment	All other [3]	Total [4]	Edu-cation	High-ways	Public welfare [4]	All other [4, 5]
1944	10,908	4,604	2,289	342	451	954	2,268	8,863	2,793	1,200	1,133	3,737
1946	12,356	4,986	2,986	422	447	855	2,660	11,028	3,356	1,672	1,409	4,591
1948	17,250	6,126	4,442	543	592	1,861	3,686	17,684	5,379	3,036	2,099	7,170
1950	20,911	7,349	5,154	788	593	2,486	4,541	22,787	7,177	3,803	2,940	8,867
1952	25,181	8,652	6,357	998	846	2,566	5,762	26,098	8,318	4,650	2,386	10,744
1953	27,307	9,375	6,927	1,065	817	2,870	6,253	27,910	9,390	4,987	2,914	10,619
1954	29,012	9,967	7,276	1,127	778	2,966	6,898	30,701	10,557	5,527	3,060	11,557
1955	31,073	10,735	7,643	1,237	744	3,131	7,583	33,724	11,907	6,452	3,168	12,197
1956	34,670	11,749	8,691	1,538	890	3,335	8,467	36,715	13,224	6,953	3,139	13,399
1957	38,164	12,864	9,467	1,754	984	3,843	9,252	40,375	14,134	7,816	3,485	14,940
1958	41,219	14,047	9,829	1,759	1,018	4,865	9,701	44,851	15,919	8,567	3,818	16,547
1959	45,306	14,983	10,437	1,994	1,001	6,377	10,514	48,887	17,283	9,592	4,136	17,876
1960	50,505	16,405	11,849	2,463	1,180	6,974	11,634	51,876	18,719	9,428	4,404	19,325
1961	54,037	18,002	12,463	2,613	1,266	7,131	12,562	56,201	20,574	9,844	4,720	21,063
1962	58,252	19,054	13,494	3,037	1,308	7,871	13,488	60,206	22,216	10,357	5,084	22,549
1963	62,891	20,089	14,456	3,269	1,505	8,722	14,850	64,815	23,776	11,135	5,481	24,423
1962–63	62,269	19,833	14,446	3,267	1,505	8,663	14,556	63,977	23,729	11,150	5,420	23,678
1963–64	68,443	21,241	15,762	3,791	1,695	10,002	15,952	69,302	26,286	11,664	5,766	25,586
1964–65	74,000	22,583	17,118	4,090	1,929	11,029	17,251	74,678	28,563	12,221	6,315	27,579
1965–66	83,036	24,670	19,085	4,760	2,038	13,214	19,269	82,843	33,287	12,770	6,757	30,029
1966–67	91,197	26,047	20,530	5,825	2,227	15,370	21,198	93,350	37,919	13,932	8,218	33,281
1967–68	101,264	27,747	22,911	7,308	2,518	17,181	23,599	102,411	41,158	14,481	9,857	36,915
1968–69	114,550	30,673	26,519	8,908	3,180	19,153	26,117	116,728	47,238	15,417	12,110	41,963
1969–70	130,756	34,054	30,322	10,812	3,738	21,857	29,973	131,332	52,718	16,427	14,679	47,508
1970–71	144,927	37,852	33,233	11,900	3,424	26,146	32,372	150,674	59,413	18,095	18,226	54,940
1971–72	167,535	42,877	37,518	15,227	4,416	31,342	36,156	168,549	65,813	19,021	21,117	62,598
1972–73	190,222	45,283	42,047	17,994	5,425	39,264	40,210	181,357	69,713	18,615	23,582	69,447
1973–74	207,670	47,705	46,098	19,491	6,015	41,820	46,542	199,222	75,833	19,946	25,085	78,358
1974–75	228,171	51,491	49,815	21,454	6,642	47,034	51,735	230,722	87,858	22,528	28,156	92,180
1975–76	256,176	57,001	54,547	24,575	7,273	55,589	57,191	256,731	97,216	23,907	32,604	103,004
1976–77	285,157	62,527	60,641	29,246	9,174	62,444	61,125	274,215	102,780	23,058	35,906	112,472
1977–78	315,960	66,422	67,596	33,176	10,738	69,592	68,435	296,984	110,758	24,609	39,140	122,478
1978–79	343,236	64,944	74,247	36,932	12,128	75,164	79,822	327,517	119,448	28,440	41,898	137,731
1979–80	382,322	68,499	79,927	42,080	13,321	83,029	95,467	369,086	133,211	33,311	47,288	155,276
1980–81	423,404	74,969	85,971	46,426	14,143	90,294	111,599	407,449	145,784	34,603	54,105	172,957
1981–82	457,654	82,067	93,613	50,738	15,028	87,282	128,925	436,733	154,282	34,520	57,996	189,935
1982–83	486,753	89,105	100,247	55,129	14,258	90,007	138,008	466,516	163,876	36,655	60,906	205,080
1983–84	542,730	96,457	114,097	64,871	16,798	96,935	153,571	505,008	176,108	39,419	66,414	223,068
1984–85	598,121	103,757	126,376	70,361	19,152	106,158	172,317	553,899	192,686	44,989	71,479	244,745
1985–86	641,486	111,709	135,005	74,365	19,994	113,099	187,314	605,623	210,819	49,368	75,868	269,568
1986–87	686,860	121,203	144,091	83,935	22,425	114,857	200,350	657,134	226,619	52,355	82,650	295,510
1987–88	726,762	132,212	156,452	88,350	23,663	117,602	208,482	704,921	242,683	55,621	89,090	317,527
1988–89	786,129	142,400	166,336	97,806	25,926	125,824	227,838	762,360	263,898	58,105	97,879	342,479
1989–90	849,502	155,613	177,885	105,640	23,566	136,802	249,996	834,818	288,148	61,057	110,518	375,094
1990–91	902,207	167,999	185,570	109,341	22,242	154,099	262,955	908,108	309,302	64,937	130,402	403,467
1991–92	979,137	180,337	197,731	115,638	23,880	179,174	282,376	981,253	324,652	67,351	158,723	430,526
1992–93	1,041,643	189,744	209,649	123,235	26,417	198,663	293,935	1,030,434	342,287	68,370	170,705	449,072
1993–94	1,100,490	197,141	223,628	128,810	28,320	215,492	307,099	1,077,665	353,287	72,067	183,394	468,916
1994–95	1,169,505	203,451	237,268	137,931	31,406	228,771	330,677	1,149,863	378,273	77,109	196,703	497,779
1995–96	1,222,821	209,440	248,993	146,844	32,009	234,891	350,645	1,193,276	398,859	79,092	197,354	517,971
1996–97	1,289,237	218,877	261,418	159,042	33,820	244,847	371,233	1,249,984	418,416	82,062	203,779	545,727
1997–98	1,365,762	230,150	274,883	175,630	34,412	255,048	395,639	1,318,042	450,365	87,214	208,120	572,343
1998–99	1,434,029	239,672	290,993	189,309	33,922	270,628	409,505	1,402,369	483,259	93,018	218,957	607,134
1999–2000	1,541,322	249,178	309,290	211,661	36,059	291,950	443,186	1,506,797	521,612	101,336	237,336	646,512
2000–01	1,647,161	263,689	320,217	226,334	35,296	324,033	477,592	1,626,066	563,575	107,235	261,622	693,634
2001–02	1,684,879	279,191	324,123	202,832	28,152	360,546	490,035	1,736,866	594,694	115,295	285,464	741,413
2002–03	1,763,212	296,683	337,787	199,407	31,369	389,264	508,702	1,821,917	621,335	117,696	310,783	772,102
2003–04	1,887,397	317,941	361,027	215,215	33,716	423,112	536,386	1,908,543	655,182	117,215	340,523	795,622
2004–05	2,026,034	335,779	384,266	242,273	43,256	438,558	581,902	2,012,110	688,314	126,350	365,295	832,151
2005–06	2,197,475	364,559	417,735	268,667	53,081	452,975	640,458	2,123,663	728,917	136,502	372,004	886,240
2006–07	2,335,894	389,573	439,586	289,827	60,592	467,949	688,367	2,262,900	774,373	144,713	389,394	954,419
2007–08	2,425,778	409,686	448,689	304,627	57,810	481,380	723,587	2,404,966	826,063	153,515	409,346	1,016,042

[1] Fiscal years not the same for all governments. See Note.

[2] Excludes revenues or expenditures of publicly owned utilities and liquor stores and of insurance-trust activities. Intergovernmental receipts and payments between State and local governments are also excluded.

[3] Includes motor vehicle license taxes, other taxes, and charges and miscellaneous revenues.

[4] Includes intergovernmental payments to the Federal Government.

[5] Includes expenditures for libraries, hospitals, health, employment security administration, veterans' services, air transportation, water transport and terminals, parking facilities, transit subsidies, police protection, fire protection, correction, protective inspection and regulation, sewerage, natural resources, parks and recreation, housing and community development, solid waste management, financial administration, judicial and legal, general public buildings, other government administration, interest on general debt, and other general expenditures, not elsewhere classified.

Note: Except for States listed, data for fiscal years listed from 1962–63 to 2007–08 are the aggregation of data for government fiscal years that ended in the 12-month period from July 1 to June 30 of those years; Texas used August and Alabama and Michigan used September as end dates. Data for 1963 and earlier years include data for government fiscal years ending during that particular calendar year.

Data prior to 1952 are not available for intervening years.

Source: Department of Commerce (Bureau of the Census).

[Billions of dollars]

End of year or month	Total Treasury securities outstanding [1]	Marketable							Nonmarketable				
		Total [2]	Treasury bills	Treasury notes	Treasury bonds	Treasury inflation-protected securities			Total	U.S. savings securities [3]	Foreign series [4]	Government account series	Other [5]
						Total	Notes	Bonds					
Fiscal year:													
1972	425.4	257.2	94.6	113.4	49.1				168.2	55.9	19.0	89.6	3.7
1973	456.4	263.0	100.1	117.8	45.1				193.4	59.4	28.5	101.7	3.7
1974	473.2	266.6	105.0	128.4	33.1				206.7	61.9	25.0	115.4	4.3
1975	532.1	315.6	128.6	150.3	36.8				216.5	65.5	23.2	124.2	3.6
1976	619.3	392.6	161.2	191.8	39.6				226.7	69.7	21.5	130.6	4.9
1977	697.6	443.5	156.1	241.7	45.7				254.1	75.4	21.8	140.1	16.8
1978	767.0	485.2	160.9	267.9	56.4				281.8	79.8	21.7	153.3	27.1
1979	819.0	506.7	161.4	274.2	71.1				312.3	80.4	28.1	176.4	27.4
1980	906.4	594.5	199.8	310.9	83.8				311.9	72.7	25.2	189.8	24.2
1981	996.5	683.2	223.4	363.6	96.2				313.3	68.0	20.5	201.1	23.7
1982	1,140.9	824.4	277.9	442.9	103.6				316.5	67.3	14.6	210.5	24.1
1983	1,375.8	1,024.0	340.7	557.5	125.7				351.8	70.0	11.5	234.7	35.6
1984	1,559.6	1,176.6	356.8	661.7	158.1				383.0	72.8	8.8	259.5	41.8
1985	1,821.0	1,360.2	384.2	776.4	199.5				460.8	77.0	6.6	313.9	63.3
1986	2,122.7	1,564.3	410.7	896.9	241.7				558.4	85.6	4.1	365.9	102.8
1987	2,347.8	1,676.0	378.3	1,005.1	277.6				671.8	97.0	4.4	440.7	129.8
1988	2,599.9	1,802.9	398.5	1,089.6	299.9				797.0	106.2	6.3	536.5	148.0
1989	2,836.3	1,892.8	406.6	1,133.2	338.0				943.5	114.0	6.8	663.7	159.0
1990	3,210.9	2,092.8	482.5	1,218.1	377.2				1,118.2	122.2	36.0	779.4	180.6
1991	3,662.8	2,390.7	564.6	1,387.7	423.4				1,272.1	133.5	41.6	908.4	188.5
1992	4,061.8	2,677.5	634.3	1,566.3	461.8				1,384.3	148.3	37.0	1,011.0	188.0
1993	4,408.6	2,904.9	658.4	1,734.2	497.4				1,503.7	167.0	42.5	1,114.3	179.9
1994	4,689.5	3,091.6	697.3	1,867.5	511.8				1,597.9	176.4	42.0	1,211.7	167.8
1995	4,950.6	3,260.4	742.5	1,980.3	522.6				1,690.2	181.2	41.0	1,324.3	143.8
1996	5,220.8	3,418.4	761.2	2,098.7	543.5				1,802.4	184.1	37.5	1,454.7	126.1
1997	5,407.5	3,439.6	701.9	2,122.2	576.2	24.4	24.4		1,967.9	182.7	34.9	1,608.5	141.9
1998	5,518.7	3,331.0	637.6	2,009.1	610.4	58.8	41.9	17.0	2,187.7	180.8	35.1	1,777.3	194.4
1999	5,647.2	3,233.0	653.2	1,828.8	643.7	92.4	67.6	24.8	2,414.2	180.0	31.0	2,005.2	198.1
2000	5,622.1	2,992.8	616.2	1,611.3	635.3	115.0	81.6	33.4	2,629.3	177.7	25.4	2,242.9	183.3
2001 [1]	5,807.5	2,930.7	734.9	1,433.0	613.0	134.9	95.1	39.7	2,876.7	186.5	18.3	2,492.1	179.9
2002	6,228.2	3,136.7	868.3	1,521.6	593.0	138.9	93.7	45.1	3,091.5	193.3	12.5	2,707.3	178.4
2003	6,783.2	3,460.7	918.2	1,799.5	576.9	166.1	120.0	46.1	3,322.5	201.6	11.0	2,912.2	197.7
2004	7,379.1	3,846.1	961.5	2,109.6	552.0	223.0			3,533.0	204.2	5.9	3,130.0	192.9
2005	7,932.7	4,084.9	914.3	2,328.8	520.7	307.1			3,847.8	203.6	3.1	3,380.6	260.5
2006	8,507.0	4,303.0	911.5	2,447.2	534.7	395.6			4,203.9	203.7	3.0	3,722.7	274.5
2007	9,007.7	4,448.1	958.1	2,458.0	561.1	456.9			4,559.5	197.1	3.0	4,026.8	332.6
2008	10,024.7	5,236.0	1,489.8	2,624.8	582.9	524.5			4,788.7	194.3	3.0	4,297.7	293.8
2009	11,909.8	7,009.7	1,992.5	3,773.8	679.8	551.7			4,900.1	192.5	4.9	4,454.3	248.4
2010	13,561.6	8,498.3	1,788.5	5,255.9	849.9	593.8			5,063.3	188.8	4.2	4,645.3	225.0
2009: Jan	10,632.1	5,749.9	1,798.6	2,826.0	594.6	516.7			4,882.2	193.8	5.0	4,406.0	277.3
Feb	10,877.1	6,012.4	1,985.6	2,892.0	609.4	511.5			4,864.8	194.1	5.0	4,391.4	274.3
Mar	11,126.9	6,266.1	2,033.6	3,084.9	620.5	513.1			4,860.8	194.0	6.0	4,388.7	272.2
Apr	11,238.6	6,363.4	1,994.5	3,204.5	620.5	529.9			4,875.2	194.0	7.0	4,403.9	270.3
May	11,321.6	6,454.3	2,065.4	3,211.3	632.5	531.0			4,867.3	193.9	6.5	4,399.4	267.6
June	11,545.3	6,612.1	2,006.5	3,417.7	643.7	532.3			4,933.2	193.6	6.0	4,468.6	265.0
July	11,669.3	6,782.8	2,020.5	3,547.5	654.8	548.0			4,886.5	193.3	5.5	4,431.8	256.0
Aug	11,812.9	6,939.2	2,068.5	3,638.6	667.8	552.4			4,873.6	192.8	4.5	4,425.9	250.4
Sept	11,909.8	7,009.7	1,992.5	3,773.8	679.8	551.7			4,900.1	192.5	4.9	4,454.3	248.4
Oct	11,893.1	6,947.6	1,858.5	3,818.2	691.9	567.1			4,945.5	192.2	4.4	4,501.1	247.8
Nov	12,113.0	7,174.6	1,850.5	4,039.8	704.9	567.5			4,938.5	191.8	4.4	4,497.4	244.9
Dec	12,311.4	7,272.5	1,793.5	4,181.1	717.9	568.1			5,038.9	191.3	4.4	4,597.1	246.0
2010: Jan	12,278.6	7,226.6	1,689.5	4,229.5	731.4	564.3			5,052.1	190.9	5.4	4,616.2	239.6
Feb	12,440.1	7,406.4	1,736.5	4,337.3	749.2	571.4			5,033.7	190.7	5.4	4,601.8	235.8
Mar	12,773.1	7,757.0	1,843.5	4,566.1	762.4	573.2			5,016.1	190.3	4.9	4,580.6	240.3
Apr	12,948.7	7,901.3	1,847.5	4,704.3	776.3	561.2			5,047.5	190.1	4.5	4,611.7	241.2
May	12,992.5	7,958.4	1,855.5	4,734.0	793.7	563.2			5,034.2	189.9	4.4	4,598.7	241.1
June	13,201.8	8,102.4	1,782.5	4,938.4	806.8	564.5			5,099.4	189.7	4.0	4,669.9	235.8
July	13,237.7	8,178.9	1,790.5	4,981.4	819.8	576.9			5,058.9	189.4	3.4	4,638.6	227.4
Aug	13,449.7	8,404.5	1,825.5	5,148.3	836.8	583.6			5,045.2	189.0	4.2	4,627.5	224.5
Sept	13,561.6	8,498.3	1,788.5	5,255.9	849.9	593.8			5,063.3	188.8	4.2	4,645.3	225.0
Oct	13,668.8	8,542.7	1,768.5	5,296.3	863.0	604.7			5,126.1	188.7	4.2	4,706.4	226.9
Nov	13,860.8	8,748.3	1,775.5	5,467.8	879.5	615.4			5,112.5	188.4	4.2	4,693.9	226.0
Dec	14,025.2	8,863.3	1,772.5	5,571.7	892.6	616.1			5,162.0	188.0	4.0	4,745.2	224.7

[1] Data beginning with January 2001 are interest-bearing and non-interest-bearing securities; prior data are interest-bearing securities only.

[2] Data from 1986 to 2002 and 2005 to 2010 include Federal Financing Bank securities, not shown separately.

[3] Through 1996, series is U.S. savings bonds. Beginning 1997, includes U.S. retirement plan bonds, U.S. individual retirement bonds, and U.S. savings notes previously included in "other" nonmarketable securities.

[4] Nonmarketable certificates of indebtedness, notes, bonds, and bills in the Treasury foreign series of dollar-denominated and foreign-currency-denominated issues.

[5] Includes depository bonds; retirement plan bonds; Rural Electrification Administration bonds; State and local bonds; special issues held only by U.S. Government agencies and trust funds and the Federal home loan banks; for the period July 2003 through February 2004, depositary compensation securities; and beginning August 2008, Hope bonds for the HOPE For Homeowners Program.

Note: Through fiscal year 1976, the fiscal year was on a July 1–June 30 basis; beginning with October 1976 (fiscal year 1977), the fiscal year is on an October 1–September 30 basis.

Source: Department of the Treasury.

TABLE B–88. Maturity distribution and average length of marketable interest-bearing public debt securities held by private investors, 1972–2010

End of year or month	Amount outstanding, privately held	Within 1 year	1 to 5 years	5 to 10 years	10 to 20 years	20 years and over	Average length [1]
		Maturity class					
		Millions of dollars					Months
Fiscal year:							
1972	165,978	79,509	57,157	16,033	6,358	6,922	39
1973	167,869	84,041	54,139	16,385	8,741	4,564	37
1974	164,862	87,150	50,103	14,197	9,930	3,481	35
1975	210,382	115,677	65,852	15,385	8,857	4,611	32
1976	279,782	150,296	90,578	24,169	8,087	6,652	31
1977	326,674	161,329	113,319	33,067	8,428	10,531	35
1978	356,501	163,819	132,993	33,500	11,383	14,805	39
1979	380,530	181,883	127,574	32,279	18,489	20,304	43
1980	463,717	220,084	156,244	38,809	25,901	22,679	41
1981	549,863	256,187	182,237	48,743	32,569	30,127	43
1982	682,043	314,436	221,783	75,749	33,017	37,058	43
1983	862,631	379,579	294,955	99,174	40,826	48,097	44
1984	1,017,488	437,941	332,808	130,417	49,664	66,658	49
1985	1,185,675	472,661	402,766	159,383	62,853	88,012	54
1986	1,354,275	506,903	467,348	189,995	70,664	119,365	59
1987	1,445,366	483,582	526,746	209,160	72,862	153,016	65
1988	1,555,208	524,201	552,993	232,453	74,186	171,375	66
1989	1,654,660	546,751	578,333	247,428	80,616	201,532	70
1990	1,841,903	626,297	630,144	267,573	82,713	235,176	70
1991	2,113,799	713,778	761,243	280,574	84,900	273,304	70
1992	2,363,802	808,705	866,329	295,921	84,706	308,141	69
1993	2,562,336	858,135	978,714	306,663	94,345	324,479	69
1994	2,719,861	877,932	1,128,322	289,998	88,208	335,401	66
1995	2,870,781	1,002,875	1,157,492	290,111	87,297	333,006	63
1996	3,011,185	1,058,558	1,212,258	306,643	111,360	322,366	62
1997	2,998,846	1,017,913	1,206,993	321,622	154,205	298,113	64
1998	2,856,637	940,572	1,105,175	319,331	157,347	334,212	68
1999	2,728,011	915,145	962,644	378,163	149,703	322,356	72
2000	2,469,152	858,903	791,540	355,382	167,082	296,246	75
2001	2,328,302	900,178	650,522	329,247	174,653	273,702	73
2002	2,492,821	939,986	802,032	311,176	203,816	235,811	66
2003	2,804,092	1,057,049	955,239	351,552	243,755	196,497	61
2004	3,145,244	1,127,850	1,150,979	414,728	243,036	208,652	59
2005	3,334,411	1,100,783	1,279,646	499,386	281,229	173,367	58
2006	3,496,359	1,140,553	1,295,589	589,748	290,733	179,736	59
2007	3,634,666	1,176,510	1,309,871	677,905	291,963	178,417	58
2008	4,745,256	2,042,003	1,468,455	719,347	352,430	163,022	49
2009	6,228,565	2,604,676	2,074,723	994,688	350,550	203,928	49
2010	7,676,335	2,479,518	2,955,561	1,529,283	340,861	371,112	57
2009: Jan	5,240,192	2,336,980	1,606,687	773,459	360,343	162,724	47
Feb	5,505,374	2,543,863	1,659,311	776,904	358,535	166,761	47
Mar	5,759,710	2,601,163	1,790,274	833,981	357,717	176,575	47
Apr	5,800,248	2,601,043	1,792,321	875,653	376,004	155,227	47
May	5,815,164	2,660,158	1,762,985	856,311	367,098	168,612	47
June	5,943,636	2,611,596	1,891,559	900,239	361,806	178,436	47
July	6,065,512	2,636,005	1,964,000	916,972	360,698	187,837	48
Aug	6,179,984	2,669,429	2,014,501	951,363	352,756	191,935	48
Sept	6,228,565	2,604,676	2,074,723	994,688	350,550	203,928	49
Oct	6,138,187	2,481,261	2,073,386	1,019,124	349,077	215,339	51
Nov	6,386,026	2,462,190	2,259,073	1,084,264	349,156	231,343	51
Dec	6,483,901	2,415,461	2,337,392	1,137,420	349,280	244,348	52
2010: Jan	6,412,960	2,324,877	2,334,184	1,147,170	349,376	257,353	54
Feb	6,591,769	2,372,965	2,420,971	1,173,496	342,995	281,343	54
Mar	6,968,331	2,492,450	2,579,109	1,258,977	343,413	294,381	54
Apr	7,112,555	2,496,967	2,644,691	1,320,051	343,461	307,386	54
May	7,139,816	2,493,411	2,659,209	1,324,688	353,276	309,233	55
June	7,315,100	2,432,122	2,800,261	1,406,962	353,499	322,256	55
July	7,360,528	2,453,077	2,797,309	1,421,267	353,608	335,267	56
Aug	7,607,853	2,504,906	2,922,651	1,481,051	341,136	358,109	56
Sept	7,676,335	2,479,518	2,955,561	1,529,283	340,861	371,112	57
Oct	7,659,482	2,470,906	2,930,452	1,537,902	338,278	381,945	57
Nov	7,827,328	2,510,845	3,012,545	1,572,551	334,655	396,733	57
Dec	7,831,450	2,544,760	2,981,135	1,568,471	330,178	406,906	57

[1] Average length calculations are to call date. Treasury inflation-protected securities—notes, first offered in 1997, and bonds, first offered in 1998—are included in the average length calculation from 1997 forward.

Note: Through fiscal year 1976, the fiscal year was on a July 1–June 30 basis; beginning with October 1976 (fiscal year 1977), the fiscal year is on an October 1–September 30 basis.

Data shown in this table are as of January 21, 2011.

Source: Department of the Treasury.

TABLE B–89. Estimated ownership of U.S. Treasury securities, 1997–2010

[Billions of dollars]

End of month	Total public debt [1]	Federal Reserve and Intragovernmental holdings [2]	Held by private investors									
			Total privately held	Depository institutions [3]	U.S. savings bonds [4]	Pension funds		Insurance companies	Mutual funds [6]	State and local governments	Foreign and international [7]	Other investors [8]
						Private [5]	State and local governments					
1997: Mar	5,380.9	1,928.7	3,452.2	317.3	182.6	141.7	211.1	181.8	221.6	248.1	1,157.6	790.4
June	5,376.2	1,998.9	3,377.3	300.2	182.7	142.1	214.9	183.1	216.4	243.3	1,182.7	711.9
Sept	5,413.1	2,011.5	3,401.6	292.8	182.7	143.0	223.5	186.8	221.3	235.2	1,230.5	685.9
Dec	5,502.4	2,087.8	3,414.6	300.3	181.2	144.1	219.0	176.6	232.3	239.3	1,241.6	680.2
1998: Mar	5,542.4	2,104.9	3,437.5	308.3	181.2	141.3	212.1	169.5	234.6	238.1	1,250.5	701.9
June	5,547.9	2,198.6	3,349.3	290.9	180.7	139.0	213.2	160.6	230.8	258.5	1,256.0	619.8
Sept	5,526.2	2,213.0	3,313.2	244.5	180.8	135.5	207.8	151.4	231.7	271.8	1,224.2	665.4
Dec	5,614.2	2,280.2	3,334.0	237.4	180.3	133.2	212.6	141.7	257.6	280.8	1,278.7	611.7
1999: Mar	5,651.6	2,324.1	3,327.5	247.4	180.6	135.5	211.5	137.5	245.0	288.4	1,272.3	609.4
June	5,638.8	2,439.6	3,199.2	240.6	180.0	142.9	213.8	133.6	228.1	298.6	1,258.8	502.7
Sept	5,656.3	2,480.9	3,175.4	241.2	180.0	150.9	204.8	128.0	222.5	299.2	1,281.4	467.3
Dec	5,776.1	2,542.2	3,233.9	248.7	179.3	153.0	198.8	123.4	228.7	304.5	1,268.7	528.8
2000: Mar	5,773.4	2,590.6	3,182.8	237.7	178.6	150.2	196.9	120.0	222.3	306.3	1,085.0	685.7
June	5,685.9	2,698.6	2,987.3	222.2	177.7	149.0	194.9	116.5	205.4	309.3	1,060.7	551.7
Sept	5,674.2	2,737.9	2,936.3	220.5	177.7	147.9	185.5	113.7	207.8	307.9	1,038.8	536.5
Dec	5,662.2	2,781.8	2,880.4	201.5	176.9	145.0	179.1	110.2	225.7	310.0	1,015.2	516.9
2001: Mar	5,773.7	2,880.9	2,892.8	188.0	184.8	153.4	177.3	109.1	225.3	316.9	1,012.5	525.4
June	5,726.8	3,004.2	2,722.6	188.1	185.5	148.5	183.1	108.1	221.0	324.8	983.3	380.2
Sept	5,807.5	3,027.8	2,779.7	189.1	186.5	149.9	166.8	106.8	234.1	321.2	992.2	433.1
Dec	5,943.4	3,123.9	2,819.5	181.5	190.4	145.8	155.1	105.7	261.9	328.4	1,040.1	410.6
2002: Mar	6,006.0	3,156.8	2,849.2	187.6	192.0	152.7	163.3	114.0	266.1	327.6	1,057.2	388.8
June	6,126.5	3,276.7	2,849.8	204.7	192.8	152.1	153.9	122.0	253.8	333.6	1,123.1	313.7
Sept	6,228.2	3,303.5	2,924.8	209.3	193.3	154.5	156.3	130.4	256.8	338.6	1,188.6	296.9
Dec	6,405.7	3,387.2	3,018.5	222.6	194.9	153.8	158.9	139.7	281.0	354.7	1,235.6	277.4
2003: Mar	6,460.8	3,390.8	3,070.0	153.6	196.9	165.8	162.1	139.5	296.6	350.0	1,275.2	330.2
June	6,670.1	3,505.4	3,164.7	145.4	199.2	170.2	161.3	138.7	302.3	347.9	1,371.9	327.8
Sept	6,783.2	3,515.3	3,267.9	146.8	201.6	167.7	155.5	137.4	287.1	357.7	1,443.3	371.0
Dec	6,998.0	3,620.1	3,377.9	153.1	203.9	172.2	148.6	136.5	280.9	364.2	1,523.1	395.4
2004: Mar	7,131.1	3,628.3	3,502.8	162.8	204.5	169.8	143.6	172.4	280.8	374.1	1,670.0	324.8
June	7,274.3	3,742.8	3,531.5	158.6	204.6	173.3	134.9	174.6	258.7	381.2	1,735.4	310.1
Sept	7,379.1	3,772.0	3,607.1	138.5	204.2	174.0	140.8	182.9	255.0	381.7	1,794.5	335.5
Dec	7,596.1	3,905.6	3,690.5	125.0	204.5	173.7	151.0	188.5	254.1	389.1	1,849.3	355.4
2005: Mar	7,776.9	3,921.6	3,855.3	141.8	204.2	177.3	158.0	193.3	261.1	412.0	1,952.2	355.5
June	7,836.5	4,033.5	3,803.0	126.9	204.2	181.0	171.3	195.0	248.7	444.0	1,877.5	354.4
Sept	7,932.7	4,067.8	3,864.9	125.3	203.6	184.2	164.8	200.7	244.7	467.6	1,929.6	344.3
Dec	8,170.4	4,199.8	3,970.6	117.1	205.2	184.9	153.8	202.3	251.3	481.4	2,033.9	340.6
2006: Mar	8,371.2	4,257.2	4,114.0	113.0	206.0	186.7	153.0	200.3	248.7	486.1	2,082.1	438.1
June	8,420.0	4,389.2	4,030.8	119.5	205.2	192.1	150.9	196.1	244.2	499.4	1,977.8	445.6
Sept	8,507.0	4,432.8	4,074.2	113.6	203.7	201.9	154.7	196.8	235.7	502.1	2,025.3	440.3
Dec	8,680.2	4,558.1	4,122.1	114.8	202.4	207.5	156.2	197.9	250.7	516.9	2,103.1	372.5
2007: Mar	8,849.7	4,576.6	4,273.1	119.8	200.3	221.7	158.3	185.4	264.5	535.0	2,194.8	393.2
June	8,867.7	4,715.1	4,152.6	110.4	198.6	232.5	159.3	168.9	267.7	580.3	2,192.0	242.7
Sept	9,007.7	4,738.0	4,269.7	119.7	197.1	246.7	138.9	155.1	306.3	538.5	2,235.3	332.0
Dec	9,229.2	4,833.5	4,395.7	129.8	196.5	257.6	141.6	141.9	362.9	537.6	2,353.2	274.6
2008: Mar	9,437.6	4,694.7	4,742.9	125.3	195.4	270.5	142.0	152.1	484.4	531.0	2,506.3	335.8
June	9,492.0	4,685.8	4,806.2	112.7	195.0	276.7	141.8	159.4	477.2	519.9	2,587.4	336.1
Sept	10,024.7	4,692.7	5,332.0	130.0	194.3	292.5	143.9	163.4	656.1	503.2	2,802.4	446.2
Dec	10,699.8	4,806.4	5,893.4	105.0	194.1	297.2	146.4	171.4	768.8	485.5	3,077.2	647.9
2009: Mar	11,126.9	4,785.2	6,341.7	129.1	194.0	330.9	150.2	191.0	716.0	516.9	3,265.7	848.0
June	11,545.3	5,026.8	6,518.5	140.7	193.6	353.4	159.9	200.0	695.7	514.4	3,460.8	800.0
Sept	11,909.8	5,127.1	6,782.7	199.3	192.5	398.1	167.3	210.2	644.9	504.4	3,570.6	895.4
Dec	12,311.3	5,276.9	7,034.4	206.4	191.3	429.8	174.5	222.0	666.3	505.9	3,685.1	953.1
2010: Mar	12,773.1	5,259.8	7,513.3	274.4	190.3	462.2	179.7	229.8	649.7	506.4	3,877.8	1,143.2
June	13,201.8	5,345.1	7,856.7	270.1	189.7	531.9	184.5	240.0	634.5	511.8	4,002.9	1,291.4
Sept	13,561.6	5,350.5	8,211.1	337.5	188.8	587.5	187.8	254.5	607.9	508.7	4,257.1	1,281.2
Dec	14,025.2	5,656.2	8,368.9	....	188.0	....	....	....	....	....	....	....

[1] Face value.

[2] Federal Reserve holdings exclude Treasury securities held under repurchase agreements.

[3] Includes commercial banks, savings institutions, and credit unions.

[4] Current accrual value.

[5] Includes Treasury securities held by the Federal Employees Retirement System Thrift Savings Plan "G Fund."

[6] Includes money market mutual funds, mutual funds, and closed-end investment companies.

[7] Includes nonmarketable foreign series, Treasury securities, and Treasury deposit funds. Excludes Treasury securities held under repurchase agreements in custody accounts at the Federal Reserve Bank of New York. Estimates reflect benchmarks to this series at differing intervals; for further detail, see *Treasury Bulletin* and http://www.treas.gov/tic/ticsec2.shtml.

[8] Includes individuals, Government-sponsored enterprises, brokers and dealers, bank personal trusts and estates, corporate and noncorporate businesses, and other investors.

Note: Data shown in this table are as of January 25, 2011.

Source: Department of the Treasury.

Corporate Profits and Finance

Table B–90. Corporate profits with inventory valuation and capital consumption adjustments, 1962–2010

[Billions of dollars; quarterly data at seasonally adjusted annual rates]

Year or quarter	Corporate profits with inventory valuation and capital consumption adjustments	Taxes on corporate income	Corporate profits after tax with inventory valuation and capital consumption adjustments		
			Total	Net dividends	Undistributed profits with inventory valuation and capital consumption adjustments
1962	62.3	24.1	38.3	15.0	23.2
1963	68.3	26.4	42.0	16.2	25.7
1964	75.5	28.2	47.4	18.2	29.2
1965	86.5	31.1	55.5	20.2	35.3
1966	92.5	33.9	58.7	20.7	38.0
1967	90.2	32.9	57.3	21.5	35.8
1968	97.3	39.6	57.6	23.5	34.1
1969	94.5	40.0	54.5	24.2	30.3
1970	82.5	34.8	47.7	24.3	23.4
1971	96.1	38.2	57.9	25.0	32.9
1972	111.4	42.3	69.1	26.8	42.2
1973	124.5	50.0	74.5	29.9	44.6
1974	115.1	52.8	62.3	33.2	29.1
1975	133.3	51.6	81.7	33.0	48.7
1976	161.6	65.3	96.3	39.0	57.3
1977	191.8	74.4	117.4	44.8	72.6
1978	218.4	84.9	133.6	50.8	82.8
1979	225.4	90.0	135.3	57.5	77.8
1980	201.4	87.2	114.2	64.1	50.2
1981	223.3	84.3	138.9	73.8	65.2
1982	205.7	66.5	139.2	77.7	61.5
1983	259.8	80.6	179.2	83.5	95.7
1984	318.6	97.5	221.1	90.8	130.3
1985	332.5	99.4	233.1	97.6	135.6
1986	314.1	109.7	204.5	106.2	98.3
1987	367.8	130.4	237.4	112.3	125.1
1988	426.6	141.6	285.0	129.9	155.1
1989	425.6	146.1	279.5	158.0	121.5
1990	434.4	145.4	289.0	169.1	120.0
1991	457.3	138.6	318.7	180.7	138.0
1992	496.2	148.7	347.5	188.0	159.5
1993	543.7	171.0	372.7	202.9	169.7
1994	628.2	193.1	435.1	235.7	199.4
1995	716.2	217.8	498.3	254.4	243.9
1996	801.5	231.5	570.0	297.7	272.3
1997	884.8	245.4	639.4	331.2	308.2
1998	812.4	248.4	564.1	351.5	212.6
1999	856.3	258.8	597.5	337.4	260.1
2000	819.2	265.1	554.1	377.9	176.3
2001	784.2	203.3	580.9	370.9	210.0
2002	872.2	192.3	679.9	399.3	280.6
2003	977.8	243.8	734.0	424.9	309.2
2004	1,246.9	306.1	940.8	550.3	390.5
2005	1,456.1	412.4	1,043.7	557.3	486.4
2006	1,608.3	473.3	1,135.0	704.8	430.3
2007	1,510.6	445.5	1,065.2	794.5	270.7
2008	1,262.8	308.4	954.4	797.7	156.7
2009	1,258.0	254.9	1,003.1	718.9	284.2
2010 ᵖ				732.6	
2007: I	1,515.5	474.1	1,041.4	756.5	284.9
II	1,565.3	467.9	1,097.4	804.4	293.0
III	1,501.0	431.0	1,070.0	809.7	260.2
IV	1,460.8	408.8	1,052.0	807.4	244.6
2008: I	1,376.3	356.7	1,019.6	812.7	206.9
II	1,329.0	343.0	986.0	802.1	183.9
III	1,350.8	313.3	1,037.5	798.4	239.0
IV	995.0	220.4	774.6	777.5	-2.9
2009: I	1,138.2	222.0	916.2	747.8	168.5
II	1,178.0	222.8	955.3	719.7	235.5
III	1,297.5	255.7	1,041.8	699.6	342.2
IV	1,418.2	319.1	1,099.2	708.5	390.6
2010: I	1,566.6	403.2	1,163.3	720.3	443.0
II	1,614.1	405.6	1,208.5	728.4	480.1
III	1,640.1	429.4	1,210.7	736.5	474.2
IV ᵖ				745.3	

Source: Department of Commerce (Bureau of Economic Analysis).

TABLE B–91. Corporate profits by industry, 1962–2010

[Billions of dollars; quarterly data at seasonally adjusted annual rates]

Year or quarter	Total	Corporate profits with inventory valuation adjustment and without capital consumption adjustment												Rest of the world
		Domestic industries												
		Total	Financial			Nonfinancial								
			Total	Federal Reserve banks	Other	Total	Manufacturing[1]	Transportation[2]	Utilities	Wholesale trade	Retail trade	Information	Other	
SIC:[3]														
1962	57.0	53.3	8.6	0.9	7.7	44.7	26.3	8.5	....	2.8	3.4	....	3.6	3.8
1963	62.1	58.1	8.3	1.0	7.3	49.8	29.7	9.5		2.8	3.6		4.1	4.1
1964	68.6	64.1	8.8	1.1	7.6	55.4	32.6	10.2		3.4	4.5		4.7	4.5
1965	78.9	74.2	9.3	1.3	8.0	64.9	39.8	11.0		3.8	4.9		5.4	4.7
1966	84.6	80.1	10.7	1.7	9.1	69.3	42.6	12.0		4.0	4.9		5.9	4.5
1967	82.0	77.2	11.2	2.0	9.2	66.0	39.2	10.9		4.1	5.7		6.1	4.8
1968	88.8	83.2	12.8	2.5	10.3	70.4	41.9	11.0		4.6	6.4		6.6	5.6
1969	85.5	78.9	13.6	3.1	10.5	65.3	37.3	10.7		4.9	6.4		6.1	6.6
1970	74.4	67.3	15.4	3.5	11.9	52.0	27.5	8.3		4.4	6.0		5.8	7.1
1971	88.3	80.4	17.6	3.3	14.3	62.8	35.1	8.9		5.2	7.2		6.4	7.9
1972	101.6	92.1	19.2	3.3	15.8	72.9	42.2	9.5		6.9	7.4		7.0	9.5
1973	115.4	100.5	20.5	4.5	16.1	80.0	47.2	9.1		8.2	6.7		8.8	14.9
1974	109.6	92.1	20.2	5.7	14.5	71.9	41.4	7.6		11.5	2.3		9.1	17.5
1975	135.0	120.4	20.2	5.6	14.6	100.2	55.2	11.0		13.8	8.2		12.0	14.6
1976	165.6	149.1	25.0	5.9	19.1	124.1	71.4	15.3		12.9	10.5		14.0	16.5
1977	194.8	175.7	31.9	6.1	25.8	143.8	79.4	18.6		15.6	12.4		17.8	19.1
1978	222.4	199.6	39.5	7.6	31.9	160.0	90.5	21.8		15.6	12.3		19.8	22.9
1979	232.0	197.4	40.4	9.4	30.9	157.0	89.8	17.0		18.8	9.9		21.6	34.6
1980	211.4	175.9	34.0	11.8	22.2	142.0	78.3	18.4		17.2	6.2		21.8	35.5
1981	219.1	189.4	29.1	14.4	14.7	160.3	91.1	20.3		22.4	9.9		16.7	29.7
1982	191.1	158.5	26.0	15.2	10.8	132.5	67.1	23.1		19.6	13.5		9.3	32.6
1983	226.6	191.5	35.5	14.6	21.0	156.0	76.2	29.5		21.0	18.8		10.4	35.1
1984	264.6	228.1	34.4	16.4	18.0	193.7	91.8	40.1		29.5	21.1		11.1	36.6
1985	257.5	219.4	45.9	16.3	29.5	173.5	84.3	33.8		23.9	22.2		9.2	38.1
1986	253.0	213.5	56.8	15.5	41.2	156.8	57.9	35.8		24.1	23.5		15.5	39.5
1987	306.9	258.8	61.6	16.2	45.3	197.3	87.5	42.4		19.0	24.0		24.4	48.0
1988	367.7	310.8	68.8	18.1	50.7	242.0	122.5	48.9		20.4	21.0		29.3	57.0
1989	374.1	307.0	80.2	20.6	59.5	226.8	112.1	43.8		22.1	22.1		26.7	67.1
1990	398.8	322.7	92.3	21.8	70.5	230.4	114.4	44.7		19.6	21.6		30.1	76.1
1991	430.3	353.8	122.1	20.7	101.4	231.7	99.4	53.8		22.2	27.7		28.7	76.5
1992	471.6	398.5	142.7	18.3	124.4	255.8	100.8	59.2		25.5	29.2		41.1	73.1
1993	515.0	438.1	133.4	16.7	116.7	304.7	116.8	70.2		26.7	40.6		50.4	76.9
1994	586.6	508.6	129.2	18.5	110.7	379.5	150.1	85.2		31.8	47.2		65.2	78.0
1995	666.0	573.1	160.1	22.9	137.2	413.0	176.7	87.9		28.0	44.8		75.5	92.9
1996	743.8	641.8	167.5	22.5	144.9	474.4	192.0	93.7		40.6	53.7		94.5	102.0
1997	815.9	708.3	187.4	24.3	163.2	520.9	212.2	86.5		48.2	65.9		108.1	107.6
1998	738.6	635.9	159.6	25.6	134.0	476.2	173.4	81.1		51.7	74.7		95.5	102.8
1999	776.6	655.0	190.4	26.7	163.8	464.6	174.6	59.1		51.7	75.6		103.6	121.5
2000	755.7	610.0	194.4	31.2	163.2	415.7	166.5	45.8		55.6	71.4		76.4	145.6
NAICS:[3]														
1998	738.6	635.9	159.5	25.6	133.9	476.4	155.8	21.3	33.5	52.8	67.3	21.9	123.7	102.8
1999	776.6	655.0	189.3	26.7	162.6	465.7	148.8	16.5	33.7	54.8	65.7	12.5	133.6	121.5
2000	755.7	610.0	189.6	31.2	158.4	420.4	143.9	15.2	25.6	58.7	60.7	−15.5	131.8	145.6
2001	720.8	551.1	228.0	28.9	199.1	323.1	49.7	1.2	25.2	51.3	72.6	−24.4	147.4	169.7
2002	762.8	604.9	265.2	23.5	241.7	339.7	47.7	−.1	12.3	49.1	81.6	−3.8	153.0	157.9
2003	892.2	726.4	311.8	20.1	291.8	414.6	69.4	7.4	12.4	54.8	88.9	4.9	176.7	165.8
2004	1,195.1	990.1	362.3	20.0	342.3	627.8	154.1	14.4	19.4	75.6	93.4	45.6	225.2	205.0
2005	1,609.5	1,370.0	443.6	26.6	417.0	926.4	247.2	29.0	29.8	92.2	122.6	81.3	324.3	239.4
2006	1,784.7	1,527.8	448.0	33.8	414.1	1,079.9	304.5	42.1	54.4	103.7	133.2	92.4	349.6	256.8
2007	1,691.1	1,340.2	345.5	36.0	309.5	994.7	271.3	27.7	50.3	99.9	117.8	93.6	334.2	350.9
2008	1,289.1	877.8	139.9	35.1	104.9	737.9	183.7	28.1	28.3	84.0	75.0	75.2	263.6	411.3
2009	1,328.6	976.3	258.0	47.3	210.6	718.4	150.9	24.7	30.0	80.4	99.0	83.5	250.0	352.3
2008: I	1,406.1	976.0	253.5	33.3	220.2	722.5	196.7	22.7	15.6	58.1	71.2	93.3	264.9	430.1
II	1,353.3	941.1	242.5	33.6	208.9	698.6	161.6	30.3	−18.0	65.4	74.0	106.8	278.5	412.3
III	1,376.0	931.8	116.5	35.0	81.5	815.3	211.2	29.3	66.0	88.2	74.2	80.1	266.3	444.2
IV	1,021.0	662.5	−52.7	38.4	−91.1	715.2	165.2	30.0	49.6	124.5	80.4	20.7	244.8	358.5
2009: I	1,223.0	873.8	141.6	43.6	98.0	732.3	141.0	26.9	37.7	103.9	97.7	69.6	255.4	349.1
II	1,249.8	916.6	243.4	47.0	196.4	673.2	139.7	20.3	33.4	73.8	99.7	74.0	232.1	333.2
III	1,360.5	996.2	300.2	49.2	251.0	696.0	151.8	22.0	22.4	70.8	101.3	81.3	246.6	364.2
IV	1,481.2	1,118.6	346.7	49.6	297.1	771.9	170.9	29.5	26.4	73.0	97.1	109.0	266.0	362.6
2010: I	1,736.5	1,348.0	362.7	56.9	305.8	985.3	250.4	39.4	41.5	91.5	129.1	112.9	320.4	388.5
II	1,784.7	1,393.4	359.4	60.3	299.1	1,034.0	277.1	52.4	32.8	107.7	126.7	104.9	332.5	391.3
III	1,809.3	1,427.0	393.7	59.0	334.6	1,033.3	269.2	54.3	35.2	90.2	123.2	114.6	346.6	382.4

[1] See Table B–92 for industry detail.
[2] Data on Standard Industrial Classification (SIC) basis include transportation and public utilities. Those on North American Industry Classification System (NAICS) basis include transporation and warehousing. Utilities classified separately in NAICS (as shown beginning 1998).
[3] SIC-based industry data use the 1987 SIC for data beginning in 1987 and the 1972 SIC for prior data. NAICS-based data use 2002 NAICS.

Note: Industry data on SIC basis and NAICS basis are not necessarily the same and are not strictly comparable.

Source: Department of Commerce (Bureau of Economic Analysis).

TABLE B–92. Corporate profits of manufacturing industries, 1962–2010

[Billions of dollars; quarterly data at seasonally adjusted annual rates]

Year or quarter	Total manu-factur-ing	Corporate profits with inventory valuation adjustment and without capital consumption adjustment											
		Durable goods [2]							Nondurable goods [2]				
		Total [1]	Fabri-cated metal products	Ma-chinery	Compu-ter and elec-tronic products	Elec-trical equip-ment, appli-ances, and compo-nents	Motor vehi-cles, bodies and trailers, and parts	Other	Total	Food and bever-age and tobacco products	Chem-ical products	Petro-leum and coal products	Other
SIC: [3]													
1962	26.3	14.1	1.2	2.4	....	1.5	4.0	3.4	12.3	2.4	3.2	2.2	4.4
1963	29.7	16.4	1.3	2.6	....	1.6	4.9	4.0	13.3	2.7	3.7	2.2	4.7
1964	32.6	18.1	1.5	3.3	....	1.7	4.6	4.4	14.5	2.7	4.1	2.4	5.3
1965	39.8	23.3	2.1	4.0	....	2.7	6.2	5.2	16.5	2.9	4.6	2.9	6.1
1966	42.6	24.1	2.4	4.6	....	3.0	5.2	5.2	18.6	3.3	4.9	3.4	6.9
1967	39.2	21.3	2.5	4.2	....	3.0	4.0	4.9	18.0	3.3	4.3	4.0	6.4
1968	41.9	22.5	2.3	4.2	....	2.9	5.5	5.6	19.4	3.2	5.3	3.8	7.1
1969	37.3	19.2	2.0	3.8	....	2.3	4.8	4.9	18.1	3.1	4.6	3.4	7.0
1970	27.5	10.5	1.1	3.1	....	1.3	1.3	2.9	17.0	3.2	3.9	3.7	6.1
1971	35.1	16.6	1.5	3.1	....	2.0	5.2	4.1	18.5	3.6	4.5	3.8	6.6
1972	42.2	22.9	2.2	4.6	....	2.9	6.0	5.6	19.3	3.0	5.3	3.4	7.7
1973	47.2	25.2	2.7	4.9	....	3.2	5.9	6.2	22.1	2.5	6.2	5.4	7.9
1974	41.4	15.3	1.8	3.3	....	.6	.7	4.0	26.1	2.0	5.3	10.9	7.3
1975	55.2	20.6	3.3	5.1	....	2.6	2.3	4.7	34.5	8.6	6.4	10.1	9.5
1976	71.4	31.4	3.9	6.9	....	3.8	7.4	7.3	39.9	7.1	8.2	13.5	11.1
1977	79.4	38.0	4.5	8.6	....	5.9	9.4	8.5	41.4	6.9	7.8	13.1	13.6
1978	90.5	45.4	5.0	10.7	....	6.7	9.0	10.5	45.1	6.2	8.3	15.8	14.8
1979	89.8	37.2	5.3	9.5	....	5.6	4.7	8.5	52.6	5.8	7.2	24.8	14.7
1980	78.3	18.9	4.4	8.0	....	5.2	-4.3	2.7	59.5	6.1	5.7	34.7	13.1
1981	91.1	19.5	4.5	9.0	....	5.2	.3	-2.6	71.6	9.2	8.0	40.0	14.5
1982	67.1	5.0	2.7	3.1	....	1.7	.0	2.1	62.1	7.3	5.1	34.7	15.0
1983	76.2	19.5	3.1	4.0	....	3.5	5.3	8.4	56.7	6.3	7.4	23.9	19.1
1984	91.8	39.3	4.7	6.0	....	5.1	9.2	14.6	52.6	6.8	8.2	17.6	20.1
1985	84.3	29.7	4.9	5.7	....	2.6	7.4	10.1	54.6	8.8	6.6	18.7	20.5
1986	57.9	26.3	5.2	.8	....	2.7	4.6	12.1	31.7	7.5	7.5	-4.7	21.3
1987	87.5	41.3	5.5	5.6	....	6.1	3.8	17.7	46.2	11.2	14.6	-1.4	21.9
1988	122.5	54.8	6.6	11.3	....	7.8	6.3	16.7	67.7	9.7	18.8	12.9	26.4
1989	112.1	51.8	6.4	12.4	....	9.5	2.8	14.3	60.3	11.2	18.3	6.6	24.2
1990	114.4	44.5	6.1	12.0	....	8.7	-1.8	16.1	69.9	14.4	17.0	16.5	22.0
1991	99.4	35.1	5.3	5.8	....	10.2	-5.3	17.5	64.3	18.3	16.3	7.4	22.3
1992	100.8	41.2	6.3	7.6	....	10.6	-.9	17.6	59.6	18.4	16.1	-.8	25.9
1993	116.8	56.5	7.4	7.6	....	15.4	6.1	19.6	60.4	16.5	16.0	2.8	25.0
1994	150.1	75.8	11.2	9.3	....	23.2	8.0	21.7	74.3	20.4	23.6	1.5	28.9
1995	176.7	82.3	11.9	14.9	....	22.0	.2	26.1	94.4	27.6	28.2	7.4	31.2
1996	192.0	92.0	14.6	17.0	....	20.7	4.5	29.5	99.9	22.7	26.6	15.3	35.3
1997	212.2	104.8	17.1	16.9	....	26.0	5.2	33.3	107.4	25.2	32.4	17.6	32.3
1998	173.4	86.7	16.1	19.6	....	9.1	5.9	29.8	86.6	22.0	26.2	7.1	31.4
1999	174.6	77.9	16.1	12.0	....	5.3	7.5	34.8	96.6	28.1	24.8	4.6	39.2
2000	166.5	64.6	15.5	16.2	....	5.1	-1.4	28.1	101.9	26.0	15.3	29.7	30.9
NAICS: [3]													
1998	155.8	82.7	16.4	15.3	4.2	6.2	6.4	34.2	73.1	22.1	25.0	5.3	20.7
1999	148.8	71.2	16.4	11.7	-6.8	6.4	7.7	35.9	77.6	30.9	22.8	2.2	21.7
2000	143.9	60.0	15.8	7.7	4.2	5.9	-.7	27.1	83.9	26.0	13.8	27.6	16.5
2001	49.7	-26.9	9.8	2.0	-48.6	1.9	-8.9	16.8	76.6	28.2	11.6	29.7	7.1
2002	47.7	-7.7	9.1	1.4	-34.4	.0	-4.5	20.7	55.4	25.3	17.8	1.3	11.0
2003	69.4	-4.3	8.0	1.0	-14.7	2.2	-11.7	10.8	73.8	24.0	18.9	23.5	7.4
2004	154.1	40.7	12.2	7.1	-4.3	.6	-6.8	31.9	113.4	24.3	24.7	49.1	15.3
2005	247.2	95.6	18.1	14.5	9.0	-1.4	1.1	54.2	151.7	27.3	25.7	79.4	19.3
2006	304.5	118.9	18.7	19.2	17.4	11.5	-6.8	58.9	185.7	32.5	52.5	76.6	24.0
2007	271.3	96.1	20.5	22.1	11.0	-1.2	-16.4	60.2	175.2	30.7	48.3	73.5	22.7
2008	183.7	51.4	16.6	15.6	8.9	3.6	-34.6	41.3	132.3	28.4	22.2	78.2	3.4
2009	150.9	53.3	16.4	12.4	13.4	6.1	-23.5	28.5	97.5	35.4	36.4	15.7	10.1
2008: I	196.7	76.4	17.3	16.8	14.1	.5	-22.8	50.6	120.3	23.2	15.1	72.6	9.4
II	161.6	35.9	12.7	13.5	5.1	4.1	-43.3	43.7	125.7	28.4	33.3	60.3	3.8
III	211.2	65.6	14.7	13.7	6.6	6.8	-24.3	48.0	145.5	32.7	25.1	89.5	-1.8
IV	165.2	27.5	21.6	18.3	9.8	3.1	-48.0	22.8	137.7	29.4	15.4	90.6	2.3
2009: I	141.0	30.7	21.5	12.6	5.3	7.1	-47.1	31.4	110.3	35.3	29.4	38.6	7.0
II	139.7	43.6	17.6	11.1	11.4	5.6	-30.5	28.4	96.1	36.7	42.2	6.4	10.9
III	151.8	55.0	14.4	11.4	12.9	5.6	-11.9	22.5	96.7	38.1	38.8	8.1	11.7
IV	170.9	83.9	12.0	14.3	24.1	6.3	-4.6	31.8	87.0	31.5	35.1	9.7	10.7
2010: I	250.4	140.1	17.4	19.9	44.8	9.2	5.7	43.2	110.3	36.6	28.7	33.5	11.6
II	277.1	147.0	17.0	23.3	51.2	9.6	8.4	37.6	130.1	35.1	30.6	55.2	9.2
III	269.2	160.5	19.6	29.1	54.6	9.4	9.8	38.1	108.7	34.0	38.4	22.7	13.6

[1] For Standard Industrial Classification (SIC) data, includes primary metal industries, not shown separately.
[2] Industry groups shown in column headings reflect North American Industry Classification System (NAICS) classification for data beginning 1998. For data on SIC basis, the industry groups would be industrial machinery and equipment (now machinery), electronic and other electric equipment (now electrical equipment, appliances, and components), motor vehicles and equipment (now motor vehicles, bodies and trailers, and parts), food and kindred products (now food and beverage and tobacco products), and chemicals and allied products (now chemical products).
[3] See footnote 3 and Note, Table B–91.

Source: Department of Commerce (Bureau of Economic Analysis).

TABLE B–93. Sales, profits, and stockholders' equity, all manufacturing corporations, 1968–2010

[Billions of dollars]

Year or quarter	All manufacturing corporations				Durable goods industries				Nondurable goods industries			
	Sales (net)	Profits Before income taxes[1]	Profits After income taxes	Stockholders' equity[2]	Sales (net)	Profits Before income taxes[1]	After income taxes	Stockholders' equity[2]	Sales (net)	Profits Before income taxes[1]	After income taxes	Stockholders' equity[2]
1968	631.9	55.4	32.1	265.9	335.5	30.6	16.5	135.6	296.4	24.8	15.5	130.3
1969	694.6	58.1	33.2	289.9	366.5	31.5	16.9	147.6	328.1	26.6	16.4	142.3
1970	708.8	48.1	28.6	306.8	363.1	23.0	12.9	155.1	345.7	25.2	15.7	151.7
1971	751.1	52.9	31.0	320.8	381.8	26.5	14.5	160.4	369.3	26.5	16.5	160.5
1972	849.5	63.2	36.5	343.4	435.8	33.6	18.4	171.4	413.7	29.6	18.0	172.0
1973	1,017.2	81.4	48.1	374.1	527.3	43.6	24.8	188.7	489.9	37.8	23.3	185.4
1973: IV	275.1	21.4	13.0	386.4	140.1	10.8	6.3	194.7	135.0	10.6	6.7	191.7
New series:												
1973: IV	236.6	20.6	13.2	368.0	122.7	10.1	6.2	185.8	113.9	10.5	7.0	182.1
1974	1,060.6	92.1	58.7	395.0	529.0	41.1	24.7	196.0	531.6	51.0	34.1	199.0
1975	1,065.2	79.9	49.1	423.4	521.1	35.3	21.4	208.1	544.1	44.6	27.7	215.3
1976	1,203.2	104.9	64.5	462.7	589.6	50.7	30.8	224.3	613.7	54.3	33.7	238.4
1977	1,328.1	115.1	70.4	496.7	657.3	57.9	34.8	239.9	670.8	57.2	35.5	256.8
1978	1,496.4	132.5	81.1	540.5	760.7	69.6	41.8	262.6	735.7	62.9	39.3	277.9
1979	1,741.8	154.2	98.7	600.5	865.7	72.4	45.2	292.5	876.1	81.8	53.5	308.0
1980	1,912.8	145.8	92.6	668.1	889.1	57.4	35.6	317.7	1,023.7	88.4	56.9	350.4
1981	2,144.7	158.6	101.3	743.4	979.5	67.2	41.6	350.4	1,165.2	91.3	59.6	393.0
1982	2,039.4	108.2	70.9	770.2	913.1	34.7	21.7	355.5	1,126.4	73.6	49.3	414.7
1983	2,114.3	133.1	85.8	812.8	973.5	48.7	30.0	372.4	1,140.8	84.4	55.8	440.4
1984	2,335.0	165.6	107.6	864.2	1,107.6	75.5	48.9	395.6	1,227.5	90.0	58.8	468.5
1985	2,331.4	137.0	87.6	866.2	1,142.6	61.5	38.6	420.9	1,188.8	75.6	49.1	445.3
1986	2,220.9	129.3	83.1	874.7	1,125.5	52.1	32.6	436.3	1,095.4	77.2	50.5	438.4
1987	2,378.2	173.0	115.6	900.9	1,178.0	78.0	53.0	443.3	1,200.3	95.1	62.6	456.6
1988[3]	2,596.2	215.3	153.8	957.6	1,284.7	91.6	66.9	468.7	1,311.5	123.7	86.8	488.9
1989	2,745.1	187.6	135.1	999.0	1,356.6	75.1	55.5	501.3	1,388.5	112.6	79.6	497.7
1990	2,810.7	158.1	110.1	1,043.8	1,357.2	57.3	40.7	515.0	1,453.5	100.8	69.4	528.9
1991	2,761.1	98.7	66.4	1,064.1	1,304.0	13.9	7.2	506.8	1,457.1	84.8	59.3	557.4
1992[4]	2,890.2	31.4	22.1	1,034.7	1,389.8	−33.7	−24.0	473.9	1,500.4	65.1	46.0	560.8
1993	3,015.1	117.9	83.2	1,039.7	1,490.2	38.9	27.4	482.7	1,524.9	79.0	55.7	557.1
1994	3,255.8	243.5	174.9	1,110.1	1,657.6	121.0	87.1	533.3	1,598.2	122.5	87.8	576.8
1995	3,528.3	274.5	198.2	1,240.6	1,807.7	130.6	94.3	613.7	1,720.6	143.9	103.9	627.0
1996	3,757.6	306.6	224.9	1,348.0	1,941.6	146.6	106.1	673.9	1,816.0	160.0	118.8	674.2
1997	3,920.0	331.4	244.5	1,462.7	2,075.8	167.0	121.4	743.4	1,844.2	164.4	123.1	719.3
1998	3,949.4	314.7	234.4	1,482.9	2,168.8	175.1	127.8	779.9	1,780.7	139.6	106.5	703.0
1999	4,148.9	355.3	257.8	1,569.3	2,314.2	198.8	140.3	869.6	1,834.6	156.5	117.5	699.7
2000	4,548.2	381.1	275.3	1,823.1	2,457.4	190.7	131.8	1,054.3	2,090.8	190.5	143.5	768.7
2000: IV	1,163.6	69.2	46.8	1,892.4	620.4	31.2	19.3	1,101.5	543.2	38.0	27.4	790.9
NAICS:[5]												
2000: IV	1,128.8	62.1	41.7	1,833.8	623.0	26.9	15.4	1,100.0	505.8	35.2	26.3	733.8
2001	4,295.0	83.2	36.2	1,843.0	2,321.2	−69.0	−76.1	1,080.5	1,973.8	152.2	112.3	762.5
2002	4,216.4	195.5	134.7	1,804.0	2,260.6	45.9	21.6	1,024.8	1,955.8	149.6	113.1	779.2
2003	4,397.2	305.7	237.0	1,952.2	2,282.7	117.6	88.2	1,040.8	2,114.5	188.1	148.9	911.5
2004	4,934.1	447.5	348.2	2,206.3	2,537.3	200.0	156.5	1,212.9	2,396.7	247.5	191.6	993.5
2005	5,411.5	524.2	401.3	2,410.4	2,730.5	211.3	161.2	1,304.0	2,681.0	312.9	240.2	1,106.5
2006	5,782.7	604.6	470.3	2,678.6	2,910.2	249.1	192.8	1,384.0	2,872.5	355.5	277.5	1,294.6
2007	6,060.0	602.8	442.7	2,921.8	3,015.7	246.8	159.4	1,493.1	3,044.4	356.1	283.3	1,428.7
2008	6,374.1	388.1	266.3	2,980.4	2,969.5	97.7	43.3	1,480.6	3,404.6	290.4	223.1	1,499.8
2009	5,109.1	360.5	287.3	2,782.7	2,427.2	85.0	55.8	1,343.8	2,682.0	275.6	231.5	1,438.9
2008: I	1,566.4	150.0	117.3	3,086.3	740.5	58.6	44.8	1,551.0	825.9	91.3	72.6	1,535.3
II	1,724.2	142.7	109.4	3,082.7	780.4	47.6	31.4	1,544.8	943.7	95.1	78.0	1,537.9
III	1,682.3	165.5	123.6	3,059.7	757.9	54.6	36.0	1,538.9	924.4	110.9	87.6	1,520.8
IV	1,401.3	−70.1	−84.0	2,692.9	690.7	−63.2	−68.8	1,287.6	710.5	−7.0	−15.1	1,405.3
2009: I	1,196.7	48.5	33.8	2,598.4	584.1	−6.4	−10.2	1,239.7	612.6	54.9	44.0	1,358.7
II	1,253.8	80.8	60.0	2,647.9	592.3	11.7	3.4	1,250.1	661.5	69.1	56.6	1,397.8
III	1,305.9	120.5	98.1	2,870.6	613.2	40.6	32.6	1,412.1	692.6	79.9	65.5	1,458.5
IV	1,352.8	110.7	95.4	3,013.8	637.6	39.0	30.0	1,473.4	715.2	71.7	65.4	1,540.4
2010: I	1,350.1	137.8	108.0	3,051.3	628.7	59.5	46.0	1,499.2	721.4	78.4	62.0	1,552.0
II	1,457.9	149.9	126.2	3,116.3	689.4	81.4	65.8	1,535.3	768.5	68.5	60.4	1,581.0
III	1,465.2	153.2	126.1	3,214.8	699.9	75.1	61.3	1,584.6	765.3	78.1	64.9	1,630.2

[1] In the old series, "income taxes" refers to Federal income taxes only, as State and local income taxes had already been deducted. In the new series, no income taxes have been deducted.

[2] Annual data are average equity for the year (using four end-of-quarter figures).

[3] Beginning with 1988, profits before and after income taxes reflect inclusion of minority stockholders' interest in net income before and after income taxes.

[4] Data for 1992 (most significantly 1992:I) reflect the early adoption of Financial Accounting Standards Board Statement 106 (Employer's Accounting for Post-Retirement Benefits Other Than Pensions) by a large number of companies during the fourth quarter of 1992. Data for 1993 (1993:I) also reflect adoption of Statement 106. Corporations must show the cumulative effect of a change in accounting principle in the first quarter of the year in which the change is adopted.

[5] Data based on the North American Industry Classification System (NAICS). Other data shown are based on the Standard Industrial Classification (SIC).

Note: Data are not necessarily comparable from one period to another due to changes in accounting principles, industry classifications, sampling procedures, etc. For explanatory notes concerning compilation of the series, see *Quarterly Financial Report for Manufacturing, Mining, and Trade Corporations*, Department of Commerce, Bureau of the Census.

Source: Department of Commerce (Bureau of the Census).

TABLE B–94. Relation of profits after taxes to stockholders' equity and to sales, all manufacturing corporations, 1960–2010

Year or quarter	Ratio of profits after income taxes (annual rate) to stockholders' equity—percent [1]			Profits after income taxes per dollar of sales—cents		
	All manufacturing corporations	Durable goods industries	Nondurable goods industries	All manufacturing corporations	Durable goods industries	Nondurable goods industries
1960	9.2	8.5	9.8	4.4	4.0	4.8
1961	8.9	8.1	9.6	4.3	3.9	4.7
1962	9.8	9.6	9.9	4.5	4.4	4.7
1963	10.3	10.1	10.4	4.7	4.5	4.9
1964	11.6	11.7	11.5	5.2	5.1	5.4
1965	13.0	13.8	12.2	5.6	5.7	5.5
1966	13.4	14.2	12.7	5.6	5.6	5.6
1967	11.7	11.7	11.8	5.0	4.8	5.3
1968	12.1	12.2	11.9	5.1	4.9	5.2
1969	11.5	11.4	11.5	4.8	4.6	5.0
1970	9.3	8.3	10.3	4.0	3.5	4.5
1971	9.7	9.0	10.3	4.1	3.8	4.5
1972	10.6	10.8	10.5	4.3	4.2	4.4
1973	12.8	13.1	12.6	4.7	4.7	4.8
1973: IV	13.4	12.9	14.0	4.7	4.5	5.0
New series:						
1973: IV	14.3	13.3	15.3	5.6	5.0	6.1
1974	14.9	12.6	17.1	5.5	4.7	6.4
1975	11.6	10.3	12.9	4.6	4.1	5.1
1976	13.9	13.7	14.2	5.4	5.2	5.5
1977	14.2	14.5	13.8	5.3	5.3	5.3
1978	15.0	16.0	14.2	5.4	5.5	5.3
1979	16.4	15.4	17.4	5.7	5.2	6.1
1980	13.9	11.2	16.3	4.8	4.0	5.6
1981	13.6	11.9	15.2	4.7	4.2	5.1
1982	9.2	6.1	11.9	3.5	2.4	4.4
1983	10.6	8.1	12.7	4.1	3.1	4.9
1984	12.5	12.4	12.5	4.6	4.4	4.8
1985	10.1	9.2	11.0	3.8	3.4	4.1
1986	9.5	7.5	11.5	3.7	2.9	4.6
1987	12.8	11.9	13.7	4.9	4.5	5.2
1988 [2]	16.1	14.3	17.8	5.9	5.2	6.6
1989	13.5	11.1	16.0	4.9	4.1	5.7
1990	10.6	7.9	13.1	3.9	3.0	4.8
1991	6.2	1.4	10.6	2.4	.5	4.1
1992 [3]	2.1	−5.1	8.2	.8	−1.7	3.1
1993	8.0	5.7	10.0	2.8	1.8	3.7
1994	15.8	16.3	15.2	5.4	5.3	5.5
1995	16.0	15.4	16.6	5.6	5.2	6.0
1996	16.7	15.7	17.6	6.0	5.5	6.5
1997	16.7	16.3	17.1	6.2	5.8	6.7
1998	15.8	16.4	15.2	5.9	5.9	6.0
1999	16.4	16.1	16.8	6.2	6.1	6.4
2000	15.1	12.5	18.7	6.1	5.4	6.9
2000: IV	9.9	7.0	13.9	4.0	3.1	5.1
NAICS: [4]						
2000: IV	9.1	5.6	14.3	3.7	2.5	5.2
2001	2.0	−7.0	14.7	.8	−3.3	5.7
2002	7.5	2.1	14.5	3.2	1.0	5.8
2003	12.1	8.5	16.3	5.4	3.9	7.0
2004	15.8	12.9	19.3	7.1	6.2	8.0
2005	16.7	12.4	21.7	7.4	5.9	9.0
2006	17.6	13.9	21.4	8.1	6.6	9.7
2007	15.2	10.7	19.8	7.3	5.3	9.3
2008	8.9	2.9	14.9	4.2	1.5	6.6
2009	10.3	4.1	16.1	5.6	2.3	8.6
2008: I	15.2	11.5	18.9	7.5	6.0	8.8
II	14.2	8.1	20.3	6.3	4.0	8.3
III	16.2	9.3	23.0	7.3	4.7	9.5
IV	−12.5	−21.4	−4.3	−6.0	−10.0	−2.1
2009: I	5.2	−3.3	13.0	2.8	−1.7	7.2
II	9.1	1.1	16.2	4.8	.6	8.6
III	13.7	9.2	18.0	7.5	5.3	9.5
IV	12.7	8.1	17.0	7.1	4.7	9.1
2010: I	14.2	12.3	16.0	8.0	7.3	8.6
II	16.2	17.2	15.3	8.7	9.5	7.9
III	15.7	15.5	15.9	8.6	8.8	8.5

[1] Annual ratios based on average equity for the year (using four end-of-quarter figures). Quarterly ratios based on equity at end of quarter.
[2] See footnote 3, Table B–93.
[3] See footnote 4, Table B–93.
[4] See footnote 5, Table B–93.

Note: Based on data in millions of dollars.
See Note, Table B–93.

Source: Department of Commerce (Bureau of the Census).

TABLE B–95. Historical stock prices and yields, 1949–2003

Year	Common stock prices [1]									Common stock yields (Standard & Poor's) (percent) [5]	
	New York Stock Exchange (NYSE) indexes [2]						Dow Jones industrial average [2]	Standard & Poor's composite index (1941–43=10) [2]	Nasdaq composite index (Feb. 5, 1971=100) [2]	Dividend-price ratio [6]	Earnings-price ratio [7]
	Composite (Dec. 31, 2002= 5,000) [3]	December 31, 1965=50									
		Composite	Industrial	Transportation	Utility [4]	Finance					
1949		9.02					179.48	15.23		6.59	15.48
1950		10.87					216.31	18.40		6.57	13.99
1951		13.08					257.64	22.34		6.13	11.82
1952		13.81					270.76	24.50		5.80	9.47
1953		13.67					275.97	24.73		5.80	10.26
1954		16.19					333.94	29.69		4.95	8.57
1955		21.54					442.72	40.49		4.08	7.95
1956		24.40					493.01	46.62		4.09	7.55
1957		23.67					475.71	44.38		4.35	7.89
1958		24.56					491.66	46.24		3.97	6.23
1959		30.73					632.12	57.38		3.23	5.78
1960		30.01					618.04	55.85		3.47	5.90
1961		35.37					691.55	66.27		2.98	4.62
1962		33.49					639.76	62.38		3.37	5.82
1963		37.51					714.81	69.87		3.17	5.50
1964		43.76					834.05	81.37		3.01	5.32
1965		47.39					910.88	88.17		3.00	5.59
1966	487.92	46.15	46.18	50.26	90.81	44.45	873.60	85.26		3.40	6.63
1967	536.84	50.77	51.97	53.51	90.86	49.82	879.12	91.93		3.20	5.73
1968	585.47	55.37	58.00	50.58	88.38	65.85	906.00	98.70		3.07	5.67
1969	578.01	54.67	57.44	46.96	85.60	70.49	876.72	97.84		3.24	6.08
1970	483.39	45.72	48.03	32.14	74.47	60.00	753.19	83.22		3.83	6.45
1971	573.33	54.22	57.92	44.35	79.05	70.38	884.76	98.29	107.44	3.14	5.41
1972	637.52	60.29	65.73	50.17	76.95	78.35	950.71	109.20	128.52	2.84	5.50
1973	607.11	57.42	63.08	37.74	75.38	70.12	923.88	107.43	109.90	3.06	7.12
1974	463.54	43.84	48.08	31.89	59.58	49.67	759.37	82.85	76.29	4.47	11.59
1975	483.55	45.73	50.52	31.10	63.00	47.14	802.49	86.16	77.20	4.31	9.15
1976	575.85	54.46	60.44	39.57	73.94	52.94	974.92	102.01	89.90	3.77	8.90
1977	567.66	53.69	57.86	41.09	81.84	55.25	894.63	98.20	98.71	4.62	10.79
1978	567.81	53.70	58.23	43.50	78.44	56.65	820.23	96.02	117.53	5.28	12.03
1979	616.68	58.32	64.76	47.34	76.41	61.42	844.40	103.01	136.57	5.47	13.46
1980	720.15	68.10	78.70	60.61	74.69	64.25	891.41	118.78	168.61	5.26	12.66
1981	782.62	74.02	85.44	72.61	77.81	73.52	932.92	128.05	203.18	5.20	11.96
1982	728.84	68.93	78.18	60.41	79.49	71.99	884.36	119.71	188.97	5.81	11.60
1983	979.52	92.63	107.45	89.36	93.99	95.34	1,190.34	160.41	285.43	4.40	8.03
1984	977.33	92.46	108.01	85.63	92.89	89.28	1,178.48	160.46	248.88	4.64	10.02
1985	1,142.97	108.09	123.79	104.11	113.49	114.21	1,328.23	186.84	290.19	4.25	8.12
1986	1,438.02	136.00	155.85	119.87	142.72	147.20	1,792.76	236.34	366.96	3.49	6.09
1987	1,709.79	161.70	195.31	140.39	148.59	146.48	2,275.99	286.83	402.57	3.08	5.48
1988	1,585.14	149.91	180.95	134.12	143.53	127.26	2,060.82	265.79	374.43	3.64	8.01
1989	1,903.36	180.02	216.23	175.28	174.87	151.88	2,508.91	322.84	437.81	3.45	7.42
1990	1,939.47	183.46	225.78	158.62	181.20	133.26	2,678.94	334.59	409.17	3.61	6.47
1991	2,181.72	206.33	258.14	173.99	185.32	150.82	2,929.33	376.18	491.69	3.24	4.79
1992	2,421.51	229.01	284.62	201.09	198.91	179.26	3,284.29	415.74	599.26	2.99	4.22
1993	2,638.96	249.58	299.99	242.49	228.90	216.42	3,522.06	451.41	715.16	2.78	4.46
1994	2,687.02	254.12	315.25	247.29	209.06	209.73	3,793.77	460.42	751.65	2.82	5.83
1995	3,078.56	291.15	367.34	269.41	220.30	238.45	4,493.76	541.72	925.19	2.56	6.09
1996	3,787.20	358.17	453.98	327.33	249.77	303.89	5,742.89	670.50	1,164.96	2.19	5.24
1997	4,827.35	456.54	574.52	414.60	283.82	424.48	7,441.15	873.43	1,469.49	1.77	4.57
1998	5,818.26	550.26	681.57	468.69	378.12	516.35	8,625.52	1,085.50	1,794.91	1.49	3.46
1999	6,546.81	619.16	774.78	491.60	473.73	530.86	10,464.88	1,327.33	2,728.15	1.25	3.17
2000	6,805.89	643.66	810.63	413.60	477.65	553.13	10,734.90	1,427.22	3,783.67	1.15	3.63
2001	6,397.85	605.07	748.26	443.59	377.30	595.61	10,189.13	1,194.18	2,035.00	1.32	2.95
2002	5,578.89	527.62	657.37	431.10	260.85	555.27	9,226.43	993.94	1,539.73	1.61	2.92
2003 [3]	5,447.46		633.18	436.51	237.77	565.75	8,993.59	965.23	1,647.17	1.77	3.84

[1] Averages of daily closing prices.
[2] Includes stocks as follows: for NYSE, all stocks listed; for Dow Jones industrial average, 30 stocks; for Standard & Poor's (S&P) composite index, 500 stocks; and for Nasdaq composite index, over 5,000.
[3] The NYSE relaunched the composite index on January 9, 2003, incorporating new definitions, methodology, and base value. (The composite index based on December 31, 1965=50 was discontinued.) Subset indexes on financial, energy, and health care were released by the NYSE on January 8, 2004 (see Table B–96). NYSE indexes shown in this table for industrials, utilities, transportation, and finance were discontinued.
[4] Effective April 1993, the NYSE doubled the value of the utility index to facilitate trading of options and futures on the index. Annual indexes prior to 1993 reflect the doubling.
[5] Based on 500 stocks in the S&P composite index.
[6] Aggregate cash dividends (based on latest known annual rate) divided by aggregate market value based on Wednesday closing prices. Monthly data are averages of weekly figures; annual data are averages of monthly figures.
[7] Quarterly data are ratio of earnings (after taxes) for four quarters ending with particular quarter-to-price index for last day of that quarter. Annual data are averages of quarterly ratios.

Sources: New York Stock Exchange, Dow Jones & Co., Inc., Standard & Poor's, and Nasdaq Stock Market.

TABLE B–96. Common stock prices and yields, 2000–2010

| Year or month | Common stock prices | | | | | | | Common stock yields (Standard & Poor's) (percent) [4] | |
| | New York Stock Exchange (NYSE) indexes (December 31, 2002=5,000) [2,3] | | | | Dow Jones industrial average [2] | Standard & Poor's composite index (1941–43=10) [2] | Nasdaq composite index (Feb. 5, 1971=100) [2] | Dividend-price ratio [5] | Earnings-price ratio [6] |
	Composite	Financial	Energy	Health care					
2000	6,805.89				10,734.90	1,427.22	3,783.67	1.15	3.63
2001	6,397.85				10,189.13	1,194.18	2,035.00	1.32	2.95
2002	5,578.89				9,226.43	993.94	1,539.73	1.61	2.92
2003	5,447.46	5,583.00	5,273.90	5,288.67	8,993.59	965.23	1,647.17	1.77	3.84
2004	6,612.62	6,822.18	6,952.36	5,924.80	10,317.39	1,130.65	1,986.53	1.72	4.89
2005	7,349.00	7,383.70	9,377.84	6,283.96	10,547.67	1,207.23	2,099.32	1.83	5.36
2006	8,357.99	8,654.40	11,206.94	6,685.06	11,408.67	1,310.46	2,263.41	1.87	5.78
2007	9,648.82	9,321.39	13,339.99	7,191.79	13,169.98	1,477.19	2,578.47	1.86	5.29
2008	8,036.88	6,278.38	13,258.42	6,171.19	11,252.62	1,220.04	2,161.65	2.37	3.54
2009	6,091.02	3,987.04	10,020.30	5,456.63	8,876.15	948.05	1,845.38	2.40	1.86
2010	7,230.43	4,744.05	10,943.85	6,230.62	10,662.80	1,139.97	2,349.89	1.98	....
2007: Jan	9,132.04	9,575.21	11,381.56	7,083.45	12,512.89	1,424.16	2,453.19	1.81	....
Feb	9,345.98	9,732.63	11,658.11	7,174.03	12,631.48	1,444.79	2,479.86	1.82	....
Mar	9,120.57	9,342.66	11,503.16	6,997.30	12,268.53	1,406.95	2,401.49	1.89	5.85
Apr	9,555.98	9,658.88	12,441.16	7,332.01	12,754.80	1,463.65	2,499.57	1.84	....
May	9,822.99	9,864.01	13,031.00	7,474.48	13,407.76	1,511.14	2,562.14	1.81	....
June	9,896.98	9,754.29	13,639.81	7,268.42	13,480.21	1,514.49	2,595.40	1.81	5.65
July	9,985.42	9,543.66	14,318.49	7,210.07	13,677.89	1,520.70	2,655.08	1.80	....
Aug	9,440.44	8,963.67	13,250.28	6,957.87	13,239.71	1,454.62	2,539.50	1.92	....
Sept	9,777.59	9,060.63	14,300.99	7,138.20	13,557.69	1,497.12	2,634.47	1.88	5.15
Oct	10,159.33	9,390.30	14,976.30	7,231.60	13,901.28	1,539.66	2,780.42	1.84	....
Nov	9,741.15	8,522.71	14,622.23	7,127.40	13,200.58	1,463.39	2,662.80	1.95	....
Dec	9,807.36	8,447.99	14,956.77	7,306.60	13,406.99	1,479.23	2,661.55	1.93	4.51
2008: Jan	9,165.10	7,776.77	14,222.14	7,068.98	12,538.12	1,378.76	2,418.09	2.06	....
Feb	9,041.52	7,577.54	13,931.92	6,674.75	12,419.57	1,354.87	2,325.83	2.10	....
Mar	8,776.21	7,155.51	14,000.91	6,318.44	12,193.88	1,316.94	2,254.82	2.17	4.57
Apr	9,174.10	7,579.73	15,159.35	6,381.98	12,656.63	1,370.47	2,368.10	2.09	....
May	9,429.04	7,593.63	16,365.23	6,405.40	12,812.48	1,403.22	2,483.24	2.07	....
June	8,996.98	6,798.20	16,272.67	6,243.42	12,056.67	1,341.25	2,427.45	2.15	4.01
July	8,427.37	6,207.89	14,899.86	6,412.48	11,322.38	1,257.33	2,278.14	2.27	....
Aug	8,362.20	6,304.58	13,772.04	6,618.92	11,530.75	1,281.47	2,389.27	2.23	....
Sept	7,886.29	6,159.18	12,562.82	6,316.05	11,114.08	1,217.01	2,205.20	2.36	3.94
Oct	6,130.39	4,733.74	9,515.71	5,434.03	9,176.71	968.80	1,730.32	2.83	....
Nov	5,527.63	3,779.86	9,262.07	5,088.99	8,614.55	883.04	1,542.70	3.11	....
Dec	5,525.70	3,673.95	9,136.33	5,090.83	8,595.56	877.56	1,525.89	3.00	1.65
2009: Jan	5,477.14	3,337.14	9,295.97	5,256.13	8,396.20	865.58	1,537.20	3.01	....
Feb	5,051.42	2,823.74	8,785.04	5,106.78	7,690.50	805.23	1,485.98	3.07	....
Mar	4,739.72	2,633.65	8,266.81	4,596.81	7,235.47	757.13	1,432.23	2.92	.86
Apr	5,338.39	3,313.47	8,839.95	4,771.71	7,992.12	848.15	1,641.15	2.60	....
May	5,823.10	3,819.95	9,848.66	5,051.78	8,398.37	902.41	1,726.08	2.41	....
June	5,985.64	3,924.19	10,189.64	5,224.16	8,593.00	926.12	1,826.99	2.35	.82
July	6,026.55	4,000.66	9,765.09	5,410.22	8,679.75	935.82	1,873.84	2.31	....
Aug	6,577.18	4,646.60	10,295.91	5,706.96	9,375.06	1,009.72	1,997.16	2.12	....
Sept	6,839.88	4,844.93	10,791.73	5,838.22	9,634.97	1,044.55	2,084.75	2.06	1.19
Oct	6,986.35	4,918.07	11,342.57	5,931.28	9,857.34	1,067.66	2,122.85	2.02	....
Nov	7,079.38	4,848.04	11,486.95	6,155.21	10,227.55	1,088.07	2,143.53	1.99	....
Dec	7,167.51	4,734.07	11,335.23	6,430.25	10,433.44	1,110.38	2,220.60	1.95	4.57
2010: Jan	7,257.37	4,795.75	11,548.08	6,523.83	10,471.24	1,123.58	2,267.77	1.92	....
Feb	6,958.36	4,567.29	10,840.96	6,320.43	10,214.51	1,089.16	2,194.44	2.00	....
Mar	7,349.86	4,942.17	11,194.52	6,453.81	10,677.52	1,152.05	2,362.24	1.90	5.21
Apr	7,607.49	5,187.03	11,690.25	6,391.99	11,052.15	1,197.32	2,475.72	1.84	....
May	7,010.08	4,689.81	10,491.24	5,929.68	10,500.19	1,125.06	2,319.24	1.98	....
June	6,767.75	4,484.05	9,960.54	5,838.56	10,159.27	1,083.36	2,235.23	2.09	6.51
July	6,814.61	4,553.76	10,007.16	5,867.77	10,222.24	1,079.80	2,210.27	2.10	....
Aug	6,922.30	4,588.87	10,186.03	5,939.69	10,350.40	1,087.28	2,205.28	2.10	....
Sept	7,149.32	4,694.66	10,423.43	6,208.29	10,598.07	1,122.08	2,298.35	2.06	6.30
Oct	7,482.15	4,778.71	11,164.11	6,456.56	11,044.49	1,171.58	2,441.30	1.97	....
Nov	7,608.40	4,770.65	11,639.37	6,389.44	11,198.31	1,198.89	2,530.99	1.94	....
Dec	7,837.43	4,875.84	12,180.49	6,447.34	11,465.26	1,241.53	2,631.56	1.90	....

[1] Averages of daily closing prices.
[2] Includes stocks as follows: for NYSE, all stocks listed (in 2010, over 2,300); for Dow Jones industrial average, 30 stocks; for Standard & Poor's (S&P) composite index, 500 stocks; and for Nasdaq composite index, in 2010, over 2,600.
[3] The NYSE relaunched the composite index on January 9, 2003, incorporating new definitions, methodology, and base value. Subset indexes on financial, energy, and health care were released by the NYSE on January 8, 2004.
[4] Based on 500 stocks in the S&P composite index.
[5] Aggregate cash dividends (based on latest known annual rate) divided by aggregate market value based on Wednesday closing prices. Monthly data are averages of weekly figures, annual data are averages of monthly figures.
[6] Quarterly data are ratio of earnings (after taxes) for four quarters ending with particular quarter-to-price index for last day of that quarter. Annual data are averages of quarterly ratios.

Sources: New York Stock Exchange, Dow Jones & Co., Inc., Standard & Poor's, and Nasdaq Stock Market.

TABLE B–97. Farm income, 1950–2010

[Billions of dollars]

Year	Income of farm operators from farming							Net farm income
	Gross farm income						Production expenses	
	Total [1]	Cash marketing receipts			Value of inventory changes [3]	Direct Government payments [4]		
		Total	Livestock and products	Crops [2]				
1950	33.1	28.5	16.1	12.4	0.8	0.3	19.5	13.6
1951	38.3	32.9	19.6	13.2	1.2	.3	22.3	15.9
1952	37.8	32.5	18.2	14.3	.9	.3	22.8	15.0
1953	34.4	31.0	16.9	14.1	−.6	.2	21.5	13.0
1954	34.2	29.8	16.3	13.6	.5	.3	21.8	12.4
1955	33.5	29.5	16.0	13.5	.2	.2	22.2	11.3
1956	34.0	30.4	16.4	14.0	−.5	.6	22.7	11.3
1957	34.8	29.7	17.4	12.3	.6	1.0	23.7	11.1
1958	39.0	33.5	19.2	14.2	.8	1.1	25.8	13.2
1959	37.9	33.6	18.9	14.7	.0	.7	27.2	10.7
1960	38.6	34.0	19.0	15.0	.4	.7	27.4	11.2
1961	40.5	35.2	19.5	15.7	.3	1.5	28.6	12.0
1962	42.3	36.5	20.2	16.3	.6	1.7	30.3	12.1
1963	43.4	37.5	20.0	17.4	.6	1.7	31.6	11.8
1964	42.3	37.3	19.9	17.4	−.8	2.2	31.8	10.5
1965	46.5	39.4	21.9	17.5	1.0	2.5	33.6	12.9
1966	50.5	43.4	25.0	18.4	−.1	3.3	36.5	14.0
1967	50.5	42.8	24.4	18.4	.7	3.1	38.2	12.3
1968	51.8	44.2	25.5	18.7	.1	3.5	39.5	12.3
1969	56.4	48.2	28.6	19.6	.1	3.8	42.1	14.3
1970	58.8	50.5	29.5	21.0	.0	3.7	44.5	14.4
1971	62.1	52.7	30.5	22.3	1.4	3.1	47.1	15.0
1972	71.1	61.1	35.6	25.5	.9	4.0	51.7	19.5
1973	98.9	86.9	45.8	41.1	3.4	2.6	64.6	34.4
1974	98.2	92.4	41.3	51.1	−1.6	.5	71.0	27.3
1975	100.6	88.9	43.1	45.8	3.4	.8	75.0	25.5
1976	102.9	95.4	46.3	49.0	−1.5	.7	82.7	20.2
1977	108.8	96.2	47.6	48.6	1.1	1.8	88.9	19.9
1978	128.4	112.4	59.2	53.2	1.9	3.0	103.2	25.2
1979	150.7	131.5	69.2	62.3	5.0	1.4	123.3	27.4
1980	149.3	139.7	68.0	71.7	−6.3	1.3	133.1	16.1
1981	166.3	141.6	69.2	72.5	6.5	1.9	139.4	26.9
1982	164.1	142.6	70.3	72.3	−1.4	3.5	140.3	23.8
1983	153.9	136.8	69.6	67.2	−10.9	9.3	139.6	14.3
1984	168.0	142.8	72.9	69.9	6.0	8.4	142.0	26.0
1985	161.1	144.0	70.1	73.9	−2.3	7.7	132.6	28.5
1986	156.1	135.4	71.6	63.8	−2.2	11.8	125.0	31.1
1987	168.4	141.8	76.0	65.8	−2.3	16.7	130.4	38.0
1988	177.9	151.3	79.6	71.6	−4.1	14.5	138.3	39.6
1989	191.6	160.5	83.6	76.9	3.8	10.9	145.1	46.5
1990	197.8	169.3	89.1	80.2	3.3	9.3	151.5	46.3
1991	192.0	168.0	85.8	82.2	−.2	8.2	151.8	40.2
1992	200.6	171.5	85.8	85.7	4.2	9.2	150.4	50.2
1993	205.0	178.3	90.5	87.8	−4.2	13.4	158.3	46.7
1994	216.1	181.4	88.3	93.1	8.3	7.9	163.5	52.6
1995	210.8	188.2	87.2	101.0	−5.0	7.3	171.1	39.8
1996	235.8	199.4	92.9	106.5	7.9	7.3	176.9	58.9
1997	238.0	207.8	96.5	111.3	.6	7.5	186.7	51.3
1998	232.6	196.5	94.2	102.2	−.6	12.4	185.5	47.1
1999	234.9	187.8	95.7	92.1	−.2	21.5	187.2	47.7
2000	241.7	192.1	99.6	92.5	1.6	23.2	191.0	50.7
2001	249.9	200.0	106.7	93.4	1.1	22.4	195.0	54.9
2002	230.6	194.6	93.9	100.7	−3.5	12.4	191.4	39.1
2003	258.7	216.0	105.7	110.3	−2.7	16.5	197.7	61.0
2004	294.9	237.9	123.5	114.4	11.2	13.0	207.5	87.4
2005	298.5	240.9	124.9	116.0	−.4	24.4	219.7	78.8
2006	290.2	240.6	118.5	122.1	−3.1	15.8	232.7	57.4
2007	339.5	288.5	138.5	150.1	.6	11.9	269.2	70.3
2008	379.6	318.3	141.5	176.8	6.6	12.2	293.0	86.6
2009	343.2	283.4	119.8	163.7	4.5	12.3	281.0	62.2
2010 p	368.2	312.9	139.8	173.1	−.1	12.4	286.6	81.6

[1] Cash marketing receipts, Government payments, value of changes in inventories, other farm-related cash income, and nonmoney income produced by farms including imputed rent of operator residences.

[2] Crop receipts include proceeds received from commodities placed under Commodity Credit Corporation loans.

[3] Physical changes in beginning and ending year inventories of crop and livestock commodities valued at weighted average market prices during the year.

[4] Includes only Government payments made directly to farmers.

Note: Data for 2010 are forecasts.

Source: Department of Agriculture (Economic Research Service).

Table B-98. Farm business balance sheet, 1952–2010

[Billions of dollars]

End of year	Total assets	Assets									Claims			
		Physical assets					Financial assets				Total claims	Real estate debt [5]	Non–real estate debt [6]	Propri-etors' equity
		Real estate	Non–real estate				Total [4]	Invest-ments in coopera-tives	Other [4]					
			Live-stock and poultry [1]	Ma-chinery and motor vehi-cles	Crops [2]	Pur-chased inputs [3]								
1952	133.1	85.1	14.8	15.0	7.9	....	10.3	3.2	7.1		133.1	6.2	7.1	119.8
1953	128.7	84.3	11.7	15.6	6.8	....	10.3	3.3	7.0		128.7	6.6	6.3	115.8
1954	132.6	87.8	11.2	15.7	7.5	....	10.4	3.5	6.9		132.6	7.1	6.7	118.8
1955	137.0	93.0	10.6	16.3	6.5	....	10.6	3.7	6.9		137.0	7.8	7.3	121.9
1956	145.7	100.3	11.0	16.9	6.8	....	10.7	4.0	6.7		145.7	8.5	7.4	129.8
1957	154.5	106.4	13.9	17.0	6.4	....	10.8	4.2	6.6		154.5	9.0	8.2	137.3
1958	168.7	114.6	17.7	18.1	6.9	....	11.4	4.5	6.9		168.7	9.7	9.4	149.6
1959	172.9	121.2	15.2	19.3	6.2	....	11.0	4.8	6.2		172.9	10.6	10.7	151.6
1960	174.4	123.3	15.6	19.1	6.4	....	10.0	4.2	5.8		174.4	11.3	11.1	151.9
1961	181.6	129.1	16.4	19.3	6.5	....	10.4	4.5	5.9		181.6	12.3	11.8	157.5
1962	188.9	134.6	17.3	19.9	6.5	....	10.5	4.6	5.9		188.9	13.5	13.2	162.2
1963	196.7	142.4	15.9	20.4	7.4	....	10.7	5.0	5.7		196.7	15.0	14.6	167.1
1964	204.2	150.5	14.5	21.2	7.0	....	11.0	5.2	5.8		204.2	16.9	15.3	172.1
1965	220.8	161.5	17.6	22.4	7.9	....	11.4	5.4	6.0		220.8	18.9	16.9	185.0
1966	234.0	171.2	19.0	24.1	8.1	....	11.6	5.7	6.0		234.0	20.7	18.5	194.8
1967	246.1	180.9	18.8	26.3	8.0	....	12.0	5.8	6.1		246.1	22.6	19.6	203.9
1968	257.2	189.4	20.2	27.7	7.4	....	12.4	6.1	6.3		257.2	24.7	19.2	213.2
1969	267.8	195.3	22.8	28.6	8.3	....	12.8	6.4	6.4		267.8	26.4	20.0	221.4
1970	278.8	202.4	23.7	30.4	8.7	....	13.6	7.2	6.5		278.8	27.2	21.3	230.3
1971	301.8	217.6	27.3	32.4	10.0	....	14.5	7.9	6.7		301.8	28.8	24.0	248.9
1972	339.9	243.0	33.7	34.6	12.9	....	15.7	8.7	6.9		339.9	31.4	26.7	281.8
1973	418.5	298.3	42.4	39.7	21.4	....	16.8	9.7	7.1		418.5	35.2	31.6	351.7
1974 [7]	449.2	335.6	24.6	48.5	22.5	....	18.1	11.2	6.9		449.2	39.6	35.1	374.5
1975	510.8	383.6	29.4	57.4	20.5	....	19.9	13.0	6.9		510.8	43.8	39.8	427.3
1976	590.7	456.5	29.0	63.3	20.6	....	21.3	14.3	6.9		590.7	48.5	45.7	496.6
1977	651.5	509.3	31.9	69.3	20.4	....	20.5	13.5	7.0		651.5	55.8	52.6	543.1
1978	777.7	601.8	50.1	78.8	23.8	....	23.2	16.1	7.1		777.7	63.4	60.4	653.9
1979	914.7	706.1	61.4	91.9	29.9	....	25.4	18.1	7.3		914.7	75.8	71.7	767.2
1980	1,000.4	782.8	60.6	97.5	32.8	....	26.7	19.3	7.4		1,000.4	85.3	77.2	838.0
1981	997.9	785.6	53.5	101.1	29.5	....	28.2	20.6	7.6		997.9	93.9	83.8	820.2
1982	962.5	750.0	53.0	103.9	25.9	....	29.7	21.9	7.8		962.5	96.8	87.2	778.5
1983	959.3	753.4	49.5	101.7	23.7	....	30.9	22.8	8.1		959.3	98.1	88.1	773.1
1984	897.8	661.8	49.5	125.8	26.1	2.0	32.6	24.3	8.3		897.8	101.4	87.4	709.0
1985	775.9	586.2	46.3	86.1	22.9	1.2	33.3	24.3	9.0		775.9	94.1	78.1	603.8
1986	722.0	542.4	47.8	79.0	16.3	2.1	34.4	24.4	10.0		722.0	84.1	67.2	570.7
1987	756.5	563.7	58.0	78.7	17.8	3.2	35.2	25.3	9.9		756.5	75.8	62.7	618.0
1988	788.5	582.3	62.2	81.0	23.7	3.5	35.9	25.6	10.4		788.5	70.8	62.3	655.4
1989	813.7	600.1	66.2	84.1	23.9	2.6	36.8	26.3	10.4		813.7	68.8	62.3	682.7
1990	840.6	619.1	70.9	86.3	23.2	2.8	38.3	27.5	10.9		840.6	67.6	63.5	709.5
1991	844.2	624.8	68.1	85.9	22.2	2.6	40.5	28.7	11.8		844.2	67.4	64.4	712.3
1992	867.8	640.8	71.0	84.8	24.2	3.9	43.0	29.4	13.6		867.8	67.9	63.7	736.2
1993	909.2	677.6	72.8	85.4	23.3	3.8	46.3	31.0	15.3		909.2	68.4	65.9	774.9
1994	934.7	704.1	67.9	86.8	23.3	5.0	47.6	32.1	15.5		934.7	69.9	69.0	795.8
1995	965.7	740.5	57.8	87.6	27.4	3.4	49.1	34.1	15.0		965.7	71.7	71.3	822.8
1996	1,002.9	769.5	60.3	88.0	31.7	4.4	49.0	34.9	14.1		1,002.9	74.4	74.2	854.3
1997	1,051.3	808.2	67.1	88.7	32.7	4.9	49.7	35.7	13.9		1,051.3	78.5	78.4	894.4
1998	1,083.4	840.4	63.4	89.8	29.9	5.0	54.7	40.5	14.2		1,083.4	83.1	81.5	918.7
1999	1,138.8	887.0	73.2	89.8	28.3	4.0	56.5	41.9	14.6		1,138.8	87.2	80.5	971.1
2000	1,203.2	946.4	76.8	90.1	27.9	4.9	57.1	43.0	14.1		1,203.2	84.7	79.2	1,039.3
2001	1,255.9	996.2	78.5	92.8	25.2	4.2	58.9	43.6	15.3		1,255.9	88.5	82.1	1,085.3
2002	1,259.7	998.7	75.6	96.2	23.1	5.6	60.4	44.7	15.8		1,259.7	95.4	81.9	1,082.5
2003	1,383.4	1,112.1	78.5	100.3	24.4	5.6	62.4	45.6	16.9		1,383.4	83.2	81.0	1,219.2
2004	1,588.0	1,305.2	79.4	107.8	24.4	5.7	65.5	....	....		1,588.0	95.7	86.3	1,406.1
2005	1,779.4	1,487.0	81.1	113.1	24.3	6.5	67.5	....	....		1,779.4	104.8	91.6	1,583.0
2006	1,923.6	1,625.8	80.7	114.2	22.7	6.5	73.7	....	....		1,923.6	108.0	95.5	1,720.0
2007	2,055.3	1,751.4	80.7	114.7	22.7	7.0	78.8	....	....		2,055.3	112.7	101.4	1,841.2
2008	2,023.3	1,703.0	80.6	123.4	27.6	7.2	81.6	....	....		2,023.3	133.6	109.1	1,780.6
2009	2,057.1	1,727.2	79.8	126.0	32.9	7.2	84.1	....	....		2,057.1	134.5	110.8	1,811.8
2010 [p]	2,120.1	1,781.9	81.4	129.1	35.6	7.2	84.9	....	....		2,120.1	132.3	108.0	1,879.9

[1] Excludes commercial broilers; excludes horses and mules beginning with 1959 data; excludes turkeys beginning with 1986 data.
[2] Non–Commodity Credit Corporation (CCC) crops held on farms plus value above loan rate for crops held under CCC.
[3] Includes fertilizer, chemicals, fuels, parts, feed, seed, and other supplies.
[4] Beginning with 2004, data available only for total financial assets. Data through 2003 for other financial assets are currency and demand deposits.
[5] Includes CCC storage and drying facilities loans.
[6] Does not include CCC crop loans.
[7] Beginning with 1974 data, farms are defined as places with sales of $1,000 or more annually.

Note: Data exclude operator households.
Data for 2010 are forecasts.

Source: Department of Agriculture (Economic Research Service).

TABLE B–99. Farm output and productivity indexes, 1950–2008

[1996=100]

Year	Farm output				Productivity indicators	
	Total	Livestock and products	Crops	Farm-related output	Farm output per unit of total factor input	Farm output per unit of labor input
1950	43	52	39	30	45	14
1951	45	54	41	30	46	15
1952	46	55	42	28	47	16
1953	46	55	42	27	47	17
1954	47	58	42	26	49	17
1955	48	59	43	28	49	18
1956	49	61	42	30	49	20
1957	48	60	42	31	49	21
1958	51	62	46	35	51	24
1959	53	65	47	45	52	24
1960	55	65	49	46	54	27
1961	56	68	49	45	56	28
1962	56	69	50	44	56	28
1963	58	71	52	46	57	30
1964	57	72	50	42	57	32
1965	59	71	53	42	59	33
1966	59	73	52	40	58	36
1967	61	74	54	40	60	40
1968	62	74	56	39	61	40
1969	63	74	58	37	61	42
1970	62	77	55	33	60	43
1971	67	79	62	34	65	47
1972	68	81	62	35	64	48
1973	70	81	66	42	66	50
1974	65	78	60	41	62	47
1975	70	75	68	38	68	51
1976	71	79	68	40	67	53
1977	75	80	74	42	70	57
1978	76	80	76	45	67	59
1979	80	81	83	46	69	61
1980	77	82	75	43	67	60
1981	83	83	86	36	75	65
1982	84	83	87	72	77	71
1983	73	84	67	73	67	63
1984	83	83	84	67	79	73
1985	87	85	88	80	84	83
1986	84	86	83	76	83	79
1987	85	87	83	84	84	78
1988	81	88	73	99	81	73
1989	86	88	84	102	87	81
1990	90	90	89	96	91	91
1991	90	92	89	97	91	91
1992	96	95	97	91	98	98
1993	91	96	88	95	93	98
1994	102	101	104	92	99	95
1995	97	102	92	104	92	89
1996	100	100	100	100	100	100
1997	105	103	105	111	102	106
1998	105	104	104	122	101	111
1999	107	108	105	128	102	115
2000	107	107	107	118	107	128
2001	108	107	106	123	108	128
2002	106	109	102	117	106	124
2003	108	110	106	109	110	131
2004	113	108	116	118	117	142
2005	111	110	112	110	114	141
2006	112	113	111	118	116	152
2007	114	113	115	109	112	151
2008	113	113	113	110	119	154

Note: Farm output includes primary agricultural activities and certain secondary activities that are closely linked to agricultural production for which information on production and input use cannot be separately observed. Secondary output (alternatively, farm-related output) includes recreation activities, the imputed value of employer-provided housing, land rentals under the Conservation Reserve, and services such as custom machine work and custom livestock feeding.

See Table B–100 for farm inputs.

Source: Department of Agriculture (Economic Research Service).

Year	Farm employment (thousands) [1] Total	Self-employed and unpaid family workers [2]	Hired workers [3]	Crops harvested (millions of acres) [4]	Total farm input	Capital input Total	Durable equipment	Labor input Total	Hired labor	Self-employed and unpaid family labor	Intermediate input Total	Feed and seed	Energy and lubricants [5]	Agricultural chemicals	Purchased services
1950	9,283	6,965	2,318	345	97	118	90	305	268	323	53	59	73	21	45
1951	8,653	6,464	2,189	344	98	120	100	293	259	311	55	61	76	21	49
1952	8,441	6,301	2,140	349	98	122	109	287	253	304	55	60	80	23	52
1953	7,904	5,817	2,087	348	98	123	114	275	246	289	55	61	81	23	50
1954	7,893	5,782	2,111	346	96	124	120	269	232	288	53	58	81	24	49
1955	7,719	5,675	2,044	340	99	124	123	263	228	281	58	65	83	24	51
1956	7,367	5,451	1,916	324	100	124	124	247	208	266	60	68	83	26	53
1957	6,966	5,046	1,920	324	99	123	123	229	199	244	62	71	82	25	54
1958	6,667	4,705	1,962	324	100	121	121	218	201	226	66	76	80	26	56
1959	6,565	4,621	1,944	324	102	121	121	217	196	227	68	77	81	30	76
1960	6,155	4,260	1,895	324	101	121	123	205	196	208	68	77	82	30	73
1961	5,994	4,135	1,859	302	100	121	121	200	195	201	68	76	84	31	72
1962	5,841	3,997	1,844	295	102	120	119	200	195	202	70	79	85	34	72
1963	5,500	3,700	1,800	298	102	120	119	192	195	190	72	82	86	37	71
1964	5,206	3,585	1,621	298	100	121	121	180	175	182	71	79	88	41	68
1965	4,964	3,465	1,499	298	100	121	123	176	165	181	72	79	89	41	70
1966	4,574	3,224	1,350	294	101	121	126	163	149	170	76	85	91	45	70
1967	4,303	3,036	1,267	306	101	122	131	154	138	161	78	86	90	52	73
1968	4,207	2,974	1,233	300	102	123	136	153	134	162	78	87	90	52	71
1969	4,050	2,843	1,207	290	103	123	139	150	135	158	81	91	92	58	69
1970	3,951	2,727	1,224	293	103	122	140	144	136	147	83	92	92	72	65
1971	3,868	2,665	1,203	305	104	121	142	142	134	145	85	94	90	79	66
1972	3,870	2,664	1,206	294	105	121	142	141	134	144	88	98	89	85	65
1973	3,947	2,702	1,245	321	106	120	145	140	136	141	90	97	90	98	70
1974	3,919	2,588	1,331	328	105	121	153	139	145	136	88	94	86	101	68
1975	3,818	2,481	1,337	336	103	123	159	137	147	131	83	91	102	75	71
1976	3,741	2,369	1,372	337	106	124	163	135	149	127	89	94	114	89	75
1977	3,660	2,347	1,313	345	106	126	169	131	145	124	89	94	120	91	74
1978	3,682	2,410	1,272	338	113	127	173	129	136	125	101	105	126	96	89
1979	3,549	2,320	1,229	348	116	128	179	131	141	125	104	109	115	103	94
1980	3,605	2,302	1,303	352	115	130	186	128	140	121	102	109	112	105	85
1981	3,497	2,241	1,256	366	111	129	187	127	140	121	97	103	108	98	81
1982	3,335	2,142	1,193	362	110	127	184	118	125	114	98	106	101	89	88
1983	3,282	1,991	1,291	306	109	125	176	117	138	106	97	106	98	83	87
1984	3,091	1,930	1,161	348	105	121	168	113	129	105	94	99	102	95	85
1985	2,760	1,753	1,007	342	103	119	159	105	117	98	93	99	91	89	87
1986	2,693	1,740	953	325	101	115	148	106	112	103	91	100	85	88	80
1987	2,681	1,717	964	302	101	112	137	108	115	105	92	99	95	87	83
1988	2,727	1,725	1,002	297	100	109	130	110	118	105	92	99	95	82	83
1989	2,637	1,709	928	318	99	107	125	106	111	103	91	95	94	90	89
1990	2,568	1,649	919	322	99	106	121	99	111	93	96	101	94	95	85
1991	2,591	1,682	909	318	100	105	118	100	110	94	97	101	94	99	89
1992	2,505	1,640	865	319	97	104	114	97	104	94	94	101	92	87	85
1993	2,367	1,510	857	308	99	103	110	93	104	88	98	103	93	92	95
1994	2,613	1,774	839	321	102	102	106	107	101	111	101	103	95	94	100
1995	2,597	1,730	867	314	105	101	103	108	105	110	105	109	100	93	105
1996	2,433	1,602	831	326	100	100	100	100	100	100	100	100	100	100	100
1997	2,432	1,557	875	333	103	100	98	99	100	96	105	105	102	103	106
1998	2,284	1,405	879	326	104	99	98	94	107	87	110	111	103	104	113
1999	2,239	1,326	913	327	105	99	98	93	112	84	113	116	105	104	117
2000	2,126	1,249	877	325	101	98	98	84	94	79	109	114	103	104	107
2001	2,084	1,211	873	321	100	98	98	84	95	78	108	111	100	102	110
2002	2,115	1,243	872	316	99	98	99	85	96	79	106	110	109	99	104
2003	2,066	1,181	885	324	98	97	100	82	94	76	105	114	91	94	101
2004	2,012	1,188	824	321	96	97	103	79	87	75	103	112	98	96	98
2005	1,988	1,208	780	321	97	98	107	79	87	74	106	113	91	100	103
2006	1,900	1,148	752	312	97	98	109	74	83	69	107	114	87	102	105
2007	1,832	1,082	750	322	102	97	109	76	90	68	116	118	100	115	115
2008	1,786	1,054	732	327	95	97	111	73	86	67	104	110	88	92	107
2009	1,757	1,018	739	319	....	....	....	....	....	....	....	....	....	....	....
2010 p	....	....	....	322	....	....	....	....	....	....	....	....	....	....	....

[1] Persons involved in farmwork. Total farm employment is the sum of self-employed and unpaid family workers and hired workers shown here.
[2] Data from Current Population Survey (CPS) conducted by the Department of Commerce, Census Bureau, for the Department of Labor, Bureau of Labor Statistics.
[3] Data from national income and product accounts from Department of Commerce, Bureau of Economic Analysis.
[4] Acreage harvested plus acreages in fruits, tree nuts, and vegetables and minor crops. Includes double-cropping.
[5] Consists of petroleum fuels, natural gas, electricity, hydraulic fluids, and lubricants.

Source: Department of Agriculture (Economic Research Service).

TABLE B–101. Agricultural price indexes and farm real estate value, 1975–2010

[1990-92=100, except as noted]

Year or month	Prices received by farmers			Prices paid by farmers											Addendum: Average farm real estate value per acre (dollars)[3]
				All commodities, services, interest, taxes, and wage rates[1]	Production items									Wage rates	
	All farm products	Crops	Livestock and products		Total[2]	Feed	Livestock and poultry	Fertilizer	Agricultural chemicals	Fuels	Farm machinery	Farm services	Rent		
1975	73	88	62	47	55	83	39	87	72	40	38	48		44	340
1976	75	87	64	50	59	83	47	74	78	43	43	52		48	397
1977	73	83	64	53	61	82	48	72	71	46	47	57		51	474
1978	83	89	78	58	67	80	65	72	66	48	51	60		55	531
1979	94	98	90	66	76	89	88	77	67	61	56	66		60	628
1980	98	107	89	75	85	98	85	96	71	86	63	81		65	737
1981	100	111	89	82	92	110	80	104	77	98	70	89		70	819
1982	94	98	90	86	94	99	78	105	83	97	76	96		74	823
1983	98	108	88	86	92	107	76	100	87	94	81	82		76	788
1984	101	111	91	89	94	112	73	103	90	93	85	86		77	801
1985	91	98	86	86	91	95	74	98	90	93	85	85		78	713
1986	87	87	88	85	86	88	73	90	89	76	83	83		81	640
1987	89	86	91	87	87	83	85	86	87	76	85	84		85	599
1988	99	104	93	91	90	104	91	94	89	77	89	85		87	632
1989	104	109	100	96	95	110	93	99	93	83	94	91		95	668
1990	104	103	105	99	99	103	102	97	95	100	96	96	96	96	683
1991	100	101	99	100	100	98	102	103	101	104	100	98	100	100	703
1992	98	101	97	101	101	99	96	100	103	96	104	103	104	105	713
1993	101	102	100	104	104	102	104	96	109	93	107	110	100	108	736
1994	100	105	95	106	106	106	94	105	112	89	113	110	108	111	798
1995	102	112	92	109	108	103	82	121	116	89	120	115	117	114	844
1996	112	127	99	115	115	129	75	125	119	102	125	116	128	117	887
1997	107	115	98	118	119	125	94	121	121	106	128	116	136	123	926
1998	102	107	97	115	113	111	88	112	122	84	132	115	120	129	974
1999	96	97	95	115	111	100	95	105	121	94	135	114	113	135	1,030
2000	96	96	97	119	115	102	110	110	120	129	139	118	110	140	1,090
2001	102	99	106	123	120	109	111	123	121	121	144	120	117	146	1,150
2002	98	105	90	124	119	112	102	108	119	115	148	120	120	153	1,210
2003	106	110	103	128	124	114	109	124	121	140	151	125	123	157	1,270
2004	118	115	122	134	132	121	128	140	121	165	162	127	126	160	1,340
2005	114	110	119	142	140	117	138	164	123	216	173	133	129	165	1,610
2006	115	120	111	150	148	124	134	176	128	239	182	139	141	171	1,830
2007	136	142	130	161	160	149	131	216	129	264	191	146	147	177	2,010
2008	149	169	130	183	190	194	124	392	139	344	209	146	165	183	2,170
2009	131	150	112	179	182	186	115	275	150	228	222	159	178	187	2,110
2010	145	158	131	184	187	184	133	246	146	283	228	164	191	189	2,140
2009: Jan	139	161	114	180	184	189	120	340	142	204	214	160	178	189	2,110
Feb	126	146	109	179	183	187	119	325	148	198	219	159	178	189	....
Mar	126	147	108	180	184	185	119	320	151	191	220	159	178	189	....
Apr	129	151	112	180	185	185	122	322	152	200	220	159	178	188	....
May	129	149	113	180	184	192	119	301	153	207	220	159	178	188	....
June	133	157	111	180	184	196	112	271	148	238	220	160	178	188	....
July	130	149	112	178	182	189	113	258	149	232	226	159	178	184	....
Aug	126	145	109	177	180	184	111	241	145	243	226	159	178	184	....
Sept	126	141	108	176	179	180	109	234	147	246	226	159	178	184	....
Oct	134	151	110	177	179	181	110	232	148	252	225	159	178	189	....
Nov	136	154	115	178	181	183	113	231	153	264	226	158	178	189	....
Dec	135	150	119	178	181	182	114	230	150	264	225	158	178	189	....
2010: Jan	140	152	122	183	186	186	121	230	159	278	227	163	191	191	2,140
Feb	135	147	123	182	185	178	126	238	145	272	227	163	191	191	....
Mar	141	154	128	182	184	175	131	238	144	276	226	164	191	191	....
Apr	139	150	128	183	186	172	140	245	144	287	226	163	191	187	....
May	141	152	131	183	186	173	137	247	144	286	227	164	191	187	....
June	138	147	129	182	185	173	134	244	144	274	227	165	191	187	....
July	142	150	132	182	185	175	135	240	144	271	228	165	191	186	....
Aug	145	156	134	182	186	178	133	238	144	277	227	165	191	186	....
Sept	148	159	135	183	187	185	130	242	144	277	228	165	191	186	....
Oct	155	168	134	186	190	194	132	251	145	289	229	164	191	192	....
Nov	159	177	136	188	193	203	134	262	146	297	231	164	191	192	....
Dec	160	179	135	191	197	214	140	273	147	305	233	164	191	192	....

[1] Includes items used for family living, not shown separately.
[2] Includes other production items, not shown separately.
[3] Average for 48 States. Annual data are: March 1 for 1975, February 1 for 1976–81, April 1 for 1982–85, February 1 for 1986–89, and January 1 for 1990–2010.

Source: Department of Agriculture (National Agricultural Statistics Service).

TABLE B–102. U.S. exports and imports of agricultural commodities, 1950–2010

[Billions of dollars]

Year	Exports Total [1]	Feed grains	Food grains [2]	Oilseeds and products	Cotton	Tobacco	Animals and products	Imports Total [1]	Fruits, nuts, and vegetables [3]	Animals and products	Coffee	Cocoa beans and products	Agricultural trade balance
1950	2.9	0.2	0.6	0.2	1.0	0.3	0.3	4.0	0.2	0.7	1.1	0.2	−1.1
1951	4.0	.3	1.1	.3	1.1	.3	.5	5.2	.2	1.1	1.4	.2	−1.1
1952	3.4	.3	1.1	.2	.9	.2	.3	4.5	.2	.7	1.4	.2	−1.1
1953	2.8	.3	.7	.2	.5	.3	.4	4.2	.2	.6	1.5	.2	−1.3
1954	3.1	.2	.5	.3	.8	.3	.5	4.0	.2	.5	1.5	.3	−.9
1955	3.2	.3	.6	.4	.5	.4	.6	4.0	.2	.5	1.4	.2	−.8
1956	4.2	.4	1.0	.5	.7	.3	.7	4.0	.2	.4	1.4	.2	.2
1957	4.5	.3	1.0	.5	1.0	.4	.7	4.0	.2	.5	1.4	.2	.6
1958	3.9	.5	.8	.4	.7	.4	.5	3.9	.2	.7	1.2	.2	*
1959	4.0	.6	.9	.6	.4	.3	.6	4.1	.2	.8	1.1	.2	−.1
1960	4.8	.5	1.2	.6	1.0	.4	.6	3.8	.2	.6	1.0	.2	1.0
1961	5.0	.5	1.4	.6	.9	.4	.6	3.7	.2	.7	1.0	.2	1.3
1962	5.0	.8	1.3	.7	.5	.4	.6	3.9	.2	.9	1.0	.2	1.2
1963	5.6	.8	1.5	.8	.6	.4	.7	4.0	.3	.9	1.0	.2	1.6
1964	6.3	.9	1.7	1.0	.7	.4	.8	4.1	.3	.8	1.2	.2	2.3
1965	6.2	1.1	1.4	1.2	.5	.4	.8	4.1	.3	.9	1.1	.1	2.1
1966	6.9	1.3	1.8	1.2	.4	.5	.7	4.5	.4	1.2	1.1	.1	2.4
1967	6.4	1.1	1.5	1.3	.5	.5	.7	4.4	.5	1.1	1.0	.2	1.9
1968	6.2	.9	1.4	1.3	.5	.5	.7	5.0	.6	1.3	1.2	.2	1.2
1969	5.9	.9	1.2	1.3	.3	.6	.8	5.0	.7	1.4	.9	.2	1.0
1970	7.2	1.1	1.4	1.9	.4	.5	.9	5.7	.7	1.6	1.2	.3	1.5
1971	7.7	1.0	1.3	2.2	.6	.5	1.0	5.8	.7	1.6	1.2	.2	1.9
1972	9.4	1.5	1.8	2.5	.5	.7	1.1	6.4	.8	1.9	1.3	.2	2.9
1973	17.6	3.6	4.7	4.4	.9	.7	1.6	8.4	1.0	2.6	1.7	.3	9.3
1974	21.9	4.7	5.4	5.8	1.4	.8	1.8	10.2	1.0	2.2	1.6	.5	11.7
1975	21.9	5.2	6.1	4.6	1.0	.9	1.7	9.3	1.1	1.8	1.7	.5	12.6
1976	23.0	6.0	4.7	5.2	1.1	.9	2.4	11.0	1.2	2.4	2.9	.6	12.0
1977	23.6	4.9	3.6	6.8	1.5	1.1	2.7	13.4	1.5	2.4	4.3	1.0	10.2
1978	29.4	5.9	5.5	8.4	1.7	1.4	3.1	14.8	1.8	3.1	4.1	1.4	14.6
1979	34.7	7.7	6.3	9.4	2.2	1.2	3.8	16.7	2.0	3.9	4.2	1.2	18.0
1980	41.2	9.8	7.9	10.0	2.9	1.3	3.8	17.4	2.0	3.8	4.2	.9	23.9
1981	43.3	9.4	9.6	10.1	2.3	1.5	4.3	16.8	2.5	3.5	2.9	.9	26.6
1982	36.6	6.4	7.9	9.8	2.0	1.5	4.0	15.2	2.8	3.7	2.9	.7	21.4
1983	36.1	7.3	7.4	9.4	1.8	1.5	3.8	16.6	2.9	3.8	2.8	.8	19.5
1984	37.8	8.1	7.5	9.1	2.4	1.5	4.3	19.3	3.7	4.0	3.3	1.1	18.5
1985	29.0	6.0	4.5	6.4	1.6	1.5	4.2	20.0	4.1	4.2	3.3	1.4	9.1
1986	26.2	3.1	3.9	7.3	.8	1.2	4.6	21.4	4.2	4.4	4.6	1.1	4.8
1987	28.7	3.8	3.8	7.2	1.6	1.1	5.2	20.4	4.3	4.8	2.9	1.2	8.3
1988	37.1	5.9	5.9	8.5	2.0	1.3	6.5	20.9	4.4	5.1	2.5	1.0	16.2
1989 [4]	40.0	7.7	7.1	6.4	2.2	1.3	6.4	21.9	4.8	5.1	2.4	1.0	18.2
1990	39.5	7.0	4.8	5.7	2.8	1.4	6.6	22.9	5.5	5.7	1.9	1.1	16.6
1991	39.4	5.7	4.2	6.4	2.5	1.4	7.0	22.9	5.4	5.5	1.9	1.1	16.5
1992	43.2	5.8	5.4	7.3	2.0	1.6	7.9	24.8	5.5	5.7	1.7	1.1	18.5
1993	43.0	5.0	5.7	7.3	1.6	1.3	8.0	25.1	5.6	5.9	1.5	1.0	17.9
1994	46.2	4.7	5.3	7.2	2.6	1.3	9.2	27.0	6.0	5.8	2.5	1.0	19.1
1995	56.2	8.1	6.7	8.9	3.7	1.4	10.9	30.3	6.5	6.0	3.3	1.1	26.0
1996	60.4	9.4	7.4	10.8	2.7	1.4	11.1	33.5	7.5	6.1	2.8	1.4	26.9
1997	57.1	6.0	5.3	12.1	2.7	1.5	11.3	36.1	7.8	6.5	3.9	1.5	21.0
1998	51.8	5.0	5.0	9.5	2.6	1.5	10.6	36.9	8.4	6.9	3.4	1.7	14.9
1999	48.4	5.5	4.7	8.1	1.0	1.3	10.4	37.7	9.3	7.3	2.9	1.5	10.7
2000	51.3	5.2	4.3	8.6	1.9	1.2	11.6	39.0	9.3	8.4	2.7	1.4	12.3
2001	53.7	5.2	4.2	9.2	2.2	1.3	12.4	39.4	9.7	9.2	1.7	1.5	14.3
2002	53.1	5.5	4.5	9.6	2.0	1.0	11.1	41.9	10.4	9.0	1.7	1.8	11.2
2003	59.4	5.4	5.0	11.7	3.4	1.0	12.2	47.4	11.6	8.9	2.0	2.4	12.0
2004	61.4	6.4	6.3	10.4	4.2	1.0	10.4	54.0	13.1	10.6	2.3	2.5	7.4
2005	63.2	5.4	5.7	10.2	3.9	1.0	12.2	59.3	14.4	11.5	3.0	2.8	3.9
2006	70.9	7.7	5.5	11.3	4.5	1.1	13.5	65.3	15.8	11.5	3.3	2.7	5.6
2007	90.0	10.9	9.9	15.6	4.6	1.2	17.2	71.9	18.1	12.4	3.8	2.7	18.1
2008	114.8	14.9	13.6	23.7	4.8	1.2	21.3	80.5	19.5	12.0	4.4	3.3	34.3
2009	98.5	9.4	7.7	24.1	3.3	1.2	18.0	71.7	18.9	10.1	4.1	3.5	26.8
Jan-Nov:													
2009	88.5	8.7	7.1	20.6	3.0	1.0	16.4	65.4	17.1	9.2	3.7	3.0	23.1
2010	103.3	9.5	8.3	23.6	4.8	1.1	20.2	74.6	19.3	10.2	4.4	3.9	28.8

* Less than $50 million.

[1] Total includes items not shown separately.

[2] Rice, wheat, and wheat flour.

[3] Includes fruit, nut, and vegetable preparations and fruit juices.

[4] In 1989, the World Customs Organization established new trade codes that harmonized reporting of commodity trade around the world. Significant changes were made in individual commodity groupings. Those changes are reflected in the data from 1989 forward.

Note: Data derived from official estimates released by the Department of Commerce, Census Bureau. Agricultural commodities are defined as (1) nonmarine food products and (2) other products of agriculture that have not passed through complex processes of manufacture. Export value, at U.S. port of exportation, is based on the selling price and includes inland freight, insurance, and other charges to the port. Import value, defined generally as the market value in the foreign country, excludes import duties, ocean freight, and marine insurance.

Source: Department of Agriculture (Economic Research Service).

TABLE B–103. U.S. international transactions, 1952–2010

[Millions of dollars; quarterly data seasonally adjusted. Credits (+), debits (−)]

Year or quarter	Goods[1]			Services				Income receipts and payments			Unilateral current transfers, net[2]	Balance on current account
	Exports	Imports	Balance on goods	Net military transactions[2]	Net travel and transportation	Other services, net	Balance on goods and services	Receipts	Payments	Balance on income		
1952	13,449	−10,838	2,611	528	83	309	3,531	2,751	−555	2,196	−5,113	614
1953	12,412	−10,975	1,437	1,753	−238	307	3,259	2,736	−624	2,112	−6,657	−1,286
1954	12,929	−10,353	2,576	902	−269	305	3,514	2,929	−582	2,347	−5,642	219
1955	14,424	−11,527	2,897	−113	−297	299	2,786	3,406	−676	2,730	−5,086	430
1956	17,556	−12,803	4,753	−221	−361	447	4,618	3,837	−735	3,102	−4,990	2,730
1957	19,562	−13,291	6,271	−423	−189	482	6,141	4,180	−796	3,384	−4,763	4,762
1958	16,414	−12,952	3,462	−849	−633	486	2,466	3,790	−825	2,965	−4,647	784
1959	16,458	−15,310	1,148	−831	−821	573	69	4,132	−1,061	3,071	−4,422	−1,282
1960	19,650	−14,758	4,892	−1,057	−964	639	3,508	4,616	−1,238	3,379	−4,062	2,824
1961	20,108	−14,537	5,571	−1,131	−978	732	4,195	4,999	−1,245	3,755	−4,127	3,822
1962	20,781	−16,260	4,521	−912	−1,152	912	3,370	5,618	−1,324	4,294	−4,277	3,387
1963	22,272	−17,048	5,224	−742	−1,309	1,036	4,210	6,157	−1,560	4,596	−4,392	4,414
1964	25,501	−18,700	6,801	−794	−1,146	1,161	6,022	6,824	−1,783	5,041	−4,240	6,823
1965	26,461	−21,510	4,951	−487	−1,280	1,480	4,664	7,437	−2,088	5,350	−4,583	5,431
1966	29,310	−25,493	3,817	−1,043	−1,331	1,497	2,940	7,528	−2,481	5,047	−4,955	3,031
1967	30,666	−26,866	3,800	−1,187	−1,750	1,742	2,604	8,021	−2,747	5,274	−5,294	2,583
1968	33,626	−32,991	635	−596	−1,548	1,759	250	9,367	−3,378	5,990	−5,629	611
1969	36,414	−35,807	607	−718	−1,763	1,964	91	10,913	−4,869	6,044	−5,735	399
1970	42,469	−39,866	2,603	−641	−2,038	2,330	2,254	11,748	−5,515	6,233	−6,156	2,331
1971	43,319	−45,579	−2,260	653	−2,345	2,649	−1,303	12,707	−5,435	7,272	−7,402	−1,433
1972	49,381	−55,797	−6,416	1,072	−3,063	2,965	−5,443	14,765	−6,572	8,192	−8,544	−5,795
1973	71,410	−70,499	911	740	−3,158	3,406	1,900	21,808	−9,655	12,153	−6,913	7,140
1974	98,306	−103,811	−5,505	165	−3,184	4,231	−4,292	27,587	−12,084	15,503	−9,249	1,962
1975	107,088	−98,185	8,903	1,461	−2,812	4,854	12,404	25,351	−12,564	12,787	−7,075	18,116
1976	114,745	−124,228	−9,483	931	−2,558	5,027	−6,082	29,375	−13,311	16,063	−5,686	4,295
1977	120,816	−151,907	−31,091	1,731	−3,565	5,680	−27,246	32,354	−14,217	18,137	−5,226	−14,335
1978	142,075	−176,002	−33,927	857	−3,573	6,879	−29,763	42,088	−21,680	20,408	−5,788	−15,143
1979	184,439	−212,007	−27,568	−1,313	−2,935	7,251	−24,565	63,834	−32,961	30,873	−6,593	−285
1980	224,250	−249,750	−25,500	−1,822	−997	8,912	−19,407	72,606	−42,532	30,073	−8,349	2,317
1981	237,044	−265,067	−28,023	−844	144	12,552	−16,172	86,529	−53,626	32,903	−11,702	5,030
1982	211,157	−247,642	−36,485	112	−992	13,209	−24,156	91,747	−56,583	35,164	−16,544	−5,536
1983	201,799	−268,901	−67,102	−563	−4,227	14,124	−57,767	90,000	−53,614	36,386	−17,310	−38,691
1984	219,926	−332,418	−112,492	−2,547	−8,438	14,404	−109,073	108,819	−73,756	35,063	−20,335	−94,344
1985	215,915	−338,088	−122,173	−4,390	−9,798	14,483	−121,880	98,542	−72,819	25,723	−21,998	−118,155
1986	223,344	−368,425	−145,081	−5,181	−8,779	20,502	−138,538	97,064	−81,571	15,494	−24,132	−147,177
1987	250,208	−409,765	−159,557	−3,844	−8,010	19,728	−151,684	108,184	−93,891	14,293	−23,265	−160,655
1988	320,230	−447,189	−126,959	−6,320	−3,013	21,725	−114,566	136,713	−118,026	18,687	−25,274	−121,153
1989	359,916	−477,665	−117,749	−6,749	3,551	27,805	−93,142	161,287	−141,463	19,824	−26,169	−99,486
1990	387,401	−498,438	−111,037	−7,599	7,501	30,270	−80,864	171,742	−143,192	28,550	−26,654	−78,968
1991	414,083	−491,020	−76,937	−5,274	16,561	34,516	−31,135	149,214	−125,084	24,130	9,904	2,898
1992	439,631	−536,528	−96,897	−1,448	19,969	39,164	−39,212	133,766	−109,531	24,234	−36,636	−51,613
1993	456,943	−589,394	−132,451	1,385	19,714	41,041	−70,310	133,057	−110,741	25,316	−39,812	−84,806
1994	502,859	−668,690	−165,831	2,570	16,305	48,463	−98,493	166,521	−149,375	17,146	−40,265	−121,612
1995	575,204	−749,374	−174,170	4,600	21,772	51,414	−96,384	210,244	−189,353	20,891	−38,074	−113,567
1996	612,113	−803,113	−191,000	5,385	25,015	56,535	−104,065	226,129	−203,811	22,318	−43,017	−124,764
1997	678,366	−876,794	−198,428	4,968	22,152	63,035	−108,273	256,804	−244,195	12,609	−45,062	−140,726
1998	670,416	−918,637	−248,221	5,220	10,210	66,651	−166,140	261,819	−257,554	4,265	−53,187	−215,062
1999	698,034	−1,034,345	−336,310	−7,245	6,836	72,481	−264,239	293,925	−280,037	13,888	−50,428	−300,779
2000	784,181	−1,230,413	−446,233	−6,610	2,714	71,349	−378,780	350,918	−329,864	21,054	−58,645	−416,371
2001	730,277	−1,152,257	−421,980	−8,398	−3,217	69,201	−364,393	290,797	−259,075	31,722	−64,487	−397,158
2002	696,268	−1,171,613	−475,345	−12,761	−4,334	71,916	−420,524	280,942	−253,544	27,398	−64,948	−458,074
2003	728,258	−1,269,802	−541,544	−17,062	−12,249	76,671	−494,183	320,456	−275,147	45,309	−71,794	−520,668
2004	819,870	−1,485,501	−665,631	−17,232	−15,328	88,846	−609,345	413,739	−346,519	67,219	−88,362	−630,488
2005	909,016	−1,692,817	−783,801	−15,512	−13,121	98,258	−714,176	535,263	−462,905	72,358	−105,772	−747,590
2006	1,035,868	−1,875,324	−839,456	−11,652	−9,743	101,611	−759,240	682,221	−634,136	48,085	−91,481	−802,636
2007	1,160,366	−1,983,558	−823,192	−10,701	4,576	127,217	−702,099	829,602	−730,049	99,553	−115,548	−718,094
2008	1,304,896	−2,139,548	−834,652	−13,375	19,103	130,122	−698,802	796,528	−644,554	151,974	−122,026	−668,854
2009	1,068,499	−1,575,443	−506,944	−13,378	14,951	130,463	−374,908	588,203	−466,783	121,419	−124,943	−378,432
2009: I	255,044	−376,241	−121,197	−4,014	2,537	32,235	−90,439	143,356	−118,747	24,609	−29,747	−95,577
II	254,021	−367,528	−113,507	−3,101	4,064	32,104	−80,441	142,281	−115,995	26,286	−30,292	−84,447
III	268,858	−400,977	−132,119	−2,283	3,849	31,231	−99,322	146,584	−111,127	35,457	−33,638	−97,503
IV	290,576	−430,698	−140,121	−3,980	4,501	34,893	−104,707	155,982	−120,914	35,068	−31,268	−100,907
2010: I	305,640	−456,961	−151,321	−3,479	5,288	35,062	−114,451	161,268	−121,108	40,160	−34,867	−109,158
II	316,163	−485,734	−169,571	−3,126	5,475	34,143	−133,078	163,871	−120,857	43,014	−33,151	−123,214
III p	323,061	−494,218	−171,157	−2,765	4,978	34,549	−134,396	165,528	−124,473	41,055	−33,886	−127,227

[1] Adjusted from Census data to align with concepts and definitions used to prepare the international and national economic accounts. The adjustments are necessary to supplement coverage of Census data, to eliminate duplication of transactions recorded elsewhere in the international accounts, to value transactions according to a standard definition, and for earlier years, to record transactions in the appropriate period.

[2] Includes transfers of goods and services under U.S. military grant programs.

[3] Consists of gold, special drawing rights, foreign currencies, and the U.S. reserve position in the International Monetary Fund (IMF).

See next page for continuation of table.

[Millions of dollars; quarterly data seasonally adjusted. Credits (+), debits (−)]

Year or quarter	Capital account transactions, net	U.S.-owned assets abroad, excluding financial derivatives [increase/financial outflow (−)] Total	U.S. official reserve assets [3]	Other U.S. Government assets	U.S. private assets	Foreign-owned assets in the U.S., excluding financial derivatives [increase/financial inflow (+)] Total	Foreign official assets	Other foreign assets	Financial derivatives, net	Total (sum of the items with sign reversed)	Of which: Seasonal adjustment discrepancy
1952			−415								
1953			1,256								
1954			480								
1955			182								
1956			−869								
1957			−1,165								
1958			2,292								
1959			1,035								
1960		−4,099	2,145	−1,100	−5,144	2,294	1,473	821		−1,019	
1961		−5,538	607	−910	−5,235	2,705	765	1,939		−989	
1962		−4,174	1,535	−1,085	−4,623	1,911	1,270	641		−1,124	
1963		−7,270	378	−1,662	−5,986	3,217	1,986	1,231		−360	
1964		−9,560	171	−1,680	−8,050	3,643	1,660	1,983		−907	
1965		−5,716	1,225	−1,605	−5,336	742	134	607		−457	
1966		−7,321	570	−1,543	−6,347	3,661	−672	4,333		629	
1967		−9,757	53	−2,423	−7,386	7,379	3,451	3,928		−205	
1968		−10,977	−870	−2,274	−7,833	9,928	−774	10,703		438	
1969		−11,585	−1,179	−2,200	−8,206	12,702	−1,301	14,002		−1,516	
1970		−9,337	2,481	−1,589	−10,229	7,226	7,775	−550		−219	
1971		−12,475	2,349	−1,884	−12,940	23,687	27,596	−3,909		−9,779	
1972		−14,497	−4	−1,568	−12,925	22,171	11,185	10,986		−1,879	
1973		−22,874	158	−2,644	−20,388	18,388	6,026	12,362		−2,654	
1974		−34,745	−1,467	366	−33,643	35,227	10,546	24,682		−2,444	
1975		−39,703	−849	−3,474	−35,380	16,870	7,027	9,843		4,717	
1976		−51,269	−2,558	−4,214	−44,498	37,839	17,693	20,147		9,134	
1977		−34,785	−375	−3,693	−30,717	52,770	36,816	15,954		−3,650	
1978		−61,130	732	−4,660	−57,202	66,275	33,678	32,597		9,997	
1979		−66,054	−1,133	−3,746	−61,176	40,693	−12,526	53,218		25,647	
1980		−86,967	−8,155	−5,162	−73,651	62,037	16,649	45,388		22,613	
1981		−114,147	−5,175	−5,097	−103,875	85,684	6,053	79,631		23,433	
1982		−127,882	−4,965	−6,131	−116,786	95,056	3,593	91,464		38,362	
1983		−66,373	−1,196	−5,006	−60,172	87,399	5,845	81,554		17,666	
1984		−40,376	−3,131	−5,489	−31,757	116,048	3,140	112,908		18,672	
1985		−44,752	−3,858	−2,821	−38,074	144,231	−1,119	145,349		18,677	
1986		−111,723	312	−2,022	−110,014	228,330	35,648	192,681		30,570	
1987		−79,296	9,149	1,006	−89,450	247,100	45,387	201,713		−7,149	
1988		−106,573	−3,912	2,967	−105,628	244,833	39,758	205,075		−17,107	
1989	−207	−175,383	−25,293	1,233	−151,323	222,777	8,503	214,274		52,299	
1990	−7,220	−81,234	−2,158	2,317	−81,393	139,357	33,910	105,447		28,066	
1991	−5,130	−64,388	5,763	2,924	−73,075	108,221	17,389	90,833		−41,601	
1992	1,449	−74,410	3,901	−1,667	−76,644	168,349	40,477	127,872		−43,775	
1993	−714	−200,552	−1,379	−351	−198,822	279,758	71,753	208,005		6,314	
1994	−1,111	−178,937	5,346	−390	−183,893	303,174	39,583	263,591		−1,514	
1995	−222	−352,264	−9,742	−984	−341,538	435,102	109,880	325,222		30,951	
1996	−7	−413,409	6,668	−989	−419,088	547,885	126,724	421,161		−9,705	
1997	−256	−485,475	−1,010	68	−484,533	704,452	19,036	685,416		−77,995	
1998	−8	−353,829	−6,783	−422	−346,624	420,794	−19,903	440,697		148,105	
1999	−4,176	−504,062	8,747	2,750	−515,559	742,210	43,543	698,667		66,807	
2000	−1	−560,523	−290	−941	−559,292	1,038,224	42,758	995,466		−61,329	
2001	13,198	−382,616	−4,911	−486	−377,219	782,870	28,059	754,811		−16,294	
2002	−141	−294,646	−3,681	345	−291,310	795,161	115,945	679,216		−42,300	
2003	−1,821	−325,424	1,523	537	−327,484	858,303	278,069	580,234		−10,391	
2004	3,049	−1,000,870	2,805	1,710	−1,005,385	1,533,201	397,755	1,135,446		95,107	
2005	13,116	−546,631	14,096	5,539	−566,266	1,247,347	259,268	988,079		33,758	
2006	−1,788	−1,285,729	2,374	5,346	−1,293,449	2,065,169	487,939	1,577,230	29,710	−4,727	
2007	384	−1,475,719	−122	−22,273	−1,453,324	2,107,655	481,043	1,626,612	6,222	79,552	
2008	6,010	156,077	−4,848	−529,615	690,540	454,722	550,770	−96,048	−32,947	84,991	
2009	−140	−140,465	−52,256	541,342	−629,552	305,736	450,030	−144,294	50,804	162,497	
2009: I	−20	112,726	−982	244,102	−130,394	−111,916	107,912	−219,828	7,221	87,565	7,761
II	−29	31,734	−3,632	193,750	−158,384	−28,348	128,667	−157,015	11,275	69,815	−1,796
III	−36	−276,241	−49,021	57,736	−284,956	342,385	96,616	245,769	11,496	19,899	−19,298
IV	−56	−8,685	1,379	45,754	−55,817	103,615	116,835	−13,220	20,812	−14,779	13,336
2010: I	−3	−301,389	−773	9,433	−310,048	320,217	72,507	247,710	15,838	74,494	11,715
II	−2	−141,177	−165	−2,441	−138,572	162,096	43,568	118,528	10,048	92,249	−4,273
III p	−8	−324,506	−773	571	−323,981	506,126	141,614	364,512		−54,385	−19,773

Note: Data are on a balance of payments basis. Beginning with data for 1999, exports of goods under the U.S. Foreign Military Sales program and imports of petroleum abroad by U.S. military agencies are included in goods and excluded from net military transactions. Beginning with data for 1999, fuel purchases by air and ocean carriers in foreign ports are included in goods exports and imports and excluded from net travel and transportation.

Source: Department of Commerce (Bureau of Economic Analysis).

TABLE B–104. U.S. international trade in goods by principal end-use category, 1965–2010

[Billions of dollars; quarterly data seasonally adjusted]

Year or quarter	Exports							Imports						
			Nonagricultural products							Nonpetroleum products				
	Total	Agricultural products	Total	Industrial supplies and materials	Capital goods except automotive	Auto-motive	Other	Total	Petroleum and products	Total	Industrial supplies and materials	Capital goods except automotive	Auto-motive	Other
1965	26.5	6.3	20.2	7.6	8.1	1.9	2.6	21.5	2.0	19.5	9.1	1.5	0.9	8.0
1966	29.3	6.9	22.4	8.2	8.9	2.4	2.9	25.5	2.1	23.4	10.2	2.2	1.8	9.2
1967	30.7	6.5	24.2	8.5	9.9	2.8	3.0	26.9	2.1	24.8	10.0	2.5	2.4	9.9
1968	33.6	6.3	27.3	9.6	11.1	3.5	3.2	33.0	2.4	30.6	12.0	2.8	4.0	11.8
1969	36.4	6.1	30.3	10.3	12.4	3.9	3.7	35.8	2.6	33.2	11.8	3.4	4.9	13.0
1970	42.5	7.4	35.1	12.3	14.7	3.9	4.3	39.9	2.9	36.9	12.4	4.0	5.5	15.0
1971	43.3	7.8	35.5	10.9	15.4	4.7	4.5	45.6	3.7	41.9	13.8	4.3	7.4	16.4
1972	49.4	9.5	39.9	11.9	16.9	5.5	5.6	55.8	4.7	51.1	16.3	5.9	8.7	20.2
1973	71.4	18.0	53.4	17.0	22.0	6.9	7.6	70.5	8.4	62.1	19.6	8.3	10.3	23.9
1974	98.3	22.4	75.9	26.3	30.9	8.6	10.0	103.8	26.6	77.2	27.8	9.8	12.0	27.5
1975	107.1	22.2	84.8	26.8	36.6	10.6	10.8	98.2	27.0	71.2	24.0	10.2	11.7	25.3
1976	114.7	23.4	91.4	28.4	39.1	12.1	11.7	124.2	34.6	89.7	29.8	12.3	16.2	31.4
1977	120.8	24.3	96.5	29.8	39.8	13.4	13.5	151.9	45.0	106.9	35.7	14.0	18.6	38.6
1978 [1]	142.1	29.9	112.2	34.2	47.5	15.2	15.3	176.0	42.6	133.4	40.7	19.3	25.0	48.4
1979	184.4	35.5	149.0	52.2	60.2	17.9	18.7	212.0	60.4	151.6	47.5	24.6	26.6	52.8
1980	224.3	42.0	182.2	65.1	76.3	17.4	23.4	249.8	79.5	170.2	53.0	31.6	28.3	57.4
1981	237.0	44.1	193.0	63.6	84.2	19.7	25.5	265.1	78.4	186.7	56.1	37.1	31.0	62.4
1982	211.2	37.3	173.9	57.7	76.5	17.2	22.4	247.6	62.0	185.7	48.6	38.4	34.3	64.3
1983	201.8	37.1	164.7	52.7	71.7	18.5	21.8	268.9	55.1	213.8	53.7	43.7	43.0	73.3
1984	219.9	38.4	181.5	56.8	77.0	22.4	25.3	332.4	58.1	274.4	66.1	60.4	56.5	91.4
1985	215.9	29.6	186.3	54.8	79.3	24.9	27.2	338.1	51.4	286.7	62.6	61.3	64.9	97.9
1986	223.3	27.2	196.2	59.4	82.8	25.1	28.9	368.4	34.3	334.1	69.9	72.0	78.1	114.2
1987	250.2	29.8	220.4	63.7	92.7	27.6	36.4	409.8	42.9	366.8	70.8	85.1	85.2	125.7
1988	320.2	38.8	281.4	82.6	119.1	33.4	46.3	447.2	39.6	407.6	83.1	102.2	87.9	134.4
1989 [1]	359.9	41.1	318.8	90.5	136.9	35.1	56.3	477.7	50.9	426.8	84.6	112.3	87.4	142.5
1990	387.4	40.2	347.2	97.0	153.0	36.2	61.0	498.4	62.3	436.1	83.0	116.4	88.2	148.5
1991	414.1	40.1	374.0	101.6	166.6	39.9	65.9	491.0	51.7	439.3	81.3	121.1	85.5	151.4
1992	439.6	44.1	395.6	101.7	176.4	46.9	70.6	536.5	51.6	484.9	89.1	134.8	91.5	169.6
1993	456.9	43.6	413.3	105.1	182.7	51.6	74.0	589.4	51.5	537.9	100.8	153.2	102.1	182.0
1994	502.9	47.1	455.8	112.7	205.7	57.5	79.9	668.7	51.3	617.4	113.6	185.0	118.1	200.6
1995	575.2	57.2	518.0	135.6	234.4	61.4	86.5	749.4	56.0	693.3	128.5	222.1	123.7	219.0
1996	612.1	61.5	550.6	138.7	254.0	64.4	93.6	803.1	72.7	730.4	136.1	228.4	128.7	237.1
1997	678.4	58.5	619.9	148.6	295.8	73.4	102.0	876.8	71.8	805.0	144.9	253.6	139.4	267.1
1998	670.4	53.2	617.3	139.4	299.8	72.5	105.5	918.6	50.9	867.7	151.6	269.8	148.6	297.7
1999	698.0	49.7	648.4	143.7	311.2	75.3	118.2	1,034.3	71.8	962.6	156.3	295.7	177.5	333.0
2000	784.2	52.8	731.4	168.4	357.0	80.4	125.7	1,230.4	125.8	1,104.6	181.9	347.0	194.1	381.6
2001	730.3	54.9	675.4	154.6	321.7	75.4	123.6	1,152.3	109.1	1,043.2	172.5	298.4	187.9	384.4
2002	696.3	54.5	641.8	151.4	290.4	78.9	121.0	1,171.6	108.9	1,062.7	164.6	283.9	201.9	412.3
2003	728.3	60.9	667.4	167.5	293.7	80.6	125.6	1,269.8	139.9	1,129.9	181.4	296.4	208.2	443.8
2004	819.9	62.9	756.9	199.1	327.5	89.2	141.1	1,485.5	189.9	1,295.6	232.5	344.5	226.1	492.4
2005	909.0	64.9	844.1	230.8	358.4	98.4	156.5	1,692.8	263.7	1,429.2	272.7	380.7	237.3	538.5
2006	1,035.9	72.9	963.0	275.0	404.0	107.3	176.7	1,875.3	317.0	1,558.3	300.1	420.0	254.3	584.0
2007	1,160.4	92.1	1,068.3	315.4	433.0	121.3	198.6	1,983.6	347.6	1,636.0	308.4	446.0	256.7	624.9
2008	1,304.9	118.0	1,186.9	389.5	457.7	121.5	218.3	2,139.5	477.6	1,661.9	333.1	455.2	231.2	642.4
2009	1,068.5	101.0	967.5	294.5	390.5	81.7	200.9	1,575.4	267.4	1,308.1	209.1	369.7	157.6	571.6
2007: I	275.3	20.2	255.2	72.9	105.1	28.7	48.4	478.6	74.3	404.4	74.5	109.8	63.3	156.8
II	284.7	21.2	263.5	78.2	106.1	30.6	48.6	490.3	81.9	408.5	79.1	110.8	64.0	154.5
III	294.6	24.3	270.3	79.7	109.9	31.0	49.7	499.1	86.5	412.6	78.8	112.6	66.0	155.2
IV	305.7	26.4	279.3	84.6	111.9	31.0	51.8	515.5	105.0	410.5	75.9	112.8	63.4	158.4
2008: I	323.5	29.7	293.8	95.1	113.9	30.8	54.0	539.1	118.3	420.8	82.3	115.0	63.1	160.6
II	342.6	31.2	311.4	105.6	117.9	32.1	55.8	565.3	131.0	434.3	87.6	118.8	63.5	164.5
III	345.1	31.1	314.0	107.7	118.2	32.2	56.0	567.4	138.3	429.1	90.6	116.0	57.5	164.9
IV	293.7	26.0	267.7	81.2	107.7	26.4	52.5	467.8	90.1	377.7	72.7	105.5	47.1	152.4
2009: I	255.0	23.8	231.2	66.3	98.5	17.5	49.0	376.2	55.3	320.9	55.1	91.7	32.0	142.1
II	254.0	25.0	229.0	68.6	94.1	17.3	48.9	367.5	60.1	307.4	47.2	87.7	32.5	140.0
III	268.9	24.6	244.3	77.0	95.8	21.9	49.6	401.0	72.5	328.5	50.3	92.0	44.0	142.1
IV	290.6	27.6	263.0	82.5	102.1	25.0	53.4	430.7	79.4	351.3	56.5	98.4	49.1	147.3
2010: I	305.6	28.8	276.9	89.4	105.9	27.1	54.4	457.0	89.5	367.4	63.4	101.9	50.4	151.7
II	316.2	26.0	290.2	96.2	110.6	28.3	55.0	485.7	89.6	396.1	67.9	112.2	57.6	158.4
III [p]	323.1	27.8	295.2	96.8	113.8	27.9	56.7	494.2	86.6	407.6	67.4	116.3	60.0	163.9

[1] End-use commodity classifications beginning 1978 and 1989 are not strictly comparable with data for earlier periods. See *Survey of Current Business*, June 1988 and July 2001.

Note: Data are on a balance of payments basis. Beginning with data for 1999, exports of goods under the U.S. Foreign Military Sales program are included in "other" exports and imports of petroleum abroad by U.S. military agencies are included in imports of petroleum and products; prior to 1999, these transactions are included in services. Beginning with data for 1978, re-exports are assigned to detailed end-use categories in the same manner as exports of domestic goods.

Source: Department of Commerce (Bureau of Economic Analysis).

Table B–105. U.S. international trade in goods by area, 2002–2010

[Millions of dollars]

Item	2002	2003	2004	2005	2006	2007	2008	2009	2010 first 3 quarters at annual rate [1]
EXPORTS									
Total, all countries	696,268	728,258	819,870	909,016	1,035,868	1,160,366	1,304,896	1,068,499	1,259,819
Europe	164,691	174,413	193,481	212,395	246,229	287,410	330,526	263,065	281,817
Euro area [2]	106,141	113,829	126,800	137,556	155,182	179,630	202,524	164,214	173,125
France	19,147	17,178	21,047	22,470	23,832	27,020	29,497	26,856	26,289
Germany	26,546	28,909	31,646	34,702	41,666	49,831	55,058	43,781	47,504
Italy	10,017	10,534	10,859	11,568	12,678	14,294	15,683	12,384	14,155
United Kingdom	33,219	33,863	36,007	38,680	45,404	50,840	54,665	46,713	49,212
Canada	160,887	169,992	190,042	212,340	231,346	249,818	262,282	205,455	249,480
Latin America and Other Western Hemisphere	148,797	149,557	172,436	193,426	222,948	243,799	290,422	240,262	295,645
Brazil	12,381	11,210	13,849	15,316	18,972	24,266	32,415	26,092	34,871
Mexico	97,415	97,395	110,739	120,317	133,833	136,173	151,995	129,682	159,188
Venezuela	4,038	2,840	4,782	6,429	9,001	10,207	12,642	9,352	10,195
Asia and Pacific	190,779	203,106	225,505	242,917	278,814	310,121	337,398	290,066	357,660
China	22,277	28,577	34,723	41,728	54,591	64,038	71,013	70,323	85,491
India	4,129	5,036	6,165	8,007	9,764	15,042	17,859	16,509	19,095
Japan	51,068	51,610	53,215	54,525	58,913	62,398	66,753	52,622	60,897
Korea, Republic of	22,891	24,787	26,750	28,534	33,376	35,719	36,589	29,586	39,587
Singapore	16,284	16,456	19,432	20,541	23,888	25,598	28,216	22,366	29,260
Taiwan	19,081	17,766	22,139	22,652	23,638	26,640	25,952	19,238	25,747
Middle East	19,775	19,894	24,322	32,097	37,679	45,391	55,747	44,990	48,328
Africa	11,339	11,296	14,083	15,841	18,852	23,824	28,522	24,662	26,884
Memorandum: Members of OPEC [3]	18,695	17,447	22,538	31,729	39,192	48,643	65,357	50,464	53,716
IMPORTS									
Total, all countries	1,171,613	1,269,802	1,485,501	1,692,817	1,875,324	1,983,558	2,139,548	1,575,443	1,915,884
Europe	262,725	287,207	324,201	359,499	387,921	416,059	448,850	334,041	382,097
Euro area [2]	173,611	189,236	211,502	231,786	248,980	271,528	282,448	214,395	241,896
France	28,476	29,409	31,871	34,267	37,496	42,000	44,743	34,468	38,636
Germany	62,619	68,360	77,647	85,443	89,759	95,057	98,648	71,876	81,404
Italy	24,239	25,485	28,226	31,210	32,846	35,271	36,593	26,670	28,392
United Kingdom	40,967	43,067	46,818	52,048	54,725	57,929	60,334	48,116	51,449
Canada	211,742	224,630	259,726	294,465	306,436	320,260	342,664	227,902	281,813
Latin America and Other Western Hemisphere	206,062	219,099	257,787	297,428	337,113	351,256	382,607	288,512	362,483
Brazil	15,824	17,986	21,249	24,598	26,578	25,874	30,794	20,221	23,892
Mexico	136,133	139,750	158,330	173,486	201,997	214,848	220,336	179,211	230,272
Venezuela	15,109	17,154	24,951	34,020	37,222	40,019	51,568	28,163	33,249
Asia and Pacific	434,150	464,469	545,359	612,851	689,572	724,108	736,697	601,714	725,988
China	125,399	152,811	197,204	244,293	288,718	322,329	338,843	297,112	357,401
India	11,830	13,082	15,612	18,878	21,944	24,201	25,850	21,302	29,972
Japan	122,362	119,211	131,428	140,242	150,670	148,070	142,192	97,600	119,500
Korea, Republic of	35,861	37,611	46,670	44,043	46,266	48,504	49,150	39,771	48,541
Singapore	14,953	15,345	15,623	15,447	18,230	18,742	16,703	16,130	17,585
Taiwan	32,663	32,201	35,076	35,207	38,516	38,607	36,640	28,539	35,347
Middle East	34,810	42,333	52,745	63,261	73,701	79,671	114,970	60,691	76,853
Africa	22,125	32,065	45,682	65,313	80,581	92,203	113,759	62,583	86,649
Memorandum: Members of OPEC [3]	53,673	69,010	95,244	125,595	146,619	176,331	245,536	113,323	153,720
BALANCE (excess of exports +)									
Total, all countries	−475,345	−541,544	−665,631	−783,801	−839,456	−823,192	−834,652	−506,944	−656,065
Europe	−98,034	−112,794	−130,720	−147,104	−141,692	−128,649	−118,324	−70,976	−100,279
Euro area [2]	−67,470	−75,408	−84,702	−94,229	−93,798	−91,898	−79,924	−50,181	−68,768
France	−9,329	−12,231	−10,825	−11,796	−13,664	−14,980	−15,246	−7,612	−12,347
Germany	−36,073	−39,451	−46,001	−50,741	−48,093	−45,226	−43,591	−28,096	−33,900
Italy	−14,222	−14,952	−17,367	−19,642	−20,168	−20,977	−20,910	−14,286	−14,239
United Kingdom	−7,749	−9,205	−10,811	−13,369	−9,321	−7,089	−5,669	−1,403	−2,237
Canada	−50,855	−54,638	−69,684	−82,125	−75,089	−70,442	−80,383	−22,447	−32,331
Latin America and Other Western Hemisphere	−57,265	−69,542	−85,350	−104,002	−114,165	−107,457	−92,185	−48,250	−66,837
Brazil	−3,442	−6,776	−7,400	−9,281	−7,607	−1,608	1,621	5,871	10,979
Mexico	−38,718	−42,355	−47,591	−53,169	−68,164	−78,675	−68,341	−49,528	−71,085
Venezuela	−11,071	−14,315	−20,169	−27,591	−28,220	−29,812	−38,926	−18,811	−23,055
Asia and Pacific	−243,371	−261,363	−319,855	−369,934	−410,758	−413,986	−399,299	−311,648	−368,328
China	−103,121	−124,234	−162,481	−202,565	−234,126	−258,291	−267,831	−226,788	−271,911
India	−7,701	−8,045	−9,447	−10,871	−12,179	−9,159	−7,992	−4,793	−10,877
Japan	−71,293	−67,601	−78,213	−85,717	−91,757	−85,672	−75,439	−44,978	−58,604
Korea, Republic of	−12,970	−12,824	−19,920	−15,509	−12,889	−12,784	−12,561	−10,185	−8,955
Singapore	1,331	1,112	3,809	5,095	5,659	6,855	11,513	6,235	11,675
Taiwan	−13,583	−14,435	−12,937	−12,555	−14,878	−11,967	−10,689	−9,301	−9,600
Middle East	−15,034	−22,439	−28,423	−31,164	−36,023	−34,281	−59,224	−15,701	−28,525
Africa	−10,786	−20,769	−31,599	−49,471	−61,730	−68,379	−85,238	−37,922	−59,765
Memorandum: Members of OPEC [3]	−34,978	−51,563	−72,706	−93,865	−107,427	−127,688	−180,179	−62,858	−100,005

[1] Preliminary; seasonally adjusted.

[2] Euro area consists of: Austria, Belgium, Cyprus (beginning in 2008), Finland, France, Germany, Greece (beginning in 2001), Ireland, Italy, Luxembourg, Malta (beginning in 2008), Netherlands, Portugal, Slovakia (beginning in 2009), Slovenia (beginning in 2007), and Spain.

[3] Organization of Petroleum Exporting Countries, consisting of Algeria, Angola (beginning in 2007), Ecuador (beginning in 2007), Indonesia (ending in 2008), Iran, Iraq, Kuwait, Libya, Nigeria, Qatar, Saudi Arabia, United Arab Emirates, and Venezuela.

Note: Data are on a balance of payments basis. For further details, and additional data by country, see *Survey of Current Business,* January 2011.

Source: Department of Commerce (Bureau of Economic Analysis).

U.S. international trade in goods on balance of payments (BOP) and Census basis, and trade in services on BOP basis, 1981–2010

[Billions of dollars; monthly data seasonally adjusted]

Year or month	Goods: Exports (f.a.s. value) [1,2]							Goods: Imports (customs value) [6]							Services (BOP basis)	
	Total, BOP basis [3,4]	Census basis (by end-use category)						Total, BOP basis [4]	Census basis (by end-use category)						Exports [4]	Imports [4]
		Total, Census basis [3,5]	Foods, feeds, and beverages	Industrial supplies and materials	Capital goods except automotive	Automotive vehicles, parts, and engines	Consumer goods (nonfood) except automotive		Total, Census basis [5]	Foods, feeds, and beverages	Industrial supplies and materials	Capital goods except automotive	Automotive vehicles, parts, and engines	Consumer goods (nonfood) except automotive		
1981	237.0	238.7	....	....	....	....	....	265.1	261.0	....	....	....	....	....	57.4	45.5
1982	211.2	216.4	31.3	61.7	72.7	15.7	14.3	247.6	244.0	17.1	112.0	35.4	33.3	39.7	64.1	51.7
1983	201.8	205.6	30.9	56.7	67.2	16.8	13.4	268.9	258.0	18.2	107.0	40.9	40.8	44.9	64.3	55.0
1984	219.9	224.0	31.5	61.7	72.0	20.6	13.3	332.4	7,330.7	21.0	123.7	59.8	53.5	60.0	71.2	67.7
1985	215.9	8,218.8	24.0	58.5	73.9	22.9	12.6	338.1	7,336.5	21.9	113.9	65.1	66.8	68.3	73.2	72.9
1986	223.3	8,227.2	22.3	57.3	75.8	21.7	14.2	368.4	365.4	24.4	101.3	71.8	78.2	79.4	86.7	80.1
1987	250.2	254.1	24.3	66.7	86.2	24.6	17.7	409.8	406.2	24.8	111.0	84.5	85.2	88.7	98.7	90.8
1988	320.2	322.4	32.3	85.1	109.2	29.3	23.1	447.2	441.0	24.8	118.3	101.4	87.7	95.9	110.9	98.5
1989	359.9	363.8	37.2	99.3	138.8	34.8	36.4	477.7	473.2	25.1	132.3	113.3	86.1	102.9	127.1	102.5
1990	387.4	393.6	35.1	104.4	152.7	37.4	43.3	498.4	495.3	26.6	143.2	116.4	87.3	105.7	147.8	117.7
1991	414.1	421.7	35.7	109.7	166.7	40.0	45.9	491.0	488.5	26.5	131.6	120.7	85.7	108.0	164.3	118.5
1992	439.6	448.2	40.3	109.1	175.9	47.0	51.4	536.5	532.7	27.6	138.6	134.3	91.8	122.7	177.3	119.6
1993	456.9	465.1	40.6	111.8	181.7	52.4	54.7	589.4	580.7	27.9	145.6	152.4	102.4	134.0	185.9	123.8
1994	502.9	512.6	42.0	121.4	205.0	57.8	60.0	668.7	663.3	31.0	162.0	184.4	118.3	146.3	200.4	133.1
1995	575.2	584.7	50.5	146.2	233.0	61.8	64.4	749.4	743.5	33.2	181.8	221.4	123.8	159.9	219.2	141.4
1996	612.1	625.1	55.5	147.7	253.0	65.0	70.1	803.1	795.3	35.7	204.5	228.1	128.9	172.0	239.5	152.6
1997	678.4	689.2	51.5	158.2	294.5	74.0	77.4	876.8	869.7	39.7	213.8	253.3	139.8	193.8	256.1	165.9
1998	670.4	682.1	46.4	148.3	299.4	72.4	80.3	918.6	911.9	41.2	200.1	269.5	148.7	217.0	262.8	180.7
1999	698.0	695.8	46.0	147.5	310.8	75.3	80.9	1,034.3	1,024.6	43.6	221.4	295.7	179.0	241.9	267.9	195.8
2000	784.2	781.9	47.9	172.6	356.9	80.4	89.4	1,230.4	1,218.0	46.0	299.0	347.0	195.9	281.8	286.4	219.0
2001	730.3	729.1	49.4	160.1	321.7	75.4	88.3	1,152.3	1,141.0	46.6	273.9	298.0	189.8	284.3	274.6	217.0
2002	696.3	693.1	49.6	156.8	290.4	78.9	84.4	1,171.6	1,161.4	49.7	267.7	283.3	203.7	307.8	281.2	226.4
2003	728.3	724.8	55.0	173.0	293.7	80.6	89.9	1,269.8	1,257.1	55.8	313.8	295.9	210.1	333.9	291.6	244.3
2004	819.9	814.9	56.6	203.9	327.5	89.2	103.2	1,485.5	1,469.7	62.1	412.8	343.6	228.2	372.9	338.7	282.4
2005	909.0	901.1	59.0	233.0	358.4	98.4	115.3	1,692.8	1,673.5	68.1	523.8	379.3	239.4	407.2	372.2	302.5
2006	1,035.9	1,026.0	66.0	276.0	404.0	107.3	129.1	1,875.3	1,853.9	74.9	602.0	418.3	256.6	442.6	416.9	336.7
2007	1,160.4	1,148.2	84.3	316.4	433.0	121.3	146.0	1,983.6	1,957.0	81.7	634.7	444.5	256.7	474.6	488.3	367.2
2008	1,304.9	1,287.4	108.3	388.0	457.7	121.5	161.3	2,139.5	2,103.6	89.0	779.5	453.7	231.2	481.6	534.1	398.3
2009	1,068.5	1,056.0	93.9	296.7	390.5	81.7	150.0	1,575.4	1,559.6	81.6	462.5	369.3	157.6	428.4	502.3	370.3
2009: Jan	84.3	83.2	7.2	22.2	33.1	5.6	11.5	130.2	128.8	6.9	38.1	31.7	11.3	35.8	41.2	31.3
Feb	85.9	85.0	7.3	22.2	33.2	5.9	12.7	122.6	121.5	6.8	34.6	30.0	10.1	34.8	41.0	30.7
Mar	84.8	84.1	7.4	22.7	32.2	6.0	12.3	123.4	122.3	6.8	34.7	29.8	10.6	35.4	41.2	30.6
Apr	82.7	81.4	7.6	21.5	31.1	5.9	11.9	122.1	120.9	6.8	33.9	29.1	10.6	35.8	41.4	30.5
May	84.8	83.7	7.8	23.3	31.3	5.7	12.2	120.7	119.6	6.8	33.1	29.3	10.5	35.2	41.1	30.0
June	86.6	85.5	8.0	24.5	31.6	5.8	12.2	124.8	123.7	6.8	37.1	29.3	11.4	34.1	41.3	30.2
July	88.2	87.5	7.7	24.7	32.1	6.9	12.5	132.0	130.8	6.8	38.8	30.5	13.8	35.6	41.4	30.7
Aug	88.6	87.6	7.7	25.8	31.0	7.4	12.3	130.7	129.2	6.7	37.6	30.3	14.6	35.2	41.7	30.7
Sept	92.0	91.0	7.4	27.0	32.7	7.6	12.7	138.3	136.9	6.7	42.7	31.1	15.7	35.5	42.2	31.1
Oct	95.2	94.3	7.9	27.4	33.5	7.9	13.6	139.2	137.6	6.8	41.0	32.0	16.0	36.7	42.9	31.2
Nov	95.7	94.3	8.9	27.0	33.5	8.3	12.9	142.8	141.2	6.7	43.4	32.6	16.1	37.5	43.3	31.5
Dec	99.6	98.3	9.0	28.3	35.1	8.8	13.2	148.7	147.2	6.9	47.4	33.7	17.0	37.0	43.7	31.8
2010: Jan	100.4	99.4	8.9	29.1	34.9	9.0	13.6	147.6	145.8	7.3	46.7	33.5	16.8	36.5	44.1	31.7
Feb	100.2	99.2	8.5	29.6	35.0	9.0	13.2	151.8	150.0	7.2	49.3	33.9	16.0	38.3	44.2	32.5
Mar	105.1	104.4	8.5	31.7	36.0	9.1	13.9	157.5	155.6	7.5	52.1	34.4	17.6	38.9	44.9	32.2
Apr	104.1	103.2	7.9	32.3	36.0	9.3	13.2	156.9	155.0	7.5	52.2	36.0	17.3	37.4	43.6	31.7
May	107.1	106.1	7.9	32.9	38.0	9.4	13.5	161.7	159.8	7.7	50.1	37.9	19.5	40.0	44.9	32.5
June	104.9	104.0	7.6	31.8	36.6	9.7	13.6	167.1	165.0	7.7	49.9	38.3	20.8	43.1	45.2	33.1
July	107.7	106.9	7.5	32.4	38.8	9.3	13.6	167.2	160.8	7.6	49.4	37.7	20.0	41.1	45.4	33.3
Aug	107.6	106.6	8.7	32.9	37.4	9.4	13.7	166.6	164.6	7.8	49.6	38.6	20.7	42.6	45.4	33.2
Sept	107.8	107.1	9.2	32.1	37.6	9.3	13.8	164.9	162.9	7.8	49.7	39.9	19.3	41.0	46.0	33.5
Oct	112.2	111.4	9.9	34.7	38.0	9.7	13.9	163.2	161.1	7.7	47.9	39.0	19.4	41.9	46.2	33.6
Nov p	113.5	112.3	10.5	35.0	38.2	9.1	14.9	164.7	162.7	7.9	49.8	40.0	18.9	41.0	46.2	33.3

[1] Department of Defense shipments of grant-aid military supplies and equipment under the Military Assistance Program are excluded from total exports through 1985 and included beginning 1986.

[2] F.a.s. (free alongside ship) value basis at U.S. port of exportation for exports.

[3] Beginning with data for 1989, exports have been adjusted for undocumented exports to Canada and are included in the appropriate end-use categories. For prior years, only total exports include this adjustment.

[4] Beginning with data for 1999, exports of goods under the U.S. Foreign Military Sales program and fuel purchases by foreign air and ocean carriers in U.S. ports are included in goods exports (BOP basis) and excluded from services exports. Beginning with data for 1999, imports of petroleum abroad by U.S. military agencies and fuel purchases by U.S. air and ocean carriers in foreign ports are included in goods imports (BOP basis) and excluded from services imports.

[5] Total includes "other" exports or imports, not shown separately.

[6] Total arrivals of imported goods other than in-transit shipments.

[7] Total includes revisions not reflected in detail.

[8] Total exports are on a revised statistical month basis; end-use categories are on a statistical month basis.

Note: Goods on a Census basis are adjusted to a BOP basis by the Bureau of Economic Analysis, in line with concepts and definitions used to prepare international and national accounts. The adjustments are necessary to supplement coverage of Census data, to eliminate duplication of transactions recorded elsewhere in international accounts, to value transactions according to a standard definition, and for earlier years, to record transactions in the appropriate period.

Data include international trade of the U.S. Virgin Islands, Puerto Rico, and U.S. Foreign Trade Zones.

Source: Department of Commerce (Bureau of the Census and Bureau of Economic Analysis).

TABLE B–107. International investment position of the United States at year-end, 2003–2009

[Millions of dollars]

Type of investment	2003	2004	2005	2006	2007	2008	2009 p
NET INTERNATIONAL INVESTMENT POSITION OF THE UNITED STATES	−2,093,794	−2,253,026	−1,932,149	−2,191,653	−1,915,685	−3,493,882	−2,737,846
Financial derivatives, net [1]	....	....	57,915	59,836	71,472	159,635	127,934
Net international investment position, excluding financial derivatives	−2,093,794	−2,253,026	−1,990,064	−2,251,489	−1,987,157	−3,653,517	−2,865,780
U.S.-OWNED ASSETS ABROAD	7,638,086	9,340,634	11,961,552	14,428,137	18,339,872	19,244,875	18,379,084
Financial derivatives, gross positive fair value [1]	....	....	1,190,029	1,238,995	2,559,332	6,127,450	3,512,007
U.S.-owned assets abroad, excluding financial derivatives	7,638,086	9,340,634	10,771,523	13,189,142	15,780,540	13,117,425	14,867,077
U.S. official reserve assets	183,577	189,591	188,043	219,853	277,211	293,732	403,804
Gold [2]	108,866	113,947	134,175	165,267	218,025	227,439	284,380
Special drawing rights	12,638	13,628	8,210	8,870	9,476	9,340	57,814
Reserve position in the International Monetary Fund	22,535	19,544	8,036	5,040	4,244	7,683	11,385
Foreign currencies	39,538	42,472	37,622	40,676	45,466	49,270	50,225
U.S. Government assets, other than official reserve assets	84,772	83,062	77,523	72,189	94,471	624,100	82,775
U.S. credits and other long-term assets [3]	81,980	80,308	76,960	71,635	70,015	69,877	71,830
Repayable in dollars	81,706	80,035	76,687	71,362	69,742	69,604	71,557
Other [4]	274	273	273	273	273	273	273
U.S. foreign currency holdings and U.S. short-term assets [5]	2,792	2,754	563	554	24,456	554,222	10,944
U.S. private assets	7,369,737	9,067,981	10,505,957	12,897,100	15,408,858	12,199,593	14,380,499
Direct investment at current cost	2,054,464	2,498,494	2,651,721	2,948,172	3,552,902	3,742,835	4,051,191
Foreign securities	2,948,370	3,545,396	4,329,259	5,604,475	6,835,079	3,985,712	5,470,998
Bonds	060,940	904,970	1,011,554	1,275,515	1,507,009	1,237,204	1,493,505
Corporate stocks	2,079,422	2,560,418	3,317,705	4,328,960	5,247,990	2,748,428	3,977,413
U.S. claims on unaffiliated foreigners reported by U.S. nonbanking concerns [6]	594,004	793,556	1,018,462	1,184,073	1,173,731	794,699	794,225
U.S. claims reported by U.S. banks and securities brokers, not included elsewhere [7]	1,772,899	2,230,535	2,506,515	3,160,380	3,847,146	3,676,347	4,064,085
FOREIGN-OWNED ASSETS IN THE UNITED STATES ..	9,731,880	11,593,660	13,893,701	16,619,790	20,255,557	22,738,757	21,116,930
Financial derivatives, gross negative fair value [1]	....	....	1,132,114	1,179,159	2,487,860	5,967,815	3,384,073
Foreign-owned assets in the United States, excluding financial derivatives	9,731,880	11,593,660	12,761,587	15,440,631	17,767,697	16,770,942	17,732,857
Foreign official assets in the United States	1,569,845	2,019,508	2,313,295	2,832,999	3,411,831	3,939,998	4,373,839
U.S. Government securities	1,186,500	1,509,986	1,725,193	2,167,112	2,540,062	3,264,139	3,592,397
U.S. Treasury securities	986,301	1,251,943	1,340,598	1,558,317	1,736,687	2,400,516	2,871,052
Other	200,199	258,043	384,595	608,795	803,375	863,623	721,345
Other U.S. Government liabilities [8]	23,702	23,896	22,869	26,053	31,860	40,577	98,767
U.S. liabilities reported by U.S. banks and securities brokers, not included elsewhere	201,054	270,387	296,647	297,012	406,031	252,608	187,457
Other foreign official assets	158,589	215,239	268,586	342,822	433,878	382,674	495,218
Other foreign assets	8,162,035	9,574,152	10,448,292	12,607,632	14,355,866	12,830,944	13,359,018
Direct investment at current cost	1,580,994	1,742,716	1,905,979	2,154,062	2,410,520	2,521,353	2,672,786
U.S. Treasury securities	527,223	561,610	643,793	567,861	639,755	850,921	826,192
U.S. securities other than U.S. Treasury securities	3,422,856	3,995,506	4,352,998	5,372,339	6,190,018	4,620,798	5,287,163
Corporate and other bonds	1,710,787	2,035,149	2,243,135	2,824,871	3,289,070	2,770,606	2,841,236
Corporate stocks	1,712,069	1,960,357	2,109,863	2,547,468	2,900,948	1,850,192	2,445,927
U.S. currency	258,652	271,953	280,400	282,627	271,952	301,139	313,771
U.S. liabilities to unaffiliated foreigners reported by U.S. nonbanking concerns [9]	450,884	600,161	658,177	799,471	864,585	731,539	665,477
U.S. liabilities reported by U.S. banks and securities brokers, not included elsewhere [10]	1,921,426	2,402,206	2,606,945	3,431,272	3,979,036	3,805,194	3,593,629
Memoranda:							
Direct investment abroad at market value	2,729,126	3,362,796	3,637,996	4,470,343	5,274,991	3,103,704	4,302,851
Direct investment in the United States at market value	2,454,877	2,717,383	2,817,970	3,293,053	3,596,885	2,552,572	3,120,583

[1] A break in series in 2005 reflects the introduction of U.S. Department of the Treasury data on financial derivatives.

[2] U.S. official gold stock is valued at market prices.

[3] Also includes paid-in capital subscriptions to international financial institutions and resources provided to foreigners under foreign assistance programs requiring repayment over several years. Excludes World War I debts that are not being serviced.

[4] Includes indebtedness that the borrower may contractually, or at its option, repay with its currency, with a third country's currency, or by delivery of materials or transfer of services.

[5] Beginning in 2007, includes foreign-currency-denominated assets obtained through temporary reciprocal currency arrangements between the Federal Reserve System and foreign central banks.

[6] A break in series in 2003 reflects the reclassification of assets reported by U.S. securities brokers from nonbank-reported assets to bank-reported assets, and a reduction in counterparty balances to eliminate double counting. A break in series in 2005 reflects the addition of previously unreported claims of U.S. financial intermediaries on their foreign parents associated with the issuance of asset-backed commercial paper in the United States.

[7] A break in series in 2003 reflects the reclassification of assets reported by U.S. securities brokers from nonbank-reported assets to bank-reported assets.

[8] Includes U.S. Government liabilities associated with military sales contracts and U.S. Government reserve-related liabilities from allocations of special drawing rights (SDRs).

[9] A break in series in 2003 reflects the reclassification of liabilities reported by U.S. securities brokers from nonbank-reported liabilities to bank-reported liabilities and a reduction in counterparty balances to eliminate double counting.

[10] A break in series in 2003 reflects the reclassification of liabilities reported by U.S. securities brokers from nonbank-reported liabilities to bank-reported liabilities.

Note: For details regarding these data, see Survey of Current Business, July 2010.

Source: Department of Commerce (Bureau of Economic Analysis).

TABLE B-108. Industrial production and consumer prices, major industrial countries, 1984-2010

Year or quarter	United States[1]	Canada	Japan	France	Germany[2]	Italy	United Kingdom
	Industrial production (Index, 2007=100)[3]						
1984	53.9	61.7	71.4	72.7	59.8	71.1	76.0
1985	54.5	64.8	74.1	73.2	62.8	72.1	80.2
1986	55.0	64.3	73.9	74.1	64.0	75.0	82.1
1987	57.9	67.0	76.5	75.5	64.3	77.2	85.4
1988	60.9	71.5	83.8	78.6	66.5	82.2	89.6
1989	61.4	71.2	88.7	81.5	69.7	85.1	91.4
1990	62.0	69.3	92.3	87.1	73.3	85.4	91.2
1991	61.1	66.8	93.9	86.7	78.2	84.5	88.1
1992	62.8	67.7	88.2	85.0	76.5	83.6	88.4
1993	64.9	70.9	84.9	81.5	70.7	81.6	90.3
1994	68.3	75.4	85.7	85.0	72.8	86.6	95.2
1995	71.5	78.8	88.3	87.0	73.6	91.7	96.9
1996	74.7	79.7	90.1	86.7	73.6	90.2	98.2
1997	80.1	84.2	93.8	89.9	75.8	93.7	99.6
1998	84.8	87.2	87.2	93.2	78.6	94.9	100.6
1999	88.4	92.3	87.6	94.6	79.4	94.6	102.1
2000	92.0	100.3	92.2	98.1	83.9	98.6	104.0
2001	88.9	96.3	86.2	99.0	84.2	97.5	102.4
2002	89.1	97.8	85.1	97.2	83.3	96.0	100.7
2003	90.2	97.9	87.6	96.1	83.7	95.4	100.1
2004	92.3	99.5	91.8	97.3	86.3	95.2	101.2
2005	95.3	101.4	93.2	97.6	89.2	94.7	99.9
2006	97.4	100.8	97.1	98.8	94.3	98.1	99.9
2007	100.0	100.0	100.0	100.0	100.0	100.0	100.0
2008	96.7	94.4	96.6	97.3	100.0	96.2	96.9
2009	87.7	84.3	75.5	85.3	83.6	78.7	87.1
2010 p	92.8						
2009: I	88.2	85.8	69.1	84.8	82.1	78.7	87.7
II	85.9	82.9	73.6	83.7	81.7	76.9	87.5
III	87.6	83.1	77.5	86.1	84.9	78.9	86.5
IV	89.1	85.4	82.1	86.5	85.9	80.2	86.9
2010: I	90.6	88.0	87.8	89.1	87.8	81.4	87.9
II	92.2	89.8	89.1	90.2	92.2	82.9	88.8
III	93.7	90.0	87.5	90.6	93.9	83.9	89.3
IV p	94.3						
	Consumer prices (Index, 1982-84=100)						
1984	103.9	104.7	102.1	108.0	102.7	111.5	104.8
1985	107.6	108.9	104.2	114.3	104.9	121.8	111.1
1986	109.6	113.5	104.8	117.2	104.7	128.9	114.9
1987	113.6	118.4	105.0	121.1	105.0	135.0	119.7
1988	118.3	123.2	105.7	124.3	106.3	141.9	125.6
1989	124.0	129.3	108.1	128.7	109.2	150.8	135.4
1990	130.7	135.5	111.4	133.1	112.2	160.5	148.2
1991	136.2	143.1	115.0	137.3	116.7	170.6	156.9
1992	140.3	145.2	117.0	140.6	122.7	179.4	162.7
1993	144.5	147.9	118.5	143.6	128.1	187.3	165.3
1994	148.2	148.2	119.3	146.0	131.6	194.9	169.4
1995	152.4	151.4	119.2	148.6	133.9	205.2	175.1
1996	156.9	153.8	119.3	151.5	135.8	213.3	179.4
1997	160.5	156.2	121.4	153.3	138.4	217.7	185.0
1998	163.0	157.8	122.2	154.3	139.7	221.9	191.4
1999	166.6	160.5	121.8	155.2	140.5	225.6	194.3
2000	172.2	164.9	121.0	157.8	142.5	231.3	200.0
2001	177.1	169.1	120.0	160.3	145.3	237.8	203.7
2002	179.9	172.9	119.0	163.4	147.4	243.6	207.0
2003	184.0	177.7	118.7	166.9	148.9	250.1	213.0
2004	188.9	181.0	118.7	170.4	151.4	255.7	219.3
2005	195.3	185.0	118.3	173.4	153.7	260.7	225.6
2006	201.6	188.7	118.6	176.3	156.2	266.2	232.8
2007	207.342	192.7	118.7	178.9	159.7	271.1	242.7
2008	215.303	197.3	120.3	184.0	163.9	280.1	252.4
2009	214.537	197.9	118.7	184.1	164.5	282.3	251.1
2010 p	218.056	201.4	117.9	186.9	166.3	286.6	262.7
2009: I	212.015	196.4	119.0	183.3	164.0	280.8	247.8
II	214.263	198.1	119.0	184.3	164.3	282.3	249.7
III	215.718	198.3	118.7	184.2	164.7	282.9	251.9
IV	216.152	198.6	118.1	184.7	164.9	283.2	254.8
2010: I	217.020	199.6	117.6	185.7	165.3	284.4	257.6
II	218.051	200.9	117.9	187.3	166.0	286.2	262.6
III	218.254	202.0	117.7	187.0	166.6	287.5	263.7
IV p	218.898	203.1	118.2	187.8	167.3	288.3	266.7

[1] See Note, Table B-51 for information on U.S. industrial production series.
[2] Prior to 1991 data are for West Germany only.
[3] All data exclude construction. Quarterly data are seasonally adjusted.

Note: National sources data have been rebased for industrial production and consumer prices.

Sources: As reported by each country, Board of Governors of the Federal Reserve System, and Department of Labor (Bureau of Labor Statistics).

TABLE B-109. Civilian unemployment rate, and hourly compensation, major industrial countries, 1984–2010

[Quarterly data seasonally adjusted]

Year or quarter	United States	Canada	Japan	France	Germany [1]	Italy	United Kingdom
Civilian unemployment rate (Percent) [2]							
1984	7.5	10.9	2.8	8.9	7.1	5.9	11.8
1985	7.2	10.1	[3]2.5	9.5	7.2	6.0	11.4
1986	7.0	9.2	2.7	9.5	6.6	[3]7.5	11.4
1987	6.2	8.4	2.6	9.6	6.3	7.9	10.5
1988	5.5	7.4	2.4	9.3	6.3	7.9	8.6
1989	5.3	7.1	2.2	8.6	5.7	7.8	7.3
1990	[3]5.6	7.7	2.0	8.3	5.0	7.0	7.1
1991	6.8	9.8	2.0	8.5	[3]5.6	[3]6.9	8.9
1992	7.5	10.6	2.1	9.4	6.7	7.3	10.0
1993	6.9	10.8	2.4	10.5	8.0	[3]9.8	10.4
1994	[3]6.1	[3]9.6	2.6	10.9	8.5	10.7	9.5
1995	5.6	8.6	2.9	10.3	8.2	11.3	8.7
1996	5.4	8.8	3.1	10.8	9.0	11.3	8.1
1997	4.9	8.4	3.1	10.9	9.9	11.4	7.0
1998	4.5	7.7	3.8	10.4	9.3	11.5	6.3
1999	4.2	7.0	4.2	10.0	[3]8.5	11.0	6.0
2000	4.0	6.1	4.4	8.5	7.8	10.2	5.5
2001	4.7	6.5	4.5	7.7	7.9	9.2	5.1
2002	5.8	7.0	4.9	7.9	8.6	8.7	5.2
2003	6.0	6.9	4.6	8.4	9.3	8.5	5.0
2004	5.5	6.4	4.2	8.8	10.3	8.1	4.8
2005	5.1	6.0	3.8	8.8	[3]11.2	7.8	4.9
2006	4.6	5.5	3.6	8.7	10.4	6.9	5.5
2007	4.6	5.3	3.6	7.9	8.7	6.2	5.4
2008	5.8	5.3	3.7	7.4	7.5	6.8	5.7
2009	9.3	7.3	4.8	9.1	7.8	7.9	7.7
2010	9.6	....	....	....	....	....	....
2009: I	8.2	6.9	4.2	8.6	7.5	7.4	7.1
II	9.3	7.5	4.8	9.1	7.9	7.6	7.8
III	9.7	7.6	5.1	9.1	7.9	8.1	7.9
IV	10.0	7.5	4.9	9.5	7.8	8.4	7.8
2010: I	9.7	7.4	4.6	9.5	7.7	8.5	8.0
II	9.6	7.1	4.9	9.2	7.4	8.5	7.8
III	9.6	7.1	4.8	9.3	7.2	8.3	7.8
IV	9.6	....	....	....	....	....	....
Manufacturing hourly compensation in U.S. dollars (Index, 2002=100) [4]							
1984	48.9	64.7	31.6	37.8	32.1	43.4	30.8
1985	51.4	64.6	32.7	39.9	32.8	44.8	32.7
1986	53.8	64.6	48.2	54.2	46.3	61.2	40.3
1987	55.6	69.3	57.8	65.1	58.4	75.9	49.9
1988	57.5	78.1	66.8	68.0	62.2	81.2	57.9
1989	59.3	85.0	65.7	66.9	61.1	85.0	56.9
1990	62.1	91.9	66.8	81.9	76.4	104.8	69.3
1991	65.8	100.2	76.6	83.7	79.1	110.1	77.2
1992	68.9	99.5	84.3	93.8	92.0	118.0	77.1
1993	70.5	94.3	98.9	91.6	92.2	96.3	68.5
1994	72.2	91.6	109.5	97.0	98.4	99.1	71.7
1995	73.4	93.4	123.1	111.1	117.4	103.7	75.2
1996	74.6	95.4	107.3	110.3	117.0	115.5	74.2
1997	76.5	96.3	99.7	99.5	103.4	109.5	81.3
1998	81.2	94.5	94.4	99.3	103.4	105.5	88.6
1999	84.8	96.4	108.6	98.2	101.4	103.3	91.8
2000	91.3	99.5	113.9	89.6	92.4	91.9	91.0
2001	94.8	98.1	102.3	89.3	92.4	92.0	90.6
2002	100.0	100.0	100.0	100.0	100.0	100.0	100.0
2003	108.0	116.6	105.7	122.5	122.4	124.2	114.2
2004	108.9	130.3	114.3	138.8	135.2	141.2	133.8
2005	112.5	146.2	113.2	144.0	137.1	145.9	140.7
2006	114.7	162.3	106.1	151.0	144.0	150.4	150.3
2007	118.5	177.6	103.1	168.9	158.8	168.8	168.9
2008	123.2	179.3	119.7	186.4	175.0	187.4	159.6
2009	129.6	167.1	130.7	179.5	173.9	186.8	138.5

[1] Prior to 1991 data are for West Germany only.

[2] Civilian unemployment rates, approximating U.S. concepts. Quarterly data for Germany should be viewed as less precise indicators of unemployment under U.S. concepts than the annual data.

[3] There are breaks in the series for Canada (1994), Germany (1991, 1999, and 2005), Italy (1986, 1991, and 1993), Japan (1985), and United States (1990 and 1994). For details, see *International Comparisons of Annual Labor Force Statistics, Adjusted to U.S. Concepts, 10 Countries, 1970–2009*, June 2, 2010, Appendix B, at http://www.bls.gov/fls/flscomparelf/notes.htm#country_notes.

[4] Hourly compensation in manufacturing, U.S. dollar basis; data relate to all employed persons (employees and self-employed workers). For details on manufacturing hourly compensation, see *International Comparisons of Manufacturing Productivity and Unit Labor Cost Trends, 2009*, December 21, 2010.

Source: Department of Labor (Bureau of Labor Statistics).

[Foreign currency units per U.S. dollar, except as noted; certified noon buying rates in New York]

Period	Australia (dollar)[1]	Canada (dollar)	China, P.R. (yuan)	EMU Members (euro)[1,2]	Germany (mark)[2]	Japan (yen)	Mexico (peso)	South Korea (won)	Sweden (krona)	Switzer- land (franc)	United Kingdom (pound)[1]
March 1973	1.2716	0.9967	2.2401	....	2.8132	261.90	0.013	398.85	4.4294	3.2171	2.4724
1990	.7807	1.1668	4.7921	....	1.6166	145.00	2.813	710.64	5.9231	1.3901	1.7841
1991	.7787	1.1460	5.3337	....	1.6610	134.59	3.018	736.73	6.0521	1.4356	1.7674
1992	.7352	1.2085	5.5206	....	1.5618	126.78	3.095	784.66	5.8258	1.4064	1.7663
1993	.6799	1.2902	5.7795	....	1.6545	111.08	3.116	805.75	7.7956	1.4781	1.5016
1994	.7316	1.3664	8.6397	....	1.6216	102.18	3.385	806.93	7.7161	1.3667	1.5319
1995	.7407	1.3725	8.3700	....	1.4321	93.96	6.447	772.69	7.1406	1.1812	1.5785
1996	.7828	1.3638	8.3389	....	1.5049	108.78	7.600	805.00	6.7082	1.2361	1.5607
1997	.7437	1.3849	8.3193	....	1.7348	121.06	7.918	953.19	7.6446	1.4514	1.6376
1998	.6291	1.4836	8.3008	....	1.7597	130.99	9.152	1,400.40	7.9522	1.4506	1.6573
1999	.6454	1.4858	8.2783	1.0653	....	113.73	9.553	1,189.84	8.2740	1.5045	1.6172
2000	.5815	1.4855	8.2784	.9232	....	107.80	9.459	1,130.90	9.1735	1.6904	1.5156
2001	.5169	1.5487	8.2770	.8952	....	121.57	9.337	1,292.02	10.3425	1.6891	1.4396
2002	.5437	1.5704	8.2771	.9454	....	125.22	9.663	1,250.31	9.7233	1.5567	1.5025
2003	.6524	1.4008	8.2772	1.1321	....	115.94	10.793	1,192.08	8.0787	1.3450	1.6347
2004	.7365	1.3017	8.2768	1.2438	....	108.15	11.290	1,145.24	7.3480	1.2428	1.8330
2005	.7627	1.2115	8.1936	1.2449	....	110.11	10.894	1,023.75	7.4710	1.2459	1.8204
2006	.7535	1.1340	7.9723	1.2563	....	116.31	10.906	954.32	7.3718	1.2532	1.8434
2007	.8391	1.0734	7.6058	1.3711	....	117.76	10.928	928.97	6.7550	1.1999	2.0020
2008	.8537	1.0660	6.9477	1.4726	....	103.39	11.143	1,098.71	6.5846	1.0816	1.8545
2009	.7927	1.1412	6.8307	1.3935	....	93.68	13.498	1,274.63	7.6539	1.0860	1.5661
2010	.9200	1.0298	6.7696	1.3261	....	87.78	12.623	1,155.74	7.2053	1.0432	1.5452
2009: I	.6644	1.2455	6.8361	1.3035	....	93.78	14.384	1,415.27	8.4107	1.1487	1.4344
II	.7609	1.1682	6.8293	1.3619	....	97.42	13.315	1,282.78	7.9239	1.1123	1.5502
III	.8332	1.0980	6.8306	1.4304	....	93.54	13.261	1,237.55	7.2907	1.0623	1.6410
IV	.9090	1.0557	6.8271	1.4762	....	89.88	13.062	1,166.70	7.0114	1.0219	1.6335
2010: I	.9041	1.0401	6.8271	1.3821	....	90.66	12.759	1,142.84	7.1928	1.0583	1.5575
II	.8842	1.0273	6.8237	1.2740	....	92.08	12.553	1,164.80	7.5737	1.1073	1.4931
III	.9062	1.0386	6.7680	1.2938	....	85.74	12.789	1,181.06	7.2501	1.0308	1.5521
IV	.9879	1.0129	6.6570	1.3586	....	82.54	12.388	1,132.58	6.7842	.9741	1.5803

Trade-weighted value of the U.S. dollar

	Nominal				Real[7]		
	G-10 index (March 1973=100)[3]	Broad index (January 1997=100)[4]	Major currencies index (March 1973=100)[5]	OITP index (January 1997=100)[6]	Broad index (March 1973=100)[4]	Major currencies index (March 1973=100)[5]	OITP index (March 1973=100)[6]
1990	89.1	71.41	89.91	40.10	91.22	85.01	109.56
1991	89.8	74.35	88.59	46.70	89.68	83.32	108.58
1992	86.6	76.91	87.00	53.14	87.79	82.20	104.96
1993	93.2	83.78	89.90	63.37	89.13	85.46	102.33
1994	91.3	90.87	88.43	80.54	88.96	85.10	102.34
1995	84.2	92.65	83.41	92.51	86.51	81.24	102.40
1996	87.3	97.46	87.25	98.24	88.52	86.14	99.40
1997	96.4	104.43	93.93	104.64	93.23	93.41	100.45
1998	98.8	115.89	98.45	125.89	101.20	98.47	113.61
1999	....	116.15	97.05	129.20	100.28	98.14	112.03
2000	....	119.56	101.75	129.83	103.97	104.75	111.82
2001	....	126.05	107.86	135.92	109.93	112.18	116.30
2002	....	126.83	106.17	140.43	110.09	110.57	118.73
2003	....	119.27	93.15	143.61	103.43	97.56	120.31
2004	....	113.77	85.51	143.42	98.81	90.58	118.90
2005	....	110.85	83.85	138.92	97.16	90.37	115.23
2006	....	108.71	82.58	135.45	96.04	90.28	112.54
2007	....	103.58	77.94	130.28	91.46	86.12	106.97
2008	....	99.89	74.40	126.83	87.61	83.16	101.72
2009	....	105.62	77.66	135.91	91.15	86.29	106.09
2010	....	101.97	75.36	130.61	87.12	83.96	99.71
2009: I	....	111.22	82.92	141.21	95.63	91.37	110.34
II	....	107.07	79.59	136.32	92.24	88.16	106.39
III	....	103.50	75.38	134.35	89.59	84.18	105.02
IV	....	100.81	72.86	131.80	87.12	81.45	102.62
2010: I	....	102.15	74.85	131.84	87.91	83.56	101.92
II	....	103.79	77.57	131.47	88.80	86.47	100.64
III	....	102.55	75.89	131.13	87.54	84.66	99.85
IV	....	99.37	73.00	127.93	84.25	81.18	96.42

[1] U.S. dollars per foreign currency unit.
[2] European Economic and Monetary Union (EMU) members consists of Austria, Belgium, Cyprus (beginning in 2008), Finland, France, Germany, Greece (beginning in 2001), Ireland, Italy, Luxembourg, Malta (beginning in 2008), Netherlands, Portugal, Slovakia (beginning in 2009), Slovenia (beginning in 2007), and Spain.
[3] G-10 index discontinued after December 1998.
[4] Weighted average of the foreign exchange value of the U.S. dollar against the currencies of a broad group of major U.S. trading partners.
[5] Subset of the broad index. Consists of currencies of the Euro area, Australia, Canada, Japan, Sweden, Switzerland, and the United Kingdom.
[6] Subset of the broad index. Consists of other important U.S. trading partners (OITP) whose currencies do not circulate widely outside the country of issue.
[7] Adjusted for changes in consumer price indexes for the United States and other countries.

Source: Board of Governors of the Federal Reserve System.

[Millions of special drawing rights (SDRs); end of period]

Area and country	1982	1992	2002	2007	2008	2009	2010 October	2010 November
World [1]	368,041	760,933	1,893,573	4,305,690	4,841,655	5,482,014	6,057,712	6,178,188
Advanced economies [1]	214,025	557,602	1,159,659	1,585,920	1,672,189	1,951,893	2,172,306	2,195,555
United States	29,918	52,995	59,160	46,820	52,396	85,519	88,267	87,304
Japan	22,001	52,937	340,088	603,794	656,178	652,926	691,149	700,171
United Kingdom	11,904	27,300	27,973	31,330	29,142	35,881	42,651	42,964
Canada	3,439	8,662	27,225	25,944	28,426	34,601	37,414	36,982
Euro area (incl. ECB) [1]	....	....	195,986	148,714	154,253	192,559	204,594	206,548
Austria	5,544	9,703	7,480	7,079	6,101	5,491	6,327	6,275
Belgium	4,757	10,914	9,010	6,827	6,306	10,403	11,034	10,973
Cyprus	490	764	2,239	3,888	416	524	386	316
Finland	1,420	3,862	6,885	4,525	4,587	6,250	5,265	4,854
France	17,850	22,522	24,268	31,855	24,630	32,487	35,549	37,431
Germany	43,909	69,489	41,516	31,896	31,846	42,059	43,477	43,983
Greece	916	3,606	6,083	526	350	1,118	957	961
Ireland	2,390	2,514	3,989	499	572	1,245	1,237	1,252
Italy	15,108	22,438	23,798	20,721	26,838	31,955	33,690	33,991
Luxembourg	....	66	114	93	220	469	470	462
Malta	999	927	1,625	2,396	239	340	333	337
Netherlands	10,723	17,492	7,993	7,198	8,140	12,088	13,140	12,800
Portugal	1,179	14,474	8,889	1,226	1,281	1,996	2,889	2,854
Slovak Republic	....	....	6,519	11,450	11,631	477	500	502
Slovenia	....	520	5,143	624	567	620	575	594
Spain	7,450	33,640	25,997	7,582	8,376	11,930	12,646	12,855
Australia	6,053	8,429	15,307	15,764	20,015	24,935	25,189	25,221
China, P.R.: (Hong Kong)	....	25,589	82,308	96,593	118,468	163,152	169,851	174,315
Czech Republic	....	....	17,342	21,878	23,812	26,268	27,759	26,802
Denmark	2,111	8,090	19,924	20,663	26,347	47,464	53,293	47,341
Iceland	133	364	326	1,634	2,284	2,435	2,620	2,969
Israel	3,518	3,729	17,714	18,047	27,601	38,663	44,287	44,748
Korea	2,556	12,463	89,272	165,908	130,607	172,201	186,603	190,171
New Zealand	577	2,239	3,650	10,914	7,175	9,947	10,044	....
Norway	6,272	8,725	23,579	38,500	33,079	31,166	31,834	....
San Marino	....	....	135	410	459	504	....	....
Singapore	7,687	29,048	60,478	103,121	113,092	119,796	140,857	142,561
Sweden	3,397	16,667	12,807	17,281	16,967	27,481	27,949	27,691
Switzerland	16,930	27,100	31,693	29,432	30,426	63,810	143,018	147,411
Taiwan Province of China	7,866	60,333	119,381	171,532	189,864	222,586	244,679	249,043
Emerging and developing economies	124,025	196,245	730,037	2,715,994	3,165,706	3,526,565	3,881,639	3,978,890
By area:								
Developing Asia	44,490	63,596	368,403	1,355,157	1,654,381	1,973,094	2,188,197	2,250,984
China, P.R. (Mainland)	10,733	15,441	214,815	969,055	1,266,206	1,542,335	....	....
India	4,213	4,584	50,174	169,356	161,036	169,782	176,514	177,868
Europe	5,359	13,811	108,246	505,671	482,760	502,935	560,096	557,768
Russia	....	....	32,840	295,872	267,908	266,503	295,924	295,011
Middle East and North Africa	63,843	45,316	107,687	480,435	602,421	597,551	632,979	655,195
Sub-Saharan Africa	4,387	8,421	27,000	92,324	102,255	102,159	104,651	107,094
Western Hemisphere	25,563	65,102	118,700	282,407	323,888	350,826	396,133	408,265
Brazil	3,566	16,457	27,593	113,585	125,239	151,448	180,390	186,150
Mexico	828	13,800	37,223	55,128	61,766	63,536	73,772	76,747
Memoranda:								
Export earnings: Fuel	69,744	40,861	131,380	793,421	900,348	868,188	931,065	950,512
Export earnings: Nonfuel	54,282	155,384	598,657	1,922,573	2,265,357	2,658,378	2,950,574	3,028,378

[1] Includes data for European Central Bank (ECB) beginning 1999. Detail does not add to totals shown.

Note: International reserves consists of monetary authorities' holdings of gold (at SDR 35 per ounce), SDRs, reserve positions in the International Monetary Fund, and foreign exchange.

U.S. dollars per SDR (end of period) are: 1.10310 in 1982; 1.37500 in 1992; 1.35952 in 2002; 1.58025 in 2007; 1.54027 in 2008; 1.56769 in 2009; 1.57179 in October 2010; and 1.52578 in November 2010.

Source: International Monetary Fund, *International Financial Statistics.*

TABLE B–112. Growth rates in real gross domestic product, 1992–2011

[Percent change]

Area and country	1992–2001 annual average	2002	2003	2004	2005	2006	2007	2008	2009	2010 [1]	2011 [1]
World	3.2	2.9	3.6	4.9	4.6	5.2	5.3	2.8	−.6	5.0	4.4
Advanced economies	2.8	1.7	1.9	3.2	2.7	3.0	2.7	.2	−3.4	3.0	2.5
Of which:											
United States	3.5	1.8	2.5	3.6	3.1	2.7	1.9	.0	−2.6	2.8	3.0
Euro area [2]	2.1	.9	.8	2.2	1.7	3.0	2.9	.5	−4.1	1.8	1.5
Germany	1.7	.0	−.2	1.2	.8	3.4	2.7	1.0	−4.7	3.6	2.2
France	2.1	1.1	1.1	2.3	2.0	2.4	2.3	.1	−2.5	1.6	1.6
Italy	1.6	.5	.0	1.5	.7	2.0	1.5	−1.3	−5.0	1.0	1.0
Spain	3.0	2.7	3.1	3.3	3.6	4.0	3.6	.9	−3.7	−.2	.6
Japan	0.9	.3	1.4	2.7	1.9	2.0	2.4	−1.2	−6.3	4.3	1.6
United Kingdom	2.9	2.1	2.8	3.0	2.2	2.8	2.7	−.1	−4.9	1.7	2.0
Canada	3.3	2.9	1.9	3.1	3.0	2.8	2.2	.5	−2.5	2.9	2.3
Memorandum:											
Newly industrialized Asian economies [3]	5.5	5.8	3.2	5.9	4.8	5.8	5.8	1.8	−.9	8.2	4.7
Emerging and developing economies	3.8	4.8	6.2	7.5	7.3	8.2	8.7	6.0	2.6	7.1	6.5
Regional groups:											
Central and eastern Europe	2.8	4.4	4.8	7.3	5.9	6.5	5.5	3.0	−3.6	4.2	3.6
Commonwealth of Independent States [4]	−3.1	5.2	7.7	8.1	6.7	8.8	9.0	5.3	−6.5	4.2	4.7
Russia	−2.9	4.7	7.3	7.2	6.4	8.2	8.5	5.2	−7.9	3.7	4.5
Developing Asia	7.3	6.9	8.2	8.6	9.5	10.4	11.4	7.7	7.0	9.3	8.4
China	10.3	9.1	10.1	10.1	11.3	12.7	14.2	9.6	9.2	10.3	9.6
India	5.7	4.6	6.9	8.1	9.2	9.7	9.9	6.4	5.7	9.7	8.4
Latin America and the Caribbean	3.0	.5	2.1	6.0	4.7	5.6	5.7	4.3	−1.8	5.9	4.3
Brazil	2.6	2.7	1.1	5.7	3.2	4.0	6.1	5.1	−.6	7.5	4.5
Mexico	3.0	.8	1.7	4.0	3.2	4.9	3.3	1.5	−6.1	5.2	4.2
Middle East and North Africa	3.4	3.8	6.9	5.8	5.3	5.8	6.0	5.0	1.8	3.9	4.6
Sub-Saharan Africa	2.8	7.4	5.0	7.2	6.3	6.4	7.0	5.5	2.8	5.0	5.5

[1] All figures are forecasts as published by the International Monetary Fund. For the United States, advance estimates by the Department of Commerce show that real GDP rose 2.9 percent in 2010.

[2] Euro area consists of: Austria, Belgium, Cyprus, Finland, France, Germany, Greece, Ireland, Italy, Luxembourg, Malta, Netherlands, Portugal, Slovak Republic, Slovenia, and Spain.

[3] Consists of Hong Kong SAR (Special Administrative Region of China), Korea, Singapore, and Taiwan Province of China.

[4] Includes Georgia and Mongolia, which are not members of the Commonwealth of Independent States but are included for reasons of geography and similarities in economic structure.

Note: For details on data shown in this table, see *World Economic Outlook* and *World Economic Outlook Update* published by the International Monetary Fund.

Sources: Department of Commerce (Bureau of Economic Analysis) and International Monetary Fund.